EDWARD LANSDALE

BOOKS BY CECIL B. CURREY

Road to Revolution
Code Number 72
The Craft and Crafting of History
Reason and Revelation
Guide to Images of America
Self-Destruction
Follow Me and Die
With Wings as Eagles
Edward Lansdale: The Unquiet American

EDWARD LANSDALE

THE

UNQUIET

AMERICAN

Cecil B. Currey

HOUGHTON MIFFLIN COMPANY

Boston 1988

For information about permission to reproduce selections from
this book, write to Permissions, Houghton Mifflin Company,
2 Park Street, Boston, Massachusetts 02108.

Library of Congress Cataloging-in-Publication Data

Currey, Cecil B.
Edward Lansdale, the unquiet American / Cecil B. Currey.
p.   cm.
Bibliography: p.
Includes index.
ISBN 0-395-38510-5
1. Lansdale, Edward Geary, 1908–1987.   2. Generals — United States —
Biography.   3. United States.   Army — Biography.   4. United States —
History, Military — 20th century.   5. Vietnamese Conflict,
1961–1975 — United States.   I. Title.
E745.L36C87   1988   88-18998
973.9'092'4 — dc19   CIP

Printed in the United States of America

KR 10 9 8 7 6 5 4 3 2 1

For my father

CHALMERS CECIL CURREY
1895–1937

and my mother

EDITH ESTELLE BARR CURREY
1895–1985

Ed Lansdale was never happy with rigid military practices or rules of thinking. He opposed all kinds of them from close-order drills to tactics and strategy. He much preferred to apply the psychology he had learned in advertising: to learn what motivates people, what they want, and how to give it to them without compromising ideals.

He was always a revolutionary — not the kind who seems to be against everything and nothing, nor the kind who revolts against the establishment in hopes of destroying it. Rather Ed revolted against traditional ways of doing things, feeling there were better ways of doing most any job if we only search them out and apply our natural intelligence.

This is a constructive type of revolution that doesn't just run against the stream for the sake of being different, nor the turncoat type that breaks away from a system once accepted and which provided nourishment. Lansdale instead wanted a revolution forced from accelerated evolution; one that sees reasonable objectives which, given time, will likely develop in any case but which can occur now if pushed for in an appropriate way.

This approach, gradually honed to a finer edge over the years, was developed when Lansdale worked in advertising in . . . San Francisco. While advertising agencies are often well manned by conventional types who play it safe by imitating existing trends in the business and aping approaches of others (or even of themselves), there are also some [employees] like Ed. Generally they are highly intelligent and imaginative people with a keen sense of perception. To them each new campaign on behalf of a client presents a challenge to be met in a way unique to the product or service to be sold. Standard formulae do not satisfy such people. They seek better ways to motivate the public into purchasing what their clients have to offer.

Ed also learned the importance of consistency and perseverance, qualities of inestimable importance in the advertising business. No ad campaign will be successful without them. Later on, while serving in Asia, he discovered or intuitively realized that such qualities are as applicable to politics and military activities as they are to advertising and applied these important factors in efforts to achieve his goals.

— Tribute to Edward Geary Lansdale
by Benjamin Carroll Lansdale
1 May 1978

CONTENTS

FOREWORD

"The Quiet American," "the Ugly American," one of "the greatest spies in history," a confidant of presidents, an Air Force major general. Could all these be one man? They were, and his name was Edward Geary Lansdale, who played a major role in American policy in East Asia in the post–World War II era. The image is of a swashbuckling hero figure immersed in "dirty tricks" and derring-do, a kingmaker and intriguer manipulating and crushing Asians for the greater glory of the American empire. To revisionists and antiwar activists of the 1970s, this image personifies their criticisms of American policy during that era.

But they did not know the man. Quiet and contained, he took his place at the edge, not the center, of a crowd. He gave no bombastic speeches and led no flamboyant attacks. His battles were over ideas, and his weapons were the tools to convince, not kill. His influence with Asians came more from his preference to listen to them than from a compulsion to tell them, an unfortunately rare attribute among the other Americans they knew. He was more interested in their songs and stories than in their armaments and believed the people's rich traditions and history were more important than their military stockpiles in the long run. The one thing that brought him out of himself was his harmonica, which he used to evoke warm and happy moments in the atmosphere of struggle and pain he shared.

His accomplishments were the stuff of legends. He befriended and helped perhaps the best president the Philippines ever had. He turned American policy away from support of French colonial rule in Vietnam to support of a noncommunist nationalist leader who had little other hope in 1954 and 1955. And he preached (Oh, how he preached!) the need for America to support Vietnamese who were willing to fight to keep themselves free of communist domination rather than to push them aside so the Americans could apply all the technology of modern war against enemies who simply melted out of their gunsights.

Lansdale was a maverick, and big bureaucracies do not suffer mavericks kindly. He was inclined to leap over the bureaucrats, military and civilian, to convince the highest official possible of any idea that he thought should be applied. When an order appeared wrong, he simply ignored it and went on doing what he thought right (and frequently it *was*). His style made him few friends among the more traditional bureaucrats and, more seriously, kept him from appointment to the kind of leadership positions where he might have been able to make major changes in American foreign policy and, quite possibly, in the history of Southeast Asia.

But he left a legacy. He inspired many with his empathy for Asians, particularly the simplest Asians in the rice paddy or at the street stall. He was a patriot for all that is best in America — its freedoms, its compassion, its respect for the dignity of every citizen. And he was a fighter in the cause of helping people to strive for these same values against those who would deny them, but he believed that the people should fight within the traditions and circumstances of their own culture, not within an American construct imposed on them by professionals. Some of his ideas were mistakes, but most were not — a pretty good record for any man. And since the ones that were right were very, very right, those will be the ones we remember him for. We are all in Cecil Currey's debt for assembling the story of Lansdale and his ideas and for giving us a full picture of this most interesting American hero.

WILLIAM E. COLBY
Former director, Central Intelligence Agency

PREFACE

Driving along Dolley Madison Boulevard through McLean, Virginia, in February 1984, I passed under a road sign, hung on a high overhead framework, that bore the letters "CIA." An arrow pointed to the left. Following directions offered by that sign I came upon a narrow, tree-shaded lane bordered by high cyclone wire fencing topped by strands of barbed wire. No more signs appeared as I continued. I stopped just short of a formidable-looking gate and guardhouse. I asked a question of the guard: "This *is* CIA headquarters, isn't it?" The man impatiently replied, "I'm not allowed to say." "How can one find out?" I wondered out loud. "Call their downtown telephone number, I suppose," he grumbled. We exchanged stares of resignation and frustration. I drove slowly away.

It took me three more years to get inside the main gate, to drive along perimeter roads through the parklike CIA grounds, to see the vast building construction projects, to walk past the statue of Nathan Hale and into the glass-fronted lobby. (When William Casey took over as director of Central Intelligence, he saw Hale's statue and allegedly said, "Get rid of it. We sent him on only one mission and he couldn't even complete that successfully!") I stood in front of the mosaic seal of Central Intelligence embedded in the floor of the white marble lobby and examined the bas-relief profile of Allen Dulles on the wall to the right. It faces toward the "wall of stars" commemorating those who have died in the line of duty. To the left, high on the wall, is an inscription from the New Testament Gospel according to John, the eighth chapter, thirty-second verse: "Ye shall know the truth and the truth shall make you free."

My three-year effort to visit CIA headquarters stands as a parable for the writing of this book. I found many obstacles. The White House, CIA, and State Department were unwilling to cooperate in my research or to release pertinent documents, some of which dated back more than forty years (and thus were hardly still crucial to the nation's security). Many officials with whom I wanted to talk evinced suspicion and caution, inbred by decades of working within the shadows of intelligence careers. The Socialist Republic of Vietnam was unwilling to allow me entry to schedule interviews with those who once had to contend with the actions of the subject of this book. Vietnamese émigrés who came to settle in the United States after the fall of Vietnam were reticent about being interviewed or responding to my correspondence, despite my being armed with recommendations from friends of theirs of many years' standing. On some future day the government will release documents unavailable to me, and researchers will then be able to flesh out aspects of this story. Yet, despite the government's lack of cooperation, just as in the case of my 1984 attempt to visit CIA headquarters, my persistence finally allowed me to get inside much of what happened in the life of this man.

Since McLean is so close to the Langley location of CIA, many former employees have retired there. Some of those retirees frequent a local hangout near the village center, built alongside Old Dominion Road, the main street, and unknowing customers rub elbows with those who once were active in this nation's intelligence service. I first went there in the company of a former agent and, in later visits, sat and talked with several ex-CIA men. They are quiet people constrained by pledges and years of experience from engaging in activities that would draw inappropriate attention to themselves and from revealing much about their former duties. Older men, they focus their public conversation on sports, automobiles, local politics, and opportunities to buy cartons of cigarettes for two dollars each ("They aren't hot, but they are a little nervous") rather than on tradecraft stories of the past.

Farther south, one of the more peaceful streets in McLean meanders off Kirby Road. Lush trees hang overhead and, in the spring, a profusion of flowers — lilacs, azaleas, pink and white dogwoods, tulips, irises — scents the air and overwhelms the senses. Undeveloped countryside lies just behind back yard fences enclosing neatly tended yards. The street climbs a hill, almost impossible to navigate during winter storms, and then slopes downward. On the lee side of the hill sits a low white house fronted by a broad lawn from which juts a simple flagpole. The American ensign flew there every day the owner was in residence. For at that house lived an old-fashioned and patriotic citizen of this nation who proudly began his day by raising the flag and who ended it by carrying the colored bunting safely back within his home to rest on a hall table during the night.

The householder was a retired Air Force officer who never piloted a plane or served in maintenance yet who rose to the rank of major general. He spent his military career in service to the Office of Strategic Services (OSS), Central Intelligence Agency (CIA), and the Department of Defense (DOD). He worked in close relationship with three presidents — Eisenhower, Kennedy, and Johnson. He wandered the globe from the Philippines to Vietnam to South America, carrying out duties of national and international importance. Novelist Graham Greene castigated him in the fictional character of Alden Pyle in his book *The Quiet American*. William Lederer and Eugene Burdick depicted him favorably as Lieutenant Colonel Edwin Barnum Hillandale in their work *The Ugly American*. His real name was Edward Geary Lansdale; his life, his work, and his contributions to the field of intelligence are the subject of this story. Millions of Americans knew of Lansdale from those books and from occasional newspaper articles that recounted certain aspects of his career, but few really understood him. By choice, he seldom emerged from the shadows of his profession.

His was indeed an odd calling, summarized in part by Charles McCarry, a former intelligence agent and now senior assistant editor for *National Geographic* magazine: "Everything an intelligence agent does is illegal except that it is sanctioned by his own government and authorized by executive authority. Take the simple act of recruiting foreign contacts. The task is to persuade them to commit treason to their own duly constituted government. No matter how they may rationalize or dress up their decision, . . . that is what they have done. Living within such a system in which activities like these are normal creates unusual stresses upon any intelligence agent."[1]

In his book *Intrepid's Last Case*, William Stevenson quotes a comment by William Hood, a former CIA executive, that amplifies McCarry's view: "Like war, spying is a dirty business. Shed of its alleged glory, a soldier's job is to kill. Peel away the claptrap of espionage and the spy's job is to betray trust. The only justification a soldier or a spy can have is the moral worth of the cause. . . . When an ordinary man puts his life at stake for a political cause, and has an impact on history, the story is worth telling."[2]

This story is particularly worth telling, for throughout his career Lansdale retained a sense of personal honor and ethics; he prized his own honesty, forthrightness, and independence during the years when he strove to advance the national purposes of the United States in countries overseas. To this day legions of Filipinos and Vietnamese treasure his memory and count themselves fortunate to have been his friends, companions, and co-workers; just as many former antagonists still revile him. Within

CIA his accomplishments and adventures became legends that were duly passed on to new recruits. McCarry recalled his own days of training as a young employee of CIA: "Some of the teaching was based on the exploits of Edward Lansdale. While his name was not specifically joined to the teaching points, we later came to understand he was the one our instructors had in mind. His career was well and favorably known throughout the Agency."[3]

I am not the first writer of nonfiction to recognize Lansdale's importance. William E. Colby, former director of Central Intelligence, has written that Lansdale's "political imagination and warm empathy with Southeast Asian leaders and peoples helped democratic alternatives to emerge between corrupt colonialists and ruthless terrorists. His assistance to President Ramón Magsaysay in the Philippines and nationalist President Ngo Dinh Diem in Vietnam were of critical importance to American policy in those areas." Colby regarded Lansdale as one of the ten greatest spies of all time.[4]

It took months for me to gain Lansdale's trust. His lips were secured by a lifetime of caution and by a pledge of silence he had given long years before to CIA. Colby has written about CIA's procedure of exacting that pledge. "I could not be accepted as an intelligence officer until I signed the secrecy agreement (which binds me still) that stated I would not reveal, without the CIA's authority, any secrets I would learn while working for the Agency."[5] Philip Burnett Franklin Agee, author of *CIA Diary: Inside the Company* and a man detested within the ranks of CIA, spoke of that oath as applying in a "permanent, eternal and universal" way to everything an operative learned while working for the Agency.[6]

Lansdale felt bound by his pledge. At our first meeting, in 1984, he set forth a caution to me: "Before we get started, I want to say something. I'm concerned about a biography [because of] my connections with CIA. . . . I gave my word years ago. They helped me tremendously. I think highly of what they did and their reasons for doing it and I have no sensitivities on that at all. But I don't want to say what my connections were."[7]

In all the years of his career and retirement Lansdale maintained his silence. I soon learned how frustrating that silence could be. Through long hours of taping sessions, he would begin a comment, falter, and then fall silent after observing, "I've never told anyone about that" or "Even my wife doesn't know that" or "I pledged never to tell that." Information came forth only in pieces, a little at a time. It was not until early in 1986 that he finally opened up. "I checked with Bill Colby," he said, "on an old oath we both took some years ago. He feels that I should ignore the part of it that has to do with my association with

CIA. And, he kindly called upon some of the CIA folks to back up his judgment. They all voted with him. So I will now admit publicly that I served with CIA, as an Air Force officer on regular Air Force pay, on volunteer duty, for the years 1950, 1951, 1952, 1953, 1954, 1955, and 1956. Just those years, no more. And, for most of the time, I was ranked as Colonel."[8] I had at last gotten "inside" in my study of this fascinating man. A year and a month later, he was dead.

Many worthy people have given their time and effort to help me in the preparation of this study. The most important, of course, was General Lansdale, who agreed to talk with me whenever I asked. He sat with me for hours at a time when his health was poor, when he would perhaps rather have been doing other things than answering the questions of a curious author. He vouched for me to those who called him asking if it was "safe" to talk with me. He wrote letters of recommendation, shared lists of names, wrote out responses to written queries I sent him, invited me to his birthday party, visited me in my home, and lectured to my students. I am very grateful to him for his help.

Nor will I forget his brothers, Phil Lansdale of Corona Del Mar, California, and David Lansdale of Media, Pennsylvania, who spoke with me at length about their memories of the general when all were younger and who read and criticized sections of this work. I appreciate their efforts and their interest. I am also much obliged to Pat Lansdale, the general's Filipina wife, for seeing that I never tired the general out *too* much. After his death she welcomed me back to McLean and set up a special room in her home so that I might come and go as I wished while studying the general's personal papers. She sent me off to Manila with a case full of goodies for her grandchildren and with an introduction to her daughter and son-in-law, Patricia and Ramón Pelaez, who waited long hours to meet me in the hurly-burly of Manila's airport, located me, lost me again in the crowd, and, without despairing, searched until they found me again and saw me safely to my quarters in the Manila Hotel. They fed and entertained me and introduced me to other people and shared with me their own view of a Philippine nation without Ferdinand and Imelda Marcos. My thanks to them and to Pat Lansdale. I am grateful.

I will not forget the interest, helpfulness, and hospitality of the late Mrs. Dorothy Bohannan, resident of Manila, who opened her heart and home to me during research trips there in 1985 and 1986. She kindly arranged tens of interviews on my behalf with individuals whose stories were helpful to the telling of this one. I met on her lanai a score and more of interesting people who talked at length with me: Emma Benitez

Valeriano, Ceferina Yepez, José Banzon, Johnny "Frisco" San Juan, Senator Manuel Manahan, Edmundo Navarro, Colonel Medardo Justiniano, Captain Frank Zaldarriaga, Proculo Mojica, Vicente O. Novalez, Henry "Hank" Pascal, Charles Glazer, Rico T. José, and J. Morton "Jock" Netzorg. I even received through her graces an invitation to attend the birthday celebration of Mrs. Luz Magsaysay, widow of the late president. I am glad for the help offered by each one.

I also value the time given me in Manila by the kindly Peter C. Richards, O.B.E., lifelong expatriate from England, who in two successive years offered me the hospitality of his home, introduced me to his gentle Dolly, and shared with me his many memories and extensive files. From Mr. Richards I gained an invaluable series of letters from Edward Lansdale that explained many of the general's actions and feelings during crucial moments of his career.

Thanks must also be given to Elena Danielson, Ernie Tompkins, and Ronald M. Bulatoff, archivists at the Hoover Institution on War, Revolution and Peace at Stanford University in Palo Alto, California. They were unfailingly courteous and helpful to me and my wife as we spent day after day going through the Lansdale Papers at the Hoover during July 1985 and through the C.T.R. Bohannan and Samuel Tankersley Williams Papers during July 1986. Of inestimable value to me have been two research assistants: Milly V. St. Julien and Nancy Callaghan, who willingly gave unflagging energy to projects that required long hours of library research and who performed numerous errands on my behalf. I also hold in high esteem Anna S. Cleveland, who faithfully and carefully transcribed my many interview tapes with the utmost accuracy and who learned to cope with military jargon and foreign names and phrases with equal facility. My thanks as well to Anne Estelle Currey, who transcribed the first few interview tapes for me.

As always, my longtime friend Lieutenant Colonel John Spencer, who at the time of my research was assigned to the National Guard Bureau in the Pentagon, provided me a place to lay my head on trips to Washington. He offered good fellowship, and I thank him and his wife, Carolyn (and especially baby James Benjamin for sharing his bedroom with me), for loaning me a car and allowing me to stay in their Springfield home on repeated occasions.

I was pleased to find much helpfulness within the intelligence community. William E. Colby is as much a gentleman in person as he appears to be in his writings. Lucien Conein and Joseph Baker searched their minds and files on many occasions to supply me with needed material and reminiscences of events, names, dates, and places. Baker kindly gave me many of the illustrations that appear in this work, and both were unfailingly helpful. Herbert H. Becker allowed me the use of a "spare" bedroom on my last trip to McLean (and only later did I discover he was spending the nights in a sleeping bag on the floor of his study!). Thank you, Herb. I am also grateful for the correspondence of John A. Bross, Lyman B. Kirkpatrick, Jr., and Ray S. Cline. I salute the "silent ones" who, because of their oaths, preferred not to be named but who shall not be forgotten.

I also acknowledge the help given me by Randy Mack of Manhattan, Kansas, who searched through the archives of the Dwight D. Eisenhower Presidential Library at Abilene on my behalf, and Jon Adelstein, graduate student at Stanford University, who ate with me, challenged my ideas, and loaned me a copy of his graduate paper on Lansdale. I also appreciate Professor Harvey Nelsen, my colleague at the University of South Florida, for helpful advice and the loan and gift of books requisite to this study. He also served as a reader. Another who scanned these pages for errors in fact, interpretation, or style was Professor Gary Mormino of the history faculty, University of South Florida. Others who have given me valuable advice include Sterling Seagrave of the Netherlands (author and son of the late "Burma Surgeon"); Professor Philip Towle of the faculty of history, Cambridge University, England; Professor Rico José of the University of the Philippines; and J. Morton Netzorg of Detroit. My thanks for their labors, their comments, and their aid in saving me from egregious errors.

The Faculty Research and Development Program of the Division of Sponsored Research, University of South Florida, Tampa, made two grants to me during 1985, and the College of Social and Behavioral Sciences made one available, all of which helped pay for travel and for the completion of other essential research activities. I am grateful to Vince Pedula for his photograph and to Laura's Timothy Nathan Tack for his genealogical insights. My thanks go also to the people at Automated Office Systems in Tampa, Florida, who sold me the Olivetti Word Processor ETV-300 on which this has been written, who freely gave of their supplies, and who convinced me that I, too, could learn modern technology.

I am particularly appreciative of my agent, Russell Galen of the Scott Meredith Agency. He has soothed me, comforted me, encouraged me, praised me, throughout this long process from initial query letter and first prospectus to final product. Thank you, Russ.

As always, I thank one who is both first and last — my wife, L. G. Currey. She inevitably reads and challenges my manuscripts. This time her professional schedule allowed her to do what she last did in 1964. She went with me on my research trips to the Hoover Institution. Day after day, from 0800 to 1630 she sat side by side with me, turning the folio sheets contained in dozens of boxes of the Lansdale, Bohannan, and Williams Papers, extracting material on note cards and filing photocopy requests. Her assistance cut my research time there by half. Her acuity saved me from conceptual and writing mistakes. She is a jewel.

CECIL B. CURREY
June 1987
Lutz, Florida

ODYSSEY TO CALIFORNIA

ROBERT MCNAMARA, President John Kennedy's new secretary of defense, had barely settled into his office on his first day at the Pentagon in January 1961 when he telephoned one of his assistants, Brigadier General Edward G. Lansdale, who had only recently returned from an inspection trip to Vietnam. McNamara told Lansdale to come to his office immediately and give him a ten-minute briefing on Vietnam. Lansdale, who served as assistant to the secretary of defense for special operations, hung up his telephone and gathered a load of Viet Cong weapons that lay stacked around his desk. He had brought them back from the Orient and intended to give them to Special Forces Command at Fort Bragg for inclusion in a museum of guerrilla weapons — rusty old French Lebel rifles, iron and bamboo punji stakes with dried blood and mud still clinging to them, homemade pistols, knives, swords, and pikes.

General Lansdale tucked the odd assortment of weaponry under one arm, closed his office door, and walked down the Pentagon corridor to McNamara's nearby office. Lansdale entered the new secretary's spacious and luxuriously appointed working area, crossed the room, and dumped the weapons on McNamara's polished desk. The secretary's astonished gaze shifted from the deadly clutter in front of him to Lansdale and back. Not pleased with his subordinate's showmanship, McNamara demanded to know the reason for this odd display.

Lansdale's briefing was direct. "The enemy in Vietnam use these weapons . . . . Many are barefoot or wear sandals. They wear black pajamas with tatters or holes in them. I don't think you'd recognize any of them as soldiers, but they think of themselves that way. The people . . . on our side are being supplied with our weapons and uniforms and good shoes and all of the best that we have, and we're training them. Yet the enemy is licking our side. Always keep in mind about Vietnam that the struggle goes far beyond the material things of life. It

doesn't take weapons and uniforms and lots of food to win. It takes
. . . ideas and ideals . . . . Let's at least learn that lesson." Lansdale
watched the secretary closely as he spoke. "I got the feeling that he
didn't understand me. Too unconventional."[1] In not listening, McNamara
made a mistake for which the nation would pay dearly in the years
ahead, but he scorned Lansdale's lesson, more interested in establishing
"statistical indicators of success" to mark American progress than in
knowing the enemy the United States faced in Vietnam.

The general soon realized that he felt neither affection nor respect for
his superior, and his opinion was not heightened by frequent contact
with the secretary of defense. "I didn't get along with [him] at all. We
were civil to each other," Lansdale recalled, "but that's about it." Despite
his reservations, Lansdale continued his efforts to educate the secretary.
A year after their first encounter, early in 1962, Lansdale stood in McNamara's office, holding papers that needed the man's signature. The secretary had graph paper strewn across his desk and he was writing on the
sheets with a hard lead pencil. He handed Lansdale one page, which
contained a list of entries as if for an accounting. The tallies included a
wide range of headings for the conflict in Vietnam, from villages pacified
to the number of roads and bridges controlled by friendly forces. Prominent
in the secretary's list was a column for calculating the number of enemy
dead.

When McNamara asked him what he thought of the list, Lansdale
replied that it wouldn't give him an honest understanding of the progress
of the war in Vietnam because the most important factor was missing.
McNamara asked what he meant. Another column was needed, Lansdale
replied. "You might call it the 'X factor.' It's missing." McNamara
wrote it down. "What is it?" he asked.

Lansdale told him the "X factor" represented the feelings of the Vietnamese people. "That is the vital element in a people's war." Without
that, Lansdale continued, all the secretary's other tallies would be false
and misleading. McNamara grimaced at this suggestion and, after a pause,
sarcastically asked how he could get a reading on people's feelings.
Not interested in pursuing an answer, he erased the "X factor" notation
from his sheet. Lansdale begged McNamara not to codify the war, but
the secretary's attention had already returned to body counts and preemp-
tive strikes. After a few desultory comments, the meeting broke up.[2]
Lansdale returned to his own office despairing of his ability to persuade
the secretary to understand the real meaning of the war, an insight he
had himself achieved some years earlier in a different time and place.

In those early days of the Kennedy administration, many attempted
to gain the ear of Robert McNamara and to persuade him of the validity

of their own approach to the conflict in Vietnam. The secretary of defense would have been well served, however, to ignore the rest and to listen to General Lansdale, who was America's preeminent authority on the needs of strife-torn Asian countries. The public knew little about Lansdale save what they might have gained from two novels wherein he had served as a role model for major characters. In one he was a "quiet" American with "an unmistakably young and unused face flung at us like a dart. With his gangly legs and his crew-cut and his wide campus gaze he seemed incapable of harm." In another he was an "ugly" American, "one of those happy, uninhibited people who can dance and drink all night and then show up at eight fresh and rested."[3]

As one might expect from novels, neither portrait was particularly accurate or expressive of this man's real knowledge and experience in Asia. In acquiring that background, Lansdale had spent half his lifetime working with governments of the Orient. He knew the people of those lands, had walked the dikes of their rice paddies and squatted beside their cooking fires. He had drunk their liquor, sung their songs, played their tunes on his harmonica, eaten their *adobo* and *pancit* and *nuoc mam*. Lansdale, a serving military officer who seldom wore his uniform, became counselor and confidant of Asian leaders such as Ramón Magsaysay in the Philippines and Ngo Dinh Diem in Vietnam. He possessed a wealth of information gained at first hand — and Robert McNamara scorned his offers of help.

Edward Geary Lansdale came from a family with no military traditions of service to country. They had been farmers, construction workers, laborers, and proprietors of small businesses. Half-memories of stories retold down through the generations recalled that one ancestor was Charles Carroll of Carrollton, Maryland, the longest surviving signer of the Declaration of Independence and the only Roman Catholic to sign that document. The family's earliest ancestors to migrate to the English colonies of the New World were two brothers who arrived around 1690, settling close by the present site of the District of Columbia.[4]

General Lansdale's father, Henry, known all his life as Harry, was born in 1883 in Washington, D.C., one of eleven children. As a young adult, Harry worked as personal secretary for John Henry Patterson, president of National Cash Register Company. While so employed he met and fell in love with Sarah Frances Philips, who had spent her childhood in San Francisco and on California ranches. Her father sent her "back East" to finish high school and be properly tutored in the manners then thought to be necessary and appropriate for maturing young ladies. There she met Harry Lansdale; the two were married in 1905 and moved to Dayton, Ohio, to set up housekeeping in the city where Harry worked.

On 15 July 1906, Sarah gave birth to the first of the four sons she would carry, Henry Philips Lansdale, known as Phil. Harry was Roman Catholic, his wife a member of the Christian Science Church. As a compromise on their religious differences, Harry had their young son baptized in a local Episcopal church. Sarah was not pacified and continued her efforts to convert her husband to her own denomination. On 6 February 1908 a second son, Edward Geary, was born. Sarah named the baby Edward in honor of her own father. Only eleven months later, on 24 March 1909, a third baby boy, Benjamin Carroll, was added to their brood. Then on 31 December 1916, after seven barren years, Sarah gave birth to their fourth son, whom they named David Brooke.

Harry Lansdale quit his job with National Cash Register in 1906. Possessed by a restless spirit of entrepreneurship, he became an executive in the young automobile industry. His ambition drove him from job to job, venture to venture. While his four sons were growing up, he went from the Cadillac Company to Regal to Fiat to the Krit Motor Car Company to Denby Trucks to Packard to Hare Motors (which produced Locomobile, Mercer, and Crane-Simplex cars and Kelly-Springfield trucks). These moves caused the family to relocate regularly: from Dayton to Detroit, to Berkeley, California, to Los Angeles, to Poughkeepsie, New York, to Philadelphia, to Detroit, to Highland Park, Michigan, to Bronxville, New York, to Los Angeles once again. In later years Harry became a dealer for Hartford Shock Absorbers and meanwhile backed a local inventor who developed an automatic automobile starter, the Startomatic, which Harry peddled to Bendix Corporation. His last career move came when a struggling automobile parts wholesalers group in Detroit asked him to become its manager. The group called itself the National Automotive Parts Association and Harry restructured NAPA into a very successful operation. He eventually became its vice president and general manager, building it into a billion dollar a year business.[5]

Married to a man in the automotive industry, Sarah quickly became infected by his enthusiasm for the cranky machines and mastered the art of driving. When not doing housework, supervising maids, or changing diapers, Sarah loved to pack her sons into the family car for long drives along dirt lanes that then passed for roads. One of the cars she drove was a Hudson with a muffler cutout that made it roar like a race car. Her great pleasure was to race interurban trolley cars that plied their way across the countryside at about sixty miles an hour. Sarah inevitably came in second.[6] Not many Americans in the first two decades of the twentieth century owned automobiles, so a woman driver was a particularly rare sight and Sarah was often the recipient of curious stares from those who saw her speeding by.

All of their moves meant that the Lansdales had a busy and mobile upper-middle-class home life. Edward Geary Lansdale grew up as a typical American boy of his time. He was a Boy Scout, had a paper route, worked on a bread route, fought and played with his brothers, sold the *Saturday Evening Post* on street corners, held minor jobs as a grocery store sack boy, a hotel bellhop, a drugstore soda jerk, and a chauffeur, and made a B average in school. He read Zane Grey and Edgar Rice Burroughs as did many of his generation, but he also read Ambrose Bierce, pored over his father's collection of the works of the Polish historical novelist Henryk Sinkiewics, and devoured Harry's set of green leather-bound books containing the papers of early American revolutionary leaders. Through the remainder of his life he felt the effect of the teachings and lives of those men. When he had exhausted the supply of his father's books, Ed turned to the local public library and brought home armloads of other stories.[7]

In 1922, when Ed was fourteen, his parents packed their belongings as they had so many times and moved from Bronxville to Los Angeles, settling in a hip-roofed bungalow at 739 South Grammercy Drive. Along with Phil, he enrolled in Los Angeles High School and in September 1923 joined the junior ROTC, the high school program of the Reserve Officer Training Corps, continuing to participate until the summer following his graduation from high school. It was his first taste of military life and Ed found it enjoyable. He rose to the rank of cadet major, the top student post. He also participated in CMTC, Citizens Military Training Corps, and for three summers attended its exercises at Camp Del Monte near Monterey, a few miles southwest of what is now Fort Ord.[8]

Lansdale graduated from high school at the end of 1926. He had worked on the student newspaper and the yearbook's production staff. He loved the printed word, had a flair for sketching pictures, and enjoyed writing. He set his sights on a career as a journalist and enrolled in the University of California at Los Angeles (UCLA) for the spring term of 1927, thus becoming part of the class of 1931. The school had not yet developed a specific major in journalism so Lansdale chose to concentrate in English. His college career proved to be indifferent in the classroom but fairly eventful outside it. He picked whatever courses struck him as interesting — one in creative writing and one in magnetics, for instance — but he refused his adviser's urging to take a language course, despite the fact that every student at UCLA needed that credit to graduate. He had no aptitude for languages, and the only foreign phrases he had picked up in high school were the curses of his Mexican classmates. Inability to master *any* foreign language would be a lifelong problem for Lansdale.[9]

Lansdale spent his first two years at the old UCLA campus on North Vermont Avenue while the state government developed additional property in then rural Westwood — a portion of an old ranch owned by the Janss family — for use as a new site for UCLA. On this land the regents laid out a hilltop campus. Construction began on essential buildings, designed in Romanesque architecture. In the fall of 1929, UCLA moved to the new site. Students were proud to be starting their own traditions at a new location. The campus was still mainly raw virgin ground with no trees. Wind from the Pacific Ocean blew in and whistled past the few completed buildings. Young men soon found a favorite location on campus at the foot of Janss stairway, which led from Westwood Boulevard up to the campus. Because of the wind and its effects on girls' dresses, males enjoyed congregating at the bottom of the stairs to enjoy the scenery.

Lansdale became great friends with a fellow graduate from Los Angeles High School, Hubert Roberts, called Pooley by his friends. Both expected one day to go into journalism and, in the way freshmen have, spoke of those future days when they would become famous. The two friends became pledges of Delta Rho Omega fraternity, which later became a campus chapter of the national Phi Gamma Delta, called Fiji by its members. DRO members were active in campus activities: they wrote many university songs, ran the plays, headed publications. Their interests lay largely in three areas: literary activities, for many saw themselves as future writers; the law, for numbers of graduates enrolled later in law schools; and the military, inasmuch as most members belonged to the local Reserve Officer Training Corps. Pledging DRO was a natural choice for Ed Lansdale.[10]

Lansdale saw Pooley on campus one day and said, "Do you know that we're going to have a new college humor magazine?" "No," Roberts replied. "That's great news." The magazine's publisher, Rehbock Lewis, chose Lansdale to serve as editor and he in turn persuaded Lewis to hire Pooley as associate editor. The golden bear was the symbol of the University of California, and the bruin reigned at UCLA — thus *The Claw* was born. "It was a lousy name," Lansdale remembered, but putting it out on time offered real challenges to the young men involved in its production. Lansdale wrote jokes and drew cartoons for the magazine. (Example: "Question: What do you call passengers who ride on Wilshire buses? Answer: You don't call them. They have to ring for their own stops.") It appeared once a month during the two school semesters and quickly became a campus favorite.[11]

Lansdale was inevitably without funds, as were most college students of the late 1920s and early 1930s, so he developed his cartooning skills and sold his artwork in the neighborhood or traded cartoons to local business establishments in return for haircuts, clothing, and meals. "It was a great racket," Lansdale explained.[12] Still with empty pockets and belly, he augmented his meager income by waiting on tables at Bultram's, a local Hungarian restaurant, which required him to dress in formal wear while on duty. On Tuesdays and Thursdays, he attended his afternoon biology lab wearing his tuxedo and at 5:00 P.M. he began to sprint across campus to Westwood Village and down the main street toward the restaurant. Arriving out of breath and sweating, he put a broad smile on his face, quickly straightened his black bow tie, and went to work. At least twice a week this job easily made him the best-dressed man on campus.[13]

The father of Walt Purdom, one of Lansdale's fraternity brothers, was head of Hollywood's Central Casting Bureau and most of the Delta Rho Omegas had jobs in the movies from time to time when college-age men were needed as extras in a film. Lansdale got such work perhaps a dozen times while in college. "We loved musicals," he recalled. "We'd get to dress up, sing songs, dance with nice-looking girls, get a meal and something to drink, and get paid for it. Great fun. Great work." There were other, more adventurous moments as well. Somewhere on some dusty studio shelf there may still be a reel of a Cecil B. De Mille film showing Ed Lansdale as a reform school inmate wearing ill-fitting prison garb, his hair shaved in a *V,* bolting down a stairway amid smoke and flying rubble.[14]

Having enjoyed junior ROTC and summer CMTC training exercises in high school, so Lansdale enjoyed the college military training program, despite his scant interest in weaponry. He never qualified with a rifle on any firing range during his ROTC days (or at any later time, for that matter), and he was awarded only a marksman badge for his pistol scores — the lowest of three possible grades, above which are sharpshooter and expert.[15] This was symptomatic of attitudes he carried throughout his career. He never developed any affection for weaponry as did so many of his compatriots and inevitably preferred to find solutions to problems that did not involve the use of firepower.

Weapons were not the only thing Lansdale regarded with a jaundiced eye. "[W]e had riding boots which those in the Infantry had to wear," he remembered, "but you can't walk in the goddamned things. They're lousy wear on rough ground but look good in parades when they're polished. I became a lousy boot polisher. Hated them with a passion."[16] What he did excel at were unconventional ideas about scouting and patrolling. After he became a ROTC cadet colonel, he invented a game of "hunters and hunted" wherein a hunter who spotted a man hiding in the underbrush would hit him with a dried mud clod. Lansdale's men rapidly learned a good deal about the art of cover and concealment.[17]

The commander of the UCLA ROTC unit was Colonel Perry L. Miles, at the time the highest-ranking field grade officer in the Army. Some of Miles' attitudes toward Cadet Lansdale can be seen in the efficiency reports he placed in his student's personnel file. In 1929 he wrote that Lansdale was "a level-headed and intelligent officer who will improve." The following year he described Lansdale as "a promising young officer of ability, efficient in the things he applies himself to, but inclined to take on too many activities." In his last evaluation, dated 22 August 1931, Miles wrote prophetically: "This officer is a sane thinker possessed of balanced judgment. Better equipped by temperament for cerebrations than action." At the age of twenty-one, Lansdale was commissioned a second lieutenant of infantry.[18]

Lansdale's work and extracurricular activities — part-time jobs, campus politics, fraternity life, ROTC, *The Claw* — all took too much time away from his studies and were a formidable obstacle to his college work. There was hardly time left after his various activities to go to class or to study. He was fed up with living so meagerly, so near the edge of poverty. Part-time work was also becoming increasingly difficult to find as financial hard times descended on the country. But the biggest menaces were those irregular verbs and bizarre idioms of a foreign tongue. The dreaded language requirement still faced him. It all finally became too much. So at the height of the Great Depression, Lansdale made up his mind. "I decided to quit school and get on with my life."[19]

2

PEACE AND WAR

IN SEPTEMBER 1931, Edward Lansdale left Los Angeles, which had been his home since 1922, for a new life on the eastern seaboard. He took with him vague plans of graduate work in journalism at Columbia University and, more immediately, family friends had given him contacts with two New York City newspapers. Editors at both newspapers had offered him a job. Out of meager funds, Lansdale bought himself a train ticket for the trip across America. The journey was a tiresome one as he sat in his day-coach seat looking out the window during daylight hours watching the endless miles of continent unfold. At night he lay sprawled across his wicker seat trying to sleep. Nearly penniless, Lansdale finally arrived at New York's Grand Central Station, his journey completed.[1]

Lansdale's hopes for newspaper work were quickly dashed. One daily folded even before he arrived in the city. The other — the *New York World-Telegram* — hard hit by the Depression, was laying off employees instead of hiring. Lansdale learned of this measure only when he walked in the front door planning to go to work.[2] Alone and frightened, he turned to a family friend, A. H. "Harry" Greenly, a Christian Scientist, whom Lansdale remembered from earlier years when the two families lived near each other, the Lansdales in Bronxville and Harry, a bachelor, in the Gramercy Park section of Manhattan.

Greenly was now chairman for the railroads' Official Classification Committee, which established basic tariff rates for all long- and short-haul carriers and shipping lines throughout the United States, and he made a place for Lansdale in his office. Lansdale found the work deadly and the salary minute, but he put forth his best effort and, in the course of time, Greenly promoted him to chief clerk. "Years later, I called that place," Lansdale remembered. "I think I was a major general by that time, about ready to retire from the service and . . . all the old gang was still working there, still doing the same thing. God! It was lousy work.''[3]

Lansdale periodically made the rounds of newspaper hiring offices in hope of finding a job but each one turned him away. Newspapers were operating on too thin a margin to take on a new, inexperienced man. Perhaps he might be able to make his way as a freelance writer and cartoonist. In evening hours, Lansdale wrote plays and submitted them, but to no avail. He drew cartoons and sent them to humor magazines of the day, such as *Judge*. ''Those plagued editors,'' as Lansdale called them, laughed at his cartoons, said they were good, but had no money to buy them. ''Yet they urged me to keep on with what I was doing. But I just gave it up; it wasn't worth all the effort.''[4]

Lansdale joined the local unit of the Army Reserve as a second lieutenant, but he was scornful of the kind of training it offered. Only thirteen years had passed since the end of World War I and all training in the unit was conducted by veterans who had little or no experience in newer techniques. His superior officers seemed not to understand how to correlate infantry with tanks and airplanes, signal corps, or heavy artillery. They still considered the horse cavalry and the horse artillery as prime units to be used in support of doughboys who in some future war would once again slog along on foot at a snail's pace. They were, Lansdale objected, teaching men to fight yesterday's war all over again. Lansdale's attitude eventually brought him into conflict with other officers in the unit who enjoyed their drill sessions and did not want to change what they had been taught.

A visiting officer tried to persuade Lansdale to transfer to a tank outfit and took him to look at a machine of the kind that had been used on the Western Front during the Great War. ''I took one look at the goddamned tank,'' Lansdale remembered, ''and said, 'Jesus! This is a stinking gasoline pot; this would be no fun. It's not for me.' '' Despite his less than enthusiastic attitude, Lansdale received promotion to first lieutenant on 17 June 1932.[5]

Lansdale made his home in a Manhattan apartment house at 288 West Fourth Street. After several months in the city, he met Helen Batcheller, who shared an apartment with some other young women at 25 Fifth Avenue. She was a year older than he and thus, in that year of 1931, had already passed her twenty-fourth birthday. Destined to become prematurely gray, Helen's hair already contained scores of glistening white strands. A petite girl with a pretty face, she stood a slight five feet three. She worked as a secretary for a hardware corporation and had only recently come to the city from her home in Dunkirk, a bustling town on the shores of Lake Erie.[6]

Ed and Helen soon became fast friends despite having quite different personalities. Lansdale was a handsome young man, outgoing, with a sometimes raucous sense of humor, who sincerely enjoyed the company of other people. Helen was a serious girl, sober and quiet, most comfortable when the two were alone. She sometimes seemed to resent the time and attention Lansdale gave others, believing it would be better spent on her. Many years later, David Lansdale asked his brother what had brought the two of them together, for Helen was "not a very warm-natured person, not a fun-loving gal at all." Ed responded quietly, "We were both very lonely." "I think that [loneliness] paired them up," David observed. It was a fairly typical Manhattan story. Ed and Helen were comfortable with each other. "So we became close," Lansdale recalled, and when they were married in 1932 it was "just for companionship."[7]

The marriage ceremony was held in the Church of the Ascension on lower Fifth Avenue, almost across the street from where Helen lived. They made their home in Greenwich Village and then moved to an address on West Fourth Street, remaining there until they moved from the city. Both continued to work at their jobs in lower Manhattan, and their combined income and occasional pay increases began to give them a more certain feeling of security. Yet it was a time of doldrums for Lansdale — he was bored with his deadly dull job and disgusted with the Army Reserve. He finally abandoned the monthly evening training sessions, although he maintained his reserve officer commission by completing occasional correspondence courses. Lansdale was ready for a change.[8]

In California, his brother Phil was suffering another kind of boredom. Phil had found an entry-level job in advertising at Bullock's, a small Los Angeles retail store. As quickly as possible he accepted a better position at Silverwood's, a men's clothing firm that operated five outlets in the city. He found much of his time taken up with chores that seemed onerous and that someone else could easily perform. Silverwood's had a regulation prohibiting the simultaneous employment of relatives, but Phil had never been particularly impressed with other people's rules. He offered Ed a job as his assistant at fifteen dollars a week and the use of an apartment in his own home. Phil's only stipulation was that Ed should "try to get out [into another job] within a year because I am not supposed to hire you." His offer was a powerful one. For Ed it would mean an opening into a career with more promise.[9]

Ed was tempted by Phil's offer to learn advertising while working for him, although there were drawbacks to the idea. The job would not pay as much as Ed and Helen's combined income. Ed's wages alone now amounted to nearly three thousand dollars a year and, with Helen's wages added in, the young couple lived at an acceptable level. But he decided that the California job was a chance well worth taking. He talked it over with Helen, urging that they both quit their jobs and move to California. When she agreed with some reluctance, he gave notice to his boss, Harry Greenly, who arranged free rail transportation for them from New York to Los Angeles. The young couple made the long trip across America in the summer of 1935.

Ed soon found that working for Phil was not the best possible arrangement. He described his salary as "horrible." Phil didn't sympathize too strongly. "Ed didn't get a whole lot of recognition while he was [at Silverwood's]," Phil said, "but hell, I didn't bring him there to make a career out of being my assistant."

Lansdale's old college friend Pooley Roberts came to Ed and Helen's apartment for occasional evening meals and fellowship. Pooley found Helen to be "an excellent cook and a very quiet, home-type young woman who didn't have much to say. She usually left us alone after meals." Phil's impressions of Ed's wife were not so equable. He observed that although his wife, Kay, and Helen spent a lot of time together, Helen seldom helped Kay with housework or cooking, preferring instead to spend much of her time reading. "She resented my relationship with Ed," Phil recalled. "Once in a while when I got home before he did, she would bawl me out. Said I was making more money than he, so I should have stayed at work to earn it." Phil was not amused. As head of advertising at Silverwood's, "I could leave at noon if I wanted." Angry with her brother-in-law, Helen would occasionally "simmer and sizzle" at him. "She seemed to think I was somehow buying Ed cheap and he was worth more than he was being paid, which he was." Helen chose not to work, so the two made less money than they had in New York and couldn't afford many of the things they wanted. One person with whom Helen spent much time was her mother-in-law, Sarah Philips Lansdale. Through Sarah's evangelistic efforts, Helen converted to the elder Lansdale's religion, Christian Science.[10]

Despite low pay and long hours, Lansdale enjoyed his work at Silverwood's. For the first time since college he had opportunity to use his talents and try out his ingenuity. He quickly learned many of the essentials of advertising — writing radio commercials and newspaper ads, learning engraving processes and short cuts, letterpress and offset printing, gravure bindery work, electrotyping, typography, and addressing operations.[11]

While at Silverwood's, Lansdale decided that fellow employees might well have unsung experiences. Even shirt and shoe salesmen had real lives outside store hours, and telling some of their stories might be worthwhile. Ed launched publication of a storewide employee magazine in each issue of which he wrote a capsule biography of a different employee. This feature became a favorite among employee readers. Before long many people with no relationship to Silverwood's were requesting copies, and Lansdale had to produce more copies than he had originally intended. One man who saw several issues and was impressed by what he read was Leon Livingston, a San Francisco advertising man. He would soon become an important factor in Ed Lansdale's life.

The job at Silverwood's no longer seemed as good to Ed as it had from three thousand miles away, and his weekly salary gave little promise of better things in the future. Lansdale was also burdened by having to make time to complete the correspondence courses necessary to maintain his Army Reserve membership. Finally, on 19 May 1937, he wrote to the commanding general of the First Reserve Area at the Presidio of San Francisco: "I do not desire reappointment in the ORC [Officer Reserve Corps]. Private and business affairs take so much of my time that I would be a very inefficient addition to any army. I sincerely regret having to do this." His request was duly approved and the commission of First Lieutenant Edward G. Lansdale was shortly withdrawn.[12]

Tension also continued to increase between Ed and Phil both at work and at home. Even when Ed and Helen found a place of their own at 2457 West Eleventh, problems continued at work. Ed concluded that there would be no further progress at Silverwood's without taking over Phil's position, a most unlikely possibility. David Lansdale recollected that the reason for the difficulty was that "nobody can work with Phil. He was continually bugging Ed to do things his way." Phil finally decided that Ed should seek employment elsewhere: "I finally said, 'Go out and get another job,' so he went up to San Francisco a couple of weekends, got a job there, and left."[13]

In late summer 1937, Lansdale drove to San Francisco carrying letters of introduction to advertising contacts there. He arrived on a Saturday for a noon appointment with an agency located in the Flatiron Building at 544 Market Street. A little early for his meeting, Ed watched people leaving their offices for the weekend. He observed them as they walked along the street to the ferry building at the foot of Market to take the boat across the bay to homes in Oakland or Marin County. "I'd been used to crowds in New York," he said, "but it was the first time I had seen a happy working crew. . . . These were happy people . . . in San Francisco. I decided I wanted to work there."[14]

Lansdale was interviewed by Theodore H. Segall, head of a small agency. During their conversation, Segall said that he worked very hard and needed to take some time off. He closed the meeting by telling Lansdale to show up for work the following Monday. On Sunday, Segall decided that since he had hired a top-level assistant, he might as well begin his vacation immediately.

When Lansdale arrived at the agency office on Monday, a curious situation confronted him. He saw a secretary, a couple of artists, a production manager, and a few other employees sitting around doing nothing. "Who are you?" someone asked. "I'm supposed to go to work here today," Lansdale replied. No one knew why Segall was late or where he might be, and Lansdale was unsure how to begin his work. Finally the telephone rang. It was Segall calling. "I've gone on a vacation for three or four weeks," he said to Lansdale. "Please run my agency while I'm away." Lansdale wondered how he could do that. "I don't even know who your clients are," he said to Segall. Segall persisted and Lansdale found himself thrown full tilt into his new job. He asked the secretary to identify the firm's clients for him and he then spent the next few days going to their offices, introducing himself as Segall's alter ego and the new boy on the block.

Segall was pleased upon his return. Lansdale had performed even better than he had hoped, keeping current clients satisfied and gaining a few new ones. When Lansdale felt that his new job would last, he asked Helen to join him in San Francisco and they found a house at 830 Thirty-fourth Avenue. Helen was impressed by her husband's new responsibilities and by the increase in their income, for Ed's starting salary at Segall's was three thousand dollars yearly, a significant improvement over his earnings at Silverwood's.

After a few months of watching the work of his young employee, Segall spoke to Lansdale about the possibility of his becoming a partner. The idea was attractive to Ed, but the two men were unable to agree on terms. "I wanted a fifty-fifty partnership," Ed said, "and that wasn't his idea. He thought I should get about ten percent, so it didn't work out."

Two years after their arrival in San Francisco, Helen Lansdale gave birth on 2 June 1939 to their first child, whom they named Edward Russell. Ed and Helen were now in their early thirties and the arrival of Ted filled both with pride and pleasure.

Life was not as pleasant for Lansdale at work. He and Segall often differed over proper approaches to business. "We used to argue all the time," Lansdale recalled. Perhaps, he concluded, it was time for a change, even though he was earning more than ever before. By the summer of 1941, his income was four thousand dollars yearly plus a percentage of all agency profits.[15]

In the course of his work at Segall's, Lansdale had met most of the other men working in advertising in the city. One such man was Leon

Livingston, who some years before had seen a copy of Lansdale's store magazine at Silverwood's and who had followed Lansdale's career since his arrival in San Francisco. In July 1941, Livingston needed a replacement for one of his account executives. He spoke with Lansdale about taking over the position at a salary of one hundred dollars a month more than he was making plus a fifteen-hundred-dollar annual bonus. Lansdale accepted. It was a happy move from the Flatiron Building to the penthouse suite at the Mills Building on Montgomery Street. Clients quickly came Lansdale's way and soon he handled such firms as the Wells Fargo Bank, the Union Trust Company, Levi Strauss and Company (which then still primarily manufactured overalls), the Morris Plan, Nestlé's Nescafé instant coffee, and Italian Swiss Colony wines.[16]

Lansdale soon learned that Livingston was as eccentric as Segall. A brilliant man, Livingston claimed that Lansdale was discourteous and talked back to him too often. When he came into Lansdale's office he regularly found Ed leaned back in his chair, his feet crossed at the ankles and propped on top of the desk, his eyes closed. "You aren't getting paid for sleeping here," Livingston would growl. "Leon," his employee replied, "you're disturbing my thoughts. I'm thinking. Get out!" Livingston complained bitterly that no one else had ever dared talk like that to him but found Lansdale so valuable that such impertinence went unpunished and the employee unfired.[17]

Levi Strauss was one of the agency's better accounts. In the late 1930s the company was still primarily local, its sales concentrated in the West. In the fall of 1941 Lansdale came to believe that the time was right for the firm to extend its sales territory and enter markets east of the Mississippi. He had not yet shared these ideas with his boss when he and Livingston one day attended a meeting of the company's board of directors. When it came time for Livingston to present his concept for future advertising plans, he conservatively suggested a continuation of billboard posters. His new assistant interrupted.

"No," Lansdale said to the Levi Strauss directors. "Don't do that. Put your money into salespeople to get in and hit all the major eastern outlets and get them lined up before you launch any major advertising campaigns." That would take weeks of preparation and, in effect, Lansdale was suggesting that no appreciable amount of money be spent on advertising until that effort was complete. Livingston was aghast at what he heard. He envisioned thousands of commission dollars thrown away by Lansdale. Yet the firm's officers liked Lansdale's idea and decided to try it out.

Following the meeting, Livingston scolded Lansdale as the two walked back to the agency office: "You're a fool for the way you talked back there." "No," Lansdale replied. "That was honest advice. I believe what I told them." Livingston became so angry he crossed to the other side of Montgomery Street, refusing even to walk alongside Lansdale. Later that day, an official at Levi Strauss called Livingston with additional information. As it turned out, the firm was happy with both ideas. Although they intended to follow through on Lansdale's suggestion, they had also decided to continue billboard advertising and wanted to increase their budget for such expenditures. This prospect mollified Livingston's ire at Lansdale. Lansdale was thus responsible for getting the Levi Strauss Company started on a course of advertising that it followed for many years, helping it to broaden its western base into a national posture.[18]

Ed and Helen found a home that they liked more than the one on Thirty-fourth Avenue and moved to Larkspur, a suburb north across the bay from San Francisco, where they settled at 15 Alexander Avenue. Now Lansdale commuted to work by ferry. While living in Larkspur, on 7 November 1941, their second son, Peter Carroll, was born.[19] The Lansdales spent Sunday afternoon, 7 December 1941, in the back yard of their Larkspur home enjoying the good weather. Helen sunned and occasionally fussed after four-week-old Peter, who sat in his baby carriage, eyes squinted in the bright light, happy in the warmth of the day. Lansdale puttered at lawn work, dressed, naturally enough, in Levis, and Ted toddled after him, desperate to help. The quiet of the day was broken forever when a friend, Cliff Spooner, ran into their back yard shouting for them to turn on their radio. While out driving, Spooner had heard news bulletins about a Japanese attack on the Hawaiian Islands. They talked back and forth, trying vainly to adjust to what they had heard, to come to a realistic appraisal of what an American war would mean to their lives.

At first the idea of a war seemed to be no more than an interesting diversion from the stress and hard times of the Great Depression, which still had a choke hold on some portions of the economy. As the day wore on, however, Lansdale began to have a growing feeling "that it was a time when all Americans had to get into the fight for our country — and that included me. The more I thought about it the more it took shape as an iron-clad duty, not to be questioned."[20] That day and that attitude marked the beginning of a career for Edward Lansdale that would span thirty years and bring him to positions of national importance and international influence.

Lansdale informed Livingston the next day that he was going to try to get his Army commission reactivated. "What's wrong?" Livingston asked. Thinking the young man could not possibly be serious about going to war, Livingston made a joke. "If you want to fight someplace, go join the Russian army. They have better-looking uniforms." Lansdale thought the remark was bad humor and insisted that he had to help defend his nation. Livingston suddenly became angry. "You're crazy," he shouted, "and you're also fired!" Lansdale didn't argue. He simply cleaned out his desk and went home. He had been fired, he said, for thinking "dirty thoughts."[21] Wanting to do something helpful immediately, Lansdale signed up on 12 December with the local Office of Civil Defense for any available assignment. On his application form he claimed — with real exaggeration — to read both Spanish and French in "fair" fashion.[22]

At the same time Lansdale made a formal request to the Army for reinstatement of his commission and for immediate entrance into service. He could, he wrote, be of most use as a public relations officer inasmuch as he had "5 years [experience] handling large advertising accts." A secondary interest, he added, was the field of intelligence because years earlier he had served as a combat intelligence officer for the 32d Infantry Regiment as a college ROTC student. He then turned in his paperwork. He was told the matter would be taken under advisement. Now all he could do was wait.[23]

It was a frustrating time. While the Japanese besieged an American army on Bataan in the Philippines and Rommel rolled back the British Eighth Army in Libya, Lansdale did odd jobs and fretted. He was jobless, with a family to house and feed. He felt he was a "hostage to fortune" and so set out to look for work. Other advertising agencies retracted offers of a position when he told them he was trying to get back into the Army and would quit any job he had as soon as he could do so. One firm, McCann Erickson, gave him temporary employment after calling Livingston for a reference. Livingston already regretted his angry firing of Lansdale. "Grab that guy," he told the caller from McCann Erickson, "and don't let him get away. He was the most original thinker I ever had here."[24] How quickly circumstances had changed. Just a few months before, Lansdale had been a well-paid advertising executive in a peaceful country. Now the nation was at war and he was on the sidelines with neither job nor Army commission.

It is not only the mills of the gods that grind slowly. By the end of 1942 Lansdale still had no firm response from the Army on his request to get back into uniform. Then during a routine physical examination late that year a military physician discovered that Ed had a "moderate enlargement thyroid gland caused by colloid goiter." The Army ruled that Lansdale's health was impaired, insufficiently rigorous to allow him to serve as an officer, and his draft board changed his registration classification under Selective Service to III-A: deferred by reason of physical impairment. Lansdale appealed to the surgeon general of the Army in late December asking for a health waiver.[25] In February 1943, the Army finally relented and published special orders #54, reappointing Lansdale as a first lieutenant, serial number O-26236. He was assigned to the San Francisco field office of the Army's Military Intelligence Service (MIS) — "for limited service only."[26] He was once again a first lieutenant, but at thirty-five he was much over normal age for such a rank.

Those orders gave recognition that Lansdale had already found a way to serve his nation in wartime that should not be compromised by Army duties. For Lansdale had not been content to wait idly during the long months while his request for reinstatement was considered. Quite a bit of Lansdale's success throughout his career rested on having a friend in just the right place. As 1942 began, with no word from the military, Lansdale turned to such a person, Carroll T. Harris, former president of a local typographic firm, who now held a lieutenant colonel's commission and who was assigned to the San Francisco branch office of the Army's Military Intelligence Service. With no apparent progress toward a commission, Lansdale told Harris of his difficulties and explained that his lack of a job also meant that he was hard-pressed for money. Harris listened and replied that he had to make a trip to Washington. He would be back in a week. In the meantime he would see what he could do to help.

When Harris and Lansdale got together after Harris' trip, the colonel said that he had urged his friends at the War Department to rescue Lansdale's commission from oblivion. He had also talked to other Washington friends whose work was similar to military intelligence. They would be able to use Lansdale's services if he was interested. The money would not be great but should be sufficient for the Lansdale family to squeeze by on. Lansdale wanted to know more. What did the group do?

Harris wondered if Lansdale had ever heard of William J. "Wild Bill" Donovan. Lansdale knew the name. Donovan, a New York lawyer, had been a colonel during World War I who planned an operation to kidnap the kaiser as a way of ending that conflict, only to be stopped by the authorities. One and the same, proclaimed Harris. Donovan was a friend of Franklin Delano Roosevelt, and the president had named him head of something called the Office of Strategic Services (OSS), an intelligence-gathering organization that also planned to conduct operations behind enemy lines. The two men talked for some time about the possibilities that might exist for Lansdale within the OSS.

Someone at OSS had suggested that Lansdale be hired as a civilian worker, under contract with the organization but attached to Harris' MIS office. He could do occasional chores for OSS under Harris' guidance.

Lansdale found the idea fascinating and quickly agreed. In the next days Harris introduced him to William Vanderbilt, a former governor of Rhode Island and a captain in the Navy Reserve who had arrived in San Francisco to start a branch office of OSS there. Lansdale and Vanderbilt quickly became close friends. Even after Lansdale's commission was reactivated, he continued to work for OSS while performing his "limited service" for MIS. As he recalled, "I was doing some things for OSS and they wanted me to continue." Lansdale commented that "I was told at one time by Wild Bill Donovan . . . that I was the only individual so employed by both services at the same time."[27]

This was the first, but would not be the last, time that Lansdale would choose to disguise his tracks in intelligence by working under the cover of an intelligence operative. In 1942, ostensibly working for military intelligence, he served behind the scenes for the Office of Strategic Services. Nearly a decade later he would go to the Philippines as a member of an organization so secret that its existence was not acknowledged by the American government for many years thereafter; Lansdale's cover was that he was a serving Air Force officer assigned to intelligence work. Perhaps one of those stories Lansdale had read and enjoyed as a youth was Edgar Allan Poe's "The Purloined Letter." It may have taught him that the best way to hide a thing completely is to put it out in plain sight for all to see. As with so many of Lansdale's unorthodox approaches to the secret shadow world of intelligence, his scheme worked.

The next step in Lansdale's introduction to OSS was to meet some of its officials. They wanted to see this new employee with an advertising background and ordered him to report to Washington. Lansdale arrived in the nation's capital and sought out OSS headquarters.

In the first days of OSS in early 1942, the organization had difficulty finding office space. Archibald MacLeish, the librarian of Congress, offered Donovan his help. MacLeish supplied names of scholars willing to help in research activities and provided a library annex in which they could work. It was, one author has said, a good place to sit and read while awaiting the results of their security checks. Donovan located the first home for OSS in an old apartment house at Twenty-third and E streets, N.W. As his group grew, Donovan took over some red brick and gray stone buildings that had been used by the National Institutes of Health. Then OSS sprawled over into several jerrybuilt wooden buildings thrown together at the start of the war. These gray structures were located behind the old Heurich brewery at the end of Rock Creek Drive near the Potomac. Yet no matter where a man might be assigned within the OSS complex, his work address was always the same: that of the apartment building at 2430 E Street, N.W.[28]

When Lansdale arrived in Washington he was directed to the group of wooden buildings behind the abandoned Heurich brewery. Security was strict and visitors were required to sign in, procure badges, and receive permission to move into other parts of the complex. Lansdale's orders instructed him to report to the unit's executive officer. As a lark, he decided to ignore procedures and see what he could get away with. "I walked in through all that," Lansdale said, "using a little misdirection, getting guards interested in other things while holding out to them what looked a little like a pass. Found the office I was to report in at and walked in." Lansdale introduced himself to the man inside, a regular Army colonel, who was quite taken with Ed's initiative. Looking sternly at Lansdale, the man scolded him. "You think you're very tricky and clever, don't you?" "No sir," Lansdale responded. "It was just sort of fun to see what I could get away with. Suppose I was a German."

The colonel waved away further discussion of the matter. "You caught me at a busy time," he said. He explained that he was immersed in work on OSS personnel files, which filled several cabinets lining the wall behind him. He was, he said, trying to familiarize himself with their contents. At that point his secretary interrupted them and informed the colonel that he was wanted on the telephone in another room. The officer asked Lansdale to wait for his return. As the door closed behind the colonel, Lansdale moved quickly to the files, found the "L" drawer, pulled it open, and located a file bearing his name. He pulled it out to skim the enclosed documents just as the colonel walked back into the room. Holding a stop watch in one hand the colonel reached out with the other to take the file away from Lansdale. "That's the fastest time I've seen anybody do that. You were moving even before I left the room." Lansdale was embarrassed. "I thought I was very clever. Very good," he said. If it was a test, had he passed or failed? Lansdale stubbornly tried to salvage something from the moment. "Let me look at my file," he said. "I want to see what you guys have in there about me."[29] OSS had recruited a very unusual man.

The two men talked for some time. The colonel questioned Lansdale about activities on the West Coast and spoke of the need to set up OSS training courses. The organization was just then, in the first weeks of the war, working out plans for providing recruits with the rites of passage from their old civilian world to the shadowed lands of intelligence work. They discussed the need for imagination and rigor, and Lansdale found himself increasingly interested in the challenge of helping launch such a program. He soon found himself doing precisely that. His new OSS duties required him to make frequent trips from San Francisco to Washington and New York as he helped set up the training program.[30]

Lansdale's superiors put him to work immediately without requiring him to go through a single day of training. He never learned the reason for this exemption. Perhaps they believed his earlier ROTC and Army Reserve training was sufficient to familiarize him with weapons and discipline. He may have simply slipped through in the confusion of the organization's first days. Or his superiors may have decided that his own native intelligence and cleverness were already acceptably well honed for intelligence operations. "I don't know why," he later said. "I was always going off doing things that would interest me. [Maybe] they figured I didn't need training. . . . I don't know."[31]

Lansdale was very interested in the psychological stresses felt by recruits during their training. After some weeks of classroom work recruits were sent out on field exercises. One assignment given regularly was an order for them to find and "kill" a "German" agent in the New York subway or some other location. The story, of course, was faked but was presented in a deadly serious manner to each trainee. Its purpose was to discover "if the guy would actually take a knife and go out to do it." Superiors tracked the trainee as he sought to carry out his assignment and then intervened at the last minute. Those who performed in a dedicated way passed that portion of their schooling. One recruit refused to believe his superiors when they called off his assigned assassination. He thought they were trying to trick him and kept right on looking for his target. "They [finally] had to kick him out of the OSS," Lansdale said. "He was a real wild man."[32]

Lansdale gained something of the same reputation. "I was always figuring out wild moves to do and then volunteering for them," he said. One result of his casual penetration of security at OSS headquarters was his assignment to do the same at other restricted facilities. "I guess [it was] to pay me back for what I'd done," he said. One day he received orders to penetrate security provided by a number of armed guards at a Navy ordnance depot in Oakland. His OSS superiors simultaneously decided to play a joke on Lansdale that "damn near got me shot and killed." After he left for Oakland, someone at his office called the depot to warn the officer in charge that a "German secret agent" was in the area. Lansdale remembered that day: "I was already inside the place. . . . Then the guards found me and asked who I was. I told them and they wouldn't believe me, so I told them to call my office." They did and were told, "No, there's no Lansdale here. We've *never* had anyone here by that name."

"They really fixed me," Lansdale admitted. "It took an awful argument to get out of it. Those clowns were mad at me, with loaded rifles pointed at my guts, their fingers on the triggers. They were nervous, too." Talking rapidly, Lansdale finally convinced the guards to let him make a telephone call. He managed to contact Captain William Vanderbilt. "Look," he said excitedly. "Get me again some other time but get me out of this now!" Vanderbilt did.[33]

Not all Lansdale's days were quite so exciting. Mostly he collected intelligence and continued to put together training courses, writing out programs of instruction and lesson plans. "I wrote some of them for OSS," he said later, "not knowing a goddamned thing, of course."[34] OSS officials put them to use in the classroom and on field exercises. When opportunities arose, he also recruited others to serve as OSS agents. He later described his duties as consisting of "special intelligence assignments, collection and dissemination of information, recruiting for secret operations and secret intelligence." A report from that period noted that Lansdale interviewed selected subjects to obtain information of military value; acted as a liaison with universities and libraries for research purposes; prepared intelligence reports based on published information and available documents; contacted and cultivated businessmen able to furnish sources of military information; and edited intelligence reports submitted by private individuals. Lansdale worked on these activities from July 1942 until February 1943.[35]

It did not take Lansdale's superiors in the OSS long to learn he had a special facility for dealing with other people. "[A]n individual has always been an individual regardless of the color of his skin or his race or his language," Lansdale observed. "I grew up in California, in a place where the Asians were a minority that had a very rough time. And I presume [my] not having joined in with the majority's denigration of the minority and having known a number of Japanese and Filipinos when I was in school — along with Mexicans and all the rest of the minority groups . . . and still treating them as individuals — this helped."[36]

During 1942 native Sumatran crews aboard Dutch ships that were helping the Allied effort heard about President Roosevelt's proclamation of the "four freedoms" in his 1941 State of the Union address. The president called for "freedom of speech and expression, freedom of religion, freedom from want, freedom from fear." These crewmen decided "to go home and have their own freedom." The Navy called on Lansdale for help "since I seemed to get along very well with Asians." Lansdale met with various crew members and had "drinking bouts with them and at one of these I was rather exuberantly made a member of the Batok tribe of Sumatra." He also persuaded them to continue helping in the Allied war effort "until the day of victory."[37]

Lansdale also made contact with a number of Andalusian emigrants who opposed Spanish cooperation with the Axis nations of Germany and Italy and who were willing to help the Allied war effort. Lansdale found that a number of them had jobs as "chauffeurs and house boys and gardeners . . . to very significant and prominent leaders of various . . . ambassadors and consul generals . . . whose households were suddenly no longer safe for secrets." Throughout the course of the war Lansdale recruited several such networks, which he then turned over to other agents to run. "They kept using me to go out getting new information and meet[ing] new people all the time," Lansdale recalled, "which seemed to be my forte."[38]

Working out of the San Francisco office of OSS at 54 New Montgomery Street, Lansdale spent most of his days on less exciting pursuits, such as quietly gathering various kinds of information helpful to his agency and to the war effort. "The Army had great demands for information and we were trying to satisfy those as well," he said. "So I was sort of the handyman [for both OSS and MIS]."[39] He searched through libraries for maps of overseas areas that would clearly show roads, trails, rail lines, and other information important to the war effort. He traveled to universities, to learned societies, to locations of any kind where he might find Americans or resident aliens with broad travel experiences. "Part of the work," Lansdale reflected, "was almost like being an editor of the *National Geographic* magazine in that we collected photographs of not only airstrips and beaches for landings but also roads and bridges . . . . details on people who lived in [other] places, their potentials for helping our troops."[40]

His work regularly took him to locations along the West Coast from Seattle to Los Angeles. "I met some very fascinating people: geologists, explorers, volcanologists, an ichthyologist," Lansdale recalled. Such work taught him how valuable research was and how helpful experts in their own fields could be to an intelligence operative. "World War II taught me that you can, if you look hard enough, find Americans who have been every place and are very knowledgeable, savvy. I found [people] who had been all over the far Pacific basin, Kamchatka south through China. . . . [They could] describe almost every inch of the ground and had [their own] connections." When Lansdale pushed them for further information, they regularly referred him to still others who might help.[41]

"I did a study [with an ichthyologist] on the poisonous and venomous fishes of the seas," Lansdale remembered, "with warnings to our troops in the Pacific. He had been an official of a fishery out in the Philippines before the war. He'd gone on foot practically throughout the islands. He knew the people there extremely well, the common stories they'd tell, their superstitions." One day while they were making small talk, the man regaled Lansdale with a scam he'd encountered in the Philippines. He told Lansdale of an old woman who lived in a cave in the mountains and traveled from place to place selling little vials of "urine from Mary, the Mother of God." Lansdale was highly amused. "I thought that's a wonderful place, to live among people like that."[42] He would soon get his wish.

Lansdale enjoyed such interviews. It was great, he believed, to have a chance "to know places and peoples and what was going on there and what made them tick and the economies, the value of life and the structure of societies." He took real satisfaction from knowing that each individual with whom he talked "was a gold mine [of information] if the interviewer was a good miner." He also believed in his own personal efforts. They provided information that when edited, compiled, and forwarded to higher headquarters was helpful to America's war machine.[43]

Lansdale's military orders came through at last, and on 28 February 1943 he again became a member of America's uniformed services. His work with OSS, however, prevented Lieutenant Lansdale from full-time duty with the Army. Despite that fact, on 23 December 1943, First Lieutenant Edward Lansdale was promoted to captain.[44]

His duties during those months are shrouded by shadows. His brother Phil recalled receiving a telephone call from Ed during 1943 that he believed originated in London. Ed's tinny voice over the transcontinental cable asked Phil if he might be interested in a dangerous assignment that could involve a parachute jump behind enemy lines into occupied Europe. Phil's reaction was quick. Their mother had raised no fools and he was not about to jump out of an airplane for any foreseeable reason![45] Lansdale never admitted to any such telephone call, insisted he had never been to England, and, when pressed, Phil had no way of proving his brother's call came from London; it was only an impression he had retained for the forty-two years since the event.[46]

The mystery deepened when, on 16 May 1984, in a discussion of his service during the war years, Lansdale said he spent "practically" all of that time within the United States except that "I got out twice on very short trips out in the Pacific. . . . I got once as far as New Zealand and one trip into China, but it was very brief. I didn't do anything. I mean, I might just as well not have gone, I felt. Except it was sort of fun traveling around."[47] He did not elaborate.

What might have taken an OSS agent into the Pacific during World War II? As early as the fall of 1941, General Douglas MacArthur insisted that there was no reason for the creation of a new intelligence service under Wild Bill Donovan, with whom he had served in World War I. MacArthur later rejected an OSS plan for guerrilla operations in the

Philippines but was willing to allow it to gather information in the Netherlands East Indies. By late February 1942, however, MacArthur gave an order that would last throughout the war — OSS would not be welcome anywhere within the Pacific theater of operations. Despite several OSS attempts to circumvent him, MacArthur remained adamant.

Donovan countered this exclusion of OSS from the Pacific by establishing a Chinese base for his Asian activities. After President Roosevelt gave oral permission, Donovan and Secretary of the Navy William Franklin Knox signed a secret agreement with the Chinese government that set up a joint secret service known as the Sino-American Cooperative Organization (SACO). SACO was to provide training for guerrillas, to conduct sabotage and espionage, and to intercept Japanese radio transmissions. The Chinese government would provide SACO with manpower and facilities; the United States would send arms and equipment.[48]

When asked again on 19 December 1984 about his trips to New Zealand and China, Lansdale insisted he had made no such trips. "Not [to] New Zealand?" "No," he said. "How about China?" "No. No," he answered. "I got a lot of Chinese map materials during the war but that was just through connections I had made in San Francisco. And I was dealing with an awful lot of problems over on the Asian mainland, but all from the Pacific coast." He was insistent on this matter, later claiming that he had made "no [such] trips. I must have been dreaming while talking to you. . . . Just damn dreaming!"[49]

There the matter might have rested except for a conversation with Lee Telesco, a Manila businessman and a retired colonel in the U.S. Army. Telesco served during World War II with the Allied Intelligence Bureau (AIB), a unit set up by General MacArthur and composed of U.S., New Zealand, Australian, and Dutch personnel. Among other tasks the AIB ran coast watcher stations in New Guinea and, by airplane and submarine, sent advisers and intelligence teams into the Philippines — from Luzon in the north all the way down to the Sulu archipelago — to work with guerrillas there.

Telesco worked in the headquarters of AIB on Queens Street in Brisbane, Australia. "So we did know what went on at all times," he said. He remembered a day in 1943 when a young officer just in from the United States came to AIB headquarters and said he had an appointment to speak with Allison Ind, the AIB executive officer and Telesco's superior. Would Telesco find Ind for him? "I took him and introduced him to Allison." The visitor's name was Edward Lansdale. Telesco did not stay to hear the ensuing conversation. "I excused myself for I didn't feel it was proper. . . . I wasn't invited to stay. . . . Later I got to know Ed real well. Yes, yes, absolutely." Telesco also recalled another fact about that incident. "There was a trip to China that Allison told me they were going to make, but I have no details about how that trip went off but I did hear that there was a trip going into China. . . . Now I can remember there was some talk of someone going into China and I believe it was Lansdale if I'm not mistaken."[50]

These stories of wartime missions overseas are so different from one another. Telesco knew Ed Lansdale for forty years and was hardly likely to forget where he first met him. Phil Lansdale spoke on many overseas telephone calls. Were they both mistaken? Yet Lansdale himself adamantly insisted that he never left the United States during the war. The real story of those events may never be learned.

The War Department closed down the San Francisco office of Military Intelligence in June 1944. Presumably with the concurrence of OSS the Army then transferred Lansdale to New York City where he remained until 20 August 1945.[51] Neither Helen nor Ed wanted to be apart for such a long time, so Helen, Ted, and Peter traveled east and the family lived together in New York for a little more than a year.

The year 1945 saw first the defeat of the Germans in Europe during May and then, in August, the capitulation of the Japanese empire following the dropping of nuclear bombs on Hiroshima and Nagasaki. For the nation the war was finally over. But for Edward Lansdale, his own battles on behalf of the country had only just begun; they would continue without surcease until 1968.

In the same month that Japan sued for peace Lansdale received orders for overseas duty. He was assigned to the Philippines as chief, Analysis Branch, Intelligence Division, in the headquarters of Armed Forces Western Pacific (AFWESPAC). Lansdale wound up his assignment in New York and on 21 August 1945, with Helen, Ted, and Peter in tow, boarded a train for the journey back to California. His War Department orders called for him to leave the United States on 22 September. The Lansdale family spent the precious intervening month at their home in Larkspur.[52]

While Lansdale waited for his shipping date, the vagaries of war's end allowed him a reunion with his brother Ben, who worked for Army Ordnance with a courtesy rank of major. Ben had returned from duty in the Philippines for some badly needed surgery. They met in San Francisco and spent long hours talking about their war experiences and what might lie in store for Ed in the far waters of the Pacific. Ed asked Ben if he could remember any tunes he might have heard Filipino soldiers singing. When Ben could not, Ed pulled out his pocket harmonica. Harry Lansdale had showed him how to play the instrument years before and he enjoyed it sufficiently to carry one around with him. Ed played a couple of songs and asked if they sounded familiar. Ben confessed he had been listening to other things while on duty in the archipelago. "Since that wasn't part of my military duties," Ben later recalled, "I hadn't paid any attention. I wondered why he cared." Ed suggested that such things might be important. He wanted to understand and communicate with Filipinos and one way would be to know "their songs, something they hold dear to their hearts." Many years later Ben remembered the incident and gave it perhaps more meaning than it had at the time: "He wasn't going out there to shoot at people or to try to make them change their minds by force, but rather to understand them and to help guide them into a type of democracy that would live and have meaning."[53]

On 22 September Lansdale bade goodbye to his two sad little boys and a tearful wife. He boarded the troopship USS *Uruguay,* just one of forty-five hundred other officers and enlisted men. Most of them stood at the rail waving to loved ones and watching the land until it sank below the horizon. As time passed, Lansdale got to know some of his fellow passengers, a few of whom were also members of the intelligence community. One man, Lieutenant Colonel Wayne E. Homan, would be his boss in Manila. Another shipmate was Captain Edmundo Navarro, a Filipino on duty with the U.S. Army, on his way back home. Navarro remembered, "We spent about nineteen days aboard that ship and together suffered seasickness that occurred when we hit the tail of a very, very strong typhoon in October. We were in the middle of the Pacific . . . so we thought we were going to sink."[54]

After finally arriving weary and seasick in the Philippines, Lansdale began his intelligence duties on 19 October. His days were filled to bursting. One responsibility in early November required him to untangle a bewildering situation involving doubtful nationality of nearly three hundred persons of Japanese, Chinese, German, and Filipino ancestry. These people had been interned in Japanese prisoner of war camps. Now released, they asserted claims that were sometimes difficult to substantiate. Lansdale characteristically "found the roots of the trouble quickly, then pulled, kicked and pounded his way through obstacles of inertia, high politics, pomposity and ignorance, and soon had an honest system operating smoothly" that was capable of determining the nationality of those involved and resolving their troubles.[55]

In his first weeks Lansdale also submitted twenty-seven staff studies required by his headquarters or by the War Department general staff at the Pentagon. He also distributed a weekly "Philippine Press Analysis," an encapsulation of news stories dealing with American activities; reported on Japanese hostile stragglers and Filipino political dissidents; and wrote reports on military, political, and economic developments in the little-known northern Ryukyu Islands located between Okinawa and Japan.[56]

The United States government still had not installed a military government in the Ryukyus and needed to know more about existing problems among those island peoples before it could do so. In May 1946, Lansdale was ordered to go there to survey several remote islands not previously visited by other military teams. He selected three men to accompany him: James Clark, an agent of the Army's Counter Intelligence Corps (CIC); Technician Fifth Class David Greene, a photographer; and Technician Fourth Class Matsue Yagawa, a Nisei interpreter. They left Manila aboard a slow propeller-driven military airplane bound for Okinawa.[57]

In the harbor at Okinawa, Lansdale commandeered a small wooden Japanese fishing vessel, the *Kee-mura,* and its crew for his team to use on their trip north. The outer fringes of a typhoon damaged the wallowing craft, forcing Lansdale and his men to change ships and proceed finally on the *Taekeku-maru.* When they reached the island of Amami-O-Shima they landed at a small coastal settlement north of the principal town of Naze, going ashore from the fishing vessel by rowboat. Very typically, Lansdale's first interest was in the people there. He was appalled at the condition of the inhabitants. "The people were very badly . . . undernourished . . . eating grass and making soup out of grass. It was all they had." Where, he wondered, were their regular food supplies? He learned that although the Japanese government had shipped quantities of rice to the island, the official in charge, thirty-eight-year-old Kinoje Degushi, had taken them for his own use to sell at a profit on the black market. Lansdale promptly confiscated all food stocks he could locate and saw to it that they were distributed to the hungry islanders.[58]

An angry Major Lansdale then called for a public meeting in a little schoolhouse to discuss what should be done with Degushi. In Lansdale's mind, the primitive building was transformed into a courthouse and the meeting became a trial. Men and women crowded into the building to learn what their conquerors were going to do to them. They saw the once-powerful Degushi sitting forlornly at the desk where a teacher normally sat. Lansdale stood at the front of the room, leaning against a table. Through his interpreter, Matsue Yagawa, Lansdale spoke to the assembled crowd. He began by asking Degushi about his supplies — "who he was supposed to give them to and what his orders were with them and how come I'd found them all there and had to distribute them to the people. . . . he wasn't very good at doing his job."[59]

Yagawa sidled up to Lansdale and whispered that Degushi had inched open a drawer in the desk at which he sat. "He's got a revolver in there," Yagawa said, "and he's looking at it and . . . trying . . . to get it." Lansdale, who wore an Army .45-caliber automatic pistol in an armpit holster, replied without hesitation. "Tell him I know he's got a gun in there and I'm waiting for him to get it," he told Yagawa. "Tell him I want him to . . . take a shot at me so I can kill him right in front of the people." T/5 David Greene, the photographer, heard this exchange and nervously asked Lansdale, "Sir, do you think I better go back and make sure our rowboat is safe?" "Yeah, go back and take care of it," Lansdale replied. Concern now showed on the face of James Clark, the CIC man. "I think I better help him," Clark added. Lansdale agreed, adding, "Make sure we got a way to get out of here." The two men hurriedly departed while Yagawa spoke Lansdale's warning to Degushi.

When the official heard Lansdale's speech, he jumped up from the desk. "I don't have a gun. I don't have a gun," he shouted. Lansdale arrested him on the spot. Unfortunately the nearest jail was to the south along the coast in a sheltered harbor at the town of Naze. "You'll have to come . . . with us on the fishing boat and we'll go to Naze and I'll put you in jail there," Lansdale told the frightened official. "I'll have to file charges with the Japanese government." Degushi walked out of the schoolhouse guarded by Lansdale and his interpreter. "How fast are you on the draw?" Yagawa asked the major. He was extremely disconcerted by Lansdale's reply. "I don't know," Lansdale said. "I've never tried one of these shoulder holsters before." He reached to draw his weapon but the holster clung to the gun so tightly he was unable to pull it free. "I couldn't tug it loose," Lansdale later recalled. "I couldn't get the goddamned .45 out." "Oh, Jeez," Yagawa moaned. "I thought you were lightning fast. . . . You'd have been creamed on the spot."[60]

One result of the episode may have been that Lansdale began to take marksmanship more seriously. A pistol record card among his papers dating from about that time shows that his scores on the target range improved drastically from those he made during his ROTC days. At "slow fire," he scored 84 percent; at "rapid fire" an acceptable 63 percent; and at "quick fire," he achieved an amazing 93.3 percent.[61]

Modern communications no longer existed in that part of the Ryukyus because of the war's devastation. The civilian population had no telephones, no telegraph system, no radios. Although the *Taekeku-maru* was slow, Lansdale recalled, it still moved faster than local boats on its way to Naze. Thus when they slipped past other fishing boats, Lansdale was surprised to see fishermen waving and yelling at them. T/4 Yagawa translated their comments for the major. "They were shouting, 'Thank you for arresting him,' " Yagawa said. "It was a very popular thing to do." How, Lansdale wondered, did they even know about it, given the sorry state of communications?[62]

After he put Degushi in jail at Naze, local people came to Lansdale to show their appreciation for his help. Many brought gifts, and the mayor presented him with a scroll. The local geisha whorehouse girl — "[only] one bad girl for all those islands out there," Lansdale said — gave Lansdale a nicely folded silk handkerchief. When he opened it he found it was illustrated "with dirty pictures," an advertisement of her prowess and profession. "We don't do this for gifts," Lansdale told those who had come to him, "and I can't really accept them." But he kept the handkerchief.[63] He had no time to enjoy the gratefulness of the Ryukyu people because he needed to return to Manila. He did allow his sense of humor to surface on the return trip. Stopping at one tiny island in the northern Ryukyus, Lansdale gathered some children around him and taught them — knowing that other Americans would soon be arriving — that the proper way to greet GIs was to shout at them: "My papa Major Lansdale!"[64]

Shortly after his return to Manila Lansdale turned in a request for home leave. It was granted and he departed for San Francisco on 16 July, not to report back for duty at AFWESPAC until 23 October 1946.[65] Upon his return he would begin the most successful work of his career.

3

BIRTH OF A LEGEND

MAJOR EDWARD LANSDALE arrived back in the United States pleased
to be beginning a long leave that would last through the summer and
early fall of 1946. The prospect of spending a lengthy period with his
family was a joy. Arriving at his home in Larkspur he found a smiling
Helen and two wildly happy boys who were overjoyed that their daddy
was with them again. Peter, the younger son, remembered that his father
always wanted to make up for time spent away. "When he was home,
my dad made every effort to be a father in every sense," Peter said,
"from playing with us to taking us camping. Sometimes it was almost
like, damn it, we are going to have fun whether you like it or not."[1]

Time was always so short that every moment had to be used to the
fullest. Peter recalled that his father liked to cook. "[M]y father will
do it in excess. He will make chili and it will be there for two months.
It is always like [he is] trying to feed an army." On one camping trip,
Peter remembered, "It was really a nice time, just the three of us. Mom
stayed home. He made enough rice pudding for the week (which my
brother and I couldn't stand to begin with). So all we did was eat rice
pudding!" Those times, Peter said, were "nice bonding occasions."
Duties may have prevented Ed from spending much time with his family,
but his boys knew that when he did come home "he always had time
for us to get out and do things."[2]

Ed and Helen had long conversations about their future during those
weeks he spent at home in 1946. Lansdale had come to enjoy and appreciate
the Army during his years of service since 1943. At a time when grateful
millions had already been discharged and when those men still in the
service were clamoring for their own speedy release, Ed Lansdale found
that he had no real desire to lay away his uniform and return to the
world of advertising. Helen was not happy to hear him talk that way.
She wanted her husband home again. She despised enforced separations

of thousands of miles and did not like the thought of empty arms and ringing silences. Her days were punctuated not by a husband's voice calling as he arrived home from work but only by the shouts of two growing boys whose father was half a world away. Far better would it be, she urged, for Ed to come home to her. Why could he not work again in some advertising firm in San Francisco? Then they could live a normal life.

Helen's pleas and arguments were unconvincing. Ed remained firm. He would not leave the Army. Furthermore, he was going to apply for a transfer from the Army Reserve to the Regular Army. Ed's promise to bring her and their sons out to the Philippines as soon as that could be arranged did not mollify Helen. In many ways Ed's decision changed their relationship forever, and it was not a contented wife who bade him goodbye at the end of his leave.

Lansdale arrived back in Manila during the afternoon of 23 October 1946. After dropping his bags in his quarters on General Solano Street near Malacañang Palace, he decided to go to his G-2 headquarters office and sign in from leave. His headquarters was then located on the campus of the University of the Philippines in Quezon City, a Manila suburb. Unfortunately he could find no transportation to get there. Looking around the parking lot at his quarters, he spied a nearby jeep, its hood up and a uniformed man working on its innards. The man had not noticed Ed until Lansdale announced in a demanding tone, "I must go to G-2" (G-2 is the intelligence section of the armed forces).

First Lieutenant Charles T. R. Bohannan, who regularly answered to the nickname Bo, looked out from under the hood. A lanky, rail-thin man who stood well over six feet, Bo stared at the newcomer. "Oh?" he grunted and returned to his work. The stranger spoke again, imperiously insisting that he must go to G-2, and Bo repeated his response. "Oh?"

Lansdale looked around to see if there was anyone else who might help him. There was no one. So he tried a new approach with the "shade-tree mechanic." He politely informed the man at the jeep, "I have just arrived from the States and it is very, very important that I get to G-2 headquarters as soon as possible. They are expecting me. Do you have any suggestions as to how I can get there?" "Well, since you put it *that* way," Bo responded, "if you'll just wait a minute or two until I get this monstrosity fixed, I'll be glad to take you there myself." And that was the beginning of a long and close friendship between the two men.[3] They liked each other immediately. Interested in many of the same things, both unorthodox in their approach, they became fast — perhaps even inseparable — friends. Bo would work with Lansdale throughout the remainder of his days in the Philippines and then would follow him to Vietnam for additional years of service there.

In the weeks following his return, Lansdale fit back into his work as deputy assistant chief of staff for intelligence (G-2) at AFWESPAC and continued in the same capacity after 1 January 1947 when a reorganization changed the unit's name from AFWESPAC to the Philippines-Ryukyus Command (PHILRYCOM). One of Lansdale's first acts upon his return was to submit an application for a commission in the Regular Army, as he had told Helen he planned to do. His boss at G-2, Colonel George A. Chester, wrote a letter of support: "This officer is one of the most able I have ever met, combining idealism, ability and aggressiveness. An 'all around' type excelling at staff work or command. A definite asset for the Regular Army." The Department of the Army approved Lansdale's request and in orders dated 19 June 1947 gave him his coveted new appointment.[4]

Ed was gratified that he received almost immediate approval for another request he submitted that allowed Helen, Ted, and Peter to join him early in the fall. They remained with him in the Philippines until 13 December 1948. Ed and Helen enrolled their sons in the American School operated by the U.S. government on behalf of the Departments of State and Defense for American dependents in the Philippines. For a time the Lansdale family stayed in a Quonset hut at Military Plaza, a U.S. Army compound where several other families of AFWESPAC/PHILRYCOM staff officers also lived, all protected by barbed wire and an MP. Later they moved into a house in reasonable condition in one of the embassy compounds located between Pilar and A. Mbini off Dewey (later renamed Roxas) Boulevard along Manila's seafront. It also had a protective fence.[5]

Helen was horrified by what she saw when she arrived in the Philippines. Manila lay in near total destruction; only the Polish capital city of Warsaw had suffered more damage during World War II. Nearly one hundred thousand Filipinos died in the crossfire between Japanese and American forces. Street fighting in the last days of the conflict had reduced this "pearl of the Orient" to rubble. William Manchester has written, "Seventy percent of the utilities, 75 percent of the factories, 80 percent of the southern residential district, and 100 percent of the business district were razed." Streets were impassable or had disappeared entirely under heaps of masonry. Most buildings lay in collapsed heaps; those that still stood were gutted. Squatters nested wherever they could find shelter among the ruins. Frantic for housing, people were trying to restore buildings that Americans would consider unsafe to tear down. Hungry people and starving dogs roamed the streets. Water mains were broken and the only available electricity was supplied by a ship anchored offshore. It was not a place where Helen wanted to live or raise her boys. The destruction, the heat, and the dirt were all part of a tremendous culture shock created by this ravaged and very different environment. From the first days after her arrival she yearned to return home to the safety and comfort of California.[6]

Home life for Ed and Helen was often strained. Even their friends noticed. Bo Bohannan's wife, Dorothy, quit her job as a junior high school science teacher in Georgetown, Virginia, and joined her husband, traveling across the Pacific aboard the SS *General Hodges*. She arrived in August 1947 in the midst of a typhoon. While settling in, she and Bo received a dinner invitation to the Lansdales'. As they left home for that evening Bo told Dorothy, "If you should ever act like [Helen], it is divorce for us." Dorothy thought Helen was striking: "a platinum blonde with a blue hair rinse and with beautiful, brilliant blue eyes. She was very straight . . . and slender."

During the meal Dorothy exclaimed that the food was "delicious," but Helen made it clear that it was not she but Ed who had cooked it. Other topics were introduced but died quickly. Ed, who seemed so full of fun away from home, was strangely subdued in Helen's presence. Conversation lagged and the evening was long. Dorothy remembered that in the months thereafter "Helen didn't make too many friends" save for a few wives of Filipino officers. "They were great at gossiping," Dorothy said. "Filipinos call it *tsismis*. . . . She was not a happy woman."[7]

Under strain with his wife, Ed spent much time with his sons during off-duty hours. Like his own father, Lansdale was not much given to small talk with them. In response to a question one day he sat Ted and Peter down and explained to them about life. They asked more questions, which he answered, and then one of the boys asked how babies were made. Ed explained conception in some detail. The two children sat silently looking at him with startled faces. Finally, one of them said with complete disbelief, "Did you do that to Mother?"[8]

If things were less than perfect at home, Lansdale's career was blossoming. He found a home in the Philippine archipelago that warmed the cockles of his heart. "Filipinos and I fell in love with each other," he said. "There was . . . tremendous brotherly love on both parts. It was an ideal situation."[9] From the first days of his assignment to AFWESPAC's G-2 shop Lansdale made a persistent effort to learn as much as he could about the people, their land, history, culture, and customs.

The Philippines was a troubled land, its physical plant in ruins, its economy destroyed. Those who had fought the Japanese clamored for reward and place while those who had collaborated sought to rationalize their actions. As early as April 1945, General Douglas MacArthur began to interfere in local politics to manipulate his friend Manuel Roxas — for whose inauguration Lansdale had planned security during the previous

July — into the presidency of the newly freed nation. Roxas' background was mixed. He had served as minister without portfolio and chairman of the Economic Planning Board of the Japanese puppet government in Manila following the capture of the islands early in World War II. Other individuals with similar records of collaboration were detained at war's end in the name of military security, but not Roxas. While his less fortunate colleagues were imprisoned at Iwahig Penal Colony, Mac-Arthur's Office of War Information announced that the general's old friend had been "liberated." MacArthur restored Roxas' rank as a one-star general and assigned him to work in the G-2 section of United States Armed Forces Far East (USAFFE).[10]

Roxas had more than the support of MacArthur, although that was crucial. He also controlled extensive landholdings in central Luzon through his wife's family. He could count on support for political financing from friends and sympathizers both in business and among landed interests in any campaign he might mount against the serving president, Sergio Osmeña. Roxas additionally had support from the newly appointed U.S. high commissioner for the Philippines, Paul V. McNutt, who made little effort to hide his dislike of the Osmeña government. It was McNutt who lobbied the U.S. Congress in 1946 to pass the Bell Trade Relations Act and the Tydings Rehabilitation Act, signed by President Harry Truman in April despite Osmeña's protest that they were a "curtailment of Philippine sovereignty and a virtual nullification of Philippine independence."[11]

The Bell Act made the Philippines dependent on a few agricultural export crops tied to the U.S. market and allowed American businesses to operate Filipino public utilities and to dispose, exploit, develop, and utilize "all agricultural, timber and mineral lands of the public domain, waters, minerals, coals, petroleum and other mineral oils, all forces and sources of potential energy, and other natural resources of the Philippines." It also decreed that "the value of Philippine currency in relation to the United States dollar shall not be changed, the convertibility of pesos into dollars shall not be suspended, and no restrictions shall be imposed on the transfer of funds from the Philippines to the United States, except by agreement with the President of the United States."[12] The act made certain that the new nation would remain an economic colony of the United States.

The Tydings Rehabilitation Act provided for $620 million in war damages to be paid to the stricken Philippines. There were again, however, strings attached: "no amount in excess of $500 would be given unless and until an agreement had been reached by the Presidents of the Philippines and the United States regarding trade relations between the two countries." Payment of war damages was thus premised on Filipino approval of the Bell Trade Relations Act with its gift of extraordinary rights to American businessmen. Two Filipino historians likened the effect of the laws to that of "a man who, having been aided by a friend who lost everything in defense of the former, now brashly demanded that he be given the right to live with his friend's wife in exchange for his financial help."[13]

Osmeña had become vice president on the Manuel Quezon ticket in 1935. During the years of Japanese occupation, Osmeña remained part of the government-in-exile located in Washington, D.C. Upon Quezon's death in August 1944, Osmeña became president, returning to his homeland even before the fighting ended there. Before the American liberation of Luzon in 1944, Osmeña governed from a temporary capital at Tacloban on the island of Leyte. When Manila was freed, Osmeña moved there, found it destroyed, and tried ineffectually to remedy the chaos into which his country had fallen. His protests against the Bell Act and the Tydings Rehabilitation Act soured the Truman government on him. One writer commented that "Osmeña's great dilemma was that he could neither compete with Quezon, a dead hero mourned by the people, nor with MacArthur, a living symbol already revered as a demigod."[14]

Urged on by Americans at the embassy and his own supporters, Roxas chose to run for the presidency. He knew he could count on favorable publicity for he had a controlling interest in three major newspapers: the *Daily News, Balita,* and *Light.* He actively courted other prominent dailies as the 1946 campaign heated up, asking editors and reporters who came to him for interviews how they were getting along financially and generously offering his assistance in procuring newsprint and sometimes making cash loans to them.[15]

Roxas' forces in the Philippine Congress were able — through fierce lobbying — to obtain the three-fourths majority vote necessary to approve the Bell Trade Act and to pass the Parity Amendment to the Constitution, which gave American businessmen economic rights equal to or better than those enjoyed by Filipino citizens.[16]

Perhaps the result was foregone. With Elpidio Quirino as his vice presidential candidate, Roxas easily won over Osmeña in the 1946 election. Roxas then immediately left on a twelve-day mission with McNutt to the United States looking for loans and other forms of war relief. Roxas thus became a captive president of a new and weak nation ravaged by war. He owed his freedom and exoneration to MacArthur and his position as president to McNutt and American support. The extent of his subservience can be seen in his Independence Day speech — which Lansdale, far back in the crowd, listened to — when he assented that the safest course for the Philippines was to follow "in the glistening wake of America whose sure advance with mighty prow breaks for smaller craft the waves of fear.''[17] Perhaps Roxas felt he had no alternative.

In March 1947 Roxas signed the Military Bases Agreement, which provided a safe future for such American bases as Clark Field and Subic Naval Station. He also agreed to a Military Assistance Pact with the United States to create a Joint United States Military Advisory Group (JUSMAG) capable of Americanizing the infant Filipino armed forces, teaching them modern strategic and tactical concepts and supplying them with equipment.[18] America got these treaties at bargain basement prices.

Roxas inherited a government faced with a nationwide revolt concentrated on the central Luzon plain. As early as the 1930s, peasants who labored there as sharecroppers on vast haciendas owned by wealthy landlords became easy targets for communist and socialist organizational activities. Those workers abandoned their international ideologies in favor of armed resistance when Japan invaded their homeland. Unlike many other Southeast Asians, Filipinos offered strong resistance to the warriors of Nippon. After the fall of Bataan and Corregidor in April 1942, some of those who had fought the Japanese organized themselves into guerrilla bands to continue the fight.

One group in central Luzon called itself the People's Anti-Japanese Army, or, in the Filipino Tagalog language, Hukbo ng Bayan Laban Sa Hapon, the acronym for which is Hukbalahap or, in shortened form, Huk. The several Filipino guerrilla bands organized by various groups throughout the archipelago killed many Japanese soldiers and tied up others who had been forced into chasing them through the swamps and forests of the Philippines. The Huks fought with amateur intensity, despised wealthy fellow countrymen who collaborated with their enemies, and assassinated many collaborationists. By war's end the Huks had seized most of central Luzon's large estates and established a regional government there strong enough to collect taxes and administer its own laws.

Leaders of the returning American Army in 1944 became suspicious of the Huks because of their communist leadership, and this attitude was shared by Osmeña's government-in-exile on its return. General Douglas MacArthur, however, told his staff that

> Tarlac marks the border between the sugar economy and the rice country [in Luzon]. North of there the people grow rice, and most of them own small areas of land. Did you notice how many schools there are up there, how the people dressed, looked happy, kind of prosperous? Do you see that hangdog look they have here, resentful, poorly dressed? They don't even look clean. That country north of Tarlac is a good strong country of democracy, small landowners, opportunity for education and what goes

with it. Down here most of this land is owned in Madrid or Chicago or some other distant place. . . . This is really absentee ownership. No pride, few schools — little participation in government. This is where they become utterly hopeless, and organizations like the Hukbalahaps are born and get their strength. They tell me the Huks are socialistic, that they are revolutionary . . . . If I worked in those sugar fields I'd probably be a Huk myself.[19]

Lansdale was not as sympathetic as MacArthur. In a report that he wrote in 1946 while serving as G-2 of AFWESPAC, Lansdale described Hukbalahap leaders as "Communist-inspired" and "true disciples of Karl Marx." They believed, he wrote,

in revolution instead of evolution. They have made their boast that once their membership reaches 500,000 their revolution will start. Meanwhile, in the provinces of Pampanga, Nueva Ecija, Tarlac, Bulacan, and Pangasinan, they are establishing . . . a reign of terror. So ironclad is their grip and so feared is their power that the peasants dare not oppose them in many localities.[20]

At war's end tension grew between the Huks and the restored government of the Philippines over the issue of surrendering weapons. The Huks had on hand about 500,000 rifles and stocks of ammunition, left over from old American Army supplies or seized from Japanese occupation troops. All of it was hard-won. They were reluctant to turn their weapons over to a government they believed to be corrupt and oligarchic. The Huks participated in the April 1946 election won by Manuel Roxas. Luis Taruc, a Huk leader known to his followers as El Supremo, even won a seat in Congress but was arbitrarily prevented from participating.

President Roxas announced immediately after independence that his policy toward the Huks would be one of a "mailed fist." At that point the Huks retreated to the jungle again and began a long rebellion that would not be quelled until 1954. For a time in 1950 they came reasonably close to a victory over government forces arrayed against them. This success came, in part, because of low morale among government soldiers and their indiscriminate retaliations against villagers suspected of sympathy toward the Huk movement.[21]

Lansdale wanted to see firsthand why Huks so easily acquired such steadfast loyalty from the common man — Juan de la Cruz — in the backcountry barrios of the Philippines. He could easily have stayed in his office and read reports about the dissidents written by others. He chose not to do so. While serving as G-2, he occasionally sent some of his own men to accompany Philippine army units as they conducted operations against the rebels.

Lansdale then, in 1945, made a decision that would influence his thinking for the remaining years of his career. Knowing that his men would give him accurate reports of official plans and actions, Lansdale decided he needed an additional dimension of knowledge. He would study the conflict from the inside, from the rebel standpoint. When he found later that his observations gave him an acute level of information that others did not possess, he simply incorporated this modus operandi into his pattern of analysis and continued to regard it as an essential part of his process for the next twenty and more years.

Privy to operations plans of the Philippine Army, Lansdale studied his maps, pinpointing on them the locations where government forces planned to lay traps for the Huks. He then examined his maps to determine the most likely paths Huk bands might take as they fled for safety when confronted by superior numbers of Filipino soldiers. "I would figure out the high ground they were heading for up in the mountains," Lansdale said, "and [then] just camp out on their trail and talk to them [when they appeared]." Although it took a great amount of courage for him to track Huks in such a way, Lansdale felt it was the best approach to learning more about them. "I have always felt that, if you are going to report on something," he insisted, "don't take the word of other people. Go out and eyeball it and see and talk to people. You get a far different feeling for the problem and the situation."[22]

Lansdale always insisted that his actions were not so dangerous as they might seem. "I was [just] one person sitting there and they were an armed group. [I] would smile and give them something else to think of fast. I would ask them if they needed cigarettes or some food or did anybody want a drink? They would come up [to me] and say, 'Yeah, I'd like a cigarette' instead of shooting me. You don't kill a guy laughing, being nice to you."[23]

Lansdale remembered that he got "very close" to some of those Huks. "I'd talked to their leaders, gone out and watched their troops operate. I'd been out at night on the trail." Such knowledge ultimately paid off. "It set me apart in the Philippines whether I liked it or not. It gave me a great deal of say [among a lot of people]."[24] Before many months passed Ed met a woman who gave him even more help in getting to know the barrio people.

A Filipino friend of Lansdale's, Johnny Orendain, served as press secretary for President Roxas. One evening he stopped by Lansdale's quarters, parked his jeep outside, and knocked on the door. When Ed came to greet his friend, Johnny introduced him to a tiny, pretty Filipina, a war widow, sitting in the jeep. Her name was Patrocinio Yapcinco Kelly, and Ed learned that Pat worked as a correspondent for a local newspaper, the *Advocate,* which had been publishing only since the end of the war.[25]

Over the next several weeks they encountered one another on several occasions. Their work sometimes brought them together, for Ed spent much time with the Manila press corps, and they saw one another at occasional parties. Ed learned that Pat was of Chinese ancestry, as were many Filipinos. Born in 1915 in the Visayan Islands where her father was employed as a cadastral surveyor,[26] she was from an upper-middle-class Pompanga family that later moved to Tarlac, a province north of Manila. When she was twenty-six and working as a reporter, Pat married red-haired James Kelly, of Filipino-Irish ancestry, just before the outbreak of the war in 1941. Following the Japanese invasion and occupation of the islands, Kelly became ill. No medicine or food was available and he died. James and Pat had been married less than a year. Widowed, with a four-month-old baby daughter named Patricia, Pat went back to live in her father's house, as was the custom in the Philippines. At war's end she resumed her work as a political reporter for the *Advocate* and as correspondent for U.S. newspapers. She also worked occasionally captioning photos for *Time* and *Life* magazines.[27]

The increasing threat from the Huk rebellion gave Pat added opportunities as a reporter, one denied to many of her fellows. "I used to cover Taruc the Huk," she said. "I had an entry to him that others didn't. *I knew him.* Taruc was in the same high school that I attended [and] married Ena Cura, a friend of mine from Tarlac." They had been in different grades — Pat was younger — and Taruc had not noticed her in any particular way. "I was one of the young teenaged girls," Pat said, "more interested in high school social doings. He was more serious." Nevertheless, Taruc "carried on a war correspondence with me" that was helpful to her newspaper work. In later years she protested, "I wasn't that interested [in the Huk uprising]. It was just another revolution. I was too young to be interested. . . . I wasn't politically minded [as a girl]."[28]

Ed became captivated by the vivacious and flirtatious young woman. "She was full of fun," he recalled with a smile, "so I think Johnny [Orendain, who had introduced them] was my best friend in the Philippines by far."[29]

Only a little to the north of Manila were areas so wild that going into them was like stepping into the past. There were high mountains something like those Ed remembered from California. Climate zones ranged from temperate to tropical and encompassed a variety of trees from palmetto and lush palms to pines and hardwoods. At higher elevations in Mountain Province it sometimes became quite cold, and one could encounter frost early in the mornings. Lansdale wanted to see that country and meet its peoples.

He particularly wanted to meet the Negritos, small tribal people who lived in the mountains north of Clark Air Force Base and who still lived in the Stone Age. Pat Kelly learned of his interest and told him, "I'll show you ways of getting back up in there."[30] She did, and Lansdale got his opportunity. As a town girl from the provinces Pat knew many of the back trails in the mountains, and she invited Ed to explore them with her. On one trip she showed him an isolated spot and said, "This is where some Americans hid after Bataan until they were finally caught and executed by the Japanese."[31] Ed valued her as a guide. "She showed me . . . things in the Zambales Mountains that I would never have known otherwise," he acknowledged. One site she pointed out to him was a macabre one. Shortly after the Lingayen landing in 1945, American artillery shelled a Japanese armored column back in the hills. "Their skeletons were [still] sitting there," Ed recalled. He and Pat made camp for the night nearby. "[A] bobcat came up in the moonlight from these [wrecked] tank [hulls] and sat on the hood of my jeep looking down where I was sleeping . . . . To me he looked like a giant . . . . It was spooky enough with these Japanese dead around."[32]

On one trip with Pat into Negrito country Ed met a tribal leader who lived just beyond the bombing range near Clark AFB. They walked into his campsite toward evening and Ed cooked dinner for them on an old gasoline stove. The only English the Negrito leader knew was "OK," and Ed's few words of Tagalog didn't help, for the Negrito didn't speak that language. "So we had a time in trying to talk," Lansdale said. They finally made progress by drawing pictures in the sand and by acting out parts as if they were playing charades:

I finally gathered that Americans had done something to his daughter . . . to [her] belly. . . . Some GI must have really been hungry for a girl . . . . But after three or four hours of talk he started shaking his head, his daughter wasn't pregnant. . . . Americans had set up 155 artillery and had been killing this armored column that was going up into the Zambales range. . . . [H]is daughter had been out getting vegetables and a 155 [shell] went right through her belly and she had been killed.[33]

Lansdale was proud of this ability to communicate without words and relied on it throughout his career. At the same time he felt defensive about his inability to learn other languages and so felt it necessary — on a fairly regular basis — to defend his ability to speak without words. About this occasion, Ed bragged that his "conversing" with the Negritos "astounded Pat because she couldn't do so [but] I sat with their leader

and had a long discussion . . . . [Pat] was amazed that I could understand, come away as friends at the end of the thing. . . . I've learned
you can use sign language for a great deal. The look in your eyes and
your shoulders and your hands tell a lot when you're really concentrating.
People can tell whether you are interested or not, just by your attitude
and the attention you pay."[34] On another occasion Ed insisted that he
had a "very bad ear" and a "very bad tongue" for languages. "I've
had to depend a great deal on a look of empathy, a physical look, and
an ability to try to communicate without words . . . . [P]eople respond
. . . to an interest in their well-being even if you can't speak their
way." He may have been correct, but his approach certainly wasted a
lot of time: a translator could have told him what the tribal leader was
saying in a minute or two. Lansdale didn't accept such criticism. His
response was that at times he used "interpreters who were almost bilin-
gual . . . and yet their empathy was flat. . . . [T]heir manner caused
people to freeze up."[35]

As Lansdale became more interested in the Huk rebellion he told Pat
that he would very much like to have the opportunity to talk with Taruc.
Her reaction startled him. "OK," she said. "You come with me. I'll
show you." They took Ed's jeep and traveled to Candaba, which was
then about a three-hour trip along country roads. Despite Pat's best efforts,
they were unsuccessful either that day or later in locating or talking
with Taruc. Ed never did get to meet and talk with El Supremo, although
on one attempt he came very close.[36]

Lansdale learned a lot about Pat Kelly on such trips. Many years
later he confessed that he believed she herself was one of the Huk rebels.
"Now one of the things I have never told anybody," he said, "Pat
showed me a lot of the backcountry the Huks went through and she
doesn't know that I knew she was . . . helping them out from time to
time, just being fellow townsmates, sympathetic towards them as individuals and carrying messages."[37] Such suspicions did little to blunt his
growing feelings for her.

Not all of Ed's trips were with Pat. After she introduced him to the
backcountry, he struck off alone or in company with other men. He
came to know some Filipino Army people who worked in intelligence
in the provinces of Zambales and Tarlac, including a young member of
the Philippine Constabulary, Napoleon Valeriano. Val was a frustrated
man who wanted reassignment from an office desk to the field. He was,
he told Lansdale, bored to tears. He wanted to get up close to the Huks
and fight them in an effective way. Lansdale knew Val's commanding
general and persuaded him to let the young officer form a fighting group;
it was known as the Nenita Unit, a company-sized band of highly dedicated

volunteers. "He picked Mount Arayat for his headquarters, in Pompanga, and put a camp up there and lived there with his men and fought the Huks," Lansdale recalled.[38]

One day late in 1946, Lansdale drove out from Manila for one of his periodic visits to Valeriano's camp. He didn't stay long for he had another destination that day. He still hoped for a chance to meet with Taruc and knew that El Supremo's sister lived in a little town just a few miles down the road from the Nenita Unit's headquarters. Lansdale had heard rumors that she was pregnant and was losing her teeth from a lack of calcium in her diet. On his way out of Manila he stopped at an Army hospital and got a supply of calcium tablets, hoping she would welcome the gift and agree to introduce him to her brother. As he drove into her town he saw Constabulary troops patrolling the streets while others searched houses.

Lansdale located the house of Taruc's sister. It was dark inside, the front door ajar. He stopped outside momentarily to pull off his shoes. "Filipina housewives are like Japanese women," he said. "They want you to take your shoes off so you won't get their floors muddy." Sticking his head in through the open door, he called out, "Anybody home?" Lansdale realized he had made a bad mistake when a rifle snout poked at his head and a shadowy man motioned him inside. Other guns jabbed at him. Taruc's bodyguard was in the house. One of the men spoke to Lansdale: "You're a spy!"

The only thing Lansdale could think to say was "Don't shoot. Look at the floor. You'll get it bloody and she'll have to clean it up! If you're going to shoot me, do it outside." The armed men relented momentarily, remembering their own mothers' dire warnings about keeping floors clean. "I didn't say it to be a smart aleck," Lansdale told them. "I was well brought up, too." The men began to interrogate him.

Lansdale was convinced that his very life depended on his next words. He had to say something to convince his captors that he would be more valuable alive than dead. "Let me explain something to you," he said to them. "I'm with G-2 of the U.S. Army. Let me tell you what that is. At your own headquarters you write news releases and get couriers to take them into the Manila papers to be printed in the press. They risk their lives going on bus rides through military lines and checkpoints to get your version of things printed . . . . Your very good stories get picked up by the Associated Press or United Press, translated, and sent on to the U.S. If they are very good the president of the U.S. reads them and you get your story before him in that way."

Lansdale stopped to draw breath. "What I do, I write reports on what people here tell me and send them on to the Pentagon. If the stories are good or unusual they get before the president much faster than news stories do.'' The men listened solemnly to his story and then lowered their rifle muzzles. Lansdale hoped they had understood his explanation. He took out a pad of paper and pencil. "What do you want me to tell the president of the United States?" he asked. So they began talking, explaining their policies and why they supported the rebellion. Lansdale took it all down on his pad. When they finished he told them he had come hoping to see Taruc's sister.

Lansdale found the woman in the back bedroom, quite visibly pregnant and not looking well. He introduced himself and gave her the calcium tablets. It was obvious that Taruc had left through a back window of the house, perhaps even while his men had kept Lansdale occupied in the front room. Lansdale always wondered why the Constabulary troops had not searched that house. "Even I, a dumb American, knew that would be the place he'd head for." All his life he remained wistful that he was unsuccessful in meeting Taruc. "I would really have liked to know the guy — what worried him, what made him happy — to give me some clues [as] to what I did right and what I did wrong. What I thought was [a] brilliant [action] might have been a stupid mistake. [To meet him] would have been a good education."[39]

Lansdale's trips out of Manila were only infrequent. He was too busy learning the corridors of power in the capital city. One young man with whom he became fast friends was Manuel Manahan, a journalist who in later years would serve in the Philippine Senate and run as a candidate for president. Manahan recalled that "Ed was hooking up with everybody. . . . He mixed with all elements [of the population] he possibly could. . . . He was very well liked, accepted by all. . . . I think Ed foresaw that he came in a period when there was still a great wealth of good feeling between Americans and Filipinos. We had learned democracy the right way. We believed in your heroes because our general education was framed in the American system. I knew more about how Washington chopped the cherry tree than about Emilio Aguinaldo or Rizal or the story about the moth and the lamp. And from Ed I learned about Tom Paine. He made great use of this. He was very smart in understanding this."[40]

Others also talked about how Lansdale fit himself within the Filipino culture. Medardo "Med" Justiniano met Lansdale while serving as a member of the Filipino military police command under AFWESPAC. The two became good friends. Lansdale appealed to Justiniano because of the way he acted toward others. "He would *always* say things in such a nice, disarming and charming way," Med recalled. "He never ordered but only asked, 'What do you think about doing it this way?'

or 'Don't you think this is how we should treat the problem?' It was so very hard to deny him, to discuss with him in an ugly way." But it was also more than that. Med respected Lansdale not only as a man but as a military officer. "All that he would [have] need[ed] to do would be to sit . . . in a beautiful office, read reports, perhaps place them on the map and then evaluate them and make some report. Lansdale was different. He placed more emphasis on . . . seeing actually what is on the ground, what the people think on the ground, what is the situation on the ground, which is not revealed in the technocratic maps that adorn an office of the military establishment."[41]

Another friend was Frank Zaldarriaga. Although he later became a newspaper publisher, at the end of the war he served with the American Army, attached to the Psychological Warfare Bureau within the Office of War Information. "My office was in the Escolta," Zaldarriaga said, "and Ed's was almost in front of mine on the other side of the hall. We used to have cup coffee. We became very good friends. . . . [H]e used to travel [to] the real backbone of the country . . . the remote barrios. . . . [H]e used to carry a harmonica in his pocket. . . . He could make a friend of everybody except Satan, I think. . . . He was a very good listener. He had an analytical mind and he could foresee things. . . . He knew this country actually better than a lot of Filipinos. This man was a legend. Wherever I went he was known." On his own travels people would sometimes ask Zaldarriaga, "Do you know Lansdale?" He often muttered in response, "This son of his mother got ahead of me again!"[42]

A longtime associate, José Banzon, described Lansdale as "very soft-spoken with lots of initiative, new ideas."[43] Edmundo Navarro, who had come over with Lansdale aboard the USS *Uruguay*, knew Lansdale was a friendly, "very unassuming" man; he seemed in some ways to be a "loner" who worked better when no one stood over him telling him what to do or how to do it. Navarro believed that Lansdale had a real knack for picking people to work with him. "[T]hey became very, very loyal to him and would die for him. He has been retired for several years and . . . I [still] look upon him as my patron, *patron,* and of course my loyalty to him will never diminish."[44]

Peter C. Richards, an expatriate Englishman and Reuters correspondent, had been imprisoned by the Japanese throughout the war. Released from internment he came to know Lansdale. "He was young, a nice chap, friendly, life of the party," Richards said. "That is what he was paid for. He made friends with everybody. But the secret of his success is that he was a man who could disappear. He wasn't in the room, but he was. You get ten people in a room and he could make himself completely disappear. Other people would be talking and he would be on one side [of them but] you didn't see him. Amongst Filipinos, he was the shape, size, and coloring that needn't be there.'' Richards had put his finger on a key point. In the aftermath of war and the birth of their nation, many Filipinos felt they had been influenced by America long enough. They were prickly with pride, resenting and resisting American advisers and suggestions. In those difficult circumstances, Lansdale could practice his craft without giving offense. He was "invisible."[45]

Lansdale also became acquainted with Americans working in the Philippines. One friend was Spence Davis, chief of the Associated Press bureau there from 1946 until early 1950. "Ed and I became acquainted first after a story I had written regarding the way surplus Army supplies were being spirited out of U.S. Army dumps there. . . . [H]e invited me to go up to central Luzon where the campaign was being conducted against the Hukbalahaps. We went, the two of us. I made several trips with him. He was interested in the reaction of the people in the countryside. . . . Ed thought going to the grass roots helped him. He had . . . a good touch with people."[46]

As a result of his efforts, Lansdale learned a lesson he always remembered. "We have got to be very careful in how we handle the Filipino people. They are very sensitive with their pride [but] they share the same ethics we do, the same principles and dreams, ideals, including democracy."[47]

Lansdale's intimate knowledge of the Filipino people brought him an unexpected visitor. In early June 1947, Major General Paul J. Mueller flew in from Tokyo. Deputy commander at General Headquarters for the Far East Command (FECOM), Mueller served as General MacArthur's chief of staff. He had come to Manila at the behest of MacArthur, who was troubled by news from the Philippines. MacArthur had issued standing orders that all of the leading Manila daily newspapers were to be flown to him at his Tokyo headquarters. For some time the autocratic old general had been concerned about recurring anti-American stories featured on front pages and in editorial columns. There was plenty of justification for such stories in the press. All too many GIs were misbehaving, drinking, whoring, fighting, and generally making nuisances of themselves during off-duty hours. Log books of civilian police were filled with entries reflecting arrests of GIs from the night before.

MacArthur saw those stories, carefully marked them, and then spoke with Mueller. It was a major concern for him, he said. He was very worried about PHILRYCOM's public information officer (PIO), a full colonel on the staff. He ordered Mueller to fly to Manila and find an officer who would be an effective PIO, who could change the attitude of the Philippine press — a man capable of getting Americans mentioned favorably on the front pages of Manila newspapers. A few days after his arrival, General Mueller walked into Major Lansdale's office. Without preliminaries he told Lansdale what was on his mind. "I have checked [with] the top [members] of the Philippine government, with newspapers, with top social people, with top businesspeople, and with Filipino friends of mine," he said. "The only American in this command they all know is you. Everybody from Malacañang Palace on down knows you. The only one they speak favorably [about] as someone they can talk to is you. None of them know the [present] PIO or his staff, not even the editors of the papers or the radio stations. They all know you as a friend, yet you're in intelligence work."

"General," Lansdale replied, "I like the people and get close to them. I'm keeping tabs on what's going on around here." The two men talked for a few more minutes. Then General Mueller left Lansdale's office and was soon on his way back to Tokyo.

"That's all he said to me," Lansdale claimed. Although flattered by the general's remarks, Lansdale was uncertain why he had dropped by to talk to him. He returned to his duties as PHILRYCOM's deputy G-2. A few days later he began getting calls from radio and newspaper staffers asking about press matters and he referred them all to the serving PIO. When such calls continued, he made an appointment to see the commanding general of PHILRYCOM, Major General George F. Moore. "I'm sort of concerned [about] getting these calls," Lansdale told General Moore. "They ought to go to the PIO."

"Didn't we tell you?" the general replied. "You are the PIO now because MacArthur wants it that way." Lansdale protested that since he was only a major his rank was too low to allow him to perform the PIO's duties properly. He knew there was no possibility he could function as PIO without real support from PHILRYCOM headquarters. "I can't do it," he insisted.

The general became angry and told Lansdale that if he were properly patriotic he would do as he had been told. Lansdale stood his ground. "I went into this Army for patriotic reasons and I'll leave for the same goddammed reasons. I'll quit. Resign the Army. It's up to you." The general was unused to having majors speak to him that way and settled back to listen.

Lansdale told him his conditions for accepting the job. "Some of the Gs [G-1, administration; G-2, intelligence; G-3, operations; G-4, quartermaster; G-5, civil affairs] are general officers, and if I have to deal with them to straighten [things] out I'm going to need some backing. If I'm talking to some general and get in an argument with him, or some of the subordinate commands [of PHILRYCOM] headed by generals, and say that certain things have to be changed, you'll have to back me. If I call you from some guy's telephone, I want you to tell him right then over the phone that you back me up.'' General Moore agreed, but even that was not enough for Lansdale. He went back to his office and wrote up a contract outlining the terms he had given the general and insisted that both the commanding general and his chief of staff sign it. "They told me they'd never done that before," Lansdale said with a smile.[48] He officially began his new job as PIO for PHILRYCOM on 14 June 1947 and remained in that position for a little more than a year, until 19 November 1948.[49]

"That arrangement," Lansdale claimed, "let me really operate. . . . It changed [the situation] almost overnight."[50] He set up a new PIO office in downtown Manila away from PHILRYCOM headquarters, close to the hub of business activity. Commensurate with his new responsibilities, Major Edward Lansdale received promotion to lieutenant colonel on 25 June 1947, only nine days after beginning his work as PIO.[51]

Lansdale was very effective in his new duties. Soon many Filipinos came to look upon his PIO office, rather than military headquarters or the embassy, as the heart of the American presence in their country. Those with information or questions called or stopped by. Lansdale always tried to respond quickly. Only a few days after beginning his work, he was able to change the minds of several editors and thus stop the rash of anti-American stories in the press. When the press did print such material they checked with Lansdale to ensure the accuracy of their reports. "Editors took material from me because I'd go after the truth real hard," Lansdale said. "We had a police beat. We'd check the blotters every morning for American misbehavior and follow up on any problems very quickly." Lansdale believed that as a result of that work, "I got very close to Philippine officials, journalists, businessmen, until I had thousands of friends there." Other Americans were impressed with what Lansdale was doing and both the newly created Air Force and the embassy sent officers to learn from Lansdale and to work out of his office.[52]

Lansdale met frequently for breakfast with a group of editors and writers at a nearby drugstore. There they would sit drinking coffee and talking. One day a waiter interrupted the conversation. There was a phone call for Colonel Lansdale; his general wanted to speak to him. To the amusement of his friends, Lansdale replied, "Tell him I'll call him back. I'm busy right now." The Filipinos at the table thought that was great fun and Lansdale was glad that his general was "a very decent guy."[53]

Once again, however, Lansdale was becoming restless. He thought seriously about leaving the Army, which had just given him a regular commission, to serve with the infant American Air Force. Like many others of that time it seemed to Lansdale that the Air Force was on the cutting edge of America's military; its doctrine about the new "air age" fascinated him. Lansdale believed the Air Force had forward-looking ideas, unbound to rigid traditionalism. Perhaps it was new enough to allow someone with "realistic, practical thinking" to have "a constructive influence."[54] Convinced that a move would be fruitful, Lansdale submitted the paperwork necessary to effect a transfer from the Army. The passage of the National Security Act on 15 September 1947 set up the United States Air Force (USAF) as a separate entity. Eleven days later, on 26 September, Edward Lansdale was transferred from the Army to the Air Force. Unfortunately, he did not take all his rank with him. Despite having already been promoted to temporary lieutenant colonel by the Army the previous June, Lansdale was given only the rank of major in the Air Force.[55]

Headquarters of 13th Air Force, located at Clark Air Force Base, ordered Lansdale to close up his duties in Manila and report immediately for duty. Lansdale responded that he could not do so and put the issue bluntly to the air staff at Clark. "General MacArthur put me in this PIO spot and ordered me to do something [about the situation] here and [he] hasn't released me. . . . so if you want to reassign me, tell General MacArthur. Go and argue with him." He would go to Clark or stay in Manila but the decision was up to MacArthur, not to 13th Air Force or to him. The Air Force decided to leave him where he was. Lansdale was amused and reveled in the unorthodoxy he could afford to maintain because of his peculiar situation. "Well, this is pretty heady stuff for a major," he thought. "I didn't really go into the Air Force until I came back to the U.S. in 1948 when I went to the Strategic Intelligence School at Lowry Air Force Base in Denver, Colorado."[56]

The political situation in the Philippines was not improving. In March 1948 President Roxas outlawed the Hukbalahaps and the largest peasant organization, the Pambansang Kaisahan ng mga Magbubukid (PKM). The following month, while giving a speech at Clark AFB, Roxas collapsed and died. Elpidio Quirino now assumed the presidency. At first he tried to reverse Roxas' policies toward the Huks by offering them a general amnesty, but unrest continued in central Luzon. The Joint U.S. Military Advisory Group (JUSMAG) in Manila, commanded by General Albert M. Jones, helped Quirino plan an all-out offensive against the rebels, but the Huks only slipped away to hidden places of safety and waited, biding their time. Nor were the Huks Quirino's only problem; the economy of his nation was still chaotic, verging on bankruptcy. Unemployment soared while corruption extended through all levels of society.[57] Lansdale spent many hours following the course of the nation as it staggered from crisis to crisis.

Despite accomplishments in his career, life at home for Ed and Helen continued to be strained. In later years, recalling those days, Ed could say, "She was a good wife to put up with me." At the time life was more difficult. When Helen arrived in the Philippines, Ed explained the reasons for his erratic schedule, which took him all over the archipelago and out at night, leaving him little of the leisure other peacetime officers could spend with their families. He wasn't sure she ever believed him. *Tsismis,* gossip, was a deadly enemy. "I don't think she ever believed there were people in the world . . . like the Huks," Lansdale said. "Yet when she was over there in the Philippines, the army would escort us from parties with armor, light tanks, scout cars, and heavy weapons."

In one adventure into the backcountry with Spence Davis, Lansdale came home with bullet holes in his old staff car and tried to tell Helen what had happened. She was torn by such stories. She didn't like to hear her husband talk about anything other than his regular work. It was easier for her on those days when he was at his office from eight to five. He had a desk job, so why go on adventures if they weren't part of his duties? They put him in such danger. Couldn't he think of his wife and boys? Sometimes she asked him not to put himself at risk again. At other times she preferred to act as if his tales were simply "war stories" not to be believed. "She'd think I was making up some story . . . . So I stopped talking about it."[58]

Those tensions and misunderstandings put a continuing strain on the marriage. Neither Helen nor Ed had felt particularly close to each other for some time. Then, in late fall 1948, Ed received orders returning him to America — to the zone of the interior, as it is called in the military. Ted and Peter were happy at the thought of going home and Helen, who had never felt comfortable in Manila and who yearned to return to her former way of life, was ecstatic. Perhaps, she reasoned, a return to California and their home at Larkspur in Marin County might be just what was needed to get the marriage back on a more even keel. Ed was very fond of their home, she knew, enjoying the rambling house with its orchard of fruit trees. He felt it was "a very lovely spot to live."

Household goods were packed, items given to friends and servants, and the boys were withdrawn from their school as the family prepared to depart. Lansdale's friends gave him a *despidida,* a going-away party. His last day of duty was 19 November. The next day the family left Manila for San Francisco. Lansdale's orders gave him time for an extended leave while he awaited reassignment to new duties with the Air Force.

He would not have to report to work again until 23 February 1949. He and Helen hoped that such a time free from other duties would be good for all the family members.[59]

Somehow the hoped-for healing did not occur. Ed seemed restless, unsettled. Helen remembered the bitterness of *tsismis,* which had sometimes speculated on the reasons that her husband had been seen with other women. She recalled the frequent agony she had felt during Ed's absences and wondered why his thoughts so often seemed far away. Ed remembered good times in the Philippines with the fun-loving Pat Kelly and the excitement of exploring that strange land, scheming with its editors and businessmen and politicians, shadowing bands of Huks, and talking with Negritos. He chafed at the enforced inactivity of the winter at home and worried what his next assignment might be.

Lansdale was furious when he opened the mail at his home one day and found orders assigning him to the Strategic Studies Branch, Department of Air Intelligence Training at Lowry Air Force Base in Denver. He was going to be a teacher! The thought left him aghast. He was to report for duty as an instructor on 24 February 1949. He had not stayed in the Army or transferred to the Air Force to become a teacher. Lansdale wanted more action of the sort he had found in the Philippines where he could take satisfaction from knowing that his activities made a difference. The contemplative role was not for him. He had no desire to teach fellow officers what others were doing; he wanted to be one of the actors. The Air Force, however, was not particularly concerned with his misgivings. An order was an order.

In the quiet of their home, Ed and Helen came to a decision. Perhaps it would be good for Ed to go to Lowry alone; a trial separation might help both of them think through their feelings. Ed told at least a few close friends of their decision. Major O. J. "Mac" Magee, a friend from the Philippines, wrote him to say, "I was sorry to hear you and your wife had separated."[60] Bo Bohannan also knew. "Ed had written to us," his wife recalled, "and said, 'I know I'm a heel, but I'm leaving Helen.' . . . Shortly after that he asked Pat [to marry him] and Pat said, 'No. I don't want to hurt anybody. It would just hurt us.' "[61]

Troubled and less than enthusiastic, Lansdale reported alone for his new duties at Lowry. Then he received a letter a few days after his arrival that gave him some hope. His former boss at PHILRYCOM's G-2 section, Colonel George A. Chester, suggested he might find work for Lansdale more interesting than teaching Air Force officers. Chester wrote:

Looks more than ever as if I'll go to Washington and in something of our mutual interest — I don't mean P.R.O. [public relations officer].

You may get a note, or a call from someone there. If you do, you'll know the impetus came from here. Don't know too much definite myself, but I think you'd like it, and I'd surely like to have you with me again. . . . If you get a questionnaire (security clearance type) you can fill it out without committing yourself to accepting a job.[62]

Lansdale knew what Chester meant. There might be an opening in the field of intelligence for him once again. It was at least worth a little thought as he started his new duties at Lowry. His assignment required him to teach strategic intelligence.[63]

Lansdale encouraged class participation in his courses and some of his superiors complained that his sessions were too noisy. In his touchy frame of mind, Lansdale resented such criticism and let those who offered it know it was offensive. "I got my students thinking and talking," he said. "What can you teach in intelligence other than to look at problems and think of ways to solve them?" What his critics had in mind was that he would give lectures, tell students what the problems were, and then give them approved school solutions. For Lansdale that was nonsense. "I couldn't possibly know what problems they would run across, but I did know how to go about solving problems."[64]

Lansdale continued to run his classes his own way. Evaluators sat in on some of them to review his teaching methods and to determine whether he was following a prescribed and prepared lesson plan. In one critique, an inspector complained, "Mayhem's going on in your class." Lansdale refused to give way. He insisted he was only trying "to teach how we make U.S. policy, and why, and what the basis would be for some of our decisions. . . . I was trying to arouse them. That's all any of us can do. That's what teaching is all about."[65]

Lansdale's arguments must have been convincing. His efficiency reports while he was at Lowry from 24 February to 6 September 1949 were outstanding. One grader wrote that Lansdale accepted "without argument any responsibility or directions given him . . . thoroughly dependable. A good man for air attache, staff, or liaison duty . . . . capable of greater responsibility than that afforded by his present assignment." Lansdale must have grimaced to read those words. They said no more than he had been telling anyone who would listen ever since he had been ordered to Lowry.[66]

Perhaps because he was so obviously discontented, his superiors at Lowry decided to send Lansdale for several weeks of study in the Air Force's academic instructor course at the Special Staff School located at Craig Air Force Base near Selma, Alabama. Perhaps if he had more training in instructional arts he might become a more contented teacher. He arrived at the school on 7 September 1949. The very idea of receiving such training horrified him. He saw visions of becoming ever more mired in the field of teaching within the Air Force. One of ninety-eight officers enrolled in the course, Lansdale carefully figured out how to avoid such a fate. He didn't want to be the class goat — the student with the lowest grade average. Neither did he want to be the one with the best scores. He decided to try for the eleventh spot. That way he would get good grades, be well thought of by his instructors, but avoid being among the top ten, who would surely be selected for further teaching assignments. He could leave behind him a good record but no one would fight to keep him in the instructional field.

Most of his fellow students would not have agreed with him. Many regarded teaching as an opportunity for a stateside assignment for a reasonable length of time. They could have their families with them. If they were lucky they would be located near a university and could work on higher degrees during their spare time. Upon retirement they might then be able to find a position as an instructor at a junior college or university. "Well, that's not for me," Lansdale told them. "I don't want that."

During tests he sometimes purposely answered questions incorrectly to keep his score at a reasonable level. As he neared the end of the course Lansdale felt reasonably certain he had accomplished his mission. In later years he recalled that on graduation day he was surprised to hear his name announced as the top student in the class, "which was the last damn thing I wanted."[67] His recollection was not quite correct. Military records show that he graduated third among his group.[68] Whatever his final standing, it was too high for his liking. As far as Lansdale was concerned only one good thing came out of his course of study at Craig AFB. Shortly after he graduated he was again promoted to lieutenant colonel "for the grades I had gotten at Selma [and] for being a good teacher."[69] It was satisfying to have his rank back and it was with real pleasure that he pinned on his new silver oak leaves.

After completing his out-processing at Craig, Lansdale decided not to go directly back to Lowry. Remembering the letter he had received from Colonel Chester, he went to Washington instead. He located Chester in the Pentagon, where he was now assigned to the office of the Joint Chiefs of Staff. Lansdale told Chester his problems. "I apparently made good [at Craig]," he said ruefully, "which I hadn't wanted. Could you figure out some way I could get out of [teaching]? I'm desperate to find something else to do."

Chester's reply was encouraging. "Yes," he responded. "Something is coming up. I'll stick your name in the hopper and see [what happens]." Lansdale felt better on the trip back to Denver, where he once more settled into his routine of teaching strategic intelligence. The opportunity for different work came even more quickly than he hoped. Only a few days after his return he met with an Air Force colonel who had come from the Pentagon to see him. The man told Lansdale of a new group forming in Washington for specific duty on issues arising from the new "cold war" between the East and the West. "My ears pricked up," Lansdale said. "It sounded good." After listening to a generalized description of the group he was being invited to join, Lansdale spoke the magic words: "I'm for it. I volunteer right off." The colonel was optimistic. "I want you to know you are being . . . considered very favorably and you will probably hear right away."[70]

That conversation, culminating in Lansdale's decision to volunteer for "cold war duty," was momentous far beyond anything he could then imagine. It changed the course of his life and opened to him a career in intelligence that during the next twenty years would place him in the forefront of America's unrelenting effort to "contain" communism around the world. In the course of those years Lansdale would find it necessary to bridge the gulf between his own and three other cultures: first with his work in the Philippines and later in Vietnam and in South America. Many men have worked for the intelligence services of this nation and remained unsung. Lansdale rose above the group with which he worked. He was always more than a ubiquitous intelligence agent certain to surface in troubled waters. He was also a theorist, steeped in the doctrines of both ancient and modern warfare from Sun Tzu to Vo Nguyen Giap. He knew the political works of George Washington and Thomas Jefferson, of John Adams and Thomas Paine. He believed in his American heritage and was an old-fashioned patriot willing to fight and, if necessary, die for ideals he cherished. His beliefs were, Lansdale believed, principles for an American to live by and so he endeavored to practice those beliefs among those he met in embattled nations abroad.

Never interested in riding a desk, Lansdale showed others that the proper place for an intelligence operative is with people — sharing their dreams and fears, pleasures and sorrow. He was not overambitious for image or reputation, for accumulating prestige and place. He was content to live in his world of shadows, using what power he had in quiet ways to help those who trusted him. Irreverent toward established authority and always a maverick within his own official chain of command, he made demands on others that more staid men would have been fearful of attempting.

Enemies — as well as others who did not understand his work — would blame him for coups and triumphs, for feats of derring-do and debacles, for undue influence over governments and men in two Asian countries embroiled in revolution. In many ways his actual exploits were far more astonishing than those attributed to him, for he was always both more and less than others thought.

This one man would become, in succession, brother, friend, and dominant political counselor to leaders of two Pacific nations: Ramón Magsaysay in the Philippines and Ngo Dinh Diem in Vietnam. Both granted him their lifelong devotion. He would devise tactics in the Philippines that ensured a truly popular election there for the first (and almost the last) time in history and catapulted Magsaysay into the presidency. He would help Ngo Dinh Diem begin a nation that almost succeeded in becoming a stable state. Diem might well have triumphed had it not been for his assassination by those who could not or cared not to understand either him or the dogs of war that would be unleashed if they allowed his shaky regime to be shattered. Lansdale later taught leaders in Latin America how to understand and counter rebel-inspired revolutions.

All these things and more still lay in the future, but they were all made possible because during that conversation at Lowry AFB in Denver, Colorado, in late 1949, Lieutenant Colonel Edward Geary Lansdale volunteered for cold war duty with a new group based in Washington. He was about to enter a hidden world of secrecy and intrigue, of persuasion and power.

4

GIRDING FOR WAR

LESS THAN A MONTH after Edward Lansdale's conversation at Lowry AFB with the mysterious colonel from the Pentagon, orders arrived from Air Force headquarters in Washington. His wish for more challenging and exciting work had been granted. He was reassigned on 13 November 1949 to a new position as an intelligence officer with the Central Control Group in the nation's capital. He packed his gear and headed back to Washington for his new job. Neither the name of the organization he was assigned to nor the one for which he really worked revealed the true nature of its activities. He was now a part of an exclusively secret organization named the Office of Policy Coordination (OPC), on loan indefinitely from the Air Force. "The name [was] purposely made very obscure," he noted. "They swore me to secrecy whatever I was doing, not even to tell my own family, so I didn't."[1]

The Office of Policy Coordination was a direct descendant of the earlier Office of Strategic Services (OSS), for which Lansdale had worked during World War II. OSS was the government's first organized attempt at building a systematic intelligence organization. A few months before the Japanese attack on Pearl Harbor at Oahu in the Hawaiian Islands, President Franklin Roosevelt called Colonel (later Major General) William J. Donovan to the White House and appointed him to a new position. Donovan was to be coordinator of information with the responsibility of collecting and analyzing strategic intelligence information and furnishing the results to the president and to other interested agencies. Soon called the Office of Strategic Services, the agency combined research, foreign espionage, and special operations.[2]

As the war progressed, OSS evolved into an important and valuable intelligence-gathering organization, subdivided into several sections. Research and Analysis branch evaluated foreign newspapers and labor and business publications to derive political, social, and economic information. Secret Intelligence branch quietly collected material inside neutral and enemy nations. Special Operations branch carried out acts of sabotage and provided support for resistance groups within occupied nations. Within Special Operations, operational groups penetrated enemy territory to carry out guerrilla and sabotage activities while maritime unit members sabotaged enemy shipping. Counterespionage branch endeavored to prevent enemy infiltration of intelligence operations of the United States and its Allies. Moral Operations branch carried out covert propaganda efforts.[3]

OSS suffered both organizational and operational problems during the early war years, but experience brought about definite improvements. By the end of the conflict, some twelve thousand members — both men and women — performed a number of strategically important tasks at a budget of $57 million dollars in 1945. Donovan hoped to see OSS continue its work in the postwar world and as early as 1944 drew up plans for a peacetime centralized intelligence-gathering agency and submitted them to President Roosevelt, who in turn gave them to the Joint Chiefs and the State Department for their comments.[4] Unfortunately, Donovan lost his prime supporter with the president's sudden death in April 1945.

The new president, Harry S Truman, was confronted with a host of weighty problems ranging from the imminent end of the worst war in history to organizing the forthcoming peace in a way that would further the goals and ambitions of the several nations that had been uneasy allies against the Axis powers. This inexperienced new chief executive found his working days filled with challenges: the surrender of Germany in May 1945; plans for the invasion of the Japanese home islands; the question of whether to drop unproven atomic bombs on an unsuspecting Japanese people; the sudden disintegration of Japan following the destruction of Hiroshima and Nagasaki; advance planning for his meeting with Stalin and Churchill at Potsdam in Germany; and organization of the transition from a wartime to a peacetime economy in the United States.

Truman was as cool toward Donovan's plan for a postwar intelligence agency as he was toward the man himself. He looked upon Donovan as a possible Republican competitor in the coming presidential elections of 1948. Truman was also under pressure from the individual armed services, as well as the Department of State and the Federal Bureau of Investigation, not to adopt Donovan's plans. Those agencies worried that their own intelligence-collection efforts would be imperiled or destroyed if they were forced to compete with a postwar OSS. They found a ready ally in the Bureau of the Budget, which warned of the expensive nature of OSS. Truman listened to these voices and chose to deal with OSS by abolishing it. On 20 September 1945, President Truman wrote an Executive Order that put an end to OSS as of 1 October. In only ten days, Donovan's work of four years was dismantled.[5]

Truman's Executive Order reassigned OSS employees working on research and analysis duties to new positions within the State Department, where they were to organize peacetime intelligence collection. Unhappy with the prospect of having to absorb such interlopers, State posted them to separate duties in scattered locations throughout its organization. Paramilitary and covert agents of OSS were given only a stark choice by the President's Executive Order: they could revert to civilian status or transfer to one of the uniformed military services. Most chose civilian life.

Former OSS agents with experience in clandestine operations who decided to stay in service were reassigned to the War Department and fared somewhat better than those who went to State. They became part of a newly established Strategic Services Unit in the Pentagon that allowed them to remain in contact with existing OSS networks in China and in eastern and southeastern Europe. Many of them studied the techniques of irregular or guerrilla warfare and eventually helped bring about the creation of the U.S. Army Special Forces — the Green Berets.

One important result of the Executive Order was to separate even further those involved in the American intelligence community. Two often mutually hostile camps hardened their attitudes — those who emphasized research and analysis and those who stressed the importance of clandestine operations. That division has continued to plague U.S. intelligence activities.[6]

Hardly had the war ended when the long anticipated years of international peace and harmony began to seem ephemeral. The newly created United Nations proved itself not to be the ''parliament of man'' envisioned by Alfred, Lord Tennyson and other idealists who had followed in his train. This successor to the League of Nations proved itself unequal to the task of harmonizing national interests for the benefit of humanity. International bickering continued unabated and both East and West fell prey to mounting suspicions of one another. In March 1946 the Soviet Union adamantly refused to pull its troops out of the province of Azerbaijan in Iran. In May, communist rebel forces in Greece provoked a civil war. Jan Masaryk's suspicious ''suicide'' in Czechoslovakia presaged a communist coup there and in short order the Soviets installed puppet governments in Poland, Hungary, and Rumania and threatened the stability of Austria. The eastern zone of a divided Germany lay desolated by war damage and vengeful spoliation by Russian conquerors. Communist-inspired strikes and subversion in Italy and France delayed those countries in recovering from war and threatened to topple their pro-Western governments in favor of new ones more sympathetic to the Soviet Union.

In an address on 5 March 1946 at Westminster College in Fulton, Missouri, Winston Churchill, Great Britain's wartime prime minister, described Soviet efforts in the months since the end of the Great Patriotic

War to insulate itself and its eastern European dependencies from open and free contact with the West. Churchill's words rang through the assembly hall at the college: "From Stettin in the Baltic to Trieste in the Adriatic, an iron curtain has descended across the Continent."

Fear of communist agitation and influence grew within the United States as reports of Soviet espionage surfaced both at home and in Great Britain. Widely publicized show trials were held for Julius and Ethel Rosenberg, Klaus Fuchs, Alger Hiss, and Judith Coplon. Reporters wrote of repeated communist efforts to penetrate, subvert, and control labor and political organizations such as Henry Wallace's liberal Progressive Party and Walter Reuther's United Auto Workers. Newspapers, radio, and the infant television system repeatedly reminded Americans of the communist-led Hukbalahap rebellion in the former Commonwealth of the Philippines, now an independent nation wracked with dissension.

Faced with this turmoil, President Truman decided that he needed a central intelligence organization after all. Only months after his decision to dismantle OSS he began deliberating the advisability of setting up a new intelligence unit. As before, the Army, Navy, State Department, and FBI all generated strong opposition out of their belief that a central agency would erode their own intelligence-gathering efforts.[7] Yet no coordination existed among them, and Truman faced a long-standing intelligence quagmire. William Stevenson has written that "more than twenty different agencies competed to take up the OSS mantle," all hoping to be selected as the unit responsible for writing the president's intelligence reports.[8]

Only one precedent existed for a coordinated central intelligence unit. That was the Joint Intelligence Committee, created during World War II as an agency of the Joint Chiefs of Staff to help them function more effectively. Its members came from the Office of Naval Intelligence, the Army Military Intelligence Service, the Foreign Economic Administration, and the Office of Strategic Services. "This committee," Harry Ransom wrote, "was the wartime *ad hoc* answer to the need for centralized intelligence, although most intelligence operations were performed by its constituent members."[9]

On 22 January 1946, only four months after he had abolished OSS, Harry Truman set forth another Executive Order, this one establishing the National Intelligence Authority (NIA). This was an improvement over the wartime Joint Intelligence Committee. Its members consisted of the secretaries of war, navy, and state in addition to war hero Admiral William D. Leahy, who served as the president's personal representative. The NIA was more than an evaluative group, for it had its own operating agency, the Central Intelligence Group — eighty volunteer employees from War, Navy, and State. Having no separate budget, NIA operating expenses were *contributed* by its participating departments in whatever amount they saw fit to give!

Central Intelligence Group had several other limitations. It could conduct no investigations within the United States and it had no police or internal security or law enforcement functions. The Executive Order called for the president to appoint the director of Central Intelligence Group (DCI) and in May 1947 Truman chose Rear Admiral Roscoe H. Hillenkoetter for the position. Most of the admiral's thirty-year Navy career had been spent at sea, and when he resigned as DCI in October 1950 it was to return to another sea command.[10]

Central Intelligence Group grew slowly under Hillenkoetter's direction. In 1947 he pulled the Strategic Services Unit from the Pentagon, brought it under his control, and redesignated it the Office of Special Operations (OSO). He set up the Office of Reports and Estimates (ORE) to conduct scientific and economic research and to write daily intelligence summaries. Central Intelligence Group also took over from the FBI the task of gathering information in Latin America.[11]

Truman again strengthened America's intelligence capacity on 15 September 1947 when he signed into law the National Security Act. This important law created an independent Air Force and formed the Department of Defense to supervise the new air wing as well as the Army and Navy. It further created the National Security Council (NSC) and set up a Central Intelligence Agency (CIA) to replace the eighteen-month-old Central Intelligence Group. Unlike its predecessor, CIA was an independent department within the executive branch of government, reporting directly to the National Security Council. Since the president presided over NSC, CIA now was under direct control of — or at least had a channel to — the president of the United States. Further, CIA could hire and train its own employees and was to receive a secret budget of its own. It would no longer have to beg money from other departments of government.[12]

The duties of CIA included advising NSC on issues involving national security, evaluating and correlating intelligence data, and ensuring the proper dissemination of such information. It was also to coordinate all government intelligence activities and to carry out "services of a common concern." This last phrase was bureaucratic jargon meaning that CIA could conduct espionage and carry out clandestine counterintelligence activities.[13]

CIA did not initially have authority to carry out subversive operations overseas. Many within the intelligence camp decried this lack of authority, for they believed that covert action against the Soviets was desirable. Secret operations would frustrate Soviet ambitions more effectively than diplomatic protests and would still be short of war and thus unlikely to provoke open conflict.[14]

America's intelligence community strongly supported covert action. William Colby, former director of Central Intelligence, later asked, "How could America provide large-scale covert assistance to people who were struggling against Communist subversion and expansion in a Cold War, so that a hot war would never be needed to free them?"[15] Following coups in Iran and Guatemala, Allen Dulles, DCI under Eisenhower, expressed a similar view. In a letter to *Washington Post* correspondent Chalmers Roberts, Dulles wrote, "Where there begins to be evidence that a country is slipping and Communist takeover is threatened . . . we can't wait for an engraved invitation to come and give aid."[16] Far down the chain of command, Edward Lansdale agreed. His bosses, he said, "suddenly realized we had problems in the world we weren't prepared for."[17]

The nation was infected with fear of communist subversion, and the intelligence community certainly had no immunity from this general malady. A former CIA agent wrote of his early training and recalled that all recruits were expected to read a new book by William R. Kintner entitled *The Front Is Everywhere*:[18]

> Kintner taught us . . . that Communist conspirators were all around us . . . . [T]he view of the state of affairs in the world that was the fundamental assumption . . . was that the United States was faced everywhere with an enemy that was using an untold array of black psychwar operations to undermine the nations of the world in order to present us with a fait accompli one fine morning when we would wake up to find all these countries under Communist control. . . . [T]he spirit of the times . . . made the existence of conspiracy seem so real. It was good to feel that we were learning how to beat the Communists at their own game.[19]

Political turmoil in Italy in 1948 further whetted the desire of the American intelligence community for clandestine operations. The Soviet Union was heavily involved in Italy and provided extensive support to that nation's communist party in its campaign to win the forthcoming elections. Many anticommunists feared that Italy, which had already discarded its monarchy in a national plebiscite, would now fall to the same fate as Czechoslovakia. The Truman administration sent economic and military aid to bolster the government of Alcide de Gasperi. Private citizens of Italian origin wrote letters urging their relatives to stand firm against the communists. Drew Pearson, the muckraking columnist, made the matter a *cause célèbre* in newspapers across the country. Some in the intelligence community believed more should be done; the Italians should be given the kind of help OSS had provided during World War II to European resistance movements. These feelings were a primary moving force in the establishment of the Office of Policy Coordination.[20]

William Donovan had been the original author of an elastic catchall clause appearing in enabling documents that would later be very helpful to the intelligence community. The phrase reappeared in the charges of both Central Intelligence Group and Central Intelligence Agency: those agencies were empowered to "perform such other functions and duties related to intelligence affecting the national security as the National Security Council may from time to time direct."[21] Those words authorized clandestine subversive operations. While the existing Office of Special Operations occasionally engaged in such activities, it did so only on a very limited scale, as its primary responsibility was in the area of espionage and counterespionage. It would continue to have some covert capability but its main function would remain the gathering of intelligence.[22]

George Kennan, director of the State Department's policy planning staff, was one of those who believed that more should be done. He argued in May 1948 that the nation needed a permanent covert political action capability, and President Truman agreed. With the executive's approval, the National Security Council issued Directive 10/2 on 18 June 1948 authorizing the creation of a permanent organization established specifically to direct covert activities — political activities, psychological warfare, and paramilitary operations — including sabotage, countersabotage, and support to anticommunist guerrilla movements.[23]

CIA was an instrument of policy only, not an instigator. Its task was to suggest, on the basis of collected intelligence, specific actions that might be taken to prevent communists from further expanding Soviet political influence west of the Iron Curtain in Europe. Such projects would then be discussed by a "10/2" panel made up of State and Defense officials who would authorize actions or withhold their approval.[24]

The organization created by 10/2 to undertake these secret political and paramilitary operations was called by the euphemism Office of Policy Coordination (OPC). It would be the American government's "dirty tricks" department, carrying out a covert foreign policy in support of overt aims. Lyman Kirkpatrick wrote, "The new office was in, but not of, the CIA." This meant that OPC under the Hillenkoetter directorship did not take orders from the director of Central Intelligence, who was not even in the chain of command, but was guided by a small committee of representatives from State and Defense.[25]

One former member has said that "at the beginning OPC was only attached to CIA for quarters and rations."[26] Administratively the unit was completely separate from CIA's intelligence activities in the Office of Special Operations and from CIA intelligence analysis in the Office of Reports and Estimates. OPC was placed under the CIA umbrella because CIA's intelligence-collection activities provided OPC with necessary information. The Agency could also protect its work by providing OPC the secrecy it needed. Although it was to be funded by CIA and most of its personnel would be drawn from CIA ranks, its activities were completely independent, determined as the need arose without any requirement for CIA approval. Policy guidance thus completely bypassed the director of Central Intelligence.[27]

It was this fine line of distinction between OPC and CIA that allowed Edward Lansdale to maintain throughout his career, when asked, that he was not and had not been a member of CIA. His reasoning was rather jesuitical but technically correct. He had not belonged to CIA. He had been a regular Air Force officer on loan to OPC. After August 1952 when OPC was absorbed by CIA, Lansdale's distinction was harder to justify but even then, inasmuch as secrecy had been the *sine qua non* of his entrance into intelligence work, he could still insist truthfully enough that he had never been anything other than a simple Air Force officer.

The Office of Policy Coordination was governed by a director selected by the secretary of state (Louis Johnson served in that capacity at the time of its formation) and approved by the secretary of defense (James V. Forrestal, 1947–1949). This organization may well have been the most secret in the nation's history. William Stevenson has written that "OPC's existence was not even suspected, did not appear in official records, and was excluded from official CIA history until 1982." The earliest hint of its role may have been provided by Ray S. Cline who in 1976 published a work on intelligence matters entitled *Secrets, Spies and Scholars.*[28]

Frank Wisner became OPC's first director and, according to Lyman Kirkpatrick, was the genius behind its early successes.[29] A brilliant, hard-driving and ambitious man, Wisner was serving as an official in the State Department at the time of his appointment. A former New York lawyer, he had worked for Allen Dulles during World War II and for a time held the post of station chief in Rumania. He was one of those transferred to the State Department in 1945 when Truman dissolved OSS. While working at State he and other former OSS members tried to preserve OSS records and assets and they looked forward to a time when their services and talents might once again be better used. That opportunity came on 1 September 1948 when Wisner received appointment as assistant director for Policy Coordination. Although the director of Central Intelligence was his boss, Wisner was responsible for running

OPC and coordinating its activities — not with the DCI but with State and Defense. He had a fairly free hand to do as he wished because the guidance provided him by those two departments was very general.[30]

Wisner quickly began a major recruiting campaign for OPC and called on many former comrades from OSS to return to the intelligence fold. They gladly responded. It was what they had been waiting for since 1945. Wisner organized his work force into functional areas to deal with political, economic, and psychological warfare — including paramilitary operations — and into geographical divisions spanning the regions of the globe.[31]

William Colby later noted that OSS had been re-created in fact if not in name. "There were analysts evaluating information; spymasters and counterspies, recruiting and exploiting agents and working with foreign intelligence services," Colby wrote, "and now there were covert political and paramilitary activists, revelling in risk, commitment and secret influence." The old firm now had a new name.[32]

Wisner and those he trusted began in a small way for they believed the 10/2 committee would approve few covert activities for OPC and then only when normal diplomatic or military measures were inadequate, as was the case in Italy's election trials during 1948. Wisner was surprised at the latitude allowed him, and OPC grew rapidly in its early years. Its total personnel strength in 1949 was 302 — and that included administrative and clerical staff members. By 1952 it employed 2,812 plus 3,142 overseas contract employees. Its budget in 1949 was $4.7 million; in 1952 it was $82 million. In 1949 OPC assigned its people to only seven overseas stations. By 1952 its personnel were scattered among forty-seven locations abroad. This growth occurred because of increasing American political efforts in Europe and paramilitary programs in Asia. Millions of dollars were spent in providing money to noncommunist labor unions, church groups, newspapers, political parties, student organizations, writers, and free radio stations in Europe and elsewhere and in supporting other front groups.[33]

Tensions increased between West and East when the Korean War broke out in June 1950. A frosty cold war had warmed to a simmer. Americans proclaimed that at last there was no denying the fact of communist aggression. Because of a temporary absence of the Soviet delegate to the UN Security Council, the United States was able to persuade the United Nations to pledge resistance to the invading forces in South Korea. Americans found themselves caught up once more in a mobilization for war. Reserve and National Guard units were called to active duty and sent to the Far East. The draft was reinstated and war production plants again increased their output.

Men like Edward Lansdale who had only recently joined the work of OPC believed they were in the vanguard of the fight for freedom and democracy in the world. Membership in the covert structure was the best of available options for it allowed one to do more than serve as a combat infantryman on a battlefield. It afforded an opportunity to struggle against the Red tide with innovative and courageous enthusiasm.[34]

When the Office of Policy Coordination was formed in 1948, General Douglas MacArthur still served as Supreme Commander, Allied Powers (SCAP) in the occupation government over Japan. His power was further heightened when he became commander of United Nations forces fighting in Korea. Until he was relieved of his command by President Truman in 1951, he tried to restrict intelligence activities by agencies other than his own military G-2 units within the entire Pacific basin. Evidence suggests that he was successful in excluding both OSO and OPC from the Far East until at least 1950, refusing to concede any jurisdiction to civilian agencies, just as he had done with OSS during the war.[35]

It was due to MacArthur's hostility that OPC wisely concentrated initially on plans to meet the Soviet threat in Europe. Who could tell when the Russians might take it into their heads to launch a strike westward through the Hof Corridor or Fulda Gap in a sudden and mighty invasion of western Europe? Using information collected by OSO, OPC implemented propaganda targeted at the USSR and engaged in political and paramilitary projects on the Continent. William Colby summed up well the spirit of that time: "In a time of fierce anti-Communist and anti-Soviet sentiment and rhetoric, covert paramilitary and political action was the name of the intelligence game."[36]

Not convinced that the United States was doing all it could to counter the steady advance of communism, the National Security Council issued in April 1950 a document known as NSC 68. It stated that the Soviets were a danger to world peace and were intent on global domination and that America must do all it could to stand as a bulwark against the flood. Since Admiral Hillenkoetter had not been a forceful director of Central Intelligence, President Truman began to look for someone who would mount a more active fight against communism.

In October 1950 the chief executive named General Walter Bedell Smith to replace Hillenkoetter as director of Central Intelligence. A tiny but tough and brilliant man, Smith was Eisenhower's former chief of staff and for several years had served President Truman as the American ambassador to Moscow. Of the senior ranking military officers serving in the government, Smith was one of the most highly regarded. Some voices in America were already crying that the Democratic administration was soft on communism. Senator Joe McCarthy proclaimed that communists, bent on the destruction of this nation, were ubiquitous both in and out of government. Truman's appointment of the highly regarded Smith was a way of responding to such hyperbole.[37]

Never one to favor jurisdictional sloppiness, whether earlier within the Army or now in his CIA command, Smith believed it was anomalous to have the Office of Special Operations under CIA and the Office of Policy Coordination in but not under it. As the new director he insisted that it was illogical to have two divisions doing much the same thing, often in competition and always in rivalry with one another. He believed that if he bore responsibility for OPC's support and maintenance then he ought to have complete authority over it. There was, he felt, a better way to organize those offices and he had the support of the president. Using that authority he began persistently prodding OSO and OPC toward a more coordinated and centralized structure. Despite his authority and intentions it took Smith two years to accomplish a merger of the two divisions, but at length intelligence collection and covert action were brought under his supervision.[38]

Smith began this consolidation by approaching the secretary of state and the secretary of defense, advising them that he was taking over the direction of OPC and planned to incorporate it into CIA as one of the directorates. Under such an arrangement Defense and State would exert policy guidance over OPC through the director of Central Intelligence rather than directly through Frank Wisner, the director of OPC. There is no indication that either secretary had objections in the midst of the messy Korean War. They accepted the new arrangement on 12 October 1950, and in January 1951 Smith appointed Allen Dulles as his deputy director for plans, with responsibility for coordinating OPC and OSO operations. Despite this change both OPC and OSO continued their rivalry for the next year and a half, working in the same places at the same times, competing for resources and personnel. Smith came to realize that more needed to be done to secure his objective.[39]

The final merger came in August 1952 when Smith made Frank Wisner of OPC the CIA's deputy director for plans. The title, like the name OPC, was a cover. Wisner was not in charge of planning but rather directed covert activities. Richard Helms, assistant director for special operations of OSO, became Wisner's second in command, with the title chief of operations. In this way both OSO and OPC disappeared, replaced by a Directorate of Plans. OPC would no longer be in but not of the CIA.[40]

As deputy director for plans, Frank Wisner commanded an organization divided into several parts; one dealt with different aspects of psychological warfare, another carried out paramilitary operations; a third supervised various regional divisions covering western Europe, eastern Europe, the Soviet Union, Africa, the Middle East, the Western Hemisphere, and the Far East. Within each of those regional divisions there was a chief, a planning staff, an operations staff, and an administrative and logistics staff, which provided field agents and stations with support in the different countries under their jurisdiction.[41]

This was the organization Lieutenant Colonel Edward Lansdale went to work for on 13 November 1949 when he was reassigned from his teaching post at Lowry AFB to the position of intelligence officer, Central Control Group, Washington, D.C.[42] At last, he felt, he was again going to have the opportunity to perform constructive work.

Ed and Helen decided to prolong their separation, so she and the boys remained in California while Lansdale moved into the bachelor officer quarters (BOQ) at Fort Myer, Virginia. The post was close enough for him to walk back and forth to work. Leaving the BOQ early each morning, he walked through Arlington National Cemetery to Memorial Drive and followed it to Arlington Memorial Bridge, which crossed the Potomac River. After reaching the east bank he found himself near the Lincoln Memorial. Offices of the OPC were nearby, located in temporary wooden buildings left over from World War II that earlier had housed a naval installation. Tucked in around the decrepit remains of the Heurich brewery were two ramshackle structures, M and Q buildings. It was at M that Lansdale arrived for work after his morning walks. The quarters were familiar to him, for he had come here when he was ordered to report to OSS headquarters back in 1942.[43]

Covert action was on everyone's mind. Lansdale's initial assignments involved working on possible ways to limit the ever-expanding empire of the Soviet Union. Many projects were small ones, such as backing the production of pro-U.S. or anti-USSR articles and books at home and abroad or furnishing money and background briefings to representatives of labor, education, press, and youth organizations. Such activities held few risks and took only small amounts of money. It was, Lansdale felt, "fascinating work."[44] Other OPC efforts were more elaborate. Some covert action programs involved secret political, paramilitary, or propaganda moves designed to support American foreign policies or to foil efforts of Soviet intelligence agents attempting to undermine the stability of countries favored by the United States.[45]

Lansdale enjoyed working on Soviet problems and believed he had been assigned to the USSR/Plans desk because while at Lowry he had taken the economy of the Soviet Union as one of his lecture subjects and thus had developed some depth in his knowledge of that nation. At Lowry he had done his research in open sources in the Denver public libraries. For some time the Air Force urged him to classify that research but he argued against doing so. "Anybody else could have done the same thing, and probably did."[46]

While the Soviet Union might well be a threat should its armies be ordered to roll west over thin NATO defending forces, Lansdale saw clearly that America faced more direct and immediate threats to its interests elsewhere. He understood earlier than most that there was not going to be a massive armed confrontation between the United States and the USSR. Competition between the two superpowers would take place in disadvantaged, third world nations where indigenous forces would act as proxies for their sponsors. Time and again Lansdale thought of the Philippines, believing it to be one such battleground. "The more I got into cold war problems the more I got to worrying about the Philippines. . . . [A]s the Army G-2 there, I had gone into the Huk problem, had been all over the battlegrounds . . . had analyzed a great deal of it, reported on it. . . . I knew a great . . . many of the problems there. So I set the fight against the communists in the Philippines as [my] number one task."[47]

To work effectively in that area required Lansdale's transfer from USSR/ Plans to Far East division (FE/Plans). FE/Plans was headed by Colonel Richard G. Stilwell, a driven and driving man, one of the youngest full colonels in the American Army. He had served in the China-Burma-India theater during World War II and had a real talent for organization. Those who worked for Stilwell gave him their unceasing loyalty. His FE/Plans was responsible for providing a psychological and political warfare plan for every nation within the Orient to thwart any emerging communist subversive efforts or guerrilla uprisings.[48] Stilwell approved the transfer and Lansdale went to work with a will.

Lansdale believed that the United States was sadly lacking in its capability to launch psychological or political operations against those who might seek to destabilize a legitimate government, as the Huks were doing in the Philippines. He recognized how successful Huk rebels had been, achieving spectacular success in selling their program to people in central Luzon. Much Huk support came straight from the hearts of its followers. Lansdale wondered why they were so successful. "I wanted to learn about psychological operations," he noted. "I knew nothing about them. There was no military school on psychological operations." All he could find were some old manuals left over from World War II that were not particularly helpful. Search as he might, Lansdale could find nothing substantial or pertinent to the Huk campaign.[49]

During the spring of 1950 Lansdale talked with friends in the Pentagon, seeking to learn of people from the war years who had practical experience in psychological warfare. He found that most were now gone from government service, but some agreed to help him out again on a short-term basis. Lansdale then approached the Philippine military attaché in Washington. How many Filipino army officers, Lansdale wondered, were then in the United States as students at one or another of the nation's military schools? The attaché informed him that about twenty-five Filipinos were currently studying in America. Lansdale challenged the attaché. "At the end of their terms can you route them through Washington? I will set up this school in the Pentagon. We will all go to it, you and me included." The attaché agreed and was as good as his word. As those army officers completed their course work they were reassigned to temporary duty in Washington.

Lansdale held his school in a borrowed Pentagon room. As instructors he used those he had earlier contacted who had agreed to share their experiences. "People came on their own, they paid their own way," Lansdale remembered, "[to] reminisce [and tell] war stories about World War II." Instruction focused on incidents where one military force had been deceived and tricked by its enemies.

Those sessions clearly taught Lansdale that psychological warfare had a very real *tactical* use. "All you have to figure out," he told his students, "is what you want the enemy to do and then use psychological means to get them to do it." One illustration Lansdale used involved an enemy in hiding: "You want him out [of his foxhole] so you can shoot him. . . . You tell him he is right within our sights. We are going to blow him out of there [but] we will give him two seconds to surrender. When he jumps up, shoot him!" During school sessions the students discussed numerous such approaches to combat. "There were a number of things like that which are universally applicable," Lansdale told them. "I had never thought much about [the subject] before, but I learned that psychological warfare was much like a machine gun or a small . . . howitzer; [it was] a support type weapon to use along with others to give a combat edge."

"A mystery started clearing away," Lansdale recalled. "I started understanding what had been happening . . . . When I eventually got out there [to the Philippines] I started psychological operations with some of these guys who had been in our school together [at the Pentagon]." From the beginning Lansdale was an eclectic thinker: "I [also] borrowed ideas from the communists."[50]

During evening hours in his BOQ room Lansdale put together a program of action for the Philippines that he felt would go far toward countering the growing Huk menace. When he completed his plan he talked with his OPC superiors, trying to get them to support his proposals. "They had approved the ideas," he noted, and "were discussing whether I should go out [to the Philippines] or not."[51]

Lansdale had just completed his recommendations when an old friend, Major Mamerto Montemayor, introduced him to a young Philippine congressman, Ramón Magsaysay, who was in Washington seeking help from the United States Congress for Philippine veterans' benefit programs. Magsaysay was tall for a Filipino, about six feet, and built strongly through the shoulders and chest. A man with a ready smile, Magsaysay was the son of a rural shopkeeper. During the war Magsaysay fought the Japanese, first as a member of Captain Ralph McGuire's West Luzon Guerrilla Force until McGuire was captured and executed by the Japanese. An American colonel, Gyles Merrill, reorganized the guerrilla force and Magsaysay served under Merrill for a time, although he also spent part of the war years in Manila. Merrill fell prey to tropical diseases while hiding out in the fastnesses of the Zambales Mountains and was forced to appoint Ramón's older brother, Jesus, as the active leader of the band. Jess, as Magsaysay's older brother was known, quickly abdicated in favor of Ramón, who he thought would be a more successful captain of the group. After the war Magsaysay entered politics, winning election to the Philippine House of Representatives in 1946. At the time of his visit to Washington in 1950 he was chairman of that body's Defense Committee.[52]

Montemayor told Lansdale that Magsaysay had good ideas about fighting the Huks and that he was a worthwhile person whom Ed would like. The two men met over dinner and Lansdale was immediately drawn to the Filipino congressman. They discussed problems besetting the Quirino government including the attitudes of the Philippine armed forces toward fighting Huks, low military morale, and the inappropriate behavior of soldiers toward their own countrymen. They found that their evaluations of various Filipino generals were similar. As they tested their ideas on one another, they discovered they were in essential agreement.[53]

After dinner the two men adjourned to Lansdale's room. Magsaysay affirmed his desire to convince President Quirino to adopt a more effective counterinsurgency program. Quirino was, in 1950, finally president in his own right, having completed the term vacated by President Roxas upon his death in 1948 while giving a speech at Clark AFB. The 1949 campaign pitted Quirino and José Laurel. During the Japanese occupation, the Philippines were governed from 1942 to October 1943 by the Japanese Military Administration, under which Laurel served as commissioner of justice. With the establishment of Philippine "independence" in October 1943, Laurel became president and Claro Recto served as foreign minister.

Laurel was an especially controversial politician for having served in that puppet position. Many Filipinos regarded him as a great hero who lightened the heavy hand of Japanese rulers during those hard times. He had adroitly avoided the Japanese demand to form a Philippine Army, which they would have sent into battle against Japan's enemies. He had refused to countenance a Filipino declaration of war against the United States and its allies. Yet when American forces returned to the Philippines, General MacArthur imprisoned Laurel and others who had collaborated with the Japanese, and Laurel remained in prison for some time. His wartime record doomed him in that 1949 election. Simply the knowledge, well circulated, that the Americans did not want him to become president was enough to ensure his defeat, and Elpidio Quirino was duly elected in what was considered the dirtiest campaign in Philippine history.[54]

Well aware of those recent events, Lansdale and Magsaysay discussed possible courses of action. As the evening wore on, Lansdale asked Magsaysay to list, item by item, what he felt should be done. Lansdale moved to his portable typewriter and as Magsaysay ticked off his ideas, Lansdale typed them up. "I put his response in my words on paper," Lansdale said. Not surprisingly, "the sequence was the same as the program I had just sold the U.S. policymakers and in the same language. Then I showed a copy of my plan to him . . . and he agreed to it."[55] Lansdale was elated.

The next day he told Colonel Stilwell about the remarkable Filipino he had just met. They discussed Magsaysay's record, his personality, and his potential. They brought Frank Wisner into the conversation and continued to explore possibilities. Lansdale had already made up his mind: "I decided he should be the guy to handle [the Huk campaign] out in the Philippines because of his feelings toward the people and toward the enemy. He understood the problem, which very few Filipinos or Americans ever did."[56]

Lansdale's listeners were more cautious and wanted to talk with Magsaysay before coming to a decision. They asked Lansdale to arrange a meeting. Lansdale set up a luncheon meeting for two days later where Magsaysay could dine with several "inside policy people." One guest was Livingston Merchant, an assistant secretary of state and that department's liaison to the Office of Policy Coordination. General Nathan Twining, vice chief of staff of the Air Force, attended. So did Colonel George Chester, who had recruited Lansdale for OPC. Lansdale's boss, Colonel Richard Stilwell, was there, as was Frank Wisner. "They [were] all familiar with what I was pushing and . . . were in agreement with it," Lansdale remembered. Lansdale presented Magsaysay to the group, told them that he had good ideas on ways to defeat the Huks, and then asked Magsaysay for remarks. It was inevitable, of course, that much of what the Filipino congressman said paralleled the proposals Lansdale had already submitted to OPC. "The others were surprised at that," although Lansdale obviously could not have been surprised for he had carefully primed Magsaysay some evenings earlier in his room. Those present were impressed with Magsaysay's speech.

At the office later, Lansdale and the others talked further. Then it was time to make a decision: should OPC support Magsaysay, backing his political career and helping him rise to a position of prominence where he could effectively act against the Huks? This might safeguard both Filipino and American interests within his nation. Or should they not? Given the cold war attitudes of the day, their final position was not surprising. They agreed to provide Magsaysay with quiet OPC support, arranged in such a way that he would not be privy to its source.

Wisner arranged for Colonel Chester and Assistant Secretary Merchant to fly to Manila, there to pressure President Quirino into appointing Magsaysay as secretary of national defense. When the two men arrived in Manila, Chester told Captain Charles Glazer, U.S. military liaison to Malacañang, that he needed to see Magsaysay. Glazer set up a luncheon meeting in an upstairs suite at the Manila Hotel. Present were Chester, Merchant, Glazer, General Peralta, who was chief of staff of the Philippine Army, and Ramón Magsaysay. They talked until about three o'clock in the afternoon. "Chester had all the authority [necessary] to make the promises. Magsaysay, whose nickname was Monching, was very happy [to know] how all this [financial] assistance would be channeled through JUSMAG for the secretary of national defense," Glazer recalled. On 1 September 1950 the Filipino president duly named Magsaysay to the desired position.[57]

After Magsaysay's return to the Philippines, Lansdale asked Stilwell to allow him to go back to Manila and try out his ideas. His boss approved and in the days that followed the OPC agent made plans to leave for his new assignment in the Pacific. He initially intended to go alone until he remembered his friend from Army intelligence Bo Bohannan who, like Lansdale, loved the Philippines and its people. He was, Lansdale knew, a very independent person, an individualist, who would provide capable help. "He was a detail man, a nuts and bolts type," Lansdale said. It took no persuasion to convince Bohannan to accompany him. "He used to reassure my wife that he knew [the Huks] and would take care of me," Lansdale recalled.[58]

Then in a planning session in OPC offices Lansdale mentioned that he had recruited Bohannan to go with him. "Then they futzed around and called . . . their approval off," he remembered. Lansdale was so appalled by this sudden change that he rose from his seat and walked to the door of the room. He stood with his back to the door and fumed at those present. "This door is going to stay closed," he growled, "until you come to a conclusion in this meeting that you are going to back me out there with your approval. If I have to come back eventually and meet with you again . . . and you haven't fully backed me, I'll have my pockets full of grenades. I'll get you all in here, lock you in and throw grenades at you." None of the OPC policymakers were used to such behavior. "They were all top policy people and said I was a wild man. . . . Anyhow, I finally got their approval."[59]

Whatever the actual words exchanged that day, Lansdale at least had what he wanted: approval to form a team for counterinsurgent activity in the Philippines and the money necessary to operate there. It was to be a small group. Lansdale and Bohannan would work alone, backed only by an Army officer on duty with CIA who was a communications expert, First Lieutenant Alger C. Ellis. Ace Ellis was to join them shortly after they arrived in Manila.[60]

Ellis' services were both important and essential. L. Fletcher Prouty, who later worked for Lansdale, has explained why:

> There are . . . times when an operator on a special project has the means to communicate with his headquarters in Washington independently of other channels. In such cases, this operator will at times bypass not only the ambassador and military hierarchy, but he may even bypass his own station chief. All of this is excused on the grounds of security and expediency. In some cases the station chief has become incensed over such actions; but . . . his anger seldom got him very far. One of the most famous of these differences occurred in the Philippines when Ed Lansdale was operating with Magsaysay and the station chief, who was on excellent terms with Magsaysay himself, was not aware of some of the operations that Lansdale and his Filipino cohorts had set in motion.[61]

Those at the Office of Policy Coordination thus considered Lansdale's work to be so secret and important that even John Richardson, the CIA station chief in Manila, could be kept ignorant of his activities.

Now Lansdale began to think about what cover he would use when he arrived in the Philippines. He needed two kinds of cover: cover for status, a tradecraft term describing an activity or occupation that gives an agent a viable reason for being in a country to disguise his actual operational movements, and cover for action, a believable story other than the truth to mask his real purposes in traveling around the country and seeing people important to him.

"The matter of cover," William Colby once wrote, "has always been difficult for American intelligence. The intelligence services of other countries . . . have always been able to provide their agents with the deepest and most protective of covers. . . . They are able to plant their agents credibly wherever they choose, fabricating for them solid false identities as foreign-service or military officers, newspaper reporters, ministry officials, or staff members of international organizations."[62] Lansdale was as aware as Colby of the difficulties of providing cover for himself in his forthcoming efforts in the Pacific. He knew his actions on behalf of OPC had to be hidden at all costs — even the very existence of such an agency was to be kept from the American people and from other nations.

While Lansdale was laying plans for his new assignment, one of his former PHILRYCOM commanders, General Jonathan Anderson, who now served as JUSMAG commander in the Philippines, returned to Washington on temporary duty. He told Lansdale that Quirino was looking for someone to advise the Philippine Army on ways to upgrade its intelligence-gathering capacity. "You would be the perfect man to go into that job," the general told Lansdale. Perhaps Lansdale remembered his World War II service, recalling the years when he quietly served OSS while also assigned as a member of the Army's Military Intelligence Service. To use such a cover again appealed to him. "Why don't you go back and tell Quirino that?" Lansdale replied. The general did precisely what Lansdale suggested. Shortly thereafter, following the application of appropriate pressure, President Quirino invited Lieutenant Colonel Edward G. Lansdale to become his adviser on intelligence matters. General Anderson also quietly informed Myron Cowen, the U.S. ambassador to the Philippines, that Lansdale would be arriving on a secret mission and that Cowen was to cooperate with any requests Lansdale might make of him.[63]

Lansdale believed his role as an Air Force lieutenant colonel would give him one level of cover; the ostensible role as intelligence adviser to the Philippine Army would provide another. Those should be sufficient, and the idea of using a cover as an intelligence officer to hide intelligence activities appealed to Lansdale's sense of humor and irony.

Only with difficulty did Lansdale persuade his OPC superiors to accept his suggested cover. During several meetings they hammered away at his resolve. "That's the lousiest cover we have ever heard of — to go out [to the Philippines] as an intelligence chief!" they argued. Lansdale's mind was made up. Throughout the discussions his response was inevitably the same: "Why not?" He would not be spending much time doing intelligence work for either JUSMAG or President Quirino.

Many members of the Philippine military intelligence community were old friends. Lansdale had helped them establish themselves in the early postwar years when the Filipino government was re-forming its army.

Using the cover of a military intelligence adviser, he would simply be "taking up old duties" among people who were "very close friends." They were, Lansdale believed, "doing an excellent job and didn't need any advice." Perhaps he might persuade Quirino to listen more carefully to his advisers than he was wont to do, but that wouldn't occupy much time. "I can do that on the side," Lansdale told those who questioned his cover. "It will all be germane." It would leave him time free to concentrate on his OPC duties. "At the same time, I will be ahead of the game." He never did quite convince his superiors. "They were all shaking their heads," Ed recalled. "[T]hey didn't want me to go at all because my cover was weak." Nevertheless, they finally agreed and Lansdale was authorized to go ahead with his departure plans.[64]

Following OPC's approval for his project in August 1950, Lansdale made plans to be in Manila by early September, only a few weeks away. With his departure for the Philippines, although he remained assigned to the USAF Central Control Group in Washington, D.C., his duty title was changed from intelligence officer to psychological warfare staff officer. He retained that title for the next seven years, until 28 February 1957, no matter what his actual duties or responsibilities and despite his reassignment on 10 September 1951 from the Central Control Group to Headquarters, 1007 Air Intelligence Squadron.[65]

Lansdale's efficiency report for the period 13 November 1949 to 28 February 1950, written by Colonel George A. Chester, noted Lansdale's superior performance of duty. "He has the highest potential value of any Air Force Officer I have known, with a steel trap mind and a driving purpose in a relaxed body. I would rather have [Lieutenant] Col. Lansdale with me than any other Officer I know."[66]

It was easier for Lansdale to receive an official transfer to the Philippines than it was for him to prepare his family for the move. Some months earlier Ed and Helen had agreed to end their separation and try once again to make a success of their marriage. With that decision made, Helen bravely sold the house in Larkspur during the summer of 1950. It had been a focal point of her security for many years. Accompanied by Ted and Peter she arrived in Washington, where Ed met them. Despite the joy of the two boys in seeing their father, it was not the happiest of reunions for the parents.

Earlier that summer, following their agreement to reunite, Ed had purchased an old house in Georgetown. In spare hours he ripped, nailed, and hammered in valiant efforts at remodeling. During those weeks Bo Bohannan was attending a counterintelligence school at Fort Holabird in Baltimore, where he studied the Japanese language. When they could take time off, Bo and Dorothy came to Georgetown to help Ed scrape paint and strip wallpaper. Dorothy remembered, "We spent much time there scraping stuff off the walls and sitting around over coffee talking [and] making plans."[67] As the time grew nearer for the two men to depart, they spent more time talking than working.

Thus when Helen arrived, the house was far from completed. When Ed drove her to the new home she was appalled at the sight. "I had only progressed as far as chopping down walls to make larger rooms and ripping out the plumbing for modernizing," Lansdale said. "Standing in the shambles, I broke the news that I was leaving within hours for . . . the Philippines. It wasn't the most pleasant moment of my life." They stayed that night in a hotel while Ed tried to help Helen understand that he had to leave. Prior to his departure he also asked Dorothy Bohannan to keep an eye on Helen and the boys. The next day he was gone.[68]

Her new home gave Helen something to focus on. She hired painters and carpenters. She painted the living room in federal blue and the dining room in a pleasant green. Kitchen cupboards were built in colonial style. Floors were polished until they shone, and area rugs were then laid on them. The old frame Georgetown house with its chimneys and fireplaces and big rooms seemed even bigger and became not only livable but charming, warm and cozy. Helen was pleased to discover she had a knack for decorating.[69]

Peter Lansdale remembered those days when his father was so often gone. His mother, he recalled, "had very old-fashioned values that children should be seen and not heard. . . . [They] were instilled in us. Without a father around, there wasn't much she could do . . . to straighten us out. She couldn't really grab us and turn us over her knee. . . . We were very much aware that she was trying to raise us by herself and I think we were smart enough to go along with that. We had a father who was [only] an image. . . . We were . . . closer to her . . . . because she was the only parent eighty-five percent of the time. . . . She would play ball and catch and throw the baseball and football around . . . . She kind of dragged us around and made life as normal as she could."

Even as a small boy Peter was aware of the tension in the household. "I don't think it was to her liking at all, the fact that Dad was gone so much. I never felt that tug in front of us but I . . . felt the trauma with Dad leaving the family [and] would, of course, obviously [become] very emotional and upset when he would go."[70]

Now Lansdale was gone once again. He had left the family home in Larkspur for his assignment at Lowry AFB in late February 1949. All through that assignment and his schooling at Selma, Alabama, he had lived apart from his wife and children. When he went to work for OPC in Washington, the separation continued until late August 1950. No sooner had the family been reunited than it was torn apart again by still another assignment taking him far away. Father and husband for only a few days since February 1949, Lansdale might well have been dismayed had he known he would remain away, except for brief intervals while on leave, until March 1957 — nearly seven years in the future. Only then would Ed and Helen again be able to have a normal, reasonably settled marriage.

5

AN HONEST ELECTION

LANSDALE'S NEW MISSION for the Office of Policy Coordination was a difficult one, and he was given only a limited time to accomplish it. In just three months, Lansdale was to protect American interests in the Philippines and to consolidate a power base for Ramón Magsaysay. He was further to provide counsel and support to the new secretary of national defense, influence the revitalization of the Philippine Army, help the government make progress in its war against the Huks, urge political reform upon the host government, and see what he could do to help Filipinos have an honest election in the November 1951 balloting. He was then to return to his work in Washington.[1] What could be done in that brief period? It was a herculean task. Yet Lansdale was enthusiastic about his coming role as Magsaysay's adviser. "I had some ideas and I had written some memos on political warfare and on psychological warfare [while on duty in Washington] . . . . So I went out to the Philippines with a pretty fuzzy but wide term of reference . . . of what my duties would be . . . to see what could be done in that situation."[2] He had not a moment to waste.

The Huk rebellion was at its peak. Some fifteen thousand organized guerrillas in the field relied on about a million supporters and sympathizers out of a total population of twenty-two million. The Huk movement was run by a Politburo composed mostly of intellectuals. The military arm, strictly controlled by the Politburo, was organized in squadrons and led by Luis Taruc, El Supremo. Rebel political indoctrination was carried on by political commissars among troop units at schools called Stalin Universities hidden deep in the hills and jungles. The insurgents made up a considerable force. Arrayed against them were the fifty thousand men of the Philippine armed forces.

Lansdale's trip to the Philippines was more comfortable than the first one had been in 1945. This time he had no need to ride a transport ship wallowing through hurricane waters. Instead he and Bo Bohannan rode first class on a Boeing B-377 Stratocruiser Pan-American Clipper flight many thousands of feet above the green Pacific. The plane landed at Nichols Field (later renamed the Manila International Airport) late in the first week of September 1950.[3]

They were met at the airport by a driver and a staff car and Lansdale was taken directly to his billet, an empty two-story bungalow in an upper-middle-class housing compound just outside the Manila city limits, in an area built up since the end of World War II. (The area later became known as Heroes' Hills.) Many American officers were billeted there. The housing area, surrounded by barbed wire and patrolled by guards, featured sentries from the Philippine Army standing watch at gate areas. Nearby, in a building that had formerly served as the offices of a real estate development firm, lay the headquarters of the Joint United States Military Advisory Group (JUSMAG).[4]

Lansdale's first two days, filled with protocol visits, demonstrated that his military rank no longer accurately reflected the authority he possessed, as would be true for years to come. His position was more important than his rank, for this agent from the Office of Policy Coordination bore the authority of both the State and Defense departments. Lansdale not only knew, but was favored by, those at the very top of the nation's intelligence system. Armed with their authority, his own modest rank was unimportant. In some ways his position was like that of an enlisted military policeman who finds it necessary to apprehend a high-ranking officer. Should the officer attempt to order the MP to leave him alone, the customary response follows: "Sir, don't confuse your rank with my authority."

And Lansdale's authority was great. He commanded a highly classified project of major importance to the United States and was able to carry it to success. In the process, several senior government officials placed themselves under Colonel Lansdale's leadership and carried out his orders.[5] For long years — as a major, lieutenant colonel, and colonel in the Philippines, in Vietnam, and in the Department of Defense's Office of Special Operations — Lansdale's rank was never commensurate with his authority, but he projected an aura of power.

As a result of his work in the Philippines and later, Lansdale became known as a man who could get things done, who could achieve success with programs he espoused. Some who opposed him feared to show their antagonism too openly because of his highly placed backers. Others, who saw his successes, gravitated toward him and lent him their loyalty and support because power itself holds a strong attraction for many. And this strong-willed, independent-minded man continued to devote his time and attention to those issues that seemed to him to be in the best interests of the United States.

Officers with the rank of lieutenant colonel are not normally entitled to wield great authority, nor are they generally waited on by those in high position, yet Lansdale was quickly received by the major general who now commanded JUSMAG, Leland Hobbs. The general was one of those senior officials who now followed Lansdale's leadership, but still he greeted Lansdale warmly on his arrival, promising to help in any way he could. Hobbs knew well that Lansdale came to Manila not only with the blessing of the Air Force but with the political support of the executive branch of the American government.

Ambassador Myron Cowen was another who knew of Lansdale's credentials and who followed his leadership. He personally met Lansdale at the embassy to escort this lieutenant colonel through the various departments there, introducing the staff to him so that they might brief him on the current situation in the host country. When Lansdale later arrived at Malacañang Palace he learned that President Elpidio Quirino was at that moment presiding over a cabinet meeting, and Lansdale settled down to wait. An aide informed the president of Lansdale's presence and Quirino interrupted that meeting to greet his visitor who, despite his lack of high rank, represented the very highest echelons of the American government. Quirino invited Lansdale to "come right in and sit down."

Lansdale later drove to Camp Murphy to talk with the chief of staff of the Philippine Army, General Mariano Castañeda, who welcomed him warmly and extended his hospitality and offers of help. "In other words," Lansdale later wrote, "my first hours . . . were spent with most of the top officials of a country that had been independent for just four years and with the top local officials of the country that had given this newly independent nation its tutelage in self-rule."[6] It was a heady time for a lieutenant colonel.

While Lansdale made that first flurry of protocol visits, Bo Bohannan hired the servants necessary to run their bungalow household in the JUSMAG housing area. Bo knew where to look. An infantryman who had fought at Buna in New Guinea and elsewhere, he had been sent into the Philippines ahead of the American invasion to work with guerrilla forces in Leyte. Those guerrillas had recognized his bravery and effectiveness and had quickly given him their highest respect. Bohannan now called on former Leyteños guerrillas he knew and soon had a houseboy and guards on duty, but no cook.[7] Lansdale discovered that their next door neighbor had a Filipino cook with a reputation for being able to prepare American-style food. Lansdale managed to hire the man away from his neighbor. One day Bo told the cook, "I would like to have some codfish cakes'' — fried patties of fish flakes mixed with crumbled crackers and egg. The cook acknowledged that he would make them. Days went by but no menu featured codfish cakes. Bo put pressure on the cook without visible results. A grumpy Bohannan finally gave the man an order: "You *will* serve codfish cakes for supper tonight!" "Oh, yes, sir," the cook replied. At suppertime there were no fish cakes. "Where the hell is my codfish cake?" Bohannan thundered. "Yes, sir, coming up." The cook smiled as he brought in a codfish-flavored layer cake covered with icing and garnished with cherries. Bohannan had finally gotten what he asked for! A very confused cook was soon on his way back to his former place of employment. Bo called in one of his men from Leyte. "Andres, do you know how to cook?" Bo asked. "Oh, no sir," the man answered. "Well, find out in a hurry," Bohannan added, "because you now are one!"[8]

Lansdale had more than food to think about. Only short weeks before he returned to the Philippines, the Huks had committed their "Makabulos massacre" of 20 August. They had attacked a small hospital at Makabulos, killed the staff of administrators, doctors, and nurses, and then had fallen upon the patients, even including those helpless in bed. Ammunition was in short supply so the rebels hacked away with bolos and bayonets in a brutal display of butchery. Military reports and the Manila press claimed that the wanton savagery of the attack that day had started a strong tide of popular revulsion against the Huks.

Lansdale read the reports and wondered. He decided to visit Makabulos and talk to people there and compare their comments with official views. He drove to the community, which was located on the outskirts of Tarlac town, and spoke with people there. "Yes," they said, "we regret the killing but this was war." Lansdale was amazed to learn that the most vivid memory of the people he talked to was how polite and thoughtful the Huk guerrillas had been. Rebels had started filtering into town in the early afternoon. Some had even gone to the movies while waiting for time to pass. At first dark they had quietly taken over the streets, asking people to please remain indoors so they wouldn't get hurt. Then the slaughter at the hospital began. Yet it was the polite and courteous warnings of the armed Huks, many of them relatives, that people remembered.[9] Lansdale was glad he had not trusted official or press stories. They were so much wishful thinking!

The Huk rebellion had made such inroads that even the Filipino president lived in fear of his life. Armored cars sat on the grounds of Malacañang Palace day and night to protect Quirino from any sudden rebel attack. "They never got that far," Lansdale noted, "but he was afraid of it."[10] Gunfire could regularly be heard in the outskirts of the capital city.

Lansdale wondered how the rebels could have done so well. The more he studied it the more convinced he became that the Huk campaign was classic in the way it demonstrated the military principle of economy of force[11] and in its application of effective strategy and tactics. Much of the responsibility for coping with the rebellion was in the hands of the secretary of the interior, whose militant arm was the Philippine Constabulary, the national police force. Local control of the Constabulary, however, was mostly the political prerogative of the governor of the province to which the troops were assigned. The Philippine Army, Navy, and Air Force, under the authority of the secretary of national defense, were no help. They devoted almost full-time efforts to ready themselves to resist an invasion by hypothetical external forces and paid scant attention to the internal Huk threat.[12]

There should have been enough Constabulary troops to keep the Huks on the run. In previous years the Constabulary had used tactics right out of instructional manuals. According to existing doctrine, they should have won. They had not even come close, however, and Lansdale put his finger on the reason: while Huks were running a revolution, the Philippine government was fighting them as though they were formal enemy armed forces.[13] Even worse, actions of Filipino soldiers were themselves one of the main Huk recruiting forces. The growth of Huk sentiment arose in large part out of the Constabulary's unsoldierly behavior.

Soldiers seemed to believe, Lansdale pointed out, that the main purpose of having a gun was to use it to shoot people. "Now 'people' meant . . . villagers," Lansdale said. The Huks were carefully following Mao's dictum of getting close to those who lived in the countryside, helping them, doing political and social work to gain popular support. "So when troops . . . misbehaved around villagers," he noted, "the Huks would point out 'They aren't your friends; they are the enemies of all of us, but *we'll* help you.' "[14]

Nor did the Philippine troops seem to limit their misbehavior to the poor and powerless. Lansdale one day encountered the daughter of a colonel in the Philippine armed forces. When he asked her why she was crying, she said she had just ridden into Manila with some friends on a bus from one of the provinces. At one security checkpoint along the highway a soldier boarded the bus and ordered all passengers to get out so they could be searched. Two of the girl's young companions had moved too slowly and the soldiers had beaten them. Lansdale could only sympathize with her and promise that things would get better. It was for him another indication that those in the military essentially saw themselves as separate from their own people. That attitude had to be changed if any headway was to be made against the Huks.[15]

Lansdale made other trips into the countryside to observe havoc wrought by the Huks and to watch the Constabulary at work. Factual background information, reports, and statistical data prepared by others never satisfied him. He always wanted to see things at first hand. General Hobbs, the JUSMAG commander, had standing orders that Americans were not to go into the hinterlands, and most U.S. personnel traveled only between the JUSMAG housing compound, the JUSMAG officers club compound, and the JUSMAG headquarters compound. Some advisers traveled a mile or so up the road to the Philippine armed forces headquarters area where they joined their counterparts for discussions and office work. Lansdale refused to abide by such restrictions. He insisted to Hobbs that he and his assistants would travel whenever and wherever they felt it necessary to give the best advice they could to the embattled Filipinos. The general made an exception for Lansdale and agreed he could move about the countryside as he wished. Lansdale knew he had to make observations at first hand if he really wanted to know what was happening. It was not until well over a year later that Hobbs finally allowed other JUSMAG officers to go out in the field.[16]

Throughout his life Lansdale excoriated the notion that Americans in Asia could take appropriate actions without an immediate knowledge of the area to which they were assigned. Effective programs, he stated, required the guidance of informed judgments. "Maybe we should be more cautious in our listening to 'experts' and pay more heed to how they have come to know that of which they speak," he later wrote. "Observing the surface of a nation, even in minute detail, is no guarantee that what lies below the surface is seen also." Lansdale's personality was tailor-made for such an approach. Offices bored him and routine dulled his senses. Staff meetings left him feeling stultified while administrative hierarchies stifled his ingenuity and constrained his imagination. He was at his best while operating on his own, subject only to broad and generalized directions that allowed him to mingle with the common people of Asia.[17]

It was essential to have qualified American advisers. Yet most Americans, he feared, remained comfortably circumstanced in Manila or Saigon or Phnom Penh where they stayed largely isolated from the real culture and spirit of the people they were sent to serve. "When was the 'expert' last invited to be a guest in an 'average' Filipino household to share a meal? When did he last spend a night with Filipinos in the provinces? When did he last travel . . . in a manner permitting the gathering of real opinions? . . . [D]oes he honestly know whereof he speaks? Or, does he merely know Manila, the largest city, and a coterie of acquaintances? . . . City views become even less meaningful in a country that is largely agrarian. . . . Working . . . close up is one hell of a lot different than sitting in an office reading information from 'objective' aloofness or of learning the scene second-hand through a few selected contacts who specialize in scandal and gossip.'' There was no substitute for firsthand knowledge. It was also important to be prepared in another way. Americans abroad must have a real dedication to high principles. Without such strength, ''all else that we possess and do will be without lasting meaning.''[18]

Never for a moment, however, did Lansdale believe he was one of the "little guys" of America. He knew his path had taken him among the politically powerful; he faced opportunities affording him great influence. He also knew he was going to act according to his own best estimates of what might be needed rather than blindly follow the instructions of others. They weren't on the scene. They might not be aware of what was needed. He was and he would act as he saw best.[19]

President Quirino had not objected too strongly when George Chester and Livingston Merchant urged him to appoint Magsaysay as secretary of national defense, particularly when their voices were joined by that of another man he trusted — young Charles Glazer, an American adviser and liaison officer who lived in Malacañang Palace.[20]

Magsaysay was part of a Filipino middle class on the rise — a rather energetic and aggressive group — which was increasing its power and attempting to carry out reforms of recognized problems. They were a very different breed from the older ruling class even though some were sons of that group. Several had attended Ateneo de Manila University or the University of the Philippines, where they acquired a social conscience. Others were in high school or college ROTC at the beginning of World War II and as idealistic students had gone with some of their instructors into the hills. They fought the invading Japanese and continued to resist the subsequent occupation of their nation. They fought all through the war with a goal, a dream, in mind: after the war ended and America gave them their independence, they were going to make their land a better place to live. That future was worth risking their lives for.

They were very much concerned with the lot of farmers and the labor movement, and in the postwar period as they began their careers they entered the ranks of reform movements in both political and economic affairs. Some of these men worked in every conceivable way to better the lot of tenants who labored on their own families' sugar plantations. Sugar barons and families of planters were some of the most reactionary people in the archipelago. Yet now their own sons were deserting family interests to campaign for landholdings for peasant farmers, for agricultural cooperatives, for cooperative sugar mills, for sugar planting associations. Magsaysay came out of the middle-class part of that general movement.

Magsaysay, proud of his progress in life, was now in a position where he could make a real difference. He had determination, drive, and an ability to find solutions to problems, to move obstacles, and to get things done.[21] As his career blossomed, other reformers rallied to his cause. His spirit of reform was so palpable they knew it was not faked. And so they joined him to carry out land reform measures, to persuade civil service employees to become true public servants, to clean out the corruption in the customs office, to reinvigorate morale within the military, to carry the war to the Huks.[22]

In his new position as secretary of national defense, Magsaysay had authority to reorganize and reform the Philippine Army and Constabulary. He could travel freely throughout his nation on military inspection trips, promote or relieve officers on the spot, and order transgressors to be tried by courts-martial. Medals, promotions, and cash were the rewards he handed out to those who fought well against the Huks. He paid bounties for dead Huks — in money for enlisted men, in promotions for officers.

Magsaysay was a man worth knowing, as Lansdale had recognized when he met him during his visit to Washington. Lansdale's chance to become close to Magsaysay came about during Magsaysay's first days as defense secretary. Stories made the rounds about how the Huks had sent trigger squads into Manila in efforts to liquidate Magsaysay. His family home seemed insecure and he feared for his wife, Luz, and his children, Teresita, Milagres, and Ramón, Jr. Magsaysay sent his family for an extended vacation to Luz' family home in Bataan and, at Lansdale's invitation, moved in with Lansdale and Bohannan in their bungalow in the JUSMAG compound. Some other American officers who lived with their dependents in that compound asked General Leland Hobbs to order Magsaysay to leave since his presence might endanger their own families' safety. Hobbs replied that they could send their families back home to the United States if they wanted to do so but Magsaysay could remain as long as he wished.[23]

Magsaysay and Lansdale got along magnificently, and Lansdale knew clearly what he wanted the secretary of national defense to do. The first step was simply to be his friend. They shared a room with two beds. Lansdale acted the part of a good listener and friend who let his roommate talk out his problems. He singled out the salient features of such conversations and summarized the problems burdening Magsaysay, adding his own values, the principles involved, and suggesting solutions. When Magsaysay made his decisions he was inevitably influenced by Lansdale's views. The relationship "was roughly the way two friends would talk with each other," Lansdale said.[24]

The opportunity to spend long hours with Magsaysay was Lansdale's first break on his mission to the Philippines. "We were like brothers," Lansdale remembered. "That got known all over Asia. It gave me a chance to be myself and be a little different than others. . . . In the Philippines they said they expected an American to behave the way I did. I displayed characteristics they had wanted to see in an American. It reassured them, so when I suggested things they listened and tried to do them."[25] Some years later, Ramón's brother, Jess, wrote Lansdale that he still recalled those days: "whether it was in Baguio or in Zambales or in Manila . . . you were *always* there to provide him [Magsaysay] with the unselfish advice that you *always* had ready."[26] One of Lansdale's longtime Filipino associates, José Banzon, reminisced that Lansdale and Magsaysay "had similar tastes; one is innovative, the other one is very receptive."[27]

Manuel Manahan, a Filipino journalist and publisher, was deeply committed to political reform. He observed the relationship between Magsaysay and Lansdale and realized that Magsaysay was Lansdale's "apt pupil." He further agreed with the American that Magsaysay, while untutored, had great qualities of leadership and was a man of action, sensitive to the needs of his people. Magsaysay saw the people's potential. His basic rule was that "those who have less in life must have more in law."[28]

Thus Lansdale's first stroke of good fortune came with the opportunity to have Magsaysay move into his quarters so the two could become "brothers." The second came about because Magsaysay chose to do much of his official business in the bungalow where they lived. A stream of officers from Philippine Army headquarters came to the JUSMAG compound to see Magsaysay and he started off each day using Lansdale's breakfast table as an office desk. His aides were in attendance as were members of the Army staff, and the defense secretary began each day by talking with those who had come to confer with him. Many — both from the Army and from civilian life — who had reason to see Magsaysay waited inside the bungalow until their turn came. They were, Lansdale knew, concerned about what was happening and had ideas on how to improve existing practices. All of them wanted to share their thoughts with the defense secretary.

In addition to those waiting to see Magsaysay, Lansdale also had visitors of his own, including some field commanders of the armed forces whom he had met during his earlier posting to the Philippines. These men often came to his quarters for a few hours of relaxation. As they visited they told him what was happening in their areas of operation, often "looking for a little bit of hand-holding or a pat on the head or understanding for what they were going through in combat [against the Huks]."[29]

The visitors — a mix of headquarters and field soldiers of all ranks ranging from unit commanders down to platoon sergeants — sat and talked with Lansdale and drank his coffee while others nearby were doing business with the secretary of national defense. Lansdale felt that a "lot of ideas" were generated during those "kaffee klatsch" sessions. This was, Lansdale admitted, an unusual way of working out military problems, and yet it worked so well he continued to use that approach in later years in Vietnam and elsewhere. It was, he insisted, the most "simple and natural way of working in the world." He was convinced that he was able to suggest many good ideas for fighting the Huk rebellion during those meetings in his house.

There is little doubt that Lansdale planned those sessions that took place so near where Magsaysay sat working, yet in a disingenuous disclaimer he insisted that the practical result was unintentional. "As we got to talking," Lansdale said, "sometimes we'd forget that the Secretary of Defense was sitting at the breakfast table trying to do business a few yards away. Our voices would rise up a bit and the next thing we knew, Magsaysay would come out and have a cup of coffee with us. So here we were getting ideas presented at his level . . . And every so often he'd say, 'Well, let's try that.' Then he would go down to Malacañang Palace and talk to the President and the Cabinet and get government backing for a project."[30] Such a setting was simply a way for American advisers, as interested friends, to bring men in key positions together in an informal atmosphere so they might develop winning tactics to use against the insurgents.[31] Thus Lansdale not only was a "brother" to Magsaysay but had a perfect way to draw his attention to problems that needed addressing.

Emma Valeriano, a Filipina who was one of Lansdale's friends, recalled that he was always low-key, letting others exploit ideas he planted. Asians loved him for he had great respect for their dignity. Mrs. Valeriano described Lansdale's manner of offering advice, which he must have used time and again with Magsaysay. "He would sit quietly . . . listen to you talk [and] speak out." Then he would sum up in his own words and with his own emphasis what had been said. "Suddenly you are getting a revelation. You think, 'Oh my God. Why didn't I think of this?' I am getting the light. Then I made my own judgment. Where did that come from? From myself! But he helped! That's why I would trust a man like him. . . . I never once distrusted what Lansdale had to tell me." Her words help explain why Lansdale's advice to Magsaysay was so valuable. "Everybody who worked with him knew they could trust Ed — still knowing or suspecting that he was an intelligence officer. That's unique. That's a trust. I knew he had some things he wanted to do and was not going to tell me but I trust that man. Even if it's for the U.S. government, I'm almost sure that's the same thing I want for the Filipinos."[32]

One suggestion that Lansdale gave Magsaysay in those days was to ensure that those who were fighting the Huks remembered at the same time to respect the rights of their own countrymen. Magsaysay agreed and soon ordered a reorganization of the armed forces. The Constabulary became part of the military establishment under the new secretary of national defense, and Magsaysay's department of government now took over the main responsibility for countering the Huks. The Constabulary force of company-sized units was replaced by battalion combat teams, which from that time on bore the brunt of the fighting.

Lansdale and Magsaysay spent much time traveling in the field on inspection trips of the newly organized forces. Most of Magsaysay's initial visits were begun in early morning, and he requested that Lansdale accompany him. "I was present at most of [them]," Lansdale said, "and very often during them I could tip him off to what a good inspector would spot and see in a unit and he would very quickly pick up the behavior patterns." In his usual public disclaimer of any importance of his own role, Lansdale added that Magsaysay "would have done the same whether anybody had been around or not." Lansdale recalled that on those visits his friend didn't look like the secretary of national defense. Wearing slacks and a wild aloha sport shirt, Magsaysay looked like someone right out of the provinces. Few who saw him guessed that he held an important government position.

Frequently the two men traveled by air to an inspection. Leaving the plane in the care of the pilot, Lansdale and Magsaysay walked to the nearest road, whereupon the secretary stuck out his thumb in a hitchhiker's gesture to passing cars. Lansdale usually wore his uniform and when a driver stopped Lansdale explained who his companion really was. He also frequently had to do the same to incredulous troops and officers when they finally located the unit they were seeking. Lansdale commented that his own role was a small one: "He quickly became known [on his own] of course."[33]

Both men soon came to the conclusion that the Philippine government had lost its own people, at least in Tarlac. Numerous visits to other towns and provinces confirmed this finding. While in the field with military units, Lansdale often watched Magsaysay wander away from where troops were deployed to nearby civilian nipa huts and their charcoal cooking fires. Invited inside, he asked question after question about the family, their crops, income, and debts to money lenders. He occasionally peered inside the pot on the fire to see what they had to eat. He noticed their scanty food and the poverty in which they lived.

One day in Aglao, his home barrio, he was confronted with the horrifying sight of the bodies of women and children he had known who had been murdered in a Huk raid to intimidate him into resigning as secretary. For the first time the real savagery of the Huk guerrillas came home to him and yet, despite it all, he remained capable of having compassion for Huk prisoners.

Manahan spoke to this point. He remembered that Magsaysay often pondered why a Huk became a rebel. Why was he ready to sacrifice his life? When a man was prepared to give up his life to overthrow a government, he must first have suffered greatly. Magsaysay was always struck by the emotion in the voices of those captured insurgents who talked of injustices in their lives.[34]

These constant surprise visits by Magsaysay and Lansdale to troops in the field kept both officers and men in a better state of readiness. The secretary checked everything. He looked at the cardboard soles of troopers' worn-through boots and wondered about the system of supply. He found a medium tank broken down during combat because of faulty spark plugs and, under fire, tried to fix it, knowing all the while that someone had stolen supplies of new plugs to sell on the black market. He determined to stop the practice. He caught officers at their command posts sleeping late in the morning after a long night of poker or mah-jongg and cashiered or demoted them on the spot. He saw at first hand evidence of an army not ready for combat with the enemy and he quickly followed his inspections with actions to remedy the problems he found. As he went from combat areas to his office, to cabinet meetings, to congressional hearings, to staff councils, Magsaysay began to think and speak and decide with more sureness, with the authority of someone who knew whereof he spoke, who had witnessed problems at first hand and was determined to correct them.[35] Magsaysay was rapidly growing to meet the demands of his job and Lansdale was there to help him.

How did others see Lansdale's role? Those at the Office of Policy Coordination were not given to public acclamation for the work of their agents. Richard Stilwell, head of FE/Plans and Lansdale's immediate superior, some years later spoke openly of Lansdale's work without actually mentioning his name. Lansdale was, Stilwell admitted, "organizationally my subordinate but, in terms of the military ideal, vastly my superior." He described Lansdale as sitting "unseen at the right hand" of Magsaysay. Lansdale, according to Stilwell, "was the primary factor" in the Philippine conquest of the Huks, and he then went on "to groom" Magsaysay for the presidency of his nation. "Yes," Stilwell said, "this officer was a king maker."[36]

Reuters news correspondent Peter C. Richards, a cynic in the English fashion, suggested that Magsaysay was entirely Lansdale's creation. Richards knew the characters in this play and shared some experiences with them. He watched as Lansdale went out to the provinces with Magsaysay and realized that attention was always focused on Magsaysay — no one noticed Lansdale. His biggest asset was this natural camouflage while he directed affairs. "Ed was . . . telling Magsaysay exactly what to do. There is no question of that. He was just somebody you wouldn't notice. . . . He didn't embarrass anybody by his presence." Richards did not suggest that Lansdale's influence was necessarily overt. It came from the long hours they spent together. "His instruction of Magsaysay was subliminal, over the days, over the weeks, over the evenings, over the nights. By the time Magsaysay stood up somewhere to speak, he knew what he had to say. It was subliminal, but it was there."

Richards had "unrestrained praise" for the skill and efficiency with which Lansdale executed the instructions he received from his superiors. "I always maintain that, in his day, Lansdale could have placed my houseboy on the throne, if that had been desired and if he had been correspondingly instructed to do so."[37] Richards spoke those sentiments in the summer of 1985, but he had held them for a long while. Nearly twenty-five years earlier he had chided a newspaper editor for the small credit given Lansdale in an article about Magsaysay's creation, elevation, and election. "I believe the same treatment could have turned my or your houseboy into hero and president (with no worse results)," Richards wrote.[38] The editor replied that although some believed that "Americans" had made Magsaysay president, the charge was not true. "It was mainly Lansdale."[39]

There were others who believed Lansdale had created Magsaysay. In 1957, a Filipino friend, Albino Z. SyCip, wrote to Lansdale: "You have succeeded in creating for the Philippines a man like the late President Magsaysay. I hope you will also succeed in your efforts to help us make the Philippines a Citadel of Democracy."[40] Newspapers also held forth on Lansdale's influence: an article in the London Times proclaimed that "Magsaysay was discovered, tutored and skilfully built up as a national leader by one of Washington's cloak-and-dagger operators, the mysterious and powerful Air Force Colonel Edward Lansdale."[41] A few years later a Filipino columnist, Renato Constantino, charged that Magsaysay's "rise to the presidency had been master-minded by Lansdale." Another columnist, I. P. Soliongco, believed that from the time Magsaysay was appointed secretary of national defense to the day he was killed "he was literally under the guidance, if not under the custody, of the then Col. Landsdale [sic]."[42]

Lansdale was only too keenly aware of such charges. To a friend he once wrote, "Some of the more errant Filipino nationalists . . . like to picture Magsaysay as a not too bright gent completely under my thumb. (Some of the kindlier ones teased us by nicknaming me 'Frank' and nicknaming Bo as 'Stein,' the implication of course being that Magsaysay was . . . 'Frank and Stein's monster.') The Philippines is hard up for decent heroes and I am not about to aid and abet Magsaysay's detractors. While he did need some hand-holding, and while perhaps his Presidential record might have been a bit more substantive if I could have stayed on close by, he was a big boy in his own birthright.''[43]

Lansdale insisted to Bo Bohannan that ''We [must] give all the credit to the Filipinos who were doing this. It is their fight. They are risking their lives.'' Bohannan kept that faith. In a speech he gave at the University of the Philippines, Bo charged, ''The first damn lie . . . which I wish to nail is the story that Magsaysay was a puppet, a *tuta* [puppy], of the Americans. Not by a damn sight. He welcomed information, he welcomed advice, but he most assuredly made up his own mind and acted on his own perceptions, not infrequently to our consternation.''[44] At another time Lansdale commented that some seemed ''to describe a mysterious role for me which I don't deserve. Magsaysay and I were as close as brothers . . . but he was more than able to make up his own mind, do his own planning, and do battle for the things he believed in.'' There were those, Lansdale wrote, who ''simply cannot conceive of an Asian being a real man in his own right,'' but Magsaysay was a man among men and an authentic hero.[45]

Many years later, while speaking obliquely to a friend about his days with Magsaysay, Lansdale described a book he had written. ''Of course I tell some white lies in it,'' he said, ''mainly to give Asians some sorely-needed heroes from among their own.''[46] He wrote to Bo Bohannan in a similar vein: ''Our friends come out smelling like roses, untainted and heroic in it and against a proper background. As you know from long ago, I decided that Asia needed its own heroes — so I've given them a whole bookful of them, with us'uns merely being companionable friends to some great guys.''

Lansdale was always reticent about revealing the extent of his work in the Philippines because of his OPC connection, which demanded secrecy from him and which was in competition with CIA. From the beginning there was a barrier of considerable animosity between the enthusiastic oddball experts of the Office of Policy Coordination and the then small CIA organization whose people looked upon themselves as intelligence craftsmen and who seemed horrified by the horde of eager and bumbling OPC types heading out all over the world to change the status quo. Many within OPC came from the foreign service and from all the regular military services — including several who later became general officers in Vietnam — with a sprinkling of civilian volunteers. It was their horror of this upstart program that led to CIA's desire to weed out what it deemed a bunch of amateurs turned loose upon an unsuspecting world. In turn, many of those in OPC had a dimmer view of CIA's professionalism than CIA itself held. All of this exacerbated the uneasy relationships between the two organizations.

Walter Bedell Smith replaced Admiral Hillenkoetter as director of Central Intelligence in October 1950, only one month after Lansdale was sent to the Philippines. No sooner was Smith in office than he began to prod the Office of Special Operations and the Office of Policy Coordination into a more coordinated relationship. Neither group was particularly happy about the restructuring; it took a few more months — until January 1951 — before Smith was able to begin his merger by appointing Allen Dulles as his deputy director for plans, responsible for coordinating both the quarreling and the jealous rivals.[47]

"My own difficulties with CIA through the years," Lansdale later said, "probably had their genesis in CIA's attitude toward OPC."[48] Thus when Lansdale was sent to Manila as chief of OPC in the area, he carried with him a heightened suspicion of his sister organization. He agreed with his OPC superiors that rebuilding nations was part of their job. His approach, however, lay in allowing a country's people to do the job themselves with Americans in the background offering a helping hand. Opponents in CIA had a cruder view. More interested in securing victories in military terms than in political or psychological ones, they were quite willing to blast and destroy their opposition on cold war battlefields. Lansdale had brought Ace Ellis to the Philippines to operate his private communications channel to OPC so it would not be necessary to work through the CIA station chief in Manila, who remained blithely ignorant of much of the real purpose for Lansdale's activities during the next three years.[49]

After OPC and CIA were merged by Smith in August 1952, Lansdale continued to work for the Agency and thus fell under its secrecy requirement. "They were the ones that came to me and asked me to swear never to tell anybody," Lansdale said. "I can see why — the other things they were doing!" Lansdale, however, believed the later reputation of CIA to be, in part, unfair. "They've done many brave, wonderful, altruistic things that Americans could be very proud of."[50] Lansdale always kept his distance from CIA, firmly convinced he was always his own man and never the creature of any other person or institution. "I had a very clear notion of who I was and always have had. I told presidents of the U.S. not to ask me to do certain things if it went against my understanding of what the U.S. was all about and what those of us in the service to it are all about. I have done the same thing to the Air Force and to the CIA. They all know that and respected it. I never played games with anybody."[51]

Lansdale always kept a very tight rein on allowing anyone to know what his real mission and motives were during all the years of his career. "I haven't talked about things. . . . I haven't gone around saying, 'I did this [and I did that].' I used to beg Bo, 'Don't tell people what you are doing.' "[52]

There were reasons for such secrecy. To allow the public access to information about the OPC and CIA role in guaranteeing free elections in the Philippines in 1951 and 1953, Lansdale believed, was "too damn sensitive," for it bespoke a time when the United States actually interfered in the political process of a foreign country.[53] He ruminated further on the matter: "Also, if these people went to cheat, to print false ballots, well, to have a fire in the printing plant was —" and he paused for a long time before adding, "and all the ballots burn up in there, the warehouse, who else is going to do it [except some group like OPC]? How openly do you ever talk about something like that? Yet it is a big plus on the right side of things and well worth doing."[54]

Lansdale added a final word on the subject. "Filipinos still scream a lot [that] they don't want any CIA interference. Well, goddamn it, if I were a citizen of a foreign [third world] country and got decent elections with [CIA] help, I would ask for them. 'Would you please come in and keep an eye on these rascals running things here?' "[55] Lansdale admitted that OPC/CIA "let me know they thought very highly of some of the projects I was pushing people into and were trying to make work."[56]

Lansdale was pleased that he was able to help Filipinos run an honest election where votes were counted fairly. "I got CIA to very quietly fund certain organizations, give them enough money to get going and come to life. . . . I tried to set up ways that citizens could keep their freedom free and untainted. The U.S. can't do it otherwise. We have no means to do it but in this way. [It is] a way of operating."[57]

One way to assess the importance of Lansdale's effectiveness with Magsaysay is to look at the goals Lansdale then had and to lay them side by side with the official programs espoused and inaugurated by Magsaysay. A close correspondence of the two would surely be indicative that either Magsaysay suggested goals to Lansdale or that Lansdale influenced Magsaysay's political reform programs.

Was Lansdale Magsaysay's *éminence grise?* What were Lansdale's goals? As suggested earlier, they were above all else (1) to protect American military and economic interests in the Philippines. This could best be achieved by actions (2) to advance Magsaysay's political career by encouraging and supporting him in his role of secretary of national defense, which in turn would (3) allow Magsaysay to reform and revitalize the Philippine armed forces and thus (4) move closer to a military victory over the Huk rebels. Success there would (5) improve Magsaysay's political standing by fostering the interest of his countrymen in this young member of government, providing him with a sure platform from which he could work for needed reforms in the government, making it more sensitive to the needs of its own citizenry. With such help freely given, Magsaysay's pro-American attitudes would be vastly strengthened, thus securing American military and economic interests in the Philippines into the foreseeable future.

What were the elements of the program Magsaysay came to support?

1. High visibility for himself.
2. Protection of U.S. interests, both military and economic.
3. Reform of the armed forces.
4. Improved maneuver warfare and psychological warfare against Huk rebels.
5. Increased government concern for the welfare of its citizens, including such innovations as the Civil Affairs Office, programs of land for the landless, the use of military lawyers to protect the interests of the poor, the launching of the ten-centavo telegrams to register complaints against officials out of which ultimately came the Presidential Complaints and Action Committee, the National Movement for Free Elections (NAMFREL), and others.
6. His decision to campaign for the presidency and his ensuing pro-American positions.

The correlation is a close one. Thus Lansdale began the process that made Magsaysay a national hero and president and brought to Lansdale the reputation of an authority on combating insurgency.

Lansdale believed the first turning of the tide in the war against the Huks came when he convinced Magsaysay that Filipinos must do all they could to help themselves. He suggested that Magsaysay should build up a sum of money available to use to counter the insurgency. In turn Magsaysay worked with then Vice President Fernando López, who consented to become chairman of a fund-raising effort called the Peace Fund.[58] Using techniques developed by American community chest and Red Cross drives, the group raised about a million dollars' worth of pesos. These became Magsaysay's contingency funds, used to pay rewards for actions against Huk leaders, to purchase firearms from citizens in the provinces, to prevent weapons from falling into the hands of the Huks, and to finance operational intelligence. Magsaysay made good use of this money.[59]

Lansdale also insisted to Magsaysay that defeat of the Huk rebels would take more than traditional military assaults on their positions. He pushed for an ever-increasing use of psychological warfare — "psywar," he called it — in a multiphase approach. To basic military operations of searching out and destroying concentrations of Huk soldiers, Lansdale added a new dimension. He saw to it that the Philippine Army developed and trained a large psychological warfare unit and incorporated into its responsibilities almost everything he could think of that might confuse and befuddle the insurgents. He studied the history and traditions of people in areas with heavy concentrations of Huks to learn appropriate appeals with which to wean people from their devotion to the Huk cause.[60]

Lansdale reveled in propaganda operations. One idea he tried to develop during late September and early October 1950 involved borrowing an American Navy submarine. He recalled that during World War II Filipino guerrillas were always entranced when a submarine surfaced in their coastal waters to bring them advisers or supplies. Perhaps, he thought, Huk leaders would feel the same way about a "Soviet" submarine, arriving to reward them for their good works. They could be given false information about arrival times and location and identification codes. After clambering aboard expecting to hear speeches and receive medals, they could be seized and arrested, thus wiping out a large part of the enemy leadership. He and Bohannan practiced Russian phrases so they could pose as Soviet deck officers. Lansdale tried to convince his superiors that he needed a submarine and that his scheme would work.

Lansdale sent a message to OPC asking to be met on Guam for a discussion of the plan. He talked a pilot into flying him there on an available C-47. Unfortunately his bosses at OPC refused to make the trip and the C-47 conked out while still over Philippine air space. Lansdale had to cancel his trip. He ruefully commented that his plot convinced OPC personnel in Washington that he had gone insane. He later met Admiral Arleigh Burke, who had come from Korea for a short visit to the Philippines. They talked one day at a lunch with Ambassador Myron Cowen. "You got submarines up there I can borrow?" Lansdale asked the admiral. "You're damn right," Burke responded. "Just yell at me. I'll get them down here fast. That's a good idea you got. Whether it works or not, let's try it." Despite the admiral's enthusiasm, OPC refused to countenance the operation. Lansdale continued to believe that the plan might have worked.[61]

At about the same time that Lansdale was exploring his submarine scheme he also coordinated a plan with Magsaysay and the Philippine military intelligence people that resulted in an early morning raid on 18 October 1950. Having found the clandestine location of Huk politburo members in Manila, armed teams launched a surprise sally against their hiding places. They arrested 105 people, including many of the movement leaders, and seized five tons of documents. The move crippled the Huk resistance within the capital city.[62]

Lansdale's three months of temporary duty were coming to an end and he was far from having achieved all he wanted. He had begun work with the Philippine Army to help it organize an airborne battalion, which he believed would be a sufficiently mobile strike force that it could raise havoc among rebels scattered across the countryside. No equipment was available nor were there funds to purchase what was needed. Lansdale decided that when he got back to Washington he would try to get his orders extended and at the same time round up necessities for his airborne troops. There was little difficulty in arranging for the cutting of new orders extending his service in the Philippines. General Walter Bedell Smith, director of Central Intelligence, wrote to Major General Leland Hobbs, JUSMAG commander, that he believed Lansdale's efforts were of cardinal importance if Magsaysay was to be properly directed. Smith wrote that he was "pleased to be of service to you in extending the orders of Lieutenant Colonel Edward G. Lansdale to make his tour of duty a full year. . . . I agree with you. He is almost indispensable where he is."[63]

While in Washington Lansdale tried without much success to locate surplus equipment to outfit his Filipino airborne unit. Then he went to see General George C. Marshall, the secretary of defense, in an effort to elicit his support. Marshall and Dean Acheson, secretary of state, conferred frequently and informally about problems facing the nation. The two men had a friendly rivalry as to which one presided over more talent. During Lansdale's Washington visit, General Marshall told Lansdale one day to wait in the Pentagon corridor outside his office. Acheson was inside and the secretary of defense insisted to his adversary that military people were far more intellectually capable than those who served in the ranks of the foreign service. He promised that they could walk out into the corridor, stop the first officer they found there, and that man would be able to give a knowledgeable account of many of America's overseas policies. Acheson scoffed and so the two secretaries walked out into the corridor. They spied Lansdale loitering there and Marshall invited Acheson to ask him questions. The secretary of state was so impressed with Lansdale's responses that he invited him to give an address to staffers at the State Department. Lansdale chose as his topic a new treaty just signed between the United States and the Philippines.[64]

Marshall was so pleased with his little ploy that he gave Lansdale his support in procuring equipment for the airborne battalion. Lansdale returned to the Philippines with parachutes for all his men and instructors to teach jump techniques. Despite his efforts, however, little came of the unit and it was never used in combat against the Huks.[65]

Back in the Philippines once again, Lansdale redoubled his efforts on behalf of Magsaysay. He persuaded the secretary to establish a Psychological Warfare Staff division within the Department of National Defense. Its name was soon changed to Civil Affairs and its purpose was to promote "civic action" within the Army. "We started with discipline and getting them [soldiers] to act helpful [to their own people]. We started Civic Action which is now part of military actions in the U.S. Army." This civic action program employed the military in a variety of public works projects. It also devised strategy to shape the political impact of military operations. All its activities were given maximum publicity to strengthen their psychological impact on both the citizenry and the rebellious Huks.

Another innovation instituted a reward system — financed by the Peace Fund — for information leading to the capture or killing of Huks. This increased rebel fears of betrayal and caused them to minimize their contacts with barrio people upon whom they had previously relied. At the same time Magsaysay held out to all insurgents the possibility of a pardon if they surrendered. He proclaimed his program toward the Huks: "all out friendship or all out force."[66]

Lansdale helped begin another program that used Army lawyers to help farmers fight for their legal rights. Tenant farmers inevitably lost court claims because they could not afford to hire legal counsel. Too often a farmer would stand with his hat in his hand before a judge trying to get justice for a claim, never understanding what lawyers were saying, and losing his rights in the process. With Magsaysay's enthusiastic concurrence, the judge advocate of the Philippine Army sent out-of-uniform lawyers to provincial courts to offer free counsel for farmers and other poor people. "We changed the outlook of the government towards [its own] people," Lansdale proudly stated.[67]

One evening Magsaysay came back to Lansdale's quarters in the JUS-MAG compound with a broad smile on his face. He had just made a major speech in which he promised that every Huk rebel who came over to the cause of the government would be given a home, land, and support. The country boy from Iba, the impoverished capital of the poor province of Zambales, knew well the hunger of rural Filipinos for land. "If a farmer owns his own piece of property," Magsaysay said, "he will resist anyone who tries to take it away from him." Lansdale and Bohannan exchanged worried glances. The secretary had no authority to make such a statement. There were no funds or facilities to support the project. It looked impossible to make his word good. If made good the deed would constitute a major psychological victory for the government; if not, it would be a resounding defeat.

Magsaysay had already experimented with such a program in a very small way. A few Huk prisoners had asked Magsaysay for a chance to redeem themselves and he had helped them incorporate and start a carpenter shop in which they made barracks furniture that the Department of Defense bought.

Magsaysay, Lansdale, and others talked extensively at their morning kaffee klatsches about how to make the secretary's promise a reality. Someone recalled a practice of the ancient Roman military *colons*. The original Roman concept was used to raise personnel for imperial legions by enticing men into ten years of military service. These legions were then stationed in remote or trouble-ridden areas to enforce Roman law and authority. While in service, those legionnaires developed the locality in which they were billeted and, upon discharge, were given title to lands there. Magsaysay and his advisers decided to develop a modern version and named it the Economic Development Corporation (EDCOR).

The Philippine EDCOR plan was similar to the Roman plan but less ambitious. Magsaysay obtained land in the public domain that was considered suitable for homesteading. The secretary then ordered the formation within the Army of new battalions headed by senior commissioned and noncommissioned officers who were approaching retirement age, and the ranks were filled by one-year draftees. After six months' training, these units were stationed in remote areas capable of development, where they established home sites of from fifteen to twenty acres. After their discharge, this land became the homes and farms of the members of those battalions. In addition they received a house, a *carabao* (Asian water buffalo), farm implements, and seeds. Those who improved their land would later be given title to it. By a certain amount of distortion, this program was made the vehicle for fulfilling Magsaysay's promise to the Huks, for on those remote lands, in the midst of loyal settlers, the government would also relocate a number of Huk prisoners. Only those who had been neither indicted nor convicted by a civil court were eligible, and they also had to declare that they wished to be "reeducated in the democratic, peaceful, and productive way of life." This program was a powerful attraction to both Huks and Huk sympathizers. Magsaysay not only offered them something they desired more than a fight with the Philippine Army but gave them a reason to defend their new lands against former comrades still loyal to the rebel cause who might try to attack their new settlements. This basic program was popularized through government use of films, special radio programs, and other propaganda.[68]

It was a tremendous counter to the Huk rallying cry of "land for the landless." The Huk cause might never be in a position to implement its slogan; the government was already doing so. EDCOR was formally launched on 15 December 1950 and by 22 February 1951 the first EDCOR farm was established on some four thousand acres of land at Kapatagan, Lanao, on the island of Mindanao. The first settlers, including fifty-six former Huks, arrived in May.[69]

Criticism of the program centered on two points. Few Huks were resettled — perhaps no more than two hundred families. The other main criticism was that more non-Huks than Huks were resettled. The second charge is easily answered. It would have been dangerous to create settlements composed solely of Huks, for those areas could have become centers for reactivation of their movement, now spread to new locations by the government itself. Then there was the justifiable and natural jealousy of civilians who had never joined the insurgency and of retired military personnel who had fought the rebels. Neither group would be joyous to see their enemies given privileges they themselves did not enjoy. For these reasons a rough rule of thumb was established: in each colony one-third of the population would be Huks, one-third would be farmers of established loyalty, and one-third would be ex-soldiers.

Another reason few Huks were resettled was basically economic. The government simply could not afford to subsidize a mass population relocation. A conservative estimate was that it cost twelve thousand pesos to establish a colonist family on Mindanao. The number of Huks who surrendered was 9,458; if each Huk and his family had been transported to Mindanao the total cost would have been 113,496,000 pesos! With absolutely no funds legally available, an expenditure of that magnitude was impossible.

Yet Huks who came over to the government because of Magsaysay's pledge were indeed given a chance for house and land. Why then were so few resettled? In the prison camps where they were temporarily quartered, training schools were set up, mostly in carpentry and mechanics. Captured Huks were offered their choice between vocational training and resettlement. Rumors were rife in the camps about the distance to Mindanao and about how primitive EDCOR settlements were. Other rumors were about hazards posed by bloodthirsty Moros, snakes, and a hostile environment. The great majority of captured Huks chose educational training.[70]

The settlements were successful and the former Huks were pleased with their new circumstances. The word-of-mouth "bamboo telegraph" carried news of this experiment all over Asia. The British in Malaya later told Lansdale that people being relocated there asked for electric lights in the new villages because they had heard that EDCOR communities had them.[71]

Civic action programs multiplied. Magsaysay made arrangements so that anyone who wanted to could send him a telegram at a price of only ten centavos. Hundreds of telegrams came daily. Each one was quickly checked out for accuracy and was promptly acted on. People began to feel that if the secretary of national defense was interested in their problems, then perhaps his soldiers might also really be on their side.

In military actions against guerrilla bands there were often civilian casualties, caused when people were caught in the crossfire of battle. Magsaysay ordered such casualties to be treated at military aid stations and, if their wounds were serious enough, in military hospitals. Civilians were given the same prompt treatment as members of the armed forces. Such action may not have compensated for injuries but was a boost to people who had no other access to medical care. People came away from such facilities feeling that the Army really did concern itself with what happened to them.[72]

Lansdale knew that civic action programs by themselves were not enough. The Army had to take the fight directly into Huk fortresses and destroy insurgents on their home ground. One objective was to clear the guerrillas' main headquarters in the foothills of Mount Pinatubo overlooking Clark AFB. Pilots of U.S. fighter aircraft taking off from the runway at Clark never knew they made their first climbing turn almost directly over this Huk headquarters. Squadrons of insurgents also roamed the bombing range and back areas within the perimeter of the U.S. base and in other, more remote locations. During the first months of 1951 Lansdale and Magsaysay spent much time on the road in this area, observing the Army in battle with Huk squadrons and exhorting soldiers to even greater efforts.[73]

One of Lansdale's favorite military units was the 7th Battalion Combat Team (BCT) commanded by Colonel Napoleon D. Valeriano. This outfit was famed (and feared by the Huks) for its utter dedication to destroying the insurgency and for its fearlessness in combat. Early in 1951 Valeriano called for volunteers from within the BCT who would form a special Charlie Company in which they would be trained to pose as Huk rebels. Its members enthusiastically adopted Huk ways, going barefoot, dressing as Huks did, speaking in the jargon of dialectical materialism, and using Huk equipment. They were usually accepted by real Huk groups as one of their own until it was too late and befuddled rebels died under withering fire from men who, from their looks and actions, should have been their comrades. The only serious problem occurred when the members of Charlie Company came under fire from another BCT which, fooled by their disguises, attacked them. When this happened, Charlie Company rapidly withdrew from the area to regroup and count losses.[74]

Lansdale knew many of the folk stories of the Filipino barrios, their lore, taboos, and myths. In an effort to exploit some of the information he had acquired, he obtained some excess Navy loud-hailers used by beachmasters during World War II, which he brought back with him from Washington. He believed they could be used as air-to-ground communications gear. Each of the Filipino BCTs was equipped with light L-5 Piper liaison airplanes and he distributed his loud-hailers to those units. Pilots then flew their aircraft over areas where Huks were known to be hiding and broadcast curses in Tagalog on any barrio inhabitants who provided rebels with food or shelter. Lansdale actually succeeded in starving some Huk units into surrender by these means. He called this concept the "eye of God" and played it out in many variations.[75]

Pleased by that success, Lansdale shifted his focus from barrio people to rebels. When the location of a Huk squadron was pinpointed, Army intelligence officers would review all the order of battle information they had on that particular group to determine unit size, designation, and names of personnel. Armed with that information and his loud-hailer, the BCT psywar officer boarded an L-5 and flew to the appropriate location. Circling overhead, the psywar officer spoke through his bullhorn to those on the ground: "You hiding down there. We see you. Yes, I mean you in Squadron 17. I mean you, Commander Sol. I mean you, Juan Santos. And you, Bulacan Boy. And you, Pepe and Ramón and Emiliano. Borro and Dario, Carmelo and Baby. We know all about you. We are coming to kill you. Stay there. And now I must go while our troops are coming to attack you. To our secret friend in your ranks I say thank you! Run and hide so you won't be killed. Sorry I can't call you by name but you know who I mean. Thank you and goodbye." There was, of course, no "friend in the ranks." The order of battle information had come from many sources, but such broadcasts from the air often stampeded the guerrillas and they left on the run.

Then suspicion began to work on their minds. Who was this "friend in the ranks"? Which of those milling in confusion was really a secret enemy spy? One or more of the guerrillas undoubtedly looked suspicious enough to qualify and were quickly judged guilty and executed by a kangaroo court of their fellows. Thus some adroitly used information often brought about as many enemy casualties as could be inflicted by a BCT unit chasing a guerrilla band in a running fight.[76]

In another version of the eye of God, troops of the Philippine Army crept into barrio villages by night and painted large staring eyes on the sides of houses. Newly awakened Huks found those eyes the next morning and knew their enemy had been among them while they slept. Properly used, the tactic made many insurgents feel they were helpless victims of an all-seeing and all-powerful enemy.[77]

Another psychological operation Lansdale conceived had a touch of the macabre. Huk raids on various towns in one particular area continued to be a problem despite efforts by the BCTs to prevent them. Provincial governors demanded that the Philippine Army station more troops in their communities to prevent such attacks. In some localities the Huks felt so secure they simply took over in certain villages after the sun set each day. In such places legal government authority shriveled as clandestine Huk governments provided the real rule in secret night meetings: court trials, punishments, taxes, even marriages. The oft-heard aphorism that "the night belongs to the enemy" seemed to be more true than ever. Something had to be done. There had to be a way to prevent rebels from exercising such power and authority. Lansdale decided to take the night hours away from them. A possibility suggested itself to him.

Lansdale ordered Army teams to spread rumors in markets, barber shops, and other public places. Their information was not to be given in complete form but only in snatches, allowing listeners to piece the parts together. The stories were based on the reputed sayings of a noted soothsayer of Ilocos Norte, an old woman who had established her reputation by predicting the death of President Roxas. She was now supposedly predicting that men with evil in their hearts would become the victims of a terrifying local vampire, an *asuang*. Nearby Huk hideaways were named as the *asuang*'s territory. People would be foolish to believe such tales, but then, who knew for certain? Roxas had not believed the soothsayer and what happened to him? He died of a stroke! Right in the middle of a speech he was delivering at Clark Air Force Base.

Lansdale's men busied themselves planting the elements of this tale. That night Huks came into town and local people passed on to them what they had heard. The second night an Army patrol staked out the trail into the barrio. After the fall of darkness they watched as a group of Huks made their quiet, stealthy way along the path. As the last man in the Huk column cautiously passed the ambush point, the waiting men silently grabbed him, punched two holes in his throat, held him up by his heels and drained his body of blood. They then carefully placed the corpse back in the middle of the trail and departed as silently as they had come.

Hours later the Huks slipped out of the village to return to their daytime hideout. Some, perhaps, were wondering what had happened to their absent comrade. Then they stumbled upon his still body lying on the trail. He was dead. There was no blood on or around him. The only wounds were those two tiny holes in his neck. They immediately recalled the stories they had heard of the soothsayer and the *asuang*. The vampire evidence seemed compelling. The darkness that wrapped itself around them no longer seemed so comforting or protective. It now felt dangerous, eerie, and threatening. Eyes darting toward every sound, they pressed on to their base camp, rapidly packed their belongings, and abandoned their jungle area before dawn. It would be a long time before any of them had much stomach for night operations again.[78]

On another occasion in northern Luzon a Huk unit occupied a strong position in the mountains. They relied for logistical support on a small village of farmers in the lowlands below them. The only avenue of approach to the Huk bivouac area from the village was such that the rebels could ambush any company-sized or larger unit of the Philippine Army that might be sent in pursuit. In an effort to dislodge the Huks, Lansdale suggested to the psywar officer of a BCT that he scout around the farming village to see what he could learn. The officer changed to civilian clothing and set off. He discovered a local superstition: if a villager performed a wicked deed and was buried in the local cemetery, his voice might well speak from the grave.

Armed with this knowledge, the nearest BCT unit captured a Huk courier descending from the mountain stronghold to the village. After questioning, the courier, who was a native of the village, woefully confessed his errors in helping the Huks. His testimony was tape-recorded and enhanced to sound as if it emanated from a tomb. The man was then killed and his body left near the village. BCT members in civilian clothes dropped rumors in the village to the effect that the Huks had killed the courier. The villagers recovered the courier's body and buried it.

That night Army patrols infiltrated the cemetery and set up audio equipment, which began broadcasting the dead Huk's confession. By dawn the entire village of terror-stricken peasantry had evacuated. In a few days the Huks were forced to descend the mountain in search of food and were quickly captured or killed by the waiting BCT.[79]

One member of Lansdale's team, Colonel Napoleon Valeriano, blossomed under Lansdale's tutelage and also became fond of psychological warfare. In one operation Valeriano found a way to discredit part of the Huks' civil infrastructure. In one village lived a mayor who was a known Huk sympathizer but who was safe from Army retribution because he had great political support and influence with the Quirino government in Manila. After a running encounter by the military with a rebel band just outside that village, Valeriano gave orders that the bodies of the two Huk casualties were to be brought into the village and displayed. A large crowd gathered and even the pro-Huk mayor came to inspect the bodies. Valeriano then stepped up to him and loudly and publicly thanked the mayor for providing vital information used to attack the rebel band. The mayor was appalled, having had no contact with Valeriano whatsoever. Afraid for his safety in the midst of Huk country, he fled to Manila the next day. When Lansdale heard this tale he was vastly amused and pleased to hear that his methods were catching on.

Some of those with whom he worked, unlike Valeriano, seemed slow to understand what was needed. Some years earlier the U.S. Army had produced a pamphlet on unconventional warfare. Lansdale had a draft version of the booklet and made copies for use by Filipino leaders in their fight against the Huks. At one point Lansdale rode in a jeep with the chief of staff, General Mariano Castañeda, past a line of troops marching along the roadway. Lansdale saw his companion reach for a rifle and aim it toward the ditch, ready to open fire. He knocked the weapon out of Castañeda's hands and the general turned to him and demanded to know why he had done so. He was only following directions in the unconventional warfare publication, which recommended firing along the sides of roads when passing through ambush territory. Lansdale patiently explained that he was sure the authors didn't intend that anyone shoot at his own troops.[80]

Slowing the Huk rebellion often seemed a herculean task to Lansdale. Civic action helped and he was glad Magsaysay was receptive to such an approach. More effective military pursuit of rebel groups by battalion combat teams also played havoc with those Huk squadrons that could be located and destroyed. Used singly, each was of some utility, and when joined in a two-pronged government approach they were surprisingly effective. Yet something more was needed and Lansdale often sat lost in thought as he pondered the problem, for despite his efforts the rebellion had not collapsed. For several years the insurgency had steadily grown in size and threat.

Lansdale thought of the Huks' past deeds. He recalled that many Filipinos were heartsick when, in 1948, Mrs. Aurora Quezon, a presidential widow and one of the most admired and popular figures in the country, was targeted and killed by a Huk ambuscade of some two hundred insurgents led by Alexander Viernes, alias Commander Stalin. Despite the distaste many felt for that act, the Huks kept recruiting after her death, and their forces even grew larger. Lansdale also knew that their support within the civilian population continued and increased even after that attack, although much of it may well have arisen from coercive Huk activities.[81]

The Huks had recruited much of their strength and their huge sympathetic following by exploiting the 1949 presidential election in the Philippines. The overwhelming majority of Filipinos realized how crooked that election had been. Huk propagandists made the most of it. They insisted, correctly enough, that the Quirino administration had come to power through cheating at the ballot box. People had simply been robbed of their votes by manipulation of the ballots. Lansdale recalled going upcountry to see a friend who had run for public office in that election. "Is it true that they cheated?" he asked. "Let me put it this way," his friend replied. "They either robbed me of my vote last time or the vote of my poor old mother, for I ran for a seat, both of us voted, and yet they only counted one person as having voted for me!" This cynical attitude ran throughout the Filipino population and did much to swell Huk ranks.[82]

In effect, this attitude made a fine constitution and an enlightened electoral code just scraps of paper rather than firm political tenets in which voters could believe. Huk propaganda proclaimed: "Your ballot isn't counted. Join us and use a gun to get a new government. It's the only way."

Magsaysay concurred with Lansdale that this situation clearly prevented the military from making further gains against Huk rebels and greatly lessened the effectiveness of civic action projects. The failure of the government to implement needed reforms was plain to everyone. Support even for Magsaysay's programs of civic action was nearly nonexistent outside the Philippine Department of Defense. So long as the government remained corrupt, the Huk cause would endure. Further use of the military simply meant that soldiers would continue to kill brother Filipinos who felt, properly enough, that they were willing to die if that would help change the government of their country for the better. Both the constitution and the electoral code had to be brought back to life for all Filipinos.

In the last busy months before Lansdale returned to Washington, he and Magsaysay talked of the forthcoming off-year elections, to be held in November 1951 when a third of the national Senate and many local officials would be voted into office. Perhaps a clean election and the placing of reform-minded candidates would bring about a decline in the fortunes of the Huk insurgency. The two men decided to focus their efforts on the election.

Lansdale asked the Office of Policy Coordination for reinforcements. Des Fitzgerald, Lansdale's boss at OPC, had recently recruited Gabriel Kaplan, a New York lawyer and politician. Fitzgerald now sent Kaplan to join the work in the Philippines and, with Lansdale, Magsaysay, and others, planned for the November election. Kaplan had experience dealing with civic organizations, such as chambers of commerce, veterans' groups, and Rotary Clubs. He sought out Filipinos and urged them to unite their local chapters into a nationwide coalition to educate voters on the importance of honest, free elections. He taught practical measures that could be used in the upcoming election to ensure that vote manipulation was kept minimal. Lansdale was also interested in that aspect of the work and had prepared himself (during his earlier trip to Washington) by long discussions with General Harry Malony, a former division commander, and a Greek and Latin scholar who was noted within the Pentagon for his political acuity. Malony tutored Lansdale in ways to police elections to ensure honest balloting and listed the sorts of tricks that could be used to persuade people to vote in certain ways and to skew elections. "It was a nut-shell course in political realities," Lansdale later claimed.[83]

Kaplan also shared with Filipinos the ways by which groups and even individuals with little political base could act as watchdogs of an election. His listeners were enthusiastic and agreed to do what they could to prepare for November. Their coalition came to be known as the National Movement for Free Elections (NAMFREL). It was a popular move. Filipinos from many organizations filled both the ranks and leadership posts of NAMFREL, but it was actually run by Gabriel Kaplan and funded by OPC through Lansdale. Prominent Filipino sponsors included Eleuterio Adevoso, Jaime Ferrer, and Frisco San Juan — all of whom had been national commanders of the Philippine Veterans Legion and members of the Hunters ROTC guerrillas during World War II. Ferrer became NAMFREL's director. Manuel Manahan was another supporter, as was Frank Zaldarriaga, who often turned up at Lansdale's JUSMAG quarters for conferences with Lansdale, Bo, Magsaysay, Manahan, and Kaplan and for the "good coffee and good Scotch."[84] Manahan had good reason for joining the crusade. "Quirino was a very vain man who surrounded himself with evil men," he believed. "Their motto was 'what are we in power for except to line our pockets?' And they did."[85]

NAMFREL chapters appeared everywhere. Spokesmen publicized the necessity for preventing tricks at the polls by members of the Quirino administration. Voters were shown how to make thumbprints on their ballots, which was the system used to verify registration certificates. In the past those who wished to manipulate votes had often claimed that ballots were invalid because of illegible thumbprints. Many times these same people did a little smudging on their own whenever possible, and people were alerted to look out for such tactics. Others were taught photography and instructed to take pictures of people entering polling places so as to identify for later prosecution those who voted more than once. A second team of photographers was instructed to take pictures of any strong-arm tactics bullies used to prevent voters from participating.[86]

Lansdale saw in the election a real opportunity to demonstrate to Filipinos that the ballot was better than a bullet to achieve change in government. He also saw it as a chance to discredit the Huk leadership, which advocated armed rebellion as the only possible solution to the country's problems. To those ends he launched a black psychological operation so skillful it took Huk leaders a year and a half of careful analysis to learn what actually happened in this attack on their cause.

Intelligence agencies divide propaganda operations into three types. White propaganda is that done by and on behalf of American positions, such as broadcasts by the Voice of America. Gray propaganda puts praise of the United States in the mouths of those whom others would not recognize as normal American conduits — a refugee from Cuba, perhaps, who condemns the Castro regime while carefully concealing that he has long been on the CIA payroll. Black propaganda is an action made to appear as if done by enemies but harmful to them. To be believable, it must support some position that is in opposition to the United States, the better to hide that it has actually been an American operation. Such black activities can often be very effective when based on solid information.

One former CIA operative has revealed how such black propaganda efforts were conducted in the Philippines:

If we simply said, in a newspaper story or column, that William Pomeroy, a renegade American leader among the Communist Huks . . . was planning to massacre all the women and children in the next village that the Huks attacked, it would anger the Filipinos who were anti-Huk, alarm a lot of people who were fence-sitters, but be denounced as just another piece of anti-Huk propaganda by sophisticates who were tired of the fighting. If we produced a copy of an order to massacre and mailed it to the Manila *Times,* ostensibly from a disillusioned Huk, we would gain a lot more credibility. The editor of the paper could take the message to the authorities, presumably, but they would be convinced of its authenticity if the job was well done, and the paper could then run a photo of the message along with the story of its grisly threat. . . . [T]his would shut up the skeptics unless they were prepared to yell "fake," which they might not be inclined to do since this would label them as more than skeptics. Most people would then consider them to be out-and-out Huk sympathizers and sympathetic to the cause of a band of butchers.[87]

One of Lansdale's urgent needs in early 1951 was for assistance with black propaganda, leaflets that the Communist guerrillas would accept as their own.[88] Lansdale trekked to Clark AFB to talk with specialists at the Air Resupply and Communications Service (ARC) about his need for some forged but authentic-looking Huk propaganda leaflets. At Clark there were four ARC Wings, predecessors to the Air Commandos and the Special Operations Force. One of those ARC Wings was assigned clandestine and psychological operations in enemy territory in support of conventional military actions then ongoing in Korea. The ARC Wing had a wide variety of equipment for printing propaganda leaflets and news sheets, including photo labs and airborne public address systems. Lansdale grumbled that despite efforts of the ARC Wing personnel, they couldn't get away from printing "by the numbers." There was an obvious "Made in USA" appearance to their work. The quality of paper, artwork, and printing was too good for a poor man's war being fought by local folks. Leaflets they produced looked foreign and thus not credible. What was needed was lowly but artful deception. Lansdale was forced back on other resources.[89]

Using local craftsmen, Lansdale carefully prepared his leaflet, using a captured Huk typewriter and mimeograph machine. It was printed on paper like that used in Huk propaganda broadsides. The finished product was introduced into a Huk cell, located on the northern outskirts of Manila, which had been penetrated by a special intelligence unit. The broadside pointed out the rampant cheating in the 1949 election and predicted that a disgusted electorate would gladly join the Huks' armed struggle after the voting when they once again found their ballots stolen by the administration. Lansdale's leaflet proclaimed that the best way to ensure this result was to boycott the election. The work was so authentic that members of the cell adopted it as their own idea and distributed copies throughout Manila, some even reaching the politburo headquarters and Luis Taruc in the hills of Luzon.

The Huk politburo rebuked the Manila cell for taking independent propaganda actions, scolding that such plans should be submitted to head-quarters for consideration and approval. Nevertheless, it was such a good idea that the politburo adopted the boycott. Soon regional and squadron commanders were arguing this approach in their own areas and the entire Huk cause became closely identified with the movement to boycott the election. Lansdale was elated with the success of his efforts. The Huks talked themselves out of participating in the election; they threw away their own votes.[90]

As November's election drew closer, Lansdale concluded that it would be a good idea if the Army helped oversee the voting. Administration politicians wanted to use the Constabulary to guard ballot boxes as they had in the past and thus, as they had done previously, change the results to suit their whims. This could be forestalled, Lansdale believed, by substituting the Army for the Constabulary. Lansdale knew that the Philippine Commission on Elections was constitutionally an independent body, tied neither to party nor to political administration. Its function was to supervise elections and ensure that they were carried on fairly. Best of all, it was empowered to request assistance when needed. While President Quirino and a number of the key members of his administration were out of the country on a visit to Spain, Lansdale told Magsaysay about the commission. He then quietly suggested to the Commission on Elections that it ask for the army's help in making the election a clean one. The commission did so, to the consternation of those in the Quirino administration still in the country. Magsaysay, as secretary of national defense, quickly gave his approval and ordered the military establishment to help during the coming election.

Plans were drawn up to use soldiers, reinforced by ROTC cadets, to patrol polling places, to ensure protection of candidates and the electorate from harassment, and to provide truly secret balloting and an honest count. They also guarded public meetings to guarantee free speech. Participating high school and college ROTC cadets were taken to precincts by army transport or by members of NAMFREL. NAMFREL poll watchers, under the direction of the Commission on Elections, were scheduled to serve on the day ballots were cast. Foreign newspaper publishers assigned correspondents to cover the election and to act as eyewitnesses at possible trouble spots.[91]

President Quirino returned from his visit to Spain the day before the election. When he learned that the Commission on Elections had asked the Army to supervise a free election, he tried to put a stop to such use of his military forces. Lansdale was in the office of the deputy chief of staff when Colonel Jesus Vargas received a telephone call from Malacañang Palace. Vargas suddenly stood to attention at his desk, crisply replying "yessir" and "nossir" to the speaker at the other end of the line. "I knew," Lansdale said, "that he was talking either to God or to the President."[92]

Quirino tried to persuade Vargas to move troops out of some precincts in Caloocan, a populous Manila suburb critical to Quirino's presidential prospects. If he did not do so Vargas would never become a general. Vargas refused. Unwilling to be browbeaten, he valiantly stuck to his agreement to help the Commission on Elections. He replied, "The Commission asked me to do that and I am going to do so." When he hung up the phone he turned to Lansdale and said, "That was —" "I know," Lansdale interrupted. "Congratulations." He shook the colonel's hand and said, "You did the right thing." Vargas gave a wry grimace and asked, "Can I get a new job tomorrow? The President will kick me out of here." "Yes, you'll have a job," Lansdale replied, "and you'll have a place in this country."[93]

On election day an amazing result was tallied, due in large measure to Lansdale's efforts and the success of his operations. Those in opposition to Quirino won seat after seat. Out of some five and a half million registered voters, about four million actually cast ballots — a million more participated than had done so in the election of 1949. Throughout the Philippines people gave the credit for the surprising vote to the army. The military had given their government back to them. Their votes counted for something. Suddenly it became a government of, by, and for the people. Voters showed their pleasure in different ways.

In Pampanga, central Luzon Huk country, a military convoy stopped along a road shortly after the election so soldiers could relieve their bladders. Other troops manned machine guns, keeping an eye out for Huks. People from a nearby village saw the troops and everyone — men, women, and children — came running to hug and kiss the soldiers, who stood there hastily trying to fasten their pants. Suddenly soldiers who had been so feared only a few months earlier were now heroes.[94]

"We made a very honest election," Lansdale noted. "People recognized its honesty. They won against the administration. It became very obvious that the Huks had been wrong in boycotting it." His comment to Filipinos thereafter was "Do you still trust the Huks?" In this war of minds, Lansdale learned well the lesson of the election: "Our ultimate objective is always a political one."[95] Lansdale continued his thought, "Any people . . . if they feel their government is really trying to help them, are going to respond to it. If they think it doesn't care, they will not. If there is someone around saying, 'Your government doesn't care about you but we do — turn to us instead,' that has an influence too."[96]

Much of the credit for the victory on election day, Lansdale believed, was due to his introduction of psychological warfare into the troubled Filipino political scene. It was not a new weapon, he said. Aside from bare hands, it was perhaps man's oldest battle technique. "[T]he important thing to remember is that it is a *weapon*. . . . [It] is used to make people *do* something." He developed a precept: the more clearly you know what you want your enemy to do, the more effective will be your use of this weapon. Be fuzzy about this and your results will be fuzzy.[97] America has not learned this telling lesson to this day.

Lansdale realized that this defeat of the Huks had come about as much or more from political weapons as from military strength. Their slogans, recruiting, and organizing of the population had all been countered by government actions and, as a result of the election, that government was now in the process of reforming itself. If the Philippine government had been true to its own rules in earlier days, if it had been truly interested in the welfare of its own citizens, no group would have tried to overthrow it. Now progress was being made. The election proved that orderly ways existed for changing society and government. No grievances existed that could not be met by peaceful means, and the rebels suddenly seemed little different from bandits and racketeers.

Should the government actually succeed in reforming itself it would take away the Huks' very *raison d'être*. The rules the government and military began to follow were set forth in the nation's constitution and its electoral code, part of the documents Filipinos themselves had created to govern their nation. In effect, Lansdale realized, the Huks started on the road to defeat the moment the government actually began to follow its own rules. "We took the revolution away from [them]," Lansdale said. "They were fighting what they called a people's war and we took the people away from them."[98]

Lansdale was now absolutely certain that military counterguerrilla operations, no matter how successful, could never be enough in and of themselves to defeat insurgents. Striking against an enemy was one thing; defeating him was quite another. As he later phrased it, "It's not enough to be *against* Communism; you have to be *for* something."[99] By the end of 1951 many Huks began leaving their usual haunts. Hundreds surrendered to the Army or simply slipped back into their civilian lives. Others who continued to resist were driven into ever more remote areas and continued to be harassed by military units. "That's when it became hard for them to sleep at night," Lansdale remembered. "We had a victory in the making."[100]

6

"MY GUY MAGSAYSAY"

EXCEPT AMONG MEMBERS of the Quirino administration, there was celebration following that Philippine congressional election in November 1951. There were NAMFREL parties and joyous gatherings at the Civil Affairs offices. Victorious candidates held their own galas. JUSMAG officers gathered at their club and hoisted a few brews in honor of their victorious friends. Friends and celebrants wandered in and out of an ongoing function at the Lansdale-Bohannan quarters in Heroes' Hills. Some Filipinos danced in the streets while their more sober brethren gathered in the churches of the land to offer their thanks to the Almighty.

In the midst of such festivities, after a suitable number of bottles had been poured and hands shaken and stories told, Lansdale and those closest to him began once more to plan ahead. There was still a war against the Huks waiting to be fought, and the political situation in the Philippines needed serious consideration. Having engineered the course of the elections just past, Lansdale now turned his full attention to the subject of politics. His next step was to prepare for the next presidential electoral race only two years hence. What should be done about President Elpidio Quirino? Another in the line of venal men who have so often risen to power on the backs of their own people, Quirino's administration was riddled with graft and corruption. He commanded little trust or confidence from his own people and he was no longer particularly useful to the American government. In Lansdale's mind the man was already discredited, yet it was clear he planned to run for office again in 1953.

Who should be the next president? Not Quirino. Magsaysay was not experienced enough for a position of that magnitude. One possible candidate was José Laurel, but U.S. support for him was unlikely because of the continuing controversy surrounding his actions while head of the Filipino puppet republic the Japanese had installed during their occupation. There was little chance that American policymakers would choose to back a man with such a history.

One possible candidate for American support was Senator Lorenzo Tañada. A member of the Free Philippine Forces during World War II and the recipient of a Distinguished Service Cross, he was appointed to the position of solicitor-general in September 1945. He then served in the Senate as a member of the Liberal party but in 1949 changed parties because of his opposition to Quirino. It was not long before Manila insiders gossiped that the American government had selected Tañada as Quirino's successor. Observers noted how regularly the senator played tennis and badminton with Ed Lansdale in Malacañang's courts. They spread the word that this was an indication that he was being groomed for the presidency in 1953. Then one day in early 1952 Tañada delivered a carefully prepared public oration on why he believed American bases should be removed from Philippine soil. Suddenly he no longer seemed such a worthy possibility for the presidency to those in Washington who heard of his speech. Angered by his independence, U.S. policymakers sent word through channels to Lansdale to drop Tañada and look for a replacement candidate. Lansdale began to search for another Filipino with the appropriate stature and talents to run against Quirino. It did not take him long to reevaluate Magsaysay and to determine that he was the man.[1] Soon Lansdale was often seen playing tennis with Magsaysay, never with Tañada.

Lansdale notified OPC that his choice was Ramón Magsaysay and Washington agreed. It was now time to build up the reputation of the secretary of national defense. Lansdale introduced him to foreign correspondents and visiting journalists. Articles glamorizing Magsaysay began to appear in major American publications. The operation involved the *New York Times,* the Philippine-American Chamber of Commerce in New York, the *Washington Post, Time, Newsweek,* and *Fortune* magazines, the *Saturday Evening Post, Cosmopolitan* magazine, *Reader's Digest,* the *Los Angeles Herald,* the *San Francisco Chronicle,* the United States embassy in Manila, Ambassador Raymond Spruance (the successor to Myron Cowen), the Manila American Chamber of Commerce, and General Albert Pierson, JUSMAG commander (who had replaced Leland Hobbs). All this activity prompted the local Philippine press to fasten on Magsaysay and afford him the same treatment he was being accorded by the Americans.[2]

It was not difficult to find ways to popularize Magsaysay and to reach out to the heads and hearts of Filipinos. Three major Manila newspapers were American-owned and got a major share of their advertising revenue from U.S. firms. American-owned wire services filtered news of the world outside the Philippines, and local newspapers that could not afford wire services used a United States Information Service (USIS) press service. Of forty-one radio stations, twelve were owned by Voice of

America. Sixty percent of the films shown were imports from the United States.[3]

Magsaysay's Civil Affairs Office (CAO) also became busy. This office not only carried on a massive propaganda effort against the Huk rebels but managed to bring Magsaysay's name and activities before other Filipinos on a regular basis. In two years it created and distributed more than thirteen million propaganda leaflets and other printed materials. It sponsored some six thousand public meetings with audiences of some million and a half people. USIS provided free literature and films for use by CAO and set up a regional production center in Manila for propaganda materials — posters, pamphlets, leaflets — in various Philippine dialects. CAO sponsored a variety of activities such as anticommunist forums in universities and patriotic writing contests in high schools and colleges. It also distributed materials in elementary schools.[4] Lansdale took credit for this effort. Some time later he admitted that he "helped organize CAO and a school to train personnel." What they did, he said, was "civic action," and the name and concept was later adopted by armies in other countries.[5]

CAO provided hungry and thirsty members of the press with liquor, food, entertainment, transportation, gifts, and sometimes even salaries. Members of the Filipino press watched carefully as the American press chorus began its campaign of vilification against Quirino. Local columnists of the Philippine press, considered the freest in Asia, then joined in with their own invective, accusing the Quirino administration of corruption and graft and of having falsified the election returns in 1949 that brought Quirino to power. Exercising real restraint, President Quirino refused to take government action against the press for such stories. In 1952, one of his most virulent critics, Arsenio Lacson, was elected mayor of Manila.

Thus the picture of Magsaysay that appeared in Philippine newspapers had its origin in Lansdale's work. Using advertising techniques he had learned long ago, Lansdale applied what textbooks describe as "symbol manipulation" and "motivation analysis" to enhance the status of the secretary of national defense. His activities, Lansdale believed, were all part of psychological warfare. That field was, Lansdale insisted, one very effective arrow in the quiver of modern statecraft and even of battle. No one should dismiss psywar as a "non-military item invented on Madison Avenue and belonging in the category of, say, PX officers or the school for cooks and bakers." He advised others, "Get your activating idea across in terms and in a way [such] that the receivers will understand, accept, and react in the way you desire. . . . [S]killed playing on [selected themes] increases the effectiveness of the psychological weapon."[6]

As this publicity campaign gathered steam, Lansdale continued to ponder ways to enhance Magsaysay's image as a man of presidential timber.

He concluded that it would be necessary to introduce his friend onto the world scene as a sober and responsible major figure. Public appearances outside his own country would be a step in the right direction. So Lansdale talked with Manuel J. "Dindo" Gonzalez, president of the Manila Lions Club, and through him persuaded officials of Lions International to invite Magsaysay to deliver the keynote address for their 1952 convention to be held in Mexico City.

In most published accounts, this 1952 trip by Magsaysay is described as a triumphal tour by an important statesman. The reality was something less, although the publicity trappings were certainly grand. President Quirino was suspicious of the entire affair and feared the political motivations behind it. Lansdale and Gonzalez were to accompany Magsaysay. Gonzalez' brother Chito was married to the president's daughter Vicky, and Quirino sent Chito and Vicky along as members of the official party. Quirino told his daughter, "I want you and your husband to accompany Magsaysay and keep your eyes on him. I want you to report back to me everything that happens on this trip."

Dindo was the last to board the airplane that would take them first to the United States and then to Mexico. Quirino, who had come to the airport, grabbed Gonzalez and said, "Dindo, watch out for that fellow Lansdale. He will try to put a lot of fancy ideas into Magsaysay's head. Look out for him!"[7] Once the group reached the United States they traveled on a private four-engine Constellation placed at Magsaysay's disposal. Upon reaching New York City, they were met by General Leland Hobbs, who was then with First Army. Magsaysay visited him on Governor's Island and received a nineteen-gun salute. Between the efforts of Hobbs and George Peabody, who handled public relations for the Philippine Association, Magsaysay's visit to the city caught the interest of many Americans. The secretary of national defense received an honorary degree from Fordham University courtesy of Jesuit backers, and he met with publishers and editors to feed them material about the campaign against the Huks.

The group then went on to Washington, D.C., where Lansdale arranged closed-door meetings for Magsaysay with President Truman, Secretary of State Dean Acheson, and Secretary of Defense George Marshall as well as with top officials of the Office of Policy Coordination. During a meeting at the Pentagon, Magsaysay asked for financial help to equip his forces with bulldozers and road graders and to purchase other items that would be helpful in his civic action projects. Surprised at his modest request, officials gave him $500,000 to use for counterinsurgency purposes, the sum quietly transferred to JUSMAG where he could draw upon it as he needed without having to account for it.[8]

Lansdale was beginning to tire of his work in the Philippines. In private meetings, Lansdale spoke with his OPC superiors in an effort to convince them that it was time he received a transfer to a new assignment. He argued that the Huk campaign was well in hand and could be dealt with from that point on by Filipinos themselves. "My arguments fell on deaf ears," Lansdale claimed. He had the opportunity during that week in Washington for a brief reunion with Helen, Ted, and Peter, although his wife reminded him that in their new house both the roof and the basement leaked. Lansdale admitted that he felt depressed as he left the capital city.[9]

On the flight to Mexico City, Lansdale and Magsaysay arranged an overnight stop in El Paso, Texas, for a visit with the secretary's old wartime comrade Colonel Gyles Merrill. Then they set out for the convention. It was not a happy flight. Lansdale had written Magsaysay's speech for him and fully expected his friend to use it when they arrived. Lansdale believed that what he had prepared "just fit him to a T." As they flew southward, he was therefore surprised to see Magsaysay looking over another address that some public relations man had prepared for him. Lansdale described it as "a very conventional sort of talk against communist guerrillas, dirty Reds under every bed, stamp them out sort of thing [with appropriate] ranting and raving." It was not, he felt, a good talk for Magsaysay to use. As the two men sat in the rear of the airplane cabin, Lansdale leaned toward Magsaysay and asked, "What are you doing with that?" The Filipino replied, "I am going to give this speech down there." "The hell you are," Lansdale scoffed. "You are going to use the speech that I wrote for you . . . . It tells exactly what you have been doing and you need to let the world know. They have got to hear it from you."

Tired of the official state bustle of past days, weary of feeling ramrodded by Lansdale, Magsaysay reacted stubbornly. "All right," he replied, "I'm going back to Manila. To hell with them. I didn't want to give a speech anyhow." Lansdale was irate. "You *are* going down [there]," he shouted and reached over and snatched the substitute speech from Magsaysay's hands. Lansdale stood up and started to walk away with it. At that point a very frustrated Magsaysay shoved Lansdale, crying out, "No I am not!" Lansdale reacted without thinking. "I slugged him real hard and he went down."

Sitting in the seat across the aisle was Vicky, Quirino's daughter. She looked at Lansdale with shock and surprise and said, "Daddy told me about you." In her eyes, Lansdale was now a real villain. Lansdale was fond of telling others how he and Magsaysay were "close as brothers," so he now repeated that line to the woman. "This is a brotherly fight," he said, speaking from extensive experience with Phil and Ben. "I'm fighting because I love this guy."[10] Magsaysay later agreed with some reluctance to use the speech Lansdale had written for him.

The visit to Mexico's capital city was not entirely smooth either. At that time, E. Howard Hunt (of later Watergate fame) was working in Mexico for CIA on what he described as a "tangential special project." One of his responsibilities was to work with labor unions. He was supporting noncommunist labor leaders south of the border, for CIA was very fearful or leftist influence and worried particularly about Lombardo Toledano, a man with an extensive following both in Mexico and throughout the rest of Latin America. The labor attaché at the embassy worked on the same problems and there was friction between him and Hunt, for they sometimes found themselves stumbling over one another as they pursued their goals.

When Hunt heard that Magsaysay was coming, he arranged a meeting between the secretary of national defense and a Mexican labor leader so the Filipino could provide an anticommunist influence on the man. Hunt made his arrangements through Lansdale, who insisted that the meeting be a quiet one. Hunt then suggested that it take place at a CIA "safe" house. Lansdale concurred but then as a precaution arrived at the location early, before Magsaysay's appearance there, to check it out and to meet with the labor leader. To his surprise and consternation, secret police of the Mexican government suddenly descended on the house and arrested the labor leader, charging him with criminal activities and procommunist conspiracies. Lansdale and a companion, Anatolio Litonjua, barely made their escape, with Lansdale boldly explaining to the suspicious Mexicans that they were only tourists looking for a place to buy pornographic postcards. Afterward an angry Lansdale called Hunt at his embassy office to chide him for having set up a meeting that might have proved fatal to Magsaysay's presidential aspirations. Years later Litonjua wrote to Lansdale that "one other ineradicable incident I always tie up with you was that close shave we had with the Mexican secret service at the Plaza Zocalo . . . . Keep that harmonica untarnished."[11] Magsaysay's speech to the Lions International was well received and he, Lansdale, and the other members of the party returned to Manila on 4 July 1952.[12]

Magsaysay no longer lived with Lansdale and Bohannan, having found secure quarters for himself and his family at Camp Murphy, headquarters for the Philippine armed forces. He was a happier man after reunion with his loved ones but that didn't stop him from his inspection trips. Magsaysay and Lansdale continued their round of visits to combat areas and participated in operational planning sessions on psywar and civic action projects to use against the Huks. Lansdale later wrote in his autobiography that it was only now that he realized Magsaysay would make a good president, for he saw the sensitive way his friend dealt with people — common and elevated — who came to visit him. "I realized that, to the people, Magsaysay was becoming *the* government, *the* leader who cared about what was happening to them and who would try to right any wrongs."[13] He was not forthright in that passage or this claim, for he had already come to that decision many months earlier. As early as the previous November he not only had been convinced but had taken steps to ensure that Magsaysay would be a candidate in the 1953 elections.

In long talks with Magsaysay, Lansdale spoke about his leadership abilities, his knack for doing the right and honorable thing, his love of his people, and his interest in ending the insurgency. Gradually he began to suggest that the Philippines needed someone like Magsaysay as president. The secretary was initially shocked at such suggestions, maintaining that he had no ambitions and insufficient talents for such a heavy responsibility. He would continue to administer the office of secretary of national defense, he argued. Beyond that he might possibly run again for a seat in the Philippine House of Representatives and serve there for a term or two. His real goal, he insisted half-seriously, was to be a good mechanic. That was what he was really suited for. It was only with real reluctance and after long hours of discussion with Lansdale and others that Magsaysay finally agreed to consider becoming a candidate for the presidency.[14]

Lansdale and his team had to accomplish several old-school political maneuvers to ensure that Magsaysay was both nominated and elected. In an initial move Lansdale wrote out a plan to use as a guide for securing Magsaysay's success. This included not only promoting the man and his ideas but also safeguarding the voting as he had done for the 1951 election. Lansdale shared his views with the new ambassador, former Admiral Raymond Spruance, who enthusiastically endorsed them. He did not bother to coordinate with General Albert Pierson at JUSMAG because relations between the two men were decidedly cool. Pierson resented "cowboys" on the loose in his domain. In late January 1953, Lansdale made a trip back to Washington to set his ideas before his OPC superiors. He made the rounds of their offices, explained and defended his proposals, and received their approval. There was then time left before he had to return to Manila so, using accrued leave, he took his family for a Florida vacation where they sunned themselves on the beaches there.[15] Little did Lansdale realize as he lay in the bright sunlight that his position in the Philippines was in real danger of compromise.

Quirino's temper was on a short leash as he observed the movement on behalf of Magsaysay, and he considered taking out his frustrations on Lansdale. In 1950, on the request of George Chester and Livingston

Merchant, who represented the Office of Policy Coordination, and with the concurrence of Ambassador Myron Cowen and liaison officer Captain Charles Glazer, Quirino had agreed to invite Lansdale to come to the Philippines to advise him on intelligence matters. He was aware that, from the beginning, Lansdale had ducked the task as much as possible in order to concentrate on other, unspecified duties. As the months passed, Quirino watched Lansdale become ineradicably linked with the growing reputation of Magsaysay. Now the president found it increasingly difficult to overlook Lansdale's activities.

Matters became worse for Quirino while he was out of the country before the 1951 election. On a stopover in the United States to undergo medical treatment at Johns Hopkins University Hospital, he learned — supposedly from Allen Dulles — that Lansdale was an agent of CIA/ OPC. Although he may already have suspected as much, Quirino was furious to learn this information. He finally lost control of his emotions at a cocktail party in Manila on 27 February 1953. In an effort to undercut Magsaysay's popularity, he described his secretary of national defense to reporters who were present as a man who knew absolutely nothing about affairs of state or how to conduct them. "He is only good for killing Huks."[16]

When that story appeared in the Manila newspapers, Lansdale was still vacationing in Florida with his family. He was surprised to receive a telephone call from Secretary of State John Foster Dulles asking him to return immediately to Washington. Lansdale did so and only then learned of the new problem. Dulles explained that his brother, Allen — newly appointed director of Central Intelligence for the Eisenhower administration — had for some reason tipped Quirino off about Lansdale's real role in the Philippines. Dulles told Lansdale that he had learned of Quirino's anger from Carlos Romulo, who then served as the Philippine ambassador to Washington. Dulles continued that although both wanted to do so, "neither Quirino nor Romulo can get up the nerve to declare you *persona non grata.*" There was considerable anger among politicians in the Liberal party over Lansdale's "meddling" in the 1951 election and they might readily decide to back the president should he decide to prohibit Lansdale from returning.

Dulles reminded Lansdale that he had already given approval to Lansdale's plans for the 1953 election and would support the candidacy of Magsaysay so far as he was able. The whole plan would collapse, however, if Lansdale were to be excluded from the Philippines. Lansdale's counsel was needed there. He therefore should immediately return to Manila by the least obvious way and once back he should refrain from doing anything that might call too much hostile attention to him. "Stay as long as you can," Dulles told him. "We think you should be there through the election." He agreed that if the situation became too heated, he would set up Lansdale for an official visit to Indochina or Malaya where he might engage in some study on behalf of the U.S. government while tempers cooled in the Philippines. In the interim, Dulles promised, he would do his best to duck any diplomatic attempt by Quirino, through Romulo, to notify him officially that Lansdale was no longer welcome in the Philippines.[17]

Two days later, Lansdale arrived at Clark AFB aboard a plane from Okinawa. He hastened to Manila to meet with Ambassador Ray Spruance and JUSMAG General Albert Pierson. Spruance was understanding about Lansdale's difficulties but Pierson saw them as an opportunity to get rid of an interloper. Lansdale had to remind Pierson that he was, like Hobbs before him, under orders to support Lansdale and was not to interfere in Lansdale's mission. "I told him not to try anything," Lansdale related. "I was under very strict orders to stay. I didn't invent these orders. I was only following them. . . . This is what I'm supposed to do and I'm going to try to do it." He gave a final warning: "Don't louse it up."[18]

Magsaysay had already resigned as secretary of national defense following Quirino's outburst on 27 February. Lansdale thought it might be useful to talk with Magsaysay's successor, Oscar Castello, a former judge, and Pierson accompanied him on his visit. Castello received them graciously and even asked Lansdale to serve as his adviser. Since Lansdale knew he would no longer be acceptable at Malacañang Palace as adviser to Quirino, he desperately needed a new cover for his work in the Philippines. Why not serve as Castello's adviser? He replied that he would be happy to do so. Castello indicated that he would inform the president the next day of Lansdale's kind willingness. Lansdale and Pierson said their goodbyes and left Castello's office. On the way out of the building they encountered members of the Manila press who asked Lansdale what his plans were.

The JUSMAG chief spoke up. "Lansdale has just left JUSMAG and isn't going to be part of it anymore. I don't know what his plans are. He will probably leave the Philippines." With that explosive comment he walked away. His jaw slack with amazement, Lansdale watched him depart. He was in a real quandary. His cover had always depended on being an official part of the JUSMAG team from which General Pierson had just excluded him. His OPC assignment required that he manage the campaign of Magsaysay for the presidency of the Philippines, and Dulles had sent him back to do just that. Yet his cover was gone. What now?[19]

Lansdale conferred with Spruance and decided that maybe he would be able to find some cover position at Clark AFB. He traveled the few miles to the base and spoke with the commander there, General John Sessums, explaining as much of his situation as secrecy allowed. The general proved to be helpful. "We have a historian here," Sessums told him, "who doesn't do very much. Maybe you can . . . pose as his assistant." Needing to establish a new base as quickly as possible, Lansdale decided the scheme might work. He looked up the office of the historian and introduced himself to W.T.T. "Chips" Ward. He told Ward he needed a place "to hang my hat for a time"; he wouldn't be around very much and really needed a position that would require no work. He would occasionally stop by to give credibility to his role as "assistant historian" and Ward would have to tell anyone who inquired that Lansdale worked for him but he would not have to say more than that. Ward liked Lansdale immediately and was enthusiastic about playing even a minor role in the netherworld of American intelligence. He agreed to help.[20]

That job as "assistant historian" at Headquarters, 13th Air Force, served as Lansdale's cover for the rest of 1953. Ward recalled that "the place was a setup." He helped in any way he could, serving sometimes as "sort of a remittance man." When Lansdale needed a safe place to live, it was Ward who rented the apartment. When he desired a quiet place to meet with contacts, Ward found it for him. The historian had access to an aircraft and sometimes loaned it to Lansdale as the need arose. "Basically," Ward said, "he was moving around a great deal and not in one place too long and I was his contact. I would have done anything [for him]." Lansdale later revealed that during 1953 Ward performed services of value on certain classified projects under his direction which "contributed to attaining U.S. national policy objectives."[21] So Ed Lansdale went to "work" for Chips Ward.

Lansdale rarely struck back at those who tried to interfere with his duties, but he truly believed that General Pierson had gone beyond any forgiveness. He sent a report of the incident to CIA headquarters. "A general [who] treated me real dirty . . . was removed from his command out there [after] I finally let Washington know . . . . but I wouldn't do that very often," Lansdale remembered.[22]

During March 1953, Lansdale secured places where he might meet quietly with his contacts as he supervised Magsaysay's campaign. In addition to his quarters at Clark AFB, Ward rented him a room in Manila as well as another small *nipa* house in the town of Angeles near the air base. Lansdale learned that Tony Quirino, brother of the president, had organized a group of men to "get" him and swore he would send the

American back to the United States in a coffin. On at least one occasion, Lansdale was pursued through the nighttime streets of Manila as thugs tried to kill him. Under such circumstances, Lansdale felt safer having more than one location to call home in case trouble followed him.[23] As the April political conventions came and passed and nominees began serious campaigning, the Quirino administration became concerned with saving its own neck and eventually forgot to draw up formal papers of expulsion for Lansdale. Finally, for the first time in many weeks, Lansdale could once again concentrate on his mission.

Lansdale threw himself wholeheartedly into working on Magsaysay's campaign. His friend was now out of the Quirino administration and the next move was to secure for him a solid political base. Magsaysay was a member of the pro-American Liberal party, which had elected Roxas some years before and which Quirino now headed. Magsaysay had to leave the Liberal party and convince its rival, the Nacionalista party, that he should be its candidate. Yet such a move would face stiff resistance from two members of that group who themselves had presidential aspirations, José Laurel and Don Claro M. Recto.

Laurel and Recto had both participated in writing the constitution on the basis of which the Philippines were promised independence in 1935 by President Roosevelt and the U.S. Congress. Both had been key figures in the puppet government established by the Japanese in 1943, Laurel as president and Recto as his foreign affairs expert. Lansdale made his move to undercut their ambitions and discovered that both men were exceedingly easy to handle. In a series of conversations — carried on in large part through negotiations handled by Dindo Gonzalez — Lansdale succeeded in persuading Laurel and Recto to unite and offer Magsaysay the top position on the Nacionalista ticket. He also convinced Lorenzo Tañada to support such a move. In a meeting held on 16 November 1952 — long before Lansdale made his trip back to Washington — Laurel, Recto, Tañada, and Magsaysay met and signed a pact. The plan called for Magsaysay to resign from his cabinet position at the appropriate time, resign his membership in the ruling Liberal party, and become a Nacionalista. At the Nacionalista convention, Laurel, Recto, and Tañada would expend every effort to secure for Magsaysay the nomination of their party. They would then participate on Magsaysay's behalf in the campaigning that followed.

It is likely the three politicians agreed to this scheme for a number of reasons. Joining forces with Edward Lansdale and his American team, Laurel and Recto saw an opportunity to lay to rest their reputations as Japanese collaborators. All of them recognized Magsaysay's growing popularity among his countrymen but believed his lack of political and social credentials, coupled with his limited intellectual powers, would enable them to control him and manage his throne for the "good of the nation." For a time Magsaysay resisted the notion of cooperating with these men but Lansdale succeeded in overcoming his objections. These men and the dashing anti-Japanese guerrilla leaders who made up the bulk of Magsaysay's close followers were an odd set of political bedfellows. The "great crusade" could now be launched in earnest.

With the Nacionalista convention scheduled for April, Ramón Magsaysay used the occasion of Quirino's insult to resign from his cabinet position so as to prepare himself for the upcoming April political convention of the Nacionalista party. Lansdale's well-orchestrated planning worked without difficulty. Enthusiastic delegates chose Magsaysay to be the party's standard bearer. He could now begin his active campaigning. He chose as his theme the graft and corruption rampant within the Quirino government and the importance of forming a new and honest administration. Since there was always the possibility that some political opponent might try to do away with this upstart candidate, Lansdale set in motion an effort to provide Magsaysay with constant security. Lansdale suggested that a young acquaintance, Vicente O. Novales, would make an excellent bodyguard. Magsaysay concurred. "I stayed with him, slept near him, stayed in his house," Novales recalled. "Everywhere he went I used to be his shadow."[25]

Novales recalled that Lansdale met secretly with Magsaysay during those days. "Normally 'the Guy' [Magsaysay] used to see Lansdale not openly because he was being accused of being a tool of the Americans. There was a big cry that there were American interventions during the campaign so he was very discreet about it. . . . Every time Magsaysay goes to his place they talk for hours. Every time the president [Magsaysay] comes out, he was very happy for the ideas."[26]

Magsaysay made a formidable candidate. He was the youngest man yet to campaign for the presidency of the Philippines. At forty-six, he was seventeen years younger than the incumbent Quirino and fourteen years younger than former president Manuel Roxas had been when he became president. He was a good campaigner in the American style. He was entirely willing, even enthusiastic, about talking with voters while standing in irrigation ditches, squatting before a fire outside a *nipa* hut, or shaking the calloused hand of a farmer who was more used to guiding a *carabao* than casting a ballot. He knew when to be serious and when to add a bit of humor; when to appear presidential and when to reveal a common look.[27] His fellow countrymen loved him and it seemed every shirt soon bore a button emblazoned with the slogan "Magsaysay is My Guy."

Lansdale planted stories favorable to Magsaysay in American-owned Manila papers such as the *Bulletin* and the *Times*. "As a practical matter," wrote political analyst Joseph Alsop in the *Manila Daily Bulletin*, "Magsaysay is the American candidate."[28] Lansdale also turned for help to his old friend Manuel Manahan. Manahan was already publisher of the Tagalog-language daily newspaper, *Bagong Buhay*. At Lansdale's request he now took on the added duty of bringing out regular issues of the *Free Philippines*, an eight-page tabloid that appeared seventeen times prior to the election, each with an issue of 100,000 copies. There were several such publications with similar names, most of them sponsored by the U.S. government; one was published in Japanese. Manahan's paper reported on plans by the Quirino administration to control electoral machinery, on frauds in voter registration, and on various morale-building incidents. The name was taken from an underground newspaper Filipinos printed during the Japanese occupation, and it had a proud heritage of resistance to oppression because many of those former staff members, when captured by the Japanese, were subjected to imprisonment, torture, and even death. The copies of the new *Free Philippines* reached many hands. Total distribution of 1,700,000 copies does not tell the whole story because each newspaper was circulated from person to person and gained a huge readership.[29]

Lansdale knew full well the importance of building up the faith of voters in Magsaysay's record and convincing them of his potential. He saw to it that the report of the United States Economic Survey Mission, established in 1950 at the request of the Philippine government, received full publicity throughout the archipelago. The final report, released in 1953, stated that economic inefficiency, injustices, and official corruption within the Quirino administration were slowing and perhaps dooming the fight against the Huks. The campaign against the rebels was in danger. Four more years of Quirino might destroy the Philippines as a free nation. Magsaysay could, Lansdale argued, change the traditional pattern of Philippine politics and transform the nation into a model of democracy throughout all Asia.[30]

Others quickly joined the fray on behalf of Magsaysay. José Crisol, head of the Civil Affairs Office of the armed forces, resigned his position to launch a student organization that soon developed into a large Magsaysay for President movement. It stressed the idea that the campaign was not a partisan political one among competing parties but was a national referendum for a man above party and faction. NAMFREL, technically nonpartisan, worked quietly for Magsaysay while another group, Citizens Committee for Good Government, secretly collected political intelligence of use to Magsaysay's lieutenants.[31]

Then a wild card was played. The election race between Quirino and Magsaysay became a three-way struggle as Carlos P. Romulo threw his hat into the ring. Other than his work with the United Nations, Romulo's main claim to fame was having had his picture taken wading ashore behind Douglas MacArthur during the landing on Leyte in 1944 as the general kept his promise to return to the Philippines. Romulo later became the postwar ambassador to the United States. Back in Manila for consultations with Quirino, the two men had a falling-out and Romulo formed a new Democratic party as a vehicle for his own candidacy. His running mate was Vice President Fernando López, who broke with Quirino at about the same time and agreed to appear on Romulo's ticket. A sugar baron from the southern island of Iloilo, Lopez not only could swing votes there but brought an aura of status and riches to the new party of Romulo.

Quirino was furious about the defections of Romulo and López. A news release from Malacañang Palace revealed the extent of his irritation:

[A]side from the Liberal and Nacionalista parties, a third one is about to be born — an American Army party organized to foist "a man on horseback" on the Filipinos . . . . Whether it will continue operating . . . is not known . . . but the arrival of its "master mind" [Lansdale] who returned here a few days ago from Washington may precipitate some developments that may culminate in some sort of a political crisis. . . . The propaganda pattern is clear as evolved by the PRO colonel [Lansdale]: Main theme: U.S. security in the Pacific . . . . make of Quirino a villain, and of the U.S. Army "pet" a hero. . . . We are beginning to see the outlines of a colossal effort to interfere in our domestic affairs and make a mockery of our national sovereignty.[32]

Quirino might understandably be upset. His Liberal party had now been split twice: once by those who followed Magsaysay into the Nacionalista party and now again by those who joined with Romulo to form the Democratic party. After that press release appeared, Lansdale must have feared that his days in the Philippines were numbered. He might have to call on John Foster Dulles for a quick trip out of the country after all.

Romulo's new party was never really able to generate much enthusiasm for his candidacy. When Romulo found his crowds dwindling to ever smaller groups of bystanders, his older brother suggested that he withdraw from the race and try to make a political arrangement with Magsaysay. Romulo concurred, and in exchange for Magsaysay's promise to reappoint him ambassador if he won the election, Romulo and López disbanded the new Democratic party, which was supported by many sugar planters, and merged it with the Nacionalista party. On 21 August Romulo announced that he was quitting the race. Shortly thereafter he was named campaign manager of the "coalition campaign." Sugar money now went to swell the coffers of Magsaysay's campaign fund.[33]

American money also helped boost Magsaysay's cause. *Time* magazine reported that "U.S. business interests in the islands anted up some $250,000 at a time when Magsaysay's Nationalist Party was seriously short of funds." Other money also seems to have been available. On 11 June, Lansdale wrote to former ambassador Myron Cowen: "One of the difficulties is getting the funds [raised in the United States] into the Philippines (which I think I can solve). Another is that local managers of U.S. firms want to help, but are damn afraid they will be found out. . . . I'm just about ready to privately guarantee delivery for such folks, promising not to name them to the candidate (will do it only for Magsaysay or Romulo, not Quirino) until told to by the donor. I've been told not to do any politicking by folks in Washington, but hellsfire, this is a real political battle going on out here and you don't win battles by sitting around."[34]

In later years Lansdale would insist that "[t]he U.S. government gave no funds, secret or otherwise, to any of the candidates in the 1953 Presidential election . . . . However, some private American citizens did contribute rather small sums to Magsaysay and to Romulo, out of friendship or belief in what these candidates stood for."[35] His letter to Cowen seems to belie that claim. In that document, he refers to the difficulties in handling two categories of "gifts": how to get money into the Philippines from the United States and how to handle money raised in the Philippines by donations from American firms doing business there. He promised that he could handle money from both sources.

That Lansdale was involved in such financing may be seen in a statement he made in 1975: "At one meeting in Washington, at the top policy level [CIA] . . . I was asked about the need of candidates for funds. . . . I recall that those present at the meeting didn't agree with me that such organizations [as NAMFREL] should get U.S. financial help."[36] Lansdale's manner of responding to queries about his activities was inevitably jesuitical. When asked whether the United States gave financial help to Magsaysay in the 1953 election, Lansdale would recall, "There were rumors in the Philippines that I had given Magsaysay 'a million' or 'millions' of U.S. dollars for his campaign. These rumors were untrue."[37] It was a clever way of handling questions. Instead of answering, he misdirected attention by responding to a question of his own devising. He had not been asked about rumors in the Philippines but about practices by the American government. Further, no one had asked him what *he* gave to the campaign, but what the U.S. government had done. It was a favorite device that he continued to use in later years.[38]

Asked about his "politicking" in the Philippines, he recalled that "all U.S. officials . . . including me" were told to keep away from campaigning candidates. Then once again he answered by misdirection:

"I heard many stories that I had been seen on the platform with Magsaysay during the campaign. They were untrue. I never was on the platform with him during the campaign. I imagine that one of his mestizo aides might have been mistaken for me, at a distance."[39] Having denied sharing a platform with Magsaysay, he then went on to admit that he had indeed worked closely with organizations supporting the candidate. It was a great answer. He had not been queried as to whether he shared speaking platforms with Magsaysay, but about the extent of his participation in the election, and to that question he gave no answer. We know from the testimony of Magsaysay's bodyguard, Vicente Novales, that during the campaign the candidate often met with Lansdale for lengthy periods. We know that Lansdale had several safe houses available to him at which such meetings could take place. So even if he didn't go to political rallies with Magsaysay, Lansdale still had frequent opportunities to talk with him and counsel him on political matters.

It is also interesting to note from the Cowen letter that Lansdale was willing to channel funds to either the Magsaysay or the Romulo campaign. This may be an indication that the United States was unwilling to back only one candidate, preferring to spread its largesse so that no matter which man won, he would owe a debt of gratitude to America.

It seems highly questionable that U.S. officials would order Lansdale to refrain from politicking since he had no other function in his assignment to the Philippines. If he was not to participate in the election campaign, why had he earlier drawn up his plan for the 1953 election? Why had he gone back to Washington to seek its approval at his headquarters? Why had he been called back to Washington by John Foster Dulles from his Florida vacation? Why had Dulles been so concerned about the danger of Lansdale being declared *persona non grata* by Elpidio Quirino? Why had Dulles told Lansdale during one of their meetings, "We think you should be there through the election"? Why would Dulles promise to do all he could to support Lansdale's election plan and avoid officially receiving a declaration of expulsion from the Philippines for Lansdale? Why would Dulles order him to return immediately to Manila and to stay in the Philippines as long as he could? Why would Dulles tell Lansdale he would arrange a short official study trip for him to Malaya or Indochina during the coming months if feelings against him in the Philippines became too strong? For Lansdale to then come under an order to avoid politicking makes no sense at all. Much more likely, and this would have been consonant with his orders, he was to avoid the *appearance* of interfering in the election, and that Lansdale did indeed endeavor to do.

Only a few days after his letter to Cowen, Lansdale seems to have felt it necessary to call upon Dulles' promise of a trip outside the Philippines. Although he claimed that progress in the election campaign was going well, he may also have concluded that a short break from his activities would benefit everyone concerned. In his autobiography, Lansdale claimed, "I was able to accept an invitation to join a small U.S. group headed by General John W. 'Iron Mike' O'Daniel which . . . was to meet [in Indochina] with French General Henri Navarre, for any counseling he wished and to examine his needs for resources. . . . The visit of about six weeks gave me a unique introduction to the affairs of Indochina."[40]

Lansdale always claimed that his participation in the O'Daniel mission was a chance one, but its destination of Indochina and Dulles' earlier promise of a study trip to that region makes for high odds against pure coincidence. The O'Daniel group made an overnight stop at Clark AFB on 19 June 1953 on its way to Indochina and the general contacted Lansdale, indicating that he wanted to talk with him about guerrilla wars. They talked for hours. About eleven o'clock that night, according to Lansdale, O'Daniel asked him if he wanted to go on the trip. "Even though I was quite busy in the Philippines I said . . . I'd come along," he replied. The general told him they would leave early the next day: "Wheels up at six in the morning."[41]

Lansdale left the Philippines on 20 June and was gone from the country about six weeks, returning around the end of the first week in August. When the members of the mission landed in Saigon some French personnel in the welcoming delegation were surprised to see Lansdale. Lansdale described them as "appalled." A few of them had earlier visited the Philippines to observe the contest there with the Huks and had gotten to know Lansdale. "The American egalitarian political views I held were ones they were afraid would rub off somehow or other on the Vietnamese," Lansdale observed. They demurred about his inclusion in the mission and wanted him to leave, but General Navarre overrode such objections and personally extended his own welcome.

At an official luncheon the following day Navarre revealed that he was working on a new plan for countering the Viet Minh uprising against the French colonial government in Vietnam. He said to Lansdale, "I would value any of your notes and ideas on fighting the Viet Minh guerrillas. Would you help me with the supplementary parts of my plan on intelligence, psychological warfare and clandestine operations?"[42]

Navarre agreed that Lansdale should have a firsthand look at the countryside prior to offering any observations, so Lansdale traveled freely throughout the three Associated States of Vietnam, Laos, and Cambodia. He visited headquarters, combat areas, and training camps and talked with members of local political groups. As usual, he relied on interpreters, sign language, and a pocket dictionary. He became aware of how strikingly different the Vietnamese were from his Filipino friends. Lansdale scheduled a trip to a Foreign Legion outpost on the Plaine des Jarres in Laos to observe a scheduled attack on the Viet Minh that was canceled at the last moment. He also made a formal call on Prince Norodom Sihanouk in Phnom Penh. (Sihanouk later starred in a movie he wrote and produced in which he bested a villainous American spy who was a caricature of Lansdale.) Lansdale visited the Hanoi area and became friendly with a group of French paratroopers there and talked at length with them about irregular operations. He visited with General René Cogny and members of his staff. He also visited Dien Bien Phu. "The French took me up there to take a look at it," Lansdale said. "They wanted me to see what one of their outposts looked like. . . . They already had some fortifications built." He went on reconnaissance flights that allowed him to inspect the area near the Chinese border.[43]

Lansdale didn't like what he saw. He inspected many of the dozens of French forts dotting the countryside, from large complexes to little ones capable of housing only a squad of soldiers. He noted that the French were using a static defensive posture based on those forts, leaving the countryside to the Viet Minh. He observed that Frenchmen held all top-level positions of administration within the government and felt that they needed to allow more Vietnamese into such jobs.

Then he wrote the annexes that General Navarre had asked of him. They were, Lansdale said, "a mixed bag of clandestine operations and secret missions and intelligence collection. He pointed out that the French idea of using paratroopers and other elite troops on commando raids was hardly a good example of unconventional warfare. Such soldiers raided settlements suspected of harboring or sympathizing with the Viet Minh. Troops would "shoot everything in sight . . . and leave a scorched earth behind." Such attacks did nothing for the French cause because they made "all the people hate those who had brought them about." The enemy, on the other hand, based their support on the people of the countryside. "So in effect these commando raids, which were looked on as very unconventional, were causing great conventional harm to the cause of the French."[44]

Lansdale was pessimistic about any French success in retaining Indochina as a colonial area. He submitted his reports to Navarre and gave copies to personnel at the American mission in Saigon — the minister and the CIA station chief. He also handed to the CIA man pictures of French intelligence agents swimming nude, which he had taken on an outing at the beach of Cap St. Jacques near Vung Tau. The man was not amused. "You wanted to know something about them," Lansdale said with a smile. "Well, here are pictures of the bunch."[45] He stayed up his last night in Saigon writing his report for General O'Daniel, only finishing it the next day during the flight over the South China Sea on his way back to the Philippines. Sometime around 8 August 1953 Lansdale returned to his work on the Philippine election.

Thanks to Lansdale, Kaplan, and American-style electioneering, Magsaysay's allies at NAMFREL and in the press were of great help in ensuring a large turnout of voters. NAMFREL used members of the Philippines Veterans Legion as volunteers to organize voters in every precinct of every province throughout the country. Other civic groups also offered their help: Catholic Action, the Jaycees, Rotary, the Lions, the League of Women Voters, and the Committee for Good Government all joined NAMFREL in its efforts.[46]

Correspondents from other Asian countries and from the United States served as informal observers, and the Philippine News Service used thousands of willing hands to cover all aspects of the campaign. With help from the Manila CIA station and CIA's FE/Plans desk, NAMFREL and the Magsaysay for President movement concentrated on blocking any attempt at electoral fraud. They hoped that under the eyes of so many volunteers they might frighten Quirino out of any last-minute efforts to steal the election. Journalists constantly monitored events, ever ready to file a good story or two about corruption in the Philippines.[47]

To the very end Lansdale felt he should monitor Magsaysay's actions and ideas. Bohannan wrote that when Magsaysay did not accept such advice, "his actions were often good, sometimes well intentioned but injudicious, occasionally outright nonsense."[48]

The United States Navy and JUSMAG let their presence be felt right up to the last moment on election day in an effort to bolster Magsaysay's candidacy. Only a few days prior to the election U.S. warships arrived in Manila Bay. American officers observed the behavior of Filipino Army men watching the polls during the balloting. Lansdale planned for Magsaysay and other key candidates to stay at Subic Bay Naval Base on election day out of concern for their safety.[49] The candidate instead chose to be a houseguest of a friend, J. Antonio Araneta.

Magsaysay's election was a landslide. He received more than double the number of votes cast for Quirino — 2,912,992 to 1,313,991. As the one-sided voting was reported, Magsaysay and Araneta went to the Malate Church where a *Te Deum* was sung. Later he went to the grounds of the American embassy and met with Ambassador Raymond Spruance and Lansdale. Lansdale's advice to be careful of his safety finally convinced Magsaysay and, along with others, he boarded the yacht of a

U.S. admiral and cruised around Manila Bay. They were enjoying this ride over the rolling waters of the bay when they heard a news flash that President Quirino had conceded the election.[50]

As the final vote was announced, the Indian ambassador to the Philippines told reporters that the results "should cause a certain American colonel to change his name to 'Landslide.' " The nickname dogged Lansdale for the remainder of his years. To both friend and foe he would thereafter be Colonel Landslide.[51]

Following the election, Magsaysay decided it was time for a vacation after all the recent hectic weeks. Lansdale went with him to the farm home of Magsaysay's father in Zambales. There they went swimming in the nude, ate roasting ears and fried fish, celebrated with evening songfests, and slept late in the mornings. The two settled into a familiar routine. "He would expound his ideas," Lansdale recalled, "and I would ask questions to be certain that he had considered the alternatives that awaited his decision. The decisions themselves were his alone to make." One of Lansdale's suggestions was that Magsaysay should remember the success he had had with the ten-centavo telegram program and try to find a way to work it into his administration of the presidency.[52]

Magsaysay's first executive order created the office of Presidential Complaints and Action Commission (PCAC). His lieutenant, the publisher Manuel Manahan, congratulated him for his act and talked of going back to the newspaper work that he had abandoned for more than a year. That would have to wait. Magsaysay named Manahan to head PCAC and he oversaw the resolution of some twenty-seven thousand cases, recommending remedial action on behalf of concerned or grieved individuals and checking on compliance by the responsible government officials or agencies. When Manahan left the office he was succeeded by Frisco San Juan.[53] This program enhanced an already rosy image of Magsaysay as champion of the common *tao*.

To maintain his reputation as a reformer, Magsaysay worked at keeping excellent relations with the press. He gave his press secretary cabinet rank within the government and named journalists, their families, and friends to government positions. He participated in raising funds for the New National Press Club building in downtown Manila and directed his administration to minister to the wants of journalists and "to be nice to them." It is little wonder that members of the press responded by providing the new president with consistently friendly coverage.[54]

Lansdale had succeeded in his goal of helping elect to the presidency a Filipino politician who would favor the American position on questions of policy. Magsaysay favored U.S. retention of its military bases at Clark and Subic. He upheld the continuation of the Bell Trade Act when he signed the Laurel-Langley Agreement into law in December 1954.[55] Magsaysay also backed an adequate system of defense for his "exposed and threatened sector" of the world and sponsored the Manila Pact. Formed by representatives of the Philippines, the United States, the United Kingdom, France, Australia, New Zealand, Thailand, and Pakistan, the pact aimed at securing collective defense of Southeast Asia against armed external aggression and subversion. Out of this pact came the anticommunist Southeast Asia Treaty Organization (SEATO), which formally came into being in February 1955.[56]

Lansdale thought back over his activities in the Philippines since his arrival as an OPC agent in September 1950. "Fortunately there wasn't a lot of attention given to [my activities] and there wasn't [always] a journalist with space in American papers looking over my shoulder," he said. "So we could make mistakes and do better next time and teach ourselves. . . . The war was going on in Korea and, thank God, that kept all the military brass [from] looking at what we were doing. . . . We had to do it on our own and with our own wits, much as the guerrillas did. It worked. We got down to fundamentals and principles that really worked."[57]

What had he done? He later wrote that, among other things, "I acted as sort of a catalyst to bring together some solutions to problems with American experts who could help. This involved a number of intelligence activities; the socio-economic aspects of EDCOR; the organization, training, and deployment of Scout Rangers; a wide spectrum of psychological operations; the popular cut-rate telegrams to the Secretary; the organization and training of the airborne battalion; the deceptive tactics of units such as Charlie Company, 7th BCT, and so forth."[58] In a letter to his friend Robert Shaplen, Lansdale offered another synopsis of his role. "Somebody had to do the strategic planning, keep Washington firm enough on backing the play, and ride herd on the tactical implementation while building up a local national hero."[59]

The reports Lansdale had filed, his brief trips back to the United States to discuss his activities with his superiors, orders he gave to others — such as the ambassador and the JUSMAG generals — who in turn sent forward their own reports, his success with Magsaysay, and his advice on countering the Huk insurgency — all of this established Lansdale's reputation within America's intelligence world as a guerrilla-buster, expert on revolutionary war, and kingmaker. He would be measured and weighed in this balance for the rest of his career.

Tired of the Philippines, Lansdale hoped to return to the States as soon as Magsaysay was inaugurated. That event came on 30 December 1953 and soon afterward he finally convinced his superiors that his mission in Manila was completed. He flew back to the United States in January 1954, home at last. He knew how his lengthy absences hurt his boys. "My kids missed having a father during the days when they'd be going to Boy Scouts," Lansdale recalled. "And I missed having them. They should have grown up hating my gut. Maybe they do. I don't think so. I tell them they're better fathers than I was. They're both very much closer to their children than I ever was to them."[60] Now he could be a family man again.

7

ON TO SAIGON

DURING HIS FIRST DAYS HOME following his Philippine sojourn Ed Lansdale was happy to fit himself back within his family circle. Ted and Peter pranced around him, excited and nervous about this tall and friendly man who was sometimes their father. Helen was a little anxious for it had been a long time since they had spent much time together and she was used to her own routine. Ed had frequently seen his Filipina, Pat Kelly, during the Manila years despite the busy nature of his assignment there, and he missed her, but he was determined to do the best he could with his family. He brought little gifts for the boys and treasures for Helen and there was happiness in the large house.

Lansdale's duties at CIA headquarters during those early days of January 1954 were pleasant ones. They consisted primarily of briefing other agents and writing reports about his past activities. He had left Bo Bohannan to oversee American interests in the Philippines, and Bo promised to keep Magsaysay on "the straight and narrow."[1] Lansdale's reputation as a psywar expert grew steadily among his peers. One man described him as a "fountain of all knowledge in such matters."[2] Yet while Lansdale basked in his newly minted reputation, portentous events occurred elsewhere that would soon bring him back into the heat of cold war politics.

Dwight Eisenhower had been president of the United States for one year when Lansdale returned home, and the former general faced serious criticism from many Americans who believed that too much had been lost to the worldwide communist menace. Some wondered if the Eisenhower administration, like its predecessor, was "soft on communism." The Nationalist Chinese Kuomintang government had fallen to Mao's communist forces in 1949. The conflict in Korea remained unsettled as a dreary round of truce negotiations continued at Panmunjom. Now President Eisenhower was under great pressure to intervene in Indochina on behalf of the faltering French efforts there as the French struggled to regain a firm hold on their colonies of Tonkin, Annam, and Cochinchina.

Since the time of President Truman, the U.S. government had borne an increasing share of France's expenses in its struggle with Ho Chi Minh's guerrilla warriors, and Eisenhower was only too aware that Beijing had extended diplomatic recognition to Ho's movement as early as January 1950 (and Moscow would later follow its example). Dean Acheson, who had served as Truman's secretary of state, described that event as removing "any illusions as to the 'nationalist' nature of Ho Chi Minh's aims and reveals his true colors as the mortal enemy of native independence in Indochina."[3]

In an effort to forestall further advances by Ho Chi Minh, Truman agreed in August 1950 to establish a Military Assistance and Advisory Group (MAAG) to work with French forces in Indochina. The problem was left in Eisenhower's lap as Truman left the presidency in January 1953. The Pentagon sent General John W. "Iron Mike" O'Daniel to inspect conditions in Vietnam during the summer of 1953; in Manila he added Lansdale to his entourage and thus Lansdale had gotten his first opportunity to visit that beleaguered land. O'Daniel returned home with a report that held a measured optimism. He believed that the approach of French General Henri Navarre to the problems of insurgency and rebellion in Vietnam was a positive one. Navarre would achieve the "decisive defeat" of Viet Minh guerrilla forces by 1955, O'Daniel predicted.

Lansdale had not been optimistic about what he saw. He believed the French had little idea of the nature of their enemy or the sort of war they were engaged in. A few months after his visit, Lansdale wrote to his family that O'Daniel did not understand that "we are nearing the final stages of World War III." Oriental insurgencies had their own "tactics, losses and gains (some of which are staggering)." There were new rules of warfare and combat to learn. "The rules are as different as the difference between Wars I and II. Because so many of us haven't understood the rules, we have lost thousands upon thousands of square miles of real estate, millions of people have been brought under subjection by the enemy, and we have expended great material wealth in the struggle. . . . [T]he little guys, the rice paddy farmers, know far more than the policymakers. [Theirs] is the simplified wisdom of the victim."[5] As he left Vietnam in 1953, Lansdale filed a copy of his report with the CIA station chief in Saigon. Thus he may bear part of the responsibility for the Agency warning that contradicted O'Daniel's optimism. CIA forewarned Washington that even if the United States sent troops to fight alongside the French and even if the Viet Minh field forces were defeated, "guerrilla action could probably be continued indefinitely."[6] Warfare was soon to have a different set of rules.

On 8 January 1954, about the time Lansdale returned to Washington,

President Eisenhower called to order a meeting of the National Security Council (NSC). On the agenda was the issue of French problems in Indochina. Twenty-seven men attended, including the secretaries of defense and state, the director of Central Intelligence, the chairman of the Joint Chiefs of Staff, and the chiefs of each of the uniformed services. Speaking with real vehemence, President Eisenhower addressed those present. "There is just no sense in even talking about United States forces replacing the French in Indochina. If we did so, the Vietnamese could be expected to transfer their hatred of the French to us. I cannot tell you how bitterly opposed I am to such a course of action. This war in Indochina would absorb our troops by divisions."[7]

While unwilling to commit ground forces to Indochina, the president believed that he had to do something. Both he and his secretary of state, John Foster Dulles, were impressed by Ramón Magsaysay's successful campaign against Huk rebels in the Philippines. They thought the same tactics might work in Vietnam. Dulles knew that Lansdale had served as Magsaysay's adviser and was inevitably impressed with what he had to say. John Foster and his brother Allen, who served as director of Central Intelligence, began to think of using Lansdale in Vietnam in a capacity similar to his role in the Philippines. They wondered what would happen if once again Lansdale received great authority and wide latitude and was turned loose in a country to effect his magic.[8]

On 14 January, at a meeting of the NSC, those present agreed that the director of Central Intelligence, in cooperation with the secretary of state, should develop contingency plans for American action in Indochina. The Dulles brothers talked further about Edward Lansdale.[9] On 29 January 1954, the president's Special Committee on Indochina met to talk over plans for helping the French.[10] Lansdale was present, as were Admiral Arthur S. Radford, chairman of the Joint Chiefs of Staff, and the Dulles brothers. Radford warned his listeners that the United States could not afford to let the Viet Minh take the Tonkin Delta. If it were lost, so also would be Indochina, and then the rest of Southeast Asia would fall.[11] Allen Dulles wondered if "an unconventional warfare officer, specifically Colonel Lansdale," might not be sent to work in Indochina, and Admiral Radford thought that might be done.[12]

John Foster Dulles then turned to Lansdale and said, "We're going to send you over there." "Not to help the French!" Lansdale exploded. "Hell, the goddamn French *colons* with their colony." The secretary of state responded patiently. "No, I [only] want you to do what you did in the Philippines." Lansdale calmed down. "Well, if it means helping the Vietnamese, sure, but there's a lot I have to learn about the place. I have to learn the language and read up on Vietnamese affairs." That conversation, Lansdale would later state, formed the basis for his subsequent actions in Vietnam. "That's as clearly defined as anything ever was."[13]

Lansdale was gratified when he learned later that both Iron Mike O'Daniel, who had since returned to Vietnam as commander of the MAAG unit there, and Ambassador Donald Heath had requested his services. Their interest in having him join them reinforced his enthusiasm for the orders given him in Washington. The situation in Indochina deteriorated apace.

In an effort to salvage something from the wreckage of their empire in Indochina, the French had created a basically fictitious and very fragile government there called the State of Vietnam headed by the aging playboy emperor Bao Dai. Although it had a governing body called the Chamber of Deputies, none of its members had any real constituency. Since 2 September 1945 when Ho Chi Minh proclaimed the Independent Democratic Republic of Vietnam, the xenophobic Vietnamese had only two choices: support Ho's Viet Minh republic or their French colonial masters. They sided overwhelmingly with Ho. Certainly most Vietnamese felt little loyalty to Bao Dai, who lived in France and cavorted on the Riviera, and they hated the French. That was the political climate into which Lansdale had been ordered.

It was with some trepidation that Lansdale informed Helen of his new overseas assignment. He had been back only scant weeks. CIA was sending him to Indochina, he told his suddenly frosty wife. He tried to soften the news by promising that he would not have to leave for some time, perhaps two months or more. In the meantime he would carry on with regular office hours and study of the French language. His home life seems never to have been a smooth one; the fates conspired against all his plans to make things easier for Helen.

A letter from a friend was an intimation that his schedule would not hold up. "General Romulo called me," George Peabody wrote, "and asked me where he could reach 'General Landslide,' and as he seemed so adamant about this, I gave him your number. Incidentally, I never heard so many laudatory comments as he made about you. . . . [H]e will work hard to have you returned to the Philippines as you were such a good influence on Mr. Magsaysay."[14]

One evening a few days later, after Lansdale had gone to bed, the telephone rang, waking him from his sleep. Drowsily holding the receiver against his ear, he listened to the voice of Ramón Magsaysay. The Philippine president asked him to return to Manila; he needed help implementing his reforms. Trouble loomed with his Congress, particularly the Senate. He needed Lansdale's help. Wide awake, Lansdale replied that he had other pressing duties, a different country to go to, a language and history to study. Lansdale had been in the Philippines long enough. He was not even vaguely tempted by Magsaysay's cry for help. Magsaysay refused to give up. He called again the following evening and then repeatedly over the next several days. Each time Lansdale demurred. Lansdale's father, Harry, was visiting and finally asked, "Who's that fellow who keeps calling every night?" His son said, "Oh, some guy out in the Philippines."[15]

Stymied by Lansdale's stubbornness and a little angry, Magsaysay telephoned President Eisenhower and explained his problem. The White House notified the Department of Defense, and the Pentagon contacted Lansdale. They were sympathetic to Magsaysay's plea. Lansdale was to leave for Manila without argument or delay. He begged his superiors to let him return to the United States after this new work in the Philippines to provide him with a little time to study French before he went to Vietnam. He was told his request would be taken under consideration.[16]

Ed told Helen that he had no choice. There would be no delay of two or three months. There was nothing more he could do. Ted and Peter were as glum as their mother as they watched Ed pack for his trip. Then the telephone rang. By this time Lansdale was thoroughly suspicious of the instrument. What new message of disaster would it bring? His misgivings were well placed. The voice at the other end was his brother Phil, calling from Los Angeles. Their beloved mother, Sarah, had just died. Like his brothers, Ed was close to his mother and the news struck with devastating effect. Numbed by his loss, he changed his flight plans to allow for a stopover in California for the funeral.

Aboard his airplane at Washington National Airport, Lansdale was dismayed when there was a lengthy delay in takeoff. He joined with other passengers in their grumbling. Then he noticed Carlos P. Romulo, the Philippine ambassador to the United States, coming down the aisle. Romulo had learned of Lansdale's loss and had asked the airline to delay the plane long enough for him to get to the airport and offer his condolences. "It was a nice gesture on his part," Lansdale remembered. The reunion of the Lansdale brothers was a sad one.[17]

The weeks passed quickly in the Philippines, where Lansdale was assigned to temporary duty at 13th Air Force on loan to President Magsaysay. Work helped dull his grief over the loss of his mother and still another separation from his family. Before he quite realized how time was passing, it was late May. Events west across the South China Sea continued to shake the French colonial empire. General Henri Navarre, who had been so cordial to Lansdale during his visit there in the summer of 1953, believed he knew the way to destroy the Viet Minh as a fighting force.

He would entice them into a "set piece" battle where the superior training and firepower of French troops could be brought into play and smash the insurgents, speeding the inevitable French victory. Navarre ordered fifteen thousand troops two hundred miles behind enemy lines to a small community twelve miles from the Laotian border known as Dien Bien Phu. Bunkers were constructed, trenches dug, fortifications strengthened. Mortars and machine guns were zeroed in, and artillery pieces sited. The only way calamity could befall the French was if the Viet Minh came equipped with artillery. That was clearly impossible, for there were no roads, no transport, and no artillery available to the insurgents. On 13 March 1954, while Lansdale labored in the Philippines, forty thousand Viet Minh irregular warriors pitted themselves against Navarre's soldiers. They came equipped with artillery that they had dismantled and carried on their backs or tied on to reinforced bicycles through the long stretches of inhospitable terrain. After only five days of combat, when Viet Minh shells made the French airstrip unusable, it was clear that Navarre's forces were doomed. Once again the French petitioned the United States for assistance.

President Eisenhower wondered what his options were. The Joint Chiefs of Staff briefed him on two possibilities: wage another traditional-style Korean War or implement the administration's own policy of massive retaliation. The Pentagon argued for the second. Use atomic weapons on Haiphong. Launch combined Franco-American ground armies against the Viet Minh. Blockade the Chinese coast and neutralize Hainan Island. Unleash Chiang Kai-shek's soldiers in assaults on mainland China.

The American president likened the situation in Indochina to a set of dominoes. "[K]nock over the first one and what will happen to the last one is the certainty that it will go over very quickly."[18] John Foster Dulles urged Eisenhower toward a martial response, but the old soldier had seen enough of war. He decided not to intervene on behalf of the beleaguered French. On 26 April a conference opened in Geneva, attended by the United States, Great Britain, the Soviet Union, mainland China, France, and representatives from France's former Indochinese colonies — Ho's Democratic Republic of Vietnam, Bao Dai's State of Vietnam, Laos, and Cambodia. While delegates met at Geneva on 7 May, the Viet Minh overran the fortress of Dien Bien Phu. The French agreed to relinquish their colony. On 20–21 July the Geneva Conference ended, having partitioned Vietnam along the 17th parallel and having recognized the legitimacy of Ho's northern government above the 17th parallel and Bao Dai's State of Vietnam as sovereign in the south — a temporary division pending a nationwide election to be held in the summer of 1956.

In the aftermath of the fall of Dien Bien Phu, Lansdale received his orders from Allen Dulles: to proceed without delay by the first available transport to Saigon and begin his mission there. There would be no time for him to return to Washington and learn French or read history. Dulles' orders ended with a strange notation: "God bless you." Lansdale wondered at the unusual garnish of flowery hope.[19]

Within a few hours, Lansdale departed Manila en route to Saigon aboard an air-sea rescue amphibious airplane belonging to the 31st Air Squadron at Clark AFB. It was 1 June 1954. His orders called for him to serve as assistant air attaché on embassy duty. That was his cover. His real mission was to assist in the birth of a southern government that could successfully compete with and oppose Ho's Democratic Republic of Vietnam. He was authorized to put together a small team to help him. The group would be known as the Saigon Military Mission and was run under CIA auspices. Upon his arrival Lansdale reported for duty to General O'Daniel, who invited him to bunk in his quarters that night. During the dark hours they were awakened by the sounds of explosions. Viet Minh forces had raided a French ammunition dump on Saigon's outskirts. Once again Lansdale was in the midst of a world at war.[20]

The next day was no more auspicious than the night had been. As a courtesy, Lansdale reported to the embassy to speak with the air attaché, who was, like himself, a lieutenant colonel. Lansdale introduced himself, spoke of his cover assignment as assistant air attaché, and explained as much of his mission as he could. "I'm coming in as your assistant," Lansdale related, but because of the nature of his assignment he promised that he would be no trouble at all. "It is just a convenience to me, a place where I can hang my hat." The attaché was incensed. He was certain Lansdale was only a CIA man masquerading as a regular Air Force officer. "Who are you," he demanded, "to bring all this [spy agency] crap in here?" He thought a moment and then added, "If you *are* a real officer, I outrank you." Now Lansdale became angry. "No, I outrank you," he insisted. The squabbling became petulant as Lansdale insisted that the attaché check his copy of the Air Force registry to determine which of them held the earliest date of rank. Lansdale smiled when the attaché was forced to admit that he was outranked. Lansdale remembered that the "son of a bitch" wouldn't give him a chair to sit on, let alone use of a desk in his office. "I had to operate out of my hat. Very shabby treatment," he recalled.[21] Disgruntled by the confrontation, Lansdale next sought out the U.S. Information Service chief, George Hellyer, who proved to be much more helpful. "[He] was a real nice guy," Lansdale stated. "I liked him and we became friends . . . . He let me use part of his desk to file my papers in."[22]

From that point on, the day slid downhill again. Indochina was one of the few places in the world where two CIA stations existed simultaneously. Lansdale's Saigon Military Mission carried on its activities while a civilian operation under the regular station chief worked concurrently on its own assignment. A great rivalry began that day between the two groups that often would become bitter. In a comment straight out of the old Lone Ranger radio program, Lansdale told how he was in charge of the CIA that wore "white hats" while the Saigon station chief was in charge of the CIA that wore "black hats" in Vietnam. "Lansdale was sort of out there on the end of the line," Joe Baker, a team member, related. "A lot of people were envious of Ed because he used to have a direct line to Allen Dulles and through Allen to John Foster Dulles, which made a lot of people antsy. But he was always sort of a loner. Never had the military or the Agency or State Department back of him."[23]

When Lansdale made his next stop that second day of his tour in Vietnam the result was the beginning of that rivalry. He sought out Emmett McCarthy, a large ex-OSS sergeant in constant battle with the bottle, a conflict he finally lost. At the time he served as CIA station chief in Saigon.[24] Here, as in the office of the air attaché, professional jealousy interfered with cooperation. Lansdale thought McCarthy treated him "like dirt" and resented it when the man made him stand at attention. Nor did he like McCarthy's mannerisms or attitude. McCarthy told Lansdale he was a "stupid goddammed amateur." He elaborated: "[You] get out of our way and let us pros really move the pieces around on this chessboard here." Lansdale lamented that McCarthy refused to be of any help. Both were proud men. Lansdale, accustomed to an extreme degree of independence, insisted that he reported only to Allen Dulles, while McCarthy asserted that the Saigon Military Mission would report to Washington through him. Unfortunately there was no way for Lansdale to avoid capitulating on this point; he had no separate communications channel to use as he had had in the Philippines. All secret messages to Washington had to go through McCarthy and the facilities at Saigon station. Communications would be a continuing sore point.[25] It got worse.

Lansdale claimed that McCarthy stubbornly resisted even limited cooperation; his reluctance held up progress on Lansdale's assignment. Most of the time they refused to speak to each other. But one day Lansdale dropped in to McCarthy's office to snoop for evidence of certain things he suspected the station chief to be doing. On his desk was a pile of mail and cablegrams that Lansdale wanted to eyeball. Behind McCarthy were his office files. Lansdale noticed that the "H" file was so situated that McCarthy would have to turn his back to open that drawer, so Lansdale demanded technical and detailed information about the Hoa Hao religious sect. While McCarthy reluctantly looked up the answers,

Lansdale picked up and leafed through the pile of mail on his desk looking for any evidence he could use against him. Unaware of Lansdale's busy fingers, McCarthy "continued to lecture me about what an amateur I was." Finally Lansdale wrote to Washington: "Fire that son of a bitch. Get him out of here." McCarthy was replaced by John Anderton and he and Lansdale cooperated amicably.[26]

In his autobiography, Lansdale disingenuously admitted only that "I had been posted to Saigon as an assistant air attache."[27] He neglected to describe his real role as chief of the CIA's Saigon Military Mission. Why had he been ordered there? According to one author, CIA assets were the only ones America had that could deal with the situation in Vietnam by the early summer of 1954. CIA manpower was all the government had to fill the gap between the language of "massive retaliation," which the United States threatened against Russian and Chinese enemies, and the reality of the forces and arms that were actually available. Tired from the recent conflict in Korea, America had neither energy nor resources available for another massive effort in Vietnam nor did it have the enthusiasm necessary to bolster a French struggle to subdue colonial insurgents. What it did have were CIA agents who could provide those in the south of that divided land with the assistance they needed to combat the network of informers, the hidden insurgent infrastructure, and the armed guerrillas the Viet Minh forces had left behind. It was hoped that Lansdale could organize and supervise the creation of a government for the area south of the 17th parallel.[28]

The first requirement was to acquire a place to call home, an operational base. For a time Lansdale stayed in a vacant room at the MAAG bachelor officers quarters courtesy of General O'Daniel, who also provided him with the use of a tiny Citroën 2-CV automobile. Then he lived for a time in a small bungalow on rue Miche, near the center of Saigon. Later Lansdale managed to rent a large, two-story house at 51 rue Duy Tan to serve as home and office. Within the walled compound on rue Duy Tan was a smaller building for the servants' living quarters, and the driveway was large enough to allow parking for five or six cars. A security man from the Philippines, Proculo L. Mojica, presided over this domain. He watched for intruders, ensured that cars parked in the driveway remained free from booby traps, and traveled as Lansdale's driver and bodyguard. When Lansdale learned that Proc played the guitar, he dug out his harmonica and the two amused themselves and guests by playing duets.

Wherever Lansdale went, Proc acted as his shadow — on picnics, on shopping trips in the markets, or on an expedition to the Waico River in Tay Ninh to watch Vietnamese efforts to recover the bodies of three

Filipina nurses who drowned while swimming. During walks through the shops of the central market, Lansdale occasionally asked Proc if he had sufficient ammo. "Open your eyes wide, Proc," Lansdale said. "Don't hesitate to pull that trigger if you see anything funny." Mojica surveyed the passing throngs through his smoked glasses, his hand on the Colt revolver in his pocket. "There were times we would go outside the city [into guerrilla territory]," Mojica recalled, "and there is where I begin to have goose flesh."[29] It was an exciting time.

During his first days Lansdale spent a great deal of time talking to others in a frantic effort to learn as much as he could about the history of Vietnam. He regretted that circumstances had prevented him from doing so before his arrival and he also felt his lack of the language, which kept him mute without a translator present. "Most of what I learned came to me . . . through questioning knowledgeable Americans, Vietnamese, and Frenchmen. Increasingly, I was awed by the complexity of this small country . . . I managed to travel to each region of the country that June [1954]."[30]

Vietnam consists of the easternmost portion of a long peninsula at the southeastern tip of Asia and is shaped like a giant letter *S*, which juts south out of China into the South China Sea. The northern part of the land contains the heavily populated, highly cultivated and productive delta of the Red River. Moving south, those northern flatlands give way to a long, undulating coast with occasional small, fertile plains interrupted by rocky promontories that reach into the sea. Farther south the thin coastal strip widens as it falls toward the rich alluvial soil of the Mekong River delta. Inland mountains form the Annamite chain, which merges with high plateaus. This high country, from north to south, parallels the coast.

Chinese and European names were given to this land. The French renamed the north Tonkin, the central area Annam, and the south Cochinchina. The very name Vietnam derived from Nam Viet, or *Yueh-nan* in Chinese, an ancient term for the South Chinese province of Kwangtung. The term meant "south of Yueh," or "land of the south," or simply "distant south."

For a thousand years Vietnam endured Chinese control, and during that period the Vietnamese absorbed the wisdom of Confucius. They based much of their society on his doctrines and from them worked out well-ordered patterns of life that remained largely unchanged for dozens of generations. Law and custom kept everyone in his or her rightful and proper place. Primary loyalty was to the family — the living as well as the dead, for ancestors were not really dead and were never forgotten.

Ancestors played important roles in family life, and fathers periodically consulted with them in hopes of protection and helpful advice. Family obligations were revered and connections maintained even with remote cousins. At all levels, the Vietnamese honored respect: brother to elder brother, wife to husband, son to father, all to ancestors. Obedience, status, and loyalty were social bywords.

The land was sacred. It provided food and cradled ancestral graves, family huts, the hamlets composed of several nearby families, and villages made up of two or more hamlets. Modern Vietnam had some seventeen thousand hamlets formed into roughly two thousand villages. There were no isolated farms, for people went out from their hamlet homes to the land and worked long hours on land their ancestors had toiled over for a thousand years. Women and children often walked long distances for cooking and drinking water, even farther during dry seasons if a local well drew salty liquid from the aquifer. Clothing was simple: black pajama-like garments; shoes were unknown to calloused feet. People lived in bamboo and straw huts with thatched roofs, furnished mainly with a table, straw sleeping mats, and cooking utensils. They had no electricity, no newspapers, no radios. Lives were simple and wealth was measured in terms of water buffaloes, which cost about fifty dollars, roughly a year's income.

Vietnamese people drew their strength from the soil on which they lived. They looked to themselves and to each other for guidance rather than toward some higher government. In home, hamlet, and village were their families and the spirits of ancestors and so they remained on the same land through many generations, linked spiritually in a continuity with the past. So tied were they to their hamlets that they seldom traveled more than a short walk from their homes throughout their lives. Often hamlets were not even connected by roads to the larger world, travel was by foot, and so their cosmos was contained by the bamboo hedge surrounding their community. And those villages survived the vagaries of war, the idiosyncrasies of emperors, and the years of French colonization.

Peasant farmers formed the lowest social class. Above them were landowners, merchants and artisans, priests, mandarin scholars, and nobles. At the very apex was the emperor, the head of state. Government within villages was exercised by fathers, by teachers, and by elected village elders. Rulers seldom tampered with such local autonomy: "The law of the sovereign gives way before the custom of the village" and "The authority of the emperor stops at the village gate."

Unlike China, Vietnam was not overburdened by its people. Its soil and the size of the area could have supported a population three times as great as it was when Lansdale arrived in June 1954. Traditional life in rural Vietnam was peaceful but not pleasant. While there were no famines such as those in more recent years in Ethiopia or Bangladesh, there were other problems. Droughts withered the land and rains flooded it. Peasants were scorched by the sun and drenched by monsoon rains. Flies swarmed everywhere — a fact of life — feasting on festering sores, creating black cloaks for fish and meat and vegetables for sale in village markets, harassing all forms of life. Rats were plentiful, large and strong enough to attack even adults. Life was tragically hard; the golden beauty of the doll-like Vietnamese children was blighted by their late twenties. Women in their mid-thirties were ageless and worn, ravaged by toil and childbirth, by disease and suffering.

Fully one-half the population was illiterate, limiting people's understanding to what they had themselves experienced. Although sensitive to basic family and kin relationships and intensely aware of hardships a greedy landlord or tax collector could impose, these Vietnamese had little conception of cold war or imperialism, democracy or communism. Such terms were meaningless. Their wider concerns focused on crops and weather, cockroaches and flies, a sick child, grinding toil in rice paddies, or the labor needed to dig a new communal well. And in his travels during that June of 1954, Lansdale saw these peoples and their plight.[31] It was an experience he would remember all the days of his life.

Lansdale also wanted to become acquainted with the sects of the land: the Hoa Hao, the Cao Dai, the Binh Xuyen. His inquiries led him to learn that they were not to be treated lightly. Each had its own private army. The Binh Xuyen, led by Le Van "Bay" Vien, had some twenty-five hundred brigand troops. The Cao Dai and the Hoa Hao fielded much larger forces, twenty and fifteen thousand, respectively.

The Binh Xuyen (pronounced "zwin") was a nonreligious sect formed about 1940 by day laborers and charcoal makers, who gave their sect the name of their neighborhood on the outskirts of Cholon, the Chinese city adjacent to Saigon. Armed by the Japanese during World War II, they afterward joined the Viet Minh fight to prevent the French from regaining control of Indochina. Turning against the Viet Minh after Bay Vien became leader, the Binh Xuyen became little more than bandits in the Saigon River delta area. They rose to more prominence and a degree of respectability when Bao Dai sold Bay Vien the rights to gambling, opium dens, prostitution, and control of the police in the Saigon-Cholon area.

The Cao Dai (pronounced "cow yie") sect, an offshoot of Buddhism, was founded in 1919 by a mystic named Ngo Van Chieu, who claimed communion with a spirit named Cao Dai. The movement became a formal religion in 1925. By 1954 it counted some two million adherents in the South, mainly from Saigon northwest to Cambodia. Organized as a hierarchy headed by a pope, the Cao Dai was eclectic, freely borrowing practices and ceremonies from many other religions, claiming what it thought to be the best of several faiths. Headquartered in Tay Ninh, the Cao Dai showed equal respect to Buddha, Jesus, Confucius, and Lao-tse and acknowledged more recent saints such as Joan of Arc, Sun Yat-sen and Victor Hugo, whose effigies stood in the elaborate main temple in Tay Ninh. In 1941 Cao Dai leaders, making the most of the weak colonial rule of the wartime Vichy government, tried to achieve independence for Vietnam but were captured and exiled to Madagascar. Other followers helped the Japanese overthrow remaining French rule in 1945 and, like the Binh Xuyen, fought with the Viet Minh to prevent any French return. In 1947 they switched sides and joined the French against their former comrades. In 1951 the chief of staff of the Cao Dai army, Trinh Minh Thé, broke from the group and formed his own Quoc Gia Lien Minh force, which fought both the Viet Minh and the French.

The third group, the Hoa Hao (pronounced "wah how"), was also an offshoot of Buddhism, and its simple faith attracted thousands of converts from among the country's poor. Founded in 1939 by Huynh Phu So, its name is that of the village in the Mekong delta where its founder was born in 1919. Centered along the Mekong and Bassac rivers, the Hoa Hao by 1954 counted some one and a half million followers who practiced an admixture of rites borrowed from Buddhism and other faiths. Huynh Phu So was a faith healer reputed to have the gift of prophecy. So may have been murdered by the Viet Minh leadership in 1947 — his followers speak of it as his "disappearance" — and the Hoa Hao thereafter became deadly enemies of the Viet Minh. When Lansdale visited the parts of Vietnam they controlled, he learned that the group was split into two major and three minor factions, each with its army.[32] None of these sects with their competing ideologies and armed camps was interested in supporting a new southern nationalist government.

In his travels into Hanoi and Haiphong, Lansdale spoke also with members of two prominent nationalist political parties, the Dai Viet and the Vietnam Quoc Dan Dang (VNQDD), whom he had first met the previous year when he had come to Vietnam as part of the O'Daniel mission. Secrecy for both groups was a way of life. French rule had prevented the formation of open political parties because *any* political activity by the Vietnamese seemed a threat to colonial authority. Those who had defied this understanding had been arrested, imprisoned, murdered, or exiled. When Lansdale suggested that now was the time for them to come out into the open, they were leery and refused even to admit that they were members of Dai Viet or VNQDD. They were afraid of open politics, more comfortable with membership in clandestine and revolutionary activities. Part of small cells, under strict discipline and led by a secret directorate, they had little faith in Lansdale's promises that a new era was opening.

Lansdale began to realize the enormity of the problems he faced. How could he help when politicians knew no way to operate save within the confines of clandestine organizations? Corruption seemed a way of life among those in influential positions. How could honest men rise to office when even their own leaders showed no interest in personal ethics? How could national unity ever be forged in the South when religious sects controlled feudal satrapies and divided up both the countryside and its people? French rule was still intact and showed little sign of leaving. How could people who had been under colonial rule for more than a century govern a nation when their rulers had seldom let even the best of them do more than clerical work?[33]

Throughout June Lansdale worked alone, waiting for other team members to arrive. The second member of the Saigon Military Mission (SMM), Lou Conein, joined him on 1 July 1954 but by early August no one else had come. According to the terms of the Geneva agreement, no other Americans could be brought into the country after 11 August, so Lansdale sought out O'Daniel. The general agreed to house ten other men under MAAG cover plus any others in the pipeline who arrived before the deadline. Lansdale selected his men and they were rushed into Saigon: Joe Baker, Rufus Phillips, Victor Hugo, Joseph Palastra, Grayson Woodbury, Joe Redick, Arthur Arundel, Robert Andrews, Frank Garber, Charles Sandman, Fred Allen, Raymond Wittmayer, Edward Williams, Luke Rogers, Gerry Morris, Gordon Jorgenson, Ed Quereau — all CIA, some on loan from active or reserve military, some career agents. For the most part they were young men, with all the energy and enthusiasms of youth.

Conein, an Army infantry major and paratrooper on loan to CIA, spoke fluent French and was the only team member with experience in Indochina, having parachuted into northern Vietnam in 1945 as liaison between French and American forces. In September of that year he had met Ho and Vo Nguyen Giap and other Viet Minh leaders. His ready leadership and scrounging ability served the team well. "Hell," one man later recalled, "everything we used was stolen." Baker, a daring Army Reserve captain who had fought in the Italian campaign during the Second World War, was always ready to do whatever was necessary. Baker served as the unit administrator. Joe Redick, a Navy Reserve lieutenant who occasionally wore his uniform as cover for his SMM activities, was also fluent in French, held both a master's and doctor's degree in languages, and also spoke Japanese, Spanish, and a little German. He was a self-proclaimed "bureaucrat," the one who "tried to keep people doing what they were supposed to, and sometimes succeeding." His teammates sometimes called him Mother Redick. Lansdale often asked Redick, a crack shot, to accompany him as interpreter and body-guard. Andrews, a loyal, hard-working active Navy lieutenant, looked like a movie star. Hugo, Palastra, and Woodbury were all eager Army second lieutenants, fresh from the same class at the United States Military Academy, the first two destined for high general officer rank.

Arundel, called Nick by his family, was a Marine lieutenant, son of well-to-do parents. Garber, an Army lieutenant, was all muscles and boasted the best physique of any team member. He greatly enjoyed his status as a paratrooper, once making thirty jumps in a single day. Allen, small and so quiet that others sometimes wondered what he did, was an Army paratroop major down from Korea. Ziggy Williams was as quiet as Allen and both were studious men, often spending their evenings reading background material on the land and its people. Two men, Witt-mayer and Andrews, were not well known by their teammates, preferring to remain aloof from much of the zest and horseplay. Phillips was a young Army second lieutenant eager to get in the fight who soon found himself assigned to the psywar component of the Vietnamese National Army. Sandman, an Army sergeant, was universally acclaimed by the others as "the mainstay of us all; always there when we needed him."

Jorgenson, an Army lieutenant colonel and the second highest ranking man of the unit, served as Lansdale's deputy. Hard-working and efficient, Jorgenson was a gentleman, helpful to those both above and below him. Morris, a Navy lieutenant, spoke fluent French; after a later Agency transfer to Germany, he spoke equally fluent German. A tight-lipped Irishman from New York and the father of two boys, Rogers also held the rank of an Army lieutenant colonel. Last, the team included Ed Quereau, an older man, a lieutenant colonel married to an English woman. Acting as liaison with Filipinos and with CIA facilities and assets in the Philippines was Bo Bohannan. These were the men who would carry out SMM missions ranging from sabotage to rigged astrological predictions in the North, from training partisans to bribing sectarians in the South.[34]

Too many men now formed the team for them all to stay with Lansdale at the big house on Duy Tan, so he rented another one on rue Tabard, called the pool house because of its swimming pool. It was large and also walled. Lansdale and Redick stayed in the house on Duy Tan and the others bunked at the pool house. Lansdale met with his men regularly and they sat talking over plans and projects. Conein commented on Lansdale's habit of thinking aloud. "Maybe a hundred of his ideas were really lousy, but one out of a hundred was absolutely brilliant."[35] Gradually the men were sorted into groups and assigned projects fitting their willingness or skills. None had the sort of psywar experience Lansdale prized but most were experienced in paramilitary and clandestine intelligence operations. The men would have been ideal as cadre to lead troops in guerrilla combat, but Lansdale wanted them to learn about the psychology of war. Conein summed up the situation. "We didn't know what we were doing or why!" Joe Redick sat at a table listening. "Let's get some order out of this," he said. "You tell us what we're going to do. I'll write it down and we'll have some orders."[36] Very soon SMM would undertake its assignment — paramilitary operations and political-psychological warfare against the Viet Minh.

During the earlier days of June while he had still waited for his team to arrive, Lansdale worried about the sort of leadership necessary to keep Bao Dai's State of Vietnam intact and free from Viet Minh influence and subversion. He wanted to talk to as many officeholders as possible, so as he waited he sought out and introduced himself to such men as Phan Huy Quat, minister of defense, and General Nguyen Van Hinh, chief of staff of the Vietnamese National Army. He had met Hinh in the Philippines in 1952 and was a friend of both Hinh's wife and his favorite mistress. He told them he was to work as an "informal liaison officer" between them and General O'Daniel at MAAG. They arranged with the French high command for Lansdale to be assigned to G-5, the psywar division of the Vietnamese Army. Lansdale thus became the unofficial adviser to one of Hinh's key supporters, Captain Pham Xuan Giai, head of G-5.[37]

Lansdale also worried about the timetable established by the Geneva Accords for a nationwide election in the summer of 1956. It would come too soon. The southern government had to reorder itself and pursue reforms in a way that would strengthen citizen loyalty toward it. Then Lansdale learned that Ngo Dinh Diem (pronounced "zee-yem") had accepted an offer from Bao Dai to serve as premier in the South. It was what Lansdale had been waiting for.

Ngo Dinh Diem was scheduled to arrive in Saigon from Paris on 26 June.[38] He was a member of the Ngo Dinh family, an old and respected Vietnamese clan. In the tenth century, one of Diem's ancestors, Ngo Quyen, commanded an army that expelled Chinese overlords from the land and reduced the influence of that giant northern neighbor. For long centuries the Ngo Dinh family served as privileged officials within the mandarinate class that formed the emperor's ruling aristocracy. Three

centuries before Diem came back to Saigon, his family converted to the
Roman Catholic faith, to which he also gave loyal assent.

Born in 1901, this short, stocky, chain-smoking man with his shock
of black hair walked with jerky movements, dressed inevitably in white,
and appeared to have been made from ivory. As a youth he studied for
the priesthood but later abandoned that goal. Yet he prized chastity and
took such a vow for himself. All his life he believed in and practiced
daily meditation after the Catholic fashion.

Diem served as a youthful mandarin official under French rule and
by 1929 became a provincial governor. For a time he served as minister
of the interior under the French-installed puppet government of Bao Dai
before quitting in disagreement and disgust. Eleven years later, in 1944,
he was asked by the Japanese to accept the office of prime minister and
he refused. Tragedy struck his family in 1945 when his brother Khoi
was killed by the Viet Minh. In 1946 Ho Chi Minh invited Diem to
become part of his provisional Democratic Republic and Diem turned
his back on the offer because he remembered the death of Khoi at Viet
Minh hands. Bao Dai asked him to become prime minister in 1949 and
again Diem refused. He would only be part of an independent, noncommunist Vietnamese government. After an unsuccessful attempt to organize
a competing political force, Diem left Vietnam in August 1950.

Thereafter he traveled widely, living in quiet, spartan style at Catholic
monasteries in Japan, in Belgium, and with the Maryknoll fathers in
their seminary in Yonkers, New York. Wesley Fishel, a Michigan State
University professor, originally induced Diem to visit the United States
and he also introduced him to Wolf Ladejinsky, an unreconstructed New
Dealer, to Leo Cherne, president of the International Rescue Committee,
and to Francis Cardinal Spellman, one of the most influential Roman
Catholics in the United States.[39] In 1953, Spellman introduced Diem to
Supreme Court Justice William O. Douglas, to senators John F. Kennedy,
Mike Mansfield, and Hubert Humphrey, and to several State Department
and White House officials. In Spellman's eyes, Diem was the only democratic alternative to a communist takeover in Vietnam.

On 18 June 1954, midway through the Geneva Conference, Bao Dai
asked Diem to become premier, and three days later Diem agreed so
long as he was granted both civil and military powers. He thus would
hold the offices of prime minister and defense minister and was supreme
commander of military forces. On 26 June he flew to Saigon, where
only a few of his Catholic supporters were on hand to welcome him.
On 7 July he formally assumed his new offices.[40]

Diem's reputation in the West following his arrival in Vietnam was
inevitably cast in negative terms. He was egocentric, humorless, stub-

bornly perfectionist, and power-hungry. Westerners laughed at him for his nonstop monologues, which might last through hours of incessant talking — often in French rather than in Vietnamese — on every topic from agriculture in Quang Tri province to meteorology. He was almost totally ignorant of the massive problems he would face in trying to organize a government. Outsiders ridiculed him for his inevitable refusal to act on any problem, no matter how trivial, without long meditation and his seeming inability to delegate power or responsibility to others. Reporters and Western officials told how suspicious he was of everyone outside his family circle. Such analyses are not entirely fair.

Those who knew him well remember another side to his personality. One Filipina described Diem as shy, sincere, "almost a saintly man, a very good man who wanted the best for his people but had to be helped to know how to do it, to express it."[41] Another Filipino remembered that Diem was somber, "a priestly fellow" who loved his people. "We likened him all the time to Gandhi."[42] Lansdale agreed. He felt that many descriptions of Diem were "pretty mean caricatures" and focused on his worst features. With all his power, Diem seemed to Lansdale to be shy, gentle, modest, a man with likable human qualities. Lansdale particularly enjoyed Diem's dry sense of humor and his inquiring mind. "This is the man I knew," Lansdale remembered. "When others talked about him I would look at them in wonder. You can't see that there are other qualities in him? He's not like that."[43]

Support for Diem, however, inevitably meant accepting his family also. His brothers came first: Nhu, Thuc, Can, and Luyen. Nhu became his shadow and constant adviser. Madame Nhu — the lovely Tran Le Xuan ("beautiful spring") — acted as First Lady and this impetuous, stubborn, and strong-willed woman became a political power in her own right. So thoroughly did the Nhus influence Diem that Americans who had to struggle with their obstinacy sometimes remarked wistfully, "No Nhus is good news." Diem unfortunately trusted Nhu totally and by 1955 Nhu was the adviser with the greatest influence, insisting that others address him as Monsieur le Conseiller. Monsignor Thuc served as Catholic archbishop, leader of Vietnam's two million Roman Catholics. Can (later executed by the Khanh administration) became a government official at the old imperial capital of Hue in central Vietnam. Luyen became Vietnam's ambassador to England's Court of St. James's. Nhu's father-in-law, Tran Van Chuong, served as ambassador to Washington while his wife, Madame Chuong, sat at the United Nations as her nation's official observer. And so Diem, with an influential and powerful entourage, was the man Lansdale would endeavor to befriend and advise as he had done with Ramón Magsaysay.[44]

Told when Diem was to arrive, Lansdale started out for the airport to watch for his plane but changed his mind and examined the people along the streets who had gathered to see the new premier pass by. Lansdale was disappointed when Diem made the trip from the airport to Norodom Palace inside a closed car that sped past, affording not even a glimpse of the new premier.[45] That evening Lansdale jotted down some thoughts on governing that he wanted to place in the hands of Diem. The next morning, accompanied by George Hellyer, who spoke French and could act as interpreter, the two men walked into Norodom Palace (which Diem quickly renamed Doc Lap or Independence Palace) and sought out Diem, whom they found working alone in an office.

With incredible chutzpah, Lansdale introduced himself. He was a colonel in the United States Air Force, he worked at the embassy, and what could he do to help? After a few moments, he handed his notes to the premier, suggesting that the notes could form the basis of their conference. With great difficulty, aided by a French-English dictionary, Diem began to read Lansdale's memo. Hellyer offered to read and translate the paper but found that he had forgotten his spectacles, so Diem loaned him his own. As Hellyer read, Diem listened, frequently nodding in agreement. "I think Lansdale surprised the hell out of him," Conein said. "I don't believe Diem thought he was going to last very long. What could he lose by talking to this man?"[46]

Diem's position at that moment could not have been worse. He had no political base at all. William E. Colby later bluntly summed up just how precarious Diem's situation was: "He only controlled the space of his [own] palace grounds."[47] Diem's problems were almost insuperable. He was premier of a country without antecedent that was nothing more than a piece of real estate south of the 17th parallel. Where was his government? At the time, Vietnamese held only four ministry offices; the others were still held by French appointees. "How can you call this a Vietnamese government?" one observer asked.[48] How is a government for a new nation created? Where was his power, his police, his army? Where even were his citizens? How does a man who has for years lived in exile return under the sponsorship of a totally foreign nation and take up the reins of authority? The French, who had provided government services and law and order, were leaving. Anarchy might well follow in their wake. All these questions were in the minds of Diem and Lansdale as they met that 27 June 1954.[49]

Within three weeks of their first meeting Diem asked Lansdale to move into Independence Palace with him. Because of his other activities with the Saigon Military Mission, Lansdale refused. It might have been hard to explain to others what he was doing. Yet he spent a great deal of time with Diem. Often calls came to Lansdale's compound late at night from the presidential palace. Would Lansdale be so kind as to pay a visit to Diem? The hours of darkness provided a measure of secrecy: fewer people would be around to observe their meetings. In a skilled flurry of activity, Lansdale would shave, dress in proper uniform, and be downstairs to his car and on the way within five minutes. "I never presume on anything except proper dress in the presence of a president," he told one observer.[50]

Their meetings lasted for hours, in part because Diem simply enjoyed talking. There may have been another reason. Diem had one top American official after another coming into Saigon telling him what he had to do. Each was supremely self-confident that he had all the technically correct information to back up his position. Each also made it plain that he controlled money and materiel destined for Vietnam and that Diem must follow his directions or he would recommend to Washington that promised largesse would be held up until an agreement could be reached. Such experts often commented grandly on issues they hardly understood, which must have given Diem a constant sinking feeling. He would then patiently try to correct their errors by providing broad background material. Of course this bored them stiff and many didn't bother to hide the fact. A number of highly placed Americans regularly sounded off with their negative opinions about Diem. Then seeing him face to face they offered treacly smiles and assurances of warm friendship. Their snide comments had already been reported to the president by his spies. "In his shoes," Lansdale asked, "what would you have done? . . . I have some sympathy for his long talking marathons. Admittedly, I'm almost a minority of one."[51]

Lansdale was not, however, just a passive listener and recorder of Diem's words. Lansdale's initial advantage was his sympathetic and receptive manner. He had great warmth for other human beings. "It really showed to Asians after having their ass kicked by the white man for centuries, yet now here was a white man who treated them with dignity and respect," team member Joe Baker later observed.[52] He knew about "face" and its importance. "Ed was more Asian than the Asians," Emma Valeriano declared.[53] "He had a rare genius. He could accommodate, could understand. If you took him into the streets [and saw there a woman], he could tell from her singsong whether her baby is happy and has eaten better than last week or whether it is because she doesn't have enough milk. That is an instinct, an understanding which he had." So insisted Michael Deutch, who served with Lansdale later in Vietnam.[54] One of Lansdale's strongest talents was his sense of timing. He always seemed to know when to offer necessary advice. As a result, "Diem trusted Lansdale about as much as he trusted any foreigner."[55]

As a sign of his trust, Diem began to include Lansdale in gatherings of the Ngo Dinh clan. He was invited to join family dinners, and he met Bishop Thuc, Nhu and Luyen and their wives, but he never met the youngest brother, Can, who lived with his mother in Hue. Lansdale believed that he achieved a number of successes because of his growing closeness with Diem. At one point he was able to persuade Diem to restrain Nhu's secret police from indiscriminate arrests of possible political opponents. "Families are coming to me," Lansdale told his friend. "What am I going to tell them? That you are worse than Adolf Hitler?" The arrests stopped.

Lansdale learned that there were many simple elements of statecraft that the contemplative president was unaware of. One day Diem asked him, "What does floating a loan mean? I had a meeting with bankers and they talked about that." Lansdale brought in people from the Agency for International Development (AID) who gave Diem a financial briefing. On another occasion the premier inquired what the phrase "chain of command" meant and Lansdale sent O'Daniel to explain it to him. Lansdale suggested to Diem that he had the power and authority to do simple, caring things for his people and Diem sent supplies of mosquito netting, blankets, and food to communities where they were needed. "I'd tip him off . . . . He used to take those actions. . . . [V]ery simple things he could act on as president." He urged Diem to travel more widely, to visit his people and inspect government projects. During one visit to central Vietnam, Filipino workers on a government project persuaded their Vietnamese friends to hoist Diem on their shoulders. Lansdale later saw a picture of the effort. People were cheering. "You could tell from their faces that it was a great moment they were sharing. He should have been yelling with them but he was looking scared." Frightened that he would be dropped, Diem grasped the hair of those holding him up. "I teased him about it," Lansdale recalled.[56]

Lansdale succeeded in persuading Diem to make frequent trips into the countryside and to show more interest in the problems of his people. On one visit Diem asked those around him about a bug infesting a field of crops. Then he squatted down and searched the base of a plant, located one of the bugs, and examined it, all the while talking about the infestation with a woman who held a naked, crying baby.[57] On another visit during rainy, muddy weather, Diem was again picked up by people at a site and carried around on their shoulders. They were dripping and muddy and soon his white sharkskin suit was covered with filth. Aides tried to brush him off later and he responded, "No, no. Leave it there." He wore the dirty suit as a kind of badge.[58]

Lansdale's biggest failure was his lack of success in easing Diem free from the iron grip of the Nhus. There may have been a special reason for their close relationship. Lansdale learned from a friend that Diem had been asked by his father, prior to his death, to look out for his younger brother Nhu. Such a family obligation might well explain why Diem insisted on maintaining such a tightly knit bond with his brother, despite pleas from advisers that Nhu's policies were harmful to Diem and his administration.[59]

For a time, however, Lansdale's mission required him to focus on other matters of more immediate importance. One provision of the Geneva Accords seemed to offer an exceptional opportunity: "any civilians . . . who wish to go and live in the zone assigned to the other party shall be permitted and helped to do so." Lansdale saw a real opportunity to use that proviso to strengthen the government of the South.[60] Such movements could take place only in the first three hundred days after the signing of the agreement in Geneva. There was no time to waste for Lansdale and the men of his Saigon Military Mission.

8

A NATION RISES

HANOI REACTED ANGRILY to the projects Edward Lansdale now began to carry out. An official history complained that "under U.S. patronage, a plot was evolved for the amputation of one half of Vietnam. . . . [Using] all kinds of deceitful manoeuvres and means of corruption, the United States set up a puppet government comprising reactionary elements most hated by the Vietnamese people . . . . [T]he U.S. 'advisers' were the real masters of the country [including] Lansdale, for the secret police."[1]

To cauterize that amputation, Lansdale wanted to encourage as many people in the North as possible to move south of the 17th parallel. It was, he believed, a real opportunity. As he compared relative populations, North and South, Lansdale believed that Ho's government had an edge in determining the outcome of the election scheduled for the summer of 1956. He was disgusted that neither Diem nor anyone else saw what could be done. Diem expected no more than ten thousand refugees from the North. Personnel at AID were calculating that they might need tenting capable of housing about the same number. Red Cross people were laying in a supply of bandages to help a few thousand. French authorities, who had agreed to help transport those who wished to move, planned to provide for no more than thirty thousand, mostly landlords and business-men.

At a meeting of the country team, Lansdale talked with impassioned fervor to O'Daniel and Ambassador Donald Heath. He told the group that they "were pretty much running out of time to get anything done."[2] His listeners scoffed when he suggested that they might persuade as many as two million people to move south. He hoped to balance the population between the two Vietnams. Lansdale finally persuaded Heath to go with him to argue with Diem. Heath served as interpreter. During the course of the conversation, Heath suddenly stopped and turned to Lansdale. "I'm the ambassador. I shouldn't be interpreting for a colonel in the Air Force on the subject of refugees; it's very embarrassing for the U.S."[3] Lansdale smiled and continued to press his case with Diem.

He pointed out that the South was totally disorganized and not ready either to help or to absorb an influx of refugees. He wanted Vietnamese to organize and bestir northerners into relocating. With the specter of Palestinian refugee camps clearly in mind, he wanted no such dismal affair in Vietnam. "I wanted farmers to get farmlands; fishermen to get into fishing again — become very useful citizens."[4] It would be necessary, he said, for Diem to organize — to name a commissioner to handle refugee movements and problems, to get the refugees settled and helped into useful lives. Diem felt no sense of urgency. He was unwilling to delegate authority and he wanted no commissioner with independent authority.

Lansdale tried more persuasive arguments. "When the plebiscite comes between North and South, we have to have more people to vote on our side. . . . It would give us a chance for the future." That was an argument Diem could understand. He finally gave his authorization to launch an effort that might persuade those in the North to abandon their homes.[5]

No one had authorized Lansdale to suggest such a movement; the action seemed to him, however, to fit within his general orders to help the Vietnamese people. "You can . . . get away with almost anything so long as it's for the right thing and you do it for the right reasons," he mused later.[6]

Lansdale was off and running. In his autobiography, in a less than forthright claim, Lansdale wrote, "I had split my small team in two. One half, under Major Conein, engaged in refugee work in the North. The other half stayed with me to help with other endeavors."[7] That was a very sanitized version. Supervising the refugee flow as part of the MAAG staff engaged in such work was only a cover for Conein and his men. Their real work was of two parts: developing a paramilitary organization in the North to be in position and ready for action when the French finally left and the Viet Minh took over, and sabotage. Conein established a headquarters in Hanoi with a branch in Haiphong.[8] Their work would keep them very busy indeed.

If people were going to be persuaded to move south, they must first become convinced that conditions where they then lived would soon become untenable. It was a challenge to Lansdale's psywar capabilities. Working closely with George Hellyer, U.S. Information Service chief, Lansdale and his team began a rumor campaign. They used Vietnamese soldiers assigned to the psywar (G-5) bureau of the Vietnamese National Army. Dressed in civilian clothes, the soldiers were sent north to spread a rumor in local marketplaces. The rumor had it that the Viet Minh had made a deal that allowed a small unit of the Chinese army into northern

Vietnam. Its troops, the rumor continued, were misbehaving, raping women, and stealing. After his men infiltrated north, Lansdale lost track of them. They failed to return, having deserted to the Viet Minh cause. Lansdale had almost forgotten about them when he received an excited query from Washington: "Would I please find out if there was any truth to the fact that two Chinese regular divisions were in North Vietnam?" After checking, he decided that his men must have carried out their orders. Like any rumor, the stories passed from mouth to mouth had drastically increased the number of Chinese miscreants from a platoon-sized force to two divisions. He wired back: "It's not true, but [was] something I started. Mea culpa."[9]

Pleased by these results, Lansdale concentrated on creating other rumors. He assigned Arundel and a Vietnamese identified only as Trieu Dinh to produce a leaflet that would inform Tonkinese how to behave when the Viet Minh takeover of Hanoi occurred in early October. The finished product included items on property and money reform and called for a three-day holiday for all workers to celebrate the event. Shopkeepers were instructed to take an inventory of their goods so that the new government would know what to confiscate. The leaflet was so well prepared that when local party officials saw copies, they assumed the broadside was authentic and insisted that shopkeepers obey its demands. The day after the leaflets were distributed, refugee registration tripled and within two days the worth of Viet Minh currency fell to half its previous value. Viet Minh authorities saw through the trick, denouncing the leaflets in radio broadcasts, but their appearance was so authentic that rank and file Viet Minh were certain that the radio denunciations were nothing more than a French propaganda trick.[10]

Around the end of September 1954 Lansdale learned that the largest printing establishment in the North intended to remain in Hanoi and do business with the Viet Minh. He instructed Conein's northern team to destroy its modern presses. This job also fell to Arundel and Trieu Dinh, but the saboteurs arrived too late. Viet Minh officials had already placed security men inside the plant and the strike had to be called off.[11] Trieu Dinh was kept busy. Lansdale next assigned him the task of working up an almanac for popular sale throughout Vietnam. Lansdale paid for the hiring of noted astrologers who predicted imminent disasters certain to befall Viet Minh leaders and who forecast a long period of prosperous unity for those in the South. While Lansdale was certain such predictions would bode ill for northern politicians, a corollary effect might well be to boost morale in the South at a critical time when Diem's political position was still precarious. Phillips worked with Trieu Dinh on this task and when they finished they shipped many almanacs by air to Haiphong where they were smuggled deep into Viet Minh territory for sale to the populace in cities and towns there. Supervised by Arundel, Trieu Dinh also produced essays extolling Vietnamese patriotism, which were then published and circulated throughout the land.[12]

Refugee registration increased dramatically in the summer of 1954 and continuing into the spring of 1955. Most northerners needed no rumors, no black propaganda tricks, to move south. Two hundred thousand were dependents of Army personnel who had cast their lot with Diem. An even greater number, 679,000, were Roman Catholics. Sixty percent of the nation's one and a half million Catholics made the journey, many from the bishoprics of Phat Diem and Bui Chu, some fifty miles from Haiphong. This last group was hastened on its way by marketplace rumors that "the Blessed Virgin Mary is going south." Such people were by-products of French colonization and enjoyed privileged status, which they hated to lose. They had raised militia units to fight with the French against the Viet Minh. Fearing reprisals now, they willingly relocated.[13]

As registrants flooded the port of Haiphong, the city soon became swamped with people unable to find shelter. Food and medicine were scarce. Several nations volunteered to help. On Lansdale's request, Ambassador Heath contacted the commander in chief, Pacific (CINCPAC) to ask for Navy assistance. Ships of the U.S. Seventh Fleet then arrived in Haiphong with tons of medicine and food supplies. O'Daniel agreed to allow some of his MAAG troops to help the refugees. Civil Air Transport (CAT) — a CIA front — asked Lansdale's help in obtaining a French contract for a refugee airlift to the South, and Lansdale was able to secure one. CAT thereafter provided Lansdale's team with means of secret air travel between Saigon and the North. Great Britain, the Chinese government on Formosa, the French, and private relief agencies all came to aid in the rescue.[14] In many ways the effort was a dramatic version of an oriental Dunkirk.

In the midst of these efforts, Filipino Oscar Arellano, vice president for Southeast Asia of the Junior Chamber International, and Bo Bohannan came to Saigon and met with Lansdale and Conein. After talking about the needs of the refugees, Arellano suggested that volunteer medical teams from the Philippines would be happy to offer help. Arellano arranged support from both his government and the Junior Chamber International. The men decided to call the effort Operation Brotherhood. Several weeks later the first group arrived — seven physicians and nurses, who set up a clinic in Saigon. Lansdale later wrote in a secret memorandum that "SMM would monitor the operation quietly in the background." He explained to one correspondent, "The CIA backing was part of U.S. support I had urged for a number of undertakings to help the people in

Asia where 'people's wars' were raging and the misfortunes of countryfolk were so exploitable . . . . completely unlike espionage or the use of force.''[15]

The size of the volunteer group sent by Arellano blossomed to 105 members who were assigned to various locations in the South. They were a great help to the refugees. The first ones to arrive lived in a house in Saigon provided by the Vietnamese government and stocked it with medicines they brought from the Philippines. They started a public health program in addition to providing refugee care. Their first effort outside Saigon was on the Camau peninsula, and later they extended their work into Cambodia and Laos. Emma Valeriano, one of the first to arrive, recalled that the Vietnamese asked why they did such things. ''Because we were trained by the Americans under their public health system,'' she replied.[16]

Just as several nations helped evacuate refugees from the North, so also did the Poles and Russians help transport those Viet Minh who wanted to leave the South. They used American ''liberty'' ships given to the Soviets during World War II, and the rusty, trampish appearance of the vessels indicated that they had apparently not been repainted since the day they left American shipyards. Northern propaganda hinted that ships used in the northern sea lifts simply disguised real American intentions to block Polish and Soviet ships from taking the Viet Minh to safety. Lansdale was amused at such tales. ''This Communist tactic was impulsive and amateurish — and just begged to be clobbered.''[17]

Lansdale wanted Viet Minh to remain south of the 17th parallel voluntarily so ''they could be [re]educated later.'' He also hoped — by getting their families to resist — to stop the abduction of other young men to the North by the Viet Minh. And if Viet Minh regulars made the trip with lowered morale, so much the better. He undertook another black propaganda campaign in the form of a leaflet that purported to be instructions from the enemy evacuation organization. Paper, printing, and language all rang true. It was distributed in Viet Minh evacuation areas by soldiers of the new Vietnamese Army. The leaflet listed the personal gear people should bring with them, urging them to include warm clothing, not only for the notably cold winters of Tonkin but also because it would be useful to those who would naturally ''volunteer'' to join with other patriots in building railroads in China! A footnote to the leaflet angrily denied that Viet Minh evacuees would be unsafe on the voyage north. Ship captains would keep them safe by restricting passengers to areas well below deck so enemy fighters couldn't strafe them, and captains would simultaneously keep keen watch for enemy submarines that might try to sink the vessels.

This scary picture came into sharp focus when evacuees reached Cap St. Jacques and saw the rust-bucket transports awaiting them. Images of being trapped below deck in floating coffins flooded the minds of those who arrived dockside. Word spread quickly, and sizable units of Viet Minh combat forces and their dependents refused to board. Intelligence reports later revealed that village and delegation committees from Viet Minh communities complained after the leaflet was distributed about "deportation" to the North.[18] Lansdale may have taken too much credit for this success inasmuch as the northern government also tried to hold down the number of Viet Minh to be transported north in order to have sympathetic agents in the South available for work in the coming elections of 1956 and for future guerrilla operations if necessary. Psywar of this type, however, appealed to Lansdale and was his way of injecting a little imagination and humor into the grim business at hand.

Only about ninety thousand Viet Minh made the trip north, compared with nearly a million who fled Ho's government. Lansdale did not get the two million refugees he had hoped for, but he believed that perhaps another four hundred thousand would have come south had the grace period not ended before they could safely do so. Another one hundred thousand refugees ultimately trickled south on their own after the deadline.[19] Lansdale was pleased with the results of his effort. "It doesn't matter who you are if you have a voice and don't let the little formalities of life stop you. You go ahead and act as the situation demands."[20]

On Lansdale's orders, his northern team, headed by Conein, organized a Vietnamese paramilitary group to use against the Viet Minh. Most of its members were drawn from the northern Dai Viets, a political party with loyalties to Bao Dai. Conein gave to the unit the cover name Binh and used the flow of refugees as a disguise for Binh activities. "It was a completely chaotic situation. Nobody knew what was going on," he said. Conein determined that his Binh men needed paramilitary training. Under control of Lieutenant Robert Andrews, thirteen of the Binh exfiltrated North Vietnam through the port of Haiphong and boarded an American naval vessel, part of Task Force 98 commanded by Admiral Lorenzo S. Sabin, Jr., which was helping evacuate refugees.[21] The Binh troops were then taken over two thousand miles eastward to Saipan in the Mariana Islands, where they received instruction at Saipan Training Station, a CIA-maintained field training base. Operated under Navy cover as the Naval Technical Training Unit, its primary mission was to provide physical facilities and competent instructors to train men in intelligence tradecraft, communication, counterintelligence, and psychological warfare techniques. Graduates worked in support of CIA activities throughout the Far East.[22]

In addition to Conein's Binh group, Lansdale ordered the formation of a second paramilitary team to plan organized resistance against the Viet Minh from secure bases in the South. He chose team leaders, working out of Saigon, to organize this second group: Raymond Wittmayer, Fred Allen, and Edward Williams. (Williams undertook double duties, working simultaneously with revolutionary political groups in the South.) The new unit was given the cover name Hao.[23] On 23 November 1954, Allen and Andrews supervised the movement of twenty-one members of the Hao team onto a U.S. Navy ship moored in the Saigon River. Dressed as coolies, they joined the throng of workers moving on and off ship and disappeared one by one. The ship then took the Haos "to an overseas point" (Saipan) for training.[24]

Lansdale realized he needed additional personnel to help with SMM duties and so added Navy Lieutenant Ed Bain and Marine Captain Richard Smith to his force. They provided him with administrative and personnel services at his Saigon headquarters, acting as paymasters, housing officers, file clerks, and mess and transport officers. They also directed clandestine introduction of paramilitary materiel into Vietnam by air, sea, and land. They became Lansdale's "official smugglers."[25]

While the Binh and Hao teams trained on Saipan at the Naval Technical Training Unit, Bain and Smith smuggled the supplies they would later need for their missions into Vietnam with the help of the Air Force's 581st Air Resupply and Communications Wing and CIA personnel in Okinawa and the Philippines.[26] As arms, ammunition, and explosives arrived in Saigon the two men stored them at SMM's pool house on rue Tabard and readied them for shipment north by the Navy task force handling refugee transport. Ships came south laden with those escaping from the government of Ho; they returned carrying supplies for the Binh and Hao teams. The pool house came to resemble a munitions depot, with tons of smuggled explosives dispersed behind the thick walls of the building. The compound was guarded day and night by SMM personnel armed with automatic weapons and grenades, for in addition to the supplies destined for the Binh and Hao teams the house also contained many working papers and secret files (all of which, Lansdale said, were prepared with explosive devices for their instant destruction if that should ever become necessary).[27]

Team members moved the arms and equipment for the Vietnamese paramilitary teams north out of Saigon, covering their movements by mingling with those working with refugees. Civil Air Transport also helped move materiel from Saigon to Haiphong. When Viet Minh security forces tightened control over shipments into Haiphong's airport, SMM changed from an air to a sea route to transport its contraband. Lansdale's men smuggled a total of eight and a half tons of supplies north for the Haos, including fourteen radios, three hundred carbines, ninety thousand rounds of rifle ammunition, fifty pistols, ten thousand rounds of handgun ammunition, and three hundred pounds of explosives. They delivered two and a half tons to Hao agents in Tonkin, the remainder cached at operational sites along the Red River by Conein and his men, with help from the U.S. Navy. They didn't worry too much about their own personal safety, for there was little danger in traveling the countryside prior to 1957. There were occasional Viet Minh ambushes along some roads, but so few occurred that, for the most part, SMM team members felt safe moving about throughout the central coast area and up into the highlands. With a few precautions, they felt able to travel anywhere. It was a reasonably peaceful time.[28] By 31 January 1955, all operational equipment for the Binh and Hoa teams had been transshipped from Saigon to Haiphong with help from Navy and Civil Air Transport personnel and hidden in operational sites that were still free from Viet Minh control.[29]

When members of the Hao team completed their training at Saipan they were then flown by the U.S. Air Force to the hidden valley camp used by Freedom Company on the back ranges of Clark AFB in the Philippines. They were held there until Lansdale thought it was time to move them back into Vietnam and send them into the North to wait for the moment when they would begin their operations against Ho's government. In mid-April 1955, they were notified that it was time for them to return, and the U.S. Navy took them to Haiphong, where they infiltrated the general population.[30]

It was also time for the Binh team to become operational. Conein briefed them and they started filtering north individually in careful stages over a thirty-day period. Once in place they adopted the pose of normal citizens, carrying out everyday civilian pursuits. And waiting.[31] According to an agreement with the French, the Viet Minh took over Haiphong on 16 May 1955. Both the Binh and Hao teams were in place, completely equipped. They had moved into position under the noses of both Ho's government and the International Commission, composed of French, Poles, and Indians, which supervised the transition from French to Vietnamese rule. Lansdale was pleased that his team members had been able to insert the two paramilitary teams without anyone noticing them.[32]

"I had responsibility for keeping those assets alive," recalled Lou Conein. "That kept me busy. They were in place when we left . . . . They didn't exist more than two years before they were wrapped up."[33] Lansdale later explained what went wrong. At the time he was recalled from Vietnam in late 1956, he turned control of the Binh and Hao groups over to CIA. Concerned that the Binh and Hao team members might have been turned and were now being run by the enemy, CIA wanted to check the situation out. Lansdale demurred, pointing out that such contact might well blow their cover. Unconvinced, CIA called some of the teams back south to check them out. "They still were good [but] they couldn't get them back [in place] after calling them south."[34]

The last days of Conein and other members of SMM working in the North were busy ones. With members of the Binh team, he wrote up detailed notes of potential targets for future paramilitary operations against Tonkin's power plants, coal mines, water systems, bridges, the communications network in Hanoi and Haiphong, and oil depots and harbor facilities at Haiphong. Dirty tricks, however, were limited because the United States maintained a very small consulate and a MAAG detachment in the North and, Conein stated, "We couldn't do anything that would jeopardize them. We could have done a lot more if they hadn't been there."[35] Rumors had it that when the French departed, so also would official America, so Conein and his men planned to hit several targets just prior to the French departure. When the consulate and the MAAG detachment remained open after the French left, "that canceled a lot of other things that could have happened."[36]

At least two efforts at sabotage were carried out. Conein's men prepared for "delayed sabotage" of Hanoi's buses and railway equipment. They were assisted in their work by special CIA technicians flown in from Hawaii and Japan. The point of the exercise was to cause engines on buses and trains to fail occasionally and gradually. Operators and inspection teams might thus not suspect sabotage.[37]

Contamination of the engine oil supply for Hanoi's city buses took place in a night operation inside an enclosed storage room. "We put certain types of acids in the oil," Conein revealed. Fumes from the oil and the contaminant came close to knocking them out. Dizzy and weak-kneed, the men breathed through their handkerchiefs and finished their job.[38] The plan to knock out railway engines was more ingenious. "For trains we had special coal bricks made up which when thrown into [burners] would blow the hell out of a train."[39] Supplies of these special bricks were intermingled with towering piles of coal in Hanoi's railroad yards. Time ran out, however, before Conein and his team could launch strikes at other targets. He and his men evacuated Hanoi on 9 October 1955 along with the last French troops.[40]

One Filipino upon whom Lansdale relied heavily during those months in Vietnam was "a very brilliant guy," José "Joe" Banzon.[41] Banzon remembers those days. "I went as observer, supposed to stay only for three months but [my tour] developed into five years."[42] Banzon proved particularly helpful when Lansdale needed to coordinate with people in the Philippines. After the first successes of Operation Brotherhood, when Lansdale deemed it time to bring other Filipinos to help the cause in Vietnam, he again turned to Banzon. The moment was propitious to create Freedom Company.

Lansdale believed that the establishment of Freedom Company was one of his greatest achievements during his Vietnam days. In his autobiography, however, he refused to take credit for it, offering instead a sanitized version of its origin. It was, he stated, a spontaneous movement on the part of Filipinos. He only learned of it during a brief visit to Manila and he did no more than "encourage" the enterprise.[43] That was an abbreviated and misdirected explanation, complicated by contrary stories he told at other times. To one man, Lansdale said that Freedom Company began in response to a request from Diem to Ramón Magsaysay for Filipino assistance.[44] Yet in his autobiography he declared, "With a grimace on his face, Diem told me that the Vietnamese didn't need the help of a bunch . . . of nightclub musicians (most of the dance bands in Asia at the time were made up of Filipinos)." Using his best efforts at persuasion, the most he could get from Diem, he wrote, was a promise to "sleep on it."[45]

Perhaps the best explanation was one Lansdale later gave to Maxwell Taylor: Lansdale believed that much of the equipment sent to Vietnam by the United States was not properly maintained, used, or stored effectively. There was a need for technicians who knew how to handle "weapons and equipment and how to maintain military hardware."[46] Working with Banzon and another Filipino friend, Frisco "Johnny" San Juan, and with help from Bohannan, Lansdale set up a private effort, which they called Operation Know How, whereby Filipino technicians would be made available for work in Vietnam if their services were requested. That parent organization, Lansdale asserted, "was founded from a suggestion of mine."[47] Out of this came Freedom Company, a nonprofit Filipino corporation backed by President Magsaysay, its honorary president. The company provided Filipino technicians who were ready to pass their experience, knowledge, and skill — whether in equipment maintenance or in fighting Huk guerrillas — on to the Vietnamese.[48] San Juan served as director and, in his words, "assisted in its introduction into Vietnam in 1955."[49]

One high official of Freedom Company told of the role played in its affairs by Lansdale. "General Lansdale was there as the guardian angel. Through him I could knock on doors. Through him I could get access to the right persons."[50] The organization's work in Vietnam began, Lansdale said, when San Juan and some other Freedom Company officials came to Saigon in 1955 "to make a survey of ways in which they might be helpful to the Vietnamese." San Juan met with José Banzon, who got him an appointment with Diem. "Before the meeting was over," Lansdale noted in a memo, "a contract was signed between the govt of Viet Nam and the Freedom Company."[51]

Expenses of company operations in Vietnam were underwritten by Diem's government and by CIA. The charter of Freedom Company stated plainly that it was "to serve the cause of freedom," but as Lansdale wrote, it also had "an almost untapped potential for unconventional warfare (which was its original mission)."[52] Lansdale later told Maxwell Taylor that he used Freedom Company as a "mechanism to permit the deployment of Filipino personnel in other Asian countries, for unconventional operations, under cover of a public service organization." He described that the people he wanted to use were "sheep-dipped" through the personnel offices of Freedom Company and then shipped abroad for work in Vietnam "and elsewhere."[53]

Freedom Company was extremely useful for Lansdale's purposes. Its first task was to help found and organize a Vietnamese Veterans Legion, a job high on Lansdale's list of necessary achievements if the Diem regime was ever going to establish a base within the Vietnamese population. "I brought in a team of veterans from the Philippines to help and paid for their way out of CIA funds. . . . I got people in Saigon listening to what veterans in the provinces were saying. It was very worthwhile."[54] Its personnel also later helped write the constitution of the Republic of Vietnam, trained Diem's Presidential Guard Battalion, and ran the counterguerrilla training camp in the hidden valley on the far ranges of Clark AFB.[55] It also provided technicians to train Vietnamese soldiers in ordnance maintenance, vehicle repairs, the use of electrical equipment, and the running of quartermaster and other depots, and from time to time it met Vietnamese requests for specialists in other areas.[56]

In 1957, following the death of Magsaysay, Freedom Company reorganized and became Eastern Construction Company (ECCOI), with San Juan as president and general manager. ECCOI negotiated a contract with the Vietnamese government whereby the new organization assumed the obligations of Freedom Company. ECCOI later extended its operations into Laos and elsewhere. One employee commented, "I had no definite information that it was [a CIA front]. However, when you see this outfit funded by the State Department, what do you think?"[57] Lansdale never concerned himself with what people might suspect but was careful to keep his real activities sufficiently hidden so that very few around him could be certain that he worked for CIA and paid for many projects with CIA money. Freedom Company was one endeavor that was worth every cent of those secret funds.

Yet Lansdale needed more than Freedom Company if he was to succeed in his mission of saving Diem. Bandits and brigands preyed upon the land, leaving disorder in their wake. Save for his family, a very few Vietnamese friends and Edward Lansdale and his Saigon Military Mission team, Diem had hardly anyone he could count on. Several months after his arrival, Diem's authority still hardly extended to Saigon's city limits and he had only one battalion of reliable troops he could count on to follow his orders. Other soldiers were deserting in company-sized units. Withdrawing Viet Minh warriors blocked roads, rivers, and canals and sabotaged railways. As the French continued to withdraw most of their public servants from their former colony, there were few well-trained Vietnamese bureaucratic or administrative personnel capable of taking their place. The situation remained chaotic.[58]

During September 1954, Lansdale learned that Army Chief of Staff General Nguyen Van Hinh was plotting to overthrow Diem. Alerted to this danger, Lansdale became concerned about the quality of Diem's presidential guards and interrogated them. They asked for technical advice on how to stop armored vehicles when all they had were carbines, rifles, and hand grenades. Lansdale told them how to build tank traps and how to use molotov cocktails. The next morning, all the guards had vanished, determined not to be caught in a fight where they might have to depend on burning bottles of gasoline.[59] Diem needed guards he could count on, so he negotiated with Trinh Minh Thé, the Cao Dai sect leader, offering him some needed financial support. In return Thé would provide Diem safe haven if he had to flee a coup. Lansdale provided Diem with CIA money for Thé, passed along by CIA station chief John Anderton.[60]

In an effort aimed at providing Diem with better palace security, Lansdale, Joe Banzon, and Bo Bohannan sought and received permission from Malacañang Palace for Napoleon Valeriano to come to Saigon to train new guards. He finally arrived in January 1955, accompanied by three junior officers, to begin his training work.[61] As Valeriano's work progressed, he arranged for Vietnamese officers to be sent to Manila, where they trained alongside Magsaysay's presidential guards. Diem was "warmly grateful for this help by Filipinos," Lansdale said, in providing a loyal and efficient guard unit "who also continuously taught our concept of loyalty and freedom."[62]

When Lansdale learned that General Hinh was continuing to toy with the idea of overthrowing Diem, he told Hinh that U.S. support would stop if he attempted a coup.[63] By October 1954, contention between the two Vietnamese leaders was murderous. Hinh refused to obey Diem's orders to move certain of his troop units to new positions. When the affected battalions attempted to make the move on their own, the general brought in special units to block them. Diem then tried to fire Hinh but he refused to give up his command and commented that he might instead fire Diem. Lansdale sought to work with both of them. "My advice to Diem was that he stop trying to play the general and start acting like a politician. . . . My advice to Hinh was that he stop trying to play the politician and start acting like a general."[64]

Hinh's forces then took over the national radio station in Saigon and began broadcasting anti-Diem material. The French high command, which still had authority over the Vietnamese Army, chose not to intervene. Lansdale prevailed upon the local U.S. Information Agency (USIA) chief at the embassy to remove radio equipment it owned from the station (an action that would have stopped the broadcasts), but those who tried could not get past Hinh's tanks parked at approaches to the station. Lansdale found a Navy lieutenant, Laurence Sharpe, a staff officer in the task force transporting refugees, who had known Hinh's officer in charge of the force that occupied the station. Lieutenant Nguyen Van Minh and Sharpe had been friends earlier when both attended a military course in the United States. Lansdale asked Admiral Lorenzo S. Sabin, Jr., Sharpe's commander, to transfer Sharpe to him for a while and Sabin did so. Lansdale and Sharpe then set out in a jeep for the radio station. They drove right up to the threatening snouts of the waiting armored vehicles. Lansdale shouted at an open window of the building: "Tell your goddamn tank to point its cannon some other direction so I can bring a friend in and we can talk to you."[65] Within two or three days after Sharpe disappeared inside, Minh and his men evacuated the station and an uneasy calm returned to Diem's Saigon.

While the Hinh affair developed during the early fall of 1954, Lansdale got his first chance to meet Trinh Minh Thé. The meeting came about because of discussions between Lansdale and Diem over ways in which the sect armies might be integrated into the Vietnamese National Army. Diem wanted Thé's force, for he knew such support would bolster his own prestige. He asked Lansdale to deliver a personal letter to Thé; the message requested the integration of their forces at the earliest possible moment. Lansdale talked over Diem's request with O'Daniel and Ambassador Heath and both men agreed he should follow through on it. When contacted, Lansdale's superiors in Washington also agreed.

Two days later, Lansdale and five of his team members left for the rendezvous. They wore civilian clothes and carried hidden guns. Their destination lay west of Saigon along Route 1, the hamlet of Bai Trai at the foot of Nui Ba Den mountain, near the Cambodian border. There they met Thé and many of his guerrilla soldiers. Lansdale and his companions followed Thé, a small, young-looking man, as he climbed to his mountain hideout. Joe Redick translated for Lansdale and Thé. Lansdale gave the sect warlord Diem's letter and, after studying it, Thé promised to support the premier. Lansdale then returned to Saigon, briefed Heath and O'Daniel, and told Diem the good news. Months later, on 13 February 1955, arrangements finally were completed for the integration of Thé's soldiers into the National Army. Thé himself received a brigadier general's commission from Diem.[66]

Lansdale knew that this small victory solved only a part of Diem's problems with the sects. He sought out other opportunities to meet with leaders of those groups. He arranged a meeting with Hoa Hao chieftains at his house on Duy Tan and also talked with Le Van "Bay" Vien of the Binh Xuyen sect. Lansdale worked out a preliminary settlement with Vien and then set up a meeting between Vien and Diem. Diem refused to be bound by Vien's offer and the Binh Xuyen remained hostile.

Despite several conversations Lansdale held with the man, General Hinh had not given up the idea of a coup against Diem. On Hinh's target date — 26 October 1954 — his forces would attack Doc Lap Palace. Two of Hinh's trusted lieutenants were LTC Lan and Captain Pham Xuan Giai. Lansdale decided to try a more innovative ploy that might doom the coup. He invited Hinh, Lan, and Giai to go with him on an "official" trip to the Philippines. They would have an opportunity to see the fight against the Huks at first hand. Hinh reluctantly turned the offer down, but Giai and Lan both agreed. General O'Daniel loaned Lansdale a MAAG C-47 and Lansdale and his guests clambered aboard. They spent 26 October in Manila. Lansdale soon returned to Saigon, leaving Hinh's officers to frolic in the fleshpots of Manila. During his brief stay, Lansdale found time to talk with Magsaysay and make firm plans allowing Valeriano to advise Ngo Dinh Diem on security measures and train his presidential guards. The trip was an obvious success. Without his key officers, there was no way Hinh could launch a successful attack on Diem's palace.[67]

Ambassador Donald Heath had been a good friend to Lansdale, and Ed was sorry to learn that he would be leaving Vietnam in early November 1954. His replacement, retired General J. Lawton "Lightning Joe" Collins, was an unknown factor. The new ambassador arrived in Saigon on 8 November to begin a mission originally planned to last about ninety days. Instead it lasted nearly seven months. Collins was a friend of the French high commander in Vietnam, General Paul Ely, and Washington believed this association might help smooth problems and solve existing disagreements between U.S. and French policy. Lansdale was not impressed with Collins.

"Age makes me more charitable," Lansdale commented many years later. "At the time I used to think he wasn't too bright and he probably wasn't. . . . Words meant one thing to an American in Washington and something very different out in Saigon. He used to fool himself with words. He would talk about 'civil service.' He never seemed to know there wasn't a civil service out there; it wasn't trained, hadn't worked together, and didn't extend beyond Saigon. . . . He talked about government as though it existed with a civil service, buildings, communications, money, and budget. . . . Collins never understood [the reality of government in Vietnam]."[68] Collins was, Lansdale believed, much like Maxwell Taylor "in their mastery of the fleeting smile, their pose of clean-cut all American boy with graying hair, gentlemanly diction, and cold-blooded arrogance with subordinates in private. Their talk with Diem was the country squire looking down his aristocratic nose at a bumpkin." Lansdale knew in his gut that such an attitude was the wrong approach. "Let's cut out the American self-delusion. We lose 'peoples wars' that way."[69]

At the very first country meeting called by Collins in Saigon, Lansdale was appalled at the ambassador's approach. Without any preliminary discussion or any attempt to learn what others were doing, Collins pontificated that as the personal representative of the American president, he would lay down rules governing how his people were to behave toward the Vietnamese and what they were to do for them. Lansdale tried to interrupt, only to be told, "Sit down. You're out of order." Lansdale sat back with a troubled face. Collins then lectured Lansdale that he had apparently forgotten his military courtesy. He was a general and Lansdale was only a colonel. Lansdale got up from his chair with a dramatic flair and said, "You claim to be representing the American president. Nobody else here seems to be representing the American people! As far as I'm concerned, that's my job. The American people and I are walking out on you." Lansdale turned and stalked from the room. Collins would have been within his rights to demand of Washington that Lansdale be recalled. Lansdale was certain that would happen. He was surprised later when Collins said only, "Gee, you're sure a hothead, aren't you?" As they talked they managed to establish a formal, though hardly friendly, working relationship.[70]

Lansdale was never short on brashness. Not long after his initial confrontation with Collins, he managed to catch Collins at an idle moment and inquired, "When do you do your thinking? Maybe I can help you with that." The ambassador replied that he did his thinking during an after-lunch nap. Lansdale was incredulous. "You mean you stay awake, just lie down on the bed, and think?" "Yes," Collins responded. Lansdale pressed on. "Do you mind if I come up after lunch and sit down next to your bed and if you've got something, you can think out loud?"

Collins reluctantly gave his permission. After a few days with Lansdale sitting owl-like beside his bed while he tried to nap, Collins put an end to the sessions. "It was a lousy idea," he told Lansdale. Lansdale guessed waspishly that Collins' reason was that "he was missing his sleep." Their relationship was never a good one. "I could always go in and talk to him . . . . But he often wound up giving me orders directly opposite to what I'd hoped he would."[71]

After learning about Hinh's abortive coup plot, Collins applied pressure on Hinh to leave the country. Bao Dai was also informed that the United States was serious about cutting off support for Vietnam unless Hinh canceled his plotting. Thereupon, Bao Dai ordered his general back to France. On 29 November 1954, Hinh left Saigon for exile in Paris, where he continued his career as a high-ranking officer in the French air force. Lansdale and Joe Redick were the only Americans who went to see him off at Saigon's airport.[72]

Following Collins' arrival and because of Collins' friendship with General Paul Ely, the commander of French forces in Vietnam, General O'Daniel was able to persuade Ely to organize a dual U.S.-French command to train Diem's National Army. The force was named the Training Relations Instruction Mission (TRIM). Ely retained overall authority but TRIM, set up on 13 December 1954, was under the immediate direction of O'Daniel, who continued to head the American MAAG unit. The organization had a carefully planned international flavor. General O'Daniel had a French chief of staff and an American deputy chief of staff. Each of the four divisions of TRIM — Army, Navy, Air Force, and National Security — had chiefs and deputies who alternated between American and French officers.

Since Lansdale's cover as an assistant air attaché at the embassy was increasingly wearing thin, he asked for and received O'Daniel's permission to head TRIM's National Security division, which would advise the Vietnamese on operations. He also asked Collins for authority to coordinate all U.S. civil and military efforts among the various American agencies working in Vietnam, and on 11 January 1955 Collins gave his approval. Joe Redick commented on the workload: "It was a little difficult to get much [SMM] work done because we spent all day on this overt job [at TRIM] working with the French and then we'd try to get our own work done."[73] Lansdale participated in frequent staff meetings of his TRIM division personnel and Vietnamese Army officers, regular briefings of various officials, repeated troop training inspections, and continued supervision of new Vietnamese training and logistic operations. It was a lot of work in addition to his SMM activities and his advisory efforts with Diem at the palace.

On 28 December 1954, the French government finally ratified the agreements that gave total independence to the Bao Dai/Diem regime. Three weeks later, on 20 January 1955, the French agreed to turn over full control of the Vietnamese armed forces within five months. Lansdale was certain the former colonial masters of Vietnam were delaying their exit as long as possible and were doing their best to undercut Ngo Dinh Diem's efforts. "At most," he wrote, "Vietnamese officials were getting sniffs, not deep breaths, of the air of freedom and independence."[74] From the time of his arrival in 1954 to the moment of the final departure of the French from Vietnam, Lansdale was suspicious of French motives, believed that they did everything possible to undercut his efforts to strengthen Diem's government, and carried on numerous feuds with various French military officials.[75]

There never seemed a time when Lansdale could sit back and relax for a few hours. Diem's situation demanded his full concentration, for the premier's position remained precarious even after Hinh's departure in November 1954. The French, so rumor had it, continued to fund sect activities, which hurt any possibility of building national unity.[76] Diem still could not count on his army to stand firm against either the sects or the Viet Minh. Bao Dai was ready to betray him. Trusted ministers and officials in Diem's cabinet resigned their posts, including Foreign Minister Tran Van Don and Minister of Defense Ho Thong Minh. Their departure left Diem with hardly the hint of a government. Although Lansdale continued to meet with them and explore ways to end their hostile boycott of Diem's regime, Hoa Hao sect forces under Ba Cut and Tran Van Soai continued to work with the Binh Xuyen in efforts to bring down his government.

One reasonably effective solution, Lansdale found, was to bribe recalcitrant sect generals. "I had ways of disarming them all, including some payoffs and some going into the army," he later admitted.[77] Upwards of ten million dollars in CIA bribe money made its way into the hands of some of those who opposed Diem in order to free them from their "principles." Thé alone received between one and two million dollars — purportedly to use to provide his men with back pay — before agreeing to rally to the government and marching into Saigon at the head of some five thousand of his black uniformed Cao Dai soldiers. When that moment finally came, Lansdale was vastly relieved and knew it had been worth all his efforts. On 13 February 1955, Ed wrote to Helen, "Today a tough little guy came down out of the hills and swore in some of his troops to the Vietnamese National Army and then had a parade past the reviewing stand."[78]

When later suspicions arose that Lansdale had bribed sect leaders he inevitably reacted angrily. In his autobiography he complained about French "soreheads," who circulated "convoluted fictions about my bribing Vietnamese with huge sums of money."[79] He asserted that the most he had ever given Thé was "a cup of coffee or a meal when he visited with me." When pressed, he did admit that he provided Thé with "a month's pay" for his troops when Thé integrated them into the Vietnamese Army.[80]

Yet payments he did make, not only to Thé but to others as well. Nguyen Thanh Phuong, a Cao Dai general, demanded and received $3.6 million for his loyalty in addition to monthly payments for his troops. A Hoa Hao warlord, General Tran Van Soai, cost three million dollars. When Bernard Fall queried Lansdale in 1964 about these bribes, Lansdale insisted that none were given; all he had ever provided was "back pay" due sect troops and he had given it in cash to their leaders.[81]

Asked again many years later about his payoff to Thé, Lansdale remained characteristically close-mouthed, falling back for explanation on a faulty memory. "I'm not ducking the truth, but I still don't remember it. I denied such a thing strongly in my book for the simple reason that I've been accused all too often of 'buying' people such as Trinh Minh Thé with huge sums of money, and know that such 'buying' is completely against my own beliefs. . . . I know the Pentagon papers included a report written a year after the event [his own diary of the period, which later appeared anonymously in the *Pentagon Papers*] saying that I had made a payment in 1954 to Thé. If I did, it has gone from my memory and worries me that it has. . . . I wonder why in hell I would do such a thing. I presume it was to help Diem at his request. . . . But, I really cannot recall the incident. . . . Makes me wonder if I have a memory block about Thé."[82]

Although considerably weakened by defections from their ranks owing to Lansdale's payments, the sects were not defeated. Indeed, the Binh Xuyen, with its monopoly on prostitution, drugs, and gambling, had little need of bribes, and this group continued to contemplate the possibility of overthrowing Diem. It was encouraged in this by the French, who thought a more pliant premier might better protect their economic interests in the South.[83] Diem finally had enough. In January 1955 he decided to provoke a confrontation with the Binh Xuyen and shut down their gambling casinos in Cholon, depriving them of their main source of income. Lansdale supported Diem in this move, convinced that the best policy was to "sink or swim with Ngo Dinh Diem." Collins did not agree. He and others at the embassy believed Diem was finished. Nor were there more than a few remaining supporters within the Eisenhower administration in Washington: the Dulles brothers, Walter Robertson, who served as assistant secretary of state for the Far East, and Kenneth Young, head of the State Department's Southeast Asia Section.

Lansdale tried to keep a close watch on the sects. Two informants were Trinh Minh Thé and Nguyen Thanh Phuong. On 5 March 1955 they stopped at his Duy Tan house in Saigon, having just come from a meeting of sect leaders. Called to order by Bay Vien, leader of the Binh Xuyen, the assemblage had decided to plan a coup against Diem, take over the government, and divide it among themselves. They then promptly organized themselves into a formal United Sects National Front.

When Lansdale heard this news, he drove the eight blocks from his house on Duy Tan to the embassy residence to tell General Collins what he had learned. Collins' response was that the information was too vague for him to take any action. Then Lansdale learned from Thé and Phuong that the United Sects Front was about to issue an ultimatum to Diem. With Redick acting as translator, Lansdale spent a long night trying to persuade Thé and Phuong to withdraw from the movement and at last they agreed.

Those remaining in the Front went ahead with their plans. On 22 March they issued an ultimatum to Diem and gave him five days to comply. The premier offered to negotiate, but the Front members refused. As the days passed, soldiers of the Binh Xuyen openly positioned mortars so they could bombard the palace if Diem allowed the deadline to pass.

Fighting began shortly after midnight, early on 26 April 1955, when Binh Xuyen troops launched a mortar attack on Doc Lap Palace. Diem ordered his men to begin counterbattery fire. Exploding rounds turned nearly a square mile of the city into a shambles. The explosions awakened Lansdale. Then his telephone rang. It was Diem, informing him that the palace was under attack. Diem next called General Ely to inform him of the Binh Xuyen mortar attack and to let Ely know that he, Diem, would resist.[84] Lansdale telephoned Collins and was told to come over to the ambassador's residence in an hour. As he drove through the city, Lansdale saw troops moving into position. He also noticed that French tanks blocked reinforcements of the Vietnamese National Army from moving into place. Explosions were constant. House-to-house combat drove thousands into the streets, and hospitals filled with casualties, civilian and military. Finally, after pressure from Collins, General Paul Ely imposed a cease-fire some three hours and fifteen minutes after the Binh Xuyen bombardment began. He ordered elements of his army to interpose themselves between the two opposing forces and an uneasy truce followed. Some thirty thousand French soldiers backed by four hundred tanks kept control of half of Saigon.

Determined to get rid of Diem, General Collins flew back to Washington to press his case. Before he left, he instructed Lansdale, with whom he now had some pointed disagreements, to continue his liaison with Diem but to minimize any further advice to him on substantive matters. The premier later told Lansdale that he knew Collins had already decided to dump him when his plane took off from Saigon.[85]

As Americans filtered into the embassy at the beginning of business on 26 April, the news on everyone's mind was the fate of the shaky Diem regime. Many argued that Diem had no chance. Even if he managed to survive the existing crisis, the United States should still look for another candidate to back because if the nationwide referendum decreed by the Geneva Accords was held in 1956, Ho Chi Minh would win handily over the tiny, white-suited premier. America should choose a winning horse to back. Lansdale disagreed. He knew the French belittled Diem's chances and insisted he could never win a contest with Ho. So what? What did they know? They were hated foreigners. Lansdale later told how he occasionally wandered the countryside driving his Citroën. "Thinking I was a lone Frenchman, even kids'd throw rocks at me." Such Vietnamese attitudes made him suspect any information that came from the French. "Diem would win a popularity contest hands down if it was an honest vote," he insisted.[86]

When Collins arrived in Washington he quickly reported his views to President Eisenhower on 27 April. Eisenhower promised to support whatever Collins recommended. Collins then went to the State Department, spoke with John Foster Dulles, and told members of the Vietnam Task Force, Eisenhower's advisory group on Vietnamese policy, about his conversation with Eisenhower. He insisted that Diem had to go.[87] Diem, however, still had a few powerful backers, men like Senator Mike Mansfield and Assistant Secretary of State Walter Robertson. With their cooperation, Kenneth Young, head of the task force, worked out a compromise that would elevate Diem to the position of president while allowing Phan Huy Quat, a former leader of the northern Dai Viets, to become premier. Mansfield and Robertson sought out John Foster Dulles to convince him to back the compromise solution. Dulles agreed and charged Young with preparing a cablegram to be sent to Saigon that would explain the new American position. Dulles signed the cable at 6:00 P.M. on 27 April.

On 28 April, while at his TRIM office, Lansdale got a call from Diem asking him to come right away to Doc Lap Palace. Redick went with him as interpreter. While on their way they observed nearby machine gun fire. The meeting with Diem took place on a long second-story porch on the eastern portico. Diem had learned that Collins had obtained Eisenhower's approval to dump him. Was this true? Lansdale responded that he didn't know, didn't believe it, but would run a radio check to make sure.[88] He encouraged Diem to persevere. He returned to Duy Tan about 1:00 P.M., and as he did, he heard the sound of explosions. The second Binh Xuyen attack on the palace had begun.

Returning later to the embassy, Lansdale found only confusion and despair. Despite some objections by others, Lansdale fired off a telegram to Dulles, stating that he not only supported Diem but had been in the streets, knew what was going on, and was convinced that Diem's little army, with the help of Thé, would defeat the Binh Xuyen forces, for they had broad popular support. Lansdale reported that Diem had established control of Saigon and that his units were driving Bay Vien's soldiers back into Cholon. He also discounted the fears of Collins and MAAG intelligence officers that Diem's troops might turn against him.[89] Joe Baker heard Lansdale argue for a particular view on several occasions. "Ed was low-key but he could always convince people. . . . God! The way Ed explained the situation in Vietnam. If we gave up, all of Asia would go down the drain. It was just remarkable. . . . Of course he was an advertising man, a salesman, very soft-spoken, very quiet, very smooth."[90] It was late in the afternoon when he left, stopping off at the pool house on rue Tabard on his way back to Duy Tan. Clouds of smoke hung over the city as a large section of Saigon burned. Thousands were now homeless, left to live in the streets. Later that night, Lansdale received his reply from Washington. The State Department wanted confirmation of his claims.

The next day, 29 March, was a busy one.[91] Lansdale made official rounds, talking with others about their assessment of the fighting. Many of them now accepted his view and were willing to notify Washington of that fact. He visited his MAAG office and talked with O'Daniel while the two listened to the sound of fighting rage outside the compound. Back at Duy Tan, he munched on a sandwich while making notes on the fighting in Saigon and on the needs of the pacification campaign in central Vietnam, having received a report on the latter from Rufe Phillips. Conein stopped by to let him know that the pool house on rue Tabard was being hit by mortar shells.

He was alone in the living room when John "Demi" Gates, who was reporting for duty, came walking in escorted by Bo Bohannan. Bo informed Lansdale that he'd heard there was some good fighting in Saigon he was missing, so he'd hopped the noon Pan Am flight out of Manila. "You couldn't have picked a better time," Lansdale told him.[92] In the afternoon, Lansdale returned to Doc Lap Palace and sadly noted the gouges cut in its walls, the shell holes and litter in the surrounding gardens. His meeting with Diem was not a happy one. The premier had received a cable from Bao Dai, the contents of which had been broadcast by a radio station controlled by Ba Cut, head of the Binh Xuyen group, even before Diem received it. Bao Dai had excoriated Diem for the blood of thousands of Vietnamese that dripped from his hands. He had been sent to help — not harm — the country. The message stunned the premier. Lansdale comforted him as best he could. "I brought his attention back . . . by asking him to tell me again the principles at stake. . . . He was on as sound moral ground as a man can be in the midst of so much tragedy."[93] Lansdale counseled him to sit tight. Then he went back to the embassy and sent another message to Washington, summing up his assessment of Diem's chances.

John Foster Dulles received Lansdale's reply while at a dinner party. After scanning it, he called his brother, Allen, discussed Lansdale's message with him, and then left for the White House to inform the president. Eisenhower decided to support Diem. Dulles then sent instructions to Saigon to disregard his previous cable. They were to continue to support Diem. Collins returned to Vietnam on 2 May. The next morning he met with his country team and found their attitudes quite changed since he had last seen them. With some asperity in his voice, Collins announced current policy — the United States would continue to support Diem. He later accused Lansdale of "mutiny," but Lansdale had secured his purpose. Diem was assured of continued backing. Collins, who had served as a special presidential envoy rather than as an appointed ambassador, had only a few more days to worry about Vietnam. He was replaced as ambassador on 10 May 1955 by George Frederick Reinhardt. Despite their differences, Collins was gracious enough to write a letter of commendation for Lansdale thanking him for his "splendid help" and his outstanding efforts "in the initial organization of TRIM and subsequently as Chief of the National Security Division [which] should be a source of great satisfaction to you."[94]

Diem moved ahead to crush the Binh Xuyen threat. The worst news for Lansdale came on 3 May when he learned that Trinh Minh Thé had been killed while trying to mop up Binh Xuyen troops. As early as 9 May all Binh Xuyen soldiers had been driven out of Saigon. By mid-May members of that sect had retreated to swamps east of Saigon, where those who continued to resist were wiped out by September. Diem's forces captured Ba Cut and publicly guillotined him. Tran Van Soai surrendered and the few remaining Cao Dai forces gave up. The sect threat had ended.[95]

For the first time since Diem returned to Vietnam, he now had an opportunity to consolidate his position. One helpful step occurred in the last week of May 1955 when France agreed to move eighty thousand troops of its expeditionary force from near Saigon to coastal embarkation zones preparatory to their withdrawal. In the process, however, they also packed up vast quantities of military supplies that should have been turned over to the Vietnamese National Army and shipped them out of the country. With the departure of those soldiers, for the first time in ninety years Vietnamese took control of Saigon.

Now that he had a little extra time, Lansdale endeavored to persuade Diem that he needed to do something about the attitudes and actions of his army. Lansdale had in mind his earlier experiences in the Philippines where he had helped transform its soldiers from scavengers and abusers of the populace into friends of the people. He wanted to see Vietnamese soldiers at work on civic action projects. Vietnamese soldiers, like too many other armies in Asia, were adept at cowing the population into feeding them and providing them with girls. Lansdale wanted to change this situation, to make Vietnamese soldiers into a real army of the people.

The army was still the only unit of government that could reach out to the populace beyond Saigon. It was the largest and most visible unit of government, had a reasonably strong organization that extended throughout all the provinces of the country, and had modern means of internal and external communication. It was the key to establishing practical governmental authority on a nationwide basis.[96]

Lansdale disagreed with advisers at MAAG who wanted to see the National Army molded into a mirror image of the American Army. Vietnamese forces, he believed, should consist of a small, mobile force highly trained in counterinsurgency and antiguerrilla tactics. This was essential. Despite recurring rumors that Ho's northern government intended to invade the South, Lansdale was convinced that Diem's new nation faced no major threat from foreign armies. He predicted that in the foreseeable future, its primary duty would be to ferret out and destroy an armed opposition composed of Viet Minh guerrillas and a political cadre left behind in South Vietnam during the days of the great migration.[97]

Lansdale had a measure of success. He convinced Diem to attend to the needs of his nation's people (although Diem was inclined to favor those who were Catholic over others) and persuaded him that those who worked with the people of the countryside must not do so just during the hours of a working day but rather must eat, sleep, and work side by side with them for extended periods of time. He also convinced Diem to implement a number of social, economic, and political reforms including building schools, repairing roads, teaching personal and public hygiene, and teaching rural inhabitants the benefits of aligning themselves with the Saigon government.[98]

In early June, the foreign minister of North Vietnam, Pham Van Dong, announced that his government was prepared to open consultations with

South Vietnam in preparation for holding nationwide elections scheduled for July 1956, as stipulated in the Final Declaration of the Geneva Accords. Dong stated that North Vietnam wanted free elections in which all political parties, organizations, and individuals could participate. Premier Diem was in no mood to put at risk a nation of which he had just gained control. In a radio broadcast the following month, Diem pointed out that his nation had not signed the Accords and hence would not be bound by them. While he did not reject the "principle" of elections, he was fearful that the Viet Minh would put the interests of communism above the interest of national community. Until they could prove otherwise, he would continue to reject holding either conferences or a plebiscite.

Lansdale began to feel that he had done as much in Vietnam as was possible, given the circumstances and the intractability of his friend Ngo Dinh Diem. Always there was Nhu to whisper behind his back and to counter the suggestions he made to the premier. He began to yearn once again for the Philippines and for happier, more fulfilling days spent there. In an effort to effect a transfer back to Manila, he contacted his old friend General Leland Hobbs, former JUSMAG commander, and requested his help. Hobbs brought the matter of a change of assignment to the attention of John Foster Dulles, who in turn spoke with the president. Dulles argued that the United States should recognize Magsaysay's dependence on Lansdale and return him to the Philippines. Eisenhower agreed that Magsaysay needed someone like Lansdale as a continuing adviser, for he was inexpert in politics and was badly harassed by Recto and others. As a compromise for the present and to test Filipino reactions, the two men decided to allow Lansdale to go back for a brief visit, using a vacation as a cover.[99]

In late July, Lansdale left for Manila. It was not a happy time. He later told a friend that he had "spent most of it shaking with malaria."[100] His reappearance brought out enmities toward his former role and influence both among Filipino politicians and within the American community there. When Dulles again spoke with Eisenhower about reassigning Lansdale to the Philippines, he related that Lansdale's trip there had been "counterproductive." Embassy personnel from ambassador to CIA station chief had reacted in a negative fashion and "there has been considerable Philippine newspaper comment along the same lines." The matter was dropped and Lansdale continued in his Vietnam duties.[101]

Once he had recovered from his bout with malaria, Lansdale effected a transfer from TRIM to MAAG, where he formed a staff section to train the new Vietnamese National Army in unconventional warfare — intelligence operations and psywar. Lansdale's work kept him busy through the summer of 1955. He encouraged an army cadre to enlist in civic action projects and sent promising candidates for training in the basics of guerrilla warfare to Freedom Company at Clark AFB in the Philippines. He also arranged for the first Vietnamese volunteers to be trained as army rangers. He established communication nets, located potential sites that might be used by stay-behind Viet Minh guerrillas, and mapped probable operational areas they might use. In addition he plotted feasible invasion routes from the north that Ho's army might use in any invasion of the South. He also maintained his schedule of advising Diem, continuing to spend time with the premier almost daily, and succeeded in persuading Diem to adopt the concept of arming hamlets and villages for purposes of self-defense.

In September, during visits with the premier, Lansdale listened to Diem ponder how best to rid the nation of Bao Dai, who from his French base still endeavored from time to time to influence events in Vietnam. Diem wondered whether it might be best for him simply to declare himself ruler of the country. Lansdale counseled him to consider another course of action: hold an election — a referendum — to determine by vote of the people who should be chief of state — Bao Dai or Diem. Lansdale was certain Diem would win such a contest, and an election would give his regime a veneer of popular legitimacy.

On 6 October 1955, Diem announced that a referendum would be held on the twenty-third of that month. Once again Lansdale counseled restraint. There should be no stuffing of ballot boxes, despite Nhu's inclination to do so. Both ballots and voting should be fair. In response to Diem's questioning look, Lansdale then suggested that if the premier felt he needed an edge, he could make use of the Vietnamese custom of considering colors to be omens of luck. Print his own ballots in red — the color for good luck and happiness — and Bao Dai's in black or blue or green. Diem decided that his opponent's ballots should be green — the color of a cuckold.

As expected, Diem won the election, and the shadow of Nhu loomed over the event. Diem received 98 percent of the overall vote and in Saigon 605,025 votes, one-third more than the total number of 450,000 registered voters. Of all those voting, 5.7 million cast ballots for Diem versus 63,000 for Bao Dai. Before the day ended, Diem proclaimed himself president of the new Republic of Vietnam.[102]

The following month, Lansdale bade goodbye to General O'Daniel and welcomed the new MAAG chief, Samuel Tankersley "Hanging Sam" Williams, who arrived on 15 November 1955.

Some measure of stability now existed in South Vietnam, and in his conversations with Diem Lansdale urged that he relax his intransigence toward other southern politicians. He warned that the country would be plagued by conspiracies if legitimate opposition figures were not allowed to operate openly. It was necessary, Lansdale argued, for nationalists who had long fought the French to have a legitimate place and role within the politics of the republic. Diem found this difficult to understand. Opposition to him *was* a danger to the country, he insisted. Instead of opening opportunities for others to push for policies different from his own, he continued to clamp down on opposition spokesmen. He was also sympathetic to Nhu's creation of the Can Lao party.

This brainchild of Nhu was a combination political party, pep rally, and secret police apparatus. It had started in 1953 when Nhu and five other men formed a political group called the Revolutionary Party of Workers and Peasants. Only a short while after its formation, they changed the name to Le Parti Travailliste (Labor party) and then later to Can Lao. Nhu was its secretary general. Every government official was pressured to join the movement. Reputedly, the initiation ceremony included kissing a picture of Diem and swearing undying fealty to him — a rite reminiscent of those demanded under the Third Reich of Germans who became members of the Nazi *Schutzstaffel*. The Can Lao later resorted to torture, terror, or murder to silence those who refused to join or who spoke out against it.

Nhu also increasingly became spokesman for an "official" philosophy for Vietnam, that of "personalism," *nhan vi.* Nhu came into contact with this philosophy, which developed in France in the 1930s, during his prewar studies at École des Chartres. He became convinced that it was capable of counterbalancing the primitive Marxism that Ho's northern government was trying to develop. The Vietnamese words used to translate the term (*nhan* means "person," and *vi* means "dignity") indicated that personalism presumably emphasized human dignity and the value of humanism in modern society as opposed to communism's treatment of human beings as "the masses."[103] It seemed increasingly clear to Lansdale that the practice of personalism — a cult of personality — provided little difference between a Vietnam run by Nhu and any other fascist state.

Lansdale was incensed by Diem's sympathies with Nhu's philosophy. Diem's acceptance of personalism and the Can Lao seemed to him a betrayal of his hopes to help create a broad-based, open society in Vietnam, one that would have a place even for opposition politicians. The Can Lao, Lansdale pleaded, would force all opposition underground; adherents would have no opportunity to vent their feelings or to speak openly on behalf of programs and policies. It would turn the republic into a battleground at a time when it needed the help and solid support of every citizen. To continue on the present course would only lead to tragedy.

Diem had never seen Lansdale so angry or insistent. Lansdale spoke with the new ambassador, George Frederick Reinhardt, about the ghastly prospect in the offing for Vietnamese politics. Reinhardt was unsympathetic. The Eisenhower administration had already made a policy decision. As president of Vietnam, Diem needed his own political party. All Americans in Vietnam were to cooperate with the Can Lao party. It was a strongly nationalist group and was just what Diem needed for support.[104]

Lansdale protested. Why had he not been asked for his opinion? He knew Diem as well as any living American. He met with him almost daily. To adopt such a policy without his knowledge or offering him an opportunity to present his views was shocking. Reinhardt called for his political experts on the embassy staff to join them. In a long angry session they tried to silence Lansdale's outbursts. They, after all, were the experts in political science. What did he know of such things?

Lansdale pointed out that the Can Lao party was in control of the civil service, the police, the officers of the military. It was striking back at opponents through midnight arrests. What might come next? Since it was organized into secret cells, so also would all other political parties have to adopt a clandestine existence. Openness was needed, not a Vietnamese gestapo! He conceded that there might even be short-term benefits, but it would cause Vietnam great and lasting harm to allow a favored party to force older parties underground.[105] He convinced no one.

So it was that in early 1956, Lansdale requested to return to Washington to present his objections there. Permission was given, but once again he argued his case without success. He had one private meeting with Allen and John Foster Dulles and asked them to apply pressure on Diem that might force him to institute real political reform. They replied that they would stand by the recommendations of their political experts; Diem was the only practical alternative to a communist takeover in Vietnam, and Lansdale *would* support him without qualification. They told Lansdale that his views were both visionary and idealistic. He found it difficult to believe that CIA and the State Department could be so adamant about something of which they knew all too little. "The real point," he insisted, "is that we don't seem to have very long memories or enough solid feeling of responsibility for our acts. . . . I cannot truly sympathize with Americans who help promote a fascistic state and then get angry when it doesn't act like a democracy."[106]

Lansdale was disheartened. Policy restrictions would not allow him to offer Diem the sort of constructive advice the man needed. There seemed little point in his continuing in his role in Vietnam, so he asked John Foster and Allen Dulles to reassign him elsewhere. "I didn't want to go on advising forever and a day. I felt I had been there long enough.

. . . The Vietnamese could take over and start running things."[107] The Dulles brothers insisted that he return, at least for the remainder of 1956. It was going to be a long year.

A Cassandra, Lansdale accurately foretold doom, but he could never convince either Diem or Washington that it was essential to grant political freedom to opposition parties. By refusing, Diem made it inevitable that a renewed insurgency would be mounted, and there did indeed appear thereafter a steady growth of violence in the South. Diem's decision played a significant role in his eventual downfall and assassination.[108]

Diem had not been happy to learn that Lansdale disagreed so strongly with him about the value of personalism and the Can Lao party; he was further aggrieved to find out that Lansdale felt it necessary to return to Washington to argue his case there. From that time on, Lansdale began to lose his influence at the palace.[109] Tran Van Don, who served for a time as foreign minister, had frequent occasion to observe Lansdale's deteriorating relationship with Diem during the last days of 1955 and through the months of 1956. He reported that in earlier days, members of Diem's staff "had orders to always put him [Lansdale] through to Diem, night or day, whatever Diem was doing. He was a great help . . . . He was a good friend to Vietnam." Toward the end of 1955 when Don did not so frequently see Lansdale by Diem's side, he asked the president what had happened. Diem answered, "Lansdale is too CIA and is an encumbrance. In politics there is no room for sentiment." Don believed that one reason for Lansdale's downfall was that he pressed too hard "to have Diem copy Magsaysay. . . . [T]his really hurt Diem's feelings."[110]

Lansdale felt he had little recourse other than to continue to press with Diem the need to have a loyal and open political opposition. He spent many hours explaining how to encourage such growth. "In this I was none too successful."[111] He watched the Can Lao party grow, act against dissent, and fill prisons with its opponents. Newspaper offices were shuttered. People lived in fear of midnight arrests. Other parties went underground and the fragile body politic of Vietnam fractured. Cadres from the North and former Viet Minh stay-behind agents, now called Viet Cong, or Vietnamese communists, by Diem, began active recruiting throughout the south. Guerrilla bands once again became active. His friend Diem was sowing a whirlwind.[112]

Diem made two mistakes that, in combination, proved fatal. Had he avoided either of them, his republic and his own administration might have survived. Lansdale counseled against both. Diem's initial mistake was to allow the formation and growth of the Can Lao party. Professionals, skilled technicians, and Buddhist religious leaders were all excluded from participation in government. They were thus placed in the same category as the Viet Cong — enemies of the nation. They could so easily have become another constituency for Diem, yet he turned his back on them.

The second mistake came when Diem turned his attention to the country-side. Any consideration of the rural South demanded that attention be given to both village democracy and land reform. What might have been twin pillars of reform turned out to be a Vietnamese Scylla and Charybdis. Diem could have ensured that his people's ancient tradition of village democracy be preserved and he could have introduced a real and thoroughgoing program of land reform. Had he done so, people would no doubt have proclaimed undying loyalty to his government. As in older days, they would have seen their ruler cloaked with the "mandate of heaven." Diem chose another course of action. In 1956 he prohibited local elections, sending his own appointees to serve as village chiefs of communities throughout the land, and he refused to adopt a program of land reform, choosing instead to support a continuation of the evils inherent in the system of absentee landlords. Other of his policies wrenched people from lands farmed by their families for a thousand years and thrust them into new settlements elsewhere, many of which were little more than concentration camps in which confused peasants huddled miserably and wondered whether the Viet Cong might not have a better idea. It is no wonder that some 70 percent of Diem's people in rural areas were either openly hostile or silently indifferent to the Saigon government.[113]

On 4 March 1956, Diem held an election in which voters chose candidates for 123 seats in the new Assembly. The candidates selected in that balloting were the men who wrote the constitution that Diem promulgated on 26 October 1956. The constitution fixed the presidential term of office at five years.[114]

Orders finally arrived at the close of 1956 ending Lansdale's Vietnam tour and returning him to the United States for a new assignment. Lansdale was overjoyed to receive the news. Prior to his departure, he and Diem vacationed at the sea coast just north of Long Hai for a couple of days. They were not as close as they had been in earlier days, but Diem still retained real affection for his American adviser and they parted on friendly terms.

In retrospect, Lansdale wished he could have accomplished more during his Vietnam tour. He had hoped to show the new government how to fight an insurgency and win, to instruct it properly in the politics and psychology of a people's war. "It was hard to teach the Vietnamese that these were important things to do, but that could have been done." As it was, Lansdale was persuaded that too many Americans were doing things that the Vietnamese should have done and in the process were taking the initiative from them. He lamented that no orderly process of succession had been instituted and that no political base within the population had been formed. Yet he had done much. He even wrote out instructions for his successors prior to his departure. "I left it on paper for people to follow through on; I left organizations intact and had Vietnamese working on them. I don't know what happened."[115]

9

BRIGHT STAR SHINING

IN EARLY 1957 Edward Lansdale finally came home. While he was not sorry to leave Vietnam, he feared that much of what he had built there might "sag from neglect."[1] He was unaccustomed to defeat, and his futile efforts to persuade the Dulles brothers to oppose the rise of the Vietnamese Can Lao party made him fearful that his days of influence might be on the wane. For years, he noted, he had been a "child of the powers . . . in Washington." Now he felt more like "a bastard child" and wondered if his sponsors wanted to drop him.[2] Most of his old team had broken up and gone home even before he left Saigon. As a matter of courtesy, Diem had asked him to stay on an additional two years, but Lansdale was glad when the Air Force refused the request, informing him that he would move to a new position in the Pentagon office of Air Operations/Plans. Having now served both in the Philippines and in Vietnam, Lansdale wondered if he would stay in Washington or be sent to some new, exotic location. "Maybe," he mused, "I'll have to get acquainted with belly dancers in the Middle East next."[3]

Lansdale brought home with him a residual bitterness for CIA and State Department policymakers. They seemed either unable or unwilling to see the reality of third world politics and to do what was actually needed. He was particularly incensed at George Aurell, in CIA's FE/ Plans, and complained that his "butt" was still "stinging from the last shaft job" Aurell had given him. He confided to Bohannan that "we'll have to horsewhip the bastard yet." It was a sorry thing, he told Bohannan, when a team member left behind in Saigon failed to convince authorities that "we should pursue our foreign policy on the assumption that right makes might and use this approach."[4] He lamented the U.S. government's lack of understanding and its insistence on the opposite approach.

Arriving in Washington in January 1957, he enjoyed a lengthy leave and a chance once again to renew his relationship with Helen and his sons. He had earned his newfound leisure. On a Sunday in late January he wrote his friend Bohannan that he was loafing around. Both he and a French poodle named Koko, which he had brought back from Saigon, were lying around the house. Hardly a change for the dog, Lansdale said, "except he's given up chewing my gloves and pissing on the floor."

Lansdale exaggerated the extent of his free time. Much of the working day and many evenings were taken up with debriefings, lectures, and seminars. He spoke at the National War College at Fort McNair, lectured on counterinsurgency at the Foreign Service Institute, and also gave a presentation to the Joint Chiefs of Staff. "The damn thing just kept going on for hours," he reported about the last meeting, which brought an interest in his ideas from those involved in special warfare. Lou Conein, serving with special warfare forces at Fort Bragg in North Carolina, told Lansdale that they needed plenty of help. "I have a hunch," Conein said, "that I'll be ganging up with them in my new job."[5]

It was not until 15 March that he had to report to his new Pentagon office for staff duty with Air Force headquarters as a "politico-military affairs officer." He told a few close friends that he had left the door to "the old shop" a little ajar and that Allen Dulles' view was that he would miss the excitement of working for CIA and become tired of staff work within a few months. Lansdale, Dulles said, would always be welcome back at CIA. "Meanwhile," Lansdale said, "I'll put on the blue costume and make like wings flapping."[6] Work in the Pentagon would last longer than he foresaw. Lansdale remained there until his retirement from active duty on 1 October 1963, "a long, long stint."[7]

Two days after Lansdale began his Pentagon staff duties, headlines in Washington newspapers proclaimed the sudden death of his friend Ramón Magsaysay in a fiery plane crash on 17 March. Lansdale was appalled at news of the catastrophe. He mourned both the death of his friend and the loss of his hopes for the Philippines. The government there, which had seemed so settled and solidly pro-American, now once again foundered as politicians fought one another to inherit Magsaysay's mantle. Some two million people attended Magsaysay's funeral. Manuel Manahan called Lansdale and, in a voice breaking with grief, told him that Magsaysay's body was nothing but "charcoal." The president had apparently been asleep in his bunk aboard the airplane when it crashed. "I sure hope he was asleep at the time," Lansdale said. "I still feel like hell over this whole thing."[8]

Friends in the Philippines wrote to Lansdale saying that they wished he could be there. He was needed "to immediately issue instructions, make plans and implement them." "A lot of things can be done," one American wrote. "[A]ll we need is support of some sort."[9] Another

warned that "we have to find the right man and the right people . . .
and see to it that only those people are in a position to run for election
in November."[10] Lansdale agreed and went to CIA to talk about possibilities. He recommended that the Agency fish in those troubled waters.
He reported to Bohannan that his efforts were unavailing. "The shoe
clerk and librarian types at the Company are puzzled and backing-offish
on the thing."[11] Lansdale told Bohannan to write to as many friends in
the Philippines as possible and to tell them they had not been forgotten.
Although he was not particularly interested in returning, he had recommended that Bohannan be sent back, but that idea had been vetoed by
George Aurell.[12]

Lansdale next learned that American congressmen were considering
establishing an archives building in Manila as a repository for Philippine
"revolutionary documents" and as a memorial for the martyred president.
Lansdale was vociferous in his opposition. "I hit the ceiling," he complained, pointing out to the idea's sponsors "the dangers of release of
documents from our archives (or how we civilized 'em with a Krag)."
He told Bohannan that the idea had been tabled while sponsors "consulted
the field."[13] Despite some government interest in returning Lansdale to
the Philippines, the resentment shown against him in his trip there the
previous summer persuaded the Dulles brothers to leave him at the Pentagon.

Lansdale was not enthusiastic about his new job as Far East action
officer in the International Branch, Directorate of Plans, Office of the
Deputy Chief of Staff for Operations, United States Air Force. That
title, he said, was "a mouthful meaning coming up with opinions on
other people's opinions." He hoped it would become more challenging,
but prospects seemed dim.[14] Those around him worked hard, coming
early and leaving late, but most of their efforts seemed inconsequential
to him. "I took on the problems in three or four countries," he told
one man, "and I discovered an hour a day will about do it."[15]

Lansdale's superiors noticed his dissatisfaction and suggested he might
be interested in specializing in North African affairs. That was an area
of French concern, Lansdale told them. He and the French had hardly
been on speaking terms during his years in Vietnam. If the Quai d'Orsay
learned that he was studying another colonial region where the government
of France still claimed sovereignty, "it would have screamed to high
heaven." His superiors' lack of understanding on such matters surprised
him and made him wonder "where in hell they've been."[16]

Many of those for whom Lansdale worked regarded him as a genius
who had performed his role in an outstanding manner, with the panache
of an artist. Now this talented man was dissatisfied, chafing at the restricted
visions of those around him in the Pentagon. "How do you deal with a

maverick-artist in a large institutional bureaucracy?" William Colby later wondered. "There aren't any easy answers. We need the large institutions; we need the discipline they have. We also need the geniuses. How do you patch them together?"[17] It was a question for which the Air Force was soon to find an answer.

Having learned of Lansdale's discontent, the Air Force chief of staff, General White, called him into his office. He told Lansdale of a new opportunity. The secretary of defense was considering him to fill a position and soon would be interviewing him. It would be good for the Air Force, White said, if Lansdale accepted the offer.[18]

A day or so later, the secretary of defense, Charles "Engine Charlie" Wilson, met with Lansdale. "We have a man on our staff we think is dishonest," the secretary said. "We want you to replace him." The man was Bill Godell, a former Marine who had been wounded in combat and who occupied a position of trust in the Defense Department's Office of Special Operations. Lansdale had known him for some time. "CIA people had been very suspicious of him; everybody in the intelligence community had been warning me against my friendship with the guy." Secretary Wilson told Lansdale that whoever held that job had to be trustworthy. "Those I've checked with all said you are honest. I would like you to take the job."[19]

Lansdale wanted to know more about the job. For many years the secretary of defense had maintained on his immediate staff an assistant who, among other things, was responsible for liaison with the White House, the State Department, CIA, the National Security Agency (NSA), and the intelligence services of the various armed forces. It was known as the Office of Special Operations and was headed by retired General Graves B. Erskine, whose nickname was the Big E. Erskine had commanded Marines at Iwo Jima and was well thought of within the Corps and at the Pentagon. Erskine's office supervised all Defense intelligence activities and other operational programs. It was almost totally focused on the field of clandestine operations, although it also handled routine intelligence matters and other related functions.

During his tenure in office, Erskine served such secretaries of defense as Charles Wilson, Neil McElroy, Thomas Gates, and, for a short time, Robert McNamara. Most of those secretaries used Erskine's office to keep close watch on operations of CIA that involved the military in some way. Whenever in Erskine's judgment a CIA plan was not sound, he would report his view to the secretary. CIA would then be told to drop its request for military support, which was normally tantamount to killing the project. Erskine's position made him a figure of great power, which he used only sparingly.

It was the opportunity Lansdale had been hoping for, and his response was quick. "I've talked to General White," he told Secretary Wilson, "and he believes it would be a good thing for the Air Force, so I accept." In this way Lansdale became Erskine's assistant with the title of deputy director, Office of Special Operations, Office of the Secretary of Defense.[20] Lansdale had come a long way, moving from a special agent for OPC to a supervisory position with authority over CIA.

Godell had been moved from his position with Erskine to another office where he worked on Defense Department research and development projects and was promoted from a GS-17 to a GS-18. It was the easiest way to get rid of him. "They made him chairman of a committee I had to deal with," Lansdale lamented. "It was the wrong thing to do, but they did it."[21]

On Lansdale's first day in the new job he walked into the office assigned to him and found Godell still there. "Bill, I'm going to take over from you," he said. Godell asked him to wait until he was finished removing his office files. At first Lansdale refused. "Don't take a [single] goddamn paper out of the safe." Godell professed shock and Lansdale finally relented. "All right," he said. "Take them out of here. Never come back." He didn't.[22]

Lansdale then called a meeting of those who worked in the office, many of whom were close friends of their former boss. "We're going to be working for Uncle Sam and the good of our American country from now on," he told them. "That's where your loyalty belongs. Not to any individual. Not to me. Not to Bill Godell. We work for our country. If you want to get out, I'll let you go now [and] even help you find a spot. I can understand it if you want to be loyal to Bill, but [if so] you can't work for me."[23] In a short while, Lansdale felt that he had overcome his staff's initial hesitancy and that they worked well together.

Lansdale was pleased with the scope of his new position. Erskine allowed him to develop a greater capacity in Defense for the sort of special operations he had run in the Philippines and Vietnam. Erskine told him to become acquainted with the special intelligence operations being run by the various armed services and by NSA. As he did so, Lansdale got to know many of those who worked on such projects at NSA, Army G-2, Air Force A-2, and Navy N-2. He also coordinated the intelligence unit of the Joint Chiefs of Staff. "[A]ll came in to work with me," Lansdale reported. "I coordinated their offices [and activities] at the policy level."[24] The Office of Special Operations directed policy for the Army, the Navy, the Air Force, for NSA, and for what later became the Defense Intelligence Agency (DIA). "We were in on all of the early developmental stuff for intelligence and hardware, of space entry and orbiting devices and listening devices. Part of the job was counterinsurgency. So I had . . . a whole grab bag of things."[25]

Lansdale was only a colonel. Erskine was a full general and the heads of the several service intelligence outfits also outranked Lansdale. His work brought him into daily contact with two- and three-star admirals and generals, yet Lansdale was their superior in terms of policy. Others might have rank. Lansdale had authority. Someone once asked Lansdale why he didn't wear his uniform at work. "You guys would see it was only a colonel talking to you, so I've got to wear civilian clothes all the time." As he thought about it, Lansdale admitted that "[i]t was embarrassing, really, to be junior to them and try to give them guidance."[26]

Lansdale's responsibilities quickly became even greater than he had imagined, for shortly after he became Erskine's deputy, his boss suffered a heart attack and was absent for an extended period. The general's initial hospitalization at Bethesda Naval Hospital was followed by a long recuperation at home. Lansdale had to carry out not only his own duties but those of Erskine as well. "I was [only] a colonel, just in from the field, and Washington was a real puzzle to me," Lansdale said.[27] He performed capably.

During Erskine's absence of nearly two years, Lansdale recalled, "He left me running the show." Soon after Erskine was taken to the hospital, Lansdale learned that Pentagon politicians had begun maneuvering to get the general replaced and that Bill Godell was involved. "Erskine had been his commanding general in the war," Lansdale fumed. "That was real disloyalty that I couldn't stomach." To block the conspirators, Lansdale visited the White House and talked with the president's military assistant. "My boss is in Bethesda with a heart problem," Lansdale told him. "I know you went through the same thing with Eisenhower. It would be very nice if the president sent him a get well note to encourage him a little bit." The man agreed to help. As a farewell comment, Lansdale said, "Get it over to me. I'll hand-carry it to Erskine."[28]

Lansdale read the get well card Eisenhower sent for Erskine and smiled at the handwritten note that ended "Get well, Gravestone," a macabre pun on Erskine's first name. Before delivering it to the hospital, Lansdale took it along to a Defense staff meeting. When asked for comments on the business at hand, Lansdale replied, "It's not business, but I have a nice note here from the president I would like to read aloud. After the meeting I'm taking it to Graves Erskine." He read the message. When the conspirators realized that Erskine was backed by the personal interest of the president, they decided to lay their efforts to rest. "They were all standing at attention and saluting . . . . That stopped all the sniping. Erskine and I became very close after that," Lansdale commented.[29]

Lansdale drew a lesson from that episode. "That's what you learn in psychological operations . . . work on the minds of your enemies. Let them scare themselves into shutting up."[30]

With Erskine gone, Lansdale became the chief Defense representative at meetings of the United States Intelligence Board (USIB). Previously known as the Intelligence Advisory Committee, the group's name was changed early in Eisenhower's administration. Serving as a centralizing and coordinating agency for America's various intelligence activities, the USIB tried to keep intelligence expenditures as low as possible. It approved or disapproved intelligence estimates from member agencies. Estimates that were approved were then sent to the president for his consideration. If a plan did not receive the approval of USIB, it was either dropped entirely or returned to the sponsoring agency for additional work. This ensured that projects sent to the president for his consideration had the backing of all member agencies of the USIB rather than just one or two.[31]

Lansdale enjoyed his position of great influence. At weekly meetings of the USIB he became one of those few government servants who participated in decisions directly affecting the formation of American policy. Those with whom he met included Allen Dulles, who served as chairman of the USIB, not as head of CIA but in his role as adviser to the president. His deputy director of Central Intelligence attended meetings as CIA's representative. Others who formed the membership of USIB included the director of NSA, the assistant to the secretary of defense for Special Operations, the director of intelligence and research at the State Department, the chiefs of the Army, Navy, and Air Force intelligence services, and the White House's national security adviser. The director of intelligence for the Atomic Energy Commission and a representative from the Federal Bureau of Investigation attended meetings when issues concerning those agencies were to be discussed.[32] Lansdale performed so well on the USIB that Erskine later wrote that he felt "particularly fortunate" in having him as his deputy.[33]

In early May 1957, Ngo Dinh Diem came to the United States on a state visit to seek additional aid for his country. During Diem's days in Washington, Lansdale (accompanied by Joe Redick) paid him a courtesy call at his quarters in Blair House. "Poor guy was desperate to see a friend," Lansdale found. "[H]e practically hugged us . . . . [while] the protocol boys frowned in the background." Lansdale was glad to see his friend despite the fact that "I got hooked for all sorts of things, including spending a hundred bucks for a uniform with tails, dammit."[34]

Diem's visit was not uppermost in Lansdale's mind. He complained that his *bête noir* at CIA, George Aurell, still hated him with an undying hate. "Have heard how he's getting drunk at cocktail parties, receptions, etc., and sounding off to all and sundry that there is a new era [at CIA] now, without the bribery that we did," he informed Bohannan. Perhaps the most exasperating part of Aurell's dislike was that he "[n]ames us as Company." Perhaps Lansdale still was, in spirit at least. He was finding it hard to remember that he now worked for Charles Wilson rather than for Allen Dulles.

Only recently he had learned of a projected purchase by four Americans of the Manila *Bulletin*. He thought CIA should know. He "told the Company lads about this" and supplied complete details. Hearing nothing further, he put his information into Defense channels on 8 May 1957. "It hit topside fast." Only then did CIA contact him. "The Company lads called up all hurt; said their field boys hadn't reported anything on it and why hadn't I given them a chance to check first! I told them I'd gotten [it] from the horse's mouth and had informed them fully and quickly; if they didn't want me to help them, kindly so state and not start griping when things started happening."[35]

One of Lansdale's staff at his Pentagon office, Leroy Fletcher Prouty, was long persuaded that Lansdale — no matter what his current assignment might be — continued to work for CIA.[36] While he was never anyone's lap dog, and while he may no longer have worked directly for CIA after his return from Vietnam, it is evident that he certainly shared information with the Agency when he believed it would be useful to them.

When Lansdale began working in the Office of Special Operations, no one had yet spelled out the nature of his activities. Because of his background and his views on people's wars, Lansdale wanted to emphasize guerrilla warfare and the role American soldiers might play as counterguerrilla fighters. "The Defense people didn't want me to," he recalled, "and I don't think anybody else wanted me to. But I insisted." Donald Quarles, deputy secretary of defense, backed Lansdale's efforts to establish Pentagon direction of counterinsurgency operations. With Quarles' support, the Operations Coordinating Board approved Lansdale's plan but it was promptly shot down by the Joint Chiefs of Staff in a rather heated Saturday afternoon session with Quarles and Lansdale in the deputy secretary's office. It seemed to Lansdale that the Joint Chiefs were uninterested in "effective, but more modest measures to help countries being subjected to a VC style of attack," for they dropped "like vultures" on any idea that went counter to their own rigid belief in conventional warfare.

Lansdale did not give up. He simply moved more quietly among the "wolves" around him. In an effort to establish a broader constituency within the armed forces, he brought selected individuals from each service to work as staff members in his office. Each man chosen had been trained by Air Force Special Operations or as a Navy SEAL (sea, air, land team member) or by Army's Special Forces.[37] He checked each man's background to determine whether any had held jobs as youngsters. If they had done so, Lansdale believed, "they were more open to understand . . . international and national policy problems and have realistic insights."[38] Such projects kept him hard at work.

Lansdale may have been busy but his thoughts often turned back to the Philippines. His home life at 4503 MacArthur Boulevard was smooth enough. It was good to be back with his family, to spend time with Ted and Peter and to watch them grow. All too soon they would be men and he hardly knew them until he returned from Vietnam. Helen was a calm, efficient mother and a trim, elegant woman. Yet a very long time had gone by since 1945 when he had first gone to Manila. Life with Helen in the twelve years since had always been on a hurried, intermittent basis, punctuated by long absences. Their differences had brought about a trial separation, now long since repaired, although both of them had grown accustomed to living alone. Whenever there was time to be together, it was almost as if they had to get to know one another all over again. Perhaps the boys, more than anything else, provided the main thread in their lives that held them together.

Lansdale's marriage was further complicated by his affection for his special Filipina friend, Patrocinio Yapcinco Kelly. Widowed during World War II, Pat had not remarried and had learned to love Ed. For long years she cared for him, seeing him when she could, writing when she could not. Yet she was half a world away and Ed's heart often remembered his "Tarlac Tease" and he missed her.[39] He had learned from a friend just before his return to America that "Pat spends all spare time in the province, overseeing her lands. Not a happy girl, I think."[40] At least Pat was able to see Lansdale occasionally while he served in Southeast Asia. After he returned to the United States, who knew whether he would remember her?

Ed was occasionally remiss in writing. Pat lamented in one letter, "It seems as if all roads lead to Washington these days. I wish I were on one too." Then a little less gently, she added, "Why do you have to send emissaries and packages? Why don't you just drop me a line, now and then? Or send me cards or just keep in touch with little notes, just to let your friends know you are not spending all your time saving this world?" As was often the case, she closed with "Love. Pat."[41]

Friends kept Lansdale abreast of Pat's activities. Jack Wachtell wrote that "Pat was over recently, took my place at mah jongg and cleaned up enough to pay the rent for at least a month."[42] When a former boss in the Defense Department planned a trip to the Orient that included a stopover in the Philippines, Lansdale suggested that if he had the time "you would enjoy meeting a remarkable Filipina gal named Pat Kelly who is the spark plug of USIS Motion Pictures at our Embassy and who is the unsung heroine of the Huk campaign (under fire with me in both the Philippines and Vietnam); she has great wit and political savvy."[43] He added a fond reminiscence. "You might ask her about two of your old military commanders who were quite taken with her in Vietnam. General John 'Iron Mike' O'Daniel used to call her 'Colonel Kelly'; she taught him to mix martinis her style and to dance the Philippine bamboo dance, the *tinikling*. General S. T. 'Hanging Sam' Williams, one of the toughest of our old Army types, even let her paint a mustache on him with eyebrow pencil (he later grew a fierce, bushy mustache of his own — so I guess he liked the effect). I doubt the Embassy suspects what an irrepressible spirit lurks beneath the surface of this remarkable Filipina employee."[44]

Lansdale suggested to a friend traveling to the Philippines that he "[b]uy her a martini for me."[45] He asked another man on his way to Manila to greet all his friends there. "Just tell 'em I love 'em and miss 'em. If you don't want to do that before a crowd, please do it with Pat in the singular."[46] When official business took Lansdale through the Philippines on his way for a brief visit to Vietnam he saw Pat for a few short hours. An old friend wrote that Pat "was jealous about how your time here was apportioned. . . . [I]t is evident that any gesture or communication from your end sets Pat up with a smile and a new air about her."[47]

Pat often teased Ed in her letters. In one she wrote, "I am off to Baguio come May 1st. Anything I can get you from there? G-string or something?"[48] Yet separation was often more hurtful than humorous. They made plans to meet at Eastertime in Hong Kong one year. "Sorry you couldn't make [it]," she wrote, but "I really didn't think you could and I was not too badly disappointed. I did some thorough touring and discovered a damn good hotel out in the country that reminded me so much of the wonderful places you have visited here. That was the only time I felt lonesome in the entire trip." Then it was time for a mild chiding. "Thanks for the tortoise shell set. I am going to wear them tomorrow evening and I am sure they will all be a success. But must you always send me gifts? I am starting to really suspect you are bribing me!" She ended plaintively. "Write when you know more about your future plans."[49]

Lansdale wrote to Pat's boss at USIS in Manila to say "thanks for Pat's promotion. Why don't the two of you, chaperoned by [your wife] Anne, come over here . . . ? This Mahomet is asking the mountain to come to him. We could have a real, old-fashioned, stomping, lease-breaking party.''[50] Nothing came of his invitation. Ed and Pat must have felt star-crossed. They had no future, little present, and a great number of past memories. Yet stubbornly they refused to relinquish one another and continued their distant courtship. Perhaps some day things would be different.

Such tugs on his heart were only occasional. For the most part Lansdale enjoyed family life during his hours at home, and while at the office he immersed himself in his work. He was fascinated by the unending variety of topics available to deal with. He exchanged letters with a Navy commander who wanted to sponsor Elvis Presley at the 1959 Vienna Youth Festival as a psywar propaganda measure.[51] He commiserated with Lieutenant General Samuel T. Williams when he learned of his reassignment from Vietnam. ''President Diem will agree with me that you are the one American official he can afford to talk to frankly and expect some understanding.''[52] He felt exasperated to learn that Major General Paul Harkins had been selected to replace Williams. The Army claimed Harkins was a proponent of counterinsurgency, yet Lansdale knew all too well how Harkins, as commandant at the Command and General Staff College in Fort Leavenworth, had sat on one of his studies for two years.[53]

Letters kept Lansdale current on Vietnamese and Philippine affairs. A friend sent him a taped copy of a Hanoi radio broadcast that recalled his work for the ''psychological warfare and information departments'' of Diem's government and assailed MAAG, the United States Operations Mission, and other agencies as ''part of the spy ring headed by Lansdale.'' Lansdale learned that there was ''an almost universal despair'' in Manila that he was no longer there, and he despaired over the tawdry heirs of Magsaysay.[54] A never-ending series of problems ranging from mainland China to Africa came across his desk.[55]

One of those problems was an unwanted and undesirable notoriety brought about by circumstances beyond his control. For the second time, Lansdale was about to become a leading player in a major novel. A few years previously, in June 1955, Graham Greene published *The Quiet American,* a novel set in Saigon during the Eisenhower administration. One of the book's two focal characters was Alden Pyle, patterned after Lansdale and other Americans Greene observed in Vietnam, and thus Greene became the first author to caricature Lansdale's real-life exploits. Greene did not like what he knew of them and he made this fact very clear in his text. He described Pyle as a young man with ''gangly legs,'' a crewcut, and an earnest, ''unused'' face. Pyle had been sent to Vietnam by his government, ostensibly as a member of the ''American Economic Mission,'' but that assignment was only a cover for his real role as a

CIA agent. His orders called for him to create a political force in Vietnam that could resist a communist takeover after the French departed. His duties included funneling money and explosives to a warlord general. He was ready for a fight to save the Vietnamese from communism and themselves. All that Pyle knew of Vietnam he had learned from books. The other character was Thomas Fowler, a middle-aged and cynical British correspondent, wise about the ways of the East, patterned after Greene himself.

In this despairing portrait, Pyle saw in Vietnam only what he chose. Impregnably armored by his ignorance and political prejudices, Pyle was the embodiment of well-meaning American-style politics, and he blundered through the intrigue, treachery, and confusion of Vietnamese politics, leaving a trail of blood and suffering behind him. He came, Thomas Fowler noted, to "win the East for Democracy."

"They don't want communism," Pyle insisted to Fowler. The British correspondent rejected such foolish thinking and burst out with a rejoinder. "They want enough rice . . . . They don't want to be shot at. They want one day to be much the same as another. They don't want our white skins around telling them what they want!" Fowler tried to get Pyle to appreciate Asia for what it was. He pointed to the pretty women on the streets in their colored silk *ao dais*, split up the thigh, and tried to get Pyle to look at them. The younger man was uninterested, "absorbed in the dilemmas of Democracy and the responsibilities of the West; he was determined . . . to do good, not to any individual person but to a country, a continent, a world."

At one point the two men were forced to spend the night high in a watchtower accompanied by two frightened Vietnamese soldiers. Fowler still retained a vague hope of making Pyle understand the futility of imposing Western concepts on such people. He turned to the Vietnamese conscripts and asked, *"La liberté — qu'est-ce que c'est la liberté?"* The men had no idea what it was he asked. Yet still Pyle would not see. The real nature of the war evaded Pyle's understanding right up to the moment that it killed him.

Lansdale was not pleased by Greene's portrayal of him, and consequently his own view of the British author was an unflattering one. "I used to see Greene sitting around the rue Catinat [later Tu Do]," Lansdale said. "He was writing for French and British newspapers." It was 1954 and two of Lansdale's friends, Peg and Tilman Durdin, a husband and wife team of American correspondents, had just returned to Saigon from an interview with Ho Chi Minh in Hanoi. Since Lansdale had helped them prepare for the trip and armed them with questions to ask Ho, the Durdins invited him to dine with them at the Continental Hotel, where they were staying. When Lansdale arrived, he saw a large group of French officers at the sidewalk terrace and Greene sitting with them. Later, as he and the Durdins were leaving, Greene said something in French to his companions and the men began booing Lansdale. The Durdins knew Greene, and Peg stuck out her tongue at him, turned and gave Lansdale a hug and kiss, and said, "But *we* love him!" For some reason Greene banged the table at which he sat. Lansdale smirked and thought, "I'm going to get written up someplace as a dirty dog." He later commented: "I had the feeling that Greene was anti-American." The rancorous feeling between the two men was mutual. Greene called the widespread notion that Lansdale provided the basic model for Pyle a "myth" and observed that he "never had the misfortune to meet" Lansdale, whom he "would never have chosen . . . to represent the danger of innocence."[56]

"Graham Greene once told someone," Lansdale commented, "that he definitely did not have me in mind when he created the character Alden Pyle. I sure hope not . . . . On the other hand, Pyle was close to Trinh Minh Thé, the guerrilla leader, and also had a dog who went with him everywhere — and I was the only American close to Trinh Minh Thé and my poodle Pierre went everywhere with me."

Reviews of *The Quiet American* were mixed. Although many praised Greene's work, others were less positive. *Christian Century* disapproved of "the malice toward the United States that controls the novel." The *Christian Science Monitor* wondered "whether the author is presenting a thesis or a burlesque," while the *New York Herald Tribune* complained that the book's "two principal characters are so fantastic that one is half inclined to suspect that the whole thing has been devised as an elaborate leg-pulling."[57]

By the time Lansdale went to work in the Pentagon the furor over Greene's book had largely subsided. Those who wanted to comment and conjecture about parallels between the fictional Pyle and Lansdale had talked themselves nearly dry. Mindful of security, Lansdale looked forward to renewed anonymity. Then a second novel featuring him was published — *The Ugly American,* written by William Lederer and Eugene Burdick. Once again Lansdale was faced with undesired publicity. When they wrote the book, Burdick was a professor of political science at the University of California at Berkeley and Captain Lederer served as assistant to Admiral Felix B. Stump, CINCPAC. Lansdale had known Lederer, a former submarine skipper, during his Philippine service days. The Navy captain's wife was a Filipina from an American family. Lansdale knew the family and occasionally saw Lederer on social occasions.

As one of the lead characters in this book, Lansdale wore a thin disguise as Colonel Edwin Barnum Hillándale, "the Ragtime Kid," a harmonica-playing American who was assigned to the Philippines as "a liaison officer to something or other," an implication that he really worked for CIA. Hillandale found Filipinos fascinating. He ate in their little restaurants, washed down large quantities of *adobo* and *pancit* and rice with cheap rum — two pesos a pint. He rode a motorcycle through backcountry barrios and studied Tagalog in his spare time at the university. Those at the American embassy thought of him as "that crazy bastard," but soon the "Ragtime Kid" was eating breakfast with the nation's leaders and they trusted him rather than the staid officials at the embassy.

Hillandale was more than a simple portrayal of Lansdale. Lansdale later reported that "Bill Lederer once told me apologetically that he had me and himself in mind while creating the Hillandale character . . . and would urge me to make use of magic tricks and necromancy — as he said he did — in dealing with Asians. I never did. Nor did I ride a motorcycle as the character did."

Tragically, during the American advisory days in Vietnam, Lansdale later commented, some Americans tried to pattern their activities on the fictional Hillandale. They rode motorcycles through the countryside and even taught themselves to play the harmonica, without getting much else done "except to wind up dead or captured by the enemy." He told one inquirer: "Yes, I used to play the harmonica at times when visiting in the provinces, to take up the tedium of long waits alone or to entertain children when they'd gather around and start asking me a lot of questions. But I always had some other purpose for being there."

Within three months of its release, *The Ugly American* moved onto the best-seller lists and remained there for seventy-two weeks; ultimately readers bought nearly five million copies. It may have sparked creation of a presidential committee — the Draper Commission — and its title became a phrase in the American language referring to the poor image Americans overseas earn for themselves by their boorish actions. Throughout its pages, the theme of the book was that the United States needed to recruit well-trained, dedicated Americans capable of living in and adapting to third world countries to which they were assigned. Southeast Asia, in particular, was a battleground between democracy and communism and the United States was faltering in those cold war battles.

Senators John F. Kennedy, Mike Mansfield, Stuart Symington, Leverett Saltonstall, Hubert H. Humphrey, William Fulbright, and others read the novel. Some liked it. Humphrey wrote to Secretary of State Christian Herter that "*The Ugly American* has served to strengthen our foreign policy in Southeast Asia." Fulbright, on the other hand, attacked the book from the floor of the Senate for nearly an hour. When Wisconsin

Congressman Henry Reuss first introduced the idea of the Peace Corps, he cited *The Ugly American* in support of his efforts. President Eisenhower, so the nation learned from CBS reporter Robert Pierpoint on the evening of 24 November 1958, had read *The Ugly American* while on vacation and was impressed with its criticism of the U.S. foreign aid program. The book may indeed have played a part in Eisenhower's creation of the Draper Commission (on which Lansdale served) to investigate overseas military aid expenditures.[58]

While Lansdale's name had never been widely known outside the intelligence community and the upper levels of American bureaucracy, publication of *The Ugly American* ended any possibility of continued anonymity. Forever after, when stories about him appeared in the press he was often saddled with the sobriquet "the Ugly American." It particularly bothered Lansdale when the term came to have its current meaning. In the late 1950s and 1960s when he was still active and serving in important overseas positions, sometimes with considerable national stakes riding on what he did, the characterization did matter and he tried — mostly unsuccessfully — to rectify false impressions fastened on him by those fictional characters. He was well into his retirement before he ceased to care whether others identified him with Pyle or Hillandale. There was a positive side as well for Lansdale in the appearance of this book. *The Ugly American* firmed his reputation as the nation's preeminent authority on rebellion, insurgency, counterguerrilla warfare, and the nature of people's wars and brought him to the attention of later sponsors such as senators John F. Kennedy and Hubert H. Humphrey. And it may well have secured for him a place on the Anderson subcommittee of the Draper Commission.

Perhaps as a result of the international publicity and the questions raised in Congress about the value of America's overseas military assistance programs which came about after publication of *The Ugly American*,[59] President Dwight Eisenhower decided to take a look at them — to determine how they were functioning and what needs might exist for them in areas where the United States was locked into the cold war struggle against communism. The group he named to perform this task was known as the President's Committee to Study United States Military Assistance Programs, or the Draper Commission, after its chairman, William H. Draper, Jr., a retired general. One subcommittee, under the leadership of Dillon Anderson, focused on military and foreign aid programs in Southeast Asia. The office of the secretary of defense posted Colonel Lansdale to the Anderson subcommittee. He was charged with examining military civic action programs in Asia. It was a field in which he not only had great experience but about which he already held firmly developed ideas. He probably could have written his final report without leaving his Pentagon desk or undergoing the rigors of a hurried tour of Asian nations. It is a certainty that his month-long trip changed none of his views.[60]

Despite the fact that his membership on the subcommittee would give him a new platform from which to present his ideas to a new audience, Lansdale regretted some aspects of the arrangement. He confided to Bohannan that he and Anderson did not get along well and that another member of the group was Lightning Joe Collins. He was determined to do his best. "Somehow, despite the formal dinners and all the briefing meetings, I'll have to wriggle away long enough to find out how a few blows can be struck for liberty — as well as exert a little cold war horse sense on the Committee." Lansdale also contacted Joe Redick and asked him to go with the group as a translator.[61]

Lansdale also wrote a friendly letter to President Ngo Dinh Diem. They would soon have a chance to see one another. "[W]ould you like to 'play hookey' from your work," Lansdale wrote, "and go swimming at Long Hai with me? . . . Please let me know if there is any errand you would like me to do for you before I leave."[62] Lansdale did more than write letters to friends. He turned his mind to ways in which military assistance programs could be used to develop national strength and stability in Southeast Asia. He was persuaded that he possessed a considerable amount of basic knowledge of ways third world leaders could use their military forces for the greater good of their nations. In a paper written prior to his departure, Lansdale wrote out a number of questions. Answers to them could pinpoint how effectively third world leaders used their own armies.

Should the loyalty and obedience of military officers be given to a commander, the chief of state, or a constitution? How certain, how incorruptible, how impersonal were military justice systems in Asia? What percentage of their pay did soldiers actually receive? Were they subjected to illegal "squeezes" by their officers? Did existing logistics systems force troops to supplement mess funds by brigandly seizures of chickens, pigs, and other food from civilians? Did high-ranking officers act as inspectors general when visiting troop units? Did they take effective steps to correct flawed practices they encountered?

In the absence of national communications systems, national police, provincial administrative units, and effective civil services, did leaders rely on their armed forces to undertake civil activities beyond the military's customary role of national defense? Was the role of armed forces understood sympathetically by the majority of a population? By civil and military leaders? By troops themselves?

Were Asian armies sympathetic to the aspirations of their nations' general population? Did soldiers in the countryside feel closer to civilians around them or to politicians at the capital? When armed forces engaged in military civic actions were there safeguards ensuring that they did not eventually supplant civil rule? What national symbols — past leaders or historic events — inspired Asia's armed forces? Were such symbols compatible with high political principles and human ethics? Could national stability in Asia be strengthened by U.S. military assistance programs? These were all old themes for Lansdale, topics in which he had been interested, which he had studied, and for which he had sought practical applications since his early days in the Philippines.[63]

The trip was a whirlwind. The men of the Anderson subcommittee left Washington on 21 January and flew toward their first stop, the Hawaiian island of Oahu, where they held meetings with the staff of CINCPAC in Honolulu. On Friday, 30 January, they arrived in Manila and remained there until 3 February. One of the people with whom Lansdale met in the Philippines was a young, reform-minded politician of the Liberal party, the minority floor leader of the House of Representatives, Ferdinand Marcos.[64]

On 4 February the subcommittee arrived in Saigon. Acquaintances got word to Lansdale of their disappointment with the group. A parade of witnesses appeared before the subcommittee. So quickly did they arrive and depart that they "felt frustrated and extremely disappointed at the absence of serious questioning and by the very short time allotted them." They felt they were only "a kind of window dressing."[65] Two days later, the subcommittee left for Bangkok, Thailand, where it remained until Sunday, 8 February. By evening of that day the group was in Vientiane City, Laos. Lansdale and his companions spent Tuesday, Wednesday, and Thursday, 10–12 February, in Phnom Penh, Cambodia. Then they traveled on to Rangoon, Burma, where they spent Friday and Saturday, 13–14 February. The group then moved on to Djakarta, Indonesia, where it stayed until 20 February, at which time the men set out on their return trip. Once again they stopped in the Hawaiian Islands and Lansdale wrote his report on the journey at CINCPAC headquarters. He returned to Washington on 24 February 1959.[66]

While in the kingdom of Cambodia, headed by neutralist Prince Norodom Sihanouk, Anderson's group found themselves in the midst of a near coup. The preceding June, some of Ngo Dinh Diem's soldiers — ignoring boundary lines between Vietnam and Cambodia — penetrated for a distance of about nine miles into the Cambodian province of Stung Treng. They showed little inclination to leave despite protests and even installed new boundary markers, placing them to Vietnam's advantage.

The commander of troops of the Royal Cambodian Army in Siem Reap province — the site of the famed temples of Angkor Wat — was General Dap Chhuon, a trusted officer of Prince Sihanouk. Chhuon and an associate, Sam Sary, were not as loyal as the prince believed; they were planning a coup. Returning from a trip abroad, Sihanouk learned that something nasty was afoot.

Sihanouk later wrote, "In early February [1959], I received reports of unusual happenings at Siem Reap. . . . On 7 February, two Chinese from the 'Kam-Wah Film Company' arrived from Hong Kong with huge cases of equipment — all installed in Dap Chhuon's villa." Sihanouk discovered that the two "Chinese" were in reality South Vietnamese. "[T]heir 'film equipment,' when assembled, turned out to be powerful radio transmitters which they . . . set up in the jungle surrounding the temples" of Angkor Wat. On 21 February 1959, at Sihanouk's order, the two radio operators were arrested at Dap Chhuon's villa. So also was the general himself, but before he could be questioned he was ordered shot by General Lon Nol, then chief of staff of the Cambodian armed forces, for fear Chhuon would implicate Nol in the coup attempt.

Sihanouk claimed that visitors of note often visited Siem Reap, the site of the Angkor temples, "but the interest displayed in Cambodian antiquities" in early February 1959 was "unprecedented." On 7 February, claimed Sihanouk, Admiral Harry D. Felt, CINCPAC, visited the temples, signed the guest registry, and set off to visit Dap Chhuon. On 17 February, Sihanouk wrote, General J. Lawton Collins, Colonel Edward Lansdale, and Admiral H. G. Hopwood, commander in chief of the Pacific Fleet (CINCPACFLT), also arrived at Angkor Wat, signed the visitors' book, looked at the temples, and had "a whisky-soda with Dap Chhuon."[67]

It is an interesting assertion. The dates almost correspond. Records of the Anderson subcommittee show that its members were in Thailand from Friday to Sunday, 6–8 February; in Laos 8–10 February; and in Cambodia 10–12 February. On Friday and Saturday, 13–14 February, the group was in Burma, and from 15 February to 20 February they were in Indonesia. It was at least possible for Lansdale and Collins to travel briefly to Cambodia apart from the rest of their group. Sihanouk charged that Admiral Felt arrived at Angkor on 7 February, joined — or followed — by Collins, Lansdale, and Hopwood on 17 February. The Anderson subcommittee spent more time in Indonesia than at any other stop along its way — five days — more than enough time for Lansdale and Collins to absent themselves for a time. It was also possible for CINCPAC and CINCPACFLT to travel from Honolulu to Angkor; both men had authority to arrange for flights wherever they wished to go.

It is clear that as head of state, Sihanouk knew of the visit to his country by members of the Anderson subcommittee and knew that Lansdale and Collins were part of the group. He was, however, out of the country when the subcommittee visited Phnom Penh, and its members met instead with such officials as the minister of state, the vice prime minister, the minister of foreign affairs, the minister of defense, and others. Perhaps Sihanouk believed the entire Anderson subcommittee trip had been set up to provide a cover for nefarious tricks to be played by the ugly and quiet American. It is also possible that Lansdale had a secret and covert agenda to complete during his time in Southeast Asia for which his subcommittee work simply served as cover. Openly signing a visitors' registry would be good misdirection. Who would suspect an undercover agent on a secret assignment if he did such a "touristy" act? It would also be good protective coloration to serve on a government committee and visit tourist sites. Lansdale did favor such misdirection. Only a few years before he had gone on a secret intelligence mission to the Philippines for OPC using as his cover an assignment as an Air Force intelligence officer. Was there an American agenda that included Dap Chhuon? Sihanouk believed there was. Lansdale insisted that there was not.[68]

Whatever happened in Cambodia, Lansdale made his presence felt on the Anderson subcommittee. One can see his influence throughout the trip, if only in the choice of people its members spoke with. Often they were longtime friends or individuals with whom Lansdale had previously worked closely: Albert and Marjorie Ravenholt, Dr. and Mrs. Juan C. Orendain, Hank and Ann Miller, and others.[69]

Lansdale's report on military civic action, which he wrote at CINCPAC headquarters in Hawaii while en route home from Southeast Asia, has been pulled from the files at the Hoover Institution by CIA and State Department censors, presumably in the "national interest." Thirty years after it was written it remains unavailable to historians! Such devotion to keeping the public ignorant is laudable indeed![70] Only a 13 March memorandum and an undated draft of another report exist to allow a glimpse of Lansdale's impressions.

The March memorandum is very cursory. In it Lansdale noted that "in the past few years, some of the armed forces in Southeast Asia evolved an operational doctrine of assisting the civilian population, to bring about a 'brotherhood' between the soldiers and the civilians . . . to win over the people to help the Army in finding and fighting an enemy who hid among the population." He listed a number of civic action projects in the countries visited and concluded that Southeast Asia offered a wide variety of military civic activities that contributed greatly to the economy, stability, and unity of nations facing conflict or terrorism. Their ideas, he wrote, "are exportable and . . . worth study."[71]

His draft memorandum is more illuminating. Therein he wrote that "most of the U.S. assistance in the area has been action to meet an emergency, and to date it has been an over-all success." He meant that nations seen by the subcommittee were still independent, their economies not yet ruined through monster inflations caused by massive American injections of money and materiel, none were as yet war-ravaged, and all were still noncommunist. Sadly, that would remain true only for a few more years. Lansdale wrote that much needed to be done in durable ways; flooding their economies with funds was not the answer.

He believed that U.S. MAAG teams had done well. "What we saw of the benefits of U.S. military training convinced us that greater emphasis should be placed on these training programs." Although his subject was civic action, Lansdale's interest in psywar crept into the memorandum. "If training in the U.S. was increased for the military in neutral nations; for example, if we trained Indonesians to fly the MIGs they have obtained from the Communist bloc, it would mean more that we had friends in the cockpit than who had supplied the aircraft." In the near future, such training programs were intensified. Foreign officers became a common sight at U.S. forts, ports, and air bases.

Reverting to one of his constant themes, Lansdale wrote, "The crying needs [in Southeast Asia] are stable governments, technical and managerial skills, and capital for [industrial] plants and tools . . . . [O]ur policy should be designed to emphasize the pump priming kind of assistance which would enable these nations to do for themselves . . . . This will require Americans of unusual ability, and patience."

Lansdale put his finger on another problem he had seen. "[W]e encountered evidence that our aid to a country was construed as insufficient because a larger amount had been given to some other country. . . . [T]he inevitable consequence will be to make our aid a growing source of envy and recrimination among recipient nations. . . . [W]e are failing to make it plain that our *purpose* . . . is not as a reward, or to buy with money what we cannot do with our political principles, but as mutual security." That, Lansdale believed, was the goal and it remained far distant.[72]

After the long journey, Lansdale was tired. In mid-March 1959 he wrote to friends, "I'm still trying to get untangled from the trip and all its angles." One problem had been resolved. "Dillon Anderson and I finally wound up as friends back in Washington."[73] There was other good news for Lansdale. A friend wrote from Vietnam that Diem was very pleased with the preliminary report of the Draper Commission. "He credits you, as he should, with these developments, and he wants you to know this!"[74] An officemate also scribbled Lansdale a note and attached a letter to it. "I thought you would be interested in seeing this handsome letter . . . commenting on your report on civic activities of the military in Southeast Asia."[75]

One of those "handsome letters" was written by Karl Harr to John N. "Jack" Irwin II, assistant secretary of defense. Harr was pleased with Lansdale's report and told Irwin, "Like the Roman legionary in his heyday, the soldiers of the underdeveloped countries can and should be used for community construction projects . . . . Failure to so use them would mean sterilizing resources which are badly needed . . . . Perhaps Defense can outline a general program of civic action . . . . for use by U.S. MAAG and mission chiefs, and by local government authorities."[76] That was high praise indeed, particularly when Lansdale learned that Irwin agreed and had forwarded a copy of his report to the Operations Coordinating Board, recommending that "the concepts applied in Southeast Asia can be adapted to other areas of the world."[77]

To continue his and Diem's running amusement over their 1956 vacation on the beach at Long Hai, Lansdale had stopped at the post exchange in Hawaii on the Anderson subcommittee trip and had purchased swimming trunks as a humorous gift for Ngo Dinh Diem. He wrote to Diem in April: "This is a gray, rainy day in Washington, which makes me feel like finding my swim trunks . . . and flying out to have that postponed swim with you at Long Hai. . . . It was really grand to have had a chance to visit with you and to see . . . continuing progress that has been made under your guidance."[78]

Such "progress" as Lansdale may have observed did not last long. By 1960 the Viet Cong controlled half the country by day, more by night. Government repression of its own citizens stalked the land. Opposition politicians planned coups. Even worse, recommendations by the full Draper Commission marked the beginning of massive military assistance programs in the Pacific. They allowed burgeoning American bureaucracies to build self-interested empires in Southeast Asia that called for ever-increasing numbers of civilian and military advisers. They ultimately led to armed American intervention in Vietnam and the national destabilization of the entire region from Thailand through Laos and Cambodia and into South Vietnam. Lansdale's interest in military civic action must have been sore-burdened as he saw his beloved Orient tumble into the abyss of holocaust.

Although Lansdale thought about problems in Southeast Asia, he did not have time to dwell on them. There was a new problem confronting the Eisenhower administration into which he was drawn shortly after his return from his tour with the Anderson subcommittee. It had been years in the making.

For some time Cuban politics had been in ferment and the government

1. Harry and Sarah Frances Lansdale
with their dog, Bruno, on the shore of
Lake Michigan, about 1910.

2. Ed Lansdale as a toddler, about 1910.

3. The Lansdale brothers—from left to right, Ed, Phil, and Ben—with
Bruno at Halloween time, about 1914.

4   5

4. Edward Lansdale at twenty-one, a newly commissioned second lieutenant in the Reserve Officers Training Corps (ROTC) program at UCLA.

5. Helen Batcheller, Edward Lansdale's fiancée, a year before they were
married in 1932.

6. A watercolor Lansdale painted in New York City in 1932. For several
years he was tempted to enter the field of commercial art.

7. Lansdale's self-portrait caricature drawn in the Philippines. He used to
brush off questions about his function by saying that he was a feather
merchant.

6

7

8. Lansdale and Patrocinio "Pat" Yapcinco Kelly on a trip to the Lingayen area of Luzon in 1946. Pat, whom Ed would much later marry, helped get him introductions to rebels in the Hukbo ng Bayan Laban Sa Hapon, or Huk, movement.

9. Lieutenant Colonel Edward Lansdale in conversation with Philippine Secretary of Defense Ramón Magsaysay in January 1951.

10. A rare photo, taken about 1953, of Lansdale's longtime friend and companion Charles T. R. Bohannan (left) with Ramón Magsaysay and Frank Wisner, CIA's Deputy Director for Plans. Bohannan had an aversion to having his picture taken and habitually turned away just as the shutter snapped.

11. Lansdale, his gaze intently focused, dressed in mufti in the Philippines in 1951.

12. Lansdale after one of his psywar victories against Filipino Huks in 1952.

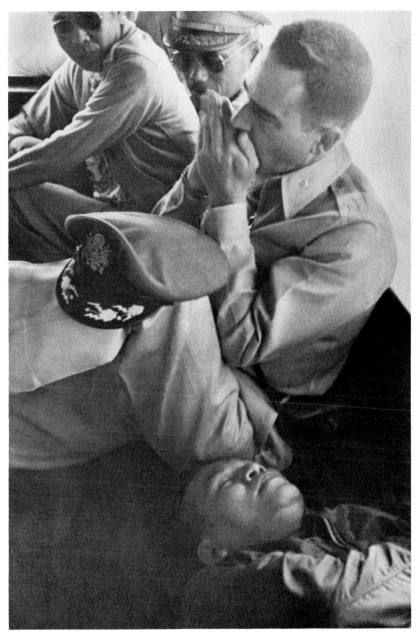

13. Waiting for the Philippine presidential election results aboard a U.S. Navy yacht in 1953. Magsaysay slept and Lansdale played the harmonica.

14. A group of young Huk rebels caught by the camera in 1954.

15. Luis Taruc, El Supremo, head of the Huk military forces (in cap), when he met with Benigno "Ninoy" Aquino in 1954. Aquino, then a newspaperman, was trying to persuade Taruc to surrender.

16. Part of the immense crowd that gathered to watch Magsaysay inaugurated as president in 1953. Lansdale (center) has made himself, characteristically, just another face in the bleachers, alone, observing rather than speaking.

17. Lansdale cooling off in a waterhole.

18. Lansdale helping to repair a wind-damaged structure in Vietnam in 1965.

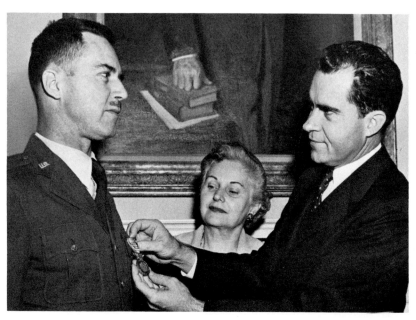

19. Colonel Edward Lansdale being decorated for his 1954–1956 work in Vietnam by Vice President Richard Nixon while Mrs. Helen Lansdale looks on.

20. Lansdale's Senior Liaison Mission headquarters at 194 Cong Ly Street, Saigon.

21. Lucien Conein and Joseph Baker, Lansdale teammates in Vietnam, relaxing.

22. Lansdale, South Vietnamese official Tran Quoc Buu, and reporter Robert Shaplen in a discussion at 194 Cong Ly Street.

23. Richard Nixon on an unofficial visit to Saigon talking with Major General Nguyen Duc Thang, Minister for Pacification, and Lansdale.

24. Ambassador Henry Cabot Lodge and Lansdale shaking hands despite their deep differences of opinion on Vietnam.

25. A reunion of the four Lansdale brothers—from left to right, Ben, Ed, Phil, and David—in Corona del Mar, California, on 15 August 1974.

26. Mrs. Pat Lansdale at home in McLean, Virginia, in 1984.

27. The Lansdale home in McLean. Lansdale flew the flag every day when he was in residence.

28. Lansdale talking to two young ROTC cadets after his lecture at the University of South Florida, 29 November 1985.

29. Lansdale on a February 1986 visit to Florida, shown with the author and his wife, Laura Gene Currey.

30. Edward Geary Lansdale as he looked in his final days.

31. General Edward Lansdale's funeral at Arlington National Cemetery, 27 February 1987.

of dictator Fulgencio Batista — which the United States supported — did not sit on nearly so firm a foundation as its leaders claimed. Batista's ultimate nemesis was a young Cuban, Fidel Castro-Ruz, born in Oriente province in 1926. Following his graduation from law school in 1950, Castro turned to politics. Disillusioned by a failure of the Batista government to effect needed reforms by constitutional means, Castro began talking about revolution. Following an abortive coup against Batista on 26 July 1953, Castro fled into the Sierra Maestra along with his brother Raúl, Ernesto "Che" Guevara, and ten other survivors. From those wilderness fastnesses, increasing numbers of Castro revolutionaries challenged Batista's right to rule, an effort that finally brought Fidel to power in a triumphal march on Havana. His forces entered the city and took control on 1 January 1959, just a few days before Edward Lansdale left for Southeast Asia.

Many Latin Americans regarded the charismatic Cuban as a hero. In Caracas, Venezuela, in 1959, Castro received a victor's parade, cheered by thronging crowds as he rode through the city in an open truck. His popularity soared everywhere throughout the region, except among CIA observers assigned to Central American postings. Reports filtered back to Langley AFB and onto the desk of Colonel J. C. King, chief of the Western Hemisphere division, warning that Fidel Castro would eventually cause the United States a great deal of trouble. King held a meeting in his office on 18 January 1960 to assess this new threat. Those who gathered discussed possibilities and the most favored option seemed to be to work through a Cuban underground to set up an internal counterrevolution. CIA had done that in Guatemala in 1954; a coup a week later unseated the government.[79] King recommended to Allen Dulles that he give consideration to eliminating Castro.

Richard Mervin Bissell, Jr., CIA's deputy director for plans, read King's memo and added his concurrence. Such views persuaded Dulles, who sought out Eisenhower and spoke with him about ways of limiting Cuban adventurism in Latin America. They agreed that something more than sabotage should be considered and Eisenhower finally told Dulles that CIA should come up with a program outlining possible courses of action. All that followed grew out of that meeting. Eisenhower, and Kennedy after him, gave little thought to ways of bringing about an accommodation between the governments of the United States and Cuba. Administration efforts under two presidents were aimed solely at isolating, weakening, toppling, and destroying Castro's regime.[80]

CIA completed its policy study on Cuba in early March 1960 and submitted its report, "A Program of Covert Action Against the Castro Regime," for consideration by the Operations Coordinating Board (OCB) of the United States Intelligence Board.[81] By virtue of his role in the Office of Special Operations of the secretary of defense, Lansdale regularly attended OCB meetings, which members referred to as the Special Group. The board members studied the CIA plan that called for establishing a Cuban government in exile, mounting an extensive propaganda effort against the Castro regime, creating and supporting a special covert action and intelligence group within Cuba, forming an outside paramilitary unit for guerrilla hit-and-run raids against the island nation, and establishing an air supply outfit in support of these activities in some nearby country under cover of a commercial airline. CIA claimed that all this could be accomplished in six to eight months.[82] Special Group accepted the plan and forwarded it to Eisenhower.

The president approved CIA's plan on 17 March 1960 and gave his permission for the Agency to use department of defense personnel and equipment in support of its project but forbade any insertion of American troops in a combat status. Despite his initial enthusiasm, Eisenhower did not provide operating funds until late summer when, on 18 August, he approved a $13 million budget for CIA to draw on.[83]

CIA selected a strange duo to spearhead its effort. The first was Gerry Droller, who had worked behind the lines in France for OSS during World War II. More recently a Swiss desk officer, he was abysmally ignorant about Latin America. The other man was E. Howard Hunt, whom Lansdale had met in Mexico City during Magsaysay's visit there. Hunt spoke Spanish and had experience south of the border, but many doubted his ability. One man remarked that Hunt was at least consistent in his judgments; he was "always wrong."[84]

Droller, Hunt, and those they worked with considered many ideas that might embarrass Castro and cause him to lose prestige. All ranged from the weird to the strange. Someone suggested dusting his shoes with thallium salts, a powerful depilatory, so his beard would fall out! (He supposedly had a weak chin, and so, the thesis went, other Latins would laugh at him.) One man advised giving him a gift box of cigars impregnated with TSD — a chemical similar to LSD — so he would get a high while smoking and make foolish judgmental errors. Why not spray his broadcasting studio with a hallucinogen, causing him to make a fool of himself while on the air exhorting the Cuban people? Perhaps it would be possible to dust the inside of his diving suit with a skin contaminant or rig a seashell with an explosive device to be placed in his favorite swimming area in Cuba's coastal waters? Another proposed to inject his cigars with botulism; that might even kill him.[85] Such infantile plans were harbingers of later ones, nearly as harebrained, and cause one to wonder why projects of national importance are ever successful, entrusted as they are to so many people who seem to have lost their grasp on reality.

While these exciting plots were under discussion, Colonel Edward Lansdale received his promotion to brigadier general in April 1960. It was a long-awaited moment. Admirers sent him their compliments. Robert Welch predicted that Lansdale might "soon be the commanding officer of some important division of our Air Force in the event of a military effort against Communism somewhere in the world."[86] Wesley Fishel asked if it were true, "as Walter Winchell hinted when he discussed you in his column the other day, that you are actually having the ceiling of your bedroom papered with stars?"[87] Kenneth T. Young, Jr., who would later serve as ambassador to Thailand, sent his congratulations on Lansdale's star: "I hope it rises over Saigon."[88] To all who sent him greetings, Lansdale replied with a nearly standard handwritten brief note: "Your taking time out to drop me a line on the occasion of my recent promotion is most deeply appreciated. Such thoughtfulness from old friends and associates is, if anything, more heartwarming than the event itself. Thanks for the lift in spirit."[89] At least he was now of sufficient rank so he would no longer have to wear civilian clothes to avoid embarrassing flag rank officers who served him in subordinate positions.

By summer 1960 neither Hunt nor Droller had been able to form a Cuban government-in-exile group strong enough or cohesive enough to challenge Castro. They then shifted their aim to generating military action. While pilots from the Alabama National Guard trained Cubans to fly at bases in Guatemala, CIA recruiters signed up other exiles now living in the United States, promising them that by forming a Cuban brigade of fighting men they could help bring down the Castro government. Through his CIA contacts, Lansdale helped get his old friend Napoleon Valeriano hired to train recruits in the swamps of Florida.[90]

Months slipped away without results. Castro still presided over his nation, still harangued his population about threats from Yankee imperialists in the colossus to the North. He and his people, he warned, would fight to the death against any American effort at armed intervention.

At a meeting of Special Group in November 1960, Undersecretary of State Livingston Merchant asked those present if plans had yet been made for positive action against Castro. General Charles P. Cabell, deputy director of Central Intelligence, responded that no such program yet existed. That situation would soon change.

During the presidential contest of 1960, Vice President Richard M. Nixon attacked his opponent, Senator John F. Kennedy, as "soft on communism." He further exclaimed that his own patience with Castro was at an end. The nation should cut away this cancer to prevent further Soviet penetration of the hemisphere. Although the Eisenhower government was contemplating several courses of action, Nixon promised to launch a total "quarantine" of Cuba if elected. Kennedy's rhetoric was nearly as lurid.[91] He was, of course, no more soft on communism than was his opponent, and he was a prisoner of existing ideas about the cold war. He agreed with Nixon that Castro's government should be overturned; the question during those weeks of the campaign was who could urge intervention in the Caribbean the loudest and most stridently. By the closest vote in the history of American presidential politics, the electorate chose Kennedy over Nixon.

Richard Bissell and Allen Dulles traveled to Palm Beach on 27 November 1960 to brief the president-elect on Cuba. They told him of their plans. An armed assault had been discussed at Langley for weeks and plans were well under way. There would be an over-the-beach landing on the island by some 600–750 men who would be supported by air strikes. Forgotten were suggestions for the infiltration of agents, guerrilla raids, air drops in support of Cuban insurgents. Incredibly, Dulles had yet to inform Eisenhower, the National Security Council, or Special Group of this plan and did not do so until two days after he met with Kennedy. Kennedy gave his approval.[92]

For armed intervention to have any chance of success, CIA needed help from the Department of Defense. Richard Bissell named Colonel Stanley W. Beerli as his liaison with Defense and Beerli soon learned that the Pentagon could be uncooperative. Beerli complained that Defense "put a price tag on everything." He had to fight "for every damn airplane, everything we wanted, every bit of the way."

The culprit was Edward Lansdale, who was trying to limit CIA's military adventurism. His influence was such that many in other offices came to share his pessimism and cooperated only slowly, if at all, with Agency requests. At one point Beerli asked for twenty-seven sergeants from Special Forces to serve as training advisers to the Cuban brigade. The Army refused to release them. CIA was forced to appeal the matter all the way to Eisenhower. Even then, Secretary of the Army Wilbur Brucker delayed as long as he could, insisting that presidential authorization allowing CIA to ask for help did not have the same force as an order from the president directing him to comply. CIA had to make a second appeal to Eisenhower. While Brucker dallied, General Lansdale went to the office of James H. Douglas, undersecretary of defense, to brief him on the sergeant's issue. During their conversation, Lansdale told Douglas of CIA plans for an over-the-beach invasion of Cuba.

Such a plan was foolhardy, Lansdale said. A force of seven hundred men could not launch a successful invasion. Three times that many would be needed, supported by additional elements and backed by much more detailed plans. Douglas was convinced: He told Lansdale he would recommend releasing the twenty-seven sergeants but at the same time would let the president know that "the Defense Department in no way approved the plan or the general feasibility of such a plan."

When next he met with Eisenhower and Allen Dulles, Douglas spoke with them about the sergeants and then added his view of the proposed invasion of Cuba. He spoke, he said, for the Department of Defense. The project was impractical and he disassociated Defense in order "to avoid any misunderstanding that making Army training personnel available to the CIA in any way implied approval of the project." He added that "there was never in my mind a present proposal [from CIA] to be taken seriously." He concluded that his boss, Thomas S. Gates, the secretary of defense, was in agreement with him.[93]

When Gates spoke with Eisenhower, he backed Douglas' position. The number of troops was "wholly inadequate." Nor was there anyone within the exile group charismatic enough to have "national appeal" to Cubans — even disaffected members of the island population. In short, he believed that anyone with the wit of a marmoset would back away from CIA's proposed invasion. President Eisenhower listened and concluded only that there ought to be better coordination on the project between CIA, State, and Defense.[94]

The president's refusal to abandon the project so infuriated Lansdale that, in a December meeting of Special Group, he spoke out heatedly against CIA's plan. As he began speaking, Dulles interrupted him. "You're not a principal in this!" Dulles said sharply. Douglas, who shared Lansdale's misgivings, defended his right to speak. Lansdale had given him a "good education" on the project's weaknesses, Douglas said, and Lansdale now wanted to go on record with his fears so the incoming Kennedy administration would not receive the impression that "this tentative CIA project" was "something that had been approved" by Eisenhower's Defense Department. Douglas asked those at the special meeting to allow General Lansdale to continue his remarks.

Lansdale commented that "in policy meetings, you have got to be very honest. You should have talk."[95] He reminded those present how the entire plan had begun. "Initially there was thought of doing what Castro had done, go up in the hills, get some people — including some who had been with him — to fight the Castro government. I went [along] with that." Yet now CIA pressed for an across-the-beach operation. "You can't do that in a country where the Army is as alert [as it is in Cuba]. We are going to get clobbered!" He spoke of CIA's expectations that Cubans would rise in revolt against Castro upon learning of the return of those exiles who had fled. Such a hope was an empty one; at the very least, insufficient facts existed to warrant basing an invasion on it. Castro held power firmly. Even as they spoke, the Cuban leader was imprisoning and executing opponents with impunity. "What's the political base for what you're going to do?" Lansdale asked Dulles. "How popular is it going to be?"

Lansdale paused for breath. "You are doing this from the wrong end," he continued. "You want to do a military operation without the where-withal to do it successfully." Lansdale knew the seriousness of the moment. He had long been close to Dulles and once had been a protégé. Dulles had supported most of his efforts in the Philippines and in Vietnam. Now they were in completely opposite camps. "CIA shouldn't ever do a military operation," Lansdale added, refusing to buckle under Dulles' glare. "A political revolution? Yes. Going up in the hills [of Cuba] again? Yes. That is your bill of goods." Adamant in his resistance, Lansdale was finally finished. He sat back in his chair, convinced that CIA was incapable of achieving its proposed objective against Cuba.

After the meeting broke up, Dulles spent a few minutes talking with Lansdale. He asked, as a favor for past efforts, that Lansdale be more discreet about any future objections he might have. At this point Lansdale was unwilling to rely on discretion.[96] Instead he was beginning to fear for his own career. "I decided to go out and visit Vietnam again. I wanted to be thousands of miles away" when CIA launched its brigade of exiles against the sandy beaches of Cuba.[97]

10

SWALLOWS AND PIGS

GENERAL EDWARD G. LANSDALE was convinced that CIA's idea for an invasion of Cuba was flawed both in conception and in planning. It would be a disaster. He had done his best, without much success, to present his views in top-level planning sessions. In his insistence, he had even crossed swords with the powerful director of Central Intelligence, Allen Dulles. Now it was time for him to back off and protect his flanks.

Shortly after his confrontation with Dulles, Lansdale sought out the man for whom he worked most directly, James H. Douglas, undersecretary of defense. Lansdale liked Douglas, describing him as "one of the most decent men I have ever known." Bearding Douglas in his office, Lansdale asked for a favor. "I see disaster ahead. I feel in my bones that something is going to go wrong. You heard my first reaction! It's still the same. I don't want any hand in this. Afterward they are going to be looking for scapegoats. . . . and I'm sure they'll . . . say I was to blame. If I'm out of the country . . . it will be very hard for them to blame me." Lansdale told Douglas that he would like to visit Vietnam and take a good hard look at its situation. "Conditions are getting worse out there. I'm concerned. Let me go and . . . spend several weeks." Douglas agreed to support an official request from Lansdale to make a brief inspection trip to Vietnam.[1]

Lansdale's wish to take a trip to Southeast Asia was not as sudden a whim as he indicated. The year before, Ngo Dinh Diem had asked President Eisenhower to allow Lansdale to visit Vietnam and he had enlarged on Diem's invitation. He worked up an itinerary that would take him — as a newly promoted brigadier general — through many nations of the Orient: the Philippines, Vietnam, Cambodia, Laos, Thailand, and perhaps others. When State learned from Douglas that Lansdale wanted to visit the Pacific area, it sent a circular telegram to a number of posts: Manila, Saigon, Bangkok, Phnom Penh, Vientiane City, and Rangoon, querying them whether they would welcome a visit by Lansdale. Only the Saigon embassy responded favorably.

When the undersecretary next saw Lansdale, he had a strange look on his face. "What's [the problem] between you and the people over at State?" he asked Lansdale. "They're acting . . . funny about your going over to visit Vietnam." Aware that such a reaction might be forthcoming, Lansdale was prepared and attempted to pass off any objections. "They have all sorts of romantic ideas [about me]," he replied. "Don't pay any attention to them."[2] Yet it was impossible for either Douglas or Lansdale to ignore State's hesitancy, which was based on lengthy objections cabled from ambassadors in the field to Washington.

Ambassador William Trimble cabled the secretary of state from Phnom Penh. He and his staff strongly urged "that General Lansdale not (repeat not) visit Cambodia." Host nation officials, Trimble insisted, strongly suspected Lansdale's involvement in the "Bangkok plots in late 1958 which they consider as precursor to Dap Chhuon uprising in February 1959." Local newspapers, Trimble reported, including *Agence Khmere de Presse,* identified Lansdale as a key figure and Southeast Asian expert in "special services" — diplomatese for CIA — and any visit by him to Cambodia "would undoubted[ly] be linked by them to some similar type US intervention in Laos and revive their suspicions of him and of us."[3]

Ambassador U. Alexis Johnson was a little more positive, but still cautious. Cabling from Bangkok, he said to the secretary of state, "While I of course well and favorably know General Lansdale and he has in past been very helpful, difficult to give [Thai] reaction [to] proposed travel without some better idea of objectives. Am willing [to] leave decision to [State] Department."[4]

Rothwell H. Brown sent a seven-page cable from Vientiane, Laos. While he would be pleased for Lansdale to visit, the trip should be made as discreetly as possible. Three days later, Brown sent a one-page addendum. "Though perfectly glad have General Lansdale visit here briefly in civilian clothes, would not wish press for his visit this region in view attitude expressed reference telegram."[5]

The attitude at the American embassy in Manila was distinctly hostile. An embassy official named Hickerson stated, "Although national elections still one year off . . . . I believe we should not give them any grounds for accusing us, even falsely, of playing any role in these activities. Visit by General Lansdale at this time would raise questions . . . and would be interpreted by many as evidence of our direct involvement [in] their present political campaign. . . . I would recommend therefore that if trip is undertaken, General Lansdale by-pass the Philippines."[6]

Only Saigon seemed to welcome a visit by Lansdale. Ambassador Elbridge Durbrow indicated his belief that Lansdale was one of a handful of Americans who could talk privately and freely with Ngo Dinh Diem, and any information Lansdale might pick up as a result could be used profitably.[7]

J. Graham Parsons, an assistant secretary of state who would later do all he could to block Lansdale from a role in American policy toward Vietnam, wrote to Lansdale about the flurry of hostile embassy reactions. "I am sorry it does not seem feasible for you to visit other posts but I feel a quiet visit to Saigon alone would be well worth the trip."[8]

Lansdale was grievously disappointed. He had planned a grand tour of the Orient as a flag officer and expert in Southeast Asian affairs. Now he was spurned by the very region in which he had spent so much time. The furor caused Lansdale to downscale his trip from a lengthy one lasting many weeks to twelve days in Vietnam — and he was lucky to get even that, for now the military began trying to modify his plans. Admiral Harry D. Felt, CINCPAC, was also opposed to Lansdale's appearing in his command. Another Navy flag officer, retired Admiral Felix B. Stump, tried to placate Felt. "Lansdale can do no harm and has a possibility of doing a great deal of good," Stump wrote to Felt. "Diem likes Lansdale, trusts him, and, I believe will listen to him, knowing that he will speak frankly and honestly. . . . President Magsaysay trusted him completely . . . . He is absolutely loyal, honest, and discreet."[9]

Felt reluctantly agreed but wanted Lansdale to understand the ground rules. He fired off a personal cable to the lowly new brigadier. "It appears," Felt sternly commented, "that we are not quite in tune as to the purpose of your trip to Viet-Nam." He was not to go for the primary purpose of getting information on the state of affairs in the Vietnamese countryside or even to sound the waters in the capital with Ngo Dinh Diem.

"I think we have adequate info in that field," Felt continued. To the contrary, Felt wanted Lansdale in Vietnam for only one reason. The admiral had drawn up his own plan for furthering American objectives in Vietnam; it was a "national plan" that had been "approved by all WASHDC agencies and which AMB DURBROW has been trying to get DIEM to do." Lansdale was to review the plan, learn it well, and realize that his mission was solely one of "furthering the objectives of that plan." He was to work on Diem, persuading him "to do things that are distasteful although essential to save his country." Felt then drew his bottom line. "If this is impossible then I would not favor a quick trip." With the United States already beginning its headlong plunge into the quagmire of Vietnam, CINCPAC arrogantly insisted that America had all the information it needed to set things right. Not additional knowledge, but syco-phantic support for Felt's ideas was needed. "I have a plan," he seemed to say. "Either support it with Diem or don't come at all."[10]

Upon receiving Felt's *diktat,* an angry Lansdale turned for support to James Douglas. On 14 December 1960, he queried his boss. In view of Admiral Felt's comments, he believed it was necessary to have the reason for his trip clarified for all concerned. "My own understanding was that I would go . . . for you and Secretary [of Defense Thomas S.] Gates, with the concurrence of Allen Dulles and of State Department officials." He had two goals: to make full use of the personal confidence Diem had in him so as to learn the facts, problems, and possible answers in Vietnam *as President Diem saw them,* and to promote Vietnamese-American teamwork. Lansdale believed it was essential to have Douglas' concurrence on both points. Since he could not make his grand tour, Lansdale wanted all parties involved — State, CIA, and Defense — to be painfully aware that he was not just another lowly general whom CINCPAC or embassies could order around but was traveling in his official capacity as deputy assistant for special operations to the secretary of defense.[11] That assurance was finally given to all interested parties.

Lansdale sighed to General O'Daniel about the conditions set on his visit: to wear civilian clothes, not to disturb the quiet existence of ambassadors anywhere, to work closely with Durbrow, not to stay too long, to keep his nose clean, and to come home promptly. "I resent being treated as a second-class citizen," he complained.[12] Lansdale also sent a message to General Lionel McGarr, MAAG chief in Saigon, that continued last-minute demands by State might delay his arrival.[13]

Others faced with such unpromising attitudes might have given up. Lansdale insisted on making the trip. He finally left Washington on a Thursday four days after Christmas, and did not return until 18 January 1961 just prior to the inauguration of the new Democratic president, John Fitzgerald Kennedy. He was in Vietnam from 2–14 January. Linguist Joe Redick accompanied him, borrowed from his CIA duties elsewhere. In the cargo compartment of Pan American flight 817, which carried Lansdale west, was a gift for Ngo Dinh Diem from the United States government — a huge desk on the base of which was a brass plate inscribed "To Ngo Dinh Diem: The Father of His Country."[14]

Lansdale traveled under severe restrictions. Although his airplane was scheduled to make a service stop in Manila, he was not to leave the terminal or to use the telephone to call friends while he waited to reboard. As anyone could have predicted who knew Lansdale, it did not work out quite that way. After Lansdale was safely airborne again, an angry Hickerson cabled the secretary of state complaining about Lansdale's patent disregard for orders. When the plane landed, the unhappy foreign service officer sniffed, Lansdale was met by "close friends" from former days who "whisked [him] out of the airport," a privilege "not normally accorded transient passengers." He was not seen again for several hours until he returned, still accompanied by friends who partied with him in the terminal until time for the plane to depart. The whole episode, Hickerson said accusingly, was obviously well planned. Several Manila newspapers carried stories about the return of the Ugly American, articles then reprinted by other journals around the rim of the Pacific basin.[15]

William Trimble, frantic and distraught, cabled the Department of State from Phnom Penh that "[a]ll local media reported Jan 4 & 5 [the story of the] incognito arrival of General Lansdale in manilla [*sic*], based on AFP dispatch . . . as 'US subversion agent en route to Laos.'" Those stories speculated that he was on an official mission to Laos to evaluate the political situation and recommend to the government necessary actions to be taken. One newspaper, Trimble said, carried a long front page editorial condemning the United States and expressing deep apprehension at Lansdale's arrival in Southeast Asia. He predicted that other newspapers would print similar articles. Trimble complained that "this augurs badly for future of Laos . . . his arrival cannot leave Cambodians indifferent." Trimble self-righteously recalled that he had earlier predicted just such a reaction and he urged State "in strongest terms" to ensure that "Lansdale not visit Cambodia."[16]

Lansdale normally preferred to ignore such carping criticism, yet he knew the incident would raise eyebrows in Washington. How he must have regretted the publication of the books by Greene and Lederer and Burdick that had destroyed his anonymity! When he arrived in Saigon Lansdale prepared an explanatory note for General Erskine (who had recently returned to duty) and sent it off to Washington with an information copy for Admiral Felt. His explanation was calm and understated. Recognized by officials at the airport, he was invited by them to have coffee in an office inside the terminal. Someone called old friends, who in turn telephoned others, and a group descended on the airport. Included among the visitors were a number of Philippine officials "from practically all political elements, including some from Malacanang Palace and opposition." Since it was breakfast time, many brought their wives and children. Ambassador Durbrow sent along a message of his own. Those who visited Lansdale at the terminal "urged he stay" in the Philippines. The conversation was social, not political, and upon his departure, reporters did not seek an interview, contenting themselves with taking pictures of the festive group. The explanation may have been good, but it was not so persuasive that State or Defense was willing to allow anything like it to happen on his return trip. Lansdale was told to route his return through Hong Kong and Tokyo to avoid any further disturbing experiences at Manila.[17]

Lansdale realized that time was his enemy. He could spend all of the next days working up explanations for the incident in Manila or he could put alibis behind him and concentrate on what he could learn from the leaders and people of Vietnam that might benefit both them and the U.S. government. There was much to absorb. Conditions had changed in the years he had been away. It became apparent to him that American officials in Vietnam believed he was there on behalf of the incoming Kennedy administration and wanted to impress him properly with their achievements. One of the first men he wanted to see was his CIA contact, William Colby, station chief in Saigon for the Agency. Reassigned from duties in Italy during Tet in 1959, Colby and Lansdale knew one another slightly. Lansdale had seen him a number of times in Washington and was impressed. Colby appreciated Lansdale's "fertile imagination" and "deep knowledge of Southeast Asia."[18] Their relationship was almost a mutual admiration society.

CIA headquarters was suspicious that Lansdale's mission represented a move by the Defense Department to assume authority over the Agency's activities and notified Colby accordingly. Colby had also heard that Lansdale was about to be named as Kennedy's ambassador to Vietnam and consequently treated him with "kid gloves." Lansdale's attitude persuaded Colby that he was "a little dubious about the CIA role" in Vietnam, so the station chief did his best to convince Lansdale that "some of our experiments were in the right direction."

Colby was not pleased with the results of his first effort, a dinner briefing for Lansdale that was also attended by the senior station officers. Colby explained the situation in Vietnam and described Agency programs there. The evening, Colby felt, "was a shambles." Lansdale acted as if he was being subjected to a "shell game" and Colby fretted because Lansdale "said hardly a word during the whole evening." Later sessions were more fruitful. "I wanted to just present our case and then let him make up his own mind."

Ultimately Colby was satisfied. The visitor from Washington's corridors of power "came away with the conclusion that I hoped he would: that the conflict was essentially a guerrilla war and that the military approach was not the answer." It would have been easier on Colby's nerves had he simply asked Lansdale for his views on first meeting him. He would not have had to play so many games. For Colby to take credit for Lansdale's view is much like a minister who preaches to his church choir; they are already among the converted. Lansdale had long been convinced that military responses were not adequate to meet the threat of a people's war. He later smiled about those encounters. "When I wrote my report, he was amazed to see that was what I was mostly concerned about."[19]

Lansdale came to understand Vietnam's gloomy prospects. In March 1960, the Viet Cong People's Liberation party had organized its action arm — the National Liberation Front (NLF) — created as a delayed response to the South's cancellation of the long-scheduled national reunification election. In September 1960, Ho Chi Minh promised to help provide the NLF with military equipment and advice and to send troops south from the People's Army of Vietnam (PAVN). The activities of the NLF became nastier and more frequent. Action teams killed perhaps six village chiefs daily, planted booby traps and mines by the thousands on paths and roads, terrorized villagers, and burned hamlets. Lansdale wanted to determine a proper response he could recommend to Diem.[20]

In his efforts to see all that he could, General Lansdale asked Diem for the loan of a helicopter. "Where are you going?" the president asked him. Lansdale wanted to go wherever the spirit led him and to travel without an entourage — American or Vietnamese — so his reply was curt. "I'll tell the pilot." Diem persisted. "What are you going to look at?" Lansdale could only shrug. "I want to see what this war's all about [that] you started. I don't think you're fighting it right." Diem remained unsatisfied and stubborn. "Where?" he demanded. "I don't know!" said Lansdale. "I'll make up my mind and tell the pilot when we're in the air. Just have a lot of gas in the helicopter." Diem threw up his hands and reluctantly agreed after Lansdale promised to take Vietnam's secretary of state, Nguyen Dinh Thuan, along with him. Redick accompanied them as translator. Diem even sent sandwiches along in case they became hungry.[21]

The diminutive president had good reason to be testy. A coup attempt the previous 11 November began at three o'clock in the morning when enemies fired machine gun rounds into his bedroom while he slept. The episode made Diem paranoid about political opponents and suspicious also of senior American officials, particularly Elbridge Durbrow. Friction between them became more evident. As Lansdale later tried to explain, "most folk . . . fail to realize that Diem is human and doesn't like the idea of people trying to kill him."[22]

On his helicopter flight over the Vietnamese countryside, Lansdale directed the pilot toward the Camau peninsula and the community of Binh Hung. The leader there was Father Nguyen Loc Hoa, a refugee from China who had been a colonel in Chiang Kai-shek's Nationalist Army before becoming a priest. In 1950 he shepherded two thousand Christian refugees from Communist China into North Vietnam. Finding themselves endangered by the war the French were fighting against the

Viet Minh, the discouraged wanderers moved on to Cambodia and lived there for seven years. When Cambodia recognized Mao's communist government in China in 1958, some of Father Hoa's flock fled to Formosa. The remaining 375 followed their leader into South Vietnam in 1959.

Although he allowed them entry, Diem did not deal too kindly with Father Hoa and his people. The land he gave them, some distance from any provincial town, was a swampy plain on the Camau peninsula infested by Viet Cong. The refugees settled in and built a community. Under the priest's watchful eye, his people laboriously dug mud from the swamp to make platforms on which they built huts. Eventually they created a square village divided by a sluggish canal. They planted rice and tended chickens and pigs they had brought from Cambodia. President Diem then gave them a special district surrounding the town to administer and defend. It was called Hai Yen, or "sea swallows." In Vietnam the swallow was known as a "guest" bird, so this was a poetic way of naming the Chinese refugees as guests in Vietnam. The Hai Yen villagers picked up the name and called themselves the Sea Swallows. Unarmed members of the community at first beat back Viet Cong (VC) attacks with farm tools. They slowly captured an assortment of odd rifles for which they made their own cartridges.

On the day Lansdale and his party arrived at Binh Hung, villagers were just returning from battle with a roving VC band. Ambushed along a canal, villagers had overwhelmed their attackers and sent them fleeing. As the helicopter landed, they returned home carrying their wounded. Lansdale told the pilot to use the machine to ferry wounded to a provincial hospital.

Lansdale stayed overnight and became friendly with Father Hoa, who invited him to attend midnight mass. People gathered at the chapel, its bells were rung, and lights turned on. "We do that for a reason," Father Hoa explained. "The VC are out there. I want to call their attention to us." During the service Lansdale heard mortar rounds exploding in the near distance. He questioned the priest as soon as mass ended. "We have scouts out," Father Hoa explained. "We turn on the lights and ring the bells to get the VC to come and attack us. We've numbered our maps with the coordinates of all the routes they might use, ranges and elevations. As soon as the scouts signal that VC are on the way in, the mortar crews open up." Sea Swallows bakers served as mortar crews and that night needed to fire only ten rounds to disperse the attackers.

Lansdale was impressed at the efficiency of the village's defense network and amused at the priest's clothing. "Never let an officer of the church see you," he told Father Hoa. "You look like a sergeant. You've got on your cassock, around that a web ammo belt with two holstered forty-fives, and you're carrying an automatic weapon!'' Father Hoa looked at him with his direct gaze. "You don't think I should dress this way? We're usually fighting every day. We've got to get respect from the other side.''[23]

As Lansdale's helicopter rose into the sky the following day, he saw villagers below saluting him; their hands formed into the three-fingered Boy Scout gesture of respect. He waved back as they disappeared in the distance. On his way back to Saigon Lansdale mused about the Sea Swallow community. He was glad to find that at least in one part of Vietnam people understood how to wage a people's war.

One incident in the Delta country saddened him. He saw a Vietnamese artillery battery firing on nearby villages suspected of harboring VC sympathizers. "In a people's war you never make war against your own people!'' he exclaimed. Rushing up to the battery commander he insisted that the tube crews be given "check fire'' orders. The officer was highly incensed at this occidental stranger's interference. Lansdale thought the man might even have tried to shoot him, but fortunately Nguyen Dinh Thuan was along and talked him out of it.[24]

In the days remaining on his abbreviated tour, General Lansdale visited as widely as possible. He spoke with Diem's vice president, Nguyen Ngoc Tho, who told him that Diem was "terrible.'' Lansdale learned that Tho and Diem had no contact with each other, so he urged the president to invite the man for dinner. "I saw them after dinner — the two were beaming and Tho was happy as a lark.''[25] He also spoke with disgruntled members of the president's administration, with officials of various political parties, and with several members of the National Assembly. All of them eagerly told Lansdale their criticisms of Diem. He brought them up short when he asked what their own program was, other than to seize power for themselves or to have him "pat them on the head'' for being critics. "Few of them,'' he thought, "had any sensible ideas.'' Lansdale softly suggested that some might consider them as acting in disloyal or treasonous ways "in a time of great national danger.''[26]

Lansdale noticed one very real difference in his relationship with Diem. It was the first time he could ever recall that brother Nhu sat with them while they were talking in personal confidence about matters of mutual concern. Nhu would sometimes answer the questions Lansdale put to Diem. More than once, Lansdale explained, "I am talking to your brother, not to you. I asked Diem what *he* thought.'' And Nhu kept supplying answers for his brother, who nodded in agreement. It was, Lansdale felt, an evil portent.[27]

It was soon time for Lansdale to return home. Depressed, he had seen little in Vietnam to give him any hope for its future. He now firmly believed that unless there was a radical change in thinking by both Vietnamese and American officials, any efforts by the United States to limit or destroy Viet Cong activity in the South were doomed to failure. On the plane ride from Saigon to Hawaii through Hong Kong and Tokyo, he jotted notes for his official report. He sensed that the American military machine was gearing up to fight a conventional war using textbook tactics for opposing Soviet massed armies. In his mind, it should have been preparing for guerrilla warfare.

When the plane reached Hawaii, Admiral Felt ordered Lansdale to remain in Honolulu briefly. Still miffed over Lansdale's ability to go over his head to insist on his own independence, Felt now felt safe to assert his own authority. "You're going to write your report here and let me see it before it goes to Washington," he ordered. "All right," Lansdale replied. "Give me a place to do it." He completed his report, with a copy for Felt, in one of the CINCPAC offices.[28]

Lansdale's conclusions, written before his return to Washington, had a doomsday ring to them. Like a funeral bell tolling the death of a loved one, so also did his report sound the beginning of a threnody for the Diem regime. The Viet Cong were much closer to their objective than he had realized from reading sterile reports in his Pentagon office. The Saigon government would be hard-pressed to do more than postpone eventual defeat. Unless they changed their entire approach, U.S. personnel in Vietnam would be unable to help with any effectiveness. Vietnam had progressed faster in material than in spiritual growth, Lansdale lamented. Armed enemies in South Vietnam numbered probably at least fifteen thousand. Viet Cong had infiltrated into even the most productive areas of the South and controlled nearly all of the land save for narrow corridors patrolled and protected by Diem's military forces. Unlike the lay of the land in Malaya or the Philippines, Vietnam's geography did not lend itself to cordoning of its borders to quarantine its political sickness.

Most political opponents of Diem believed the United States would look favorably on a successful coup. All too many Americans in Saigon, consciously or subconsciously, acted as if their efforts were doomed. That need not be, Lansdale lectured in his report. Although it was impossible to mold Ngo Dinh Diem into an Americanized modern version of the ancient Vietnamese leader and hero Le Loi, he still had potential. He had improved over the years. He had a better grasp of economic matters. He was sincere in wanting to delegate some of his daily burden of responsibility. He still had a large personal informant network. He was still honest, still moral, still dedicated, still eager to learn. Diem had not, however, ever managed to control Nhu's excesses with the

Can Lao party and elsewhere, nor had he found a way to provide for adequate land reform or a return to village democracy. There is little clear evidence that these matters were of importance to Diem.

"If the next Americal official to talk with President Diem," Lansdale wrote, "would have the good sense to see him as a human being who has been through a lot of hell for years — and not as an opponent to be beaten to his knees — we would start regaining our influence with him in a healthy way." Lansdale included a comment on their own friendship. "Our meetings [were] like the old days, with plenty of give and take, but only after I convinced him that I still had affection for the Vietnamese people and was trying to understand their problems before sounding off."

Actions could be taken. He set forth recommendations; they were neither sweeping nor grandiose. As he counseled others, so he followed his own advice: his suggestions were "bite-sized" and digestible — goals that could be met with available resources. The United States should treat Vietnam as a combat area of the cold war, an area requiring emergency treatment. A splash of iodine was insufficient. Diem must be supported while a strong executive was groomed who could legally replace him. "We have to show him by deeds, not words alone, that we are his friend," Lansdale insisted. The American government had to select personnel for service in Vietnam who were experienced in dealing with people's wars and who could be sent with appropriate authority to accomplish their tasks. They should know and like Asia and Asians. They must be willing to risk their lives for the ideals of freedom, willing to influence and guide Vietnamese toward U.S. policy objectives out of warm friendship and affection. This must be done even if it required breaking civil service and military assignment rules.

Ambassador Elbridge Durbrow, no longer effective and tired after four years' service in Vietnam, should be transferred immediately, Lansdale continued. His successor should have marked leadership talents and a capability for seeing that his country team functioned harmoniously. He must have a sympathetic understanding of Asians. He must know the tactics of Mao Tse-tung that were used by the Viet Cong in efforts to subvert the South. He who followed Durbrow must be dedicated to practical democratic means, which were the only ones capable of defeating Viet Cong tactics. This description listed what Lansdale believed were his own character and talents. Later in the report he once again described himself. "We need an American in Saigon who can work with real skill, with great sensitivity to Vietnamese feelings, and with a fine sense of the dangerous limits of Vietnamese national security in a time of emergency." There is little doubt whom he meant. It is clear that Lansdale wanted to be named as ambassador to the Diem government.[29]

While Admiral Felt's office clerks were typing and mimeographing his report, Lansdale wrote out another, separate statement of his visit to Father Nguyen Loc Hoa and the refugees of the Sea Swallows village. In Lansdale's eyes, the Sea Swallows' self-help and defense programs on the Camau peninsula were ideal counterinsurgency measures — sadly absent from other areas he visited in Vietnam. Lansdale believed it was crucially important to tell the story of this hamlet. The Sea Swallows community not only was pacified and defensible but had achieved that goal without help from the government. What was special about it? Perhaps it provided the real clue to successful pacification! He called this memorandum "Binh Hung: A Counter-Guerrilla Case Study."

Worn out from his hurried trip, Lansdale returned to Washington on 18 January 1961. He submitted his official report and its accompanying memorandum on Sea Swallows to defense secretaries Thomas Gates and James Douglas, both now in their last two days in office and soon to be replaced by John Kennedy's cabinet appointees. Douglas read it, wrote "Most excellent — should be given top level attention" in the margin. Secretary Gates concurred. He believed Lansdale's words contained wisdom that should not be lost in some administrative crack during the change in regimes. He sought out his replacement, Robert McNamara, and handed him Lansdale's report. McNamara perused it, was impressed, and quickly handed it off to Walt Whitman Rostow, Kennedy's foreign policy adviser, in the White House.

Walt Rostow read Lansdale's report and brought it to President Kennedy's attention. "Look," Kennedy grumbled. "I've only got a half-hour today. Do I have to read it all?" Rostow insisted. The president prided himself on his speed-reading ability and skimmed through the twenty-five-page report and its attached memorandum. He looked at Rostow. "Walt, this is going to be the worst one yet." After a moment of further reflection, he continued. "I'll tell you something. Eisenhower never mentioned the word Vietnam to me." He thought for a while and then added, "Get to work on this, Walt." He also asked for books on guerrilla warfare.[30]

Lansdale's report sharply contrasted with official accounts claiming that Eisenhower's nine hundred American advisers in Vietnam were doing their work well and that the Diem government was effective in its programs. Lansdale described those efforts as lacking in focus, purpose, or courage. Worst of all, they lacked understanding of either insurgency or nation-building. American efforts and prestige were sliding toward disaster. If Lansdale was correct, Kennedy feared that Nguoi Thuong Dan — the common man of Vietnam — might soon come under communist rule, and Lansdale's report had the ring of truth. Kennedy seized on the idea of counterinsurgency without really understanding it. He ordered that counterinsurgency programs be launched in Vietnam, including some forty separate projects of social and military reform. Rostow supported his boss loyally and proclaimed that the war could be won in perhaps eighteen months if only Kennedy's ideas were successfully implemented.[31] The light at the end of the tunnel never burned brighter.

Shortly after Kennedy read Lansdale's report, he telephoned him to urge that the memorandum on Binh Hung's Sea Swallows be published. When Lansdale answered the call he heard a voice with a Harvard accent asking about his visit to the Camau peninsula and Father Hoa. The voice said the memo should be printed in some popular, mass-market journal. Perhaps the *Saturday Evening Post?* Lansdale wondered which of his friends was duping him with an imitation of the president's voice. After his caller hung up, Lansdale phoned the White House and talked with a member of the military staff there. An Army aide informed him that the president had really spoken with him. Bemused by the informality of it all, Lansdale contacted the magazine's editors to persuade them to print his Binh Hung story. It appeared some weeks later, its author listed simply as "an anonymous Air Force officer" and entitled "The Report the President Wanted Published."[32]

Much like marketing a product in a competitive market, Lansdale believed that successful action in a people's war required a competition of images. He was convinced that it was possible to orchestrate images favorable to a national government with the spirit of an exuberant advertising campaign. Image manipulation, based on real and thorough reforms, could stabilize the political position of the Diem regime.[33] Lansdale knew that even the president's enthusiasm was not enough. Kennedy wanted to emphasize counterinsurgency; Lansdale wanted to understand it. It was insufficient simply to kill fanatical guerrillas. What was needed in Vietnam was an intelligent program capable of enlisting the support and sympathy of people, of bettering their lot in life, of forging their loyalty to the Saigon government. To do that would require turning America's attitudes on their heads, and not the administration nor Defense nor State was willing to take such a step.

An example: Lansdale believed America should have fewer advisers with greater authority and responsibility in Saigon; Kennedy ordered more to be sent there. As of 30 December 1960, 900 Americans served in Vietnam. A year later 3,200 were in place; by 31 December 1962, 11,300 military men were assigned there. By the time of Kennedy's death nearly 16,300 American soldiers fought in Vietnam.[34] Kennedy wanted to "kill Cong," Lansdale wanted to rebuild a nation. Their goals were not compatible.

Lansdale, however, was not a prophet. In those early hours of the Kennedy administration he could not know the future. All he knew was that Kennedy was interested in his ideas. In a private and personal letter to Diem, Lansdale told how former members of the Eisenhower administration had been of help: Gates, Douglas, General Lyman Lemnitzer, Admiral Arleigh Burke, Allen Dulles. So also would the new frontiersmen be sympathetic to Diem's plight. Robert McNamara, Roswell Gilpatric, and Paul Nitze had all talked with Lansdale about Vietnam. More to the point, "last Saturday, President Kennedy had me in for a long talk on the subject. He was warmly interested and asked many questions. I am sure that you can count upon him as an understanding friend and that you will be hearing further about this. It would have 'warmed your heart' to have heard this conversation. So, you see, you do have some sincere friends in Washington."[35]

When retired Admiral Felix B. Stump learned that some within the State and military bureaucracies dismissed Lansdale's concerns as "visionary" and "impractical," he was incensed. Such people, he told Lansdale, were "stupid." They assumed that their prestige and brains should be enough to make other people listen to them "with open mouths in awed respect." Their attitude "riles me and raises my blood pressure." The admiral believed America's objectives would be better served "if you were out there all of the time." Then the administration would soon learn that "you have good judgment and that you know what you are talking about."[36]

Stump's condemnation obviously did not include the president, for John Kennedy continued to be impressed with Lansdale's wealth of insight and experience. Lansdale felt euphoric within the warm glow of presidential approval. Perhaps something worthwhile might result — for himself, the United States, and Vietnam. Lansdale knew he could accomplish great good if he was sent back to the Orient in some high capacity. The sort of person who should be put in charge of the American effort in Vietnam, as portrayed in his recent report, clearly was a self-description. Kennedy seemed to agree. He wanted to send a man to Vietnam who not only was experienced in political maneuvering but was familiar with tactics suitable for use against an insurgency. His choice was Brigadier General Edward G. Lansdale. Even the papers for the appointment were completed and on the president's desk.

Lansdale's chance came quickly. Robert McNamara called him at home on 28 January 1961, the weekend following the inauguration, and asked him to come immediately to the White House. When Lansdale arrived he found Kennedy presiding over a meeting in progress in the Cabinet Room. In attendance were the vice president, the secretaries of state and defense, the chairman of the Joint Chiefs of Staff, the director of Central Intelligence, and their assistants — twenty to thirty men. After a brief wait while Allen Dulles finished a briefing on the proposed invasion of Cuba, Lansdale was invited in and given a seat. Kennedy had his report in front of him and told Lansdale he had read it and been impressed by it. "For the first time," he said, "it gave [me] a sense of the danger and urgency of the problem in Vietnam." Discussion centered on a new Defense/State counterinsurgency plan for Vietnam that would shift Diem's military focus from countering a possible invasion by the North to ridding the nation of VC insurgents. Kennedy asked Lansdale for his views.

Lansdale replied that the communists there thought of 1961 as their year of opportunity and the United States would have to react vigorously to oppose them. High morale, a will to win, vigor, and confidence were all needed, as were greater efforts by Americans to get close to those they advised. Diem needed to allow his political opponents some legitimate role in government. Lansdale added that Diem was convinced that State officials in Vietnam were "very close" to those who had tried to kill him during the abortive coup the previous 11 November. Lansdale had been unable to persuade him otherwise.

Then the president broke his news to the general. "Did Dean [Rusk, newly appointed secretary of state] tell you that I'd like you to go over there as the new ambassador?" Lansdale recalled being stunned by the suddenness of it all. He thought, "My gosh! The guy is asking me to go over." Despite all his previous planning, Lansdale decided to be coy. "Well," he replied, "I'm a regular military officer over at the Pentagon and it's a great honor and thank you very much, but I don't think my place is in diplomacy." The president abruptly turned his attention to other matters.

Lansdale's window of opportunity was closing. The president was an impatient man. He wanted an immediate and positive response, which Lansdale had not given. Lansdale was confused. He had wanted to be wooed, and the president wanted an eager volunteer. Later Lansdale thought about that elusive moment. "Evidently I was asked and turned it down and didn't know it," he mused. "That was a funny way to offer me a different job in some different field of work." Yet it was exactly the opportunity for which he yearned and had maneuvered and for which he would continue to harbor ambitions for some time. When later asked about that day, Lansdale could only say, "It shocked me that the president would ask me in the way he did. I still couldn't catch on that he was being serious about it. I guess he was." He ruefully added, "I didn't know him well."[37]

But the window was not quite closed. Shortly thereafter, Kennedy mentioned the matter to Rusk. The secretary of state had been surprised and annoyed when the president had offered Lansdale the ambassadorship the previous morning. As a consequence, he had returned to his offices to hold a policy meeting with subordinate administrators at Foggy Bottom. One of those who was present was later posted to the American embassy in La Paz, Bolivia. When Lansdale visited that country some years later, he and Lansdale talked about what had happened. J. Graham Parsons, assistant secretary of state, miffed by Lansdale's criticisms of State at the White House meeting, warned of the consequences of allowing a prominent "CIA agent" to become an ambassador. Others present at Rusk's meeting advised him that they would also oppose any such move on the part of the president. They reasoned that a man who had spent all his career with CIA and the military was not a likely candidate as ambassador.[38]

Queries from State to the Pentagon revealed opposition there as well. Some in Defense worried that the upstart Lansdale might act on too many of his unconventional ideas and disrupt hallowed military plans for Vietnam. Nor was Lansdale's reputation enhanced with the Joint Chiefs of Staff when President Kennedy called Admiral Arleigh Burke, chairman of the Joint Chiefs, and suggested that, as an alternative to an ambassadorship, Lansdale should be promoted from brigadier to lieutenant general (a jump from one-star to three-star rank) and sent back to Vietnam as chief, U.S. MAAG. Lansdale recalled that the Joint Chiefs "evinced as much of a tempest as State had" and promptly began scolding him for putting the president up to the scheme! Needless to say, they took no action on the suggestion.[39]

William Colby thought the Pentagon "torpedoed" Lansdale and regretted the lost opportunity.[40] Both military and civilian bureaucracies regarded Lansdale as an "unguided missile," a "maverick." Lansdale's unconventional attitudes served him well when he worked in the "irregular area" for CIA and when he later served as a presidential adviser. "I think the bureaucracy couldn't handle Ed," Colby remarked. "He made them very uncomfortable and . . . . cut across their lines of command." There was already a large organizational structure involved with Vietnam. "Nonorganizational men get ground up in huge organizational structures."[41]

Stiffened in his resolve, Rusk dug in his heels when he realized the president had not yet given up on the idea of appointing Lansdale ambassador. He told Kennedy that if Lansdale went to Vietnam as ambassador, then the president could find himself a new secretary of state. Kennedy was not sufficiently sure of himself to insist, and in the face of Rusk's adamant objections he dropped his plan. Lansdale's window of opportunity closed forever. Kennedy settled for Frederick Nolting, who went as ambassador to Vietnam in March, replacing Elbridge Durbrow.

Appointing Lansdale would have made good sense. Of all Americans, Lansdale was closest to Diem and, despite earlier failures, was possibly the only man who could have freed Diem from the deadly clutch of his brother Nhu. As in the past, he might again have convinced Diem to follow more productive paths. His knowledge of people's wars would have been invaluable in allowing him to recommend fruitful courses of action to Washington agencies. But his independent and sometimes disruptive actions made Lansdale a threat to hallowed and longstanding bureaucratic kingdoms, and thus both State and Defense combined to defeat his candidacy.

With Lansdale seemingly unacceptable to both State and Defense, Kennedy turned to retired General Maxwell Taylor, his military adviser, as his overseer for counterinsurgency efforts. Thus when Taylor gave counterinsurgency a thick dosage of conventional treatment to make it acceptable to the Joint Chiefs of Staff, Lansdale's continued critiques and suggestions on the situation in Vietnam made very little impact. By the summer of 1961 he was practically without voice on the administration's most important foreign policy problem — Vietnam. He made one more trip to Vietnam with Taylor and Rostow in the fall of that year and was then completely shut off from Vietnam affairs.[42]

Admiral Burke, still fuming over the suggestion that he elevate Lansdale to three-star rank, asked an aide to send Lansdale a memorandum in early February. Burke had heard of speeches Lansdale was making and warned that, in the future, he must curb his tongue. The entire memorandum had an obviously patronizing air: in public contacts, he was to "[s]tay away from US national policy except 'basic items' such as the Constitution." He was not to "discuss foreign affairs . . . such as 'What We Should Do.' " Burke warned that Lansdale's remarks "should be limited to military matters which you know. 'Stick to your profession.' " Nor should there be any "screaming and yelling" at or about the Soviet Union. "Read the Innaugural [*sic*] Address and State of the Union message," the memo continued, "to 'get the feel' of what can be said and how it should be said." Being put on such a tight leash after so many freewheeling days must have galled Lansdale bitterly.[43]

Yet Lansdale was not without influence, for once again he found a friend and supporter in high places. When James Douglas left office as deputy secretary of defense at the end of the Eisenhower administration, he was replaced by a Kennedy appointee, Roswell P. Gilpatric. Lansdale and Gilpatric felt an immediate empathy with one another and Ros continued to urge a role for Lansdale in Vietnam affairs. He also became

Lansdale's new boss, for McNamara chose Gilpatric to serve as his supervisor for interdepartmental intelligence operations. In later years Lansdale recalled that "largely on Kennedy's say so," McNamara then pulled him out of the Office of Special Operations and named him an assistant to the secretary of defense to work with Gilpatric. The appointment was made on 3 March 1961. It was, Lansdale remembered, an "odds-and-ends" position, which, with Gilpatric's approval, he quickly defined to cover unconventional warfare.[44] For a time, however, Lansdale's interest in unconventional warfare took a back seat to administration concerns over CIA's effort to invade Cuba at an inlet called the Bay of Pigs.

The assault on Cuba began 15 April 1961 when old American B-26s made bombing runs over the island's airfields. When news broke at the Pentagon that the invasion was under way, Lansdale held his breath. He thought the Agency's planning had been foolish and inadequate, but now that D-Day had come he crossed his fingers and — with millions of other Americans — hoped for its success. The over-the-beach assault by the Cuban 2506 Brigade struck toward the sands of Playa Girón on 18 April. Then, at the last minute, Kennedy ordered promised American air cover withheld, which in any event would only have delayed the inevitable failure of the assault. Those on the beach waited in vain, fought as best they could, and died, were captured, or managed to be evacuated.

As early as 16 April, CIA began to cover its flanks. It sent propaganda guidance cables to all its Western Hemisphere station chiefs. Those messages from Langley AFB contained instructions for answering questions about the growing calamity at the Bay of Pigs. Station chiefs were instructed to describe the incident not as an invasion but rather as an effort to resupply *insurgentes* in the Escambray mountains. There was no effort under way aimed at taking or holding any Cuban territory. They were further to claim that the resupply mission was a success.[45] Few were convinced by such disclaimers.

President Kennedy was furious over the failure. He was as concerned over the "threat" to the Western Hemisphere posed by Castro as Eisenhower had been and wanted to rid the Caribbean of its Cuban cancer. Yet the CIA effort had been a disaster. He felt his infant administration had received a severe propaganda beating. At the president's instigation, Secretary of Defense Robert McNamara ordered an investigation into the affair to determine where responsibility should fall. McNamara's Special Review Committee, on something less than solid evidence, concluded that ultimate fault lay not with CIA but with the Office of Special Operations. General Erskine was dumfounded to find his bailiwick under attack, for it had been his office — in the person of Edward Lansdale —

that had most strenuously opposed the CIA operation and that had clearly pointed out its faulty planning as early as August 1960, more than nine months before the attack and long before the sitting administration had been elected.[46]

Nevertheless, in a sudden move the day following the CIA's abortive Bay of Pigs operation, many of Erskine's staff were dispersed to other offices and duties. In his new position, Lansdale was able to bring some of them who were Special Forces or Navy SEAL-qualified onto his own staff. Erskine was dismayed by the raid on his office and observed to those who remained, "Gentlemen, we have a secretary of defense, but we sure as hell don't have a secretary of war."[47]

The Special Review Committee accepted the results of an earlier study Erskine had made in concert with CIA on U.S. intelligence needs. That report concluded that Defense needed a specific joint intelligence organization. Thus the long-planned Defense Intelligence Agency (DIA), which would guide military planning, became operational. In the administrative shuffling that followed, many members of OSO were transferred to DIA. Then the multimillion-dollar annual activities of the National Security Agency (NSA) were removed from OSO and its policy supervision became Ros Gilpatric's responsibility. The committee then recommended that OSO, stripped of its duties and personnel, be abolished.

As Gilpatric's special assistant, Lansdale acted as representative of the secretary of defense on special interdepartmental boards and committees that provided oversight for intelligence operations.[48] All CIA requests for military help on covert operations or other special projects were also routed through Lansdale's office. He supervised the activities of NSA, and, through the Joint Chiefs, the three military services. Despite his fears that he would be singled out as a scapegoat for the Bay of Pigs, Lansdale's relative standing had improved. Whereas he had previously served since 8 July 1957 as deputy to the assistant to the secretary of defense for special operations, after 3 March 1961 he became assistant to the secretary of defense for special operations.[49] He was at last in the catbird seat.

Only a month into his new job, Lansdale felt he might still get an opportunity to play a role in administration policy toward Vietnam. On 12 April 1961, Walt Rostow suggested to President Kennedy that they turn to "gearing up the whole Viet-Nam operation" and proposed that Kennedy appoint Lansdale as a "full time first-rate back-stop man."[50] Ros Gilpatric told Lansdale what was in the wind. Following a discussion with Rostow on 13 April and working closely with Gilpatric, Lansdale wrote a lengthy study that recommended that Kennedy name a task force on Vietnam. As was his custom, he built in a major role for himself —

as executive officer. "Fullest use should be made," he wrote, "of the existing position of personal confidence and understanding which General Lansdale holds with President Diem and other key Vietnamese."[51] Gilpatric would head the Vietnam Task Force, which, he proposed, should be given a continuing and dominant role in managing America's interests in Vietnam.

On 20 April, in reaction to Rostow's urgings, Kennedy directed Gilpatric to appraise the current status and future prospects of the Viet Cong movement in South Vietnam. Gilpatric named to his Vietnam Task Force representatives from State, Defense, and CIA. The group held its first meeting on 24 April at the Pentagon. Lansdale recalled that "the number two guy at State and all the desks and policy people came, along with military and economic people." During the meeting, Lansdale said, "There were some pretty sharp words against me by some . . . who were trying to be polite but letting me know that I was *shit* as far as they were concerned." To a friend, Lansdale commented that "several empurpled State officials opened the meeting with passionate speeches about my villainy." Gilpatric, who chaired the session, found "an awful lot of emotion" among those present. Nevertheless, the group recommended action programs to create an increasingly democratic government in Vietnam that could prevent communist domination. Its emphasis was, as one might expect from a group in which Lansdale sat, on stabilizing the countryside.

Gilpatric was not as enthusiastic about attending the second and subsequent meetings. He told Lansdale, "Ed, I don't think I can make this next meeting. You go in and sit in my place as chairman." Lansdale protested. "These guys hate my guts. . . . I don't know how much we're going to get done." If Lansdale's recollections were even partially accurate, what happened next is worth recalling, for these high officials of the nation were reduced by their emotions to the state of squabbling children. Lansdale opened the next session with wry drollery (or pettiness; after the passage of so many years it is difficult to tell). "I've been asked to chair this meeting. I know the feelings of some of you. If you don't mind, I'm going to take five minutes at the beginning. I'll tell you what you think of me and what I think of you. We'll get that out of the way. If you want to add something, fine. Keep it within five minutes. Then we'll get on with the business. Individual feelings shouldn't come up in policy discussions and . . . as far as I'm concerned, they don't. While I might hate the guts of some of you, it won't [alter] my thinking on the policy of the U.S."

If Lansdale said anything at all like that, his remarks were akin to throwing a pork chop into a synagogue! "That's just like you," someone rejoined. "That's the way you are!" Lansdale agreed. "Say all the nasty things you want . . . and when you're through, let me know." When the group finally began talking about Vietnam, one representative from State suggested that American policy should be like a "two-wheel bicycle." ("They *loved* figures of speech," Lansdale sneered.) Lansdale sharply rejoined. "That's great. What does a two-wheel bicycle have to do with Vietnam? And how many wheels does our bicycle have now?" The man from State complained, "You're always spoiling our political thinking." The ever-practical Lansdale came right back at the speaker. "That's not thinking at all! Come on! Let's get something down on paper, a definite program . . . we can all do and share in."

There was much of what Lansdale described as "yack, yack, yack" at the meeting. He felt they wanted to kill the whole idea of a Vietnam Task Force — and many probably did. Lansdale ascribed their motives to pettiness inasmuch as they were convinced his goal was to become secretary of state. Motions fluttered onto the table. "Let's refer it to the United Nations" or "Let's get out a form" or "We'll get international cooperation." Such tactics were, Lansdale said, their way of killing an idea. It is no wonder that he later told Gilpatric, "They felt I was very disruptive. We had the wildest damn meeting. My God!" Whatever others had said or done, by his own account Lansdale's opening speech and subsequent rejoinders were not only self-destructive but hurtful to Gilpatric's hope for a Vietnam task force that could appropriately oversee America's policy there. "We're not going to get any policy settled this way," Lansdale observed. "There's too much personal feeling showing." He was right, but much of that feeling was his own.[52]

Gilpatric still had faith in Lansdale and wanted him to go to Vietnam immediately following presidential approval of the program to consult with leaders there and to make further recommendations. So on 27 April, Gilpatric forwarded the draft document to the president. In a covering memorandum, Gilpatric wrote that his group planned "mutually supporting actions of a political, military, economic, psychological, and covert character which can be refined periodically on the basis of further recommendations from the field. Brigadier General E. G. Lansdale, USAF, who has been designated Operations Officer for the Task Force, will proceed to Vietnam immediately after the program receives Presidential approval." Lansdale was willing to compromise to receive such a plum. In his own memo on the task force he omitted many of his own views. Although he believed it essential for Diem to receive emphatic American support, only the barest hint of this view appears in the paper (and it was not even hinted at in his preliminary draft of the report distributed at the 24 April meeting). Lansdale was so confident that such high-level backing would bear fruit that he even began contacting his old teammates, including Joe Redick, the compleat interpreter of the "uninhibited communications between President Diem and myself." He also sent messages, with Gilpatric's approval, requesting various men from his former team to meet him in Saigon on 5 May.

It was not to be. McNamara made such a trip contingent on receiving an invitation from Frederick Nolting, and an invitation never arrived. Even worse, when the report landed on the desk of George Ball, then deputy undersecretary of state, he remembered the wild meeting hosted by Lansdale and simply cut out any role for him, presumably with the approval of the White House. The *Pentagon Papers* report that "State objected, successfully, to having an Ambassador report to a Task Force chaired by the Deputy Secretary of Defense, and with a second defense official (Lansdale) as executive officer." Lansdale wrote an ineffective rebuttal. "US past performance and theory of action . . . simply offers no sound basis for winning, as desired by President Kennedy." Thus in one fell swoop Lansdale alienated both Defense and State. Thereafter, despite four requests from Diem and still others from Maxwell Taylor and William Bundy, a deputy secretary of defense under President Johnson, that Lansdale be sent to Saigon, he was not reassigned there until August 1965.[53]

In those weeks it seemed to Lansdale that wherever he turned he found himself under attack. While much of it may have been the result of his own bad judgment, as when he did not immediately accept Kennedy's offer of an ambassadorship or when he exchanged sharp words with members of the Vietnam Task Force, the attacks were nonetheless alarming. Another roadblock was thrown in his path because of the nature of the job he had accepted in the office of the secretary of defense. He saw his role there, in many ways, as the apostle of unconventional warfare. His desire to emphasize and direct the development of such tactics from the secretary's office was seen by the Joint Chiefs of Staff as a direct threat. They knew Lansdale's attitude differed materially from their own. "The Chiefs finally admitted to me candidly that they didn't want the hierarchy getting into operations," Lansdale later wrote.[54] Fearing they might lose control of the war in Vietnam, the Joint Chiefs created their own agency on unconventional warfare — special assistant for counterinsurgency and special activities (SACSA). It had several temporary heads before the hard-driving and ruthless Major General Victor H. Krulak, U.S. Marines, took over the position. An astute politician able to sense the twists and turns of power in the labyrinthine corridors of Washington, Krulak was known as "the Brute."[55]

Krulak's office in the Joint Staff served as the Joint Chiefs' point of contact with related activities in the office of the secretary of defense. It also became the point of contact within the Department of Defense for CIA. Krulak and his staff had very few regular military responsibilities and only limited dealings with the armed services. Most of his energy was spent on contacts with the Army's Special Forces, with Air Force Special Air Warfare activities, and with the Navy's SEAL teams. Thus initially there was a great deal of contact between SACSA and Edward Lansdale.

Relations between Krulak and Lansdale were never good and soon turned sour. Krulak despised sharing power with Lansdale and began to undercut him at every turn. Lansdale fared so badly in these exchanges over the next several months that Krulak's allies referred to him as a "paper tiger." The more power Krulak gained, the less contact Lansdale was allowed with Vietnam. As Lansdale later recounted, "Part of my more recent agony . . . was to be up semi-close to the stumbling around on Vietnam without a chance to lend a hand in any way that was then heeded. At critical moments, I was cut out of the communications, so I couldn't even read about what was happening. . . . It was Washington at its nuttiest."[56]

Trying to be a realist, Lansdale decided to develop an interest elsewhere. He chose Israel because he wanted to know more about how Israelis used the kibbutz as a self-help, self-defense community and how that nation conducted military civic action projects. He made friends with Israeli officers in the United States and together they planned for Lansdale to make an official inspection visit to their homeland. Lansdale was working up his itinerary for the trip when, one day in early fall 1961, while speaking with the president on another matter of policy, he told Kennedy about his proposed journey to Israel. Cancel it, Kennedy interjected. "I want you to go out to Vietnam . . . just to take a look [at conditions there] for me." Lansdale was both pleased and surprised. He initially thought the president meant for him to go alone. Instead he found that he would travel as one member of a larger group, which would be headed by General Maxwell Taylor and Walt Whitman Rostow. Lansdale's mind filled with plans. Perhaps he could influence the attitudes of Kennedy's administration after all.[57]

11

ELIMINATION BY ILLUMINATION

THE DAY FOLLOWING HIS TALK with President Kennedy, General Lansdale received a call from Maxwell Taylor, who asked him to come to his White House office for a meeting. They met and Taylor outlined the scope of his mission. The Joint Chiefs of Staff had estimated at a recent meeting of the National Security Council that 40,000 U.S. troops could clean up the Viet Cong threat in Vietnam and another 120,000 would be sufficient to cope with any possible North Vietnamese or Chinese intervention. Before committing himself, Kennedy wanted more information. Thus he had decided to send Taylor to Vietnam to study the situation. Taylor held a notepad in his hand as he spoke to Lansdale and mentioned the names of others he planned to take with him. As Lansdale glanced at the paper, he saw a line drawn across the page just below the first four names.

"What's the line?" Lansdale asked. He didn't like the answer. "We'll be making protocol visits with the president of Vietnam," Taylor responded. "We're going on to Thailand after that and take a quick look there, where we'll be talking to the prime minister. All names above the line will go with me to visit the chiefs of state." The line ran across the paper just above Lansdale's name. "The rest of you won't," Taylor continued. "You'll simply be 'working party.' " The decision, Lansdale believed, was "stupid on his part" and he felt such arrangements were "embarrassing."[1]

Lansdale's experience with Vietnamese political undercurrents was greater than any other American's. His sources of information were greater.[2] To ignore this elementary fact was unwise of Taylor. So also were the duties the retired general foisted upon Lansdale. Lansdale suggested to him that he "get a hard fix on the political situation and what Diem felt he was up against." Instead, on the trip west above the Pacific, Taylor spoke with the members of his mission. "Everybody give me a list of things that you think you're qualified to look into," he told them. Lansdale gave him a long list of people he knew. By talking with them he might uncover helpful insights into current problems. When Taylor next spoke with Lansdale he ignored his wishes. "I want you to figure out a defense line so that we can put American genius to work and have an electronic line [across the 17th parallel] and then down Laos and Cambodia." Lansdale protested. "That's not my subject. I'm no good at that. . . . [It's] a waste of my time." Taylor insisted he undertake the strange duty "of noodling out the defense of the Laotian/South Vietnamese border."[3] Lansdale could only shake his head and sadly do as he was told.

When the group landed at Saigon's airport on 18 October 1961, it was met by waiting members of the press. Lansdale allowed his superiors above the line to deplane first and they were swamped by reporters. As Lansdale left the aircraft he was tugged aside by one of Diem's staff. "The president would like to see you immediately," he whispered. Lansdale tried to speak with Taylor to inform him where he was going, but Taylor was too busy to be interrupted. Finally Lansdale managed to get the attention of Walt Rostow. "Diem has invited me to the palace," Lansdale said. "I might be there for dinner. I don't know. Would you please tell the boss this isn't a protocol call? I'm just going to see an old friend."[4]

When Lansdale met with Diem, the first questions asked of him were "What's Taylor like? What does he want? What is he going to ask for?" Lansdale tried to be reassuring. "Don't be afraid of him. He's trying to figure out what you might need and how best we might help you."[5] There is no evidence that Lansdale revealed his true feelings about Taylor to Diem. It would have been inappropriate in any case. Elsewhere and later, he said of him: "Taylor is a patrician, cold, shortsighted person. He doesn't understand human beings." That was not the whole story. Lansdale admitted that Taylor could be charming. "I admit his charm, his manners, his language, and his approach to life, but he essentially turned me off at the same time. His ego got in front of his judgment at times. I was afraid of that. There was [also] a coldness that came from command for a long time, which once again turned me off."[6]

In later years Lansdale revealed what happened that day in Doc Lap Palace. "I've never told anybody this," he said. Diem admitted that he had asked the U.S. government for American combat troops to be assigned to Vietnam. Lansdale looked sadly at his friend. "Have you reached that point in your affairs that you're going to need them to stay alive?" Nhu was present and, as on Lansdale's previous trip, began to answer for his brother. Lansdale cut him off. "I asked your brother those questions, not you!" Both Vietnamese sat silently for a moment. Then Diem answered. "You mean I shouldn't ask [for troops]?" Lansdale countered with another question. "Do you *need* them?" Diem didn't respond for a time and finally said, "Well, no." Lansdale advised softly, "Stay with that then." He said later, "I was against U.S. troops going [into] combat [there]. I'd seen the French and figured we'd do much what they did — even with good intentions."[7]

Both Ngo brothers were tense, concerned about future developments. It was not a happy meeting. Dinner later was more relaxed. "He wasn't chief of state," Lansdale said of Diem, "and I wasn't an American; we were just two men who happened to know each other." Afterward Lansdale briefed Taylor on his meeting at the palace.[8] Despite Taylor's interest, Lansdale was unsure how much he understood of the nature of the unrest in Vietnam. "Very few of the military minds understood the problem they were facing or who the enemy was or how he was trying to fight, the political basis behind their military activities, the political results they were trying to achieve through their military and other psychological and economic actions. We went out to kill the enemy — a very different thing — and wouldn't try to understand him."[9]

Lansdale refused to spend much time estimating the costs of sealing off the western Vietnamese border to infiltrators. He went to MAAG headquarters and gave the task to staff officers there. "You guys are good at figuring," he said. "This is going to cost us several billion dollars. Tell me how many billions and I'll report it."[10] He later wrote to his friend, General Samuel Williams, "I had to see all these VN friends privately and unofficially, and then submit a personal report on my own, which is hardly the way to endear oneself but the only way to retain some integrity." His role in the Taylor mission, Lansdale believed, was a farce.[11]

The final report of Taylor and Rostow stated that Saigon faced a dual crisis of confidence, compounded out of doubts that the United States would continue its support for South Vietnam and doubts — arising from Viet Cong successes — that Diem's unpopular and inefficient regime would ever be able to beat back the insurgency. Taylor and Rostow urged a greater American military commitment to Vietnam and stressed that there might be a need to attack, or at least to threaten to attack, North Vietnam.[12]

Despite Lansdale's insights, the threat Taylor saw in Vietnam was not a southern insurgency but the possibility of conventional war with the North or with China. Taylor offered all the old and tired nostrums for producing victory — more firepower and mobility, more effective use of the southern army. If nothing else worked, the United States could always bomb Ho's northern government into submission.[13] Acting on Taylor's archaic advice, Kennedy made a much enlarged offer of aid to Vietnam.[14]

Taylor took his group to the White House after their return for a meeting with Kennedy. They were ushered into the president's office while Kennedy was busy elsewhere and milled about awaiting his entrance. Taylor remarked that his daughters at home would want to know something about his visit with the president so, in a moment of whimsy, he sat in Kennedy's famous leisure chair and began rocking back and forth. When the president walked in, Taylor quickly tried to rise to his feet, but his hips were caught and as he straightened, the chair began to come up with him. He had to pull himself loose in a moment rich with embarrassment while the president looked on. Lansdale thought it was highly amusing.[15]

Kennedy listened to the briefing and then asked mission members to do some further work on the recommendations they were submitting. As the meeting broke up, Kennedy asked Lansdale to wait while the others left. The president pulled him off further duties with the Taylor mission. "A crash deal was waiting for me," Lansdale later told a friend. "No rest for the weary."[16] He told Hanging Sam Williams that the new job was "probably the most frustrating damn thing I've ever tackled."[17]

It came about because the president continued to demand massive and maximum effort from his administration to restore his macho image following his disastrous gamble at the Bay of Pigs. It was an insult that needed to be redressed. During that private meeting in the presidential offices on 30 November 1961, Kennedy gave Lansdale the task of examining administration policy on Cuba and making recommendations for improving its effectiveness. Lansdale offered caveats. Any renewed effort must come from within Cuba rather than from an outside source. "Castro," he said, has "aroused considerable affection for himself personally with the Cuban population." The United States should consequently pursue "a very different course" from its earlier invasion effort.

Other attempts, Lansdale noted, that had been conceived and led by Americans were not particularly effective. Kennedy should try, he said, to help the Cuban people overthrow Castro rather than rely on another U.S.-engineered attack. To be effective, they would have to establish a strong political base among Cubans opposed to Castro within the island population. They could begin by working with exiles, particularly those with middle-class professions, who had opposed Batista and had then become disillusioned with Castro. Organize them into cells inside Cuba so they could work secretly and safely, he advised. Such a course of action would not provoke "premature actions" such as the Bay of Pigs nor was it likely to "bring great reprisals on the people there and abort any eventual success." Kennedy liked the tone of the perspicacious Lansdale.[18]

It is odd that Kennedy, distrustful of CIA in the aftermath of the Bay of Pigs, still sought out Lansdale — a former CIA agent — to help organize his next Cuban endeavor. Lansdale came to regret the choice. Decades later, in reminiscing about those days, he admitted that his Cuban efforts ultimately hurt both his career and his reputation. "I think," he said, "the thing that hurt me most in the long run was the task that Kennedy gave me on Cuba." He wished he had never become mixed up in the affair.[19]

Lansdale was not the only arrow in the president's quiver. He decided to use Special Group as the agency to make his new clandestine effort against Cuba. Relying always on Robert, the president named his brother and Maxwell Taylor, his military adviser, to the group. Brigadier General Edward Lansdale was to be executive officer and chief of operations of this new Special Group, Augmented (SGA). Other members included McGeorge Bundy, Kennedy's national security adviser; U. Alexis Johnson, undersecretary of state; Roswell Gilpatric, deputy secretary of defense; John A. McCone, director of Central Intelligence; and General Lyman Lemnitzer, chairman of the Joint Chiefs of Staff. Although Secretary of State Dean Rusk and Secretary of Defense Robert McNamara sometimes attended meetings, they were not formal members of SGA. Operational planning was known by the code name Mongoose, an animal that strikes its enemies with sudden and swift deadliness.

In an early meeting of SGA, Robert Kennedy insisted that "a solution to the Cuban problem today carries top priority." He asserted that no amount of "time, money, effort or manpower" was too great if its expenditure helped achieve Castro's downfall.[20] Lansdale was also enthusiastic. He told those assembled: "You're in a combat situation where we have been given full command."[21] He liked the feeling of power that came from belonging to SGA. "I was relaying instructions . . . from the highest authority in the land. I was often in conversation with President Kennedy and his brother."[22]

On 18 January 1962, reacting swiftly to the president's desire for anti-Castro activities, Lansdale scheduled a meeting of SGA. He assigned to its various members thirty-two planning tasks. They covered a range of activities that, if successful, might stir up an "open revolt and overthrow of the Communist regime" in Cuba. They included collection of intelligence, "defection of top Cuban government officials," propaganda operations, attacks on the "cadre of the regime, including key leaders," a schedule for "sabotage actions inside Cuba," and possible "use of U.S. military force to support the Cuban popular movement." Lansdale envisioned "a revolution that would break down the police controls of the state and . . . drive top people out of power." Such a program needed "political action cells, psychological propaganda action cells, and eventually when possible, guerrilla forces" operating within Cuba, which, like Castro's forces before them, "would eventually move into Havana and take over. So far as possible, Lansdale wanted SGA to rely on professional anti-Castro émigrés, labor leaders, youth and church groups, and "gangster elements" to carry out any tasks the group approved. In a memorandum to the group, Lansdale emphasized that "it is our job to put the American genius to work on this project, quickly and effectively. This demands a change from the business as usual and a hard facing of the fact[s]."[23]

Highly critical of American performance at the Bay of Pigs, Lansdale tried to introduce a new perspective. The administration should adopt real revolutionary tactics. The others disagreed. They had in mind commando raids and believed "a commando raid was the [only] way to fight a revolution. I couldn't disabuse them of that. They had forgotten the American Revolution; how it was fought psychologically and politically." They seemed to have little idea of the concept of a revolution. Lansdale was disgusted; perhaps he ought to start at the kindergarten level and teach other members some of what he had learned so long ago in the Philippines.[24] Others thought of flamboyant plans; Lansdale suggested choosing a simple, homely course of action. His chief goal was to erect a modest operational plan for the destabilization of Cuba.

That same day, 18 January, Lansdale transmitted a copy of his thirty-two tasks not only to the constituent agency representatives of Special Group, Augmented, but to Attorney General Robert Kennedy as well. He included a handwritten note admitting that "my review does not include the sensitive work I have reported to you; I felt you preferred informing the President privately." In later years a congressional committee investigated Mongoose activities to learn if its plans called for the assassination of Fidel Castro. Some members of that panel wanted to know if the "sensitive work" Lansdale referred to included such "executive action" plans. Lansdale denied the allegation, insisting that he "never took up [the topic of] assassination with either the Attorney General or the President."[25]

The next day, members of SGA met to confer in Attorney General Kennedy's office. Besides Kennedy and Lansdale, those present included George McManus, executive assistant to Richard Helms of CIA; General Craig, who represented the Joint Chiefs; Don Wilson of USIA; Major

Patchell from the office of the secretary of defense; and Frank Hand, CIA. Deputy Director for Plans Richard Helms probably also was present.[26]

During that meeting, Lansdale added another job to those he had previously assigned. Task 33 called for the incapacitation of Cuban sugar workers during harvest season — to sicken them temporarily and keep them away from the fields for twenty-four to forty-eight hours "without [permanent] ill effects." This would be achieved through use of nonlethal incapacitating chemicals.[27] On 30 January 1962, SGA members met to discuss Lansdale's thirty-two tasks and agreed to give them further thought. They also decided that task 33 deserved continued planning but insisted that a "policy determination" would have to be made prior to its final approval. A follow-on study concluded that the scheme was impractical and it was quietly canceled without ever undergoing final debate by SGA members.

During one of Lansdale's Mongoose visits with the president early in 1962, Kennedy remarked that Lansdale seemed to be the American counterpart of Ian Fleming's fictional character James Bond, Agent 007 of Her Majesty's Secret Service. Lansdale demurred. He suggested that a more likely candidate was a CIA agent involved with Mongoose, William King Harvey, who headed SGA's Task Force W, a CIA unit that reported directly to Lansdale.

An enthusiastic reader of James Bond's adventures, Kennedy asked Lansdale to bring Harvey to the White House. On the appointed day Lansdale and Harvey sat waiting outside the Oval Office for their meeting with the president. Struck by a sudden thought, Lansdale turned to Harvey and said, "You're not carrying your gun, are you?" The question was not unreasonable. Harvey was known at Langley as the only CIA officer who carried a weapon while on duty at headquarters. He once remarked that it was necessary. "If you ever know as many secrets as I do," said Harvey, "then you'll know why I carry a gun." Of course he was armed, Harvey responded, and began to remove his piece from its holster. Not knowing how nearby Secret Service agents might react to the sight of an armed man, Lansdale quickly told Harvey to keep the damn thing hidden.

Quietly informing the Secret Service detail that his guest would like to check a firearm, Lansdale invited Harvey to relinquish his weapon. A few moments later, as the two men prepared to enter Kennedy's office, Harvey remembered his backup piece and reached under his suit coat to whip out a .38-caliber revolver from a holster snapped to his belt in the small of his back. He handed this second weapon to some very startled Secret Service agents and the two men went into the Oval Office for their presidential chat.

Harvey later denied under oath that he had carried any firearms to the White House that day. As does any good raconteur, Lansdale enjoyed embellishing his tales to make better stories of them in the telling. The story may or may not be an invention, but it was the sort of yarn befitting the character of Bill Harvey.[28]

Meanwhile, Secretary of Defense Robert McNamara's operating style continued to displease Lansdale. He felt particularly irked at McNamara's penchant for oral rather than written orders. Duties that might expend millions of dollars were casually assigned orally. Lansdale would write his orders into memo form and would try to get McNamara's signature. It was not easy. On one occasion McNamara told him, "The president wants to talk to the Cuban people on TV. Fix it up." Lansdale grumbled to himself on his way back to his office. "How the hell does a U.S. president in Washington talk on TV to people in Cuba?" It took him almost a week, but he managed. He located scientific help from experts across the country, found a Havana television channel that could be overridden by a more powerful beam, located aircraft and airborne TV equipment, and laid in a supply of tapes. All this ran up bills and required the purchase of new equipment. Lansdale tried to secure authorization from McNamara for his expenditures. He showed the secretary an action memorandum he had written. "Just initial the corner of this memo," he requested, "so I have some means of access to a budget on this." McNamara refused. "I told you to get it done," he replied. "Bury it," he said, in some corner of the military budget. So Lansdale went to one of the Pentagon comptrollers and said, "Help me out." The comptroller charged costs of the adventure to the Navy budget. By the time Lansdale was ready, McNamara and the president had changed their minds.[29]

Frustrated though he might be from such leadership style, Lansdale's hands were full as executive officer for the Mongoose plot. Meetings came as steadily as spring rains, and during each one members floated ideas for the group to consider. Thomas Parrott, one of the men who worked on Mongoose, later claimed as "absolutely true" a story that Lansdale presented a very silly idea to an SGA meeting. Well aware of the extensive adherence to Roman Catholicism throughout Cuba, Lansdale suggested spreading a rumor among the island populace that the second coming of Christ was near and that Castro was the anti-Christ. On a specific date during black night hours, an American submarine would surface off Havana in Cuban coastal waters. The crew would shoot starshells into the dark sky, supposedly a manifestation of Christ's arrival. Rumormongers would claim that Castro was keeping Christ from landing in Cuba. Alarmed by the mysterious lights in the sky signifying the power of heaven, superstitious Cubans, in theory, would become enraged and would rise against their leader and overthrow Castro. Parrott called the zany scheme "Elimination by Illumination." Lansdale later claimed he had never heard the story until 1975, thirteen years after the fact, proclaimed that Parrott was a "jerk," and insisted the story was "a weirdo comment" and "absolutely untrue."[30]

Just as Parrott claimed Lansdale had laughable ideas, so also did Lansdale chuckle at the schemes of others. One program forwarded to him on 30 January 1962 by the Defense Department and the Joint Chiefs was called Operation Bounty. Its authors hoped it might create "distrust and apprehension in the Cuban Communist Hierarchy." The plan called for an airdrop of leaflets over Cuba that would offer rewards for assassinations: $5,000 for killing an "informer," $100,000 for each dead government official, and 2 cents for anyone who killed Castro. It was described as a way of convincing Cubans that their El Jefe was not worth much. Lansdale vetoed the plan. It was not, he believed, "something that should be seriously undertaken or supported further." He never brought Operation Bounty before SGA.[31]

Whether all ideas were sound was not the point. In focusing on intelligence collection, propaganda, and various sabotage actions, Lansdale used an approach consistent with his underlying principles and the expressed purpose of Mongoose — to build gradually toward an *internal* revolt by *Cubans*.

On 20 February, he submitted to SGA a six-phase schedule for Mongoose. He promised that if it was followed rigorously, it would result in an October 1962 "revolt and overthrow of the Communist regime" in Cuba. One of the six operations called for "attacks on the cadre, including key leaders. . . . This should be a 'Special Target' operation. . . . Gangster elements might provide the best recruitment potention for actions against police-G2 [intelligence] officials."[32] In addition to casualties that might occur in the course of the October revolt, this proposal to recruit gangsters contemplated the targeted killing of specific individuals. No one should be surprised at Lansdale's planning. He knew that in conflict men die. His president had decreed that the administration's honor, damaged at the Bay of Pigs, must be restored. Castro was believed to be a threat to the safety of the United States.

Which was better? To strike at and destroy those who would, if unchecked, provoke continued tyranny against their own populations or to wait and expend the lives of many soldiers on larger battlefields of future conflagrations that might well grow out of the activities of Castro? For Lansdale the choice was clear. He was, after all, the man who planned the *asuang* killing of Huk rebels on darkened night trails in Tarlac province half a world away and a decade and a half earlier. He was always a military man willing to spend his own or others' lives when the "national interest" demanded it.

Assassinations, or "wet" activities, would be handled for SGA by its Task Force W, headed by CIA officer William King Harvey. Funded by the Agency and staffed by its personnel, Task Force W ultimately became the largest CIA installation in the world, with several hundred people working on various planning and action phases of its assignment. Clandestine operations were based at WAVE radio station in Miami, staffed by as many as five hundred employees and case officers who controlled perhaps three thousand Cuban agents at a cost of more than $100 million annually. Harvey also got in touch with the Mafia, believing its past experiences in Cuba would prove beneficial to his work — American mafiosi must still know hit men in Cuba. They would be able to get close to Castro and his chief lieutenants. Harvey worked most closely with two mafiosi, Momo Salvatore "Sam" Giancana and Johnny Roselli. Lansdale called for widening such plans. He was not content with the existing list of "Special Target" operations. "[Soviet] Bloc technicians should be added to the list of targets." Underwhelmed by such plans, SGA members ordered them tabled at a February meeting in favor of a policy restricted only to "intelligence gathering."[33]

The door for "wet" activities was left open, however. An SGA memorandum pointed out that "any actions which are not specifically spelled out in the plan but seem to be desirable as the project progresses, will be brought to the Special Group for resolution."[34] Harvey continued his mysterious movements as winter faded into spring. On 26 April, Lansdale told SGA that Harvey was in Florida "initiating a new series of agent infiltrations" and would return to Washington on 30 April. After Harvey's return Lansdale would be able to give "more specific information on the status of agent training and operations." Maxwell Taylor wanted Harvey to attend the next meeting of SGA. On 3 May 1962, Harvey reported to SGA on the "general field of intelligence" and commented that three agent teams had infiltrated Cuba.[35] When Robert Kennedy learned in May that CIA under Eisenhower had repeatedly sought to assassinate Castro, he wanted Mongoose to emphasize such actions also.[36]

Lansdale was keenly aware of the attorney general's notions. He later testified that it was the attorney general who in midsummer 1962 ordered him to work out plans for "getting rid of" Castro. Lansdale had no doubts that "the project for disposing of Castro envisioned the whole spectrum of plans from overthrowing the Cuban leader to assassinating him."[37] Something other than casual dislike also motivated the president and his brother. Growing numbers of Soviet military advisers had arrived in Cuba. Some within the administration's inner circle were darkly suspicious that soon there might be ICBM sites planted on Cuban soil, their hostile snouts aimed at mainland U.S. targets. (CIA would confirm that fact in October.)

Lansdale exercised heavy-handed control over CIA's intelligence activities. In an SGA request to Richard Helms, he demanded an estimate "for each week as far into the next twelve months as possible . . . the numbers and type of agents you will establish inside Cuba . . . [and] brief descriptions . . . of actions contemplated." Supplying arms and equipment to resistance groups was also to be reported to SGA "for decision *ad hoc*."[38]

One CIA agent complained that Lansdale required plans "in nauseating detail down to such things as the gradients on the beach, and the composition of the sand on the beach in many cases. Every single solitary thing was in these plans, full details, times, events, weaponry."[39] SGA kept itself busy checking operational planning. Between January and early October 1962, the members held forty meetings. Both Kennedy brothers expressed their impatience. There were only delays, they complained; nothing was happening.[40] That was not quite correct. Lansdale did approve a few sabotage and paramilitary actions, including a major operation aimed at a large Cuban copper mine, blowing up bridges to stop or slow travel on the island, and blowing up certain production plants.[41]

As if he did not have enough to occupy his mind, Lansdale found himself faced with a minor tribulation. Another book had been published that featured a character modeled after him. A French author, Jean Lartéguy, published a work set in Southeast Asia entitled *Le mal jaune*. One of its minor figures was an American adviser to the president of an Asian nation, a Colonel Lionel Teryman (*terre* = land; thus, "landsman," a thin disguise for "Lansdale"). Lartéguy portrayed Teryman as a new Lawrence of Arabia, a brutal, uncouth, and violently anti-French military man who practiced a self-imposed chastity in his personal life. Once again Lansdale had to face the smiles of his fellows and hear about insinuating reviews of the book. He had almost succeeded in living down Greene's *The Quiet American* and Lederer and Burdick's *The Ugly American,* and now it began again. It did nothing to help when, a little later, Lartéguy's book was translated from the French by Xan Fielding and published in the United States under the title *Yellow Fever*.[42]

In August 1962, SGA brought intelligence collection to an end. On 10 August, members of SGA met in the office of Dean Rusk, the secretary of state. Others who gathered that day included McNamara, John A. McCone, CIA; Edward R. Murrow, director of USIA; McGeorge Bundy, Kennedy's national security adviser; Edward Lansdale; and others. They met to decide on the next phase of Mongoose. Lansdale suggested they now enter Course B, a plan to "exert all possible diplomatic, economic, psychological and other overt pressures to overthrow the Castro-communist regime, without overt employment of U.S. military." Lansdale told his fellow SGA members, "We want boom and bang on the island."[43]

Those present that day also discussed assassinating Castro. Given the Kennedys' fixation on getting rid of him and the activities of Harvey's Task Force W, it is difficult to believe that no such conversations occurred earlier. But that day is the first for which specific evidence exists. John McCone later recalled that it was one of the topics, although he claimed that he personally opposed any such action. He thought it may have been McNamara who brought it up, although the secretary of defense later claimed he could not recall any talk of assassination. Walter Elder, McCone's executive assistant, was in his boss's office when McCone telephoned McNamara shortly after the meeting broke up. Elder remembered that McCone told McNamara that "the subject you just brought up. I think it is highly improper. I do not think it should be discussed. It is not an action that should ever be condoned. It is not proper for us to discuss and I intend to have it expunged from the record."[44]

Not knowing McCone's reluctance to have anything left on paper, Lansdale prepared an action memorandum, dated 13 August, which called for the preparation of contingency plans for "Intelligence, Political (including liquidation of leaders), Economic (sabotage, limited deception) and Paramilitary."[45] He sent copies to William Harvey, to the State Department's Robert Hurwith, to General Benjamin Harris of the Defense Department, and to Donald Wilson, USIA.

Thirteen years later, the Church Committee of the United States Senate gave a long, hard look at allegations that the government of this country had been involved in various assassination attempts on leaders in other nations. The principals who were involved in Mongoose were called upon to give testimony. There was suddenly a veritable implosion of recall and memory. Few could remember anything pertinent, and those who did could do so only vaguely and with uncertainty. William Harvey had died by that time so it was acceptable to remember his efforts at planning Castro's assassination. When asked if Harvey kept him advised of what he was doing — the CIA man mounted at least eight different attempts on Castro's life — Lansdale insisted he never knew any details. "It would," he recalled, "have been highly unusual for me to know."[46] Lansdale testified before the Church Committee that "I had no knowledge of such a thing. I know of no order or permission for such a thing and I was given no information at all that such a thing was going on by people who I have now learned were involved with it."[47]

As a matter of fact, it would have been "highly unusual" had he *not* known what was planned, given his grasp of detail, his tight control over Task Force W, and his insistence on staying on top of current activity. Yet when grilled by the Church Committee, Lansdale insisted that when the subject was raised on 10 August, "the consensus was . . . hell no on this and there was a very violent reaction."[48] If that was the decision at the 10 August meeting, why then had Lansdale gone ahead to call for "liquidation" of Cuban leaders? He testified that "I thought it would be a possibility someplace down the road in which there would be some possible need to take action such as that [assassination]." His position was simple and straightforward. Every means should be explored for removing the threat posed by Fidel Castro. For that reason he instructed Harvey to develop contingency plans in order to learn if the United States had the capability for "wet" actions.[49]

Why had he circulated his memorandum? Lansdale waffled. "I don't recall that thoroughly. I don't remember the reasons why I would." Was it not his understanding that assassination efforts had already been vetoed at the 10 August meeting? "I guess it is, yes," the general replied. "The way you put it to me now has me baffled about why I did it. I don't know."[50] Lansdale added another disclaimer in his plea of innocence. Although he "had doubts" that assassination was a "useful action, and [was] one I had never employed in the past, during work in coping with revolutions, and I had considerable doubts as to its utility . . . I was trying to be very pragmatic." As a good soldier, he admitted that any responsibility must have been his own. General Benjamin Harris was a little more open. He testified that such activities are "not out of the ordinary in terms of contingency planning . . . it's one of the things you look at."[51]

Harris was correct. It was not shameful for the Special Group, Augmented to look into the possibility of assassination. In a committee composed of members of the highest level of government, it would rather be shameful had they *not* explored the subject, assigned as they were to promote the destabilization of Cuba. Whether destabilization itself was a proper subject for American attention is an altogether different question that could be fruitfully considered. That was not, however, the assignment given those men during 1962 by the American president!

When Harvey received Lansdale's memorandum, his first thought was of the danger of leaving such records for future investigative committees. He immediately called Lansdale's office and pointed out "the inadmissibility and stupidity of putting this type of comment in writing in such documents." He further added that CIA "would write no document pertaining to this and would participate in no open meeting discussing it." On 14 August, Harvey wrote Helms stating that although Secretary McNamara had brought up the topic of assassination and Lansdale had written a memorandum about it, liquidation of foreign leaders was not an appropriate subject for inclusion in official records and he further insisted the offending words be deleted from both Lansdale's memorandum and any minutes of the meeting.[52]

Lansdale later recalled only one additional contact with Harvey. He had one brief conversation with the CIA agent after the 10 August meeting. At that time Harvey stated "he would look into it [the assassination of Castro and] see about developing some plans." That, Lansdale insisted, was the last he ever heard about assassinations.[53]

On 30 August, SGA instructed CIA to come up with a list of possible sabotage targets in Cuba. The next day Lansdale called upon SGA members to approve a "stepped-up Course B plus," designed to inspire revolt against Castro. He also asked the group's support of efforts "to provoke incidents between Cubans and Bloc personnel to exacerbate tensions." His listeners changed his wording to "cause actions by Cubans against Bloc personnel" and agreed that "consideration will be given to provoking and conducting physical attacks on Bloc personnel."[54]

Nothing much happened. On 14 October, a frustrated and disappointed Robert Kennedy urged "massive activity" on the members of SGA. As a result they decided that "considerably more sabotage" should be undertaken to get "rid of the Castro regime." Now a problem unforeseen or ignored by SGA and the administration began to emerge. Its secret war against Cuba was secret only from Americans; it was certainly well known by both Cubans and their Soviet allies. In reaction to SGA activities, the Russians began rapidly increasing their support of Castro. By early October, the island contained 20,000 Soviet soldiers, 1,300 field artillery pieces, 700 anti-aircraft guns, 350 tanks, and 150 jets — all poised and waiting. U-2 spy planes then confirmed that the Soviets were constructing some half dozen launch sites for surface-to-surface intermediate-range missiles.[55]

The Kennedy administration could hardly admit publicly that SGA Mongoose activities had spurred the Soviets to increase their Cuban commitment. It was hard to do so even privately. When William King Harvey told Robert and John Kennedy that the crisis was their own fault, they removed him from Task Force W and replaced him with Des Fitzgerald.[56] Even as late as mid-October the Kennedys believed SGA might be able to solve their Cuban problems. Robert replaced Maxwell Taylor as chairman of SGA and urged greater efforts to rid the hemisphere of the Castro regime.[57]

On 30 October, however, Lansdale noted in a memorandum for the record that SGA had ordered a halt to all Cuban sabotage operations. No wonder. The Cuban missile crisis was full-blown and no one in the administration was willing to provoke the Russians more than they already were. The USSR and the United States were on the verge of war. Mongoose, Lansdale commented, was rapidly shut down as the two superpowers snarled at each other. SGA was abolished. Its parent, Special Group, chaired by McGeorge Bundy, reassumed responsibility for reviewing and approving covert actions in Cuba in conjunction with an interagency Cuban Coordinating Committee housed within the State Department. Yet Lansdale was not remorseful over SGA's efforts. Surely, he insisted, there must be room for planning "about what to do with a leader who would threaten the lives of millions of Americans" with Soviet missiles.[58]

Just a few months earlier, Lansdale had hoped for a triumphal march into Havana by Cuban *insurgentes* who would unseat the bearded one's regime. CIA managed to get agents onto the island, to recruit a few rural discontents, and to sabotage a few targets, but all else failed. No one — not even Lansdale — gave much consideration to the possibility that a successful secret war against Castro might last for a year or even ten. Clandestine raiders infiltrated onto the island looked for help that was nonexistent; those who might have offered support were already gone, now living a more tranquil life as refugees in Miami and scorned by those in their homeland as outcasts.

Lansdale's plans were also fatally flawed by the lack of consideration given to the possibility of Soviet intervention. To act as though the United States could operate with impunity in Cuba — as if it were 1898 rather than 1962 — without the Russians stepping in to help Castro counter the threat from the Colossus of the North was to risk a major East-West confrontation. Under such circumstances, to expect an open revolt and Castro's overthrow in less than a year was unrealistic. Operation Mongoose not only was a foolish and very dangerous project for John Kennedy to support, it was a time for Edward Lansdale to stand up to his superior and tell him that his dream was a fantasy. He had done so at other times. He did not on this occasion. Had he tried, the history of the United States might have been very different.[59]

Following the breakup of SGA, Lansdale tried to return to work on the problems of Vietnam, but without much success. No matter that Diem asked him to return to Southeast Asia or that Lansdale volunteered repeatedly for duty there. He regularly urged McNamara and Gilpatric to give him permission. The answer was inevitably the same. During the months of Mongoose the standard answer was "No. You keep working on Cuba. That's what the President wants." All his pleas got him nothing but "an emotionally negative response."[60] There was little more he could do. With his superiors taking such a dim view of any return to Asia, he suggested that he renew his interest in Israel, which he had begun developing before Kennedy assigned him to Mongoose. McNamara and Rusk vetoed that possibility. Finally he turned his attention to the area of Latin America. Perhaps he could carve out a new specialty.[61] It was not an entirely new area of concern. Since at least 1959 he had kept abreast of political events there. In that year he had forwarded an idea about problems in Colombia to State for its consideration. "State turned to the old Company [CIA] for help — and they turned to me."[62]

In later years Lansdale repeatedly claimed the State Department would not approve a stay lasting longer than a week for him in any Latin American country "because it takes longer than a week to run a revolution, get it started and overthrow the powers that be. They had some crazy idea that that's what I did."[63] His memories were not supported by the records, for on his first major trip to South America, his orders (dated 1 March 1963) sent him to Venezuela for fourteen days' temporary duty.[64]

General Lansdale took along Lieutenant Colonel Manuel J. Chavez as his interpreter. An Air Force intelligence officer, Chavez was stationed in Miami, seconded there to CIA. He had known Lansdale when Lansdale was still a lieutenant colonel, just back from his work in the Philippines prior to his 1954 assignment to Vietnam. In the years that followed, Chavez served as air attaché in several Latin countries. Lansdale considered him a man with good insights into Latin American political situations.[65]

Guerrilla activity in Venezuela in 1963 was intense in both the mountains and urban areas. American officials, fearing that the terrorists received their training in Cuba, agreed that Lansdale should go down for a firsthand look at the situation. He flew to Miami, met Chavez there, and the two left on 7 March 1963. They flew to the Canal Zone and met with General Andrew P. O'Meara, commander in chief, Southern Command (CINC-SOUTH). The plane from Panama to Venezuela was an old Mexican "clunker," and their flight began late after an engine caught fire as the pilot ran it up on the landing strip prior to takeoff.

They finally landed at Maiquita Airport and drove to Caracas. At Maiquita they were met by American embassy personnel and the Venezuelan defense minister, General Antonio Briceno, and other military officials. The Venezuelans saw Chavez and, ignoring Lansdale, rushed toward the former air attaché for *muchos embrazos fuertes y grandes*. The air filled with fervent cries of "Look who's here!" and "Isn't this great?" Miffed at such a breach of protocol, someone from the embassy queried Lansdale about Chavez. "I want someone who really knows these people," he replied, "who can open doors for me and tell me what I'm looking at."[66] The minister of defense later told Lansdale he had pinned Venezuelan Air Force wings on Chavez when he had been air attaché there, the first time a foreigner was so honored.[67]

Lansdale and Chavez lodged at the official military hotel and club in

Caracas, the Circular Militar. Because of the possibility of urban terrorism, guards stood watch outside the building. About three o'clock on their first night, they were awakened from their slumbers by the sounds of a racing automobile engine, just fifty or sixty feet away from the windows of their suite. Then came the muffled sounds of several gunshots. Terrorists had killed a guard, removed his sidearm, and fled the scene. For a time Venezuelan officials feared the night attack might have been an attempt on Lansdale's life but concluded its purpose had been only to seize the guard's weapon.[68]

To American businessmen in Venezuela who were concerned about the safety of their families amidst increasing incidents of terrorism, Lansdale suggested hand grenades. If dependents were threatened, they should "[t]hrow [them] out the window, duck down, be safe; scare these guys. A lot of noise and a lot of fragments fly." He toured oil drilling areas of Lake Maracaibo and examined their antiguerrilla defenses, spent some time in the Falcon Hills guerrilla area, and received briefings from the American MAAG team and Venezuelan army officials on their efforts at counterinsurgency. By then it was time to return to the States.[69]

Only a few weeks later, Lansdale once again traveled to South America, this time to Bolivia and with a different interpreter, Captain William Phillips.[70] General O'Meara, CINCSOUTH, joined Lansdale in Panama for the rest of the journey. They traveled from 25 May to 1 June, mostly in Bolivia but also visiting Peru and Brazil. Lansdale went into the jungle areas on the pretext of visiting medical teams there and spent some days along the Bolivia-Peru border. The town of Coleija made him an honorary citizen, "maybe because I was blowing kisses to all the girls out at the landing strip." He briefed the Bolivian army on the value of building schools in villages and transporting fresh water to rural areas.[71]

He wanted to visit Chile also but the foreign service ruled out such a trip. "I wish I knew what scares them so much," he wondered, "so I could do twice as much of it!" Lansdale was heartened to learn that revolutionaries in South America were still guided by the Marxist-Leninist doctrine requiring them to begin organizational efforts among proletarian workers. The populace in South America was, of course, mostly farmers. "Thank God, they missed that!" Lansdale exulted. "They still haven't caught on entirely. . . . Che Guevara, for example, was silly as a guerrilla leader [in Bolivia]. He was captured and killed [because] he had no popular base there. He was separate [from the people]."[72]

Lansdale's report on this trip to Panama, Bolivia, Peru, and Brazil has been removed from his papers at the Hoover Institution for "reasons of national security." Apparently what he wrote was unusual. In later years he recalled that State Department officials contacted embassy personnel in both Venezuela and Bolivia after his visits to those countries, requesting the American ambassadors to confirm their conclusions that his observations were superficial and incorrect. In both cases the ambassadors' responses were similar: "We are amazed he saw as much as he did. He's quite right."[73] Simply being correct was not enough to save Lansdale from his enemies; rather, it probably hastened his untimely, involuntary retirement.

Whenever he was in Washington, Lansdale continued to worry about developments in Vietnam. On 27 June 1963, President Kennedy appointed Henry Cabot Lodge as ambassador to Vietnam, replacing Frederick Nolting. Lodge was to begin his duties on 1 August. Washington insiders openly speculated that the new frontiersmen would support a coup against Diem, who continued his stubborn opposition to insistent American demands for changes.

When he learned of Lodge's appointment, Lansdale's former boss James H. Douglas wrote to the new ambassador to call his attention to "an unusually wise source of information." Lodge would find it worthwhile to spend some time with Edward Lansdale in preparation for meeting "President Djim [sic]."[74] As a consequence of Douglas' urging, Lodge met with Lansdale. On 25 July, Lansdale gave him a briefing on conditions in Vietnam as he remembered them. If he could not go to Vietnam himself, he could at least help others prepare themselves.

Lansdale told Lodge that Vietnam was a "small" nation in both geography and people — small shopkeepers, small farmers — "who will fight for what they have — if given real hope." People there, he said, had "that unique Asian radar, quick to read your inner personality — whether you genuinely like them or are merely putting on an act." He told Lodge that ambassadors lived in "a real glass fish bowl," that the "[b]amboo telegraph will spread word on you throughout Asia, unknown to you." Any condescension, even of a minor sort, would weaken Lodge's influence.[75] There is little indication from his later actions that Lodge either understood or cared about Lansdale's careful warnings.

Cut off from purposeful official actions, Lansdale floundered for an unofficial role. He wrote memoranda to Gilpatric.[76] He became acquainted with editors of *Reader's Digest*, of *Time*, and of *Life*, who sought off-the-record information about Vietnam.[77] A *Reader's Digest* editor urged him to write an article for the magazine and to visit the magazine's Pleasantville, New York, offices. Lansdale did so in the summer of 1963 and talked of American towns adopting Vietnamese hamlets as sister cities.[78] He wrote to friends, asking them to do what they could for Vietnam. He tried to reinvigorate the American Friends of Vietnam into supporting "exciting, non-partisan" activities so the group could be "real *friends* of the Vietnamese out on the firing line," but he found only a lukewarm reception.[79]

Lansdale's last major effort on behalf of Vietnam came in late summer 1963, when he was invited to have breakfast with W. Averell Harriman, undersecretary of state for political affairs. John Kenneth Galbraith, a Harvard economist serving as ambassador to India, was also present. Both were alarmed at the Diem regime's recent persecution of Buddhists. All three were well aware of recent rumors of American support for a coup in South Vietnam. "I didn't want anyone to kill [Diem]," Lansdale insisted. The talk centered on Nhu's influence over Diem. Lansdale argued that Nhu had such a close relationship because Diem had promised their dying father to look after his younger brother. That was a major reason Diem was reluctant to fire Nhu from his position as chief adviser. Harriman, Galbraith, and Lansdale agreed that the two men had to be separated.

Lansdale believed there was a way to do so. He urged Galbraith and Harriman to establish an academic position for Nhu at Harvard. "Kick him upstairs," Lansdale suggested. "Tell him he's an intellectual." Such an appeal to Nhu's intellectual pretensions, with a sojourn at Harvard, would allow him to lecture to his heart's content and get him out of South Vietnam. "Once he's away," Lansdale added, "Diem will be a very different person." Harriman liked the suggestion, but Galbraith was incensed. "He got mad," Lansdale recalled. "We don't do that at Harvard!" Galbraith said. Saving a nation would not be academically responsible.[80]

Harriman suggested that Lansdale talk over the idea with Roger Hilsman, assistant secretary of state for the Far East. "He wouldn't talk about Vietnam at all," Lansdale lamented. So he turned once again to Defense Secretary Robert McNamara. The secretary was displeased to learn that Lansdale was still trying to involve himself in Vietnam affairs but hinted at forthcoming changes in Saigon. Lansdale mustered his arguments. He asked that a coup be avoided and that the United States preserve the constitution of the Republic of Vietnam. Lansdale reminded the secretary of advice he had given in 1956 at the time the document was drafted — the need for a strong executive, the safety in a system of governmental checks and balances, the rights and obligations of individual citizens, the advantage of free elections, the necessity of allowing Chams, Khmers, Montagnards — minorities all — to participate in voting.

Lansdale admitted that violations of spirit and precepts of that constitution gradually crept into the practices of Diem's regime, until by 1963 it was little more than a historical document. He agreed that any nation's constitution remained only a piece of paper unless the deeds of both people and government honored it and brought it to life.[81] Yet he urgently counseled caution and respect for what had been accomplished there in nine short years. "I talked [to McNamara] as though they were going to overthrow Diem," Lansdale recalled. "There's a constitution" in place there, he insisted. "Please don't destroy that when you're trying to change the government. Remember there's a vice president [Nguyen Ngoc Tho] who's been elected and is now holding office. If anything happens to the president, he should replace him. Try to keep something sustained there."[82] The irony of the conversation did not escape Lansdale's attention. "Although I was McNamara's assistant on paper, he had stopped paying any attention to any advice from me."[83] He wondered what else he could do.

Probably as a result of Lansdale's persistence, in a most unusual move the Pentagon cut orders retiring him from active duty during one of his visits to Latin America. He was not consulted. He did not learn what was happening until he returned from his Bolivian trip to the headwaters of the Amazon. The orders, dated 20 May 1963, put him on the retired list as of 31 May. He did not return from Bolivia until 1 June! He was only fifty-five years old, an unseemly age for a brigadier general in good health to be involuntarily retired.[84]

Lansdale still had a few months' grace in which to wrap up his affairs. The day after his retirement he was ordered back to extended active duty (EAD) from 1 June to 30 October and appointed to the temporary grade of major general. He would not again revert to retired status until 31 October.[85] During those five months he continued to serve as assistant to the secretary of defense for special operations. Four months into the new arrangement, he knew it was not going to work. "I smelled the forthcoming action on Diem and had some hard talks at the White House and State . . . trying to prevent a tragedy, which all denied was in the wind." McNamara had long since stopped listening to his advice and had recently ordered Ros Gilpatric to terminate Lansdale at the first opportunity. "Since Curt LeMay [Air Force chief of staff] told me that I was only on duty because I was an Assistant to Sec Def, this brought about retirement willy nilly." He suggested to Gilpatric that he be fully retired. "I would stick it out longer if I thought I could serve our country that way," he said. But he found it increasingly difficult and onerous.[86]

His enemies, including General Krulak, finally succeeded in their sabotage. "The mice finally gnawed through the woodwork and got my office 'disestablished' on 30 September," he wrote a friend. Even his position as assistant to the secretary of defense for special operations was simply abolished. Lansdale sourly recalled, "A number of people ganged up on me to eliminate this office — the DIA and Joint Staff people; a special operations unit in the Joint Staff office run by a Marine [Krulak's SACSA]

I didn't like — and they came out ahead of the game."[87] Why had it happened? "I suspect my advice on getting a move on in the cold war became increasingly annoying."[88] Most of his duties went to SACSA and most of his staff was sent to DIA ("a distribution which still doesn't make sense to me").

That "disestablishment" was a little more vindictive than Lansdale admitted. Savaged and undercut by Krulak, prevented from participation in Vietnam affairs, Lansdale turned to work with Latin America. Powerful men in Washington contemplated Lansdale's career and finally shunted aside the very man who had for so long served them. President Kennedy thought of him as a character straight out of an Ian Fleming novel who had refused an ambassadorship and failed to overthrow Castro. McNamara regarded him as a grandstanding showman and resented his frequent disagreements with administration policy. The Joint Chiefs viewed him as a bizarre variation from normal officers of flag rank. Dean Rusk at State could not countenance his diplomacy of concern and friendship; such back-door approaches undercut State's own procedures. He had embarrassed State not only over Vietnam but in Latin America as well. His approach to foreign policy at once appealed to Kennedy and horrified the bureaucracy. His very effectiveness in what he did became a double-edged sword that others now used against him. When asked why the president had not intervened on his behalf, Lansdale's answer was a sour one: "Kennedy went along with the bureaucrats."[89]

As was his wont, Lansdale tried to put the best face possible on the disaster. He wrote to a friend that he was "really awfully pleased" to have been the subject of a surprise retirement, because it had ceased "to be any fun clanking around the Pentagon as a major general carrying a file of papers." He had, he claimed, turned into one of those terrible people "whose critiques and predictions kept turning out to be right — and I guess they felt like shooting me on what I had to say about Vietnam and other critical problems."[90] For his last month, Lansdale had little to do except watch others taking over from him.

Always a gentleman, Major General Edward Lansdale thought of those who had helped him. He wrote "a little word bouquet" of appreciation to the receptionist at the Pentagon's River Entrance for her daily cheerfulness to him during the past six years.[91] He also paid his respects to Eugene M. Zuckert, secretary of the Air Force:

> It takes a Service mighty big of spirit to care for a bastard child — and this bastard child returns the affection. I trust the Air Force will never get so narrow of outlook that it cannot free some of its people for individual service in the great way it has done for such a number of us in its early years. . . . While most retiring Air Force persons take with them a memory

of their brotherhood in the air, my own earth-bound career in jungles and mountains (and even my long exile in the Pentagon) had its unforgettable moments which I cherish and thank the Air Force for. I never felt alone.[92]

According to his friends, Lansdale was "the most miserable man in town" as his retirement date approached.[93] He was unsure what to do in the days ahead. He spoke of being offered "fat-cat administrative posts" but it had been too long since his advertising days in California; the business world failed to interest him. Perhaps he would just get some rest, do some writing, "and then get back into the scrap when I figure out how best to do so."[94]

On the day he vacated his office, Lansdale turned over his accumulated files to the SACSA people. They were unsatisfied and asked him for his secret intelligence files. "I didn't *have* any secret ones!" he responded. "They never understood the human relationships that went into information [gathering] about foreign countries, people, and events. [All] I kept [in my files at the office were] names of Americans, people in the service, who'd gotten very close to citizens of foreign countries."[95] Today it is called networking. So very much of Lansdale's work, his effectiveness with others, consisted not so much in *doing* as in *knowing*. He knew a multitude of people and understood how and when to put them in contact with one another. His letters emphasize the way his team expanded through one member recommending a new contact who had promise. Commonly used phrases included "Just a little note to tip you off to someone you should get to know," "Suggest you two get together," "Keep him in mind."[96] It was an attitude of heart and mind that the McNamaras, Rusks, and Krulaks of this world would never understand. And that was Lansdale's secret.

He spent some "frustrating years" trying to find an effective way of using U.S. personnel systems for selection of those people with the qualities he desired for work in special operations. He sought individuals with sensitivity, with a dedicated knowledge of principles involved in U.S. policies toward a given foreign country, with language skills, with effectiveness in dealing with foreigners in their homeland, as well as with combat and technical skills. Never very appreciative of the French, Lansdale still learned one valuable lesson from a French ministry of defense official who commented one day that he used the method adopted by Otto Skorzeny, a Nazi officer skilled in special operations.

Skorzeny's approach to selecting personnel was simple and effective. He talked to those rare individuals whom he knew personally to have demonstrated skill in special operations and asked them for the names of others. Skorzeny then studied the dossiers of those men whose names

had been given him and from them, using his own judgment, selected
the people who appealed to him. He then assigned them to field duties,
observed their performance, and made his final selection from those who
did well. "I made use of this method," Lansdale said, and over several
years compiled the names of Americans — military and civilian — who
were available for assignment. Had he been able to do so, he would
also have allowed the host country to write their efficiency reports, but
when he suggested that novel approach to Secretary McNamara, his idea
was vetoed.[97] That was the only "secret" he could have shared with
Krulak, but the Brute never asked. His approach had allowed him to do
many things others had never dared to try.

Lansdale thought of fellow officers over the years who, with jealousy
or suspicion, had asked, "How did you ever do such things? Whoever
gave you permission to act that way?" His inevitable response had been,
"That's what . . . our citizenship confers on us."[98] To those who questioned his clandestine activities he also had a ready answer: "[T]hey
were actions that essentially followed American principles. . . . [T]he
essence of the American way is . . . the status of an individual. . . .
When [that's] the basis for your actions . . . you get an awful lot of
allies and brothers with you."[99]

Now it all seemed a thing of the past. He was being put out to pasture
and he was ridden with frustration. As Lansdale thought back over the
years, he was unwilling to describe past years and his military career in
the usual way. Most retiring officers proclaimed at their retirement ceremony, "I had a wonderful career and I am very proud of it." Ed didn't
feel that way. "It didn't quite turn out that way," he admitted. "By
and large, [my work in OSD] was a bum experience."[100] But it was
over and now he could turn to new things. He retired 31 October 1963.
West of the international dateline in Vietnam, it was already 1 November.

12

INTERLUDE: A PEOPLE'S WAR

AS EDWARD LANSDALE RETURNED from Vietnam at the end of 1956, others touted him as the best man on counterguerrilla warfare within the three armed services. While the reputation was satisfying and ego-boosting, it did not tempt Lansdale to rest on his laurels. There was still more to learn. There had to be more to this business of countering guerrillas than just being *against* what they stood for. Already convinced of some of the answers, he wanted to learn others. From the time of his posting to the Pentagon in early 1957, Lansdale cast about for ways to understand guerrilla warfare, to analyze and deal with it systematically. He sifted through events in his life since his initial assignment to the Philippines in 1945, his talks with Huks, his advice to the Philippine Army and government. He recalled conversations with Magsaysay, Valeriano, Manahan, Banzon, San Juan, and other Filipinos. He remembered his days in Vietnam and reconstructed discussions with the Ngos — Diem and Nhu — with Trinh Minh Thé, Le Van Vien, Nguyen Van Hinh, and hundreds of others. He thought about his experiences with common people in the Philippines and Vietnam — the Juan de la Cruzes and Nguoi Thuong Dans.

Not content with memories alone, Lansdale began to read widely for the first time in years. Daily news summaries came automatically to his desk, so it was easy to keep up with the world scene. Struggles in China, the Ukraine, the Philippines, Malaya, Burma, Indonesia, Tibet, Iraq, Lebanon, Syria, Egypt, Cyprus, Algeria, Cuba, Greece, Hungary, Guatemala, Iran, Israel, Laos, Bolivia, Venezuela, Argentina, and Colombia — the list of troubled countries was long. It seemed as if the world everywhere was in flames.

To understand more about that unrest, Lansdale read the military teachings of Mao Tse-tung, Sun Tzu's *The Art of War,* Vo Nguyen Giap's teachings on military tactics. He perused the writings and speeches of

Edgar Snow (author of *Red Star over China* and other books), Dato Ghazali bin Shafie (permanent secretary to the Malaysian external affairs ministry), C. L. Sulzberger, Joseph Kraft, Le Duan (politburo secretary to the Democratic Republic of Vietnam), Ramón Magsaysay, Vicente Villamin (Filipino political analyst), Senator Thomas Dodd, and dozens of others.

Lansdale reflected on his youth. College courses taken in years past now proved helpful. His major in English and his stint with UCLA's humor magazine *The Claw* gave him dexterity in using words. His days in advertising also afforded him skills to draw upon. He might no longer be peddling men's trousers for Levi Strauss or wine for Swiss Colony, but he was still selling — ideas emerged that he wanted to share with others, and their presentation could be enhanced by the commercial years spent on the sloping hills of San Francisco.

Lansdale was spurred in his search for ideas by the political climate of the day and his own convictions that America was in a war to the death with communism. The cold war between East and West was intense. Fighting in Korea had ended not long before in cynical stalemate; the United States was increasingly involved in Indochina. Those Americans who visited Beijing or Moscow and who counseled restraint and moderation were somehow thought to be subversive and something less than loyal and patriotic citizens; some even categorized them as traitors willing to sell out their own country. The attorney general's list of subversive organizations remained a powerful instrument in the hands of men like Senator Joseph McCarthy and others of his ilk. One observer reminded her readers that "[o]nly a carrier of bubonic plague was more frightening than a communist."[1] In the midst of this setting, Lansdale was as opposed to communism as any American of his time, and he firmly believed that no one with a free choice would accept that system if a better alternative was available.

Certain conclusions began to emerge for Lansdale, based on his welter of memories, his experiences. They were tempered by books he had read, by lessons others shared with him, and by his own uncommonly good common sense. His job within the Office of Special Operations gave him access to many classified files and records pertinent to his studies. His work focused his mind on reflections about the nature of cold war conflicts. What emerged was a synthesis of his basic humanism, his love for Asians, his genuine enjoyment of other people, his early training as a Christian and his respect for the precepts of Scripture, his devotion to the founding principles of this nation, and his long years of serving in lands beset by insurgencies. He finally came to believe there was indeed an approach to counterguerrilla warfare that could be extremely successful but that was not yet perceived by most other Americans.

Some years later, Mary McGrory, correspondent for the *Washington Star*, wrote to him about his viewpoint. With a humorous twist she summed up Lansdale's vision. "I saw McGeorge Bundy the other night," she wrote, "and told him that of all the Vietnamese policies I had heard expounded, yours was the only one that made sense to me. I told him that while I had never recovered from the initial shock of learning from you that counter-insurgency is [only] another word for brotherly love, I was all for it."[2] That was precisely what Edward Lansdale came to believe. This man of war became convinced that while massed firepower was not effective against rebels, kindness might be!

Lansdale wanted to share his ideas with others. He thought about all the talented men and women serving in America's armed forces who were assigned to many lands around the globe — over a million troops stationed at bases, MAAGs, and missions in more than forty countries. Each one was a potential witness for American ideas of caring and concern. If properly motivated, they could accomplish much on behalf of their nation. He *knew* he had made a difference in his missions to the Philippines and Vietnam. At the end of World War II he had had no high rank. He was then only a lowly major. Yet by dint of common sense, dedication, hard work, honesty, and intelligence, he had made a difference. All he had needed was the chance. Pitting his own talents against those of the nation's enemies, he had won. And he was not unique. There were hundreds of thousands of other Americans stationed abroad. Not all of them could be Edward Lansdales, but surely some had the same deftness of mind and understanding.

Therefore, Lansdale accepted every possible invitation to speak to interested audiences. If on a lecture platform he could spread the word, say the right phrase, or pluck the correct chord in someone else's heart, then he might convert others to his own approach to people's wars. In turn they might achieve great things or work to persuade still others or, at the least, support Lansdale and his brethren in their endeavors. Every soldier was a potential recruit in Lansdale's army, a novitiate in his order. Working together, such Ugly Americans might defeat the hydra-headed monster of communism and bring a better way of life to the beleaguered of the earth. Lansdale believed individuals really could effect change and he felt his own responsibility as a change agent was heavy indeed. It was no time to slack off.

Lansdale was not timid about committing his thoughts to paper or proclaiming them in a speech. The words of most high-ranking officers tend to be ephemeral, not worth recording, and in some cases not worth listening to. They are mundane, full of jargon and catch phrases of the moment, mumbled woodenly at audiences notable only for their glazed eyes. Most generals who deliver meatier discourses are reading speeches

written for them by a staff officer. Not Lansdale. His words sprang from
his own experiences, his own thoughts, his own reading. They were
lively, cogent, pertinent, and important. He employed no ghostwriters.
Each succinct word was idiosyncratically and personally his very own.
Scores of listeners avidly sought copies of his addresses to read and
ponder, to share with still others. Printed versions of his speeches were
distributed even to the members of other countries' armed forces. The
files are full of old requests for copies of his latest talk. Unfortunately,
many of them remain sequestered for they bear a security classification
and thus are still withheld from scholars in the "interests of national
security."[3]

Lansdale's experiences in the Orient and his influential position in
the Pentagon made him a sought-after speaker, and he made the most
of it. Always good with words and skilled in arranging them, he now
became an adept speaker. As his own ideas became ever clearer to him,
he stood before audiences as an exhorter, evangelist, and missionary. It
was his purpose to convict, to convert, to persuade others to accept
truths that became ever more precious to him.

Lansdale discovered that others were hungry for words of victory.
Once a lieutenant colonel returned from his assignment with an Army
training mission in Liberia. Lansdale invited some top officials at the
Pentagon to hear him talk. They sat listening for hours. When they left
the meeting room they were surprised to discover that a fire had been
raging for some time on a lower floor. "We had just ignored all distrac-
tions!" he marveled. What had so entranced them? The speaker told
how he organized elementary studies for his mostly illiterate counterparts,
taught sanitation, diet, patriotism, responsibility, and respect for neighbor-
ing tribes, and urged an end to brigandly stealing. He preached the duty
of becoming "true brothers of their people." Lansdale was enthralled.
"This is a whole book on counter-subversion," he remarked. *"Our enemy
can be beaten."*[4]

Not long after arriving at the Pentagon, Lansdale got his first opportunity
to express his developing viewpoint. On 22 February 1957 he spoke to
instructors in the Department of Social Sciences at the Air Force Academy
in Colorado Springs. The Air Force was proud of him. "[H]is permanent
promotion to Colonel was considered a *combat* promotion on the merits
of his contribution to the eminent success" of campaigns in the Philippines
and Vietnam. Lansdale spoke twice that evening: an informal gathering
scheduled from 8:30 P.M. to midnight continued until 4:30 A.M. In his
formal presentation, Lansdale stressed the two phases of any counterguerrilla campaign: pacification and social stabilization. The first might last
up to three or more years; the second could extend for a generation. He
emphasized that rebels elsewhere might yearn for the same goals that

once motivated Americans: officers assigned in troubled areas should understand that those around them "are going through *their* 1776."[5]

This emphasis on the American Revolution and the country's Founding Fathers quickly became a recurring theme. The "liberty of individual men," Lansdale said to a panel on strategy, "is our really precious, fundamental political belief." If the United States was to help others preserve their own freedom, it must act "in the *spirit* of our own most precious beliefs." He reminded his listeners that ancient Roman soldiers brought more than roads, viaducts, and baths to areas in which they served. Many a Roman leader must have considered that his strategy and tactics might well go down in history. Yet aside from Julius Caesar, whose works provided much later torment for beginning students of Latin, most of those generals' ideas have long since been forgotten. Their heritage "was in the law and in the language." What would be the American legacy? Lansdale suggested that "the American spirit of freedom" was the best the nation could offer.[6]

It was important for Lansdale that his audiences recall the founding documents and themes of their own nation. He was not wrapping himself in the flag; he was trying to build anew on a recognizably firm foundation. If his listeners understood their own heritage they could more readily perceive the reality of modern battlegrounds. "The Continental troops at Valley Forge, the officers and men under Marion, Greene, or Wayne would have found much that was familiar to them in the *motivation* of . . . modern [insurgent] troops, in the[ir] *use of propaganda* . . . in the *covert political organs* so reminiscent of the Committees of Correspondence, the Committees of Safety, and in the *support* of our Continental troops by farmers and shopkeepers with food, money, and hard military information."[7] Lansdale had sympathy for the goals of insurgents; he simply wanted them to achieve something better than communism could offer.

Americans needed to know the promises in their own Declaration of Independence, spelled out in the first ten amendments to the Constitution. They should know and be proud of their own founding documents. "But don't confuse the mechanics of the system we Americans have developed," he warned, "with being the only way they can be used. Learn to recognize these profound truths . . . in the cultures of others."[8] In a speech he wrote for use by the deputy secretary of defense, Lansdale said that communists believed man to be a thing, a material instrument, a slave of the state. "We believe that men 'are endowed by their Creator with certain unalienable Rights.' " Thus American strength must "come from our belief in the spiritual Creator and His endowment. This is our bond with all the free people of the earth."[9]

Lansdale was always concerned to uphold the best that Americans could offer to others. One such concept was honesty, and he emphasized it over and again. In a talk to the Military Government Association held at Washington's Shoreham Hotel, he told of a U.S. colonel and his Filipino assistant inside the vaults of the Philippine National Bank as contesting armies in 1945 made a shambles of the city. The two men counted stack upon stack of money and then turned it over to the American Army for safekeeping until it could be restored to the bank. The Filipino marveled. "There we were. All alone with millions of dollars worth of money. And, doggonit, that colonel made me an honest man." Lansdale pointed out that honest men make honest elections.

He segued into a description of NAMFREL and the election that brought Magsaysay to power. An old man lay dying in a hospital in the town of San Fernando and asked to see Colonel Lansdale. Lansdale went to his bedside and held his hand. The old man was proud of his son, a Huk rebel, until time for the election. Expecting the worst, he was surprised to find that everyone he voted for won! There was thus no need for a revolution. They already had a government that cared. When a Huk squadron came into San Fernando, he shouted at them to go away and send his son home. They bayoneted him and now he was dying. But he wanted Lansdale to hear his joy over the honest election.

The only governments capable of allowing man to live with man, Lansdale lectured, were those founded on the concept of individual men with "certain unalienable rights." He ended with these words: "If the Communists fight us with seemingly infinite patience; if they use deceit and terrorism and hidden subversive organizations against us; if they cast doubt on the character or intent of any strong leaders among us; let us hold hard to this truth in all our actions."[10]

During a lecture on Southeast Asia, given at the Army War College, Lansdale noted that much military emphasis was placed on guarding against Soviet encroachment on the West. Training concentrated on preventing a Russian thrust into Germany toward the Rhine along the Hof Corridor and through the Fulda Gap — "a future war which may or may not happen." It made more sense, he told his audience, to focus "on the dirty, half-hidden war that is going on now — not on a future possibility. This war has combat rules of its own [and] offers us a chance to learn these rules." Although Southeast Asia had only six percent of the earth's total land area, it held about one-fourth of the globe's population. The real stakes there were "the people on the land," and communism sought to win them over. Lansdale reminded the senior officers — most full colonels, several of whom would soon become generals — assembled that day at the War College that "as military men, we had better learn how to cope with this formidable enemy."

Lansdale had read a considerable number of Mao's writings. He was aware that the Chinese leader once stated, "Among our enemies there were some people who guessed our thought processes and knew our combat methods. If there had been more, we would not have been so often victorious."[11] Lansdale intended to be one of those capable of peering into the innermost recesses of his enemies' minds. And he knew that one of the first requirements was to take away an enemy's supporters. The way to begin was to know an enemy — his strategies, tactics, goals, and thoughts. Only those prepared in such a way could hope to defeat communism.

To those at the Army War College, Lansdale recited Mao's deeply held beliefs about the correct way to treat people in embattled areas, his "three great disciplinary measures" and "eight noteworthy points," which had been part of strictly enforced discipline for the Chinese Eighth Route Army.

Mao's three cardinal measures were: Act in accordance with orders. Do not take anything from the people. Do not allow self-interest to injure public interest. His eight points gave followers practical advice: Put back the door [after using it as a bed]. Tie up straws [after using them for a mattress]. Talk pleasantly. Buy and sell fairly. Return everything borrowed. Indemnify everything damaged. Do not bathe in view of women. Do not rob personal belongings of captives. The purpose of such rules, Mao insisted, was to create a necessary relationship between an army and its people and could be adopted by any army. Once again Lansdale quoted from Mao: "There are those who cannot imagine how guerrillas could survive for long . . . . But, they do not understand the relationship between the people and the army. The people are like the water and the army is like the fish. How can it be difficult for the fish to survive when there is water?"[12]

This presentation makes clear that Lansdale was adding a new element to his theories. Americans should not only *understand* communist recipes for insurgency, but *use* them even more effectively than did their foes to counter their enemies' plans. His position was unusual for that era. Lansdale was a dedicated anticommunist, conservative in his thoughts. Many people of like persuasion were neither as willing to study their enemy nor as open to adopting communist ideas to use as a countervailing force. If for no other reason, this fact makes Lansdale stand out in bold relief to the majority of fellow military men who struggled on behalf of America in those intense years of the cold war.

A devotee of psychological warfare — psywar — since his first days in the Philippines, Lansdale continued to stress its importance during the years when he listed essential themes for his far-flung audiences.

He defined psywar as "an action, usually propaganda, which you take to influence the will of other people, usually the enemy, to support the gaining of your military objective in war." Several illustrations he used of successful psywar actions included Joshua's use of noise at Jericho, Chinese soldiers signaling an attack during the Korean War by blowing bugles, Timur the Lame's escorting envoys from cities he wanted to conquer to see huge piles of bones made from the slain bodies of those who resisted him, Hitler's newsreel movies of Stuka-Panzer teams in action, and Tran Hung Dao's order that his soldiers have their arms tattooed as a symbol of their will to resist the minions of Kublai Khan. Lansdale noted that even such modern slogans as "Make the world safe for democracy" and "The Four Freedoms" were examples of successful psywar actions. Tricking an enemy, he said, "aside from bare hands," was probably man's oldest weapon.

Lansdale cautioned audiences to be neither dismissive of psywar nor overenthusiastic. Think of it, he said, only as "an important *supporting* weapon." Some military people misused psywar operations, becoming fixated with the technique itself and losing sight of the desired result. "They remind me of artillerymen toiling for long hours to perfect the firing of salutes," Lansdale lectured, forgetting that the purpose of their weapons is to destroy or weaken the enemy. Practitioners of psywar should remember a few simple rules: Be certain of the objective and work toward it with "bite-sized" programs. "Be fuzzy about this," he warned, "and your results will be fuzzy . . . . There is no sense in printing leaflets for people who cannot read!" Remember to put ideas across in ways people could understand. "Remember and honor the old adage that 'actions speak louder than words.' Psychological operations aren't much good if you say one thing earnestly and then prove that you didn't really mean it by acting otherwise."[13]

On many occasions Lansdale emphasized the importance of enlisted soldiers. If used correctly, they might well be the most important asset of third world nations. An army might be the only true national entity keeping a government and nation alive. It had the only nationwide communications net. Its members were the only disciplined representatives of the central government that a citizenry came into contact with regularly. Officers came from the cream of the educated class and were outstanding young potential leaders of the government. In many places, Lansdale reported, officials elsewhere had come to realize the value of an army. In Turkey, thousands of reserve officers taught children in primary schools. In Indonesia, Army construction battalions worked in East Java on flood control projects. The Laotian army instructed Muong and Tasseng chiefs how to be good public administrators. In the Philippines, judge advocate officers provided legal counsel to the poor. Insofar as such efforts succeeded, he said, national governments were strengthened.[14]

The common combat ground of the struggle with communism, Lansdale told listeners over and again, "is among the people at a village or rice paddy." One of his inevitable themes was military civic action. A government soldier holding a shovel or offering a helping hand to other citizens of his country provided a bulwark against subversive insurgency.[15] Civic action, Lansdale insisted, had first been named by the ancient Chinese general Sun Tzu as the "moral law," "the first constant factor which governs the art of war." All actions that caused "people to be in complete accord with their ruler" illuminated that moral law. Thus, for Lansdale, the principle underlying civic action had been a prime factor for centuries. It was an excellent tool to use against communism. "[T]he way to start defeating Communist guerrilla leaders and forces is to use the same cardinal principle — *and to use it better.*"

The few real successes enjoyed by the West in the years of the cold war, Lansdale said, "have been possible only when the armed forces of free men sincerely applied this cardinal principle." The moral law, he insisted, was too important to be ignored, for to those civilians who found themselves within an insurgent combat zone, the army was inseparable from the government. It was important, then, to emphasize civic action, any deed "which makes the soldier a brother of the people, as well as their protector." When troops remembered to act in appropriate ways, government was strengthened; when they did not, guerrilla influence increased.

His examples were earthy ones. He asked others to put themselves into the shoes of beleaguered peoples. "How would you react if soldiers stole your chickens or pigs or personal belongings — maybe roughing you up and having sport with your wife or daughter in the process? How would you react if political leaders posed as men of integrity, but you saw them living high on the hog, buying property and jewelry and expensive cars — all on a low government salary — and thus obviously hoggishly corrupt?" Personal honesty and integrity were essential. No amount of fancy, showy military civic action projects could overcome a stolen chicken or a carelessly driven jeep. Soldiers and bureaucrats, right down to the lowest private and civil service grade, were visible representatives of their government. *Their* actions were the ones by which John Smith, Juan de la Cruz, and Nguoi Thuong Dan judged the real intent of their government.[16]

Lansdale regularly spoke of the importance of civic action. "A truly pragmatic American would insist that we do today what will help us tomorrow," he began. Describing himself as one who had served for many years as a public servant in Asia "*not* to an empire but to a democracy," Lansdale called on his listeners to join with him. If only "we could get just the right handful of Americans out to Vietnam," he said, then that country's fortunes would begin to improve. Acting as unselfish friends, such people would encourage the development of realizable political goals, instruct political parties how to develop a popular base, and encourage the growth of native political institutions. They would help Vietnamese find "their own true cause to fight *for,* much more than helping them to fight *against* something." Such activities would "put the war upon a sound moral and political footing."

Others sacrificed. Lansdale quoted from a current Vietnamese handbill that called for five thousand volunteer students from Saigon to work in the countryside during their summer vacation. The broadside proclaimed: "You will warm up your unfortunate comrades with humanity and love. You will throw a bridge between cities and countryside, the educated and uneducated, the privileged and ill-treated. You will build love, understanding, sacrifice, confidence, and hope. You will revive the national self-reliant spirit, the four-thousand-year-old moral tradition of Vietnam." Lansdale's voice was husky with emotion when he summarized such attitudes. "Surely," he said, "we have a bond . . . with people such as they."[17]

His concern over winning the loyalty of people to their own government grew apace. He insisted to all who would listen that "[o]f all the names given to the armed struggles in today's world — insurgency, revolution, rebellion, guerrilla warfare, brushfire wars, wars of national liberation, and low-intensity conflict — probably the name 'people's war' is the one most useful." If Americans would only think of such conflicts by that name, "our military and political leaders might awaken to how important a factor is their consideration of human behavior in the decisions they make. Ideally, each decision should be measured for its potential effectiveness by pre-action questioning of the decision. . . . 'What will the people's reaction [be] to this proposed action?' "[18]

In a country suffering from a people's war, observers should judge which of the rights of man were in good health "and which are weak, withering, or dead. These latter are the rotten spots in the political base — the ones the enemy will exploit — the ones that will sicken the morale of the government forces — the ones that will turn people away from supporting the government." It was, he argued, imperative that leaders recognize this fact and begin to heal or construct anew the rights of their own citizenry. "The very minimum, in the midst of war,[19] is that the government must at least start such reform and do so with a sincerity."[20]

Lansdale regularly sounded his most important themes: the importance of people and the necessity for improving their lives, for responsive and responsible government, for appropriate soldierly behavior. All this was necessary if ever "a political base for supporting the fight" against guerrillas was to emerge. He hammered away at the need for a wide range of social operations by the army, at the need to supervise troop behavior and to care for civilians accidentally caught in and wounded by combat's crossfire — and to do so in military hospitals. He even — dare he say it? — argued that insurgent enemies be offered "a fair chance at rehabilitation," for they also were part of a nation's people.[21]

Lansdale knew he had to make the right sounds when he spoke to politically sensitive military audiences, and he unflinchingly remembered to touch all the correct bases. At the Air Force Academy, during his introductory remarks on "The Insurgent Battlefield," he gave ardent plaudits to his own superiors. The very notion of counterinsurgency, he said truthfully enough, "has been greatly heartened by the personal interest of President Kennedy." Further, he said, "[t]he top echelon, including Secretary McNamara, Deputy Secretary Gilpatric, and the Joint Chiefs of Staff, General LeMay definitely, are dedicated to making our effort succeed." His phrases, courteous though they were, may well have caused him to choke as he uttered them. McNamara had no sympathy for or understanding of his ideas, and Curtis LeMay, the crusty old pilot who was now Air Force chief of staff, would go to his grave proclaiming "victory through air power" and "bomb insurgents back to the Stone Age." Yet Lansdale was sufficiently a politician to know it was necessary to give verbal bouquets to appropriate authorities *whether or not* they actually supported his views.

His actual address that day to the Air Force Academy may well have been one of his most insightful. Still stressing the need to gain the loyalty of a nation's people, he began with a hoary military precept: "Take the high ground." The terrain of a battlefield is inevitably of crucial importance to warring parties. It has been so throughout history. Yet on an insurgent battlefield, the dominant terrain feature was not a hill, city, river, valley, or forest. The paramount object was a country's people. The sole purpose of insurgent fighting was *"to win these people.* When the people are won, along with them go the terrain, the wealth of the land, the whole existence of the nation." If a rebel contending party obtains the loyalty of the populace and the governmental army secures for itself an overwhelming superiority in tanks, planes, artillery, and numbers of soldiers, the government will still ultimately fall. He concurred with the Old Testament prophet who proclaimed "the race is not to the swift, nor the battle to the strong."[22] In all his years of study, speaking, and writing, this appreciation may have been Lansdale's most important contribution to a proper understanding of the basic nature of people's wars.

Correct in his understanding, appreciative of the value his enemy saw in "protracted wars," Lansdale suggested to his cadet audience that they not become impatient when victory eluded their efforts year after year. Communists were willing to bide their time, to work patiently even when no end was in sight. "The Communist preparation of the battlefield in Vietnam began about 40 years ago," Lansdale remarked. If they could be patient, then we must be also.[23]

A few months later, Lansdale sounded this theme for a second time at the Army's Special Warfare School. Once again he lectured, "The Communist goal is to win control of the people. Along with them go the land, its bounty, the independent life of the nation." They could be defeated, however, if American fighting men remembered that "[y]our *means* must justify the end goal you seek." He cautioned against the uses of force. Some communities within a beleaguered foreign land might support insurgents. "[A]re those communities to be treated as part of the enemy or are they . . . part of the nation which the troops are sworn to defend?" For Lansdale there was but one answer. He called for Special Forces troops to serve wisely. "Move in [to an enemy area] with military alertness, but also with brotherly concern. . . . If you win the people over to your side, the Communist guerrillas have no place to hide." Then, Lansdale counseled, find them and, as warriors, fix and finish them.[24]

This address was important in two ways. First, it made clear that he was no dewy-eyed idealist who only urged others to do everyone a good turn. He was too realistic in his appraisals, too practical in his programs, too earthy in his tactics, too full of good common sense. He did not decry soldierly killing of fellow combatants. "We must not become so engrossed" in other activities, he warned, "that we ever forget that a fighting man must ever be ready for a fight." He only wanted such death-dealing to be effective, using tactics that avoided self-destructive and self-defeating collateral harm to civilian populations. Second, this address was a clear call for American fighting men to understand that they faced an entirely new kind of war that would not be fought with three divisions — two up and one back. He grew increasingly concerned to emphasize this fact in all his lectures. The world had turned, and tactical doctrines sufficient for World War II were no longer going to work.

Plato once described Socrates as "the best and wisest man I ever knew." This author's candidate for that place in his life is a former philosophy teacher, Dr. Samuel M. Hamilton, professor emeritus, Fort Hays State University, Hays, Kansas. Professor Hamilton once wryly observed that he was a very limited man; he had but one course in him. Those students who signed up for a second or third course simply hadn't understood him the first time! Edward Lansdale's addresses came to be much like that. He had but one set of themes and he believed them to be of crucial importance if America was ever going to learn how to fight a people's war, and he regularly despaired of that ever happening. He modified his themes occasionally as experience or study dictated, and he tailored them for individual assemblies, but he seldom varied from them. No matter the audience, the same threads of reason always showed against the fabric on the loom.

It is little wonder Lansdale felt this sense of commitment. Other military men seemed alarmingly sanguine about the course of American involvement in Vietnam. General Paul C. Harkins, chief of USMAAG, exulted, "The war is being properly managed. . . . We must keep doing what we are doing." General Maxwell Taylor commented, "I would say that our strategy today is that which I have been recommending. . . . As we get greater forces we can always move toward some objective which is so valuable to the Viet Cong that they must stand and fight." General Earle G. Wheeler argued, "[O]ur U.S. forces . . . should be able to defeat the Viet Cong and to re-establish this favorable balance that we had a couple of years ago." Admiral Ulysses G. Sharp announced, "We have stopped losing the war." General H.W.O. Kinnard reported, "[W]e are winning the war militarily and can keep on winning it militarily."

Whether on active duty or retired, other military men were optimistic. Retired brigadier general and military author S.L.A. Marshall claimed, "I think we can bring the war to a conclusion within the next year, possibly within the next six months." General William Westmoreland boasted, "We're going to out-guerrilla the guerrilla and out-ambush the ambush. . . . because we're smarter, we have greater mobility and firepower, we have more endurance and more to fight for. . . . And we've got more guts." General Harold K. Johnson reported, "We are very definitely winning in Vietnam." Admiral John S. McCain, Jr., agreed: "We have the enemy licked now. He is beaten." It was not only generals and admirals who were complacent. Colonel William Pietsch exulted that "Charlie is on the run everywhere. He's whipped."[25] It is little wonder Edward Lansdale often felt like John the Baptist, "the voice of one crying in the wilderness."[26]

Lansdale was neither willing to give up his mission of announcing what the United States needed in its efforts in Southeast Asia nor particularly respectful of the intellects of those who disagreed. Nor was he too timid to say so. He told officer students at the Air War College, "All actions in the war should be devised to attract and then make firm the allegiance of the people." If American flag officers could not understand that simple fact, then they should be "promptly retired to take up basket-weaving or anything else truly suited to [their] talents."[27]

One of those converted by Lansdale offered a plaintive echo. Lieutenant

Colonel Pete Kosutic taught at the Air Force Special Operations School at Eglin AFB in Florida. He observed, "Our major problem, as I see it, is we cannot seem to enlighten our senior officers who have little or no interest in Insurgency, Nation building, Psy Ops and civic action."[28]

On every possible occasion, Lansdale described why the United States had not done well in its military venture in Vietnam. "[E]ach side has fought a different type of war." The Viet Cong carried on an insurgency while the United States fought a "limited war." "Each side fights," he argued, "in the way most familiar to its field leaders." An American officer described the leadership of U.S. field forces: knowing what we should do, we continued to do what we were accustomed to doing. Lansdale agreed. "We label our fight as 'helping the Vietnamese maintain their freedom,' " he said. Yet too many within the U.S. military prosecuted the fight using only the "ugly mechanics of a 'limited war.' " Such an approach, Lansdale insisted, with its horrendous collateral damage in terms of both civilian property and lives, "might well provoke a man of good will to ask, 'just what freedom of what Vietnamese are we helping to maintain?' "[29]

Lansdale would have appreciated the words of Robert Taber, author of a 1965 book entitled *The War of the Flea*. Taber wrote, "There is only one means of defeating an insurgent people who will not surrender, and that is extermination. There is only one way to control a territory that harbours resistance, and that is to turn it into a desert. Where these means cannot, for whatever reason, be used, the war is lost."[30] Lansdale spoke precisely to that point in a letter to a friend. If, he wrote, the "only alternative is to kill every last person in the enemy ranks [then] I'm not only morally opposed to this alternative, but I'm convinced that it's humanly impossible."[31]

Many men echoed his words, but none were ever heard. Among them was Lieutenant Colonel Carl Bernard, assigned to Vietnam as a senior province adviser. In a paper written after his return, he stated: "The tools of the Viet Cong are primarily *non*-military . . . . The tools [of the United States] overwhelmingly are military . . . . This basic failure in . . . US . . . perception of the war has insured that the enemy becomes stronger each year . . . . The . . . US continues . . . looking for massed enemy formations. The VC continues to concentrate its talents on controlling the people. Each succeeds."[32] Few knew of Bernard and few listened to Lansdale. The crusade for understanding faced formidable obstacles and the endtime drew nearer.

In a 1964 foray into public print, Lansdale wrote a jaundiced view in *Foreign Affairs* of the progress of the war in Vietnam. He admitted that the journal was an unusual choice in which to air his views, describing the magazine as one for "stuffed shirts and intellectuals — strange company for me — but the group that has a lot to do in shaping opinion towards our policies abroad."[33] He confessed his belief to another correspondent that his efforts to bring about a change in America's approach to Vietnam "were just getting stopped by the arrogance of the policy-making intellectuals." Consequently he chose *Foreign Affairs* as a way to "strike at their thinking through one of their own bibles."[34] "The harsh fact," he wrote, "and one which has given pause to every thoughtful American is that, despite the use of overwhelming amounts of men, money and matériel, despite the quantity of well-meant American advice and despite the impressive statistics of casualties inflicted on the Viet Cong, the Communist subversive insurgents have grown steadily stronger . . . . to act at their will in the very areas of Viet Nam where . . . American efforts have been most concentrated."[35] Since wars were waged to gain political objectives, the United States needed to determine precisely what it sought and shape its strategy to those ends.[36]

Four years later an increasingly pessimistic general sent a second article to *Foreign Affairs*. In 1968 he posed again a crucial question: What did America seek in Vietnam? The question had, he said, been repeatedly asked, but the answers did not satisfy because no one ever gave a *full* response. With growing cynicism, Lansdale recalled the way his government approached the conflict in Vietnam. "[W]e concentrate on eliminating the enemy by physical means and have relied superstitiously on the magic of casualty numbers." As a consequence, the very people the United States was supposedly helping the most had suffered grievously. "We have concentrated on killing the enemy," he recalled, and despite some success, such an approach was simply not good enough to achieve the original goals to which the United States had pledged itself.

It did not take a wise man to divine that the American solutions were counterproductive. "Not enough of our aims are focused sharply," Lansdale wrote, and as a consequence "we seem to be struggling toward some day when the long war will end with a whimper instead of a bang." What is it, he asked his readers, that the United States *should* be seeking? He enumerated the goals once more: peace, fairness, the ability to choose a government freely, justice, freedom. It was time to lead the way to a true people's peace. For the first time, General Lansdale lowered his hopes and asked for a lesser goal. Let the people of Vietnam once again vote with their feet, he begged. Let the area be divided into a communist North, a center area ruled by a coalition government, and a noncommunist South: Vietnam divided into thirds (after the old French separations into Tonkin, Annam, and Cochinchina) instead of into halves. Then the citizens of that war-torn area could have a real choice.[37]

Even his hope that Vietnam, like ancient Gaul, might be divided into three parts eventually faded away and Lansdale turned his mind to ways in which America could disengage from its war of attrition in Southeast Asia. Writing in *Look* magazine during the Nixon era, he called for the nation "to de-Americanize the effort and start bringing our men back home again with honor." In that one sentence, the ever-political general captured the essence of two of his president's key slogans: the struggle must be "Vietnamized," and the war must be ended "with honor."

Fighting must be quarantined within the borders of South Vietnam; the southern government must become a "really responsible partner." Lansdale called for the withdrawal of mammoth U.S. military and civilian organizations in Vietnam, which smothered Vietnamese initiative. They should be replaced by "businesslike joint commissions" to administer needed material aid. As always opposed to large numbers of troops, Lansdale argued that such a venture would allow American forces in Vietnam to depart, with only a few left to monitor the joint commissions. By so doing, even in 1969, the American government and military might "learn a more effective way of stopping Communist 'wars of national liberation.' "

Lansdale's genuine liking for the people of Vietnam shone clearly through his words in that article. He sought to describe them in a way helpful to others. The Vietnamese common man, Nguoi Thuong Dan, was real; he was not a cardboard figure. He was "a hard worker, amazingly industrious," possessed of "great resiliency." Lansdale struggled to find appropriate words. "The sun has touched his character," he wrote. "This is clear in his love of song and poetry, in his ribald slang, in the zany spoofing of his humor. He is an immensely likable friend. His one real yearning is to have something of his own, a farm, a small business, and to be left free to make it grow as he wishes." The years of war had been "plain-shirted hell," but there was still time to help.[38]

Lansdale reflected sadly on what might have been built in Vietnam had his government seriously listened to his ideas. The real fundamental need was to construct a firm political base for all the "social-military-psychological-economic actions that we then undertook." That had not happened. Thus it was not only Diem who had been "destroyed" in 1963, but also constitutional government. The remedy for Diem's abuses lay not in replacing or assassinating him, but in reforms toward making the constitution a living document. "So if we Americans are ever to come out of the war honoring our own beliefs . . . we'd better get on with the job of encouraging the Vietnamese to bring their Constitution alive."[39]

Throughout the years of the American phase of the war in Vietnam,

Lansdale told those who listened to his addresses to "[o]pen your eyes where you serve." Uniformed Americans should not hold themselves apart. Win over the local population. Be good soldiers. See that their troops behave with true military courtesy. Accord others the dignity that is their birthright. Have empathy and humility. Act as a friend. Set an example. Offer a smile and a greeting in the language of the host country. Keep always a high code of honor. Prize integrity. Practice what you preach. Lansdale pounded home those concepts time and again.[40]

Only those who acted in such ways were "true Americans." Such persons had integrity, the courage of their convictions, with competence in a technical field, with devotion to getting things done, and with affection for their fellow man. "This strength we must have," he stated, "or all else that we possess and do will be without lasting meaning."[41]

Lansdale was elated to come across mimeographed copies of his addresses and offprints of his writings in other languages, pleased that they were receiving wide distribution. There was, he told others, a "black market" in them. Asian and Middle Eastern military headquarters translated them into local languages and circulated them to their staffs and commands without requesting permission from Lansdale or the Department of Defense. "I'm really happy about this, as long as it helps the military on our side of the struggle," Lansdale admitted.[42] It felt good to be listened to, to have others seek out written pages that encompassed his thoughts, to be unconventional. He told one correspondent of the importance of the "breed of man who undertakes the unconventional, striking out for his own independent thinking," who was willing "to depart from the ancient and conventional." Then in his characteristically subdued and self-effacing style, he poked a little fun at himself. Perhaps he was only unconventional at the moment. "The first guy who thought of putting only two units in the line while holding one in reserve probably was highly unconventional — although this is now the one most important conventional lesson most military men have learned."[43]

Lansdale believed so firmly in his ideas that, sometime in 1959, he set up a special group within his Office of Special Operations at the Department of Defense. The group, he announced, needed "practical help" in the form of ideas for civic action programs that could be submitted by any interested person within the armed forces "through military channels." Such suggestions, he said, would "reach a group now established in the highest echelons of our Defense establishment to work on how those of us in the service of our country can contribute further to this dedicated end." Ideas were to be forwarded to the "Coordinating Group, Department of Defense." The purpose? To help "build a world in which men can live as brothers . . . . This is the high endeavor we must set ourselves."[44]

In all his appearances to proclaim his ideas, Lansdale followed a pattern in his talks. Beginning with friendly greetings, he outlined his themes and then moved on to wide-ranging illustrations studded with pertinent quotes from past and present, East and West, Communist and capitalist. Success against insurgencies depended on honest and dedicated servants of the military. For inspiration he hearkened back to America's heritage: its forefathers, Declaration of Independence, Constitution, and Bill of Rights. He drew his conclusions and stopped on an upbeat or inspirational challenge to his audience.

He called himself and those who agreed with him "gremlins." Webster's *Third International Dictionary* defines the word as "an unaccountable, disruptive influence." It was precisely the role Lansdale wanted to play. To do so effectively, one had to be fearless, not only of enemies but of the received truths held by friends and superiors. To act in such a way took a tiger's strength and so Lansdale regularly addressed his audiences as "gremlins and tigers."

Possessed of a controlling personality, Lansdale knew that his own ideas were more insightful than those of most other strategists, yet this egoistic viewpoint was well hidden behind a friendly, down-home manner. He was an excellent stump speaker with rhetoric that sometimes took on sonorous, cadenced rhythms. He never was troubled by self-doubt and could, with equal facility, assume the roles of brother, father, friend, chastiser, exhorter. He basically saw himself as a good man with high ideals, striving to make them part and parcel of the fabric of his own and other societies. He *wanted* people to like and respect one another and saw himself as the "leavening in the lump." When presenting his ideas he was pleasant and low-key, no matter how serious the subject matter might be. He was never strident and could always add a wry bit of humor, a little fillip, to liven the occasion. His illustrations were in large part from his own experience, which gave his expert testimony added dimension and authority.

Lansdale targeted his audiences well. Speaking to those at the Civil Affairs School, he recalled his experiments and experiences with civic-military actions. He reminded warriors at the Special Forces School of his long support for special operations and his sponsorship of many of their programs. At war colleges, while speaking to senior officers, he emphasized his own brotherhood as a high-ranking officer. Writing for Filipinos, he reminisced of his days there. "By the caprice of Army clerks, who shuffled millions of Americans in uniform about the world at seeming random, the end of World War II found me in the Philippines." It was a good sentence. It was not accurate or historical, but it was good, as was one of those that followed: "[F]ortunate chance had put me in the right place at the right moment to experience and savor and share in a rare friendship, a brotherhood, that had flowered between two distinctively different peoples."[45] He urged students at Yale to join with him, to learn the real stakes of the conflict in Vietnam, to see it as a people's war. "This whole subject area should not be a strange one to a Yale whose Class of 1773 had its Nathan Hale."[46] He regularly used all his communicative skills to reach and persuade his audiences.

The hearts of some who heard Lansdale were warmed and stirred. One correspondent wrote that his wife urged him to *"immediately"* seek an ambassadorship in Asia as a result of Lansdale's example. "I would make many mistakes, but, by God, I'd learn the language, history, customs, economies and try to know all the people." Maybe, the man wrote, he might even accomplish some good.[47] Ellsworth Bunker, American ambassador to Vietnam from April 1967 to March 1973, wrote to compliment Lansdale. "I am delighted to know that you are pushing for more understanding of our problems in Viet-Nam in the universities and other forums as well as in articles for magazines."[48]

But not everyone who learned of Lansdale's ideas liked them. Robert Welch, founder of the John Birch Society, told readers of his newsletter, *The American Opinion,* that Lansdale "disgraced his uniform and country with antics [in the Philippines] that might have been pardoned in a vaudeville hoofer, and meddled . . . in ways that were both offensive and painfully embarrassing to our friends. Transported to Indo-China, he began to knife our supposed allies, the French."[49]

Nor did everyone who liked his ideas always approve of the way he worked to spread them. Rose Kushner, a Lansdale admirer and freelance writer who idolized him, greatly approved of his ideas on how best to combat insurgencies. She was still capable of scathing criticism. Kushner charged: "[Y]ou have *not* been 'openly critical of . . . the struggle in Viet Nam': You have been most decidedly 'closedly critical' if there is such a term. . . . Yes, I know that you are writing a book. My older son was sixteen when you started and now he is registered for the draft. . . . My second son was thirteen last June. Do you think your book will help him? . . . [H]ow many kids have come and gone since you . . . began your book?" Kushner challenged Lansdale to strive even harder to "save one life" or shorten "the damned war by only one hour."[50] Kushner's point was that much as Lansdale might write and talk about different political or military approaches to people's wars and the conflict in Vietnam in particular, he inevitably did so with circumspection, staying within the framework of the military system to which he belonged. Kushner believed it was time for him — and all Americans — to step outside systems and to oppose the war boldly with every available weapon.

Even after retirement, as he continued to write and speak, Lansdale was never able to do what Kushner called for. But he did continue to speak out. His autobiography, *In the Midst of Wars,* written in 1972, was but another illustration of themes so often expressed in earlier writings and addresses. Even the book's subtitle gave indication of his conviction that he had been called for a special purpose: *An American's* Mission *to Southeast Asia.*[51] He wrote: "In the middle years of the century the U.S. government sent me to help our Asian friends in the Philippines and Vietnam . . . . You should know one thing . . . I took my American beliefs with me into these Asian struggles, as Tom Paine would have done. Ben Franklin once said, 'Where liberty dwells, there is my country.' Tom Paine had replied, 'Where liberty dwells not, *there* is my country.' "[52]

One of Lansdale's last public proclamations was his foreword to a 1978 book about the Vietnam War. He titled the foreword "Thoughts About a Past War." As if it were still twenty years earlier, he criticized "the sheer massiveness of organizations the United States created in Vietnam." They overwhelmed "recipients with large headquarters complexes and warehouses, hordes of staff personnel, fleets of vehicles, and extensive housing." The veritable "surge of hard-charging 'can do' American advisors and field representatives spread across the military zones." They stifled Vietnamese initiative. Not only was America's bureaucracy overpowering but so also was the military effort. "American leaders relied so heavily on military solutions in a war that begged for political solutions." As he had so many times before, he pointed out, "We mostly sought to destroy enemy forces. The enemy sought to gain control of the people. . . . [W]e seemed to have lost all memory of the [necessary] political imperatives in waging war successfully."

Lansdale pointed out that overthrow of Diem broke one of the fundamental principles of war: "[W]e divided the political forces of our side in the face of an aggressive, capable enemy." He asked questions for his readers to ponder. "[S]uppose that we had waged a 'people's war,' " that we had applied "all the truth we could find and prove, to the way we waged the war?" The results would have been far different. Another strategy would have "guided us to be faithful to our own principled heritage," and America could have helped Vietnam "construct a political system that gave both basic rights and a voice in public affairs to all individual citizens." His last question was poignant. "Is this not," he asked, "what we set out to do in Vietnam?" The task would have been simpler had America only remembered "the great beliefs and principles that are our heritage."[53]

Late in life Lansdale received another chance to advise a powerful and influential American. Former President Richard Nixon, who in earlier years had known and respected Lansdale, encountered him in New York in 1984 and asked him for some brief thoughts about modern wars. Lansdale pondered the matter and wrote out a two-page response. Themes he first emphasized in talks and writings upon his return from Vietnam in 1956 seemed of enduring value to him. His words still burned with a flame that in their fervor was nearly religious. With characteristic earnestness, Edward Lansdale — now in his mid-seventies — revived lessons he had learned forty years earlier.

"[C]onventional operations," he wrote to Nixon, "are more apt to widen the problem or to be more cosmetic than a cure. . . . Essentially, in a revolutionary 'people's war,' the people of the country actually constitute the true battleground of the war. Whoever wins them wins the war. Unless a government is made up 'of the people, by the people, and for the people,' it is vulnerable." Once that was fully understood, Lansdale wrote, "we will then realize the primacy of political-psychological actions, supported by military and economic means." The United States, he warned, must never do for another people what they were capable of doing for themselves. "[N]ative leaders have to win the war. We can't do it for them. We can advise on the selection of the best native leaders for the fight and help make their leadership effective while behaving as helpful friends." The proliferation of overseas American bureaucracies should always be avoided. "We don't need a new agency to undertake [such] U.S. actions . . . . We created the C.I.A. to fight the Cold War . . . . C.I.A. seems to have forgotten what it once did so successfully. We should reform it to bring back the strengths and imagination of its earlier phase (as O.P.C. [Office of Policy Coordination])."[54]

Lansdale never constructed a systematic synthesis of his rules for successfully countering an enemy-inspired people's war. His ideas must be gleaned from a careful study of existing transcripts of his speeches and copies of his writings. From those sources one can deduce the points he deemed essential.

1. The United States is now and will continue to remain a superpower. As such it has valid national interests stretching around the globe. Those concerns will bring it into repeated conflict and contests of strength with competing powers, most often in third world nations valuable for their resources or strategic locations. Such countries will inevitably be poor and often backward, with uncertain traditions, and with weak governments pursuing policies making them easy targets for revolutionary groups inspired by America's enemies.

2. In the midst of such conflicts, the United States will decide, or be called upon, to intervene on behalf of the existing government. As

it sallies forth on an intervention, America must remain true to its own best traditions and beliefs. Citizens assigned to those troubled areas must be aware of and believe in their own heritage. Too often the national government has assigned personnel to other countries simply because they were on hand and available, without regard to their attitudes and values. Cynics, Lansdale believed, could be used elsewhere on other duties, but never in responsible positions overseas where they represent the United States. Those who serve abroad must emphasize the importance of the American heritage of the freedom, dignity, and worth of individual men and women. This, Lansdale always insisted, was America's bond with mankind everywhere.

3. The United States must call a halt to automatic support of any government or group claiming itself to be an opponent of communism. This has been an unsavory predilection of too many American administrations as they struggled to gain momentary advantage at the cost of long-term loss of America's reputation. The nation must stop automatic support for "nickel and dime" dictators or "freedom fighters" unless they are truly willing to reform their own programs and policies.

4. Do not rely on the might and strength of MAAGs and other military or civilian organizations to produce results elsewhere. Large units, with their proliferating commands and bureaucracies, stumble over themselves and are rarely effective. Too often they want to run their own programs at the expense of national ones and to adopt a "let me do it for you" stance damaging to long-term growth or improvement in the host country. They regularly stifle local initiative and too often endeavor to convert the programs of foreign nationals into mirror images of themselves. Far better to send a few individuals of strong character and well-developed commitments to America's heritage. Entrust those few with both authority and latitude. There are *always* the right kind of talented Americans available for advisory assignments in other nations.

5. Search for those who are responsive and responsible, who adhere to a high code of conduct, people who can act with unfailing courtesy, who have integrity and imagination. Let them be committed to the best of their own heritage: freedom, justice, peace, the worth of the individual, the basic rights of mankind. Choose those who retain a sense of humility, who have empathy for others, and are able to accord friendship to those with whom they will work, who are more interested in serving than being served. Find those who are imbued with thoroughgoing honesty and self-reliance, who respect fairness and are willing to sacrifice in order to serve their own country and others. Let them be tough enough to retain hope and confidence

even in the midst of travail. Only such people will have a real influence for good. Edward Lansdale was never willing to forget that "actions speak louder than words." He never wanted anyone to be able to say to him, "I cannot hear what you say because I see what you do." Perhaps, as Mary McGrory once said of Lansdale's ideas, fighting a people's war really is only another name for brotherly love.

6. Upon arrival in a host country, an adviser must examine the condition of individual citizens there. Which of their rights are healthy? Which are withering and weak? Revolutionaries will seek to exploit all conditions that cause men and women to suffer. Those are the very circumstances on which an adviser must focus. The government must be helped to understand that it must work for reform — restoration or improvement of individual rights — rather than simply fight against insurgents. It must be convinced to care for its own people or nothing it does will be availing or have lasting value. On all its policies, it must first ask, 'What will citizen reaction be to this policy?' Advisers must teach host officials a paramount lesson: their own people were the battle ground, the terrain, of the people's war facing them. Unless they won over the allegiance of those men and women, no matter how much help they received from the United States in the form of ammunition, aircraft, tanks, and helicopters, no matter the number or size of grants-in-aid, they would lose the war!

7. The host country must begin that process by building a strong political base among its citizenry. When not serving as a protector while fighting insurgent bands, the host army must be brothers to their people. Advisers must emphasize the importance of correct and appropriate military behavior toward civilians and the value of civic action programs. Choose projects wisely to provide both short- and long-term value. Work hard at them. A soldier with a shovel, hammer, or trowel, an officer teaching elementary studies, a medical team laboring to provide health care — all on behalf of their own people — are mighty bulwarks against an enemy.

8. Know the enemy's goals. Read and understand the literature of a particular opposition or insurgent movement. Analyze its background and study the lives of its leaders. Learn what motivates an insurgency. Be knowledgeable about enemy plans and objectives. Offer rebels options attractive enough to tempt them away from steadfast devotion to their cause. Help them leave the rebellion and rally to the government. Be fair even to insurgent rebel soldiers because every one of them is actually part of the population a government seeks to win. "Land for the landless," use of army attorneys to plead the cause of poverty-stricken farmers, belief that those "who have less in life must have more in law" were not empty slogans in the Philippines.

They showed all the nation that its government was beginning to care *and to reform itself.* Provide a better idea. No idea can be bombed or beaten to death. Military action alone is never enough. Without his recognition that the government had a better idea, Luis Taruc would never have come down from the hills. Without a better idea, the Viet Minh/Viet Cong were willing to fight twenty-five years against the strength of both France and the United States in order to ensure success of their own. Without a better idea, rebels will eventually win, for ideas are defeated only by better ideas.

Know that rebels can be patient, willing to wait and work for one or twenty-five years preparing for the action phase of their operation, preparing to reach their goal. Have as much patience as the enemy and persist in your cause as he does in his. People's wars are no place for the easily discouraged or the faint of heart. Use the power of government to preempt and coopt the ideas of a revolution. A government has advantages an enemy can never have: a nationwide chain of command and communications systems, vaster resources of wealth and people, control of educational, legal, and financial systems, the support of allies, and much more. A responsive government can never be defeated.

9. Use psychological warfare — psywar — to trick, harass, and confuse an enemy, to raise his fears, to expose his weaknesses. It is an important component of any campaign against insurgents. Be willing to try the unconventional. An army must comport itself not only with military alertness but with psychological insights.

10. When all else has been accomplished, few revolutionary insurgents will remain. People will look upon those they once supported as little more than bandits and will cooperate with government forces in rooting them out. Then kill them.

This nation once fought in Vietnam for many long years without avail. It ignored Lansdale's approach and his prescription for victory. The Army during those years listed meaningless "lessons learned": a soldier who carries two canteens will be less apt to become thirsty than if he carries only one; troopers who sleep beneath insect bars are less apt to be bitten by insects; PRC-10 and PRC-25 batteries deteriorate rapidly in humid, tropical climates. Those were not new lessons. Moses knew most of them when he led the Children of Israel through the desert for a generation. No American soldier should have had to relearn them. Rather, members of the armed forces should have learned lessons in fighting people's wars, and they did not. The United States now faces the possibility of increased involvement in Central America. Perhaps it is time, finally, to apply the lessons of Edward G. Lansdale.

13

BACK TO VIETNAM

WHILE LANSDALE TRAVELED in Bolivia during the June prior to his October retirement, a tragedy began building in Vietnam. On 8 May 1963 government troops fired on Buddhists in Hue as they celebrated the birthday of Gautama Siddhartha Buddha. Thich Tri Quang, a politically astute monk, used the occasion to stir resentment against Diem. A month later, on 11 June, another Buddhist monk, Quang Duc, publicly burned himself to death as a plea to Diem to show charity and compassion to his people. Duc's death was the first of several as other bonzes committed self-immolation in protest against government policies. In a fit of insensitivity, Madame Nhu referred to the burnings as "barbecues" and offered to supply matches for any others who wished to kill themselves.

On 21 August, shortly after the arrival of Henry Cabot Lodge as replacement for Ambassador Frederick Nolting, troops loyal to Diem attacked Buddhist temples and sanctuaries in Saigon, Hue, and other cities, destroying property and beating, jailing, or murdering hundreds of monks, nuns, student activists, and ordinary citizens. Diem closed universities in Saigon and Hue and, throughout the land, spontaneous demonstrations against the government filled the streets. Diem's foreign minister, Vu Van Mau, himself a Buddhist, resigned in protest as did the Vietnamese ambassador to the United States, Tran Van Chuong, who was Madame Nhu's father. He shaved his head as a monk would do and joined Mau in protest over Diem's treatment of Buddhists. Rumors of a coup increased in number and intensity.

The fragile nation that General Lansdale helped Diem to build in 1954 — only nine years earlier — was shattering like glass. Lansdale deeply desired to provide Diem with any possible help. That was the problem. At this juncture, he had very little to offer. In addition to the friendship that bound them, he had a very personal reason for wanting Diem maintained in power. Their intimate relationship remained Lansdale's conduit to influence. Diem and Lansdale depended on one another for their identities;

separated by powerful forces — military and civilian — within the American government, both lost.[1]

Lou Conein, Lansdale's longtime teammate, was in Saigon, still assigned to CIA. In July 1963 he learned from General Tran Van Don that certain officers were planning a coup. He forwarded this information to Washington. Conein also saw American officials arriving in Vietnam on inspection missions. Victor Krulak, SACSA, came in September, as did Joseph Mendenhall of the State Department. Both men reported their views to President Kennedy at a National Security Council meeting on 10 September. Krulak insisted that the war was going well; Mendenhall claimed Diem was near collapse. Kennedy quizzically asked, "You two did visit the same country, didn't you?" At the same meeting was Rufus Phillips, Lansdale's young friend and former teammate. He also had just returned from Vietnam where the strategic hamlet program he had been running had broken down. After listening to Krulak and Mendenhall, Kennedy turned to Phillips for his views.

Phillips told the president that Diem and Nhu were not in touch with either their own people or reality. A coup was inevitable unless the United States made an extraordinary effort to save Diem. Phillips recommended that effort. "This can only be done," he said, "by sending General Lansdale to Saigon. He is the only American who has Diem's trust and therefore has a chance of persuading him to exile his brother, Nhu, which would make reconciliation with the Vietnamese Army possible." He also advocated protecting the standing and reputation of the United States by separating it from Nhu's actions against Buddhists. He further suggested cutting CIA assistance to Colonel Le Quang Tung, whose Vietnamese Special Forces conducted the raid on the pagodas under Nhu's direction. Last, Phillips wanted to stop U.S. support for the local motion picture program, which had become a propaganda vehicle for Nhu. President Kennedy responded by thanking him for his recommendations, "particularly," he said, "about General Lansdale." Unfortunately, for reasons that remain obscure, Lansdale was not sent back.[2]

Diem's final moments drew closer. Lansdale later told how Diem made "loud, strong noises that he wanted me. He asked that I come to educate Americans on what was happening there." In Diem's last conversation with Lodge, he once again asked, "Please get Ed Lansdale back." No one told Lansdale. No one sent him to Vietnam. "I didn't know. I never got that [message]."[3]

Robert McNamara and Maxwell Taylor visited Saigon and found "great progress" in the war but agreed with Phillips that the United States levy sanctions against Diem for his anti-Buddhist campaign. Hearing nothing about a coup in his talks with Vietnamese Army officers, General Taylor erroneously concluded that it had been canceled and so notified the White House. Acting on that information, President Kennedy cabled Ambassador Lodge to give no more encouragement to further coup attempts although it was permissible to groom potential alternative leaders. John Richardson, CIA station chief, reported to Washington that the situation in Southeast Asia had reached a point of no return.

On 5 October 1963, Lodge cabled Kennedy that the coup was on again. General Duong Van "Big" Minh asked Conein for assurances that the United States would not block a coup, that economic and military aid would continue to be given to a new government. The United States duly convinced him it would do as he asked. Conein kept in close contact with rebels through meetings with General Tran Van Don. To make uneasy matters worse, another Buddhist monk committed self-immolation, which was followed by scores of arrests. John Richardson began to doubt the ability of Big Minh to conduct a successful coup; when he voiced his feelings, Lodge summarily sacked him. General Paul Harkins at US-MAAG informed General Don that he had learned of the coup planning and believed any such act would be a grave mistake. Don then told Conein that, because of Harkins' position, he had postponed the coup, which had been set for 26 October. Conein assured Don that Harkins' views were purely his own; the MAAG chief did not speak for the American government.

By the end of October, President Kennedy became increasingly uneasy over conflicting reports from Saigon. A coup might wreck the war effort against the Viet Cong. Kennedy's confidence was further shaken on 29 October at a National Security Council meeting when General Taylor strongly supported Diem's performance, citing messages from General Harkins. The president then cabled Lodge to ask the generals to postpone their coup. Lodge never delivered the message.

Conein remembered the fury of those days. Frederick Nolting had been a staunch backer of Diem, wanting to keep him in power no matter what. When Nolting was replaced by Lodge, that support vanished. "Here in Washington, you had a house divided; out in the field, you had a house divided," Conein said. "All these people were on different sides of everything. They couldn't make up their minds what the hell was going on." He thought for a moment and added, "Of all the people, Lansdale was probably the only one who could have salvaged anything."[4]

On 1 November, dissidents laid siege to the presidential palace. Unable to summon military reinforcements, Diem and Nhu escaped the grounds and took refuge in St. Francis Xavier Church in Cholon. At about 6:00 A.M. 2 November, Diem began negotiating with his generals. They had already assured Lodge the president's life would be spared if he capitulated. When Diem agreed to surrender, an M-113 armored personnel carrier, manned by Major Duong Huu Nghia and his bodyguard, Captain Nguyen Van Nhung, picked up the two men from the church. Only a little while later, Captain Nhung pointed his weapon at Diem and Nhu and murdered them while they were inside the personnel carrier.

Conein continued. He believed "the biggest, stupidest mistake" of Big Minh was to have Diem and Nhu shot. "The consensus of people I talked to was that prior to picking them up in the APC [armored personnel carrier], Nhung received instructions from Big Minh to get rid of them. That wasn't supposed to be. They were supposed to ask for political asylum. They would be taken to the first country — the Philippines, Taiwan — that granted it. Once a new government reestablished a certain amount of corrections, Diem was to be invited back, but without Nhu or Madame Nhu. The Archbishop [Ngo Dinh Thuc] was already in Rome; he went there way before the coup. Nobody gave a damn about him."[5]

When General Lansdale heard about the coup he was shocked. "Diem was a friend of mine, so what happened went very much against my beliefs." He chose to describe the murders in words similar to Conein's. "It was an unreasoning, stupid act."[6] Lansdale's friend Hanging Sam Williams agreed, predicting that America would one day regret the failure "to take Diem into custody, unharmed, and to ship him out of the country." Williams added another sobering thought. "Those that may think Minh will jump every time some one in Washington, or Saigon, says 'frog' are due for an awakening."[7]

The day following the coup Robert Shaplen called from the Washington Associated Press bureau wanting Lansdale's reaction to the news from Saigon. "I thought," Shaplen said, "that might have been you running the coup." With frustration edging his voice, all Lansdale replied was, "No. I just retired from the Air Force."[8]

In the days following his retirement Lansdale was at loose ends, uncertain what to do. He quickly accepted when Richard Reuter offered him a job. President Kennedy had appointed Reuter, formerly executive director of the CARE relief organization, to head Food for Peace (FFP) in mid-1962. Since it was necessary for Lansdale to be sponsored, the Department of Agriculture agreed to carry him on its rolls as an "agricultural specialist," a strange title for a retired Air Force general. Lansdale stayed with Food for Peace until sometime in the spring of 1965.[9] During his service with FFP, Lansdale lobbied Reuter to use the organization in a more political way, to "gain staunch believers in the ideals we American[s] share" while at the same time providing sustenance for the hungry. Basic American concepts, Lansdale insisted, "can be exported successfully . . . just as much as wheat or no-fat dry milk."[10]

Not heavily burdened with responsibilities in his new job, Lansdale had leisure time to pursue his own interests. Friends wondered why he served in such an obviously ill-fitting capacity. General William Yarborough, commander of Special Forces at Fort Bragg, wrote, "I am completely at a loss to understand why, with all of the talents that you have for irregular warfare, you are not somehow directly connected with our strategic mechanism in this regard?"[11] Another correspondent said that "many Vietnamese friends are eager and anxious for you to return."[12]

With time on his hands, Lansdale recalled his years of evangelism on behalf of proper ways to fight people's wars. Perhaps there was still something he might do. His memory reached back to the National Training Center at Vung Tau, his friend Nguyen Be who was the commandant there, his team member Jean Sauvageot who had once been Be's adviser, and the revolutionary development cadre turned out by the center. He thought of the Peace Corps and of West Point, Annapolis and Colorado Springs, and how those military academies produced officers dedicated to traditional military views. What was needed in America was a hybrid combination of the fervor of Vung Tau and the Peace Corps, the breadth of knowledge demanded of entrants into the foreign service, and the discipline of officers' training. Lansdale wondered whether it might be possible to launch such an enterprise.

Only twenty-eight days after his retirement he produced a lengthy memorandum; its subject was "Liberty Hall." In his introduction, Lansdale wrote that he had received offers of employment and suggestions for things to do, but "none of them exactly fills some of the outstanding needs I noted in my years in the rough and tumble of U.S. national security work, needs which a man might act to fill in the freedom of retirement."

He didn't mention communism by name, calling it only "the tyranny." We seem, he wrote, to be reluctant to use our political beliefs — the greatest strength in our national heritage — when confronted by this tyranny abroad. The nation devoted energy and money to military assistance, to economic aid, to diplomatic activities, to psywar, to collecting information — but very little to spreading America's special political insights.

Few Americans working abroad in the field of national security, Lansdale observed, seemed to understand the dynamics of the American Revolution. Some of them, he said, felt that the political beliefs that created the nation were archaic and outdated. Perhaps the situation might be improved by providing different and more extensive training to people prior to their overseas assignments. To that end, Lansdale proposed creation of Liberty Hall.

It would be a public subscription, nonprofit, public service educational corporation to be located in the Washington area. A small, permanent staff of experienced people would be augmented by adjunct lecturers drawn from the ranks of those who had served well and long in public advisory positions. This staff would be available as consultants, by invitation, to both American and foreign governments. Liberty Hall's curriculum would focus on teaching practical American political action for export abroad. Courses would examine fundamental elements of democracy and the "opposing tyranny." Working seminars would explore ways of encouraging and strengthening democratic alternatives and elements overseas. The student body would be drawn from the best of American youth, from those already working in the foreign service or military, and from interested third world nationals. All this, Lansdale said, was only a rough concept, in need of further thought and consideration by others. Yet it was a beginning. "Is this idea feasible?" he asked.

A group of backers rallied to promote Lansdale's plan. They incorporated as the Freedom Studies Center of the Institute for American Strategy. The group published a brochure with a blue and gold cover and devised a logo: a liberty torch superimposed on a globe of the earth. Illustrations pictured the school located at Boston, Virginia — a beautiful Tudor beige stone manor house of twenty-three rooms. It described itself as a "private 'West Point' of psycho-political warfare" whose purpose was "to help close the Cold War educational Gap" by training cold war leaders, studying communist strategies and tactics, and developing programs for extending the "sphere of freedom." Initially there was some rather widespread interest. Listed backers included the American Legion, Claremont (California) Men's College, Houghton College in New York, Northeastern University in Boston, San Antonio College, Kansas State University, and the departments of education of Florida, Nebraska, Oregon, and Wisconsin.

But something was lost in transition. Lansdale envisioned an institution that would be patriotic, not right-wing, a private effort to train people to serve effectively overseas. He wanted to avoid both the political left and right, to focus on those of the middle who were most apt to occupy common ground. The reality disappointed Lansdale. The organizers picked only those of a rightist persuasion. "It was almost a John Birch Society roll call," Lansdale complained. "I refused to have anything more to do with it. . . . That isn't what our country is all about. We tolerate such people — but just barely. We don't want to endow them with any ability or strength." And so he separated himself from his brainchild.[13]

Even had Liberty Hall worked out according to Lansdale's intentions, it would not have satisfied his need to avoid a normal retirement and to continue to be useful in the service of his country. So while working on Food for Peace programs, he continued to explore his options. Lansdale spent many hours lobbying with administration officials, engaging in discussions with friends, writing endless memoranda, and seeking critiques of them from allies — all aimed at finding a way to once again get back into a policymaking role. He considered the problems of Vietnam and wrote several papers describing the political needs there and the utter necessity for Washington administrators to come to grips with the real problems in Southeast Asia. He was joined in this effort by Bo Bohannan and Rufe Phillips. In a draft manuscript, Phillips wrote, "We have approached Vietnam as if it were a logistical problem left over from World War II . . . . The result has been that we have created a vast bureaucratic apparatus, a replica of Washington, D.C. in Saigon . . . almost totally insensitive and unresponsive to true Vietnamese needs . . . . We should ask ourselves what would have happened to our own Revolution had France insisted as a condition for its aid that a replica of the Court of Versailles be set up to advise General Washington."[14]

Bo joined in with a ten-page manuscript in which he asserted, "Virtually everything in the Philippine experience is applicable" to Vietnam. "[U]nless — and until — the troops . . . can persuade . . . the civilians that they . . . are their friends and protectors, the war will continue to be lost." A little later, he wrote, "Only a demonstration of our continuing belief and ability in establishing political freedom [in Vietnam] can restore our stature in the eyes of the world — and ourselves."[15] When asked for his views by James S. Killen, director of the United States Operating Mission in Vietnam, Rufe Phillips sent along a memo and an appendix "with which I entirely concur," recently prepared by a "small informal group" with extensive successful experience in Asia. He also included a draft for building a political base for government in Vietnam "prepared by a member of that same group with the collaboration of myself and others." That member was, of course, Ed Lansdale.[16]

In a flurry of statements, Lansdale and Bohannan set forth their ideas and then exchanged the papers for the other to critique. Today it is sometimes difficult to tell which was the author of a particular paper, so thoroughly are they intermixed. Yet all are the product of Lansdale's thinking and all are suffused with common themes: the American effort in Vietnam lacked appropriate leadership; current policy that focused on conventional military operations gave an unwarranted advantage to the enemy; insurgents were successfully winning the hearts and minds of people there and the United States was not; the war could not be won by conventional methods or bureaucratic systems.[17]

Lansdale claimed that his views were not those "of a professional pollyanna" but of a "tough old senior officer." In one paper he put words into the mouth of a "typical" Vietnamese who asked, "Why can't you send us back that officer and some more like him, who understand how to motivate men? We have no need for more weapons, or more troop advisers. What we need are men who understand revolution."[18] Soon Lansdale was calling for the United States to send a "first team" to Vietnam composed of "men who have proven that they can defeat Asian insurgents." The leader of that team must have authority to direct operations in the field as well as responsibility to undertake them on the spot, "not from ten-thousand miles away in Washington by a Cabinet officer." He reminded his readers that in victories over insurgencies in the Philippines from 1950 to 1953 and in Vietnam from 1954 to 1956, "the counterinsurgency leader on the scene was given great freedom of action. . . . Washington picked a man, sent him to do a job, and backed his play. This lesson needs to be heeded today." Such a leader — acting as the president's personal representative — could accomplish those firm, vigorous actions required to change defeat into victory. In a list of potential Americans to head such a "first team," General Lansdale prominently mentioned his own name.[19]

He wrote a follow-on piece in which he suggested that the existence and mission of such a team need be neither publicized nor concealed. It needed no formal accreditation or approval from the Vietnamese provided it received appropriate cooperation from U.S. leaders. It required no elaborate logistics or separate headquarters, although it would need its own communications with Washington through existing facilities. Above all, it needed the backing of the president. In a determined effort to reserve the right to choose his own men if he was authorized to head such a team, Lansdale insisted that membership in the group would be earned by those with "success at understanding and using the sound actions of free men against Asian Communist subversive insurgents."[20]

All this was preliminary to another effort by Lansdale to get back to Vietnam. He worked hard to do so. Production and critique of these papers lasted months, yet in a letter to Sam Williams, Lansdale casually told how he "spent a weekend" on a plan for a Vietnam team that he would head to save American efforts there. He suggested he did it only because by early summer 1964 the Johnson administration was apparently "reaching the end of the road" on ideas for Southeast Asia. He managed, through interested intermediaries — probably the good graces of Hubert Humphrey — to put his plan in Johnson's hands. The president thought enough of the idea to discuss it at a meeting of the National Security Council. Lansdale's enemies soon heard what had happened and rushed to seal him off from any further involvement in Vietnam.

"Next I heard," Lansdale reported, "I was being jumped for getting things [to the President] 'out of channels,' although 'channels' had been shut off for me.'' Once again his efforts had been for naught. The president sent U. Alexis Johnson and Maxwell Taylor on official inspection missions to Vietnam. Both men, Lansdale sniffed, had been vying with McNamara as the real ''experts'' on Vietnam. ''It reminded me of sending in coaches of a losing ball club, to play the team the same old way, and expect a win,'' Lansdale groused. In an effort to salvage something from the wreckage of his most recent plan, Lansdale proposed going over to Vietnam as a ''tourist'' traveling space-available on Military Air Transport Service flights, ''just to be available to Vietnamese who need an American to talk problems over with (which they obviously can't with Taylor, Johnson, etc). But it became clear, on sensitive inquiry, that Vietnamese I would contact were quite apt to get in dutch with US officials in Saigon.''[21]

Despite his weariness after years of battling bureaucrats, Lansdale was not one to admit defeat even when his efforts were thwarted. Old friends, including Democratic senators Mike Mansfield and Thomas Dodd, still rallied to his cause. An even more important supporter, however, was the new vice president, Hubert H. Humphrey, whom Lansdale had known first as senator from Minnesota. Humphrey became particularly interested in Lansdale's theories as a possible way out of the quagmire of Vietnam into which America was being ever more deeply drawn, and he supported Lansdale's pamphleteering. Lansdale, greatly heartened by Humphrey's encouragement, pressed on him copies of memoranda that he and his team had put together over the past several months. If Lansdale was ever to get back into a responsible position, it would come through the kind offices of the new vice president. In a memorandum written just after the 1964 presidential election, Lansdale again called for an experienced team armed with great authority to be sent to Vietnam. ''Success is assured,'' he claimed, ''*if* the effort is guided by advisors with proven experience in such wars who are backed by the very top.''[22]

On 8 July 1965, Maxwell Taylor resigned from his post as ambassador to Vietnam, which he had held since July 1964. For a brief moment, Lansdale and his friends hoped he would be named as Taylor's replacement. Their hopes were dashed when President Lyndon Johnson announced that Henry Cabot Lodge would fill the post. The coveted ambassadorship once again escaped Lansdale, but powerful friends and allies found a way to give him another chance. When Lodge was appointed, Vice President Humphrey met with him and urged him to take Lansdale along. Humphrey also lobbied with Johnson about the invaluable assistance Lansdale could give the administration by serving in Vietnam. Bogged down with a war he did not want, Johnson was quite willing for Lansdale to return to Southeast Asia. Additionally, the influential Senator Thomas Dodd had a long memory. He blamed Lodge for causing Diem's assassina-

tion and for the deterioration in Vietnam over the preceding two years.
He threatened to block Lodge's confirmation by the Senate Foreign Relations Committee unless Lodge allowed Lansdale to accompany him in
an official position.[23]

Lodge had to mend his fences and asked Lansdale out to lunch. After
some polite conversation Lodge informed him that he had long wanted
him to return to Vietnam. He confided how CIA strongly opposed such
a move. Was Lansdale aware that the president wanted him to go there
once again? Lansdale's reply was short. "Well he ought to ask me then;
he hasn't." Would he be interested in becoming CIA station chief in
Saigon? "I imagine they [CIA] would oppose that," Lansdale replied.
"I was an Air Force officer. I had been a member of the U.S. Intelligence
Board," directing all American intelligence operations, which were
"about ten times as big as CIA." He reflected a moment and then added,
"I imagine some people out there wouldn't like it if I go to Vietnam
again." Lodge accepted Lansdale's demurral of a CIA position but insisted
the president still wanted him on the American team. "He wants you
out there." Lodge then offered a proposition that caught Lansdale's attention. "Go with me. You'll be my assistant and take over pacification
programs in Vietnam. I'll take care of you."

Lansdale was hooked. "That's an old subject with me," he said. "I
used to run it and we won in the old days. I guess we have to do it
again. I'll try it once more." Lodge reiterated an important point. "I
will come up with a name for what you should be doing that makes
sense to everybody, but I want you to pacify the country." Many years
later, Lansdale said that accepting Lodge's offer "was a mistake. Everybody had their ideas on how to fight that war. They wanted me to do it
a certain way — the wrong way." But that was hindsight. At the time
he was elated. Once more into the fray![24]

During the third week of July, Lodge arrived in Saigon to resume
duties he was familiar with from his first stint there in 1963 and 1964.
Lansdale would shortly follow. With President Johnson's concurrence,
Lansdale was appointed special assistant to Ambassador Lodge, with
the title of Embassy Senior Liaison Officer. To the press, Lansdale admitted, "I've got an old love affair with the people of Asia and I'm going
back to see if I can help." It took him some weeks to assemble his
team and depart. He arrived in Saigon on 29 August 1965.[25]

Reporters across the nation gave free rein to speculation when they
heard the announcement. Lansdale was returning to the Far East. News-
writers filled their pages with hype that would have discouraged a lesser
man. *Newsweek* warned that his return to Asia "is hardly calculated to
please the Pentagon's organization men." South Vietnam's military rulers

were also suspicious, the magazine claimed. The *Washington Post* reported that Lansdale secured his new job only "over Pentagon objections." In a second appraisal, the paper noted that Lansdale shared characteristics with "Col. T. E. Lawrence," of World War I fame. Just as did Lawrence of Arabia, so "Lansdale has inspired admiration, ridicule — and above all, controversy. . . . Sharp disagreements [in the Pentagon] led to Lansdale's retirement" from the Air Force and his "unorthodox manner may incur the opposition of certain American officers." The *St. Petersburg* (Florida) *Times* put the matter bluntly: "He's an object of suspicion by the American military who fear his sleight-of-hand will seize some of their power. . . . He is suspected by the Central Intelligence Agency and American Foreign Service officials because they know he's a political animal."[26]

So much for placating his enemies. The press also set impossible goals for Lansdale to achieve. *Newsweek* told readers that "Lansdale is expected to push hard for a greater effort on the political and economic fronts of the war, while opposing the recent trend toward . . . bombing and the burning of villages." The *Washington Post* admitted that Lansdale "would be the first to acknowledge that a miracle is expected of him . . . and miracles in Southeast Asia these days are mighty hard to come by." The story quoted an unnamed official's comment, "If he doesn't perform a miracle, his friends will be disappointed and his enemies delighted." A Florida newspaper described Lansdale's "smoky dark eyes" and claimed his "acid face" was "as complex and nebulous as the politics of the Asian countries he has worked in." The writer exclaimed, "He's back, and he knows he has a tough row to hoe."[27]

U.S. News & World Report found it strange that General Lansdale would go back to Saigon "to work for the man generally regarded as having played a major role in the downfall of President Diem." While later claiming that Lansdale was a "miracle worker," the journal confessed it would take three hundred thousand Lansdales to make a difference in Vietnam.[28] These and other news stories forewarned Lansdale's enemies and created unreasonable expectations of what he could accomplish. They were no help to his mission.

Arriving in late August 1965, Lansdale settled into an old white stucco French villa at 194 Cong Ly Street. For the next several years it would serve as his combination office and residence. The villa was on the road from Saigon to Tan Son Nhut airport and adjacent to the information office of the Military Assistance Command, Vietnam (MACV). His two telephone lines answered to the response Tiger 433 or Saigon 25728.[29] Antonio Quintos, who had known Lansdale since his days at AFWESPAC, became chief security officer for the white clay tile–roofed building, which sat on an 800-square-meter lot enclosed by a protective wall. Lansdale ordered Quintos to leave the gate unguarded; covert security inside the building would protect team members. Since Lansdale always wanted team members close by, the villa was suitable with its large kitchen, dining area, extensive living area floored in black and white squares, and six bedrooms, each capable of accommodating two or more beds.[30]

Within a few days of his return to Saigon, Lansdale's team members began to trickle into the city. One former U.S. official recollected that "they looked like the Lavender Hill Mob, sent over from central casting."[31] It was not an accurate description. Those who came brought with them a great deal of talent and a wealth of Asian experience. Joseph Redick once again served as interpreter. Michael Deutch came as economic adviser. Bo Bohannan came from his retirement farm outside Fort Riley, Kansas. Napoleon Valeriano came upon Lansdale's request. Henry L. "Hank" Miller moved over from his work with USIA to serve with Lansdale. CIA loaned Lou Conein for an indefinite time. Joe Baker had been enjoying a comfortable CIA assignment in Paris: "I wasn't really happy about going . . . but he called me and out I went."[32] George Melvin transferred from Laos with "renewed faith in the whole Vietnam venture now that the U.S. is bringing in the first team under a winner instead of a loser."[33] For a time Rufus Phillips helped out but soon found it necessary to return to the States. While serving in Washington, Phillips "read" the team's communications and also kept the wives abreast of their husbands' activities. And the team was joined by Daniel Ellsberg, a reserve Marine officer.

Were those who belonged to CIA working for the Agency or for Lansdale? "They could have been [working for CIA]," Lansdale remembered. "I don't think they were. . . . I think CIA was very honestly letting them work hard to help us. . . . I got the CIA, Army, USIA, AID, and State to lend me personnel. I wouldn't have cared if their original outfits wanted them to do things on the side . . . as long as it didn't take away from their work and their value."[34] It was all right to work for another organization; it was not acceptable to exaggerate one's own importance. In early fall 1965, Lansdale sent a private letter to Rufe Phillips telling about recent problems with Bohannan. "Bo worries me considerably. Apparently, he tried to set up his own control net within the team. I had a straight talk with him, without mentioning that particular action, and he swore he was 100% loyal. But most of the old team members are really down on him. Luigi [Lou Conein] says Bo offered money, a car, etc, if he would report to Bo instead of me. Val[eriano] stopped him from instructing the guards to obey his orders only, not mine. Similar things with others. Damn! I feel that perhaps Bo was only trying to operate in his own old fashion, and was clumsy. Hope so."[35]

Bohannan didn't care for convention; Lansdale was unconventional. There was a difference. Bo used to anger Lansdale by the way he handled himself. Lansdale would call for Bo to appear as an expert witness to testify at a meeting. Bo would arrive barefoot and squat in a corner until it was time for him to speak. "They would look at him . . . and think he was crazy. . . . People used to ask me about him." Lansdale's response was usually, "Bo is just being himself. He knows what he is talking about." In this case, however, Bohannan's course of action "would have loused up everything," and so Lansdale asked him to leave the team. Others had recently questioned him about Bohannan: William Holbrook at the embassy, even General William Westmoreland. And so Bohannan left Saigon for Manila.[36]

Another team member, Dan Ellsberg, was a close friend of Napoleon Valeriano, who told him about the quarrel. Ellsberg later recalled, "Bohannan was at odds with most people on the team at that point. . . . [He] made a bid that undercut Lansdale in some way so he would be regarded as head of the team. . . . It was regarded as a betrayal by Ed and . . . Bohannan [was] out. . . . A couple of times [after that] Bohannan got missions out to Vietnam and would come to visit but the relations were very strained."[37] Joe Baker and Lou Conein recalled that after Bohannan's departure he acted as team liaison in the Philippines where, Conein said, "he liaised and liaised and liaised." Bohannan's ideas were out of sync with Lansdale's purposes. Always more hawklike, "he wanted to nuke the goddamn bastards."[38]

Lansdale smiled at the innocence Ellsberg displayed toward life in the Orient. "He was a complete babe in the woods, not knowing about health habits in Asia and other kindergarten lessons that we all learned so long ago that we never think about them any more."[39] He was, Lansdale believed, very naive in the face of a foreign culture. "I forgot you had to teach these kids not to drink water from the tap, not to brush their teeth in tapwater."[40] Lou Conein also felt a comradely affection for Ellsberg. "I liked Dan. He's all right. Very gung-ho. He thought it would be wonderful to be out in black pajamas and play cowboy and Indian at night."[41]

Lansdale was aware of Ellsberg's interest in combat. At the time they served together, Lansdale remembered Ellsberg as "very pro-war. He used to want to sneak off all the time and go on active duty. He'd get a rifle and want to go out on the line with the infantry." On more than one occasion, Lansdale reminded Ellsberg not to take a carbine with him on trips into the provinces and "to stop playing soldier."[42] In reality, all team members carried weapons on those occasions when they made trips into the field, and so Ellsberg's doing so was unexceptional. In this telling, as with other of his recollections, Lansdale sometimes embellished the facts to make his storytelling more dramatic.[43] Joe Baker's memory of those days was more accurate when he recalled that team members liked Ellsberg even though some regarded him as "very intense" — hardly a damning condemnation.[44]

All the team recognized Ellsberg's abilities. Baker saw him as "a tremendous writer."[45] Conein recognized his young friend as "extremely intelligent, no dumb bunny, one of the most fantastic writers I have ever seen."[46] His intelligence and grasp of information was legendary. "He could always write with unconscionable speed," one author concluded. "His ability to summon the right words under pressure had been among his most conspicuous talents."[47] Lansdale thought Ellsberg was "a brilliant guy" who "impressed me very much with his ability to argue."[48] Lansdale used him as a "bureaucratic wordsmith . . . mostly as my defense weapon in dealing with the many committees and study groups that Americans in Saigon set up to bog me down. I could use him to keep them engaged while I went ahead and got the real work done."[49]

It pleased Lansdale to observe Ellsberg talking in a meeting. "I'd send him to meetings with the political staff of the embassy to keep them occupied. He'd keep a meeting going for at least an hour." Ellsberg would ask him, "What do you want me to say?" Lansdale would reply, "Whatever comes into your mind. Keep them there. I want them out of the way not paying attention to what we're doing here for about an hour." Inevitably, Lansdale said, "He'd do it. He was very good at that."[50] Lansdale was even more pleased, when he sent Ellsberg into the provinces on errands, to learn that the young man inevitably spent time with the children he encountered.[51]

The two men were sufficiently close that Ellsberg believed he came to understand the reason for Lansdale's ability to deal successfully with people in the Orient. His "magic" was "very simply that he did not show contempt for them. It was true of . . . most other Americans [in Vietnam. They] were patronizing, condescending toward people." But not Lansdale. "He had respect for them, acted respectfully . . . . He would listen to them. . . . They really did feel they were being heard respectfully and reasonably, and that's all it took. He didn't have to speak their language . . . . Yet he did establish a rapport with them that amounted to reverence. . . . All he had to do was listen to them."[52]

Ellsberg was also impressed with Lansdale's acuity in summing up political realities. Only a couple of months after their arrival in Vietnam, Lansdale sat at his villa on Cong Ly, lost in depression. Ellsberg asked what concerned him. Lansdale spoke sadly. "I don't believe this is a government that can win the hearts and minds of the people." Later events proved the wisdom of his observation.[53]

Ellsberg continued to appreciate Lansdale's insights. In later years, he tried to sum up the way Lansdale may have seen his mission in the Orient. "The French saw their *mission civilatrice* as bringing French culture, language, and history to the world. The British saw themselves as conferring the gift of administration, law, and order. Lansdale . . . was pretty much an imperialist in the mold of the British except in his case . . . it was [to bring] democracy. He did think it was in the interest of the people he was working with, the Filipinos, the Vietnamese. At the same time he believed it was very much in *their* interest to be within the sphere of American influence; . . . that our interest was to be served . . . by fostering a kind of nationalism and a relative independence which, however, would need American aid and influence but would be independent. It was a way of extending and ensuring a sphere of American influence for the good of America but also for the good of [other] people and against communism, which he despised."[54]

Occasionally Lansdale counseled Ellsberg about matters more serious than contaminated drinking water. Having read some of Ellsberg's political memoranda, Lansdale told him his work was excellent. "I'm happy that you are recognizing the main battle-line in a people's war, its strategy and its tactics." Despite his overall appreciation, Lansdale suggested that Ellsberg "take off your dark glasses so you'll be able to see more clearly. Or did you realize how negatively you put your findings? . . . [Y]ou narrow your chances to recognize opportunities for constructive actions — which I had hoped would be the one, single most important lesson you would discover for yourself in Viet Nam. . . . I'm not suggesting that you swap dark glasses for rose-colored ones."[55] Daniel Ellsberg may well have taken Lansdale's advice. In later years he came to recognize many opportunities for constructive actions!

Prophetically (or with 20/20 hindsight), Lansdale recalled one major problem he had with Ellsberg's activities. He complained that Ellsberg "had no concept of classified documents. He used to carry secret papers in his pocket . . . . [T]hey belonged to the embassy . . . . Jesus, I used to go crazy trying to keep him clean on that."[56]

Immediately after the team's arrival, its members had quite an active social life. Joe Baker remembered, "At first everyone treated us like royalty. Here was this mystery group coming out there at the request of Hubert Humphrey and LBJ, so everyone really wanted to see who we were. . . . God! We were invited out every night, freeloading — drinks and food all the time."[57]

At an official reception, both Lodge and Lansdale met Nguyen Cao Ky, then serving as premier of South Vietnam. This flamboyant man was a fixture who first came to prominence during the Khanh regime in 1964 as commander of the air force. In a typically extravagant act, he threatened to call an air strike against the headquarters of squabbling generals. Ky became prime minister in the spring of 1965 but, despite much devious maneuvering, was never able to consolidate his power. In 1967 he became vice president under Nguyen Van Thieu and served in that position until 1971.

When Lodge and Lansdale met Ky at that 1965 reception, the premier was at the height of his popularity and power. He took pains to assure the two men how interested he was in bringing "social justice" to his country. Ky later wrote he was aware of Lansdale's reputation of being a "kingmaker" and so told him, "Now that you are here, you will have no problems [with me], because I have no intention of becoming a king."[58] Such was Lansdale's first meeting with the man who now ruled the land Diem had once governed.

The *Washington Star* reported to its readers that the Lodge/Lansdale team began with high expectations. While Lodge would provide a striped-pants facade, "exchanging smiles and shaking hands," Lansdale began working behind the scenes to replace General Ky's "national leadership committee" with a peasant-oriented indigenous civilian government. Throughout the fall of 1965, Lansdale had to try to live down Ky's worries that he was trying to overthrow his government. Yet for Lansdale, the survival or replacement of any leadership group, such as Ky's military junta, was relatively unimportant. He was more concerned about creating a social revolution to undercut Viet Cong claims. So Lansdale spent long hours with Ky, in marathon five-hour conversations, as he once had with Diem. Lansdale urged American officials in the military, information, and aid agencies to become involved, to get closer to their Vietnamese counterparts. It would, he believed, be a mistake to involve U.S. troops in pacification work. That was a task for the Vietnamese themselves. "Our job," Lansdale said, "is how to be revolutionaries without tearing up the social fabric." He tried to serve as a channel to military and political leaders of Vietnam who were unwilling to speak frankly to most U.S. officials serving there. Lansdale opened his villa to such men, in effect turning it into a sort of club where they could stop by for a drink and a casual visit. Ky and others availed themselves of this opportunity during Lansdale's first weeks in country.[59]

Soon after his arrival, Lansdale was invited to lunch at the villa of a Vietnamese general. After the meal the man took him into the gardens behind his home, far away from any possible listening device planted by an enemy. Speaking quietly, he asked Lansdale, "Where have you got him hidden?" "Who?" Lansdale asked. "Diem!" answered his host. "Don't you think it's time to bring him out again? That was a clever move!" Lansdale was perplexed until the general explained. The officer really believed Diem had not been assassinated but was only spirited away by the United States, to be kept in hiding until the time was right to bring him forth once more. "I had a hard time convincing him that none of it was true," Lansdale said.[60]

Lansdale laughed about such encounters. He was further amused to learn that many Vietnamese, including Ky, believed he still served in some high CIA capacity. During one meeting with Lodge and the CIA station chief, the Agency man reminded Lansdale to "tell people you aren't CIA." "I tell them all the time," Lansdale responded. "What's this?" asked Lodge. The CIA man explained: "Everybody thinks Ed is the head of the CIA wearing a white hat and I'm the head of the CIA wearing a black hat." Lodge turned to Lansdale. "You aren't [still] connected with CIA are you?" "No," he said, "but everybody thinks I am. That's an old rumor out in Asia. So I just go along with it. It keeps the enemy afraid to kill me. They think I've got millions of people all over in my pay. I'm happy they do. It's a good insurance policy." Lodge ordered Lansdale to disassociate himself from such claims.[61]

The Lansdale team had a honeymoon of nearly six months before bureaucratic jackals began hounding their heels. Assigned by Lodge to help South Vietnam organize and carry out a rural construction program, Lansdale aimed at nothing less than bringing a political and economic New Deal to villagers of the countryside, trying to imbue them with a sense of national allegiance to the Saigon government. Lansdale envisioned national elections and eventual replacement of the ruling generals with popularly elected civilians. From the start, Ky was understandably concerned that Lansdale might try to rid the nation of his military regime. Thus, despite embassy assurances that Ky and his generals were cooperating fully in rural construction activities, Lansdale knew Ky's heart was not in the program.

Lansdale was to work with Nguyen Tat Ung, the minister of rural rehabilitation, appointed in June 1965 to this new cabinet post. Ky believed Ung was close to the youth of the country, but Ung was essentially urban in outlook, a Buddhist and an idealist. He was a good man for the job, ready to try his utmost to help build something solid among his people. His principal means of operation was through his own cadre, a corps of whom were trained in a ten-week course at a center in Vung Tau. After much squabbling among American agency advisers who wanted final approval, these fifty-nine-member teams — trained largely in agricultural and in self-defense paramilitary skills — were to be stationed in villages across the country. They were known as "pacification teams." Most members of these teams were still in their early twenties and many were reassigned to their home villages to build roads and bridges and to teach sanitation and elementary level studies to children.

Lansdale urged Ung to get out into the countryside, to see at first hand some of the pacification problems and the solutions local leaders had devised to deal with them. One of the biggest problems, he told Rufe Phillips, was that all of Vietnam was treated as a "lush, tropical bombing range." He suggested that Ung might give support to worthy projects and get a feel for difficulties so he could discuss them more easily with Ky. Ung agreed and planned a trip into I and II Corps areas in central Vietnam. Lansdale invited Ung, his staff, agricultural and social affairs people, military officials, and their American advisers to his villa for an informal talk about problems, how to solve them, what help was available in Vietnam, and how to cut red tape to get projects moving. Ung was buoyed up. He and his staff left the next morning, 14 September 1965, on the trip. Their air transport crashed and burned. Everyone on board died.

After a brief grace period, Ky appointed a new minister, Major General Nguyen Duc Thang, a northern Catholic, an artilleryman with a bent for mathematics who used to take quick breaks when tensions became too great by hiding out in the stacks of the national library and reading books on mathematics. Thang was taller and huskier than most Vietnamese and his looks, mannerisms, and devotion to his country reminded Lansdale of Ramón Magsaysay. The two men became close, often talking far into the night at each other's home. Thang was a more forceful executive than Ung had been, quickly getting a firm grasp of his ministry, making quick trips to the provinces, energetically getting programs under way. Lansdale confided that Thang "keeps looking better as the days go on." He exulted, "We might even have a winner in him." Later he observed, "It was a long, hard grind, but the Vietnamese were learning how to run their own show, taking casualties among their cadre, but many villages were starting self-government and learning to make it work."

Lansdale and others were called back later to Washington for a discussion of how Americans should run the pacification program. He was surprised. He didn't think Americans should run it; it had to be a Vietnamese project or it would never work. There was, Lansdale knew, a deep xenophobia among Vietnamese. Americans could lead them to build a successful noncommunist Vietnam, but they would never think it was theirs, nor voluntarily risk their lives, fortunes, and sacred honor to defend it. Lansdale wondered why Americans couldn't understand this basic fact. He believed Lyndon Johnson would have been just as xenophobic if Canadians or British or the French moved in force into the United States and took charge of his dreams for a Great Society, told him what to do, and spread out by thousands throughout the nation to see that it got done.[62]

Lansdale's team was initially treated very well by the American bureaucracy in Vietnam. State Department was generous with funds and equipment. Ambassador Lodge made his personal plane available to Lansdale and key team members. The CIA station chief was helpful. On the surface, State Department, the military, and the Agency were all helpful, "but when Ed tried to deal with political powers on a political base," Joe Baker reported, "the embassy would move in to stop him." In other words, when Lansdale tried to do those things that were necessary, others obstructed his efforts.[63]

The month after Lansdale's arrival, he received a letter from Henry Kissinger, then a Harvard professor, who planned a trip to Vietnam to study the possibility of creating "a viable political structure in South Vietnam." He asked for Lansdale's help in meeting many of the different political groups who were in opposition to the Ky government. Lansdale wryly replied, "What you're seeking is right down my alley. Trouble is, it's right down several other alleys also."[64]

Those "alleys" Lansdale spoke of were narrow and tortuous. From the beginning of his mission, he found difficulties thrown in his way. William Colby later explained the reason. Lansdale's assignment, Colby said, was not a clear-cut one and caused a turf war. American bureaucracies in Vietnam were intent on preserving their own prerogatives, and Lansdale's mission cut across their territorial lines. Although assigned as Lodge's personal adviser, he didn't have a program to manage. He was a critic and "idea man" while others were program managers who were very jealous of their relationships with their Vietnamese counterparts. Nor did Lansdale have the backing he once had while working with Magsaysay. While in the Philippines he had been able to count fully on CIA backing for support, for money, for influence. In Saigon, both Americans and Vietnamese were confused about where he fit into the scheme of things.[65] What Colby described as "programs," Lansdale referred to as "empires."

"There were empires of headquarters," Lansdale related. "Combat troops had a tremendous backstopping of headquarters and supply units that staggered the imagination." There was, he insisted, too much "Americanization." "[W]e came in so powerfully as a people, as a nation, and so organized in management . . . that we overwhelmed the problem," he said. "We continued to take the initiative away from the Vietnamese, who would have to solve their own problems and did a lot of these things for very good reasons — important, high-minded reasons — but each time we did that, we took away from the Vietnamese the right to solve their own affairs." He shook his head ruefully. "I don't think we needed all that."[66]

There were so many "empires" that the Vietnamese told wry jokes about them. Americans, they claimed, were going to cement the whole country over and in that way stop the war because by then there would be cement laid over the entire nation and no people left. "Look at the airstrips," they said. "Soon we'll have a superhighway going up to Hanoi."[67]

Lansdale and his team sought to pull together the overlapping and sometimes conflicting programs of the Joint United States Public Affairs Organization (JUSPAO), the Agency for International Development (AID), the United States Information Service (USIS), the military, and others. It was his hope to make sense out of the existing bureaucratic muddle. Author Robert Shaplen, a friend of Lansdale, was optimistic and wrote enthusiastically of Lansdale's hopes.[68] His approach stood the best, and perhaps the only, chance of success. He wanted to construct a real political base for the Vietnamese government, working from the bottom up through the hamlets, villages, and districts rather than filtering all programs downward through the cumbersome and politics-ridden South Vietnamese Army with everything funneled from the central government in Saigon through the old French and mandarin bureaucracy in the country's provinces to the districts, villages, and hamlets below.

Hailed in advance as a miracle worker, a charismatic mystical mystery man with hypnotic powers, Lansdale was expected by the populace to pull a rabbit out of a hat, and that he could not do. "All the advance publicity got him off on the wrong foot with both the Vietnamese and the Americans," a team member commented. "Even though most of it was what you'd call 'favorable,' it didn't help Ed. . . . It was a superb example of the power of the written word. Before we had even landed at Tan Son Nhut, we had been labelled, tagged and pigeon-holed as boatrockers who had to be carefully watched."[69]

Unlike most Americans in Vietnam, Lansdale believed it was essential for Vietnamese leaders to claim credit for any changes and reforms. His attitude aroused antagonism in the hearts of many within the U.S. bureaucracy who didn't appreciate moving down to second place and allowing others to receive credit for successful programs — although they did not object to blaming Vietnamese leaders for projects that failed. Mission members also scoffed at Lansdale's shirt-sleeve diplomacy — his relaxed manner and hospitable entertaining of Vietnamese at his villa. They refused to acknowledge that his companionability and unorthodox methods touched a chord of harmony in the minds of many Vietnamese who were tired of dealing with strait-laced American bureaucrats unable or unwilling to hide their contempt for orientals. And so military men and bureaucrats from across South Vietnam found their way to Lansdale's home, where they could relax for a few hours, secure in their knowledge that here at least they would be treated as responsible equals.

Some at the embassy scorned the frequent "hootenannies" at Lansdale's villa, where — after the flow of talk and business finally ceased — Vietnamese, Lansdale and members of his team, labor leaders, intellectuals, Army men, visiting dignitaries from the United States, newsmen, and unknown drop-ins gathered around to sing the folk songs of both countries. There were almost nightly gatherings to drink, sing, and talk over urgent needs of the nation. Passers-by became used to the sounds of strumming guitars, a harmonica, and raucous voices raised in American and Vietnamese folk songs. Lansdale believed such songs important; they reminded participants of national heritage and patriotic themes. At the very least, they were relaxing and fun. To those outside his circle who looked for ways to criticize Lansdale's activities, such songfests were a ridiculous waste of time. What critics seemingly failed to notice was that for several months, Ky came by occasionally and Thang was a frequent visitor at the villa.

Lansdale's unconventional attitudes were always controversial. Economic aid was not a universal cure. Americans should step aside and promote Vietnamese leadership. Diplomacy was best conducted in a relaxed atmosphere among friendly equals rather than by American officials lecturing Vietnamese for their failings. Soldiers should be careful to avoid causing civilian casualties. Large troop units were not the way to fight a people's war. "If Ed had his way in Viet Nam," a reporter with years of experience in the Orient explained, "all the bureaucrats would be out of jobs. USIA, AID, CIA and the Embassy would have a fraction of the people they have on the payroll now, not to mention the Army, Air Force, Navy and Marine Corps."

Yet Lansdale did not have a program of his own and thus had no way to enforce his views. If he made a suggestion about military tactics or strategy, he was reminded to stop meddling in the domain of General William Westmoreland. If he commented on elections, he was ordered not to interfere with the job of Philip Habib, chief of the embassy's political section. If he tried to deal with psychological warfare — which had been a favorite topic with him for years — he was told the subject was the property of Barry Zorthian, JUSPAO chief. Pacification was controlled by William J. Porter, the deputy ambassador.

One of Lansdale's team lamented over such difficulties: "If we needed leaflets, that belonged to JUSPAO and psywar; if we needed charcoal or fertilizer for a certain hamlet, we had to go to AID; if a village chief died and the people wanted to choose his successor, that involved [Habib]; if we needed a helicoptor [sic] in a hurry, permission had to come from the military transport officer. It became an impossible knot to untie. The only solution would have been to cut through it, but this had to be done at the top."

Military activity. Psychological warfare. Political projects. Pacification. The U.S. Mission fought four separate and uncoordinated wars. Ambassador Lodge failed to realize that all had to be united if any were to succeed, but when Lansdale tried to so inform him, his advice was spurned.

Milton Sachs, a professor of politics at Brandeis University, described the origin of much of Lansdale's difficulties. He had the reputation of an "unconventional channel-jumper," he "short-circuited" bureaucratic procedures. "This is something that bureaucrats in any agency, civilian or military, disapprove of in principle." There was also a more deep-rooted resentment. "He was a major general who never went to West Point and [he] held the rank of Minister without coming up through the Foreign Service." No wonder there was such turmoil when he tried to assert his own views.

Leonard Unger, Lansdale's immediate superior in the State Department, lamented these difficulties. "Maybe Ed's trouble is that he's not enough of a son-of-a-bitch. Maybe if Ed beat his fist on the table and raised more hell, he would get some things done the way he thinks they should be done. But that's not his way . . . to raise that kind of hell."[69]

Occasionally, however, Lansdale did raise hell, and that was to others only further proof of his unfitness. He admitted it was a mistake to "open my big mouth" at country team meetings, but sometimes he was unable to remain silent. Even by 1965 the American war in Vietnam had become massive, a cancerous spread of U.S. agencies, services, missions, institutes, and programs — and Lansdale disagreed with the whole tenor of that approach. At one meeting he criticized the constant bureaucratic political jockeying. "We've got young Americans getting killed out there," he stormed, "and you guys are playing games and shafting each other and working behind each other's back and I think it's lousy." He hoped the others, one day, might have to "put some of our casualties in body sacks for shipment home." That might teach them what the purpose really was for their assignments to Vietnam. Lodge suggested he tame his emotions. Fighting a war, Lansdale rejoined, was "an emotional goddam business."[70]

Had he been given more support, Lansdale believed he could have achieved significant change for the better in Vietnam. Yet just the opposite happened. Despite (or because of) his objections at the pacification meeting in Washington in January 1966, Lansdale was bypassed once again. In a major embassy reorganization in mid-February 1966, Lansdale lost his chance to direct American pacification efforts in Vietnam. He would continue to serve in his ill-defined job as senior liaison officer, with no specific responsibilities. Pacification — which was what Lansdale knew best and was the reason he had come to Vietnam — would be handled by Deputy Ambassador William Porter, who formed the Office of Civil Operations (OCO) to take charge of the program. He was later succeeded by Robert Komer, who remodeled OCO into Civil Operations and Revolutionary Development Support (CORDS). Lansdale was shut out from meaningful participation in either. "A beautiful pacification ensued," he commented, but because it was not directed by Vietnamese, "it was transitory." He also gained a prime enemy in the person of Lodge's deputy, Philip Habib. He effectively undermined Lansdale's role as a political channel to the Vietnamese. Lansdale later lamented bitterly, "He was against everything I was for, and for everything I was against."[71]

Leonard Unger, Lansdale's superior in the State Department, cautioned him to "coordinate" with Habib. Lansdale replied that while Phil was a "nice boy," he really couldn't spend too much time educating him but would keep him informed on team activities. When Unger took umbrage at this show of independence, Lansdale quietly asked him, "how long do you guys want to see the shit kicked out of the U.S. to serve the career ambitions of a handful of Americans? You don't seem to understand that, if the US bureaucracies had [really] done their work, we wouldn't have over 2,000 American kids killed in combat so far!"

Lansdale continued his lecture to Unger. He pointed out that Unger and another ally, William Bundy, had let his team down. They had not backstopped him in the Washington corridors of power. On a trip to Washington in mid-January 1966, Lansdale had learned that enemies were doing their best to box him in. White House assistants, the vice president's staff, the Joint Chiefs in the Pentagon, even CIA — all told him they had not received copies of his communications to Washington. Someone was "deep-sixing" them. Lansdale promised Unger he would continue to do his best in Vietnam, "but if or when I get chopped down for it, I'm then publicly blowing the whistle on the poor work of the U.S. in Vietnam." He resented, he said, "spending most of my time explaining every last move to Lodge and Habib in kindergarten terms they would understand."[72]

After his return in early 1966 from the trip to Washington, Lansdale told his team that their political support was ephemeral, "a series of melting ice floes and [I] will keep on skipping from one to the other to keep us afloat." For a time, Lansdale said, they might be able to count on support from Walt Rostow and Robert Komer, a CIA analyst who later headed pacification programs in Vietnam. Others who could be helpful included William Bundy and Vice President Humphrey. Lansdale told his team that he warned supporters, "[W]e cannot work with our hands so tied or with the frequent knifings." Finally, Lansdale confessed, he felt "like slugging [LBJ] as a smart-aleck" for insisting on priorities and policies that simply were not going to work.[73]

Where once he had been a daily confidant of Diem and had held long talks with Ky only a few months earlier, now Lansdale found he was blocked from any meaningful contacts. When William Porter took over pacification programs, he informed Nguyen Duc Thang not to deal with Lansdale in the future because meetings with him would be outside the chain of command and might confuse matters. Thang, a strong, husky man, knuckled his fist and "corked" Porter hard on the arm. "Lansdale is my friend and I am going to see him any goddamn time I feel like it and tell him any goddamn thing I want. If he gives me any advice, I'm going to welcome it!" Porter's comment was "Ow!" Lansdale, who was present at the encounter, added, "I'm going to go on seeing him. I don't care what you say. Or else give me a ticket and get me out of Vietnam. . . . As long as I'm here and he needs help, I'm going to help him."[74] Lansdale did continue to work with Vietnamese but in many cases had to use circumvention to meet with their leaders. "When Ed wanted to see General [Nguyen Van] Thieu, he would have Lou [Conein] arrange the meeting through the back door because Lou and Thieu had been friends for years."[75] Asking for such help must have galled Lansdale bitterly. Lansdale also tried to work with Bui Diem, chief of staff and later secretary of state for foreign affairs under Ky, but found him so busy with other duties that he had little time to spare for pacification. Lansdale was a most frustrated man.[76]

It did not take waiting reporters long to sense that the bureaucracy had drawn blood from Lansdale. On 24 February 1966, only six months after Lansdale's arrival in Vietnam, Stanley Karnow trumpeted, "[I]t is widely acknowledged here [in Saigon] that Lansdale has performed no miracles. Instead, the key question is whether he had been able to do anything even remotely significant."[77]

The team vented much of its frustration and ire upon Lodge. For some, he was "Cabbagehead"; for Conein, who saw a chemical symbol in the ambassador's initials, he became "hydrochloric acid." To others,

Philip Habib became simply "that dirty little Arab."[78] Lansdale was somewhat more judicious: "I don't think he ever understood that he was dealing with real live human beings out there. Taylor never did. Westmoreland never did. That was too bad."[79]

Habib allegedly resented Lansdale's easy familiarity with so many important men in that country. Lansdale recognized Habib's personal ambitions; the job in Vietnam was just the "next big step" in his career. "He made no bones about it," Lansdale complained. "He wanted to be an ambassador when he left there. I was in his way because I was doing something that obviously was his business, *but he wasn't doing it.*" During one confrontation, Lansdale told Habib, "Look, my reputation has already been made. I've got my fame. You can have yours. I'll help you get it, but please, we're in the middle of a war and we've got to get on with helping these people."[80] Habib refused the proffered cooperation.

Daniel Ellsberg also came to hold strong views about both Habib and Porter. "Habib was stupid about Vietnam," Ellsberg later said. "He was head of the political section but he had a tin ear for anything Vietnamese. . . . [T]he Vietnamese he dealt with he just drove out of their minds." Nor was Porter any better. "I liked Porter very much. He was an intelligent, decent guy — but he hated the Vietnamese. He just couldn't stand them. In this he was like Habib. . . . Habib hated orientals, he despised them, he had contempt for them, he just couldn't stand them. He didn't make any effort to hide that."[81]

Lodge, however, was the key. Lansdale tried to do his best, but without total support from the ambassador there was little he could accomplish. Each different agency Lansdale approached was full of the fact that it could go directly to Congress for its funds. "I begged Lodge to knock their heads together, to back me up," Lansdale lamented. "He said no. You do it."[82] Nearly everyone, he observed, had an idea as to how pacification should be approached. Most of them wanted the results to have been "made in the U.S.A." and he knew that would not work. "It has to be made in Vietnam with the Vietnamese doing it their style in ways they would understand." With world-weary cynicism, he added, "They finally got me because I didn't pacify the country!"[83] From his lofty vantage point, General Westmoreland tended to agree with Lansdale's assessment. Although he had different ideas about how to rectify matters, pacification, in his view, was a mess.[84]

At a conference in the Hawaiian Islands in February 1966, President Johnson met with top leaders of South Vietnam and at the end of the meeting LBJ proclaimed the Declaration of Honolulu. While Johnson added a few touches of his own, such as a pledge to combat "hunger, ignorance and disease," and to pursue "the unending quest for peace," the key passage was written by Lansdale. It pledged America to give "full support to measures of social revolution, including land reform, based on the principle of building upward from the hopes and purposes of all the people of Viet Nam." While his ideas were accepted — at least in theory; LBJ made no pretense later of following or even understanding them — Lansdale was not given the authority, money, or power to pursue them in any practical way. At this point, he seemed very much near the end of his rope.

Then Lansdale received help from an unexpected source. The Buddhists of Vietnam began to demand that Ky follow a social revolution. Their spokesmen found out about and approved of Lansdale's program and Lieutenant General Nguyen Chanh Thi talked fondly of Lansdale, expressing a hope to work with him in the future. The lay followers of the monk, Thich Tri Quang, said that they wanted Lansdale to advise them if they achieved a Buddhist majority in the nation's Assembly. Leaders of the large Catholic refugee population also sought advice from Lansdale.[85] Consequently, he was allowed to remain in Vietnam to satisfy his diverse admirers.

By April 1966, American newspapers carried stories of Lansdale's decline. The *Washington Evening Star* described him as a "faded star and a failure . . . a straw man." The article continued with mention of the "ill concealed satisfaction" over his failures evident among his rivals at MACV, CIA, AID, and JUSPAO.[86] Even clandestine broadcasts of Liberation Radio, the voice of the Viet Cong's People's Revolutionary party, contained stories of Lansdale's lessening influence. One broadcast described Lansdale as "a mythological personage" and told how he had failed "Johnson [who] placed all his hope" in this "brigand" and "colonialist old fox Lansdale."[87] He had come back to Vietnam with high hopes. Now there was the taste of dust in his mouth.

14

"GODDAMMIT, THIEU"

LANSDALE KEPT HIMSELF and his team busy in Vietnam during the first weeks of 1966. Hubert Humphrey came on an official visit in February and his lengthy talks with Lansdale and his ever-present enthusiasm heartened Lansdale's hopes that something might still be salvageable from his mission to Vietnam.[1] But there was no discernible improvement after the vice president returned to America; Lansdale was still blocked by enemies in the embassy. As politicians will, Lodge praised Lansdale at appropriate moments but refused to provide him with real support. The ambassador, in his 1966 evaluation of Lansdale's services, referred to his "big and deserved reputation" and described Lansdale as "extraordinarily intuitive," "understanding," and a man with no apparent weaknesses.[2] Lansdale would have preferred the man's staunch backing; he got instead empty phrases.

Finally Lansdale resorted to the threat of resignation to relieve his frustration. He would either get support or go home. In April 1966, at his insistence, Lodge forwarded a cable to William Bundy: "Recommend immediate reconsideration of maintaining Lansdale team in Vietnam — U.S. prohibition against team using its known capabilities for informal contacts with Vietnamese leaders . . . makes presence Lansdale team incomprehensible."[3] And still nothing happened except bland assurances that he was "needed" in Vietnam. Lansdale felt as if he were swimming through a sea of taffy, unable either to move forward or to free himself.

The situation was bad enough; the laughter of enemies made it worse. Even the Soviets seemed to realize how little of a worthwhile nature he was allowed to do. *Komsomol Pravda* described in a neutral way "the general from CIA" on his "second secret mission." But Tass called him a "cloak and dagger knight" unable to cope "with the tasks entrusted to him," a "CIA superspy" who did not "exercise the slightest influence on the situation in South Vietnam."[4] The worst part about such jibes was that they were essentially accurate.

Perhaps the high point of 1966 came for Lansdale when his alma mater, UCLA, honored him twice within two months. In March he was selected as Alumni of the Month. Phi Gamma Delta, his fraternity, printed a story about him in its March newsletter, *The Fiji Brewin:* "The moral of his story is that, if you major in English literature at UCLA, you never know where the hell you might wind up."[5] In May the university presented him with its professional achievement award in foreign service.[6] John Doran, a former fraternity brother, wrote Lansdale a letter of congratulations and sent along a picture of the two when they were both young college studs. Lansdale's reply was businesslike: "I'm afraid that we're being taught some savage lessons about a type of warfare that the next generation or so of Americans will have to face up to on other continents as on this one; . . . I'm walking humbly in this one trying to get our folk on sounder footing."[7] Lansdale wanted to receive his award personally, so he took a brief leave of absence from Saigon to fly to Los Angeles. Following his visit to the California campus, Ed spent a few days in Washington seeing Helen and the boys and trying unsuccessfully to mend his political fences.

Prevented by bureaucratic jealousies from performing a real job, Lansdale filled his days with frenetic activity upon his return to Saigon, much like a caged animal running in an exercise wheel. The day files of the Senior Liaison Office recorded the tasks Lansdale and his team members set themselves to performing. They were interested in morals, in ethics, in eliminating or lessening private and public corruption, in promoting education and caring for refugees, in improving slum conditions. They wrote memoranda about training of rural development cadres. They composed letters to and received them from multitudes in and out of government — Vietnamese and American — those already part of the team and others who hoped to be; subordinates and superiors, politicians, members of the press (including Gloria "Glo-Glo" Emerson), job seekers, and well-wishers.[8]

Just one fat file of letters from Lansdale to William Bundy touched on such topics as rural security, veterans' benefits, conditions of docks, markets, and roads, speech writing suggestions for Nguyen Cao Ky, a possible issue of a series of Vietnamese postage stamps honoring the nation's heroes, scholarships for war orphans, orphanages, *chieu hoi* returnees, the future of war-spawned illegitimate children and Vietnamese women, and a slang dictionary of Vietnamese terms.[9]

The day files record meetings with Nguyen Duc Thang and efforts to get Vietnamese public television announcers who spoke southern, rather than northern, dialects. Lansdale was interested in establishing credit unions in rural areas. He wrote about boys' clubs, how to keep soldiers from taking food from villagers, the importance of Vietnamese folk songs and music, meetings with popular composer Pham Duy, awards for patriotism, and political maneuverings of William Porter and Phil Habib. He told of a vacation at a friend's house in Dalat, of a visit by John Steinbeck to the villa at 194 Cong Ly Street, of various acts of humanity performed by team members to U.S. personnel and Vietnamese citizens. He spoke of his concerns about marijuana use by GIs and corresponded with John Paul Vann about the difficulties of advising. There are notations of his gifts of music tapes to President Johnson and others and evidence of his continuing concern about the welfare of the Eastern Construction Company (ECCOI), which he had organized years earlier as Freedom Company. He wrote helpful letters to American graduate students working on master's theses and doctoral dissertations.[10]

Lansdale recorded his meeting with a visiting American politician named Richard M. Nixon. He worked to relocate twenty-three thousand people — forty-five hundred families — out of the war-torn demilitarized zone marking the line between North and South Vietnam. He persuaded General Westmoreland to assign Captain Hershel Goober as a "traveling troubador." He discussed with Ky the negative effects of news censorship. He sifted through the Vietnamese bureaucracy for men with favorable attitudes toward the United States and pushed them for positions of responsibility. He recorded trips made throughout Vietnam in a constant search for ways to stabilize the countryside.[11] Lansdale occasionally asked for a few days off for personal reasons.[12] He squired visiting firemen from the States[13] and described how making use of "auspicious" and "superstitious" dates on the Vietnamese calendar might help Americans who worked in Vietnam. He noted that Viet Cong bands "taxed" the highways of the land to bring in revenue for their cause, worried about juvenile delinquents, and warned of the appearance of counterfeit U.S. five-dollar bills.[14]

In all these activities — and in other unenumerated ones — Ed Lansdale was primarily concerned about the welfare of people. Such a stance made him anathema to those more concerned about search and destroy missions, agent orange, free fire zones, harassing and interdicting fires, and body counts. He stood at cross-purposes to the major American efforts in Vietnam, and the conflict left him in tears of frustration. He lamented the "considerable misunderstanding of our role, in which I have been moving in close to the Vietnamese to spark them into actions and seem to be forever stepping on American jurisdictional toes."[15]

He outlined to Rufus Phillips the "dirty power struggle" that continued "behind the scenes" among Americans. It was time, he said, for someone to "talk plain turkey" to them about real needs in Vietnam. "Everyone," he wrote, "is trying to gain brownie points for self — at the expense of the other guy. I catch most of them eyeing me . . . . Maybe my disgust shows. I just wink at them . . . . It adds to the mystique. . . . What a viper's nest!"[16] Never willing for his own men to lose sight of the noble purpose for which he had called them to Vietnam, Lansdale made certain that texts of the Declaration of Independence, the Constitution, and the Bill of Rights were available in the team office, and he periodically asked his people to reread them to refresh their memories on those basic American principles.[17]

There were occasional light moments. Lansdale was vastly amused when his friend Nguyen Duc Thang stopped by his villa one day to talk. Thang told Lansdale of his one-man crusade to get Saigon street kids to stop using American slang such as "Hello. Okay. You Number One." He told Lansdale of stopping one such boy on the street and patiently explaining to him why he should use polite Vietnamese language rather than foreign slang. The boy looked at General Thang in amazement and replied, "My! How did you American learn to speak such good Vietnamese?"[18]

Another moment of levity was provided by an article written by Phan Chan Thanh, "The Man Sentenced to Death by Ho," which appeared in Saigon's *Thoi Nay* magazine. The story told of a planned effort to assassinate Lansdale in July 1963. Nhuong Van, twenty-six years old, a member of the Binh Xuyen sect, was to carry out the act outside the American embassy on orders of Ho Chi Minh. The writer seemingly did not know that in July 1963, Lansdale was half a world away. The story breathlessly related other attempts on Lansdale's life, one by Diem's generals because they did not appreciate his support of the president, another by a hit squad of the North Vietnamese Army. "Kill Lansdale at any cost!" According to the author, "assassinations and exterminations are as often," for Lansdale, "as the meals he takes every day."[19]

Other times of relaxation and joy for Lansdale came in those evening hootenannies at his villa. As those impromptu sessions continued, Lansdale came to believe that Vietnamese music might even serve as a vehicle for strengthening the society. He began to collect songs composed, written, and performed by Vietnamese about their country, its people, and their emotions. Often at those gatherings both Americans and Vietnamese sang old, familiar tunes. On other evenings they lifted their voices in newly composed tunes, voiced for the first time among friends. Some expressed the mood of men in combat, of villagers, of cadre, of youth: commentary of the day by people caught up in war. Lansdale began taping the songs and over the months of his second Vietnam tour, his music collection grew. The songs he recorded, he believed, were part of the history of a long, long war and told the human side of that conflict.

Lansdale also met Vietnam's preeminent folk singer, a balladeer named Pham Duy, who wrote "heart songs" that spoke to his people's hunger for something spiritual. Pham Duy was one of those rare geniuses whose music was celebrated by those who heard it. One of his most hauntingly beautiful heart songs was "Rain on the Leaves," written in 1965. Lansdale first heard Pham Duy singing it to Vietnamese troops while dressed in the black pajamas of a village farmer. Lansdale knew that such music was worth saving.

He visited a group of college students in Gia Dinh who were building housing for refugees who had come from central Vietnam. Since classes would begin again in only a matter of days, the students were rushing against the clock to complete their work. While visiting there, Lansdale heard them break into a spontaneous song soon picked up by other crews in the camp until hundreds of voices carried the refrain "Viet Nam, Viet Nam," a pledged cry of young Vietnamese to the future of their country. He taped the tune.

There were many other melodies — some about the courage of Father Hoa at Binh Hung, about the bravery of those who "voted with their feet" in 1954, about the need to stand firm against insurgency and to dedicate oneself to service of country, about the beauty of a Vietnamese sunset — marching songs and ballads of love. At one point, Lansdale invited Ambassador Lodge and others to his home to sing old and new songs, and he also taped this session. As Filipino friends came to listen, Lansdale encouraged them also to sing their songs. Instruments of all kinds were used. Lansdale played his harmonica. Others joined in with guitars, mandolins, and Vietnamese zithers.

Pham Duy translated some old favorite American tunes into Vietnamese: "My Darling Clementine," "Red River Valley." He also put the song "We Shall Overcome" into his tonal language. The refrain became "We Shall Win the War." He continued to write new songs. One was a cadre tune for the young people of the National Training Center at Vung Tau: "The Enemy Is No Man — we must defeat the enemy within each of us — become pure of spirit — before we can defeat the enemy without."

Pham Duy also played and sang the songs of other nations to entertain visitors at Lansdale's home, special treats for soldiers from America, Korea, and the Philippines: "Arirang" for troops of Korea's Tiger and White Horse divisions, "Magtanim hindi biro" (Planting Rice) for employees of ECCOI, and "Hue Down upon the Perfume River" or "God Smite Thee, Barry Zorthian" for Americans.[20]

Even Nguyen Cao Ky came to sing, joining in on "Gui Gio Cho

May Ngan Day,'' a Vietnamese Air Force song likening high cloud formations to white snow. With others, he sang "Tien Em" and "Toi Co." And no matter how many songs of his were sung, Pham Duy was always ready to compose another. His talent was inexhaustible. He produced a steady stream of airs for a revolutionary nation: "Wearing the Black Pajamas," "Let's Build a New Life Hamlet," "A Bowl of Rice Is a Bowl of Sweetness," and "To Sing Often Is Better than to Sing with a Good Voice." His countrymen sang them and Ed Lansdale preserved them on tape for historians and future generations.[21]

Life might be song-filled inside Lansdale's villa; it had a harsher texture when he left the cloistered walls of his "monastery."[22] For some months Lansdale continually renewed his threat to resign unless he was given real responsibilities. In October 1966 he notified Lodge, "I wrote you some months ago suggesting that the [senior liaison] office be closed out and that we depart from Viet Nam in late 1966. I have given the matter much further thought. . . . If there is no change of the U.S. approach, then I believe that the disbandment of SLO and return home of the staff is very much in order." He sent copies to William Bundy, to Robert Komer, and to his immediate Washington superior, Leonard Unger.

On 3 November, Unger replied. His answer was not what Lansdale wanted to hear. "Basically, the question of the employment of the Senior Liaison Office must be a matter for decision by Ambassador Lodge. . . . [I]t is only the Ambassador on the scene who can make effective judgments on matters of this sort. . . . As far as my personal views are concerned . . . I have always been and remain persuaded of the major contribution you have made and can continue to make as a personal emissary to and 'persuader' of the Vietnamese leaders; the role of [your] staff in this connection is not so clear to me." Unger had protected and supported Lansdale's work in the past. Now consigned to an endless series of trivial responsibilities and cut off from any influential position, Lansdale had hoped for better. He now saw that Unger had no intention of intervening with Lodge. It was to be the ambassador's show.[23] Lansdale's frustration showed through when he wrote to Rufus Phillips that he had heard "by the grapevine" that Unger was "secretly in cahoots with Habib."[24]

In 1966 as in 1965, Lansdale went back to Washington at Christmastime, not so much for fellowship with his family as to protect his flanks and rear from attacks by political enemies. Although his old friend Hanging Sam Williams might console him by writing, "[M]y private sources . . . tell me that you . . . are doing a good job & making progress," Lansdale knew better. He understood full well how high were the obstacles and how deep the pitfalls in his path.[25] On his return to Saigon, he received another warm and friendly compliment from Lodge, who praised his work. "I would like you to keep right on as you are," the ambassador wrote, "mingling with Vietnamese of all kinds, and maintaining your many friendships, thereby providing me with valuable information on which to base important judgments."[26] Since Lansdale was aware of Lodge's longstanding refusal to accept any of his advice or pleas for help, the note sounded to him like the tolling of a death knell.

Outranked and outflanked, Lansdale was a prisoner of the bureaucracy. Under the strain, his team began to slip away, quitting the scene in disgust and frustration. By March 1967 only five — including Lansdale — remained of those who had come in 1965 to join in the good fight for a stable Vietnam.

Lansdale did not have long to wait before Lodge presented him with a more honest appraisal of his work. In March 1967, as the ambassador prepared to vacate his position in Vietnam, he called Lansdale into his office for a frank discussion. "I'd suggest you come home with me," he told his senior liaison officer. "LBJ wanted you out here with me on pacification, but you've failed on that and you better come home."[27]

Lansdale had threatened to resign often enough. Now when actually faced with the ambassador's request for him to do so, Lansdale became alarmed. "No," he insisted. "I'm trying to help a lot of Vietnamese make their constitutional form of government a reality. . . . There is a lot [to do]. I should stay here and get [it] done, just for a time, but not indefinitely." Lodge pressed the issue. He and Philip Habib had recently flown to Guam for a top-level meeting and they had talked with Ellsworth Bunker, the newly appointed ambassador. "I talked with Bunker," Lodge observed, "and he doesn't want you; he wants to save him[self] embarrassment." Lansdale stubbornly dug in his heels. "I'll ask him that when he comes."[28]

Lansdale now sought ways to circumvent Lodge's insistence on his return to America. In March 1967 he reluctantly submitted his resignation, which he left undated, to be effective whenever Lodge desired it. An accompanying letter, however, showed how strongly he was trying to dodge any effort to send him home. Lansdale stressed in his letter how the time was not right. Vietnamese politicians, he said, wanted him to stay on through the coming September elections. He asked for time to discuss his future plans with both General Westmoreland and William Bundy.[29] He also contacted Rufus Phillips in Washington and asked for his help. Phillips hastened to notify Hubert Humphrey about Lodge's demand for Lansdale to resign. He noted Lansdale's compliance with the order but insisted it was only a *pro forma* resignation. Phillips told

Humphrey he had only recently talked with Lansdale in Hong Kong and "he represents the *only* hope the U.S. has of achieving anything . . . in South Viet Nam."[30]

Phillips comforted Lansdale. All was not lost. A mutual friend had met with the newly appointed ambassador and briefed him about Lansdale's potential for service in Vietnam. "Bunker was very positive about wanting you to stay on," Phillips wrote. He added his opinion about the new man. "Bunker is a very different type from Lodge . . . [and] you will work well together."[31] When the new ambassador arrived in Saigon, Lansdale met him at the airport. He was pleased when Bunker invited him to ride in his limousine on the trip from Tan Son Nhut airport to the official ambassador's residence. He felt his morale rise for the first time in weeks when Bunker told him, "I'm very happy you're still here. I want you to stay and work with me." Lansdale replied with careful caution. "Lodge told me you had talked to him and didn't want me. If so, I will bow out right now." The elderly ambassador shook his head. "No. No. I want you to stay."[32]

As he observed the new ambassador in action, Lansdale felt better about American prospects. "He was a surprisingly candid and honest person, a true, old-fashioned gentleman whose word was as good as his bond, which wasn't true of Cabot Lodge," Lansdale later said. "Bunker tried very hard to understand Vietnam. I give him one hundred percent as ambassador — a very fine man."[33] So Lansdale stayed on in Saigon.

Lansdale supplied Ambassador Bunker with information on the Vietnamese scene as he had done for Lodge — much that was crucial for a proper understanding of its politics as well as an occasional humorous tidbit. In one instance he reminded Bunker of the difficulties inherent in the tonal language of the country. One candidate running for a seat in the September elections for the Senate was Quach Kim Long, a man of Chinese descent who spoke Vietnamese rather poorly. He stepped to the microphone during a political rally and, in a shaky voice, pleaded with voters to cast their ballots for Long. In his nervousness he not only dropped the *g* in his name but lowered his voice as well. To the astounded Vietnamese listeners, it was a plea to "vote for a vagina."[34]

Lansdale stayed on in Saigon through scheduled elections for the Lower House and through the 3 September 1967 elections for the Senate and the contest to select a new president and vice president. Nguyen Van Thieu and Nguyen Cao Ky were elected, respectively, to the two highest offices in the land, but accusations of fraud tainted the balloting. They won by only one-third of the total count and even that tally was challenged. Their victory was barely validated by a 53–48 vote of the Assembly. Lansdale observed that both men would be weak leaders. "Given their natures, I doubt that they will improve much," he said. Dispirited, Lansdale departed Vietnam for the United States two days after the 31 October 1966 inauguration of Thieu and Ky.[35]

Once again Lansdale made the rounds of his Washington contacts within the Johnson administration trying to garner support for a real role for himself in Vietnam. Despite his best lobbying efforts, he made no progress. November turned into December and still he delayed returning to Saigon. At Christmastime 1967, for the third year in a row, Lansdale spent the holidays with Helen, Ted, and Peter. As the old year ended, he still debated whether or not to return to Saigon. When friends urged him to go back, Lansdale wondered whether their counsel was like the old-time gag gift of a cigar that exploded in a smoker's face.[36] Yet a new ambassador was now on station with whom he had a good rapport. Opposed to the huge buildup of U.S. combat forces, certain that America's military leaders — and General Westmoreland in particular — had little grasp of the realities of a people's war, afraid that many more of the nation's young men would die needlessly in a war few understood, Lansdale finally decided to return. "So back into the whole damn mess I went," he told a friend. "Sentiment overcame judgment. . . . It was a heart-breaker . . . not the least being the jealousies, back-stabbings, and hinderances [sic] of the US officials there." The whole mission, he admitted, took place during "a sordid epoch."[37]

And so Lansdale returned to Saigon once again to take up his missionary tasks. This gray, unassuming man with the Mount Rushmore head may have held the keys to American success in his hands and yet no one listened. As before, he found plenty of opponents who tried to undercut him at every turn. For the most part, in face-to-face encounters, he spoke to them softly and modestly, almost in a self-effacing way, yet they were unwilling to forgive or cooperate. No matter which direction he moved, Lansdale found he stepped on someone's toes. And many who opposed him carried their peeves to listening correspondents. One freelance author put Lansdale's situation to him bluntly: "[A]ll wonder what in hell is going on up there on Cong Ly. . . . [O]pinions I have gotten from the press corps are: that you have become an alcoholic, that you are now senile and they are all covering up for you, that you are taking drugs, that you are an empty, shallow, superficial myth who somehow gave everyone a snow job, that you are under some kind of restriction to stay in your house. I have been told that no one can ever see you alone."[38]

Philip Habib, William Porter, Barry Zorthian, and others may indeed have "maliciously and with intent aforethought" worked to destroy Lansdale's position and reputation. He was an easy target because he was perhaps one of those least equipped to deal with administrative infighting. Honest, plainspoken, and direct in his dealings, he was disinclined to roll in the muck with self-serving American bureaucrats. Nor was he interested — ever — in creating an empire of his own. Even at the first he had been happy to work with only a dozen helpers, and this at a time when major American agencies counted employees by the thousands.

Yet he was not quite such a simple bumpkin as his enemies thought. Some CIA operatives, at least, saw through his unassuming ways and greatly admired Lansdale for his willingness to appear naive, obtuse, even sometimes a yokel if such a pose would help him get his job done. There was always an extreme contrast, obvious to insiders, between the way Lansdale appeared when talking with an "outsider" and with a team member. With those who worked close beside him, Lansdale was shrewd, complex, and tactical in his thinking. To members of the American establishment in Saigon, he sometimes posed as a simple romanticist about Vietnam, its culture, and people. All this was a cover, used to help him get around enemies and obstacles, to disarm or overcome them, and to drive past them toward his goals. Sometimes it worked; in Saigon his act clearly failed him.

"I was stupid enough to return for the Tet offensive [of January 1968]," Lansdale said. "God, I didn't know that was coming."[39] He was not alone. It surprised every American in Vietnam including the Marine guards at the embassy and at the ambassador's residence. They became afraid the rampaging Viet Cong attackers might target Bunker, so they slipped him out of his home and drove him to Lansdale's villa on Cong Ly.

When the attacks began, Lansdale and his team changed into black pajamas and went out to reconnoiter their neighborhood. Lansdale had previously organized Vietnamese families within a three-block radius into a network to spy out any strangers who might enter the area. As he and his men talked with contacts and watched for infiltrators, many neighborhood people sought refuge inside the walls of his villa. Some even arrived in cars and left them parked in Lansdale's yard. Throughout the grounds were nervous families, sprawled on cots or blankets, nervously starting at each new sound.

When Bunker and his Marine escort showed up, Lansdale welcomed them and gave the ambassador his bedroom. Bunker lay down and went to sleep. His Marine guards stood security watches and became ever more concerned as reports filtered in about the uprising. Later that night they moved Bunker once more, to the compound where Philip Habib lived. The Cong Ly villa sat next to the road to Tan Son Nhut, but Habib lived in a more remote location and thus, the Marines hoped, a far safer location.[40]

"We lost the war at the Tet offensive," Lansdale later realized.[41] At least one reason for that defeat, he argued, was that in defending against the unexpected Viet Cong onslaught, American commanders' ability to discriminate between friend and foe — never a very highly developed skill — was lost totally. All Vietnamese looked the same; they were all "gooks." "We are a technical nation and we love our equipment," Lansdale observed. Commanders, particularly in the infantry, tried to use firepower to cut down on casualties among their troops. They relied on artillery to keep the enemy soldiers at a distance and punish them. Their first thought seemed to be to radio for artillery support. Instead of sending troops forward against enemy fire to overrun an enemy position, commanders asked for artillery barrages. Those fire missions, Lansdale claimed, killed not only foe but huddled civilians — "innocent people, including children." American officers who acted in such ways made "hundreds of people hate Americans and be afraid of them."

Lansdale recalled a fine American Army officer he first met in Indonesia. Later promoted and transferred to Vietnam, that officer commanded a brigade located just outside Saigon during the Tet fighting. The community nearest the general's infantry brigade was Saigon's district eight. Lansdale and his team had worked with the working-class people there for several years, endeavoring to convince them to support the Saigon government, and team members reported that they were very loyal. As the Tet offensive began, some Viet Cong soldiers moved into district eight. Most of the Viet Cong were relatives or sons of friends. As they came into the community, many there argued with them. "You're on the wrong side. Come home." Only a few of the guerrillas were strangers to the people in district eight. Community leaders sought out the general and tried to explain the situation. "The enemy came in here last night. They aren't part of us. They don't belong here. We will show you where they are," they said. But the commander thought the area "was a scrawny looking place . . . so he brought in artillery and blasted all the houses down."

Twenty years later, Lansdale's voice still caught fire as he recalled the incident. "We had spent two years teaching those people how they could have a new start in life. We gave them places outside town along the [Mekong] river in the mud flats. We taught them how to dry mud [and use it] to build foundations. They built their shacks there. We started cottage industries and they started earning money. Whether the place looked awful or not, it was all these people had and they were proud they had gotten a little ahead."

During the Tet fighting, Lansdale sent team members into district eight to see what help they might offer. Enraged survivors of the artillery barrage told them to get out and never come back. "They [now] hated all Americans," Lansdale said, his voice melancholy. His team drove back to Cong Ly Street to report. "These were grown men and they'd worked two years getting those people into a better situation. And they were crying!"

Bunker called a country team meeting. Lansdale attended and listened to Westmoreland tell how his forces were pushing the enemy out of Saigon. "You've loused up one district," Lansdale cried out, "and I'm going to speak up for the people there. You are doing it wrong." The ambassador tried to calm Lansdale. "I don't know whether you ought to speak right now. [You're] so damn mad, red in the face and you're yelling at him. [Do you] really [need] to yell at somebody in this meeting?" "Yeah," Lansdale rejoined. "I've got to get it out of my system." He never did. The memories of faulty tactics remained with him the rest of his life.[42]

As the fighting moved out of Saigon, life at 194 Cong Ly slowly returned to normal. Once again came the constant procession of Vietnamese to Lansdale's villa: Catholics, Buddhists, students from the University of Saigon, Cao Dai priests, Hoa Hao believers, generals, editors, songwriters, poets, politicians. They talked endlessly and soaked up Lansdale's hospitality until early morning hours as they chain-smoked, emptied repeatedly filled glasses, and wrangled over the politics of that war-blasted land. To a lesser extent than in earlier years, Lansdale also made forays into the provinces and to other cities in his continuing search for people capable of providing responsible leadership.[43]

Lansdale continued to mourn the widening gulf between his hopes for Vietnam and its apparent political and military reality. Work as he would with American military leaders, he was never able to show them how to comprehend appropriate tactics to use in a people's war. Lansdale later recalled that he did no more than ask American generals to remember the Army's own heritage from the days of the Philippine insurrection in the early twentieth century. Lansdale reminded them of those times when soldiers with rifles in one hand worked with the other to benefit their "little brown brothers." Even when some leaders consented to try military civic action projects, they did so "by the numbers."

A military unit might survey a hamlet and decide to build a schoolhouse for the children. The night after it was finally completed, Viet Cong agents would burn it to the ground while those who lived in the community stood idly watching, unwilling to intervene. Lansdale carefully explained, time after time, why such things happened. The unit had not gotten local people involved. The building was an alien thing amidst familiar surroundings. Viet Cong cadre exhorted the dangers of such structures in speeches to community members. "The Americans are scheming to take you over. They put up this building and want to take all the kids in there to teach them how to be obedient to foreigners. We've got to burn down this dirty foreign structure." Townsmen agreed. "Yes. They won't get my child. Burn it down. I'll help."

Lansdale patiently described a better course of action. Get people involved. Ask them what they want. Help them do it at their request. Work with them, side by side. *Never* do anything for people they were capable of doing themselves. Americans should tell villagers they will help defend the project against Viet Cong efforts to destroy it. Lansdale recalled a time when he stayed overnight in I Corps area with a Marine unit. Marines there worked on several officially designated civic action programs, one of which was a medical clinic. In their spare time, some of the young men built a merry-go-round for children in the village. Lansdale saw some of them pushing laughing boys and girls around and around. Everyone was having fun. He told the commander, "That's the best damn civic action project you have here." The commander was astonished. "That's not civic action. The troops just did that for fun on their own." Lansdale disagreed. "This *is* civic action. It has let them know you're their friend and they like you and have fun on it. Villagers won't want the enemy to come in and harm you. They'll help defend this village and your men." In an unbelieving voice, Lansdale recalled how neither military nor political leaders in Vietnam could ever "catch on to the purpose of some of these activities."[44]

Lansdale was at one with the attitude held long before by President George Washington. The month following the outbreak of the January 1968 Tet offensive, a friend sent him a copy of a letter Washington had written to Henry Lee, dated 31 October 1786. In that document, Washington wisely observed: "Know precisely what the insurgents aim at. If they have real grievances, redress them if possible; or acknowledge the justice of them and your inability to do it in the present moment. If they have not, employ the force of government against them at once . . . . Let the reins of government then be braced and held with a steady hand, and every violation of the Constitution reprehended."[45]

One value of Lansdale's open-house policy was due to the Vietnamese practice of saving face by avoiding telling someone information in a straightforward manner. Ky could know that his whisper in Lansdale's ear about an embassy official's poor handling of an issue would still be sure to reach Bunker without Ky himself having to tell him. For some weeks, President Thieu made no use of Lansdale's conduits because he believed Ky had a prior claim on them. Slowly Lansdale convinced him otherwise and he finally began to make headway with the new Thieu administration. The president occasionally dropped in to one of the hootenannies. "Attuned to every nuance of power," one writer said, "the Vietnamese continue to consult Lansdale, talk to him, trust him."[46]

On 10 June 1968, General William Childs Westmoreland turned over command of USMACV to General Creighton Abrams. A few days later General Abrams asked Lansdale to have lunch with him. During the course of the meal he asked Lansdale for any suggestions he might have. Lansdale thought for a moment and then recommended that he change the procedure used by Westmoreland for his Monday meetings with the Vietnamese Army chief of staff, General Cao Van Vien. He told Abrams how "Westy" had done it. Leaving his headquarters at 0600, Westmoreland rode with his aide and bodyguards in the midst of an armed convoy — 6 × 8 trucks carrying extra guards manning mounted machine guns, jeeps filled with heavily armed soldiers, police motorcycle outriders fore and aft, sirens blazing. The motorcade drew up at General Vien's headquarters in front of Vietnamese Army troops lined up as if on parade. Vietnamese soldiers presented arms as the convoy came to a halt and as "the pro-consul of the United States" stepped from his vehicle and marched toward Vien.

The men exchanged salutes. "How are you this morning, General Vien?" "Fine, General Westmoreland. How are things with you?" The American pro-consul proceeded to tell the Vietnamese general how well everything was with the U.S. Army. Westmoreland then asked Vien how *his* army was. Half his troops might have deserted, but Vien was not about to admit of any difficulties to this overbearing and uncultured foreigner. "Fine," snapped Vien. "Things go well with my army also." General Westmoreland took his leave in the midst of a further round of salutes in time to attend one of Lodge's country team meetings. During the session he briefed those in attendance with the news that everything was going well with the Vietnamese. General Vien had just assured him so.

Lansdale's eyes twinkled as he told the story. "Now General Abrams, do you drive? If so, take a jeep and drive over to see Vien. If you feel you need to do so, take an aide along, although it isn't really necessary. Vien and all his troops will be lined up. Ask permission to park your jeep. Be a human being. Tell him you're worried about something. Pick a topic, any topic. Confess a problem with your troops. Vien'll say, 'You haven't heard anything yet. Let me tell you about *my* problem.' You'll get down to the truth very quickly. Maybe you can help each other, buck one another up. . . . It's about time human beings began talking to one another."

Lansdale had made similar suggestions to Westmoreland, but that commander didn't want to listen. "He'd just tell me to shut up," Lansdale recalled. "I'd bring a psychological warfare idea to him on, say, troop behavior. He used to tick them off in little notes on a pad: troops misbehaving. [It was] very hard to talk to him."[47]

Lodge was gone, Westmoreland had moved on to become Army chief of staff, and most of Lansdale's team was now assigned elsewhere or was in retirement. Now it was his turn. Blocked at every turn, he decided to return home. Only a few days after Westmoreland's departure, he submitted his resignation as senior liaison officer to Ambassador Ellsworth Bunker. He began to clean up his desk and pack his belongings. The hardest task was to bid farewell to his many Vietnamese friends.

On Lansdale's next to last day in Vietnam, a group of politicians from all over the nation gathered in Saigon for a meeting near Tan Son Nhut airport. They wanted to meet Lansdale, so he invited them to his villa for lunch and arranged for neighborhood women to prepare and serve the food. As guests arrived there proved to be so many that they spilled out of the house, overflowed the grounds, and puddled in small groups along the street. Lansdale listened to them make impromptu speeches and then gave one of his own. What, he asked, did they want to do for their country? What kind of a nation did they want? He confessed his disappointment in many Vietnamese politicians. "All you want to do is be president and have everybody bowing to you and cheering as you smile and wave your hand at them. It doesn't seem to go beyond that."

Somewhat chastened, the men looked around awkwardly at one another. Then one man stood and made "a stirring speech" about his country and what he wanted for it. At his conclusion, someone else congratulated him. "I didn't know you believed that. That's what I believe and [yet] you and I have been enemies for twenty years. I've fought you the last ten years. If I had known, . . . I'd have been helping you." When Lansdale heard those words, he exultantly shouted, "Well goddamn it, you people better start working together or you're going to lose your country!" Maybe — at last — some were learning the necessary lessons for building a nation. "It was," Lansdale said, "a very moving meeting."[48]

By late afternoon his guests had departed and Lansdale returned to his office inside the villa. He continued packing for his departure the next day. The telephone rang. President Thieu's voice requested that Lansdale come to Doc Lap Palace. Lansdale found the president fuming. "The police tell me you're trying to start a revolution [by meeting] with all these politicians," he said accusingly.

"Goddammit, Thieu!" Lansdale roared, angry that the man was spoiling his festive mood. He may have been the only American who had ever shouted a curse at a Vietnamese president. "You know what I was doing?" he continued loudly. "I was doing *your* job. You should do what I was doing. I'm a foreigner and you should never let a foreigner do your job as president." Lansdale proceeded to tell Thieu everything that happened at the luncheon meeting. He urged his listener to make use of those men. Call them in. Listen to them. Allow them to sound off on their ideas. If Thieu heard any good plans, reward the one who thought of it and put the idea to work. The government would be better for it. Both men eventually calmed down and they cordially bade one another goodbye, but Lansdale was pessimistic. Would Thieu never learn the art of governing? It took seven more years to learn the answer.

The next day Lansdale boarded a plane at Tan Son Nhut airport for the last time. As the aircraft lifted into the upper atmosphere on that June day, Lansdale saw through the window his last glimpse of the Vietnamese countryside. At the embassy Ellsworth Bunker decided to leave Lansdale's position vacant. The assignment had been vague even by the loose standards of the State Department, and there was little reason to name anyone else as senior liaison officer. Many members of the American country team heaved sighs of relief that at long last Lansdale was gone. Now they could conduct their affairs without having to listen to his chiding.[49]

Lansdale's plane slipped through the upper air and he nodded in his seat, thinking of the future. He expected to return in some important post, possibly even as ambassador before many months passed. The November presidential elections were drawing closer, and he had become friends with the candidates of both parties — Vice President Hubert H. Humphrey and Richard M. Nixon. Both had come to his villa at 194 Cong Ly during visits to Vietnam. Both respected him as an American legend in Asia. Both believed the conflict in Southeast Asia must be settled quickly. Both had asked his advice. No matter which man lost, Lansdale could claim the winner as his own. It was a comforting thought as the airplane thundered eastward toward Washington and home.[50]

The mission of Edward Lansdale had been doomed from the first. His ideas may well have been the only chance America had to turn the war around and salvage something from the national efforts in Southeast Asia. He went to Vietnam, however, with too little power and place. What chance did Lansdalian notions of civic action have when the dominant U.S. military doctrine was "search and destroy"? Westmoreland was enamored of his own beliefs, and staff sycophants did little to change his mind: root the enemy from the countryside by military sweeps and thus destroy opposing forces through a war of attrition. There was no way — given his lack of standing — that Lansdale could have successfully halted or modified such myopic military visions. All levels of the U.S. government and military had accepted the concept that we could win a war of attrition by simply doing more — sending more infantry, more Marines, and more supplies, ordering more bombers to drop additional bombs on questionable targets, expending more artillery rounds in savage shellings of the countryside, defoliating more acres of forest, churning more land with rome plows in hopes of uncovering tunnel systems, rousting countless more peasants from their land and turning them into homeless refugees pouring into the cities. No one wanted to listen to a quiet-spoken old retread talking about brotherly actions. It was a time for *men* and *action,* and single-minded bureaucrats — military and civilian — won the argument. At best, they had suffered Lansdale's views with singular distaste. Now he was out of it and those who remained behind could get on with what they did best.

15

HOME AT LAST

EDWARD G. LANSDALE'S LAST TRIP HOME from Vietnam in early summer 1968 was much like that of other wartime Viet Vet returnees — a sleek, comfortable ride on a modern jetliner that carried passengers on an hours-long journey spanning thousands of miles of Pacific waters. Those quick flights wrenched passengers from a war-torn land to a nation torn by war, split into divisive factions, resentful of those who had gone to fight. No friendly smiles awaited those who deplaned in California. No thankful elders rushed to shake their hands. No beery barflies set up free drinks for veterans of that conflict. No banners, no parades, no cheering throngs. Like his fellows, Lansdale simply got to his Alexandria, Virginia, home the best way he could and disappeared into the anonymity of civilian (and retired) life, there to lick his wounds for a time.

Lansdale's Asian odyssey ended on 25 June when he arrived at Washington's National Airport and greeted Helen, who had come to meet him. For a few weeks it was good to relax once again, to eat American food. He was too thin for the clothes hanging in his closet. He drank too much and chain-smoked constantly. Physically far removed from his former work as senior liaison officer, his mind refused to relinquish its thoughts of those days, as in his imagination he fought and refought the political struggles he had waged with mindless bureaucrats in Saigon. Ill at ease and restless, he devoured news of the war, noted casualty lists, studied reports of new and "winning" tactics devised by American tacticians for battlefield implementation. He cursed their lack of imagination, their inability to recognize the new face of war, and finally decided to renew his efforts.

Lansdale considered himself neither Democrat nor Republican. He was conservative on some issues, liberal on others. He had always confounded partisans in both camps. He was first of all an American. "I believe in my country very much," he once said. "I'd do anything for it. My citizenship gives me the right to be that way and to me it's very precious."[1] Yet as he listened to the campaign rhetoric of Humphrey and Nixon he came to believe that the Republican candidate for president was more realistic and might be willing to listen to advice. A few weeks after his return from Saigon, Lansdale volunteered his services to the Nixon for President campaign.

His contact within the Nixon camp was Richard V. Allen, with whom he met on several occasions to provide him with background information on Vietnam. Lansdale also wrote to Allen regularly, supplying him with various ideas Nixon might use in the area of foreign affairs. Lansdale did not wish to burn his bridges to the Humphrey camp and so Allen assured him that "[w]e understand that contact [with you] is to remain confidential."[2] Following the November election, which Richard Nixon won, and despite Lansdale's help, the new administration made no offers to send him back to Vietnam. His dreams of returning to Asia as an ambassador seemed as ephemeral as ever. Unwilling to abandon them entirely, Lansdale continued to send unsolicited letters of advice to Nixon and his foreign policy advisers.[3]

Whenever possible, Lansdale continued to express his views on Vietnamese affairs. Sometimes he did so through the printed page. When an article by David Halberstam entitled "The Americanization of Vietnam" appeared in *Playboy* magazine, Lansdale wrote to the editorial director criticizing the "unrelieved gloom" with which the author viewed the Vietnam scene. More to the point, Lansdale wrote, Halberstam was to Vietnam "what Samson was to architecture. Tumble the whole thing down."[4] More often Lansdale expressed himself from a speaker's platform.

For several years Lansdale was much in demand as a speaker at various military educational institutions: the Air War College, the army's Command and General Staff College, the Army War College, the Air Force Academy, Fort Bragg, Eglin Air Force Base. Lansdale also spoke, along with William Westmoreland, at the Fletcher School of Law and Diplomacy at Tufts University in Massachusetts. The two men delivered papers on the strategy of the Vietnam War. "I had fun writing the first paragraph," Lansdale said, "in which I pointed out that all of the Vietnamese leaders on both sides were most familiar with a 'military textbook' called *The Three Kingdoms,* with which practically none of the Americans were familiar."[5]

When Daniel Ellsberg leaked the Pentagon Papers in 1971, Lansdale had more reason than most Americans to be surprised both by the act and by the secrets the documents contained. Ellsberg wondered what effect his deed might have on Lansdale. Years later he still felt "a very respectful and loving attitude toward Lansdale . . . . I say that of not too many people. . . . Ed had quite a fatherly relation toward me."[6] Lansdale reciprocated that affection. "I like[d] Dan personally. His heart was in the right place when he was with me and he was always trying hard, so I excused all sorts of things."[7] Despite that basic warmth, Lansdale still thought of the younger man as "the self-appointed martyr of the war dealing in stolen goods. . . . I feel strongly that he broke a trust when he purveyed the papers. They simply weren't his to play God with and neither he [n]or any of us can tell the extent of harm that might result to those who trusted us."[8] As the news of Ellsberg's act continued to make headlines, Lansdale commented that Ellsberg "loved being a martyr, I'm sure."[9]

As Ellsberg continued to be featured in newspaper, magazine, and television accounts, Lansdale's opinion hardened. To Bohannan, he remarked, "Dan seems to have fallen in love with his role of crying 'mea culpa,' although his robe of martyrdom is a bit shabby by now."[10] By 1975, just prior to the fall of Vietnam, Lansdale snorted, "Ellsberg and a host of others are lobbying on the Hill now, to cut off all aid and thus stop the war. The silly bastards no longer think straight."[11] Despite such harsh conclusions, Lansdale maintained a fond and warm-hearted concern for his former teammate. The two talked on the telephone at some length only a year or so before Lansdale's death.[12]

Lansdale remained willing to help former teammates. Rufus Phillips sought Lansdale's advice when he ran for political office: for the Fairfax County board of supervisors in 1971 and for the U.S. Congress in 1974 and the U.S. Senate in 1978. He lost the last two races, for he was never able to build a base of voters to support his views.[13] International affairs, however, were of more interest to Lansdale than election races in America. He reminisced to Peter Richards that he would like to work abroad again, even in the Philippines in some official capacity, but, as he said, "I know that I've become too big a boogeyman to too many people to be really effective any more."[14]

Lansdale also had a more personal project to occupy his time. Publishers had for years — since at least 1964 — talked with him about writing a book for them about his experiences. He invariably refused. As he wrote to Peter Richards, "I am never about to write the truth of some past events — the way they turned out made nice history for the nations involved and I'm happy to keep history in the fiction class."[15] At long last, however, he decided after his return from Saigon to write a book about his experiences in the Philippines and his first tour in Vietnam and signed a contract with the publisher Harper and Row. He began work on these memoirs in 1970 and assiduously wrote page after page as faces and events flashed across his mind. It was a more wearying process than he had imagined when he agreed to tell his story, but finally, by July 1971, he could promise a friend that the book would be printed by spring 1972. His honesty about his story was open and unabashed in private letters. "Of course I tell some white lies in it," he admitted. "Not just to protect some friends, but mainly to give Asians some sorely-needed heroes from among their own. I have a hunch it will bring some knowing chuckles from you. Yet, there's a lot of hirtherto [*sic*] untold history in it which is accurate enough to ease my conscience."[16] To his friend Bo Bohannan, Lansdale confessed, "Our friends come out smelling like roses, untainted and heroic in it and against a proper background. As you know from long ago, I decided that Asia needed its own heroes — so I've given them a whole bookful of them, with us'uns merely being companionable friends to some great guys."[17] His letters were genial cynicism at its best.

Entitled *In the Midst of Wars,* the book appeared in February 1972 and immediately attracted a number of favorable reviews. Chester L. Cooper, who had been a White House assistant on Asian affairs during the Johnson administration and who had written his own book on Vietnam, *The Lost Crusade,* described Lansdale as "an imaginative, dedicated psy-warrior" who was also "intensely loyal" to those with whom he had worked. "[H]is friends can do no wrong. A mist of nostalgic affection sheathes his heroes." The book, Cooper wrote, was thus a reflection of Lansdale's own personality; it was a "contained and modest" story by a "laconic" man that did not do justice to "exciting and colorful events." Cooper noted Lansdale's work in the Philippine elections of the early 1950s. "He should have quit while he was still ahead . . . . Poor Colonel, Poor Vietnamese, poor us. If we had known then what we know now!"[18]

Peter Arnett, an Associated Press reporter who spent eight years in Vietnam, wrote a review for the *New York Times*. He called Lansdale "an idealized cold-war warrior" with "bravery, boldness and common sense" whose "legendary exploits and style became the model for the scores of young American operatives dispatched [to Southeast Asia] by various departments and agencies." Arnett was dissatisfied by Lansdale's account for, he said, even after 386 pages, Lansdale "remains as elusive as the legends" about him. The memoirs, Arnett wrote, were "like reading a history of the American Civil War that ends with the first election of Abraham Lincoln to the Presidency."[19]

Richard Critchfield, correspondent for the *Washington Star* at the height of the Vietnam conflict, called Lansdale "a fabled figure," a "legendary Asian hand." He recalled talking with Lansdale upon his taking up the position of senior liaison officer. "What does a man do," Lansdale told him, "when he returns to a country, 10 years later, with great stress on its social and political structure, great suffering, great pain. I have no great plan. One's got to move in with tremendous gentleness; these people have been divided and hurt and a lot of clumsiness could divide and hurt them more. But there isn't much time. They need rule of law, consent of the governed . . . and a life in which kids have some hope of tomorrow." *In the Midst of Wars,* Critchfield wrote, was a "discreet account," "an invaluable historical document and an exciting adventure story, and like the author himself, rugged, humorous, compassionate, baffling, naive and a little infuriating." More important, "Lansdale was perhaps the best senior American official to serve his country in Vietnam," but there was never enough time for him to achieve his goals because he was so soon stripped of any real authority.[20]

The review in the *Christian Science Monitor* would have delighted the heart of any author. Saville Davis, a special correspondent for the newspaper, listed some of the many ways others regarded Lansdale: "a folk hero, a military miracle man and a wrecker of United States policy." He was, Davis said, "a man who carefully chooses his adversaries at home and abroad and spares them no form of verbal demolition. Meanwhile he pours affection on anyone with a sense for people." The book itself was a "thriller." "It never preaches, barring a few paragraphs at the end. It explains by narrative, by one intensely gripping episode after another. It rocks you back in your chair, takes your breath away, reports crisp dialogue that is faster and more powerful than bullets, leads you through the most personal moments of guerrilla war and agony." No one, Davis said, knew Asia like Lansdale. He had learned his own lessons in the Philippines and thus was able to determine what was wrong with the American role in Vietnam long before the United States became militarily involved there. "He told us and told us and told us and only a few would understand." Since no one listened, "[w]e brought not liberty . . . but new-old forms of political repression, terror and tyranny. This was a people's war and we ourselves destroyed the only relationship — to the people — that could have enabled us to win. An artificial big-army war obsessed us and riveted our attention . . . and the real war went unnoticed."[21]

Without knowing of Lansdale's comments to friends about the self-censorship he imposed while writing *In the Midst of Wars,* Sherwood Dickerman, who had five years' experience as a foreign correspondent in Southeast Asia, believed Lansdale did not tell all he knew; "there are grounds for suspecting that he may have omitted more than he put in." Dickerman called Lansdale "a warmly sentimental man toward Asian friends, and a quick-study improviser and promoter." The book itself was "a period piece of the cold war, a nostalgic memoir" that sometimes read "like an adventure of Frank Merriwell in Asia, a daring lark for a good cause with no regard for consequences." Dickerman described the ugly and quiet American as both "ingenious and ruthless" and "idealistic and courageous." He was "the most influential single American in Southeast Asia and certainly the most controversial."[22]

Jonathan Mirsky came forth with a review quite at odds with those written by Arnett, Davis, Dickerman, Critchfield, and Cooper. The director of the East Asia Center at Dartmouth College, Mirsky found only one difficulty with Lansdale's book: "from the cover to the final pages it is permeated with lies." Wherever one turned in the book, "the accounts are likely to be lies." It was, he said, contemptible for Harper and Row to "foist such a package of untruths on the public." No good thing was to be found in this publication and Mirsky warned the book-buying public to be wary and spend their money on another title.[23] Two weeks to the day after Mirsky's review was printed, Lansdale wrote to Peter Richards in an effort to downplay its effect. Obviously incensed by the attack, he told Richards that that very morning he received a telephone call from the head of the Philippine-American Women's Association in Washington who asked him to come to the embassy for an autograph session. She explained, "We all read that wonderful review of your book in the Saturday Review and rushed out and bought copies." He pondered whether he ought to send Mirsky a thank-you note.[24]

Yet twelve years later, Mirsky's words still stung. Lansdale referred to that review as the most savage of the critiques of his book, inspired because "I didn't admit that I was a chief CIA agent out in the Far East. . . . I was writing the history I saw and the hell with what I really was. It didn't matter too much about my position, in a way."[25]

In October 1972, Lansdale received a whimsical letter from an old, old friend, O. J. "Mac" Magee, one of his companions from OSS days during World War II. Magee had just finished reading *In the Midst of Wars*. Writing the book, he claimed, had been a mistake. Transportation Corps was going to ask if Lansdale was "the same jolly major who worked for us?" "[I]f he served with us through WWII," OSS would grumble, "he was AWOL most of the time." The Infantry School and the Artillery School would check their records and find no Lansdale ever attended their courses and wonder "how in blazes he got away with advising armed units and foreign heads of state in the technical aspects of warfare." Westmoreland, Lodge, Bunker, the widows of John Foster Dulles and Adlai Stevenson would put two and two together and come up with the common opinion that "old Ed had at one time or another made damned fools of them all."

Magee mischievously continued. "They will probably keep their mouths shut, but in the darkness of the night each is bound to wake up" in the cheerless hours of dark. Lying sleepless, they would contemplate Lansdale. "Ah yes, I was one of the Washington policy-makers Ed used to call on occasionally. I see now that when he got an idea rejected overseas, he simply took off for Washington, let people know whom he saw (but not what was actually said at those conferences), returned to his overseas station and announced to a shaken US official that his original idea had been approved." Magee concluded with the thought, "Old Ed proved that in the Executive Branch of our Government it's not who you know that counts. It's who people think you know. And how well."[26]

The reviews, the acclaim, the criticism all came at a time when Lansdale had little energy left to appreciate or notice what others were saying about his memoirs. He was caught up in the midst of a personal and family disaster. In February 1972, just as *In the Midst of Wars* was about to be released, a mysterious fire broke out in the library area of the Lansdale home on MacArthur Boulevard. Helen discovered the flames before they got completely out of control and was able to call the fire department. The fire department's prompt reaction saved the home from destruction, but the library was severely damaged and hundreds of Ed's books and many of his papers were lost. Bad as that was, the loss of his library was dwarfed by injuries suffered by Helen. In former years she had been a heavy smoker but had quit a little earlier. Now, following the fire and her efforts to save the house, Helen's health rapidly deteriorated. Her lungs, harmed by years of smoking, had been grievously injured by the billowing clouds of smoke in the library as she fought the flames. During March and April, Helen experienced increasing difficulties in breathing, yet her devotion to her Christian Science faith kept her from seeking medical help. Encouraged by Ed's longtime team member Sam Karrick, a Christian Science practitioner (the sect's term for a minister), Helen refused Ed's entreaties to enter one of the nearby military hospitals for a health check. When he was unable to convince her, he then urged her to enter a nursing home where she might get proper health care. Again she refused.

Ed became nearly frantic. He had been separated from his wife because of the demands of his career for so many years. His earlier romantic feelings for his Filipina friend Pat Kelly had been carefully stored away. In the years since his return to America in 1968, Ed and Helen had reached out to one another, had rediscovered mutual interests and the joy of quiet love. Now Helen seemed to be slipping away from him and Ed could hardly bear the thought of being alone.

About the first of May 1972, Helen went into a rather unexpected decline. Ed hired Christian Science nurses who came in to care for her during the days and to do necessary housework while he watched over her at nights. Both of their sons, Ted and Pete, learned from Ed that their mother was gravely ill and came home to be with her. Twelve years later, Lansdale had not forgotten the emotions that then were so strong. In recalling those days, it was hard for him to get the words out. "She told me when she was going to die," he said and tears welled into his eyes. "We were very close. She said goodbye." His voice faded and broke, and for a moment he was unable to continue. "It was rough then," he continued and his voice strengthened a little. "She was a good wife to put up with me."[27]

All three of Helen's men — her husband, Ted, and Pete — were with her when she died on 14 May 1972. Ed told a friend that "Helen liked the idea of having all her menfolk present — and fell into a natural and peaceful sleep the last night, simply not awaking. It hit me pretty hard and I'm taking my time about getting myself oriented again." He continued to live in the house, accompanied by a large French poodle named Can Bo that he had brought back with him from Saigon, "even though [the house is] too big for one guy and his dog to rattle around in by themselves."[28] Friends and neighbors invited him to their homes and took him out to restaurants in an effort to alleviate his sorrow and to keep him from spending too much time alone. For long months he lost much of the verve that had for so long enlivened him. He conceded to friends that Helen's death had left him lonely and terribly dispirited. Despite efforts of well-wishing friends and acquaintances, he led a rather secluded existence, turning inward and remembering lost years.

Lansdale no longer found much zest in life. He was sixty-four years old, a recent widower, and was forced to face the fact that he might well spend all the rest of his years alone. For this ebullient man who loved people it was an unlikely prospect. Then suddenly Pat Kelly reentered his life.

The two had maintained a desultory correspondence. Pat occasionally included a note to Ed in letters her boss at the embassy, Hank Miller, wrote to him. She managed to let Ed know she had read his book and liked it. Lansdale was lonely and bereft and needed someone to share his time. Sometime before September 1972, he wrote Pat asking if she would like to go "culture hunting" through America in a white Mercedes, perhaps lazily floating in a boat in Florida's Everglades. By that time she had already applied for a special U.S. immigrant visa. Ready to retire from her job at the American embassy in Manila where she worked for USIS, Pat wanted to make a trip to the United States. "I thought I had better go see this America I had worked for," she recalled.[29]

By October, Ed had written two more letters to Pat and in reply she

filled him in on Ferdinand Marcos' recent declaration of martial law.
She made lists of clothing to bring to America if she was granted her
visa. "One minute I am all ready to pack up and go and the next I feel
I am crazy to leave Tarlac and the easy way of life in the province.
. . . Tell me more about the streets paved with gold."[30]

Pat dreamed of "an easy, lazy trip to nowhere" across America and
reminisced about their times together. "I can never look at a setting
sun beyond the mountains or the sea, without thinking of you and those
beach trips." She dared him "to buy me a couple of good bras . . .
white and 34-B. If you are going to dress me up, you might start from
the basic. Am I starting to frighten you?" She shared with him a rumor
circulating across Manila that he had come back for a visit, "so why
doesn't my darn phone ring?" Pat told Ed of a plan she was working
out with Ann Miller, wife of her former boss. "The scheme, if they
really get the much hated assignment in Washington, is for them to get
a house, invite me to stay with them (I simply can't stay with you, no
matter how much I would like to) and find work for me with another
Federal Agency or work with Hank in his new job."[31]

In an early November letter, Pat was incredulous. Lansdale had sent
her a check for a substantial sum to help her with expenses for her visit
to America. In her response, she addressed him as "Banker Ed" but
said she would hold it and might even send it back, "of course minus
my Christmas present." She was certain she had saved enough of her
own money for plane fare to Washington. "I am itching to . . . visit
with you . . . in some beach place with coconuts and sun all around."
A few days later she wrote, "I am envious of your trips and wish I
were there to tag along . . . but I can wait." Such a visit to America
would open a new world "for this *provinciana* from Tarlac." Pat playfully
chided Ed that she was still waiting for a "CARE package you mentioned."
Would there be a bra in it? "I remember Hong Kong . . . where you
knew that an underwear specialty shop was in that crowded arcade across
from the President Hotel."[32]

Three days later Pat wrote again, continuing her former theme "on
the subject of bra buying," interrupted by the arrival of the mail, which
contained another of Ed's letters. She had asked for a 34-B bra; if Ed
bought her a 43-D as he threatened, "then I will surely show up with a
43-D bust. I will be so top heavy, I will need lead shoes to anchor me
to the upright position." She laughed at the difficulties of writing. "This
thinking in Pompanga, talking in Tagalog and writing in English get
me all mixed up." In early December Pat announced her plans to arrive
in America about 26 January of the new year. Ed's CARE package
arrived and was opened "amidst cries of pleasures." "I can't realize

what a good bra can mean to a girl who has been using second rate copies." "Hey," she exclaimed, "with all these travel lectures you are doing, any chance of your getting invited to attend some seminar at Hawaii or California during the time I expect to pass that way? Won't it be just too wonderful if you can meet me part of the way?"[33]

A few days later Pat wrote of a dream about Ed "so real its aura is still with me, hours after I have awaken[ed]." She had finally cashed his check. Plans had not worked out. Her trip would be postponed until sometime in 1973. By February, Pat once again had an itinerary firmed up. And then finally, she started out. On 19 February 1973 at 2:45, she left Manila on Pan American flight 842 and reached Honolulu the same day at eight o'clock in the morning. Monday through Friday she spent with friends in Hawaii and then once again boarded flight 842 at 9:42 A.M., 23 February, arriving in San Francisco at 4:35 P.M.[34] After visiting friends there, Pat flew to Washington and stayed with her former boss and his wife, Hank and Ann Miller, who were longtime friends of Lansdale. Her plans to tour the country had to be laid aside. She got no further than the nation's capital city. "I was looking for work in advertising or public information. Then I saw Ed."

Lansdale was happy to see Pat. They spent time together at the Miller home and he escorted her to various tourist attractions in the Washington area. He made up his mind quickly. "Do you want to work or do you want to get married?" Pat thought rapidly. "Why should I work when I can marry him?" It was a convincing argument. They were married 4 July 1973 in Alexandria at the Good Shepherd Catholic Church. The Millers gave the bride away.[35] Lansdale cared deeply for his second wife, long thinking of her as the "eternal feminine Pat."[36]

They combined their honeymoon with a speaking trip. Ed had lecture dates in Alabama and Florida, and in sunny Florida they had a reunion with Ed's son Ted and his wife, Carolyn. On the trip south, the newlyweds rode the autotrain, accompanied by Ed's seventy-five-pound French poodle, Can Bo. When the dog tried to crawl into their roomette bed the first night, "I kicked him out. Who in hell does he think married the gal?" he wrote to a friend.[37]

The marriage infused Ed with new enthusiasm. "We are a couple of very happy people . . . busily enjoying each day," he claimed. Pat was surprised by Ed's willingness to do most of the cooking and didn't complain when he turned housekeeping and laundry chores over to her, although for a time she wondered how they could run their home "without a bunch of servants and helpers" as was usually the case in Filipino homes. Pat regularly surprised Ed on shopping expeditions by pointing to fresh cherries or peaches and unexpectedly asking, "What's that?"

To familiarize her with her new country, Ed packed lunch baskets and took her on picnics to area orchards where she could pick baskets full of fruit from the trees. Both reveled in such outings.[38]

Lansdale loved to drive cross-country and so at every opportunity he loaded Pat and Can Bo into the car and they set off. In 1974, at Pat's entreaty, they planned a trip back to the Philippines during the early fall. They began with a drive from Virginia to California and then flew to Manila for a brief vacation. It was to be Ed's last trip to the land where the myths about him had begun so many years earlier. Upon their return to America, they stopped during their trip home at Stateline on the shores of Lake Tahoe with its ultra-blue lake waters, its pine forests and mountains, to enjoy the scenery and to allow Pat to try her hand at gambling, a game she continued in Reno and Elko. The Wasatch Mountains east of Salt Lake City in Utah seemed to Ed as though "we were driving through miles of heaped up Persian rugs." They stopped to visit Ed's son Ted in Iowa and then continued through southern Indiana and West Virginia glorying in the colorful fall foliage.[39]

During the winter of 1974–75, Pat and Ed drove to Fort Leavenworth in Kansas "to give her a taste of snow and freezing weather while I lectured . . . about revolution."[40] Later that year, during the second week of June, the couple visited Ames, Iowa, to see Ed's son Ted, who was packing for an unaccompanied tour in Korea. His other son, Peter, and his family also arrived in Ames. "It will be the first time that the kids in both families will see each other — and this grandfather can't resist the impulse to see all the grandchildren together."[41] During the fall, Ed was alone once again for some months while Pat went back to the Philippines for a visit with her daughter, Patricia, and other family members there.[42]

In 1976, they drove to Media, Pennsylvania, for a family reunion at the farm home of Ed's brother Dave. While there they made a canoe trip down the Brandywine and through its mild rapids.[43] Later that year Ed and Pat drove to Canada to "goof off" on a trip that took them to Niagara Falls and down the St. Lawrence to Quebec. They returned through the Adirondack and Pocono mountains.[44] In July 1978 they drove to a family reunion in San Francisco and then to Oregon. Later that year they made a two-week trip to Colorado Springs, where Ed spoke at the Air Force Academy at a seminar on military aviation. "I wound up jumping the Air Force for not insisting upon better strategy by the U.S. in Korea and Vietnam and urged the historians present to take a hard look at what the Air Force did or didn't do . . . . My eye finally was attracted to someone glaring at me from the front row . . . . It was Curt LeMay. He probably thought I was talking about him. I guess maybe I was.'' They made a leisurely return trip by way of Taos, Santa Fe, Oklahoma City, on into Tennessee and the Smokies, and finally back home.[45] In the summer of 1981, Pat and Ed drove from Virginia to Colorado Springs where he spoke again at the Air Force Academy.[46]

Such trips then came to an end. Lansdale noted in 1982, "The lectures seem to have dried up."[47] Without invitations, the main reason for those long drives disappeared and the couple became more homebound. His last major trip came during the winter of 1982–83 when he and Pat took a trip west at her insistence to look at retirement home locations. Unused to cold weather, she pined for a more balmy climate, so they visited San Antonio, Texas, and various sites in southern California and then flew west to Honolulu. They returned home to freezing cold and snow.[48]

During 1975 three events occupied most of Ed's time. The first was the happiest. On 1 July, he and Pat moved from the old house on MacArthur Boulevard in Alexandria to a new home on Lorraine Avenue in McLean, Virginia. Situated on a quiet street on a secluded slope with wooded hills rising behind it, the house was a real improvement over the former home, although Ed wondered what snowy winter storms might do to drivers trying to guide their cars up the hilly street.[49]

The second event was the collapse and takeover of the Saigon government by North Vietnam. In the weeks prior to that fatal moment, Lansdale tried to reawaken the interest of the American government in the imminent fate of its erstwhile ally. "Vietnam," wrote Lansdale, "as far as seen in Washington, is kaput. . . . We've been in demonstrations in front of the White House, have buttonholed Congressmen, I've been on TV and radio, even had a piece in the New York Times. . . . I'm very doubtful that U.S. officials are going to get many of our Vietnamese friends out of the box they're in. . . . Hard to keep from throwing up at this spectacle."[50]

As a way to save those valiant souls in Vietnam who had struggled for so many years to build a government in the South, Lansdale conceived the idea of an evacuation zone around Saigon. American troops would be inserted there to stand guard while all those who wished to leave Vietnam could do so. He wrote to Bohannan, "The President bought my idea . . . but Congress is fighting against it." In the end, that idea also came to naught.[51]

As refugees from Vietnam arrived in the United States, Lansdale did what he could to help them settle into their new life in exile. One old friend, Bui Anh Tuan, wrote him from Camp Chaffee, Arkansas, that both his wife and son were anxious "to see the face of this legendary Colonel Landslide."[52] Lansdale confided to Bohannan that many of their friends who had escaped were still in relocation camps. Unfortunately, he noted that the entire refugee effort was thoroughly tied up in red tape and bureaucratic proceedings. "By group effort, we did get [folk singer] Pham Duy out of camp in Florida." He had recently been asked to host a meeting at his home where newly arrived refugees could organize some self-help programs. "The mob scene is to take place here on June 7."[53] By November, Lansdale was becoming discouraged. "Most — altogether too many — of the refugees are content to stay with their sponsors," he wrote Bohannan, "moan about having been taken away from home by the Americans, and are figuring out how to get food stamps and go on relief." Discouraged or not, Lansdale spent the Christmas of 1975 playing Santa Claus to refugee families in need, offering them provisions of holiday food, fruit cakes and candies.[54]

While working to help Vietnamese refugees, Lansdale was haunted by his former labors on behalf of John Kennedy. He complained in early June that a government leak had revealed his 1962 contingency plans to eliminate Fidel Castro. The leak was "aided and abetted by McNamara . . . disowning me," he told Peter Richards. "McNamara . . . told the press that I wasn't working for him back in 1962, but for a 'higher authority.' It was stupid . . . as I told him on the 'phone. I gather he was running scared of something."[55] The story about Lansdale made the front pages of local newspapers and was mentioned on TV network news programs. They featured his "admission when pressed that I might well have been planning such a thing against Fidel at a time when he was inviting the Soviets to place missiles in his country to kill off a few million Americans."[56]

In the U.S. Senate, the Select Committee to Study Governmental Operations with Respect to Intelligence Activities began looking into alleged American assassination plots against leaders of foreign countries. Headed by Senator Frank Church, a Democrat from Idaho, the group soon came to be known simply as the Church Committee. Church indicated that he might want to have Lansdale testify. Lansdale wrote to Bo Bohannan, "Guess I'll now have a part-time career when . . . the Church Committee gets after me."[57] Bo sympathized with his plight. "Would rather like to be called myself," he told Lansdale, "even though it would certainly mean some time in jail for contempt — I would consider it time well spent."[58]

When the Senate committee finally ordered Lansdale to appear during the second week of July, Lansdale wrote to Bohannan that its staff had checked out his opinion of some of their earlier witnesses. One man about whom they asked was Fletcher Prouty, "who was my earlier Dan Ellsberg on my Pentagon staff — I sure pick 'em, huh?" Lansdale told the committee staffers that "Prouty was a good . . . USAF transport pilot but with a whacky imagination; he has claimed that I invented the Huk rebellion, hiring actors to pose as guerrillas just to get RM [Magsaysay] elected."[59]

His appearance before the Church Committee, Lansdale exclaimed, "is what every red-blooded American boy should dream of doing some day. It has all the charm and fun of going to a dentist to have root canals plucked out." One major difference from the "fun and gaiety" of a visit to the dentist was that "I could talk back." He noted that "I had two long days of it — the first with staff and the committee's legal counsels and the second with the committee itself — with questions being shot at me by the majority and minority counsels as well as by 13 senators." It was, Lansdale claimed, "a couple of summer days wasted." He had real difficulty, he said, trying to remember "details of what happened 13 years ago" and was incensed when "they tried to badger and intimidate me about minutiae . . . getting sarcastic when I couldn't remember who said what at a meeting," but he was pleased that he was "apparently about the only witness who didn't bring an attorney with him."[60]

"I must admit," Lansdale confessed, that "I did a little lecturing in return, although I barely kept my temper in at some of the nastier questions, especially those from [Howard] Baker and [Lowell] Schweiker. . . . Seen up close, they're a pair of heels." Lansdale had only a little better impression of Senator Frank Church. "I got a shock when I was talking to him up close. His eyes turned me against him; they are those of an unctuous parson who goes around sniffing little girls' bicycle seats. Gives me shivers to think he might run for President. But, he was quite decent in dealing with me." As he looked around the committee room, Lansdale felt that the "most statesmenlike" members were Barry Goldwater of Arizona, Walter Mondale of Minnesota, young Gary Hart of Colorado, and Philip Hart of Michigan. For a long while Lansdale thought Philip Hart was asleep during the hearing and was surprised when he made a most adroit and balanced summing up of the facts presented at the end.[61]

Lansdale remained troubled as he completed his testimony. "Lord knows what McNamara, Bundy, Rusk, and others have said after my day at bat. Or Fletch Prouty, who made the news by telling about CIA spies in the White House. (The guy has a bad case of paranoia). A lot of people, including Penthouse magazine, want me to tell all on their pages. Which I'm not about to do."[62]

Those Senate hearings continued to haunt Lansdale for the rest of the year. He became particularly angry in November when the committee sent him a copy of the final report. One of the senators had inserted a footnote — "a weirdo comment" by Tom Parrott, who was secretary of the Special Group, Augmented for Kennedy in 1962 and who "apparently wanted to blacken my name as his defense of Kennedy — but in a crazy way." Parrott told the zany "elimination by illumination" story about Lansdale's psywar efforts while serving as executive officer for the SGA in its planning to unseat Castro. Lansdale was not amused and wrote forthwith to Senator Church and assured him that the story was absolutely untrue. He had never conceived of or proposed such a plan. "I can only guess you included this bit of fluff to give some comic relief to your report. It certainly didn't contribute any feeling of integrity to it."[63]

Lansdale wondered for a time whether he should do more to correct the record. In a reaction touched with paranoia, he decided to leave the story untouched. Then, he said, Cuban gunmen would think he was only a nut and stop trying "to blow up this nice new home of ours." Upon further reflection he admitted he was not too unhappy the news was finally out that he once tried to engineer a revolution in Cuba. It might, he hoped, give someone else the idea of trying it. "Americans sure as hell don't know how to encourage or support a revolution in a police state," he lamented. "[T]hey can just do their work in friendly places."[64]

For a time in 1976 and 1977, Lansdale and his friends talked about a new book. Ed learned that Joseph Burkholder Smith had written an exposé entitled *Portrait of a Cold Warrior* about his days as a CIA agent. Bohannan was incensed about such flagrant disregard for Agency rules of secrecy and said to Lansdale, "May Joseph Smith boil in oil. Incidentally is it a true name?"[65] Lansdale dismissed the publication as just "[a]nother silly book from a very silly ex-CIA-type. Now I await the confessions of the personnel chief at the Agency on why he hired such stupid jerks."[66] He also described it as "full of gossip about our friends." The author, Lansdale said, offered a "lightweight account of a lightweight's deeds in Singapore, Djakarta, Manila, and Mexico — but his funding of elections in Manila will make you cringe. . . . Incidentally, Bo, he tells of George Aurell getting miffed at one of my operational messages passing under his nose disguised as a housekeeping message about air conditioners. Yours? One of my few good laughs when reading the book."[67]

In the years of his retirement, Lansdale was frequently haunted by the feeling that while he yet had much to offer in service to his country, no one in any of the administrations called him back to active duty. In 1977 he decided to test the waters, to learn if he could stir up any interest in his once again serving in an overseas assignment. Lansdale felt his juices rise as the ambassadorship to the Philippines came open. Perhaps part of his interest was due to Pat's periodically urging him to move back to the Philippines so she could be closer to her family.[68] After a great deal of thought, he wrote to Averell Harriman, a longtime friend, "Although I've just turned 69, I'm in good health and spirits — and would welcome a chance to serve our country among the Filipino people, for whom I have a deep affection." So it was that some of his friends had urged him "to submit my name for consideration at the White House to be named as our Ambassador to the Philippines." If such an appointment should prove to be impossible, he would be willing to serve in some lesser capacity so long as doing so helped "strengthen our ties with the Philippines." He suggested the possibility of acting as an "ambassadorial assistant (such as I did last time in Vietnam) or as a Presidential Commission member" or even as "a special envoy" of some kind.[69]

He had, Lansdale believed, many qualifications. "I have known Ferdinand Marcos . . . for more than 30 years now." Additionally, "my wife is a Filipina, and I count among my close friends numerous Filipinos. . . . My previous experience in the Philippines has given me close personal relationships with some of the officials who are now potent." Lansdale recalled "the times when we candidly and thoroughly discussed problems regarding affairs in Asia [and so] I now come to you to seek your trusted advice and counsel." Lansdale then put the question to Harriman. "Do you think there is merit in my coming out of retirement . . . . Or would you think it will only be fighting the windmill?"[70] To Lansdale's dismay, no support for such an appointment materialized, and sadly he let the matter drop.

As the years passed, Lansdale's empathy with Vietnamese refugees and his sorrow over the fate of their country continued unabated. He was pleased, therefore, when he learned in late 1978 that Boston public television station WGBH planned a long special dealing with the Vietnam War, eventually to be shown on the Public Broadcasting System. He talked with the producer and urged him not to create a stereotype; many of the emotional traumas of the late 1960s and early 1970s desperately needed a healing touch and here was an opportunity to reach out, he argued. Lansdale was one of many scheduled to be interviewed on camera for the program. He was dissatisfied with the results of a long day's interview, just as he was when he later saw a copy of Stanley Karnow's book, *Vietnam: A History*, written as a text to accompany the television series. The book, Lansdale observed, was "an outline history of the communist disinformation campaign they ran throughout the Vietnam war out of Hanoi. All of it is . . . derogatory to the US and the Saigon government. I have a gut feeling he listens too hard to arguments from the other side; is too kindly disposed to arguments they put forth."[71]

After the camera crew packed its cases and departed, Lansdale was certain his answers had not fit in with the director's outlook. He was constantly on guard, thinking about how his answers would sound in the finished film with the camera pulling in for a head shot and then cutting to troops "beating up kids and old ladies, kids screaming, napalm." He tried to put all his answers in ways that would belie and counteract such pictures. That wasn't, he later admitted, what the camera crew was interested in.[72] When he later saw the film series, he described it as a "poisonous distortion of the truth" for not showing how hard many Vietnamese had worked to build a government in the South, how little authority the Republic of Vietnam had to begin with, and how far it developed despite constant opposition from the early days by its Viet Cong enemies.[73]

The hours of tension during the interview upset Lansdale. By afternoon he was feeling sick to his stomach. Then he developed a severe headache and suddenly became violently nauseous. He barely made it to a bathroom before he began vomiting. Worried by these symptoms, he drove to the Andrews Air Force Base hospital and asked for a physical. "The docs . . . said I was fit as a fiddle," he reported to Bohannan.[74] More likely it was a definite warning, a portent of things to come.

Although he took life easier for a few weeks, it was not in Lansdale's nature to relax and so he agreed when Pentagon officials asked him to participate on a review board evaluating the first volume of an official history of Vietnam written by Ronald Spector. Lansdale's critique of the manuscript helped send it back to the author for more work. "His animosity towards Diem, Hanging Sam and Operation Brotherhood irked me," Lansdale told Bohannan.[75]

The 1980 national political contest between Walter Mondale and Ronald Reagan failed to generate any enthusiasm in Lansdale. "Our leaders all seem to be made out of cardboard," he complained, "and watching all the candidates on TV, they seem to be made out of just different colors of cardboard."[76]

Lansdale still responded enthusiastically when called on by the Pentagon. In February 1981, he was asked to comment on the American posture toward the Central American nation of El Salvador and he was supplied with necessary study material. His conclusions were sharp and critical. He set forth a series of questions. Did the present Salvadoran government have a plan to stabilize social conditions? If so, was it a practical one? Was it true that Salvadoran army units took arbitrary actions on their own authority? Was it true that troops were misbehaving toward their own people? Was the Salvadoran military even capable of creating a motivated, disciplined force? Was there anyone who had the respect of most of the officer corps and troops? If so, how did that person feel toward a democratic form of government? Did he have any close American friends whose advice he would accept?[77] The tone of his paper was not optimistic.

All too often during the years between 1942 and 1968, the demands of Lansdale's career caused him to neglect his own elemental health needs. For decades he drank too much and chain-smoked during all his waking hours. Food was often an afterthought, picked up and eaten on the run with little thought given to proper nourishment. Getting a good night's rest was regularly impossible as he held meetings, talked with visitors, and worked on reports, memoranda, and letters until the early hours of the morning. Stress and tension were constant companions for decades. All this finally caught up with him.

During the summer of 1981, he suffered a small stroke while sitting at his desk paying bills. He noticed as he signed his name that it looked unlike his normal signature. He could not force his hand to move properly. When he told his son what had happened, Peter insisted that he go to the hospital at Andrews AFB for another check. Physicians ran a series of tests and told Ed that his heart was not behaving properly; they could hear a murmur. They put him on medication and told him to return for another EKG in six months. After a few days of bed rest and tests, the physicians said that he was well enough to leave. "I then shocked them by driving us out to Colorado, where I had a number of lectures at the Air Force Academy. . . . A loafing drive across country and back; good medicine for me."[78] Once again his body had warned him.

The next time came swiftly. As he prepared to go outside the house, he suddenly blacked out and collapsed on the floor, saved from injury by falling against an overstuffed chair. The experience frightened Lansdale sufficiently to once again seek medical advice. "I don't like this," he told the doctors. "What's wrong?" After another period of observation at the hospital at Andrews AFB the physicians informed him that the blood was flowing irregularly through his heart, caused perhaps by a faulty valve. There was little they could do about it and after a week he was released from the hospital.

Only a few days later, on 25 August 1982, at about eleven o'clock in the evening, he collapsed again, this time in a hallway of his home. He hit the floor with sufficient force to bruise his cheek badly. "It's an awful feeling," Lansdale noted, "to be going someplace and then find yourself on the floor." He made up his mind. To Pat, Ed said, "I'll go back to the hospital in the morning and get those docs to take another look." He was almost too late.[79]

The following morning, between five and six A.M., 26 August 1982, he rose from bed to go to the bathroom. As he stood up he blacked out and fell unconscious onto the floor, one hand spastically gripping the bed covers and tearing them off a sleeping Pat. His head hit a dresser and bedside table as he collapsed, breaking a rib and his nose and blackening one eye. Pat came instantly wide awake and peered at him over the side of the bed. Lansdale had fallen in such a way that most of his body now lay under the bed. Pat tried to lift the bed so he could crawl out from under it but was not strong enough to do so. She then frantically dialed the number of the emergency unit located at the McLean fire department, and an ambulance shortly screamed its way down Lorraine Avenue to the Lansdale home.

The emergency team lifted the bed off Lansdale and began checking his vital signs. "We're taking you to the hospital," one of the men told Ed. "I'm an outpatient at the Air Force hospital," he replied. "No," the medic responded. "It's going to be the nearest one — Fairfax County Hospital." They wheeled Ed to the ambulance, opened its doors, and slid his stretcher into the back. Pat climbed in with her husband. On the way to the hospital one of the medics confided to Pat that Ed was very seriously ill and it might be too late to save him. "I didn't feel that way," Ed later commented, "except I got nauseated on the way and started vomiting."

Arriving at the Fairfax emergency room, Ed was sufficiently aware to notice that a heart specialist team was waiting to attend to him. It included four very pretty nurses. "I'd never gone through anything like that before. Then suddenly, watch out, I had to heave. That was too much." Lansdale passed out. The attending physician, a heart specialist, had his family waiting in the car in the hospital parking lot. They had been about to start a vacation trip to the beach when he had been summoned to the emergency room.

"Apparently anybody who was standing around all took turns hitting me in the chest to keep my heart going." Ed remembered one of the pretty nurses. She was kneeling on the examining table, her legs straddling him, pushing on his chest. "I remember . . . she had such a determined look on her. Her lips were all screwed up." Lansdale smiled at her. "You don't know how you look when you get that real determined look on your lips," he croaked. Her response was a quick one. "The only other man who has seen it is my husband." Lansdale slid back into unconsciousness wondering what the times were like when her husband saw that concentrated look. Seconds or moments later, Ed opened his eyes again. The pretty nurse was still pushing away at his chest. "Jeez," he muttered, "I usually have more fun at a time like this," and then he was gone again.

After administering a local anesthetic, the physician emplaced a temporary pacemaker in Ed's groin. After he finished his task, the physician continued to monitor Lansdale's vital signs. He looked at Ed, who was again awake. "Your pulse is very slow," he told his patient. Ed thought for a moment and replied, "Don't worry if it's a little slow. It has been [that way] all my life. My normal pulse is 59–60. I'm quite used to that." The physician shook his head. "It's a little slower than 60. It's only 19!"

Afraid they were losing their patient, the heart team applied electric shock paddles to Ed's heart to prod it into a more normal rhythm. A little later they inserted another pacemaker in his shoulder, set to force his heart to beat ninety times a minute. Lansdale later described the situation. "A great scene on TV doctor shows, but lousy in real practice."

In the lounge area, Pat and Ed's two sons, Ted and Pete, waited anxiously for word of Lansdale's condition. Remembering she had been told that her husband might die, Pat prayed fervently. "I'll go to church regularly if you let him live," she promised. A few years later, Ed said, "That's why she goes to church all the time now, being a very good girl. She made a pact." Overhearing his comment, Pat smiled sweetly. "I've got my hold on him. Now when I get mad at him I warn him that I may not go to church anymore." "That'll teach me," Ed laughed.

The team had done its work well. Ed responded and soon his body began healing. "I looked like I had been in a barroom brawl. Broken nose, two black eyes, three broken ribs, a black and blue chest from all the hammering. I was a sight. I hadn't looked like that since a drunken brawl years ago when a gang in Los Angeles tried to beat me up."[80] Lansdale noticed differences in his body caused by the heart attack. His pulse didn't feel as strong, and he got tired more often. For the first time in his life he found it necessary to take daily naps.[81]

During his recuperation he learned that his longtime friend, William E. Colby, had recently published an entry in the Rand McNally *Almanac of Adventure* — a list of the ten greatest spies of the modern world. Lansdale ranked number ten among that select group. Colby sent a copy to Ed "With all best wishes to you and thanks for your magnificent service." In the brief article, Colby included Edward Lansdale because of his "political imagination and warm empathy with Southeast Asian leaders and peoples [which] helped democratic alternatives to emerge between corrupt colonialists and ruthless terrorists."[82] It was a gratifying moment.

More fragile now, and at seventy-four years beginning to look his age, Lansdale finally had to learn to live at a more sedate and relaxed pace. His trips became fewer and briefer, and hosting large groups of friends for a party or evening of relaxation became rarer, although he still tried to get together for periodic reunions with his brothers. Naps claimed his afternoons and when he rose in the mornings the sun rode higher in the sky. One part of his routine remained unchanged. Each morning he unfailingly raised the American flag on the tall pole in his front yard and every evening he lowered the colors and folded them protectively, laying them on a table beside his front door ready for the next day's ceremony.

Occasionally the military still called on General Lansdale for advice. In May 1983 he wrote out a position paper on Central America at the behest of Pentagon officials,[83] and in May 1984 he was part of a two-day discussion group that gathered at the Pentagon to study policy options on Nicaragua and El Salvador. Discussion focused on the question of what should be done about the Sandinista government in Nicaragua and leftist rebels in El Salvador. Lansdale spoke out against current practice, condemning it for relying on sending heavy weapons to El Salvador. "Much of the equipment was for a big war and would be counterproductive . . . . We recommended more use of their infantry; they could recruit, equip, train, and field about twelve battalions by money saved from big stuff they didn't need. We talked to the ambassador, to the CINCSOUTH, and to other military." Lansdale was pleased when one of his peers spoke up during the meeting, exclaiming, "Bombers are no damned good in a guerrilla war. It is insane to use them." Lansdale reached over and shook his hand. "I don't know," he later reflected, "Whether we impressed anybody. I suspect we didn't. They probably dismissed us as has-beens."[84] Lansdale proposed using a broad campaign of psychological operations in Central America. "I don't think the Army knows how to fight anymore. I've got a sneaking awful feeling that they've lost touch with reality. . . . I don't know why people don't remember these things."[85]

That same year of 1984, during the campaign electioneering in the Philippines between Ferdinand Marcos and Corazon Aquino, Lansdale was surprised to get a telephone call from the State Department. The speaker wanted to know whether Lansdale had secretly gone to the Philippines. "It seems," he said, "that rumors are getting active that you are out there and the U.S. embassy in Manila is getting so many inquiries about your local address there that they asked us to check and make sure where you are." Friends in the Philippines also wrote to complain that he hadn't even bothered to stop in and say hello to them during his visit there. Lansdale was amused. It was great to stir up such a fuss without even leaving home.[86]

He also learned that he had a following. There was a group of men who were impressed with his career — an identified cadre of "Lansdalians." One of them was F. Andy Messing, Jr., who first heard about Lansdale in 1970 while going through his Special Forces training. He appreciated Lansdale's insistence that the United States must use an integrated fusion of social/political/economic/military approaches in its efforts in the third world. Messing believed that the military in El Salvador was persuaded to shut down its death squads because of arguments by American advisers who cited Ed Lansdale's experiences in the Philippines during the 1950s. As the years passed, Messing came to know others; Sam Sarkesian, John Singlaub, John Waghelstein. Eventually, a young Marine lieutenant colonel named Oliver North came also to view himself as a Lansdalian, thinking of himself as a Lansdale of the 1980s.

Lansdale was interested in these folk. During the tumultuous election campaign in the Philippines between Corazon Aquino and Ferdinand Marcos, he called Messing and asked him to go there and take a look at the situation. Lansdale supplied Messing with the names of people to contact inside both political camps. Messing made the trip in January 1985 and was surprised at the responsive Lansdale network still in existence there. Upon his return, he informed Lansdale that Aquino was the person who should head the government there. "I thought so," Ed replied. Lansdale, Messing, and others lobbied the American Congress to support her and worked on members of the National Security Council to change its attitudes. Messing was pleased at the outcome of their labors and stressed that an influential Lansdale network continues to exist today.[87]

On 27 April 1985, when Ed was seventy-seven years old, the Lansdales were getting ready to make a short vacation trip. Prior to their departure, Ed went into the bathroom to empty his bladder. As he emerged, he announced to Pat, "I peed blood." They canceled their trip and Pat took Ed to Bethesda Hospital. After a round of testing, a physician informed Pat that they had discovered a cancerous growth in one of Ed's kidneys. She signed her permission and Ed was operated on, his kidney removed. Once again, Ted and Peter came to be with their father during a time of danger. Lansdale was discharged three days after the operation.

Pat worried constantly about him. "He is weak. He has no appetite. He has a heart condition. He has thyroid goiter and shortness of breath."[88] Ill health slowed but did not stop Lansdale. He and Pat made a trip to Florida on the autotrain in 1985, and a friend and his wife pushed Ed's wheelchair all over the vast grounds of Walt Disney's EPCOT Center outside Orlando one rainy day. That same year Ed served again on a government panel. Benjamin Franklin Cooling, the senior historian in the Office of Air Force History, called upon Lansdale in June to critique an official book manuscript on Air Force civic action projects during the Vietnam conflict, and Lansdale did so gladly.[89] In 1986, for the last time, Ed vacationed with his brothers in California and Oregon.

On Monday, 23 February 1987, the season's worst snowfall hit the Washington area, snarling traffic, shutting down the airports, and causing many government offices to close. When Pat awakened that morning her mood quickly turned to one of grief. Ed lay too quietly beside her. At age seventy-nine his health problems had been too much for him to endure any longer. Sometime during the previous night he had died. His sons came home once again to sit beside their father, but this time they did so in a quiet funeral home in Vienna, Virginia, where their father lay resting, wearing the Air Force uniform of a major general. Lansdale's death was noted in a front page story the following day in the *New York Times*. It noted his belief that "[t]he sure defense against [revolution] is to have the citizenry and the Government so closely bound together that they are unsplittable."[90] The *Washington Post,* in a lengthy obituary the same day, called its readers' attention to Lansdale's advocacy of the idea that communism "will not die by being ignored, bombed or smothered by us." It could best be challenged only "by a better idea."[91] On Wednesday, the *Philippine Daily Inquirer* in Manila ran a front page story on the career and accomplishments of Edward Lansdale.[92] On Thursday, 26 February, the *Washington Post* carried an editorial on Lansdale's career and his insistence that American policy must go "beyond military defense into efforts to win the 'hearts and minds' of the people."[93] On Thursday the Manila *Philippine Star* carried a column in which the writer spoke of Lansdale's contributions and announced that a funeral mass would take place in his honor at three o'clock in the afternoon the following day at the chapel located on the campus of the Philippine Women's University.[94] Other newspapers from London to St. Petersburg, Florida, carried notices of the passing of the "ugly American."

Friday, 27 February 1987, the nation's capital was cold, cloudy, dreary. By early afternoon people began to gather at Fort Myer's main post chapel, with its tall steeple pointing like a winter-chilled finger toward God. The sanctuary filled with mourners and well-wishers, most in their sixties and seventies, men and women of Lansdale's generation. Outside stood six proud heavy brown horses, shaggy in their winter coats, hitched to a black-draped catafalque. The waiting animals occasionally stomped their large steel-shod hooves, and their nostrils steamed in the cold air. At the end of the ceremony they would slowly bear Lansdale's coffined body into the snow-covered fields of Arlington Cemetery, to join other of America's fallen and honored heroes. In a little while, six Air Force men positioned near the yawning hole in the frozen ground at the grave site would move as one while thrice firing their outdated M-1 rifles into the chilly air. A bugler would sound the mournful tones of "Taps."

Also in the street, standing at attention, was a platoon-sized Air Force honor guard commanded by a full colonel. Nearby stood the members of an Air Force brass ensemble. Before the service, those musicians played hymns such as "Amazing Grace" and "God of Our Fathers." Inside the church, members of Bravo Company of the 3d Infantry "Old Guard" escorted the flag-draped coffin down the center aisle to its place of honor. The Lansdale family — widow, sons and wives, brother and wife, grandchildren, nieces, nephews — filed in from a side door and quietly took their places in a front pew. Retired Colonel Sam Karrick, a Christian Science practitioner and a member of Lansdale's old team, conducted the service and solemnly read from the words of Scripture and the writings of Mary Baker Eddy. Near the end, two men who had known Ed throughout his career came to the podium and stood gripping the lectern to render eulogies to their friend. Spence Davis, author and retired correspondent for the Associated Press, gave tribute "to Ed Lansdale, the unconventional, good American. We salute you." Rufe Phillips, his voice breaking, spoke for many when he sorrowed that "we shall not see his like again."

NOTES
BIBLIOGRAPHY
INDEX

NOTES

Edward Lansdale's papers were located in two places during my research. Some personal correspondence and papers were left by General Lansdale in his home files at the time of his death. His widow kindly allowed me to sift through them for material helpful to this biography, which I did during the week of 3 May 1987. After being shipped and catalogued, the papers will eventually become part of the Lansdale Papers at the Hoover Institution on War, Revolution and Peace at Stanford University, Palo Alto, California. The personal papers and correspondence that I consulted at Lansdale's home are identified in these notes as "Lansdale Personal Papers." The Lansdale Papers at the Hoover Institution are referred to here as "LP, THIWRP." Lansdale's military records are contained in his 201 Personnel File, United States Air Force, which is referred to here as "Lansdale 201 file."

Complete bibliographical information about works and interviews cited in these notes can be found in the Bibliography. To avoid repetition, I have used in each note a shortened form containing the author's name and a short, identifiable title.

Interviews with Edward Lansdale by Cecil B. Currey are cited in the notes as "Lansdale interview" and include the date. Interviews with Edward Lansdale by others are cited by interviewer's name. The only exception is the interview of Lansdale conducted by Major Alnwick for the U.S. Air Force Oral History Program, which is cited as "Air Force interview." All other interviews by Cecil Currey are cited by interviewee's name and date.

The Senate Select Committee to Study Governmental Operations with Respect to Intelligence Activities, chaired by Senator Frank Church, published during the first session of the 94th Congress a report entitled *Alleged Assassination Plots Involving Foreign Leaders*. This report is cited in the notes as "Church Report."

Acronyms abound for government and military offices and positions. A few acronyms recur in these notes: DOD, Department of Defense; OSO, Office of Special Operations; SLO, USE, Senior Liaison Office, U.S. Embassy; USDOD, OSD, U.S. Department of Defense, Office of the Secretary of Defense.

INTRODUCTION

1. Charles McCarry interview, 13 November 1985.
2. Quoted in Stevenson, *Intrepid's Last Case*, pp. 21–22.

3. Charles McCarry interview, 13 November 1985.
4. William E. Colby, "The Ten Greatest Spies of All Time," in Whittingham, *Almanac of Adventure,* p. 165.
5. Colby and Forbath, *Honorable Men,* p. 81.
6. Agee, *CIA Diary,* p. 21.
7. Lansdale interview, 15 February 1984.
8. Letter, Edward Lansdale to Cecil Currey, 8 January 1986.

1. ODYSSEY TO CALIFORNIA

1. Gibbons and McAdams interview. See also Adelstein, "Something Extra and Special," pp. 54–55.
2. Letter, Edward Lansdale to Cecil Currey, 27 June 1984; Gibbons and McAdams interview. Someone has written that "the war was difficult for Secretary McNamara. Vietnam was a combination of people and ideas and those were the two areas in which he was weak"!
3. See Greene, *The Quiet American,* and Lederer and Burdick, *The Ugly American.*
4. Lansdale made a desultory search into his family genealogy during his retirement years, compiling his findings into a manuscript, "The Lansdale Family." He noted in his typescript that his family may have had Scandinavian origins. Viking raiders often landed along the coastal areas of Lancashire province in England, and some may have come from the town Lønsdale, a community in Norway just above the Arctic Circle. In Lancashire, variant spellings, such as Lonsdale, Lansdell, and Lansdale, soon appeared, all associated with the small town of Kirkby Lonsdale. Lansdale's brother Phil recalled, "Some years ago [my wife] Jean and I drove through Kirkby Lonsdale intending to stop at a pub for a pint. The town looked so dull that we didn't bother." Letter, Phil Lansdale to Cecil Currey, 23 March 1986. Brother Ben was not so harsh in his judgment. He too visited Kirkby Lonsdale, staying overnight with his wife at the old Rose and Crown Hotel "in the same lumpy bed the queen slept in and except for the lumps and the pillows stuffed with hardened cement, found it a delightful place. And if you should ever visit in the springtime, walk around to the path in the back of the old churchyard cemetery and you'll find one of the prettiest scenes in England — the view into the Lune River Valley below the church." Letter, Ben Lansdale to Phil, Edward, and David Lansdale, 2 March [no year], Lansdale Personal Papers.
   Charles Wareing Bardsley, in *Dictionary of English and Welsh Surnames,* lists several early English holders of the Lansdale family name (pp. 468, 494).
5. Letter, Phil Lansdale to Cecil Currey, 20 September 1985; interviews with David Lansdale, 11 November 1985; Edward Lansdale, 15 February 1984, 12 November 1985; Phil Lansdale, 20 September 1985. See also letter, Ben Lansdale to Gary May, 28 April 1978, Box 2, LP, THIWRP.
6. Letter, Phil Lansdale to Cecil Currey, 23 March 1986; Edward Lansdale interview, 17 February 1984; David Lansdale interview, 11 November 1985; letter, Ben Lansdale to Gary May, 28 April 1978, Box 2, LP, THIWRP.

7. Lansdale interview, 15 February 1984.
8. Ibid.; Phil Lansdale interview, 20 September 1985; letter, Phil Lansdale to Cecil Currey, 23 March 1986; letter, Ben Lansdale to Gary May, 28 April 1978, Box 2, LP, THIWRP; Lansdale 201 file.
9. Hubert H. Roberts interview, 13 July 1985; John Doran interview, 11 November 1985; Lansdale interview, 15 February 1984; letter, Phil Lansdale to Cecil Currey, 23 March 1986. Lansdale never succeeded in learning any foreign language. Years later John Foster Dulles was talking with someone at the State Department about Lansdale. "Oh yes," he said, "Ed speaks all these different languages; stick him in a country and he immediately talks with people there." Not so, Lansdale later reminded him. "I can't speak a goddamn foreign language at all."
10. Hubert Roberts interview, 13 July 1985.
11. Ibid.; Lansdale interview, 15 February 1984. In 1971 Lansdale recalled that working for the humor magazine was a much more vivid memory than were the days he spent on ROTC training. "Some of the jokes that Walt Purdom, Pooley Roberts and I used to put together in drinking sessions . . . had a surprisingly long life. I used to see them in theater programs later in New York as space fillers. Walt called me by telephone out of the blue from San Francisco one day just before he died — after a couple of decades of our not seeing each other — just to reminisce about those days. They simply don't seem that long ago." Letter, Edward Lansdale to Max Buerger, 21 June 1971, Box 2, LP, THIWRP.
12. Lansdale interview, 15 February 1984; Hubert Roberts interview, 13 July 1985.
13. Letter, Ben Lansdale to Gary May, 28 April 1978, Box 2, LP, THIWRP.
14. Lansdale interview, 15 February 1984; Hubert Roberts interview, 13 July 1985.
15. Lansdale 201 file; Lansdale interview, 15 February 1984.
16. Lansdale interview, 15 February 1984; Lansdale 201 file.
17. Lansdale interview, 15 February 1984. "It was strange," he once reminisced. "A lot of the guys I went to school with . . . wound up on Bataan and others went up into the Aleutian campaign. They lost a lot of people to frostbite. I went to Letterman Hospital in San Francisco later and saw many of them. The poor guys had been training in Arizona for desert warfare in Africa and got shipped to the Aleutians without proper equipment. I don't know who it is that makes decisions like that but the Army is very good at doing it."
18. Lansdale 201 file; Lansdale interview, 15 February 1984. Miles would later be promoted to brigadier general and reassigned to command the Military District of Washington while General Douglas MacArthur was chief of staff. Miles was involved in the effort to expel veteran "bonus marchers" from the nation's capital in the summer of 1932 when twelve thousand jobless veterans marched to Washington in hopes of persuading Congress to provide them with a bonus because of their service to the country in World War I. On orders of President Herbert Hoover and under the personal direction of MacArthur, marchers and their families were driven from Washington with tear gas and bayonets and their shanties were burned.
19. Lansdale interview, 15 February 1984.

NOTES

2. PEACE AND WAR

1. Letter, Phil Lansdale to Cecil Currey, 22 March 1986; Edward Lansdale interview, 15 February 1984.
2. Ibid.; also see Lansdale 201 file.
3. Ibid.; David Lansdale interview, 11 November 1985.
4. Edward Lansdale interview, 15 February 1984.
5. Ibid.; Lansdale 201 file and certificate of promotion, dated 18 August 1932.
6. Edward Lansdale interview, 15 February 1984.
7. Ibid.; Phil Lansdale interview, 20 September 1985; David Lansdale interview, 11 November 1985.
8. Edward Lansdale interview, 15 February 1984; letter, Edward and Pat Lansdale to Dorothy Bohannan, 10 October 1985, Bohannan Collection; Phil Lansdale interview, 20 September 1985.
9. Phil Lansdale interview, 20 September 1985; Hubert Roberts interview, 13 July 1985; Lansdale 201 file.
10. Phil Lansdale interview, 20 September 1985; Edward Lansdale interview, 15 February 1984; Hubert Roberts interview, 13 July 1985.
11. Lansdale 201 file.
12. Ibid.
13. David Lansdale interview, 11 November 1985; Phil Lansdale interview, 20 September 1985; Lansdale 201 file; letter, Ben Lansdale to Gary May, 28 April 1978, Box 2, LP, THIWRP.
14. Edward Lansdale interview, 15 February 1984.
15. Ibid.; Lansdale 201 file.
16. Lansdale 201 file; Edward Lansdale interview, 15 February 1984.
17. Edward Lansdale interview, 15 February 1984.
18. Ibid.
19. Edward Lansdale interview, 15 February 1984; Lansdale 201 file.
20. Letter, Edward Lansdale to Cecil Currey, 10 July 1984.
21. Ibid.; Edward Lansdale interview, 15 February 1984.
22. Lansdale 201 file.
23. Ibid.
24. Edward Lansdale interview, 15 February 1984; letter, Edward Lansdale to Cecil Currey, 10 July 1984.
25. Ibid.; Lansdale 201 file.
26. Ibid. His orders were published by authority of General George Catlett Marshall, Army chief of staff.
27. Lansdale and Vanderbilt corresponded until Vanderbilt's death in 1981. Letter, Edward Lansdale to Cecil Currey, 10 July 1984; Edward Lansdale interview, 15 February 1984; Air Force interview.
28. This background material on OSS has been drawn from Cline, *The CIA Under Reagan, Bush and Casey,* p. 61.
29. Edward Lansdale interview, 15 February 1984.
30. Ibid.; Edward Lansdale interview, 16 May 1984.
31. Edward Lansdale interview, 15 February 1984.
32. Ibid.
33. Ibid.
34. Ibid.

35. Lansdale 201 file.
36. Air Force interview.
37. Ibid.
38. Ibid.
39. Edward Lansdale interview, 16 May 1984.
40. Air Force interview.
41. Edward Lansdale interviews, 16 May 1984, 19 December 1984; Air Force interview.
42. Edward Lansdale interview, 16 May 1984.
43. Ibid.; Air Force interview; Lansdale 201 file.
44. Lansdale 201 file.
45. Phil Lansdale interview, 20 September 1985.
46. Edward Lansdale interview, 16 May 1984. In that interview I asked, "Sometime or other during the Second World War did you ever get to the European theater?" Lansdale answered, "Never. Never. Never did." I then asked, "You spent all your time then where?" Lansdale replied, "In the U.S. and working on Asia — the Pacific area." "Where were you stationed?" I added. The general responded that his assignments had been only "in San Francisco, Washington, and New York."
47. Ibid.
48. As commander of United Nations Forces in Korea in 1951, MacArthur also objected to CIA operations in his area of command. See Smith, *OSS: The Secret History of America's First Central Intelligence Agency,* pp. 250–252.
49. Edward Lansdale interview, 19 December 1984, and later handwritten notes on an early version of this manuscript submitted to him for his comments.
50. Lee Telesco interview, 21 July 1986. Another man who knew Lansdale in those long-ago days telephoned as this was being written. William Gilday, who also worked in intelligence, first met Lansdale in Rockhampton or Brisbane, Australia (he could not remember which), in July or August 1943. He did not see him again until 1951 when their paths crossed in Manila. Gilday greeted Lansdale with "Long time, no see." Lansdale replied, "Jeez, you've gotten older." William Gilday interviews, 22 May, 4 June 1987.
51. Lansdale 201 file.
52. Ibid.
53. Letter, Ben Lansdale to Gary May, 22 May 1978, Box 2, LP, THIWRP.
54. Edmundo Navarro interview, 25 July 1985.
55. Lansdale 201 file.
56. Ibid.; letter, Edward Lansdale to Adjutant General, Lowry Air Force Base, 15 December 1948, Biographical File, Miscellaneous, LP, THIWRP.
57. Lansdale 201 file; Intelligence Report #30, "Philippines, 1945–1948; 1950–1954," Assistant Chief of Staff for Intelligence, U.S. Armed Forces Western Pacific, Box 33, LP, THIWRP; Edward Lansdale interview, 15 February 1984.
58. Edward Lansdale interview, 15 February 1984; Box 33, LP, THIWRP.
59. Edward Lansdale interview, 15 February 1984.
60. Ibid.
61. Biographical File, Box 2, LP, THIWRP.
62. Edward Lansdale interview, 15 February 1984.

63. Ibid.
64. Clippings, 1949–1963, Biographical File, Box 1, LP, THIWRP.
65. Ibid.

3. BIRTH OF A LEGEND

1. Peter Lansdale interview, 11 November 1985.
2. Ibid.
3. Dorothy Bohannan interviews, 27 July 1985, 18 July 1986.
4. Lansdale 201 file.
5. Ibid.; Peter Lansdale interview, 11 November 1985; Dorothy Bohannan interviews, 27 July 1985, 18 July 1986. Some use was also made of notes written by Edward Lansdale on an early version of this manuscript.
6. Manchester, *American Caesar*, p. 413; Dorothy Bohannan interviews, 27 July 1985, 18 July 1986.
7. Dorothy Bohannan interview, 27 July 1985.
8. Ibid.
9. Lansdale interview, 16 May 1984.
10. Abaya, *Betrayal in the Philippines*, pp. 60–68.
11. Ibid., p. 195.
12. Fernandez, *The Philippines and the United States*, p. 221.
13. Agoncillo and Guerrero, *History of the Filipino People*, pp. 495–496.
14. Steinberg, *Philippine Collaboration in World War II*, p. 103.
15. Abaya, *Betrayal in the Philippines*, pp. 172–173.
16. Abaya, *The Untold Philippine Story*, p. 26. In a March 1947 plebiscite, the Parity Amendment was accorded full legitimacy.
17. Fernandez, *The Philippines and the United States*, p. 241.
18. Ibid., pp. 330–331.
19. Manchester, *American Caesar*, p. 420.
20. Edward Lansdale, "The Philippine Presidential Campaign, II," Philippine Guerrilla Movements, Folder 8000.
21. Respect for the government in Manila steadily lessened among rural folk in central Luzon, and membership rolls of the Hukbalahap movement grew ever longer. By 1950 irregular troops of the Huks were approaching Manila; the sound of gunfire could be heard in the streets. Huk leaders decided the time was right to seize final power. They were undone by Ramón Magsaysay, first serving as defense minister and later as president. The Huk movement suffered a grievous setback when Magsaysay forces raided their secret headquarters in Manila, arresting many of them in a single night. A number of countermeasures put into effect by Magsaysay caused an increase of popular support for the government and a consequent diminution of Huk power. In 1954, El Supremo walked out of the jungle after conversations with Manuel Manahan and Benigno "Ninoy" Aquino and surrendered. Thus the Hukbalahap rebellion ended. For a skewed view, interested readers might like to consult *US Intervention in Philippine Politics*. The publisher of that book, Katipunan ng Bagong Pilipina (KnBP), might be likened to the American League of Women Voters; the Foreword of the book describes it as an organization composed of fourteen thousand women.
22. Lansdale interview, 17 December 1984.

23. Ibid.
24. Lansdale interview, 16 May 1984.
25. Patrocinio Lansdale interview, 23 June 1985; and Edward Lansdale interview, 19 December 1984.
26. The Visayan Islands are those wherein the Visayan language is spoken. They include Leyte, Samar, Bohol, Negros, and Panay.
27. Patrocinio Lansdale interview, 23 June 1985.
28. Ibid.
29. Lansdale interview, 19 December 1984.
30. Ibid.
31. Ibid.; Lansdale interview, 17 December 1984.
32. Lansdale interview, 17 December 1984.
33. Air Force interview.
34. Lansdale interview, 30 November 1984.
35. Air Force interview.
36. Patricinio Lansdale interview, 23 June 1985.
37. Lansdale interview, 17 December 1984.
38. Ibid.
39. In late November 1984, General Lansdale accepted my invitation to speak to students at the University of South Florida and made the trip south from McLean, Virginia, with his wife. He spoke twice on 29 November 1984, once at 8:00 A.M. to my class in American Military History and, later, at 2:00 P.M., to interested students and faculty in a seminar room at the University Library. Both sessions were taped and transcribed. The morning session is cited as "Military History lecture" and the afternoon meeting is cited as "Library lecture." This story is drawn from his Library lecture.
40. Manuel Manahan interview, 24 July 1985.
41. Medardo Justiniano interview, 25 July 1985. Justiniano had no more reservations about working with Americans than did Manahan. "My God," Med exclaimed, "how can we dispense [with America] when I speak your language better than I speak Tagalog? I was brought up under Americans. Here I am, part Chinese, part Filipino, but I am speaking English to you and I think you understand me!"
42. Frank Zaldarriaga interview, 26 July 1985.
43. José Banzon interview, 30 July 1985.
44. Edmundo Navarro interview, 25 July 1985.
45. Peter C. Richards interview, 23 July 1985. Richards first came to the Philippines in February 1937 and worked for various British commercial firms until 1942, when he and his wife, Dolores "Dolly" Opisso, were interned by Japanese occupation forces at the Santo Tomas University in Manila. After the war Richards returned to England for a brief stay, joined Reuters news agency, and promptly returned to Manila as bureau chief. At one time or another he also served as correspondent for the *London Times* and *London Daily Telegraph*. Some years ago he was created an officer of the Most Excellent Order of the British Empire (O.B.E.). An unusually astute man, Richards has spent decades studying the Philippine political scene.
46. Spence Davis interview, 30 January 1986.
47. Lansdale, Library lecture, 29 November 1984.
48. When Lansdale told this story nearly forty years after the event, he recalled that the general who came to see him was Lieutenant General Richard K.

Sutherland, who had indeed earlier served as MacArthur's chief of staff. By this time, however, Sutherland was back in the States and General Mueller was chief of staff for MacArthur at the headquarters of the Supreme Commander, Allied Powers (SCAP) in Tokyo. Available government documents showed Mueller signing various directives, dated 11 January 1947, 20 March 1947, 23 June 1947, and 31 December 1947, as MacArthur's chief of staff. For that reason I have corrected Lansdale's story on this point. See Lansdale interviews, 15 February 1984, 16 May 1984.

49. Major General Paul J. Mueller wrote an efficiency report on Lansdale for the period 1 July 1947 to 30 April 1948, giving high praise to Lansdale for his work. See Lansdale 201 file.
50. Lansdale interview, 15 February 1984.
51. Lansdale 201 file.
52. Lansdale interview, 16 May 1984.
53. Lansdale interview, 15 February 1984.
54. Letter, Edward Lansdale to Irving Casey, 4 May 1966, SLO, USE, Saigon, Box 51, LP, THIWRP.
55. Lansdale 201 file.
56. Lansdale interviews, 15 February 1984, 16 May 1984.
57. Abaya, *The Untold Philippine Story*, pp. 37–38, and Jesus Lava, "A Critique of Benedict J. Kerkvliet's *The Huk Rebellion: A Study of Peasant Unrest in the Philippines*," paper delivered 22 February 1978 at the College of Administration, University of the Philippines. Kerkvliet explains the Huk defeat as due to fatigue; everyone was tired after so many years of war. Preposterous!
58. Lansdale interview, 17 May 1984.
59. Ibid.; Lansdale 201 file.
60. Letter, Major O. J. Magee to Edward Lansdale, 15 July 1949, "Correspondence: Philippines, 1945–1948; 1950–1954," Box 33, LP, THIWRP.
61. Dorothy Bohannan interview, 27 July 1985.
62. Letter, Colonel George A. Chester to Edward Lansdale, 1 March 1949, "Correspondence: Philippines, 1945–1948; 1950–1954," Box 33, LP, THIWRP.
63. Lansdale interview, 16 May 1984.
64. Lansdale interviews, 16 May 1984, 17 May 1984, 17 December 1984.
65. Ibid.
66. Lansdale 201 file.
67. Lansdale interviews, 17 May 1984, 17 December 1984.
68. Lansdale 201 file.
69. Lansdale interview, 17 December 1984.
70. Ibid.

4. GIRDING FOR WAR

1. "I forever kept that [secret] to myself except right now when I am talking about it," Lansdale once noted. Lansdale interview, 17 December 1984.
2. Ransom, *Central Intelligence and National Security*, pp. 58–59, 64.
3. Leary, *The Central Intelligence Agency*, p. 17.
4. Ransom, *Central Intelligence and National Security*, p. 72.

5. Ibid., pp. 71–73, and Colby and Forbath, *Honorable Men*, p. 60.
6. Colby and Forbath, *Honorable Men*, pp. 60–62.
7. Leary, *The Central Intelligence Agency*, p. 67.
8. Stevenson, *Intrepid's Last Case*, p. xxii.
9. Ransom, *Central Intelligence and National Security*, p. 59.
10. Ibid., p. 75, and Colby and Forbath, *Honorable Men*, pp. 68–69; Leary, *The Central Intelligence Agency*, p. 23.
11. Colby and Forbath, *Honorable Men*, pp. 69–70.
12. Ibid., p. 71.
13. Ibid., pp. 70–71, and Ransom, *Central Intelligence and National Security*, pp. 75–76.
14. Colby and Forbath, *Honorable Men*, p. 71, and Leary, *The Central Intelligence Agency*, p. 38.
15. Colby and Forbath, *Honorable Men*, p. 72.
16. Marchetti and Marks, *The CIA and the Cult of Intelligence*, p. 26.
17. Lansdale interview, 17 December 1984.
18. Kintner, *The Front Is Everywhere*.
19. Smith, *Portrait of a Cold Warrior*, pp. 76, 78.
20. Colby and Forbath, *Honorable Men*, p. 72; Leary, *The Central Intelligence Agency*, p. 58.
21. Cline, *The CIA Under Reagan, Bush and Casey*, p. 125, and Colby and Forbath, *Honorable Men*, p. 73.
22. Letter, Lyman B. Kirkpatrick, Jr., to Cecil Currey, 13 February 1985.
23. Ibid. and Cline, *The CIA Under Reagan, Bush and Casey*, pp. 124–125.
24. U.S. Congress, Senate Select Committee, *Foreign and Military Intelligence*, pp. 48–49.
25. Kirkpatrick, *The U.S. Intelligence Community*, p. 32, and Cline, *The CIA Under Reagan, Bush and Casey*, p. 126.
26. Letter, John A. Bross to Cecil Currey, 1 April 1985.
27. Brian Freemantle, *CIA*, p. 29, and Cline, *The CIA Under Reagan, Bush and Casey*, p. 125.
28. Stevenson, *Intrepid's Last Case*, p. xxii, and Cline, *Secrets, Spies and Scholars*. See also Prouty, *The Secret Team*, p. 186; Colby and Forbath, *Honorable Men*, p. 73; and Smith, *Portrait of a Cold Warrior*, p. 63.
29. Letter, Lyman Kirkpatrick, Jr., to Cecil Currey, 13 February 1985.
30. Ibid. and Leary, *The Central Intelligence Agency*, p. 46; Cline, *The CIA Under Reagan, Bush and Casey*, p. 125; Prouty, *The Secret Team*, p. 209.
31. Colby and Forbath, *Honorable Men*, pp. 80–81.
32. Ibid., p. 73, and Leary, *The Central Intelligence Agency*, p. 27.
33. Smith, *Portrait of a Cold Warrior*, p. 68; Leary, *The Central Intelligence Agency*, pp. 43–44; Freemantle, *CIA*, p. 33; U.S. Congress, Senate Select Committee, *Foreign and Military Intelligence*, pp. 27, 31–32; Cline, *The CIA Under Reagan, Bush and Casey*, pp. 137, 150, 153.
34. Colby and Forbath, *Honorable Men*, pp. 76–80.
35. Leary, *The Central Intelligence Agency*, p. 47.
36. Colby and Forbath, *Honorable Men*, pp. 81–82, 92.
37. Leary, *The Central Intelligence Agency*, p. 23, and Prouty, *The Secret Team*, p. 229.
38. Kirkpatrick, *The U.S. Intelligence Community*, p. 32; Freemantle, *CIA*,

p. 31; Colby and Forbath, *Honorable Men*, pp. 92–93; Smith, *Portrait of a Cold Warrior*, p. 75.

39. Letter, Lyman B. Kirkpatrick, Jr., to Cecil Currey, 13 February 1985; letter, John A. Bross to Cecil Currey, 1 April 1985; Cline, *The CIA Under Reagan, Bush and Casey*, pp. 134–135; Kirkpatrick, *The U.S. Intelligence Community*, p. 32; Prouty, *The Secret Team*, p. 231.
40. Smith, *Portrait of a Cold Warrior*, p. 56; Colby and Forbath, *Honorable Men*, pp. 90–92; Leary, *Central Intelligence Agency*, p. 50; Freemantle, *CIA*, p. 31.
41. Smith, *Portrait of a Cold Warrior*, p. 57.
42. Lansdale 201 file.
43. Lansdale interview, 17 December 1984, and Cline, *The CIA Under Reagan, Bush and Casey*, p. 172.
44. Lansdale interview, 17 December 1984.
45. Cline, *The CIA Under Reagan, Bush and Casey*, pp. 15, 16, 204.
46. Lansdale interview, 17 December 1984.
47. Ibid.
48. Smith, *Portrait of a Cold Warrior*, pp. 57, 66.
49. Lansdale interview, 17 December 1984.
50. Ibid.
51. Ibid.
52. Lansdale interview, 30 November 1984. Also see Abueva, *Ramon Magsaysay*.
53. Lansdale interview, 17 December 1984.
54. Undated analysis of the 1949 election in the Philippines by Peter C. Richards, Richards Collection. In the 1951 election, Laurel won his seat handily with 2,200,000 votes. See Avancena and Maramag, *Days of Courage*.
55. Lansdale interview, 17 December 1984.
56. Lansdale interview, 12 November 1985.
57. Lansdale interview, 17 December 1984; Charles Glazer interview, 19 July 1986, and Lansdale, *In the Midst of Wars*, pp. 15, 19. Smith, *Portrait of a Cold Warrior*, states incorrectly that the appointment was made on 31 August 1950 (p. 92).
58. Lansdale interview, 12 November 1985. Bohannan never received the appreciation for his work in the Orient within official Washington political or military circles that Lansdale did despite the fact that "Bo was in on the development of a great deal in the Philippines. . . . They asked me [in Washington] when I was trying to push him for a top medal, 'Why do you think he is so hot? Would the Huk campaign have gone the way it did if you weren't there?' 'Well, no,' but it wouldn't have gone [the way it did] if he wasn't there, too, so you have to count him in on that.' " Despite Lansdale efforts, those who doubted Bohannan's contributions refused to change their minds. In an undated memorandum to me written in the summer of 1986, Dorothy Bohannan, Bo's widow, commented, "The powers that be may not have seen fit to give Bohannan any credits, but the Filipinos have done so in their own way. The number of families who respect and treasure his memory are astounding. Families wanting bits of his ashes to put in their sanctuaries; the friends who come back again and again to say they will never forget. Maybe this is more worthwhile than all the medals the US could ever hand out."

59. Lansdale interview, 12 November 1985.
60. Lansdale interview, 17 December 1984.
61. Prouty, *The Secret Team*, p. 231.
62. Colby and Forbath, *Honorable Men*, p. 88.
63. Lansdale interview, 17 December 1984, and Air Force interview.
64. Lansdale interview, 17 December 1984.
65. Lansdale 201 file.
66. Ibid.
67. Dorothy Bohannan interview, 27 July 1985.
68. Ibid. and Lansdale, *In the Midst of Wars*, p. 15.
69. Memorandum, Dorothy Bohannan to Cecil Currey, Summer 1986.
70. Peter Lansdale interview, 11 November 1985.

5. AN HONEST ELECTION

1. Lansdale, *In the Midst of Wars*, p. 78.
2. Air Force interview.
3. Lansdale, *In the Midst of Wars*, pp. 1–2. Specifically, the domestic airport uses one runway of what was Nichols Field, and Villamor AFB (which until recently was still known as Nichols Field) uses another. The International Airport began as a runway built by POW laborers during the Japanese occupation.
4. Ibid., p. 18, and memorandum, Dorothy Bohannan to Cecil Currey, Summer 1986. See also Dorothy Bohannan interview, 27 July 1985.
5. C. P. Cabell, deputy director, CIA, to US Air Force Chief of Staff, 30 March 1954, Lansdale 201 file.
6. Lansdale, *In the Midst of Wars*, pp. 18–19.
7. Dorothy Bohannan interview, 27 July 1985, and letter, Edward Lansdale to Douglas Valentine, 12 January 1985, Lansdale Personal Papers.
8. Ibid. and memorandum, Dorothy Bohannan to Cecil Currey, Summer 1986.
9. Lansdale, "Lessons Learned."
10. Lansdale, Military History lecture.
11. Military forces generally tend to recognize nine "principles of war": the principle of mass (use sufficient troops to get the task done); the principle of the objective (know precisely what your goal is and how you will achieve it); the principle of simplicity (keep matters as simple as possible); the principle of security (watch your rear and flanks and prevent the enemy from knowing your plans); the principle of maneuver (try to put your enemy in a position where he cannot win); the principle of offensive (generally speaking, it is better to be on the offensive than the defensive); the principle of unity of command (at any organizational level, one and only one person must be in charge); the principle of surprise (surprise the enemy); and the principle of economy of force (the other side of the principle of mass: do not use more troops than are necessary to achieve victory). The Chinese and Soviets also recognize the principle of annihilation (Colonel Chivington said it best at the Sand Creek Massacre in Colorado in 1867: "Kill them all. Nits grow into lice!"), and the British list the principle of flexibility (never be too rigid, always be prepared to adapt your tactics to changing battlefield circumstances).
12. Lansdale, "Lessons Learned."

13. Lansdale, "Introductory Comments."
14. Lansdale, Military History lecture.
15. Lansdale, "Introductory Comments."
16. Air Force interview and Lansdale interview, 17 December 1984.
17. Lansdale, "The True American." See also Adelstein, "Something Extra and Special," pp. 12–14. In the summer of 1985 Jon Adelstein, my wife, and I had a long and pleasant supper meal at an outdoor café in Palo Alto while discussing Lansdale and his impact.
18. Adelstein, "Something Extra and Special," p. 14.
19. This was not a new attitude for Lansdale. It had begun during his service in World War II. During those hectic years his superiors got wind of a new wartime project some agency was working on. They inquired about how the authorization for it had come about and were told that "Lansdale came in and told us it was important." Lansdale's superiors remonstrated: "But he was in uniform. He was only a first lieutenant." "Well," the agency spokesman rejoined, "he was talking like he was head of the whole U.S. Army, so we went ahead." Why had Lansdale assumed such authority? "I just thought this is what the U.S. and this agency should be doing. And they went ahead and did it. I spent my whole service that way," he said. He then added an observation that goes far toward explaining his freewheeling style during his years in intelligence work. "Many, many people have said [to me], 'I wish I could have done what you did in getting to do the things you wanted to do and [which] were worth doing.' And I said, 'They were there for anybody who had the nerve to do them.' My superiors used to bawl me out. I got terrible scoldings!" His response was inevitably the same. He listened and then said, "I went into the service for patriotic reasons and I'll quit for the same damn reasons. I just want to serve my country as best I can. *I'll make up my own mind what that is!*" Lansdale interview, 16 May 1984.
20. Charles Glazier interviews, 29 July 1985, 19 July 1986. A few weeks after our conversation in 1986, Glazier died of throat cancer.
21. Shalom, "Counter-Insurgency," pp. 159ff. Also see Smith, *Portrait of a Cold Warrior,* p. 201. Magsaysay's accomplishments caused his countrymen to enshrine his memory in their hearts. During the summer of 1985 in the stress-filled months just before the fall of the Marcos regime, the enthusiasm of a Manila taxi driver for the former president was so stirring that I asked him to set some of his thoughts down in a letter. This member of the capital city's underclass, a man in his mid-to-late fifties, wrote out his thoughts in marred but stirring language. "He did good things to our country. . . . He never thought to become a highest post in the government. He planned to run a contender as President just to fulfill his promise to the people. And when the election came he win by landslide. He promised the people that he will do his best to give every Filipino a descent way of living. Land for the landless, justise for all. If the people needs him in a remote area, he brings the government to the people."
  The taxi driver told how Magsaysay was concerned about all levels of governance. "Some times here in Manila he wears ragged clothes, as disguised to be apprehended by traffic policeman in the busy street of the city. And he is given ticket issued by a policeman not knowing he is the president. He signed the violation, Pres. Ramon Magsaysay. And he admires

the policeman doing his duty. And the policeman gives a salute to our guy. Recommendation of good service is being given to the policeman."

Following Magsaysay's sudden death, the cabbie recalled, "He was mourned by the people so deeply in their heart. I myself I love him so much. His grave is simple, like just for a common person. There's no other president that could ever pared him or a contender president like R.M., Our Guy. He is my only Guy, my only president like him could give every Filipino a social justice. A very good president never lives so long. Ever in my heart he is always alive. He is my idol, my only president, my only guy, R.M., Monching." Letter, Luis Paycana to Cecil Currey, 17 September 1985.

22. Air Force interview.
23. Letter, Edward Lansdale to Associate Professor José V. Abueva, chief of research, Ramón Magsaysay Research Project, University of the Philippines, 5 November 1962, USDOD, OSD, Box 36, LP, THIWRP.
24. Air Force interview.
25. Lansdale interview, 16 May 1984.
26. Emphasis added. Letter, Jesus Magsaysay to Edward Lansdale, 14 May 1957, Correspondence, USDOD, OSD, Box 39, LP, THIWRP.
27. José Banzon interview, 30 July 1985.
28. Manuel Manahan interview, 24 July 1985.
29. Air Force interview.
30. Ibid.
31. Lansdale, "The Story Ramon Magsaysay Did Not Tell," p. 7. See also Lachica, *The Huks*, p. 133. The edition of this book cited here is a word-for-word facsimile of the original Manila edition.
32. Emma Valeriano interview, 26 July 1985.
33. Air Force interview. "Magsaysay had a clear understanding of the war's objective," Lansdale recalled. The secretary of national defense knew he had "to win the people away from the other side over to the Philippine government's side. You don't do that by killing people's innocent relatives. You don't make war where it will hurt the people you are trying to win over; you try to strike an identified enemy." Likewise Lansdale believed that, ultimately, the Philippine Army came to deserve credit. They learned "when to go in and hit an area, and to know they were hitting the enemy, not civilians." See Lansdale's remarks in Peterson, Reinhardt, and Conger, *Symposium on the Role of Airpower*, pp. 57, 27.
34. Manuel Manahan interview, 24 July 1985.
35. Lansdale, "Lessons Learned: The Philippines."
36. Richard G. Stilwell, "The Challenge of the Profession of Arms," speech given to the Corps of Cadets, United States Military Academy, and letter, Richard Stilwell to Edward Lansdale, 8 February 1960, Speeches, Miscellany, 1957–1961 (i), USDOD, OSD, Box 43, LP, THIWRP. Lansdale responded a week later: "Thanks for sending me a copy of your talk. . . . even though I blushed at the personal parts of it." See also Miscellany, Philippines, 1945–1948, 1950–1954, Box 32, LP, THIWRP.
37. Letter, Peter C. Richards to Dear Sir, 27 July 1982, Richards Collection, and Peter C. Richards interview, 23 July 1985.
38. Letter, Peter C. Richards to A.V.H. Hartendorp, 24 October 1961, Correspondence, USDOD, OSD, Box 40, LP, THIWRP. Richards wrote that

"Lansdale is to my mind the most remarkable, efficient and effective man I have ever set eyes on."

39. Letter, A.V.H. Hartendorp to Peter C. Richards, 30 October 1961, Correspondence, USDOD, OSD, Box 40, LP, THIWRP.
40. Letter, Albino Z. SyCip to Edward Lansdale, 1 October 1957, Correspondence, USDOD, OSD, Box 41, LP, THIWRP.
41. *London Times,* 18 November 1954.
42. Renato Constantino, "CIA, Philippines," *Manila Chronicle,* 15 July 1971, and I. P. Soliongco, "President Magsaysay and the Americans," *Saturday Chronicle* (Manila), 8 February 1969.
43. Letter, Edward Lansdale to Robert Shaplen, 30 May 1965, Correspondence, USDOD, OSD, Box 40, LP, THIWRP.
44. Letter, Edward Lansdale to C.T.R. Bohannan, 18 July 1971, Bohannan Collection, and Lansdale interview, 12 November 1985. And see C.T.R. Bohannan, "Revisionism in Philippine History," an address to the History Department, University of the Philippines, 17 September 1979, Lansdale Personal Papers.
45. Letter, Bert J. Talbot to Edward Lansdale, 18 November 1954, and letter, Edward Lansdale to Bert J. Talbot, 21 January 1955, Correspondence, USDOD, OSD, Box 41, LP, THIWRP.
46. Letter, Edward Lansdale to Peter C. Richards, 23 July 1971, Richards Collection.
47. Memorandum, Edward Lansdale to Don Blackburn/Hans Schechter, 28 November 1972, Lansdale Personal Papers.
48. Ibid.
49. Ranelagh, *The Agency,* pp. 224–225.
50. Lansdale interview, 17 December 1984.
51. Lansdale interview, 12 November 1985.
52. Ibid.
53. Lansdale interview, 15 February 1984.
54. Lansdale interviews, 15 February 1984, 17 December 1984.
55. Lansdale interview, 16 May 1984.
56. Lansdale interview, 17 December 1984. Lansdale's father, Harry, was as unaware of the real nature of his son's mission as anyone could be yet offered a loving summation of Lansdale's mission in a letter to his daughter-in-law Helen. "Whatever Ed's activities may have been, they were for the revelation of truth and the establishment of order based on honesty and justice; and Truth always prevails and cannot be defeated." This assessment by a caring father was at least as close as many others came — then or later — to guessing Lansdale's influence on Ramón Magsaysay. See Letter, Henry Lansdale to Helen Lansdale, 26 April 1953, Correspondence, Box 4, LP, THIWRP.
57. Lansdale interview, 17 December 1984.
58. Filipinos often have difficulty speaking certain sounds in the English language. The explosive *p* sound and the softer *f* are commonly mispronounced. A tale that still makes the rounds in the Philippines is of the time Ramón Magsaysay was speaking at a large rally attended by members of the American press. He urged his listeners to contribute to the Peace Fund because the money would go a long way toward solving many problems. Very confused reporters afterward wondered why "fish ponds" would help in

actions against the insurgents. One housewife remembers that a servant once complained to her: "Mum, I haven't been faid for the fast pive faydays." An old test was to ask a Filipino to say, "Put the pickle on the plate."

59. Lansdale, "The Story Ramon Magsaysay Did Not Tell," p. 7.
60. Smith, *Portrait of a Cold Warrior*, p. 94, and Lansdale, Library lecture.
61. Lansdale interview, 17 December 1984, and Lansdale, *In the Midst of Wars*, p. 62.
62. Lansdale, *In the Midst of Wars*, pp. 63ff. William J. Pomeroy, an American who, with his wife, lived among the Huks and became one of their advisers, confirmed how those arrests crippled the Huk leadership. See Pomeroy, *The Forest*, pp. 100–101. On counterguerrilla propaganda also see Crisol, *The Red Lie.*
63. Letter, Walter Bedell Smith to Leland S. Hobbs, 9 January 1951, Correspondence, Philippines 1945–1948, 1950–1954, Box 34, LP, THIWRP.
64. Lansdale interview, 16 May 1984.
65. Lansdale, *In the Midst of Wars*, pp. 78f.
66. Lansdale, Military History lecture, and Adelstein, "Something Extra and Special," p. 8. For a much different view of those days see Pomeroy, *An American Made Tragedy.*
67. Lansdale, Military History lecture.
68. Smith, *Portrait of a Cold Warrior*, p. 95; Lansdale, *In the Midst of Wars*, pp. 52ff; Lansdale, "Lessons Learned"; Bohannan, "Revisionism in Philippine History." Rightly or wrongly, Kerkvliet maintains that the EDCOR program had "no noticeable effect" on the peasants of Central Luzon. See Kerkvliet, *The Huk Rebellion*, p. 239.
69. Lansdale, *In the Midst of Wars*, pp. 52–53.
70. Bohannan, "Revisionism in Philippine History."
71. Lansdale, "Lessons Learned."
72. Ibid.
73. Memorandum, Edward Lansdale to Don Blackburn, 11 June 1972, Lansdale Personal Papers.
74. Lansdale, *In the Midst of Wars*, p. 88.
75. Memorandum, Edward Lansdale to Don Blackburn, 11 June 1972, Lansdale Personal Papers.
76. Lansdale, "Military Psychological Operations," Part I; Lansdale, *In the Midst of Wars*, pp. 73–75; Smith, *Portrait of a Cold Warrior*, p. 85.
77. Lansdale, "Military Psychological Operations," Part I, and Library lecture.
78. This story has been told elsewhere many times. Lansdale first told it in abbreviated form in his book *In the Midst of Wars* (pp. 72–73) and in a lengthier version in "Military Psychological Operations," Part II. A Filipino reaction to the tale was given by Hilarion M. Henares, Jr., "Make My Day!" column in *Philippine Daily Inquirer*, 13 November 1986:

[The *asuang* story is one] that makes Filipinos vomit. Lansdale would never dare desecrate the body of a white American. . . . But not the Filipinos, who are dung, who are of an inferior race, and whose bodies may be desecrated, drained of blood and left to rot in the jungles. . . . It was Lansdale and the CIA who taught our armed forces that they have license to torture Filipinos who are enemies of Americans. The water cure, the electric cattle prod, the high voltage electrodes applied to testicles and nipples, the coke bottle forced into the vagina, the rubber hose and the pliers, are all techniques taught to our soldiers by US Special Forces. [Henares should make up his mind. The Special Forces? The CIA? Or Lansdale?] Now the same techniques are used by the rebels. We Filipinos devour each other fighting America's holy war. . . . It was Lansdale and the CIA who manipulated our press . . . our elections . . . our government. . . . And they still do.

79. Edward Lansdale, "Military Policy in Underdeveloped Areas," Box 12, LP, THIWRP.
80. Leites and Wolf, *Rebellion and Authority*, p. 143. Also see memorandum, Edward Lansdale to Don Blackburn/Hans Schechter, 28 November 1972, Lansdale Personal Papers.
81. Peterson, Reinhardt, and Conger, *Symposium on the Role of Airpower*, pp. 14–15. See also remarks by Colonel Ismael Lapus, part of the proceedings of a seminar on the Huk campaign given by Brigadier General Edward G. Lansdale, Colonel Ismael Lapus, Colonel Napoleon Valeriano, Major Medardo Justiniano, and Major Charles Bohannan, "Counter-Guerrilla Operations in the Philippines, 1946–1953," Fort Bragg, North Carolina, 15 June 1961.
82. Lansdale, Military History lecture.
83. Lansdale, *In the Midst of Wars*, p. 89.
84. Frank Zaldarriaga interview, 26 July 1985.
85. Manuel Manahan interview, 24 July 1985.
86. Smith, *Portrait of a Cold Warrior*, p. 97.
87. Ibid., p. 93.
88. Memorandum, Edward Lansdale to Don Blackburn, 11 June 1972, Lansdale Personal Papers.
89. Ibid.
90. Lansdale, Library lecture, and Lansdale, "Military Psychological Operations," Part II.
91. Lansdale, *In the Midst of Wars*, pp. 89, 90–91.
92. Lansdale, Military History lecture.
93. Ibid.
94. Ibid.
95. Lansdale, "Military Psychological Operations," Part II.
96. Lansdale interview, 16 May 1984.
97. Lansdale, "Military Psychological Operations," Part II.
98. Lansdale, Military History lecture.
99. Lansdale, untitled lecture, 29 March 1960, Armed Forces Staff College, Norfolk, Virginia. Emphasis in original.
100. Lansdale, Military History lecture. The success of that November 1951 election soon brought Lansdale recognition as an expert in counterinsurgency. Colonel George A. Chester filled out Lansdale's 1951 officer efficiency report, describing him as "lucid, efficient, effective, practical, and intelligent [with a] sense of idealism and loyalty [and] skillful at influencing others to do his bidding. [He has a] high sense of loyalty to his superiors, [a] highly developed political sense particularly regarding the Far Eastern area." Lansdale 201 file.

6. "MY GUY MAGSAYSAY"

1. This view is strongly held by Peter C. Richards. He adds: "In 1976 when . . . I stayed with the Lansdales at McLean, Virginia, I asked Ed what

caused him to drop Tañada. He evaded the issue and wouldn't be pushed. Later I asked his wife Pat. She replied casually that perhaps it was because Tañada had made a speech that angered the American powers-that-be. On 13 November 1982, Tañada delivered [a speech] to the Rotary Club of Manila. . . . He made it plain that he had always urged the removal [of American bases]. The speech that angered the Americans some thirty years earlier was along the same lines. . . . Tañada never became president of the Philippines." See Peter C. Richards to [?], undated, with accompanying report, Richards Collection. Also see Charles Glazer interview, 19 July 1986.

2. This contention and the list of publications have been compiled by Peter C. Richards, who adds: "I am still wondering whether the first interference, without which this second interference would not have been provoked, did more harm than good. I am referring to the 1949 elections before which Lansdale said to me 'We must not under any circumstances allow Laurel to be elected.' He used 'we' and referred to the elections in an independent nation!" See Peter C. Richards to Dear Sir, 27 July 1982, Richards Collection. Also see *US Intervention in Philippine Politics*, p. 11.

3. Shalom, "Counter-Insurgency in the Philippines," p. 159.
4. Ibid.
5. Lansdale, *In the Midst of Wars*, p. 70.
6. Lansdale, "Military Psychological Operations," Part I.
7. Romulo and Gray, *The Magsaysay Story*, p. 166.
8. Shalom, "Counter-Insurgency in the Philippines," p. 168, and Romulo and Gray, *The Magsaysay Story*, p. 169. See also letter, Edward Lansdale to José V. Abueva, associate professor, University of the Philippines, and chief of research, Ramón Magsaysay Research Project, 5 November 1962, Correspondence, USDOD, OSD, Box 36, LP, THIWRP. Abueva published his research as *Ramon Magsaysay: A Political Biography*.
9. Lansdale, *In the Midst of Wars*, pp. 98–99.
10. Lansdale interview, 12 November 1985.
11. Szulc, *Compulsive Spy*, pp. 66–67, and letter, Anatolio Lintojua to Edward Lansdale, 15 May 1960, Correspondence, USDOD, OSD, Box 38, LP, THIWRP.
12. Romulo and Gray, *The Magsaysay Story*, p. 169.
13. Lansdale, *In the Midst of Wars*, pp. 100–101.
14. Manuel Manahan interview, 24 July 1985.
15. Lansdale, *In the Midst of Wars*, pp. 104–106.
16. Ibid., p. 106.
17. Ibid., pp. 106–107, and Lansdale interview, 12 November 1985.
18. Lansdale interview, 12 November 1985.
19. Ibid.
20. Ibid.
21. W.T.T. Ward interview, 11 November 1985, and Charles Glazer interview, 19 July 1986. Strangely enough, on an earlier draft of this manuscript, Lansdale wrote the following marginalia alongside the description of Ward's services: "No, No. Nothing like that. That's news to me. He was my friend. He gave me a place to work from. Never served as a remittance man. Never needed to have an apartment rented. Didn't know he had an airplane available. Didn't need one anyway. Don't know what he was

thinking.'' In Glazer's comments of July 1986, he averred that ''Chip's description is right.'' See also letter, Edward Lansdale to Bureau of Field Services, School of Education, University of South Carolina, 3 December 1969, Box 6, LP, THIWRP, which includes a two-page review of Ward's experience and activities in Asia, and letter, Edward Lansdale to José Abueva, 5 November 1962, USDOD, OSD, Box 36, LP, THIWRP.

22. Lansdale interview, 12 November 1985.

23. Lansdale, *In the Midst of Wars*, pp. 107–108.

24. Peter C. Richards to [?], undated, with accompanying report, Richards Collection; Lansdale, *In the Midst of Wars*, pp. 104–106; Smith, *Portrait of a Cold Warrior*, p. 98; Maria Kalaw Katigbak, ''Checkpoint,'' *Weekly Nation*, 22 July 1968.

25. Vicente O. Novales interview, 27 July 1985. Novales humorously explained, ''When RM became an aspirant . . . . the late Bohannan, Ed Lansdale and Frisco San Juan looked for people who [could] be security officers. One of the criterias [sic] was [to be] intelligent so I don't know how I was selected!''

26. Ibid.

27. Smith, *Portrait of a Cold Warrior*, p. 101.

28. Quoted in Shalom, ''Counter-Insurgency in the Philippines,'' p. 170.

29. Manuel Manahan interview, 24 July 1985, and Lansdale, *In the Midst of Wars*, pp. 119–120. On the date of the last issue, Manahan had copies of all seventeen issues bound and a presentation copy made for Lansdale. On the cover, the gift was engraved ''To Col. Ed Landsdale [sic]: 'Feather Merchant' Salesman-Extraordinary of Democracy from the Free Philippines Staff, Manila, November 17, 1953.'' Box 65, LP, THIWRP.

30. Smith, *Portrait of a Cold Warrior*, p. 96. For Lansdale's view on the 1953 election and on the heritage of democracy the Philippines had received from America, see letter, Edward Lansdale to George E. Taylor, 22 October 1957, Box 13, LP, THIWRP.

31. Shalom, ''Counter-Insurgency in the Philippines,'' p. 170, and Smith, *Portrait of a Cold Warrior*, p. 250.

32. The press release was given out on 28 March 1953 at 5:00 P.M. See Richards Collection.

33. Letter, Edward Lansdale to Stephen Shalom, 20 May 1975, Lansdale Personal Papers. Also see Lansdale, *In the Midst of Wars*, p. 109, and Smith, *Portrait of a Cold Warrior*, pp. 99–100.

34. Letter, Edward Lansdale to Myron M. Cowen, 11 June 1953, quoted in letter, Stephen Shalom to Edward Lansdale, 16 April 1975, Lansdale Personal Papers.

35. Letter, Edward Lansdale to Stephen Shalom, 20 May 1975, Lansdale Personal Papers.

36. Ibid.

37. Ibid.

38. Lansdale was often asked the same kind of question about his later activities in Vietnam. Had he bought off the warlords of the feuding sect armies by transferring them huge sums of money made available by CIA so they would support the government of Ngo Dinh Diem? Lansdale's response was inevitably the same. How could he have done anything like that? It was a time when his own checking account was kept in a Washington

bank so that Helen could have access to his salary. His Air Force pay was sent directly to that bank and the one check he wrote each month for personal necessities was always small and even then written with trepidation because he had no way of knowing what his checking account balance was and he didn't want to cause an overdraft and add another burden to Helen's life. He had not been asked about his own personal finances but about CIA funds, yet those who heard his response thought they had received an answer to their question.

39. Letter, Edward Lansdale to Stephen Shalom, 20 May 1975, Lansdale Personal Papers.
40. Lansdale, *In the Midst of Wars*, pp. 109ff.
41. Ibid. See also Gittinger interview and Gibbons and McAdams interview.
42. Lansdale, *In the Midst of Wars*, pp. 110–113, Gittinger interview, and Gibbons and McAdams interview.
43. Lansdale interview, 16 May 1984.
44. Air Force interview.
45. Gittinger interview.
46. Lansdale, *In the Midst of Wars*, pp. 115ff. Voters became so excited about Magsaysay's candidacy that they went around the streets humming the tune or singing the words of such songs as the "We Want Magsaysay March":

We want the bell of liberty
Ringing for us once more;
We want the people's will to be
Free as it was before!

We want our native land to lie
Peaceful and clean again;
We want our nation guided by
God-fearing honest men!

Men who'll serve without the nerve
To cheat eternally;
Who'll do the job and never rob
The public treasury!

Only the man of destiny
Our need will satisfy;
This is the cry for you and me;
We want Magsaysay!

47. Ibid., pp. 117–122, and Smith, *Portrait of a Cold Warrior*, p. 102.
48. Letter, C.T.R. Bohannan to Mrs. Dumbach, 6 April 1977, Bohannan Collection.
49. Shalom, "Counter-Insurgency in the Philippines," p. 170.
50. Lansdale, *In the Midst of Wars*, p. 121. Smith, *Portrait of a Cold Warrior*, gives the tally as 1,688,171 to 703,398 (p. 103). See also Manahan interview, 24 July 1985, and I. P. Soliongco, "President Magsaysay and the Americans," 8 February 1969, *Saturday Chronicle* (Manila).
51. Letter, Edward Lansdale to Robert Shaplen, 30 May 1965, Correspondence, USDOD, OSD, Box 40, LP, THIWRP. The following year in Vietnam, Filipino friends one day surreptitiously changed the metal nameplate on

Lansdale's uniform to read "Landslide" and he wore it for some time
before he noticed what had been done. For instances of this use of his
nickname see Ceferina Ypez interview, 27 July 1985, Vicente O. Novales
interview, 27 July 1985, and many documents in LP, THIWRP.

52. Lansdale, *In the Midst of Wars,* p. 122.

53. Ibid., p. 123, and Manuel Manahan interview, 24 July 1985.

54. See Syjuco, *The Press in the Republic of the Philippines.*

55. Constantino, *The Making of a Filipino,* p. 223. One analysis of the agreement
criticized it strongly as "grossly detrimental to the national interest" inasmuch as it vested "in large and well-established foreign corporations the
right to operate as wholly-owned subsidiaries in all sectors of the economy
and to exclude Filipinos from their ventures." The agreement further aggra-
vated and expanded "the already dominant position of foreign interests in
[the] critical sectors" of petroleum, mining, fertilizer, drugs and pharmaceu-
ticals, chemicals, machine and construction industries and worsened the
foreign exchange problem. See "Philippine Chamber of Industries," pp.
78–84.

56. Agoncillo and Guerrero, *History of the Filipino People,* p. 596. For the
attitude of a high-ranking Filipino on the election of Magsaysay, see Espino
interview, 21 July 1986. General Romeo Espino was former chief of staff
of the Philippine armed forces.

57. Military History lecture. Lansdale said that American preoccupation with
the war in Korea kept the military from sending equipment to the Philippines.
"The Philippine Army had a Christmas catalog of U.S. equipment to ask
for. Their Navy asked for a submarine." He grimaced and added whimsi-
cally, "You know you need a submarine against guerrilla forces up in the
mountains. That's always great stuff. We said no."

58. Letter, Edward Lansdale to José V. Abueva, 5 November 1962, Box 36,
LP, THIWRP.

59. Letter, Edward Lansdale to Robert Shaplen, 30 May 1965, Correspondence,
USDOD, OSD, Box 40, LP, THIWRP. At the time he wrote, Lansdale
was in retirement and was struggling mightily to get back into action.
"It's sheer agony to be shoved to the sidelines," he said to Shaplen,
"and watch the mistakes being made by the glory-grabbers." He believed
that he had performed identical services both in the Philippines and in
Vietnam and that a description of his role in one would serve as well for
the other. "I'm amused that you saw so little similarity between a save in
the Philippines and a save in Vietnam. . . . In both instances, Asian Communist subversive insurgents took lickings — the only time the US has
been able to do so. . . . [W]e have a lot more of these wars to fight
yet."

60. Lansdale interview, 17 May 1984. Colonel Richard G. Stilwell spoke of
Lansdale's "inestimably valuable contribution to the furtherance of the
objectives of the United States Government." Not long before his retirement
as director of Central Intelligence, Walter Bedell Smith had written to the
adjutant general of the Air Force that Lansdale's service "has been superior
in every respect and of outstanding value to the Central Intelligence Agency
and the United States." See Lansdale 201 file. For what he had just achieved,
Lansdale was awarded the National Security Medal. He was told that it
was only the third one awarded; the first had gone to William Donovan
for his work with OSS; the second went to J. Edgar Hoover for his work

with the FBI; and Lansdale received the third for his Philippine efforts.
"Then they said you can't ever tell anybody what it's for and you can't
wear the medal." See Lansdale interview, 30 November 1984.

One of Lansdale's friends penned a poem in his honor entitled "Ode to
Ed Lansdale":

To the beautiful isles in the Philippine Sea
A mustachioed prophet did come.
He gave them a glance and fell in a trance
Assisted by Philippine rum.

His loftiest thought in a vision he caught
(To high things did this prophet aspire)
T'was the idea he sought and to many he taught
That the low should oughta be higher.

His words gained some credence wherever he went
Which, indeed, was so hard to explain
For some people claim he was not heaven sent
It was merely a cyst on his brain.

He prophesied wonders both cultured and wild
The miracles clicked on the hour
He was called a "Messiah" or "A natural child,"
Depending on who was in power.

There's now a new man in Malacañang
Who goes by the book as it's wrote
With his broad happy smile, he can ponder awhile
On results of a popular vote.

The old Apo now, with his offices shed
Has nightmares of fruitless travail
And the name that he screams from his Sears Roebuck bed
Is that of a Colonel Lansdale.

The mighty have fallen; the weak come to power
Ed's connection with this is not clear
But I know that if my name were Ike Eisenhower
I'd keep him the hell over here.

7. ON TO SAIGON

1. Lansdale interview, 12 November 1985.
2. Note, Bill Moore to Edward Lansdale, 22 May 1954, Vietnam Correspondence, Box 35, LP, THIWRP.
3. Quoted in Krepinevich, *The Army and Vietnam*, p. 18.
4. Gravel, *The Pentagon Papers*, I, 56.
5. Letter, Edward Lansdale to Helen, Ted, Pete, Dad, Phil, Ben, and Dave Lansdale, 13 February 1955, Correspondence 1955, Box 4, LP, THIWRP.
6. Gravel, *The Pentagon Papers*, I, 432–33.
7. "Foreign Relations of the United States: 1952–1954," Department of State, quoted in Prouty, "The CIA's Saigon Military Mission," p. 20.
8. Lansdale interview, 16 May 1984.

9. Prouty, "The CIA's Saigon Military Mission," p. 21.

10. Present at the meeting were the president's personal representative, General Walter Bedell Smith; Allen W. Dulles, director of Central Intelligence; John Foster Dulles, secretary of state; Philip Bonsal, assistant secretary of state for the Far East; Roger M. Kyes, deputy secretary of defense; Brigadier General C. H. Bonesteel III and General Graves B. Erskine for the Department of Defense; William Godell, office of the secretary of defense; Admiral Arthur S. Radford, chairman of the Joint Chiefs of Staff; and C. P. Cabell, George Aurell, and Edward Lansdale, representing CIA.

11. Gravel, *The Pentagon Papers*, I, 443–447.

12. Ibid. and Gibbons and McAdams interview; Lansdale interview, 16 May 1984; Prouty, "The CIA's Military Mission," p. 21; Prouty, *The Secret Team*, p. 193.

13. "So I went and actually tried to do my best to do what I thought I had done in the Philippines to help the Filipinos," Lansdale said. See Lansdale interview, 16 May 1984; Wise and Ross, *The Invisible Government*, p. 156; Lansdale, *In the Midst of Wars*, p. 127. See also Prados, *The Sky Would Fall*, pp. 47ff.

14. Letter, George Peabody, Jr., to Edward Lansdale, 2 February 1954, Correspondence, USDOD, OSD, Box 40, LP, THIWRP.

15. Gibbons and McAdams interview.

16. Ibid. and Lansdale interview, 16 May 1984.

17. "Her death affected me more than my father's [later] death did." See Lansdale interview, 17 December 1984.

18. Bowman, *The Vietnam War: An Almanac*, p. 35.

19. Lansdale, *In the Midst of Wars*, p. 128. And see letter, Edward Lansdale to Allen W. Dulles, 15 November 1961, Correspondence, USDOD, OSD, Box 37, LP, THIWRP.

20. Lansdale might have left the Philippines, but he never forgot Magsaysay or his other Filipino friends. His letters thereafter were reminiscent of the letters the Apostle Paul wrote to leaders of the young church in the first century. Both believed themselves to be elder statesmen. Their love for groups they had created was obvious. They were concerned that their executives remember and carry out their duties effectively and not forget how they achieved prominence or who their friends were. An example among many is a letter Lansdale wrote to Magsaysay in late 1955:

> Congratulations on the outcome of the elections. It was grand news for you, to know that you have the support of your people in what you have been trying to do for them. . . . [Y]ou are now setting about getting the men in place to help you do the job that's to be done, and I hope you keep right on with it. It's good to know that the Filipinos have not forgotten the hard lessons learned in 1953, and I know that this time you are going to remember some of the dedicated folks who helped you now when the going was rough. . . . I hope I will be able to visit Manila . . . and we can talk about some of these things. . . . All my warmest and best, as always.

Letter, Edward Lansdale to Ramón Magsaysay, 24 November 1955, Vietnam Correspondence, 1954–1956, Box 35, LP, THIWRP.

21. Lansdale interviews, 16 May 1984, 12 November 1984, 17 December 1984.

22. Lansdale interview, 17 December 1984, and Gravel, *The Pentagon Papers*, I, 575.

23. Joseph Baker interview, 23 June 1985.
24. In his autobiography, E. Howard Hunt describes Lansdale as "a brilliant but erratic CIA station chief in Saigon." See *Undercover*, p. 151. Hunt thus made the same mistake many other authors have, but Lansdale was never a station chief, in Saigon or elsewhere.
25. Gravel, *The Pentagon Papers*, I, 574. Lansdale found a way around the restrictive communications problem. To one of his team members, Victor Hugo, he said, "Anything really sensitive should come through whatever couriers can be arranged out of Clark [AFB]. However, if you can use just a bit of deception in your writing (Bo is a good one to learn it from), then you can send [information] through APO mail." See letter, Edward Lansdale to Victor Hugo, 10 August 1955, Vietnam Correspondence, 1954–1956, Box 35, LP, THIWRP.
26. Lansdale interview, 16 May 1984, and conversations with Joseph Baker, 17 May 1987, John Anderton, 22 May 1987, and Lucien Conein, 25 May 1987. It is little wonder that from the beginning of his Vietnam assignment, as one author has suggested, Lansdale "was up against formidable problems, many of which were the result of smoldering hostility." See Browne, *The New Face of War*, p. 345.
27. Lansdale, *In the Midst of Wars*, p. 127.
28. Smith, *Portrait of a Cold Warrior*, pp. 177–178.
29. Joseph Redick interview, 19 December 1984; Proculo L. Mojica interview, 28 July 1985; letter, Proculo L. Mojica to Pat Lansdale, 3 March 1987, Lansdale Personal Papers; letter, Proculo L. Mojica to Cecil Currey, 3 March 1987. When Mojica completed his tour of duty in December 1955, he was replaced by Amador Maik, another Filipino, who remained with Lansdale until Ed left Vietnam. Maik's days were "hotter" than Proc's had been, for Lansdale by then traveled through the countryside with former sect soldiers whose loyalties were still doubtful. When he was invited to a parley with sect members, Lansdale's usual order to Maik was "Lock and load." Maik carried a tommy gun. "If you see anything funny, start shooting," Lansdale told him. "Don't [wait to] ask me."
30. Lansdale, *In the Midst of Wars*, pp. 142, 145.
31. This view of the land and people of Vietnam has been drawn from Cincinnatus, *Self-Destruction*, pp. 3–5; Mecklin, *Mission in Torment*, pp. 74–78.
32. Lansdale, *In the Midst of Wars*, pp. 152–153, and Shaplen, *The Lost Revolution*, pp. 116–117.
33. Lansdale, *In the Midst of Wars*, pp. 140–150.
34. Other authors have stated that the SMM team consisted of ten, eleven, twelve, or fourteen men. If Bohannan in the Philippines is included in the tally, there were twenty members. Lansdale interviews, 18 and 19 December 1984; Joseph Redick interview, 19 December 1984; Joseph Baker interviews, 23 June 1985, 26 May 1987; Lucien Conein interviews, 24 June 1985, 27 May 1987. Also see Harrison, *The Endless War*, p. 211.
35. Lucien Conein interview, 24 June 1985, and letter, Edward Lansdale to Helen, Ted, Pete, Dad, Phil, Ben, and Dave Lansdale, 13 February 1955, Correspondence 1955, Box 4, LP, THIWRP.
36. Lansdale interview, 18 December 1984; Gravel, *The Pentagon Papers*, I, 576–577; Joseph Redick interview, 19 December 1984, and conversation with Lou Conein, 27 May 1987.

37. Gravel, *The Pentagon Papers*, I, 577–578, and Lansdale, *In the Midst of Wars*, pp. 136–137.

38. There has been some confusion about when Diem arrived. The Pentagon Papers declare that he landed in Vietnam on 7 July; Lansdale recalled that it was 25 June, as does Mecklin in his book *Mission in Torment*. Diem arrived in Saigon on 26 June 1954.

39. Diem called both Fishel and Ladejinsky to Vietnam in later years; Fishel moved into Doc Lap Palace as one of Diem's closest advisers.

40. It was not until some six months after the Geneva Conference ended that France finally transferred all the attributes of government to the Bao Dai/Diem administration. See Fall, *The Two Viet-Nams*, p. 244.

41. Emma Valeriano interview, 26 July 1985.

42. Henry Paschal interview, 29 July 1985.

43. Lansdale interview, 19 December 1984. Lansdale amused himself by teasing Diem for his bachelor status. "I asked him about girlfriends." There was one girl he had been very much interested in when he was younger. She had never married and lived in Hue. Since Diem visited that city occasionally to see his mother, Lansdale made him promise that he would call on the girl during his next trip there. "Take her for a boat ride down the Perfume River," Lansdale advised. When Diem returned, Lansdale asked if he had seen his old friend. "I went by and looked at her house," Diem replied, "but couldn't get up enough nerve to go to her door."

44. This portrayal of Diem has been drawn from many sources, including, in addition to the interviews already cited, Charlton and Moncrieff, *Many Reasons Why*, p. 43 and passim; Mecklin, *Mission in Torment*, pp. 29–51; Asprey, *War in the Shadows*, II, p. 825; Kahin and Lewis, *The United States in Vietnam*, pp. 66n, 67; Kalb and Abel, *Roots of Involvement*, pp. 94–97; Gettleman, *Vietnam*, pp. 248–251; Raskin and Fall, *The Viet-Nam Reader*, p. 72; Schlesinger, *A Thousand Days*, pp. 321, 538, 540.

45. Lansdale, *In the Midst of Wars*, pp. 156–157.

46. Shaplen, *The Lost Revolution*, p. 104, and Lucien Conein interview, 24 June 1985.

47. William E. Colby interview, 24 June 1985.

48. José Banzon interview, 30 July 1985.

49. When Lansdale left Vietnam at the end of 1956, much had been accomplished. Diem was securely in office, a constitution had been written and approved, elections held, labor unions formed, veterans' groups organized, health and self-help programs developed, and an army equipped and trained.

50. Joseph Johnson interview, 29 January 1986, and Joseph Baker interview, 23 June 1985.

51. Letter, Edward Lansdale to Robert Shaplen, 30 May 1965, Correspondence, USDOD, OSD, Box 40, LP, THIWRP.

52. Joseph Baker interview, 23 June 1985.

53. Emma Valeriano interview, 23 June 1985.

54. Michael Deutch interview, 24 June 1985.

55. Joseph Redick interview, 19 December 1984.

56. Lansdale interview, 16 May 1984.

57. Mecklin, *Mission in Torment*, p. 35.

58. Henry Paschal interview, 29 July 1985.

59. Letter, Edward Lansdale to Robert Shaplen, 30 May 1965, Correspondence, USDOD, OSD, Box 40, LP, THIWRP.
60. Lansdale, *In the Midst of Wars*, p. 165.

8. A NATION RISES

1. *Vietnam: A Historical Outline*, pp. 57, 151.
2. Lansdale interview, 16 May 1984.
3. Ibid.
4. Ibid.
5. Lansdale interview, 19 December 1984.
6. Lansdale interview, 16 May 1984.
7. Lansdale, *In the Midst of Wars*, p. 168.
8. "Lansdale Team's Report on Covert Saigon Mission in 1954 and 1955," Gravel, *The Pentagon Papers*, I, 577. Although not identified internally as such, the author of this report was Edward Lansdale. Hereafter cited as "Team Report."
9. Lansdale interview, 16 May 1984, and Team Report, p. 575.
10. Lansdale interview, 16 May 1984, and Team Report, pp. 578–579.
11. Team Report, p. 578.
12. Ibid., p. 582. One essay was supported by a front page editorial in Saigon's leading paper, operated by the Dragon Lady, "a fine Vietnamese girl" who was mistress of an anti-American French civilian. Lansdale noted, "We had helped her keep her paper from being closed by the government . . . and she found it profitable to heed our advice on the editorial content of her paper." See also letter, Rufus C. Phillips III to Cecil Currey, 16 November 1987.
13. Lansdale interview, 16 May 1984, and Scheer, *How the United States Got Involved in Vietnam*, pp. 26ff. A young Navy doctor, Tom Dooley, did much to popularize the American view that the northern government was a great evil from which the bulk of the population wanted to flee. His book *Deliver Us from Evil* did much to instill this belief in the minds of his readers. He served in Vietnam as part of the Navy rescue effort and witnessed much suffering as he worked among Catholic refugees; his anticommunism increased proportionately. His book should be read not as history but rather as a signpost of the cold war. By 1960 he was one of the nation's ten most admired citizens, and Diem — upon Lansdale's recommendation — gave Dooley Vietnam's highest award. He died from cancer not long thereafter.
14. Shaplen, *The Lost Revolution*, pp. 114–115, and Team Report, p. 576. One man who helped Lansdale in the refugee effort was Lieutenant Colonel William Rosson, who later served as a division commander, then as chief of staff and ultimately deputy to the commander of U.S. forces fighting in Vietnam. He later retired to Florida after completing his years of military service. He told Lansdale that one day, during the weeks he helped on refugee relocation, he stood in a soaking rain while supervising the unloading of a refugee ship. Someone handed him two babies to hold. "They . . . piddled all over my uniform," he said. His thoughts churned: "Goddamn Lansdale got me into this." He later said to Ed, "If you'd been there, I'd have shot you on the spot." Lansdale's response was quick. "It did you

good. You learned about people's warfare doing that.'' Lansdale interview,
16 May 1984.

Many years after those hectic days, former ambassador Donald Heath
attended a lecture Lansdale gave in New York before the Council on Foreign
Relations. In small talk following the address, Heath remarked, ''You get
aroused, Ed. You see something urgent where others look at it and think
it's something to be done next year. I thought you were going to ask all
of us in the room tonight to go out to Vietnam again with you. I'd have
found myself saying, 'Yeah, I'll go with you.' '' Lansdale interview, 16
May 1984.

15. Team Report, p. 576, and letter, Edward Lansdale to Joe Treater, 16 November 1975, Lansdale Personal Papers. One night in 1955 the folks at Operation
Brotherhood alerted Lansdale that Oscar Arellano was despondent, talking
about committing suicide. Lansdale picked him up and drove him to his
house on Duy Tan. Arellano felt that no one, particularly his family, understood or loved him. Ed plied him with whiskey and sat down at his typewriter
to write a long glowing eulogy about Oscar to his wife, Pommy. When
he finished, he handed the eulogy and a .38-caliber pistol to Arellano and
told him to read the paper before he shot himself. ''He read the letter,
wept whiskey tears over all the nice things I'd said about him, and handed
me back the gun.'' Letter, Edward Lansdale to Peter C. Richards, 30
November 1974, Richards Collection.

16. Emma Valeriano interview, 26 July 1985.

17. Lansdale, ''Military Psychological Operations,'' Part II.

18. Ibid. and Team Report, p. 579. ''To place Ed's psywar efforts against the
Viet-minh in a larger perspective,'' Rufe Phillips has written, ''he (we)
were trying to slow them down. Nobody knew whether they were going
to observe the accords or not, and as a civil war developed in the south,
the fear was that they might, with French acquiescence, simply take over
by force. Hence anything we could do to cut their morale and produce
internal problems for them seemed worthwhile. Also, when trying to undermine or slow down a communist movement, one of the most effective
tactics is to sow mistrust. Ed's tactics did that very effectively.'' Letter,
Rufus C. Phillips III to Cecil Currey, 16 November 1987.

19. Lansdale, In the Midst of Wars, p. 168. The figures for those who went
north are William Colby's. See letter, William E. Colby to Cecil Currey,
5 September 1987. Others put the estimate as high as 150,000.

20. Lansdale interview, 16 May 1984.

21. Lucien Conein interview, 24 June 1985, and Team Report, p. 578.

22. Memorandum, ''Resources for Unconventional Warfare, S.E. Asia,'' Edward Lansdale to Maxwell D. Taylor, undated [apparently July 1961],
Gravel, The Pentagon Papers, II, pp. 643–649, and conversations with
Lou Conein, 25 May 1987, and Joe Baker, 27 May 1987. Lansdale never
revealed where this training took place, referring to it only as ''the secret
training site,'' ''an overseas point,'' ''a secret training area,'' or ''some
offshore islands.'' See Team Report, p. 580, Gittinger interview, Lansdale
interview, 16 May 1984. Karnow, Vietnam, incorrectly identifies the training
site of the Binh and Hao units as Clark AFB (p. 220). That site in the
Philippines was run by Freedom Company (later Eastern Construction Company, Incorporated [ECCOI]) and located in a hidden valley in the far
ranges of Clark. Several groups of southern farmers and militia approached

Lansdale and informed him that they were migrating from Vietnam to Madagascar or elsewhere in hopes of finding a more quiet life. They were afraid of a coming Viet Minh takeover and believed they were ill prepared to resist. Lansdale offered to help train them in appropriate techniques of resistance. Bohannan and John C. Wachtell thereupon contracted with Freedom Company to establish a basic counterguerrilla training course in the Philippines and it was located on the Clark AFB reservation.

23. Team Report, p. 578.
24. Ibid. and Gittinger interview.
25. Team Report, p. 577.
26. Ibid., p. 582.
27. Ibid., p. 583.
28. Gittinger interview.
29. Team Report, p. 583.
30. Ibid.
31. Ibid.
32. Ibid.
33. Lucien Conein interview, 24 June 1985.
34. Gittinger interview.
35. Lucien Conein interview, 24 June 1985.
36. Ibid.
37. Team Report, p. 579.
38. Ibid. And see Lucien Conein interview, 24 June 1985.
39. Lucien Conein interview, 24 June 1985.
40. In my interview with William E. Colby, 24 June 1985, he talked about those days in Saigon. "Where Lansdale really put his foot in it was with some of these fun-and-games dirty tricks. . . . Those of us who have been in that kind of operation know that those things really are . . . a bloody nuisance. Once in a while they kind of work. . . . His real contribution was his positive thinking. . . . People began to identify with him, rallying, gathering strength psychologically or politically. . . . But blowing up streetcars doesn't help at all."
41. Gittinger interview.
42. José Banzon interview, 30 July 1985.
43. Lansdale, *In the Midst of Wars*, p. 213.
44. Memorandum, Edward Lansdale to Ray Male, 14 April 1967, SLO, USE, Day File, April 1967, Box 57, LP, THIWRP.
45. Lansdale, *In the Midst of Wars*, p. 214.
46. Memorandum, "Resources for Unconventional Warfare" (see note 22).
47. Memorandum, Edward Lansdale to Ray Male (see note 44).
48. Team Report, p. 580.
49. Memorandum, Edward Lansdale to Ray Male (see note 44).
50. Subject interview.
51. Lansdale, *In the Midst of Wars*, p. 214, and memorandum, Edward Lansdale to Ray Male (see note 44).
52. Memorandum, "Resources for Unconventional Warfare," p. 647 (see note 22).
53. Ibid., p. 648.
54. Lansdale interview, 17 December 1984.
55. Memorandum, "Resources for Unconventional Warfare," p. 648 (see note 22).

56. Lansdale, *In the Midst of Wars*, p. 215.
57. Edmundo Navarro interview, 25 July 1985.
58. Shaplen, *The Lost Revolution*, p. 115.
59. Team Report, p. 578.
60. Ibid. See also letter, Rufus C. Phillips III to Cecil Currey, 16 November 1987.
61. While serving in Vietnam, Colonel Napoleon Valeriano met Emma Benitez, the wife of a prominent Filipino and a nurse working with Operation Brotherhood, whom he later married.
62. Team Report, p. 582.
63. Ibid., pp. 577–578.
64. Lansdale, *In the Midst of Wars*, p. 172.
65. Lansdale interview, 17 May 1984.
66. Lansdale, *In the Midst of Wars*, pp. 189ff.
67. Team Report, p. 580.
68. Lansdale interview, 17 December 1984.
69. Letter, Edward Lansdale to Robert Shaplen, 30 May 1965, Corrrespondence, USDOD, OSD, Box 40, LP, THIWRP.
70. Gittinger interview; Joseph Baker interview, 23 June 1985; Scheer, *How the United States Got Involved in Vietnam*, pp. 23ff.
71. Gittinger interview.
72. Team Report, p. 580, and Shaplen, *The Lost Revolution*, p. 119.
73. Joseph Redick interview, 19 December 1984; Team Report, pp. 581–582; Shaplen, *The Lost Revolution*, p. 119.
74. Lansdale, *In the Midst of Wars*, p. 181.
75. Two French-language sources reveal that Lansdale's feelings about the French were by no means well hidden. "De fait le colonel Lansdale était connu pour ses sentiments francophobes." Pierre Rocolle, *Pourquoi Dien Bien Phu?*, p. 446n. "Le nom du colonel Lansdale domine cette période, comme celui d'un 'Lawrence d'Indochine' détaché auprès de Diem par la Central Intelligence Agency. Acheter le soutien des sectes, s'assurer le contrôle de l'armée nationale, sont les premières préoccupations du pouvoir et de ses influents amis." George Chaffard, *Indochine: Dix ans d'indépendance*, p. 53.
76. Shaplen, *The Lost Revolution*, pp. 110–120.
77. Gittinger interview.
78. Letter, Edward Lansdale to Helen Lansdale, 13 February 1955, Correspondence 1955, Box 4, LP, THIWRP.
79. Lansdale, *In the Midst of Wars*, pp. 218, 224, 318, and passim.
80. Shaplen, *The Lost Revolution*, p. 117.
81. Gravel, *The Pentagon Papers*, I, 278, and Fall, *The Two Viet-Nams*, pp. 245–246. Rufus Phillips has argued that no "payoffs" were ever made. "What really bothers me is that this is the one thing that will be picked up out of your book, amplified and used by Ed's detractors to discredit his career and what he stood for. Neither Joe [Redick] nor I have ever seen any evidence to support this while we were with Ed in Saigon, or later with the CIA, or afterwards." Letter, Rufus C. Phillips III to Cecil Currey, 16 November 1987.
82. Letter, Edward Lansdale to Gregory C. Lavin, 20 March 1973, Lansdale Personal Papers.

83. Shaplen, *The Lost Revolution,* p. 118.
84. Letter, Edward Lansdale to Robert Shaplen, 30 May 1965, Correspondence, USDOD, OSD, Box 40, LP, THIWRP.
85. Ibid.
86. Lansdale interview, 16 May 1984.
87. Gravel, *The Pentagon Papers,* I, p. 233.
88. Ibid., pp. 233–234.
89. Ibid., pp. 183, 234, 303.
90. Joseph Baker interview, 23 June 1985.
91. Lansdale listed some of his activities: dodging Bay Vien's moves to kidnap him, continuing supervision of a number of SMM projects, driving through firefights in Saigon and Cholon to confer with O'Daniel at MAAG, followed by a trip back to Cholon to seek logistical support for pacification work in Quang Ngai, quieting fears of some newcomers to his team who were "pop-eyed at the burning cars and dead bodies strewn around," arranging the surrender of one Binh Xuyen battalion to trigger-happy Diem supporters, getting ragged by French officers at TRIM as a murderer of civilians who hid under his bed at the sound of gunfire, and conferring with U.S. officials. See letter, Edward Lansdale to Robert Shaplen, 30 May 1965, Correspondence, USDOD, OSD, Box 40, LP, THIWRP.
92. "One Memory about Boh," Edward Lansdale to Dorothy Bohannan, 18 November 1982, Lansdale Personal Papers.
93. Letter, Edward Lansdale to Robert Shaplen, 30 May 1965, Correspondence, USDOD, OSD, Box 40, LP, THIWRP.
94. Lansdale 201 file.
95. The description of the series of events in April 1955 has been drawn from Lansdale, *In the Midst of Wars,* pp. 282–311; Shaplen, *The Lost Revolution,* pp. 121–126; Wise and Ross, *The Invisible Government,* pp. 156–157; and Doyle, Lipsman, and Weiss, *Passing the Torch,* pp. 126–129.
96. Team Report, p. 581.
97. Dawson, *55 Days,* p. 19.
98. Corson, *The Betrayal,* p. 38.
99. Memorandum, John Foster Dulles to Dwight D. Eisenhower, 7 June 1955, June 1955 File, Box 12, Dulles Papers.
100. Letter, Edward Lansdale to Ernest K. Lindsey, 5 August 1955, Correspondence, Box 35, LP, THIWRP.
101. Memorandum, John Foster Dulles to Dwight D. Eisenhower, 26 July 1955, Chronological Series, Box 12, Dulles Papers.
102. Letter, Edward Lansdale to Editor, *Washington Post,* 16 August 1971, Correspondence, Box 6, LP, THIWRP; Lansdale, *In the Midst of Wars,* pp. 313–340; Bowman, *The Vietnam War,* p. 43; Marchetti and Marks, *The CIA and the Cult of Intelligence,* p. 28.
103. Fall, *The Two Viet-Nams,* pp. 246–247.
104. Lansdale, *In the Midst of Wars,* p. 342.
105. Ibid., pp. 342–343; Stavins, Barnet, and Raskin, *Washington Plans an Aggressive War,* pp. 20–21.
106. Stavins, Barnet, and Raskin, *Washington Plans an Aggressive War,* 11.
107. Lansdale interview, 16 May 1985. Overwork, lack of proper eating habits, and neglect caused Lansdale to have trouble with his teeth in late 1955 and early 1956. He told Helen of his problem while in Washington. She

remained concerned for some time and, drawing upon her Christian Science faith, wrote him after his return to Vietnam: "To help you with your teeth think of 'acknowledgement of the perfection of the infinite Unseen' — 'the source and substance of all true being.' " See letter, Helen Lansdale to Edward Lansdale, 23 January 1956, Correspondence, Box 4, LP, THIWRP.

108. Taylor, *Snow Job,* p. 13. Again Rufe Phillips has taken exception. "[Y]ou state that by refusing Ed's advice, Diem made it inevitable that a renewed insurgency would be mounted. We know from Communist books and statements, as well as captured documents, that it was inevitable. Diem did not cause it; his failure to follow Ed's political advice [only] gave the Communists more to exploit and weakened his (Diem's) own political base." Letter, Rufus C. Phillips III to Cecil Currey, 16 November 1987.

109. Wise and Ross, *The Invisible Government,* p. 158.

110. Don, *Our Endless War,* pp. 60–61.

111. Lansdale, *In the Midst of Wars,* p. 344.

112. Ibid., pp. 344–345.

113. Stavins, Barnet, and Raskin, *Washington Plans an Aggressive War,* pp. 20–21. Once again, Rufe Phillips disagrees. "[Y]ou quote a very dubious source that 70% of Diem's people were hostile or indifferent," he wrote. "By 62–63 when I returned as Assistant Director in the AID Mission, our estimate was about 40% favorable, 40% undecided or indifferent and about 20% hostile." Letter, Rufus C. Phillips III to Cecil Currey, 16 November 1987. His concern is misplaced. AID was no more accurate in its use of statistics than were other American bureaucracies operating in Vietnam, and AID invariably erred on the side of optimism. If even AID was forced to report that no more than 40 percent of the population could be counted on, it is significant that the agency's figures and those used in this text differ by only 10 percent, and I stand by what I have written.

114. Thus there was a second presidential election in 1961, which Diem won by 88 percent of the votes cast. The many governments that followed each other so rapidly after Diem's murder in 1963 did so without any base in the electorate. In 1966 elected delegates wrote a new constitution under which were held the presidential and legislative elections of 1967. In those elections, Nguyen Van Thieu was elected president for a four-year term. See Edward Lansdale to Editor, *Washington Post,* 16 August 1971.

115. Lansdale interview, 16 May 1984.

9. BRIGHT STAR SHINING

1. Letter, Edward Lansdale to C.T.R. Bohannan, 13 November 1956, Bohannan Collection.

2. Gittinger interview.

3. Letter, Edward Lansdale to C.T.R. Bohannan, 8 November 1956, Bohannan Collection. Lansdale's "official" assignments were inevitably covers for his real activities. Throughout most of his time in the Philippines and all of the years in Vietnam, Lansdale remained assigned to Headquarters, 1007 Air Intelligence Squadron. His dates of assignment there ran from 10 Septem-

ber 1951 to 28 February 1957. On 1 March 1957 he was finally transferred to Headquarters, United States Air Force, and from 15 March to 31 May 1957 he served as a "Politico-Military Affairs Officer," Intelligence Branch, Policy Division, Headquarters, United States Air Force. See Lansdale 201 file.

4. Letter, Edward Lansdale to C.T.R. Bohannan, 23 January 1957, Bohannan Collection.
5. Ibid. and Gittinger interview.
6. Ibid.
7. Ibid.
8. Letter, Edward Lansdale to C.T.R. Bohannan, 16 April 1957, Bohannan Collection.
9. Letter, Bert Fraleigh to "Dear Folks," 24–28 March 1957, USDOD, OSD, Box 37, LP, THIWRP.
10. Memorandum, George Peabody to Edward Lansdale and Napoleon Valeriano, 26 March 1957, Correspondence, USDOD, OSD, Box 40, LP, THIWRP.
11. Letter, Edward Lansdale to C.T.R. Bohannan, 28 March 1957, Bohannan Collection.
12. Letter, Edward Lansdale to C.T.R. Bohannan, 19 March 1957, Bohannan Collection.
13. Letter, Edward Lansdale to C.T.R. Bohannan, 16 April 1957, Bohannan Collection.
14. Letter, Edward Lansdale to C.T.R. Bohannan, 19 March 1957, Bohannan Collection.
15. Gittinger interview.
16. Letter, Edward Lansdale to C.T.R. Bohannan, 23 January 1957, Bohannan Collection. Lansdale was so bored those first weeks on his new job that he signed up for a few hours of schoolwork to fill his spare hours. Between 26 and 29 March he completed sixteen credits of an eighteen credit hour course, "Formulation and Development of Foreign Policy" at the Foreign Service Institute in Washington. It was the only school he attended except when he took the course years before at Craig AFB in Selma, Alabama. See Lansdale 201 file.
17. William E. Colby interview, 24 June 1985.
18. Lansdale interview, 17 December 1984, and Gittinger interview.
19. Ibid.
20. Lansdale 201 file and Lansdale interview, 17 December 1984. The assistant to the secretary of defense for special operations, who concurrently was given the title director, Office of Special Operations, was appointed by the secretary of defense on 15 July 1953. His duties and the responsibilities of OSO were outlined in an unclassified memo of that date from Deputy Secretary of Defense Roger Keyes. The memo appointed General Graves B. Erskine, USMC (Ret.), both as assistant to the secretary and as director of OSO. The memo abolished the Office of Psychological Policy in OSD and assigned all its psywar and international information activities to the new OSO, which was further detailed to advise the secretary of defense and monitor policy on all Defense intelligence activities. This latter included membership on USIB to represent the secretary of defense and to supervise Army, Navy, Air Force, Joint Chiefs, and NSA intelligence activities.

See an undated memorandum written by Edward Lansdale entitled "OSO/OSD," Lansdale Personal Papers.

21. Lansdale interview, 30 November 1984.
22. Ibid.
23. Ibid.
24. Lansdale interviews, 12 November 1984, 17 December 1984.
25. Gittinger interview.
26. Ibid. and Lansdale interview, 30 November 1984.
27. Lansdale interview, 30 November 1984.
28. Lansdale interviews, 30 November 1984, 17 December 1984.
29. Lansdale interview, 30 November 1984.
30. Lansdale interview, 17 December 1984.
31. Kirkpatrick, *The U.S. Intelligence Community,* pp. 32–39.
32. Ibid. and Lansdale interview, 17 December 1984. The National Security Agency, set up in 1952 as a separate agency within the Department of Defense, fell under the direction, authority, and control of the secretary of defense. It provided special technical functions to support intelligence operations, usually involving communications and electronic intelligence. President Kennedy added the Defense Intelligence Agency to USIB and, in 1971, President Richard Nixon named the Treasury Department to membership on the board.
33. Lansdale 201 file.
34. Letter, Edward Lansdale to C.T.R. Bohannan, 8 May 1957, Bohannan Collection.
35. Ibid.
36. Prouty's later book, *The Secret Team: The CIA and Its Allies in Control of the United States and the World,* gives an indication of his view of Company activities. He did not hold Lansdale in high esteem. In turn, Lansdale had his own view of Prouty. "I continue to be surprised," Lansdale once wrote, "to find Fletcher Prouty quoted as an authority. He was my 'cross to bear' before Dan Ellsberg came along. Fletch is the one who blandly told the London Times that I'd invented the Huk Rebellion, hired a few actors in Manila, bussed them out to Pampanga, and staged the whole thing as press agentry to get RM [Magsaysay] elected. He was a good pilot of prop-driven aircraft, but had such a heavy dose of paranoia about CIA when he was on my staff that I kicked him back to the Air Force. He was one of those who thought I was secretly running the Agency from the Pentagon, despite all the proof otherwise." He elsewhere commented on Prouty's "whacky imagination" and lamented that "I sure pick 'em, huh?" See letters, Edward Lansdale to C.T.R. Bohannan, 2 March, 2 July 1975, Bohannan Collection.
37. Letter, Edward Lansdale to Robert W. Komer, 30 May 1971, and accompanying notes, and letter, Komer to Lansdale, 1 June 1971, Correspondence, Box 3, LP, THIWRP. And see Lansdale interview, 30 November 1984. Elsewhere Lansdale noted, "I managed to get unconventional officers assigned to OSO's staff on TDY [temporary duty] and had them write new UW [unconventional warfare] policies for their services, which later were adopted. For example, Army's Special Forces adopted their counterinsurgency doctrine at the close of the Eisenhower Administration, in 1960, based on work in OSO. As another example, CINCPAC agreed to riverine

warfare in Viet Nam, with fiberglass river boats proposed by OSO early in 1960 and used on the Mekong that year by the Vietnamese. Also, the first shipment of rifles that later became the M.16 was from OSO in 1960 to the defenders of Binh Hung in Camau.'' See memorandum, "OSO/ OSD,'' Lansdale Personal Papers.

38. Lansdale interview, 15 February 1984.
39. Letter, Edward Lansdale to Albert and Marjorie Ravenholt, 14 May 1968, Correspondence, USDOD, OSD, Box 40, LP, THIWRP.
40. Letter, Joe Tinio to Edward Lansdale, 8 November 1956, Box 35, LP, THIWRP.
41. Letter, Pat Kelly to Edward Lansdale, 9 June 1958, Correspondence, US-DOD, OSD, Box 38, LP, THIWRP.
42. Letter, John C. "Jack" Wachtell to Edward Lansdale, 28 May 1960, Correspondence, USDOD, OSD, Box 41, LP, THIWRP.
43. Letter, Edward Lansdale to James H. Douglas, Jr., 20 January 1963, Correspondence, USDOD, OSD, Box 37, LP, THIWRP.
44. Letter, Edward Lansdale to James H. Douglas, Jr., 12 February 1963, Correspondence, USDOD, OSD, Box 37, LP, THIWRP.
45. Letter, Edward Lansdale to Edward C. Bursk, Jr., 4 May 1966, Correspondence, General, SLO, USE, Saigon, April 1966, Box 51, LP, THIWRP.
46. Letter, Edward Lansdale to Henry L. Miller, SLO, USE, Saigon, Box 54, LP, THIWRP.
47. Letter, Albert Ravenholt to Edward Lansdale, 27 June 1959, Correspondence, USDOD, OSD, Box41, LP, THIWRP.
48. Letter, Pat Kelly to Edward Lansdale, 26 April 1963, Correspondence, USDOD, OSD, Box 38, LP, THIWRP.
49. Letter, Pat Kelly to Edward Lansdale, 18 April 1967, Correspondence, USDOD, OSD, Box 38, LP, THIWRP.
50. Letter, Edward Lansdale to Henry Miller, 26 September 1967, SLO, USE, Saigon, Box 54, LP, THIWRP.
51. See Daniel V. James File, 1959–1963, Correspondence, USDOD, OSD, Box 38, LP, THIWRP.
52. Letters, Edward Lansdale to Samuel T. Williams, 28 October 1957, 13 February 1958, Correspondence, USDOD, OSD, Box 42, LP, THIWRP.
53. Letter, Edward Lansdale to Robert W. Komer, 30 May 1971, and accompanying notes, and Komer to Lansdale, 1 June 1971, Correspondence, Box 3, LP, THIWRP.
54. Letter, Wesley R. Fishel to Edward Lansdale, 19 November 1957, Correspondence, USDOD, OSD, Box 37, LP, THIWRP. And see letter, Oscar Arellano to C.T.R. Bohannan, 23 November 1959, Box 17, Bohannan Papers.
55. Lansdale, memorandum, "Thoughts on China," 23 November 1959, US-DOD, OSD, Box 42, LP, THIWRP, and letter, Edward Lansdale to Richard Reuter, 2 July 1959, USDOD, OSD, Box 48, LP, THIWRP.
56. Graham Greene, *The Quiet American.* See Lansdale interview, 16 May 1984; Herbert Mitgang, "The Prophetic Quiet American," *New York Times Book Review* (8 June 1975); Edward F. Palm, "Novels of Vietnam and the Uses of War Literature," *Marine Corps Gazette* (November 1986), pp. 91–99; Critchfield, *The Long Charade,* pp. 164–170, and *London Telegraph,* 26 February 1987.

57. For Lansdale's comment, see letter, Edward Lansdale to Peter McInerney, 4 September 1980, Lansdale Personal Papers. For reviews, see *Christian Century*, 1 August 1956; *Christian Science Monitor*, 22 March 1956; *New York Herald Tribune*, 11 March 1956.

58. Lederer and Burdick, *The Ugly American*. For Lansdale's comments, see letter, Edward Lansdale to Peter McInerney, 4 September 1980, Lansdale Personal Papers. The effect of the publication of that book has been drawn from Iversen, "The Ugly American: A Bestseller Re-Examined." Also see Lansdale interview, 15 February 1984.

59. Iversen, "The Ugly American: A Bestseller Re-Examined."

60. See files of the Draper Committee, Anderson Subcommittee, Southeast Asia, USDOD, OSD, Box 43, LP, THIWRP. Hereafter cited as "Draper/ Anderson files." Members of the Draper Committee included William H. Draper, Jr., chairman, Dillon Anderson, Alfred M. Gruenther, John J. McCloy, Joseph T. McNarney, Joseph M. Dodge, Marx Leva, Arthur W. Radford, and James E. Webb. Working members of the Anderson Subcommittee included Dillon Anderson, chairman; retired General J. Lawton Collins (procedures called for the subcommittee to have one retired officer of flag rank); Colonel Edward G. Lansdale, office of the secretary of defense; Charles Wolf, Jr., Rand Corporation; Colonel Victor W. Alden, CINCPAC staff; Staff Sergeant Howard E. Jeannette, USAF, NATO Standing Group; and Joseph P. Redick, U.S. embassy, Tokyo, who worked as translator. Major Vernon J. Mouton was commander of the aircraft in which the men traveled. Kenneth Young is also listed in the files as a "consultant" but may not actually have gone along on the trip. See "People Visited, 23 January–24 February 1959," Draper/Anderson files, and Office Memorandum, Frank [?] to C.T.R. Bohannan, 26 January 1959, Box 17, Bohannan Papers.

61. Letter, Edward Lansdale to C.T.R. Bohannan, 20 January 1959, Bohannan Collection.

62. Letter, Edward Lansdale to Ngo Dinh Diem, 6 January 1959, Correspondence, USDOD, OSD, Box 42, LP, THIWRP.

63. "Thought Outline on the Development of Leadership Through MAP" [draft] by Edward Lansdale, undated, Draper/Anderson files, LP, THIWRP.

64. "People Visited by Anderson Subcommittee," Draper/Anderson files, LP, THIWRP.

65. Letter, Wesley R. Fishel to Edward Lansdale, 18 February 1959, Draper/ Anderson files, LP, THIWRP.

66. For the time schedule and itinerary of the Anderson subcommittee, see visa requests, various notes, memoranda to State Department Passport Division, tentative and actual itineraries, and so forth in Draper/Anderson files, LP, THIWRP.

67. Sihanouk and Burchett, *My War with the CIA*, pp. 102, 105, 107–108.

68. Whatever Lansdale did or did not do in 1959, Prince Sihanouk certainly viewed him as a threat. A film that Sihanouk later produced and starred in, *Shadow over Angkor*, centered on the Dap Chhuon plot in which an Army general agreed to lead a CIA plot to overthrow the Sihanouk government. The claims are curious ones.

69. In addition to meeting with government and military officials, subcommittee members also spoke with a good number of Americans holding powerful

positions in Asia: R. M. Henry, manager in Manila of the local branch of First National City Bank of New York; J. L. Manning, president of the Manila Trading and Supply Company; Earl Carroll, president of Philippine-American Life Insurance Company; B. S. Huie, general manager of the Luzon Stevedoring Company; John Oppenheimer, Southwest Pacific director for Pan American Airways. In Thailand they met with Louis Mulker of the Bank of America, G. H. Thomas of Caltex, and others. While in Burma, they spoke with Louis J. Walinski of Robert Nathan Associates. One wonders what expertise such folk had in military assistance programs or what their experience had been working in military civic action projects.

Wherever they traveled in Southeast Asia, Lansdale suggested to military officers that they visit Vietnam. There they could see how Diem's government had handled a number of civic action problems similar to their own. Many took his advice. See "People Visited by Anderson Subcommittee," Draper/Anderson files, LP, THIWRP, and letter, Edward Lansdale to Ngo Dinh Diem, 2 April 1959, Correspondence, USDOD, OSD, Box 42, LP, THIWRP.

70. The Department of State at first refused my Freedom of Information requests regarding my research; to release material about Lansdale would "not be in the public interest." I appealed and was finally told that State would indeed search its records, but I would have to pay for the time involved as well as for any duplicating costs. Once again I appealed and was finally told I would have to pay only duplicating costs. *Three* years later, as this is being written, I have yet to receive the first photocopy, although a form letter from State dated 25 February 1987 informs me that the search has been completed and my "case is currently in queue for administrative processing."

The story began in reverse fashion at Central Intelligence. The spokesman there quickly informed me that CIA would be glad to cooperate and would waive any fees. Six months later, I was told they had changed their minds. With such "cooperation," the Freedom of Information Act is sidestepped.

71. Lansdale, memorandum, "Civic Activities of the Military, Southeast Asia," 13 March 1959. Copy in author's possession.

72. "Highlights of the Findings on Southeast Asia," Draper/Anderson files, LP, THIWRP.

73. Letter, Edward Lansdale to Albert and Marjorie Ravenholt, 19 March 1959, Correspondence, USDOD, OSD, Box 42, LP, THIWRP.

74. Letter, Wolf Ladejinsky to Edward Lansdale, 22 April 1959, Correspondence, USDOD, OSD, Box 3, LP, THIWRP.

75. Note, Colonel Robert F. Evans, assistant to the director, Far East Region, Office of the Secretary of Defense, to Edward Lansdale, 24 April 1959, Draper/Anderson files, LP, THIWRP.

76. Letter, Karl G. Harr, Jr., to John N. Irwin II, 4 May 1959, S.E. Asia File, Box 6, Dulles Papers.

77. Memorandum, "Trip Report on Southeast Asia by Colonel Lansdale," John N. Irwin to Christian A. Herter et al., Operations Coordinating Board papers, Box 6, Dulles Papers.

78. Letter, Edward Lansdale to Ngo Dinh Diem, 2 April 1959, Correspondence, USDOD, OSD, Box 42, LP, THIWRP.

79. Wyden, *Bay of Pigs,* pp. 19ff.

80. Fain, Plant, and Milloy, *The Intelligence Community,* p. 802, and Wyden, *Bay of Pigs,* pp. 23–24.
81. Permanent members of the Operations Coordinating Board called their group by many names; it later became the 54/12 Group (because covert operations were conducted under the authority of National Security Directive NSC 5412/2), the Special Group, the 303 Group, the Forty Committee, or, sometimes, the Operations Advisory Group. By whatever name, it was charged with evaluating recommended covert programs to the president for his approval or disapproval. Its permanent members consisted of a deputy undersecretary of state, the deputy secretary of defense, the director of Central Intelligence, and the special assistant to the president for national security affairs. Perhaps one of the most secret operating units of government, its existence remained classified until the early 1970s. See Agee, *Inside the Company,* p. 35, and Wyden, *Bay of Pigs,* p. 24n.
82. Wyden, *Bay of Pigs,* pp. 24–25, and Gittinger interview.
83. Wyden, *Bay of Pigs,* p. 25.
84. Ibid., pp. 31–32 and passim.
85. Fain, Plant, and Milloy, *The Intelligence Community,* p. 803.
86. Robert Welch founded the John Birch Society, served as editor of its news organ, *The American Opinion,* and wrote the column "Scoreboard" in which this appeared in the issue of July–August 1961. See clippings, Box 26, LP, THIWRP.
87. Letter, Wesley Fishel to Edward Lansdale, 26 May 1960, Correspondence, US DOD, OSD, Box 37, LP, THIWRP.
88. Letter, Kenneth T. Young, Jr., to Edward Lansdale, 23 May 1960, Box 42, LP, THIWRP.
89. Many examples of this note may be found in Correspondence, Box 40, LP, THIWRP.
90. Smith, *Portrait of a Cold Warrior,* p. 342, and Wyden, *Bay of Pigs,* p. 35 and passim.
91. Wyden, *Bay of Pigs,* pp. 65–67.
92. Ibid., p. 69.
93. Ibid., pp. 71–72. See also letter, James H. Douglas to Edward Lansdale, 14 June 1976, and its accompanying memorandum, James H. Douglas to Peter Wyden, 10 May 1976, Lansdale Personal Papers.
94. Wyden, *Bay of Pigs,* p. 72.
95. Military History lecture. Lansdale commented further that honest talk was seldom allowed in such situations, a fact he found to be passing strange. He was present on several occasions when top Pentagon brass had meetings with a president. "They would talk very big [while at their offices] in the Pentagon. Then the Chairman [of the Joint Chiefs] would talk with the President or National Security Council people or in Cabinet meetings." When talking to the president, Lansdale saw the chairman of the Joint Chiefs responding with simple "nossirs" or "yessirs," crisply polite and correct, offering no opinions of his own. "Then he would go back [to the Pentagon] and report to the other chiefs: 'This is what the President wants us to do.' 'But Chief, didn't you tell him what we had discussed?' And he would respond, 'I did, but this is his decision.' Well, he *hadn't!* It used to get them [upset] when I'd be present at some of those meetings and the President asked me [for an opinion]. I'd tell him [what I believed]

point-blank. They'd come to me [later] in great shock. 'You said no to the President. You said what he wanted couldn't be done.' " Lansdale's answer was a plain one, harmonious with his temperament and personality. "This is what any citizen has to do when he gets [before] the top guy. [The President] is not an expert. He figures that I am, or at least have some knowledge [of the problem under discussion]. This is the time to be honest, before people go out and get killed trying to do the right thing for the United States!"

96. Wyden, *Bay of Pigs,* pp. 72–73; Lansdale interview, 17 December 1984, and Military History lecture.

97. Military History lecture. Shortly after the Bay of Pigs, an inquiry was held into the incident. When CIA tried to share the blame, Lansdale was incensed. He told someone at the Agency, "You sons of bitches. I'd make you stand there and take the full load [of responsibility] for the thing. If you won't stand up, the hell with you." Some suggested that Lansdale's planning had been faulty. "Hey!" he responded. "I was out of your hair by then. That's why I went out to Vietnam. I wasn't in the country when you guys were making all these decisions. My friends, I got out . . . for a reason. I knew it was going to fail. You are the guys with egg on your face and you're going to wipe it off and say somebody else has it on his face. You are going to point to me. I wasn't even present. [Furthermore] I wrote a report when [this] was planned. [I] insisted on bringing in the Joint Staff . . . to provide military input." Lansdale complained that CIA never understood it had insufficient resources to run an amphibious operation. "It was too ambitious for CIA. There were some military men in CIA whose idea it was, but none were experienced in amphibian [*sic*] operations. Someone will write a book eventually and say I was the guy who secretly tipped off Castro!" See Lansdale interviews, 16 May 1984, 17 December 1984. While Dulles may have wished Lansdale would go away, others disagreed. Lansdale received a letter in which the writer insisted that "all this country needs to win the Cold War is about thirty Ed Lansdales." Letter, W. C. Bullock to Edward Lansdale, 8 November 1960, Correspondence, USDOD, OSD, Box 37, LP, THIWRP.

10. SWALLOWS AND PIGS

1. Lansdale interviews, 16 May 1984, 17 December 1984.
2. Ibid.
3. Cable, William Trimble to Secretary of State, 28 November 1960, "Lansdale's Trip, January 1961," USDOD, OSD, Box 49, LP, THIWRP.
4. Cable, U. Alexis Johnson to Secretary of State, 28 November 1960, "Lansdale's Trip, January 1961," USDOD, OSD, Box 49, LP, THIWRP.
5. Cables, Rothwell H. Brown to Secretary of State, 26 and 29 November 1960, "Lansdale's Trip, January 1961," USDOD, OSD, Box 49, LP, THIWRP. It is unclear exactly what Brown meant by his statement "would not wish press for his visit this region." Did he mean he would not want *to* press, that is, to urge Lansdale to stop in Laos? Or did he mean he would not want press *coverage* of the visit? Some of Lansdale's friends were unenthusiastic about Brown. Retired Admiral Felix B. Stump wrote

to Lansdale a few weeks later, "I am sure you know the story on Brown in Vientienne [*sic*]. Why is he still there?" Letter, Felix B. Stump to Edward Lansdale, 26 January 1961, USDOD, OSD, Box 41, LP, THIWRP.

6. Cable, Hickerson to Secretary of State, 28 November 1960, USDOD, OSD, Box 41, LP, THIWRP.

7. Durbrow's view is quoted in letter, J. Graham Parsons to Edward Lansdale, 8 December 1960, USDOD, OSD, Box 41, LP, THIWRP.

8. Ibid.

9. Letters, Felix B. Stump to Edward Lansdale, 23 May 1960, to John M. Steeves, 23 May 1960, to Admiral Harry D. Felt, 23 May 1960, USDOD, OSD, Box 41, LP, THIWRP.

10. Cable, Admiral Harry D. Felt to Edward Lansdale, undated; information copy to James H. Douglas, USDOD, OSD, Box 41, LP, THIWRP.

11. Memorandum, Edward Lansdale to James H. Douglas, 14 December 1960, USDOD, OSD, Box 49, LP, THIWRP.

12. Letter, Edward Lansdale to John W. O'Daniel, 23 December 1960, "Lansdale's Trip, January 1961," USDOD, OSD, Box 49, LP, THIWRP.

13. Cable, Edward Lansdale to General Lionell McGarr, 23 December 1960, USDOD, OSD, Box 41, LP, THIWRP.

14. Drinnon, *Facing West,* p. 432. Prouty describes the gift not as a desk but as a desk *set;* see *The Secret Team,* p. 60. For travel arrangements, see Travel File, USDOD, OSD, Box 47, LP, THIWRP, and Cable, Edward Lansdale to Thomas S. Gates and James H. Douglas, 14 January 1961, "Lansdale's Trip, January 1961," USDOD, OSD, Box 49, LP, THIWRP.

15. Cable, Hickerson to Secretary of State, 3 January 1961, "Lansdale's Trip, January 1961," USDOD, OSD, Box 49, LP, THIWRP.

16. Cable, William Trimble to Secretary of State, 3 January 1961, "Lansdale's Trip, January 1961," USDOD, OSD, Box 49, LP, THIWRP.

17. Memoranda, Edward Lansdale to Graves B. Erskine, 6 January 1961, and Elbridge Durbrow to Secretary of State, 7 January 1961, "Lansdale's Trip, January 1961," USDOD, OSD, Box 49, LP, THIWRP. See also memorandum, Kenneth P. Landon to Bromley Smith, Operations Coordinating Board, 9 January 1961, Southeast Asia file, OCB papers, Box 6, Dulles Papers.

18. Lansdale interview, 17 December 1984, and William E. Colby interview, 24 June 1985. According to Lansdale, Colby was one of those at CIA who he could trust was telling him the truth. "You couldn't with very many of their operators. . . . I was very pleased to see that and told him as much. I always found him very honest and straightforward and that's a blessing. There's very few people in that Agency who ever got anyplace topside who were that [way]. A disease or contagion gets them. They're so used to dealing with subterfuge in their daily work it becomes a part of their character and they don't even realize it."

19. Lansdale's comment is from interview, 18 December 1984. The other quotes in this paragraph are taken from my interview with Colby and from his book *Honorable Men,* pp. 171–172.

20. Kalb and Abel, *Roots of Involvement,* p. 121.

21. Letter, Edward Lansdale to Ngo Dinh Diem, 30 January 1961, Correspondence, USDOD, OSD, Box 39, LP, THIWRP, and Lansdale interview, 16 May 1984.

22. Memorandum, "Vietnam," Edward Lansdale to Secretary of Defense

[Thomas S. Gates] and Deputy Secretary of Defense [James H. Douglas], 17 January 1961, "Lansdale's Trip, January 1961," USDOD, OSD, Box 49, LP, THIWRP.

23. Lansdale interview, 16 May 1984, and letter, Edward Lansdale to Roger W. Allen, 6 July 1983, Lansdale Personal Papers. Because of later publicity in America, the Sea Swallows community persevered in the face of great odds and even improved its situation. Lansdale's report on his Vietnam mission (part of which was printed as "The Report the President Wanted Published" in the *Saturday Evening Post*) and other publicity caused several American communities to "adopt" the Sea Swallows community and send it contributions of various commodities. Lansdale donated his fee from the *Post* article for medical supplies for Binh Hung. President Diem also increased aid to the villagers. Gradually Father Hoa built up his defense force to combat the frequent hit-and-run raids by Viet Cong against the settlement. Hoa toured Vietnam recruiting Chinese refugees for his "army." Hoa became more widely known, and the fifty-three-year-old priest was appointed a district chief and military commander of the Hai Yen Special Area, comprising more than twenty villages and hamlets in which some fifteen thousand people lived. By 1965 his defense force was some one thousand warriors strong, of whom six hundred were former members of the Nationalist Chinese army. Ultimately they were able to virtually eliminate the Viet Cong's operations in their area of the Camau peninsula. Unfortunately, Father Hoa's success and growing popularity caused him to fall from grace in the eyes of the Saigon government, and he was barred from the community he had formed. Lansdale wrote that "the local Vietnamese Division Commander has given orders that Father Hoa . . . is not to show up in Binh Hung personally, under penalty of death." Letter, Edward Lansdale to General Wallace Greene, Commandant, USMC, 11 July 1966, SLO, USE, Saigon, Box 51, LP, THIWRP. With the fall of Saigon in 1975, Father Hoa once more became a refugee and fled for his life. He later became a resident of Taiwan.

24. Gittinger interview.

25. Lansdale interview, 17 December 1984.

26. Memorandum, Edward Lansdale to Secretary of Defense and Deputy Secretary of Defense, 17 January 1961, "Lansdale's Trip, January 1961," USDOD, OSD, Box 49, LP, THIWRP.

27. Lansdale interview, 17 December 1984.

28. Lansdale interview, 16 May 1984.

29. Memorandum, Edward Lansdale (see note 26).

30. Schlesinger, *A Thousand Days*, p. 320; Kalb and Abel, *Roots of Involvement*, p. 122. Rostow wanted Lansdale to return to Vietnam. "He knew more about guerrilla warfare on the Asian scene than any other American," he said. "He had an extraordinary sensitivity and respect for the political problems of postcolonial nations and for the human beings caught up in them. No one had a better right to form an assessment of the situation in Vietnam, and to have that assessment taken seriously." See Rostow, *The Diffusion of Power*, pp. 264–265. Rostow also gave JFK the works of Mao and Guevara and passages from Krushchev's speech on 6 January 1961 on "wars of national liberation." Kennedy asked Rostow to determine how well the Army was preparing itself for insurgent warfare. Rostow

told him that Fort Bragg's Special Forces numbered fewer than a thousand men. Kennedy glanced at some of their training literature and Army field manuals and pronounced them inadequate. He then ordered the Special Warfare Center to expand its mission. The commander there, Major General William P. Yarborough, a Lansdale protégé, took him at his word and established training bases in Panama, Okinawa, Vietnam, and West Germany. See Lansdale correspondence with Yarborough, USDOD, OSD, LP, THIWRP.

Kennedy went even further. He went to Fort Bragg to see the Special Forces in action. Donald Duncan, a Special Forces trooper, described the preparation for that presidential visit:

Every enlisted man and officer . . . was affected: men were detailed to build floats, the Psychological Warfare Battalion cranked out millions of leaflets and painted huge posters and backdrops, engineers were detailed to drive huge logs into the mud of McKellar's Lake and support them with cables. Strange equipment appeared. Mock submarines were knocked together. Speeches were written and rehearsed, rewritten and rehearsed again. Sky divers practiced jumping into the lake. Mock battles, complete with ambushes, were rehearsed. A team with a "Rube Goldberg" rocket belt appeared. Hundreds of NCO's spent countless man-hours picking up bits of paper along the road leading to the lake. Then it was mass rehearsals from morning to night — talkthroughs, walkthroughs, and finally, dress rehearsals. . . . President Kennedy was coming!

On the day of the show, Kennedy was treated to a real military spectacular:

A LARK lumbered into the lake, carrying a man wearing a rocket contraption — jets roaring, he flew across the water and landed in front of the President. Scuba divers swam to shore from the dummy submarine; skydivers trailing colored smoke tracked in from fifteen thousand feet and hit the water as planned; an expert judo team brutally displayed skills; another group climbed the tall poles and made thrilling rides on a "slide-for-life" into the water. The ambush went off without a hitch — low-level passes were made with L-19s, Caribous, Mohawks, and helicopters; on cue over a thousand men who had been hiding in the brush across the lake stood and removed fatigue shirts, and in their white T-shirts, shooting off hand flares, ran screaming and yelling to the water's edge. They represented the number of guerrillas the twelve-man team can organize and direct. Hundreds of men . . . appeared elsewhere on the lake — all wearing the forbidden [green] beret. The message is clear; these are the skills that every Special Forces man has. We are ready to go. We are yours. Use us. Then millions of leaflets drop over the area — they are printed with the President's picture. . . . Much of the equipment shown, including the rocket, had never been seen before and probably would never be seen again, and much of it had no application to Special Forces anyway.

Duncan, *The New Legions*, pp. 146–148. I first encountered this delightful passage while reading an excellent new book on Vietnam by James William Gibson, *The Perfect War*, pp. 77–78. Despite predictable carping and criticism by some reviews in military publications, Gibson's book gives the keenest analyses of America's military attitudes during the Vietnam era I have yet seen.

After Kennedy's visit to Fort Bragg, counterinsurgency became a watchword within government. Within the State Department a six-week course became mandatory for those who sought career advancement; AID, USIA, and CIA became similarly involved. By the end of the year, Secretary McNamara had requested a 150 percent increase in the size of antiguerrilla forces. Special warfare had become a fetish.

Yet only a few — other than Lansdale — realized that to succeed, counterinsurgency had to have a social vision as well as military strength. One had to transform society. Killing guerrillas was not enough; their program had to be preempted as well.

31. Kalb and Abel, *Roots of Involvement,* p. 123.

32. See note 23 and Lansdale interview, 16 May 1984.

33. Adelstein, "Something Extra and Special," p. 23.

34. Cincinnatus, *Self-Destruction,* p. 233. Also see Committee of Concerned Asian Scholars, *The Indochina Story,* pp. 74–76.

35. Letter, Edward Lansdale to Ngo Dinh Diem, 30 January 1961, Correspondence, USDOD, OSD, Box 39, LP, THIWRP. Lansdale used this occasion to give Diem additional advice. It did not differ from the arguments he had used with Diem in 1956, but perhaps even repetition might be worth trying. Diem should try to soften his image, Lansdale wrote, for some felt he believed himself to be infallible; too many of his organizations — the Youth Corps, the Can Lao party — were formed by coercion. People joined because they were afraid not to rather than because they were organizations "rooted in the hearts of the Vietnamese people." He added his feeling that "Your country needs you to rouse spirits right now, the way Winston Churchill did for Britain at a dark hour." If he would only allow province chiefs, military commanders, and cabinet to speak openly and frankly, Diem would "hear many things, not only bad problems but also good ideas." Lansdale reminded Diem that he had done that once before, in February 1955, "and it was a very wise and healthy action." Diem should also allow General Lionel McGarr, MAAG chief, and William Colby to attend such meetings and take notes.

There were so many things Diem might do. He should ease existing restrictions on his political opponents. "[B]y arresting people or closing down newspapers, [you] will only turn the talk into deep emotions of hatred and generate the formation of more clandestine organizations and plots to oppose you. . . . If you could get most of the oppositionists working on a program of specific ideas to save the nation, and to work on this program freely among themselves outside of the government, you would turn the major share of their political energies into constructive work." Diem was, Lansdale asserted, "the only person who can set the proper political climate for such an action. It needs you . . . to remove the lurking fear of secret arrest at night as punishment for political activity."

36. Letter, Felix B. Stump to Edward Lansdale, 26 January 1961, USDOD, OSD, Box 41, LP, THIWRP. Stump was not the only one impressed with Lansdale's acuity. Albert Ravenholt, a longtime acquaintance from Philippine days, was also convinced that Lansdale was the man of the hour. He wrote a suggestion to Theodore H. White. If White intended to offer Kennedy constructive ideas on American efforts in Asia, then one of the most effective steps the new president could take would be the appointment of Lansdale as assistant secretary of state for the Far East. There was, Ravenholt believed, a special urgency to getting Lansdale's "wits, toughness, military experience and political breadth to bring the scattered U.S. agencies under unified control and make the State Department the director of actual American policy." See letter, Albert Ravenholt to Theodore H. White, 14 November 1960, Correspondence, Box 40, LP, THIWRP.

37. This conversation is a combination drawn from two discussions with General

Lansdale on this subject. See Library lecture and Lansdale interview, 16 May 1984. See also letters, Edward Lansdale to Samuel T. Williams, 23 December 1960, 14 February 1961, and letter, Samuel T. Williams to Edward Lansdale, 8 January 1961, Williams Papers, Box 8. In the letter of 14 February 1961, Lansdale attempted to downplay his own interest in an ambassadorship and his sense of loss. "I've been trying to wriggle out of it [the appointment] since [it was offered by Kennedy], but don't know quite what will happen." Why? Lansdale explained. "I would like to do trouble-shooting from Washington in a number of places around the world." Presumably an ambassadorship would limit his freedom to do so!

38. Lansdale interview, 16 May 1984.
39. Letter, Edward Lansdale to Robert Komer and accompanying notes, 30 May 1971, Correspondence, Box 3, LP, THIWRP.
40. Colby and Forbath, *Honorable Men*, p. 172.
41. William E. Colby interview, 24 June 1985, and Asprey, *War in the Shadows*, II, pp. 978–979.
42. Letter, Edward Lansdale to Robert Komer and accompanying notes, 30 May 1971, Correspondence, Box 3, LP, THIWRP.
43. Memorandum, Captain B. W. Spore, USN, to Edward Lansdale, 6 February 1961, Correspondence, USDOD, OSD, Box 41, LP, THIWRP.
44. Memorandum, "OSO/OSD," Edward Lansdale, undated, Lansdale Personal Papers.
45. Agee, *Inside the Company*, pp. 166–167.
46. In that August 1960 meeting of Special Group Lansdale had specified that CIA should not plan a military operation, particularly one demanding an amphibious capability. Ignoring such cavils, CIA proceeded to select Marine Colonel Jack Hawkins as military commander for the beach assault. Bissell and Dulles approved the choice. After the failure at the Bay of Pigs, Bob Amory at CIA (who had never been consulted about Hawkins and who had fought in twenty-six assault landings in the Pacific theater during the Second World War, many of which used forces as small as the unit used at Playa Girón) angrily commented that Hawkins "had made [only] one in his whole goddamn life, and that was Iwo Jima, which was three divisions abreast. . . . [H]e just didn't know beans about what a small, self-contained beachhead would be like." Wyden, *Bay of Pigs*, p. 69n.
47. Corson, *The Armies of Ignorance*, p. 390.
48. Ibid. And see U.S. Congress, Senate, Select Committee, *Foreign and Military Intelligence*, p. 144. A note in the Lansdale Papers at the Hoover Institution lists the staff of the Office of Special Operations as of November 1960, just a few months prior to its abolition. Erskine served as chief with Lansdale as his assistant. Other staff members included Winnie Balmer, Howard E. Barkey, Hollis C. Brown, Edward C. Bursk, Jr., Clyde W. Elliott, Jerom T. French, Dr. John P. Gigrich, Frank M. Hand, Enes M. Hockett, Marguerite C. Holzhauer, Sylvia C. Jenks, Lillian P. Jester, Alyce B. Jones, James J. Kelleher, Jr., Lawrence M. Knapp, Madison E. Mitchell, Betty M. Moreland, L. Fletcher Prouty, Robert E. Rich, Doris L. Scott, Franklin P. Shaw, Gerald W. Sheerer, William A. Smith, Helen H. Snably, Burns W. Spore, Floyd M. Van Hoosen, and Randolph V. Zander. See "Lists of Staff," OSO, USDOD, OSD, Box 48, LP, THIWRP.
49. See USDOD, OSD, Box 36, LP, THIWRP.

50. Gravel, *The Pentagon Papers*, II, pp. 34–35.
51. Ibid., p. 35, and U.S. Department of Defense, *United States–Vietnam Relations*, XI, p. 32.
52. The quotations are taken from Adelstein, "Something Extra and Special"; letter, Edward Lansdale to William J. Rust, 16 October 1982, Lansdale Personal Papers; Gittinger interview, and Lansdale interview, 16 May 1984.
53. Gravel, *The Pentagon Papers*, II, pp. 2, 6, 8–9, 17, 32–44, 653, and U.S. Department of Defense, *United States–Vietnam Relations*, XI, pp. 32, 42–56, 422. For other Lansdale reports and memoranda in *United States–Vietnam Relations*, see X, pp. 1307–1310, 1329–1331, and XI, pp. 1–12, 22–56, 157–158, 175–176, 427.
54. Memorandum, Edward Lansdale to Don Blackburn/Hans Schecter, 28 November 1972, Lansdale Personal Papers; memorandum, "OSO/OSD" by Edward Lansdale, undated, Lansdale Personal Papers.
55. Stavins, Barnet, and Raskin, *Washington Plans an Aggressive War*, pp. 77–78.
56. Letter, Edward Lansdale to Samuel T. Williams, 24 October 1963, Correspondence, USDOD, OSD, Box 42, LP, THIWRP.
57. Gittinger interview.

11. Elimination by Illumination

1. Gittinger interview and Lansdale interview, 17 December 1984.
2. Asprey, *War in the Shadows*, II, p. 1019.
3. Letter, Edward Lansdale to Samuel T. Williams, 10 October 1964, Williams Papers, Box 10, and Gittinger interview.
4. Lansdale interview, 17 December 1984.
5. Gittinger interview and Lansdale interview, 17 December 1984.
6. Lansdale interview, 17 December 1984.
7. Gittinger interview.
8. Lansdale interview, 17 December 1984.
9. Ibid.
10. Gittinger interview. For Lansdale's report, which he wrote at Baguio City in the Philippines, see Gravel, *The Pentagon Papers*, II, pp. 643ff.
11. Letter, Edward Lansdale to Samuel T. Williams, 10 October 1964, Williams Papers, Box 10.
12. Gravel, *The Pentagon Papers*, II, pp. 4–5.
13. Krepinevich, *The Army and Vietnam*, p. 62.
14. Gravel, *The Pentagon Papers*, II, p. 1. On 6 December 1961, before his move to State as a planner, Rostow wrote in his last memorandum to Kennedy how crucial it was to return Lansdale to Vietnam in some appropriate role. "He is a unique national asset in the Saigon setting; and I cannot believe that anything he may be able to do in his present assignment could match his value in Southeast Asia." Rostow mused that while Lansdale might have been unable to alter "the tragic course on which Diem was launched" he still represented America's "last chance" to do so. See Rostow, *Diffusion of Power*, pp. 278–279.
15. Gittinger interview.
16. Letter, Edward Lansdale to Major General Theodore R. Milton, commanding

general, 13th Air Force, 6 November 1961, Correspondence, USDOD, OSD, Box 39, LP, THIWRP.

17. Letter, Edward Lansdale to Samuel T. Williams, 10 October 1964, Williams Papers.
18. Lansdale interview, 19 December 1984, and Military History lecture.
19. Ibid.
20. Church Report, p. 141. The Church Committee compiled more than eight thousand pages of testimony from some seventy-five witnesses. Its interim report, issued 20 November 1975, was approximately 350 pages long.
21. Fain, Plant, and Milloy, *The Intelligence Community*, p. 802; Colby and Forbath, *Honorable Men*, p. 188; Church Report, p. 140.
22. *Washington Post*, 3 July 1975.
23. Church Report, pp. 142–143; Fain, Plant, and Milloy, *The Intelligence Community*, p. 803; and Rositzke, *The CIA's Secret Operations*, p. 179.
24. Military History lecture and Lansdale interview, 19 December 1984.
25. Freemantle, *CIA*, p. 156; Fain, Plant, and Milloy, *The Intelligence Community*, p. 804; Church Report, p. 144.
26. Ibid.
27. Church Report, p. 143.
28. David C. Martin, "The CIA's 'Loaded Gun,' " *Washington Post*, 10 October 1976, pp. C-1, C-2.
29. Lansdale interview, 19 December 1984. Lansdale recalled that "later, when I was in Vietnam in 1965, some [there] were jumping on me for poking my nose into other people's affairs. One of them was Barry Zorthian, the JUSPAO man, the public affairs organization which handled psychological operations there. He told me I knew nothing about [such] things. Then he brought in some aircraft to start TV programs in Saigon. He used my equipment I had developed for Havana. The pilots and other crew members saluted me. 'Well,' [they said]. 'We meet again!' And I was supposed to be the stupid guy who didn't know anything. Things like that kept happening and were gratifying."
30. Church Report, p. 142n; letter, Edward Lansdale to C.T.R. Bohannan, 22 November 1975, Bohannan Collection.
31. Fain, Plant, and Milloy, *The Intelligence Community*, p. 804; Church Report, p. 144; Freemantle, *CIA*, p. 156.
32. Church Report, p. 143.
33. Ibid.; Jeremiah O'Leary, "Lansdale Names Robert Kennedy in Castro Plot," *Washington Star*, 3 July 1975; Freemantle, *CIA*, p. 157.
34. Church Report, pp. 144–145.
35. Ibid., pp. 153–154.
36. Fain, Plant, and Milloy, *The Intelligence Community*, p. 804.
37. Church Report, p. 168.
38. Ibid., pp. 144–145.
39. Ibid., p. 144.
40. Ibid., p. 140.
41. Ibid., p. 146; Corson, *The Armies of Ignorance*, p. 393.
42. Lartéguy, *Le Mal Jaune*.
43. O'Leary, "Lansdale Names Robert Kennedy"; Church Report, p. 147; Thomas Powers, "Inside the CIA. Target: To Kill Fidel Castro," *Manila Times Journal*, 29 September 1979.

44. Church Report, pp. 164–166.
45. Ibid., pp. 161ff.; Fain, Plant, and Milloy, *The Intelligence Community,* p. 804.
46. O'Leary, "Lansdale Names Robert Kennedy."
47. Church Report, pp. 155–156, 166 and passim; Freemantle, *CIA,* p. 157; Corson, *The Armies of Ignorance,* p. 140.
48. Church Report, p. 166.
49. Ibid., p. 167; O'Leary, "Lansdale Names Robert Kennedy."
50. Church Report, 167ff.; Freemantle, *CIA,* pp. 160–161; O'Leary, "Lansdale Names Robert Kennedy."
51. Church Report, pp. 161, 161n, and interview with Lansdale by Clifton Daniel, "The Assassination Plot Rumors," *New York Times,* 6 June 1975.
52. Church Report, pp. 162, 165–166.
53. Ibid., p. 167.
54. Ibid., pp. 146–147.
55. Detzer, *The Brink,* p. 58.
56. Powers, *The Man Who Kept the Secrets,* p. 138.
57. Church Report, p. 147.
58. Ibid., pp. 167, 169, 170.
59. Corson, *The Armies of Ignorance,* p. 393.
60. Letter, Edward Lansdale to Samuel T. Williams, 24 October 1963, Correspondence, USDOD, OSD, Box 42, LP, THIWRP, and Lansdale interview, 17 May 1984.
61. Ibid. and Gibbons interview.
62. Letter, Edward Lansdale to C.T.R. Bohannan, 21 August 1959, Bohannan Collection.
63. Lansdale interview, 16 May 1984.
64. Manuel J. Chavez interview, 15 January 1986.
65. Ibid.
66. Lansdale interview, 16 May 1984.
67. Memorandum, Edward Lansdale to General Breitweiser, Air Force chief of intelligence, 21 March 1962, Operational Personnel, USDOD, OSD, Box 48, LP, THIWRP.
68. Lansdale interviews, 16 May 1984, 28 November 1984, and Manuel J. Chavez interview, 15 January 1986.
69. Lansdale interview, 16 May 1984, and letter, Edward Lansdale to Peter C. Richards, 14 January 1964, Richards Collection.
70. Letter, Edward Lansdale to William Phillips, 10 June 1963, USDOD, OSD, Box 40, LP, THIWRP.
71. Memorandum, Edward Lansdale to Lieutenant General Andrew P. O'Meara, 4 June 1963, USDOD, OSD, Box 40, LP, THIWRP. This document has been removed from the files by State for "reasons of national security." See also Travel File, Box 47 and "Trip to Bolivia, 1963," Box 45, LP, THIWRP, and Karnow, "Lansdale."
72. Lansdale interview, 16 May 1984, and letter, Edward Lansdale to Peter C. Richards, 14 January 1964, Richards Collection.
73. Lansdale interview, 19 December 1984.
74. Letter, James H. Douglas, Jr., to Henry Cabot Lodge, 19 July 1963, Correspondence, USDOD, OSD, Box 37, LP, THIWRP.
75. Briefing, Edward Lansdale for Henry Cabot Lodge, 25 July 1963, "Vietnam, General, 1961–1963," USDOD, OSD, Box 49, LP, THIWRP.

76. "We cannot brag to the Vietnamese about how much wiser than they we are, and then expect them to accept us at our own high self-estimation. Each American has to earn his own privilege of being heeded as an adviser." Memorandum, Edward Lansdale to Roswell Gilpatric, 23 August 1962, USDOD, OSD, Box 48, LP, THIWRP.
77. "I told them stories of Diem's personal life and his courage, along with some stories of today's life in Vietnam. . . . I suggested several [State] sources . . . to obtain unclassified documents." Memorandum, Edward Lansdale to Robert McNamara/Roswell Gilpatric, 11 June 1962, USDOD, OSD, Box 48, LP, THIWRP.
78. Correspondence, 1962–1963, *Reader's Digest*, USDOD, OSD, Box 49, LP, THIWRP.
79. Letter, Edward Lansdale to John O'Daniel, 5 August 1963, Correspondence, USDOD, OSD, Box 39, LP, THIWRP.
80. Gibbons and McAdams interview and Lansdale interview by Harold Morse, Honolulu *Star-Bulletin*, 7 January 1984.
81. Morse interview. Also see memorandum, "Lessons Learned: Constitution," Edward Lansdale to Henry Cabot Lodge, 9 September 1966, Day Files, SLO, USE, Saigon, Box 56, LP, THIWRP.
82. Lansdale interview, 17 May 1984.
83. Letter, Edward Lansdale to Samuel T. Williams, 10 October 1964, Williams Papers, Box 10.
84. Lansdale 201 file.
85. Ibid.
86. Ibid. and letter, Edward Lansdale to Admiral Arleigh Burke, 20 September 1963, Correspondence, USDOD, OSD, Box 37, LP, THIWRP. Also see letter, Edward Lansdale to Samuel T. Williams, 10 October 1964, Williams Papers, Box 10.
87. Letter, Edward Lansdale to Colonel E. F. Black, 14 October 1963, USDOD, OSD, Box 36, LP, THIWRP, and Lansdale interview, 30 November 1984.
88. Letter, Edward Lansdale to General C. P. Cabell, 23 October 1963, USDOD, OSD, Box 37, LP, THIWRP.
89. Adelstein, "Something Extra and Special," pp. 57–58, and Karnow, "Lansdale."
90. Letter, Edward Lansdale to Peter C. Richards, 14 January 1964, Richards Collection.
91. Letter, Edward Lansdale to Colonel Ralph H. Smith, Army Headquarters Command, the Pentagon, 24 October 1963, Miscellany, USDOD, OSD, Box 36, LP, THIWRP.
92. Letter, Edward Lansdale to Eugene M. Zuckert, secretary of the Air Force, 25 October 1963, Correspondence, USDOD, OSD, Box 42, LP, THIWRP.
93. Karnow, "Lansdale."
94. Letter, Edward Lansdale to Arthur W. Arundel, 15 October 1963, Correspondence, USDOD, OSD, Box 36, LP, THIWRP.
95. Lansdale interview, 30 November 1984.
96. See William T. "Chip" Ward file, Correspondence, USDOD, OSD, Box 54, LP, THIWRP; letter, Edward Lansdale to John M. Mecklin, counselor of embassy for public affairs, Saigon, 1 July 1963, Box 39, LP, THIWRP; memorandum, Edward Lansdale to General William Rosson, 20 December 1962, "Operational Personnel for Special Duty," Box 48 and passim, LP, THIWRP.

97. Memorandum, "Thoughts for Study," Edward Lansdale to Don Blackburn, 26 June 1972, Lansdale Personal Papers. Lansdale was the most accessible of men. He was always willing to take time to correspond with those who were interested in what he had done. Tommy Allen of Oxford, Georgia, was but one example out of hundreds. Allen, a college student, sent Lansdale a list of questions on which he needed information for a class: How was President Diem chosen? Why did we support him? Why was US support withdrawn at the end? Did the SMM's exploits in North Vietnam violate the Geneva Conference? How did he feel about American Vietnam policy before the phased withdrawal? Will the South Vietnamese be able to withstand a continued war after the withdrawal of American forces? Was Chinese intervention a threat in Vietnam? Should we have assisted the French in 1954 with ground troops? Was the "domino theory" valid? What is the value of Vietnam to U.S. security? Should the United States be the world's policeman? Should the United States return to a limited isolationism? Lansdale wrote out a careful nine-page response. See letters, Tommy Allen to Edward Lansdale, undated, and Edward Lansdale to Tommy Allen, 13 May 1975, Lansdale Personal Papers. Nor did Lansdale hold a grudge. Victor Krulak, who once occupied the Office of Special Assistant for Counterinsurgency and Special Activities, was now gone from that position, assigned elsewhere to new duties. His successor, Brigadier General Don Blackburn, was engaged in a study of past special operations and asked Lansdale for help. Lansdale spent a considerable amount of time answering Blackburn's questions between 1970 and 1972. See various citations in these notes.

98. Lansdale interview, 17 May 1984.

99. Lansdale interview, 16 May 1984.

100. Lansdale interview, 19 December 1984.

12. INTERLUDE: A PEOPLE'S WAR

1. Kushner, "General Dirty Tricks."

2. Letter, Mary McGrory to Edward Lansdale, 23 November 1965, Correspondence, SLO, USE, Saigon, Box 54, LP, THIWRP.

3. The following is a partial listing of those still-classified speeches, some of which were official briefing papers, and their classifications.

   9 June 1958. DOD Cold War Intelligence Requirements for a Contested Free World Country. [Draft.] Secret.

   15 July 1958. Pacification in Vietnam. Attachments. Secret.

   23 July 1958. The Lao National Army — Its Role in Defeating Communist Subversion in Laos. Secret.

   11 August 1958. Utilization of Foreign Manpower for Military Purposes. Top Secret.

   10 September 1958. Foreign Manpower Readily Available for Military Use. Secret.

   22 December 1958. Plan for Utilization of Foreign Manpower Air Units. Secret.

   27 April 1959. Military Assistance. Confidential.

   4 January 1960. Chinese Communist Counterguerrilla Operations. Secret.

   27 April 1960. Communist Tactics in Laos. Confidential.

   29 June 1960. Communist Operations. Secret.

29 June 1960. JCS Seminar on Collateral Activities. Secret.
25 August 1960. Leadership Training in Africa. Confidential.
21 December 1960. Defense Activities in the Cold War. Confidential.
17 January 1961. Vietnam. Secret.
3 March 1961. Unconventional Forces. Confidential.
8 May 1961. Vietnam. Top Secret.
29 May 1961. The Defense of Burma. Secret.
12 July 1961. Defense Resources for Unconventional Warfare. Secret.
19 July 1961. Communist Organization for Unconventional Warfare. Attachments. Secret.
12 September 1961. Peacetime Military Support of CIA Operations — The Damage of Confessions. Secret.
18 March 1963. Venezuela. Secret.
3 June 1963. Visit to Bolivia. Secret.
18 June 1963. Political Action Ideas, Latin America. Secret.
26 June 1963. Bolivia. Secret.
7 October 1963. Civic Action in Bolivia. Confidential.

See "out-slips" in Speeches, Miscellany, 1957–1961 (i), USDOD, OSD, Box 43, LP, THIWRP.

4. Lansdale, "The U.S. Military in Non-Military Warfare."
5. Memorandum for the record, "Military Policy in Underdeveloped Areas," 22 February 1957, Department of Social Sciences, U.S. Air Force Academy, Colorado Springs, Box 12, LP, THIWRP.
6. Lansdale, "The U.S. Military in Non-Military Warfare," and memorandum, the EUCOM Cold War Seminar, Oberammergau, Germany, 20 October 1959, Speeches, Writings, Notes/Miscellany, USDOD, OSD, Box 43, LP, THIWRP.
7. Lansdale, "The Free Citizen in Uniform."
8. Ibid.
9. "Some Thoughts for Deputy Secretary Quarles' Speech to the Chaplains," 13 April 1959, Speeches, Writings, Notes/Miscellany, USDOD, OSD, Box 43, LP, THIWRP.
10. Lansdale, "Fundamentals for Americans."
11. Quoted in "Partisan Warfare," Der Spiegel, 9 May 1962, "Vietnam Conflict, 1961–1975," Box 26, LP, THIWRP.
12. Lansdale, "Southeast Asia."
13. Lansdale, "Military Psychological Operations," Part I. See also Lansdale, "Military Psychological Operations," Part II.
14. Lansdale, "The Free Citizen in Uniform."
15. Ibid. and Conference at West Point, 1959, partial transcript, "Carlisle Barracks and West Point, 1958–1959," USDOD, OSD, Box 46, LP, THIWRP; "The Insurgent Battlefield." Copies in author's possession.
16. Ibid. and Lansdale, "People's Wars: Three Primary Lessons."
17. Lecture, Principia Conference on Vietnam, 9 April 1965, Elsah, Illinois, mimeographed, 9 pp. Copy in author's possession.
18. Lansdale, "People's Wars: Three Primary Lessons."
19. The previous year, Lansdale had completed his autobiography, which he entitled In the Midst of Wars. This sentence shows that he remained pleased with his choice of titles.

20. Lansdale, "People's Wars: Three Primary Lessons."
21. Lansdale, "Counter-Guerrilla Operations in the Philippines, 1946–1953."
22. Ecclesiastes 9:11.
23. Lansdale, "The Insurgent Battlefield."
24. Memorandum for Secretary McNamara/Deputy Secretary Gilpatric, 16 April 1962, Correspondence, USDOD, OSD, Box 40, LP, THIWRP.
25. Cincinnatus, *Self-Destruction*, pp. 111–112.
26. Mark 1:3.
27. Lansdale, "People's Wars: Three Primary Lessons."
28. Letters, Pete Kosutic to Edward Lansdale, 20 November 1970, Correspondence, Box 3, LP, THIWRP, and 7 June 1971, Insurgency and Counterinsurgency, Box 16, LP, THIWRP.
29. Lansdale, "Vietnam: Goons, Clerks and Patriots."
30. Taber, *The War of the Flea*, p. 11.
31. Letter, Edward Lansdale to Paul F. Braim, 15 April 1969, Correspondence, Box 2, LP, THIWRP.
32. Carl F. Bernard, "The War in Vietnam: Observations and Reflections of a Province Senior Advisor," U.S. Army Command and General Staff College Student Paper, 1969.
33. Letter, Edward Lansdale to Peter C. Richards, 17 October 1964, Richards Collection.
34. Letter, Edward Lansdale to Samuel T. Williams, 10 October 1964, Williams Papers, Box 10.
35. Lansdale, "Vietnam: A Test of American Understanding of Revolution."
36. Memorandum, Edward Lansdale to Don Blackburn, 11 May 1972, Lansdale Personal Papers.
37. Lansdale, "Still the Search for Goals."
38. Edward G. Lansdale, "Two Steps to Get Us Out of Vietnam," *Look*, Vol. 33 (4 March 1969), pp. 64, 67.
39. Letter, Edward Lansdale to Paul F. Braim, 15 April 1969, Correspondence, Box 2, LP, THIWRP.
40. Lansdale, "The Free Citizen in Uniform."
41. Lansdale, "The True American."
42. Letter, Edward Lansdale to Colonel Frank E. Burdell, Jr., 8 April 1963, Speaking Requests, USDOD, OSD, Box 47, LP, THIWRP.
43. Letter, Edward Lansdale to Jay Mallin, 4 February 1974, Lansdale Personal Papers.
44. "Some Thoughts for Deputy Secretary Quarles' Speech to the Chaplains," 13 April 1959, Speeches, Writings, Notes/Miscellany, Box 43, LP, THIWRP.
45. Lansdale, "Comrades," pp. 23–27.
46. Lansdale, "Vietnam."
47. Letter, [?] to Edward Lansdale, 23 January 1959, Correspondence, Box 2, LP, THIWRP.
48. Letter, Ellsworth Bunker to Edward Lansdale, 6 August 1969, Box 2, LP, THIWRP.
49. "Printed Matter, Vietnamese Conflict, 1961–1975," Box 26, LP, THIWRP.
50. Letter, Rose Kushner to Edward Lansdale, 10 February 1970. This letter is part of a bulky collection of materials Kushner put together some years ago when she planned to write a biography of Lansdale. After health problems

intervened, her interests turned to other topics and she turned this collection over to Lansdale, who stored it in his garage. He was kind enough to share these materials with me prior to his death. They form part of what I have here cited as Lansdale Personal Papers.

51. Emphasis added.
52. Lansdale, *In the Midst of Wars,* p. ix.
53. Edward G. Lansdale, "Thoughts About a Past War," Foreword to Millette, *A Short History of the Vietnam War,* pp. vi–xiv.
54. Letter and accompanying memorandum, Edward Lansdale to Richard M. Nixon, 29 September 1984, Lansdale Personal Papers.

13. BACK TO VIETNAM

1. Adelstein, "Something Extra and Special," pp. 23, 49, 66.
2. Letters, Rufus C. Phillips III to Editor, *U.S. News & World Report* and to William J. Rust, *U.S. News & World Report,* 25 October 1983. Mr. Phillips kindly provided me with copies of these letters. See also Bowman, *The Vietnam War: An Almanac,* p. 61.
3. Lansdale interviews, 16 and 17 May 1984.
4. Lucien Conein interview, 24 June 1985.
5. Ibid.
6. Letter, Edward Lansdale to Elden Aldridge, 2 November 1971, Correspondence, Box 2, LP, THIWRP.
7. Letters, Samuel T. Williams to Edward Lansdale, 14 November 1963, 16 October 1964, Correspondence, USDOD, OSD, Box 42, LP, THIWRP.
8. Lansdale interview, 17 May 1984.
9. Lansdale interview, 17 December 1984. In his 30 November 1984 interview, Lansdale recalled the date of his departure from Food for Peace as January or February 1965. Also see memorandum, Edward Lansdale to Secretary McNamara/Deputy Secretary Gilpatric, 30 July 1962, USDOD, OSD, Box 42, LP, THIWRP.
10. Memorandum, "Long Range Impact, FFP," Edward Lansdale to Richard Reuter, 7 May 1964. Also see his memorandum, "Food for Peace," 1 May 1964, Box 14, LP, THIWRP; letter, Samuel T. Williams to Edward Lansdale, 16 October 1964, Box 10, Williams Papers.
11. Letter, Major General William P. Yarborough to Edward Lansdale, 12 October 1964, Correspondence, USDOD, OSD, Box 42, LP, THIWRP.
12. Letter, Takashi Oka to Edward Lansdale, 26 March 1965, Correspondence, USDOD, OSD, Box 40, LP, THIWRP.
13. Lansdale interview, 17 May 1984; memorandum, "Liberty Hall," Freedom Studies Center, Boston, Virginia, Box 12, LP, THIWRP; letter, Philip F. Hilbert to Edward Lansdale, 12 December 1963, Correspondence, USDOD, OSD, Box 38, LP, THIWRP; Freedom Studies Center, Box 14, LP, THIWRP.
14. Untitled draft manuscript by Rufus Phillips, ca. 1964–1965, Box 17, Bohannan Papers.
15. C.T.R. Bohannan, "Phillipine Counter-Insurgency Experiences Applicable to Vietnam," ca. 1964, and C.T.R. Bohannan, memorandum, "US Options in Vietnam," 24 November 1964, Box 27, Bohannan Papers.
16. Memorandum and appendices, Rufus C. Phillips to James S. Killen, 9 July 1964, 12 pp. Copy in author's possession.

17. Draft manuscript, C.T.R. Bohannan [?], Box 17, Bohannan Papers.
18. Lansdale, "Of Course We Can Win in Vietnam," two-part outline: "Why We Are Losing in Vietnam" and "How We Can Still Win in Vietnam," ca. 1965, Box 17, Bohannan Papers.
19. Lansdale, "Concept for Victory in Vietnam," 20 May 1964. Private working paper, first draft. Copy in author's possession.
20. Lansdale, "A Catalyst Team for Vietnam," 12 June 1964, Vietnam, General, 1961–1963 (3), USDOD, OSD, Box 49, LP, THIWRP.
21. Letter, Edward Lansdale to Samuel T. Williams, 10 October 1964, Box 10, Williams Papers.
22. Lansdale, memorandum, "United States Policy Options in Vietnam," 25 November 1964. Copy in author's possession. See also Lansdale, "How to Win in Vietnam," draft, Box 17, Bohannan Papers. A more polished version dated 10 January 1965 may be consulted in "Speeches and Writings," Box 8, LP, THIWRP. For Lansdale as a Humphrey adviser, see Solberg, *Hubert Humphrey*, pp. 269–270.
23. Karnow, "On Duty, 'Dirty Tricks' and Democracy."
24. Ibid. and Lansdale interviews, 17 May 1984, 17 December 1984; Gittinger interview.
25. *Newsweek*, 30 August 1965; *Washington Post*, 29 August 1965.
26. *Newsweek*, 30 August 1965; *Washington Post*, 23, 25 August 1965; *St. Petersburg* (Florida) *Times*, 26 September 1965.
27. Ibid.
28. *U.S. News & World Report*, 6 September 1965, 5 December 1965. A few years later, Frances FitzGerald described Lansdale as "a man who never thought in terms of systems or larger social forces. . . . No theorist, he was rather an enthusiast, a man who believed that Communism in Asia would crumble before men of goodwill with some concern for 'the little guy' and the proper counterinsurgency skills. He had a talent for practical politics and for personal involvement in what to most Americans would seem the most distinctly foreign of affairs." FitzGerald, *Fire in the Lake*, p. 78. A strange comment from one who should have known better. Lansdale specifically worked his way through theoretical problems in terms of "systems" and "larger social forces" that wreaked such havoc on the nation of South Vietnam. FitzGerald could write such unabashed nonsense only because of her own tinted persuasions. Misplacing the beginning of Lansdale's second tour in Vietnam by as much as six months, FitzGerald further muddied the waters by claiming it was initiated "at the behest of the CIA" (p. 269).
29. Letter, Henry L. Miller to David L. Walton, SLO, USE, April–May, Box 51, LP, THIWRP.
30. Antonio A. Quintos interview, 26 July 1985. "We never wanted to show anybody that we are protecting the building and we are all low-key. I always situated my desk inside the house, so I have a commanding view, a full control of what is going on at the gate." Quintos thoroughly approved of Lansdale who "has in his heart the problems of us Asians. . . . [He] could get things done in his most mild-mannered ways, no matter how critical the situation and how crucial the issues were. . . . He is very much attuned to the temperament, the idiosyncrasies of the Asian people."
31. Karnow, "On Duty, 'Dirty Tricks' and Democracy."
32. Joseph Baker interview, 23 June 1985.

33. Letter, George Melvin to Edward Lansdale, 28 August 1965, Correspondence, SLO, USE, Saigon, Box 54, LP, THIWRP.
34. Lansdale interview, 12 November 1985.
35. Letter, Edward Lansdale to Rufus Phillips, 11 October 1965, SLO, USE, Saigon, Box 54, LP, THIWRP.
36. Lansdale interview, 12 November 1985.
37. Daniel Ellsberg interview, 23 September 1985.
38. Conversations with Joe Baker and Lou Conein, 3, 4 May 1987. Joe Baker served as executive officer ("Will all team members be a little more careful regarding security? Several times the young ladies in the office have found classified material on the desks after everyone has left. Also . . . please be careful when you are talking to the press or non-team members. Remember security is a personal thing and this makes you responsible"), handled logistical support, and maintained the operational diary. Conein was charged with security administration and liaison with Vietnamese Army personnel. Joe Redick was charged with personnel administration; Dan Ellsberg studied how best to fit the team within the U.S. establishment in Vietnam. Michael Deutch pondered economic matters. Prior to his departure, Bohannan worked with land reform. Hank Miller surveyed ways to improve understanding and cooperation between the Vietnamese government and its people. Napoleon Valeriano's responsibility was to determine ways in which police and army fell short of protecting their own citizens. Lawyer Charles Choate studied ways to implement the rule of law. Sam Karrick served as liaison with the U.S. military while Rufe Phillips identified emergency problems the team might have to cope with. Lansdale was always careful of public relations. He reminded Joe Baker of "stacks of unanswered mail" in the office "addressed to me from people I hardly know, or don't know. Please collect *all* unanswered mail. Then set up a system . . . and follow through to make sure an action is taken" on each letter. See, among other documents, "Establishing the Team, Memorandum. Job Description," by Napoleon Valeriano [?]; "Memorandum to All Team Members from Executive Officer [Joe Baker]"; note, Edward Lansdale to Joseph Baker, 3 November 1965, SLO, USE, Saigon, Box 50, LP, THIWRP; Michael Deutch interview, 24 June 1985.
39. Letter, Edward Lansdale to Peter C. Richards, 23 July 1971, Richards Collection.
40. Lansdale interview, 17 December 1984.
41. Lucien Conein interview, 24 June 1985.
42. Letter, Edward Lansdale to Peter C. Richards, 21 February 1972, Richards Collection.
43. Lansdale interview, 15 February 1984.
44. Joseph Baker interview, 23 June 1985.
45. Ibid.
46. Lucien Conein interview, 24 June 1985.
47. Barry Farrell, "The Ellsberg Mask."
48. Lansdale interview, 17 December 1984.
49. Letter, Edward Lansdale to Peter C. Richards, 23 July 1971, Richards Collection.
50. Lansdale interview, 15 February 1984.
51. Letter, Edward Lansdale to Marge Byers, 21 June 1971, Correspondence, Box 3, LP, THIWRP.

52. Daniel Ellsberg interview, 23 September 1985.
53. Ibid.
54. Ibid.
55. Memorandum, Edward Lansdale to Daniel Ellsberg, 10 May 1967, Day File, May 1967, SLO, USE, Saigon, Box 57, LP, THIWRP.
56. Lansdale interview, 17 December 1984.
57. Joseph Baker interview, 23 June 1985.
58. Ky, *Twenty Years and Twenty Days*, pp. 74–75. For the Vietnamese view of Lansdale, see Barry Zorthian, JUSPAO, Saigon to USIS, 5 December 1966, Lansdale Personal Papers, which includes a summary of a Lansdale meeting with Vietnamese newsmen and their resultant stories.
59. Reported in the *Washington Star*, 9 April 1967; see *Washington Evening Star*, 19 October 1965.
60. Gittinger interview.
61. Lansdale interviews, 15 February 1984, 16 May 1984.
62. Letter, Edward Lansdale to Peter McInerny, 17 July 1982, Lansdale Personal Papers. See also letters, Rufus C. Phillips to Edward Lansdale, 15 September 1965; Edward Lansdale to Rufus C. Phillips, 14 November 1965, 18 December 1965, Correspondence, SLO, USE, Saigon, Box 54, LP, THIWRP.
63. Joseph Baker interview, 23 June 1985.
64. Letter, Henry Kissinger to Edward Lansdale, 24 September 1965, and letter, Edward Lansdale to Henry Kissinger, 28 September 1965, SLO, USE, Saigon, Box 53, LP, THIWRP.
65. William E. Colby interview, 24 June 1985.
66. Lansdale interview, 16 May 1984; Morse interview.
67. Gittinger interview.
68. Shaplen, *The Road from War*, pp. 30–31.
69. The following summary of Lansdale's problems with the bureaucracy in Vietnam is drawn from Rose Kushner, "The Quiet American Comes Home," Lansdale Personal Papers.
70. Gittinger interview.
71. Karnow, "On Duty, 'Dirty Tricks,' and Democracy."
72. Letter, Edward Lansdale to [C.T.R. Bohannan?], ca. 10 January 1966, SLO, USE, Saigon, Box 54, LP, THIWRP.
73. Morse interview.
74. Lansdale interview, 17 May 1984, and Gittinger interview.
75. Joseph Baker interview, 23 June 1985.
76. Tran, *Our Endless War*, pp. 168–169.
77. *Washington Post*, 24 February 1966.
78. Lucien Conein interview, 24 June 1985.
79. Lansdale interviews, 16 May 1984, 17 December 1985.
80. Gittinger interview and Westmoreland, *A Soldier Reports*, p. 276.
81. Daniel Ellsberg interview, 23 September 1985. Ellsberg gained a great deal of respect for Lansdale. One of Lansdale's most impressive abilities, Ellsberg became convinced, was his talent for keeping secrets. "I spent an awful lot of time with him in very drunken evenings" at the villa on Cong Ly Street, Ellsberg recalled. Conversation and drinking often continued until 0300–0400 hours "with long, long tales of his derring-do in Vietnam and even the Philippines. And the word 'Cuba' was never, never mentioned. I learned [only later in 1975] that he had been head of the Cuban Task Force and Operation Mongoose. For the first time that gave me a new

insight into the meaning of the word secrecy. I would not have thought he could have kept that from me. I knew that man well enough. He not only kept it from me and Lou Conein [but from] every member of his team. . . . I did not know, for instance, that he had . . . worked for Bobby Kennedy.''

82. Lansdale interview, 17 December 1985.
83. Ibid.
84. Westmoreland, *A Soldier Reports,* pp. 276–282.
85. *Washington Evening Star,* 2 April 1966.
86. Ibid.
87. Transcript, Liberation Radio broadcast, 17 March 1966. Copy in author's possession.

14. ''GODDAMMIT, THIEU''

1. *Washington Evening Star,* 10 February 1966.
2. Administrative File, Performance Rating, 17 June 1966, SLO, USE, Saigon, Box 50, LP, THIWRP.
3. Cable, Henry Cabot Lodge to William Bundy, 5 April 1966, Box 58, LP, THIWRP.
4. ''The General from the CIA,'' *Komsomol Pravda,* February 1966, and Tass, 25 February 1966; transcripts in Lansdale Personal Papers.
5. Newsletter, *The Fiji Brewin,* March 1966, Lansdale Personal Papers.
6. Letter, Lieutenant Governor Glen M. Anderson to Edward Lansdale, 3 May 1966, Correspondence, April–May 1966, SLO, USE, Saigon, Box 51, LP, THIWRP.
7. Letter, Edward Lansdale to John W. Doran, 24 January 1966, Correspondence, December 1965, General, LP, THIWRP.
8. Letter, Edward Lansdale to Gloria Emerson, 4 September 1966, Correspondence, August/September 1966, SLO, USE, Saigon, Box 51, LP, THIWRP, and references throughout LP, THIWRP.
9. Lansdale told how the dictionary venture came about. ''I noticed . . . at big gatherings, where Americans and Vietnamese mixed at official functions, the Vietnamese-speaking Americans occasionally got baffled looks on their faces. I asked them about it and was told they simply didn't understand what was being said. I went to the Vietnamese and asked them. They told me they made up slang to get around Americans who spoke Vietnamese. I put out a dictionary with political slang in it. The Vietnamese had nicknames for all sorts of people and events and constantly added new ones. Along with general slang, they had names for leading Americans — the ambassador, the generals, the AID people. Westmoreland was 'Mr. Four Stars.' I was the 'General.' They had, I finally discovered, about six or seven of these damned nicknames for me.'' Lansdale interview, 17 February 1984. His nine-page mimeographed pamphlet listed terms from *Anh Hai* (''big brother,'' Nguyen Cao Ky's nickname among his staff) to *Xoay Xo* (''one who finds a way to get things done,'' a ''real operator''). My favorite entry is *Cao Boi,* or ''cowboy,'' an early nickname for Ky. A copy of this pamphlet is in Lansdale Personal Papers.
10. Letter, Edward Lansdale to Irving Casey, 4 May 1966, Correspondence,

April–May 1966, General, SLO, USE, Saigon, Box 51, LP, THIWRP. Casey was a student at American University. See also letters, Edward Lansdale to Karl H. Cerny, undated; Edward Lansdale to William Dickey, 14 April 1965; Bernard Fall to Edward Lansdale, 22 May 1965, Correspondence, Box 35, LP, THIWRP. Lansdale corresponded with Lieutenant William Dickey about the early days of Diem's administration and his comments brought forth a furious rejoinder from Bernard Fall, who called Dickey's thesis "a slur on my character and reputation."

11. "My visit to Quang Nam 28 February–1 March [1966] turned out to be interesting. . . . I took a look at how pacification is progressing in the Ngu Hanh Son 'national priority' area of Hoa Vang, visiting several of the hamlets." Letter, Edward Lansdale to General Wallace M. Greene, Jr., Commandant, USMC, 3 March 1966, Correspondence, March 1966, General, SLO, USE, Saigon, Box 51, LP, THIWRP.

12. "Request your permission for my taking some leave in Hong Kong from November 23 to November 28. My brother and his wife will be visiting Hong Kong at that time, and this would permit a bit of a family reunion. I would appreciate the use of the T-39 [airplane], if it is not otherwise needed." Lodge penciled in the words "by all means." Memorandum, Edward Lansdale to Henry Cabot Lodge, 7 November 1966, SLO, USE, Box 58, LP, THIWRP.

13. Letters, Barbara Price to Edward Lansdale, 14 June 1966; Henry Miller to Pat [Kelly], 17 July 1966, Correspondence, June 1966, General, Box 51, LP, THIWRP.

14. Day Files, 1965–1968, Boxes 55–58, LP, THIWRP.

15. Letter, Edward Lansdale to Major General C. K. Gailey (Ret.), Correspondence, April–May 1966, Box 51, LP, THIWRP.

16. Letter, Edward Lansdale to Rufus C. Phillips, 9 November 1966, Correspondence, Box 54, LP, THIWRP.

17. SLO Day File, May/June 1966, Box 55, LP, THIWRP.

18. Memorandum, "Thang and Cheek," Edward Lansdale to Henry Cabot Lodge and William Porter, with copies to Westmoreland, Habib, et al., 20 July 1966, Day File, July 1966, Box 56, LP, THIWRP.

19. Thanh, "The Man Sentenced to Death by Ho," transcript in Lansdale Personal Papers. Thanh presumably plagiarized an equally odd story, published in the United States and written by Jack Lasco, "America's Deadliest Secret Agent." Thanh/Lasco quote General Vo Nguyen Giap as saying, "There have been occasions when the American agent, General Lansdale, has proven to be of greater value to the enemy [South Vietnam] than the military forces of his aggressor country. He has been the cement which has held together the cracking government of the enemy."

20. Songs sung by Americans in the Vietnam War ranged from Barry Sadler's "Ballad of the Green Berets" to "The Yellow Rose of Texas." A few of the more esoteric titles and tunes Lansdale collected include "I Feel a Coup Is Coming On," "Don't Take My Counterpart Away," "O Little Town of Ban Me Thuot," "God Rest Ye, General Westmoreland," "Deck the Halls with Victor Charlie," "Mow the Little Bastards Down," "I've Pacified This Land One Hundred Times," "Landlord, Fill That Nuoc Nam Bowl," "Hang on to Your Hearts and Minds," "There's a Fireball Down There," "Where Have All the Field Reps Gone?," "The Airsick ARVN,"

and, of course, "Puff, the Magic Dragon." See "Songs by Americans in the Vietnam War," Lansdale Personal Papers.

21. Transcript, "In the Midst of War," a musical program with voice-over, Lansdale Personal Papers. Tapes were given to many visiting dignitaries: Lyndon Johnson, Richard Nixon, Hubert Humphrey, Walt Rostow, Robert McNamara, Richard Helms, Dean Rusk, and others. Some years ago Lansdale donated his master tape file to the Smithsonian Institution.

22. Vietnamese observers called the villa at 194 Cong Ly the "monastery" because unlike many other quarters inhabited by Americans there was not a constant procession of women — Vietnamese and American — moving through its gates for sexual liaisons inside.

23. Memorandum, "Future Plans," Edward Lansdale to Henry Cabot Lodge, 3 October 1966, and attached 3 November 1966 letter, Leonard Unger to Edward Lansdale, Day File, October 1966, SLO, USE, Saigon, Box 56, LP, THIWRP.

24. Letter, Edward Lansdale to Rufus C. Phillips, 9 November 1966, Correspondence, Box 54, LP, THIWRP.

25. Letters, Edward Lansdale to Samuel T. Williams, Christmastide 1966, and Samuel T. Williams to Edward Lansdale, 20 December 1966, Williams Papers, Box 10, THIWRP.

26. Memorandum, Henry Cabot Lodge to Edward Lansdale, 24 January 1967, Correspondence, SLO, USE, Saigon, Box 54, LP, THIWRP.

27. Lansdale interview, 17 December 1985.

28. Ibid.

29. Memorandum, Edward Lansdale to Henry Cabot Lodge, 7 March 1967, SLO, USE, Saigon, Box 58, LP, THIWRP.

30. Memorandum, Rufus C. Phillips to Hubert H. Humphrey, 21 March 1967, Correspondence, Box 54, LP, THIWRP.

31. Letter, Rufus C. Phillips to Edward Lansdale, 28 March 1967, Correspondence, Box 54, LP, THIWRP.

32. Lansdale interview, 17 December 1985.

33. Ibid.

34. Memorandum, "More Smoke Filled Rooms," Edward Lansdale to Ellsworth Bunker, 28 August 1967, Day File, August 1967, SLO, USE, Saigon, Box 57, LP, THIWRP.

35. Letter, Edward Lansdale to Samuel N. Karrick, Jr., 22 September 1967, Day File, September 1967, Box 57, LP, THIWRP, and Rose Kushner, "The Quiet American Returns to Saigon."

36. Letter, Edward Lansdale to Peter C. Richards, 28 December 1967, Richards Collection.

37. Letter, Edward Lansdale to Peter C. Richards, 23 July 1971, Richards Collection.

38. This document has been incorrectly identified by the archivists as from Robert Erlandson. See letter, Rose Kushner to Edward Lansdale, 13 October 1967, Correspondence, SLO, USE, Saigon, Box 53, LP, THIWRP.

39. Lansdale interview, 17 December 1985.

40. Ibid.

41. Lansdale interview, 17 May 1984.

42. Lansdale interview, 29 November 1984.

43. *Washington Post,* 29 September 1968.

44. Lansdale interview, 16 May 1984.
45. Letter, Eugene Methvin to Edward Lansdale, 23 February 1968, SLO, USE, Saigon, Box 52, LP, THIWRP.
46. Langguth, "Our Policy-Making Men in Saigon."
47. Lansdale interview, 16 May 1984.
48. Gittinger interview.
49. *Washington Post,* 29 September 1968.
50. *Christian Science Monitor,* 25 July 1968.

15. HOME AT LAST

1. Lansdale interview, 17 May 1984.
2. Letter, Richard V. Allen to Edward Lansdale, 23 July 1968, Box 5, LP, THIWRP.
3. Responses to his unsolicited advice were neutral, as when Henry Kissinger carefully replied that Nixon had read a Lansdale letter "with great interest." Letter, Henry Kissinger to Edward Lansdale, 29 January 1972, Box 3, LP, THIWRP.
4. Letter, Edward Lansdale to A. C. Spectorsky, 20 January 1970, Box 26, LP, THIWRP.
5. He continued his appearances until well into the 1980s and was saddened by the declining military interest in emphasizing ways of countering third world insurgencies and wars of national liberation. "The only remnant of the old days," Lansdale said in 1980, "is a brief, one week course on special operations, counter guerrilla, counter terror, counter revolution — just a little familiarization course. Apparently the last remnant of counterinsurgency. How times have changed." Letter, Edward Lansdale to C.T.R. Bohannan, 10 March 1980, Bohannan Collection. Also see letters, Edward Lansdale to Peter C. Richards, 8 January 1972, 12 September 1973, Richards Collection; letters, Edward Lansdale to Dorothy and C.T.R. Bohannan, 1 August 1979; Edward Lansdale to C.T.R. Bohannan, 14 June 1976, 25 March 1977, 26 February 1979, 9 January 1982, Bohannan Collection; letter, W. Scott Thompson to Edward Lansdale, 24 August 1973, Lansdale Personal Papers.
6. Daniel Ellsberg interview, 23 September 1985.
7. Lansdale interview, 17 December 1984, and letter, Edward Lansdale to the Old Team, 1 July 1971, Bohannan Collection.
8. Letter, Edward Lansdale to the Old Team, 1 July 1971, Bohannan Collection.
9. Lansdale interview, 15 February 1984.
10. Letter, Edward Lansdale to C.T.R. Bohannan, 21 October 1976, Bohannan Collection.
11. Letter, Edward Lansdale to C.T.R. Bohannan, 2 February 1975, Bohannan Collection.
12. Daniel Ellsberg interview, 23 September 1985.
13. See Box 5, LP, THIWRP.
14. Letter, Edward Lansdale to Peter C. Richards, 6 November 1972, Richards Collection.
15. Letter, Edward Lansdale to Peter C. Richards, 14 January 1964, Richards Collection.

16. Letter, Edward Lansdale to Peter C. Richards, 23 July 1971, Richards Collection.
17. Letter, Edward Lansdale to C.T.R. Bohannan, 18 July 1971, Bohannan Collection.
18. *Washington Post,* 15 March 1972.
19. *New York Times,* 9 April 1972.
20. *Washington Star,* 26 March 1972.
21. *Christian Science Monitor,* 6 April 1972.
22. *Washington Post Bookworld,* 19 March 1972.
23. *Saturday Review,* 1 April 1972.
24. Letter, Edward Lansdale to Peter C. Richards, 15 April 1972, Richards Collection.
25. Lansdale interview, 15 February 1984.
26. Letter, O. J. Magee to Edward Lansdale, 7 October 1972, Lansdale Personal Papers.
27. Lansdale interview, 17 May 1984.
28. Letter, Edward Lansdale to Peter C. Richards, 11 July 1972, Richards Collection.
29. Letter, Pat Kelly to Edward Lansdale, 8 September 1972, Lansdale Personal Papers, and interview, Pat Lansdale, 23 June 1985.
30. Letter, Pat Kelly to Edward Lansdale, 2 October 1972, Lansdale Personal Papers.
31. Letters, Pat Kelly to Edward Lansdale, 26 October, 31 October, and 5 November 1972, Lansdale Personal Papers.
32. Letters, Pat Kelly to Edward Lansdale, 10 November, 16 November, 24 November 1972, Lansdale Personal Papers.
33. Letters, Pat Kelly to Edward Lansdale, 27 November, 4 December, 6 December, 7 December 1972, Lansdale Personal Papers.
34. Letters, Pat Kelly to Edward Lansdale, 11 December, 13 December 1972, 2 February 1973, and Itinerary, Lansdale Personal Papers.
35. Pat Lansdale interview, 23 June 1985.
36. Letter, Edward Lansdale to C.T.R. Bohannan, 13 October 1975, Bohannan Collection.
37. Letter, Edward Lansdale to Peter C. Richards, 12 September 1973, Richards Collection.
38. Ibid.
39. Letter, Edward Lansdale to Peter C. Richards, 30 November 1974, Richards Collection.
40. Letter, Edward Lansdale to C.T.R. Bohannan, 21 February 1975, Bohannan Collection.
41. Letter, Edward Lansdale to C.T.R. Bohannan, 1 June 1975, Bohannan Collection.
42. Letters, Edward Lansdale to C.T.R. Bohannan, 13 October, 18 October, 4 November, 11 November 1975, Bohannan Collection.
43. Letter, Edward Lansdale to C.T.R. Bohannan, 14 June 1976, Bohannan Collection.
45. Letter, Edward Lansdale to C.T.R. Bohannan, 13 December 1978, Bohannan Collection. A copy of his address "Limited War" is in Lansdale Personal Papers.
46. Letter, Edward Lansdale to C.T.R. Bohannan, 9 January 1982, Bohannan Collection.

47. Letter, Edward Lansdale to Peter C. Richards, 14 July 1982, Richards Collection.
48. Ibid.
49. Letters, Edward Lansdale to C.T.R. Bohannan, 28 June, 12 July 1975, Bohannan Collection.
50. Letter, Edward Lansdale to C.T.R. Bohannan, 14 April 1975, Bohannan Collection. And see memoranda, Edward Lansdale to the Old Team, 29 March 1975, 7 March 1977, Lansdale Personal Papers. For two years Lansdale worked steadily on behalf of the new refugees from Asia.
51. Letter, Edward Lansdale to C.T.R. Bohannan, 14 April 1975, Bohannan Collection.
52. Letters, Bui Anh Tuan to Edward Lansdale, 30 May 1975, 1 September 1979, Correspondence, Box 2, LP, THIWRP.
53. Letter, Edward Lansdale to C.T.R. Bohannan, 1 June 1975, Bohannan Collection.
54. Letters, Edward Lansdale to C.T.R. Bohannan, 4 November 1975, 11 November 1975, 26 December 1975, Bohannan Collection.
55. Letter, Edward Lansdale to Peter C. Richards, 23 July 1975, Richards Collection.
56. Letter, Edward Lansdale to C.T.R. Bohannan, 1 June 1975, Bohannan Collection.
57. Ibid.
58. Letter, C.T.R. Bohannan to Edward Lansdale, 23 July 1975, Bohannan Collection.
59. Letter, Edward Lansdale to C.T.R. Bohannan, 2 July 1975, Bohannan Collection. In his book *The Secret Team*, Prouty argued that most political events were quietly manipulated by key industrialists, scientists, military officers, intellectuals, and highly placed individuals in the intelligence community. One such manipulated event, Prouty argued, was Ellsberg's release of the Pentagon Papers. The documents were, Prouty claimed, a "neat rewrite" of the war that carefully omitted most CIA covert activities and left the best possible impression of those that remained. By making the documents public, Prouty insisted, Ellsberg thus did an important service to his secret colleagues. See Farrell, "The Ellsberg Mask."
60. Letters, Edward Lansdale to C.T.R. Bohannan, 12 July 1975, Bohannan Collection, and Edward Lansdale to Peter C. Richards, 23 July 1975, Richards Collection.
61. Letters, Edward Lansdale to C.T.R. Bohannan, 12 July 1975, Bohannan Collection, and Edward Lansdale to James H. Douglas, 21 June 1976, Lansdale Personal Papers.
62. Letter, Edward Lansdale to C.T.R. Bohannan, 12 July 1975, Bohannan Collection.
63. Letters, Edward Lansdale to C.T.R. Bohannan, 22 November 1975, Bohannan Collection; Edward Lansdale to Peter C. Richards, 26 December 1975, Richards Collection; Edward Lansdale to Frank Church, 1 January 1976, Lansdale Personal Papers.
64. Letters, Edward Lansdale to C.T.R. Bohannan, 22 November 1975, Bohannan Collection, and Edward Lansdale to Peter C. Richards, 26 December 1975, Richards Collection.
65. Letter, C.T.R. Bohannan to Edward Lansdale, 5 December 1975, Bohannan Collection.

66. Letter, Edward Lansdale to C.T.R. Bohannan, 11 May 1978, Bohannan Collection.
67. Letter, Edward Lansdale to C.T.R. Bohannan, 5 March 1977, Bohannan Collection.
68. Letter, Edward Lansdale to C.T.R. Bohannan, 21 October 1976, Bohannan Collection.
69. Letter, Edward Lansdale to W. Averell Harriman, 26 February 1977, Box 3, LP, THIWRP.
70. Ibid., and see Edward Lansdale to W. Averell Harriman, undated rough draft, Box 3, LP, THIWRP.
71. Lansdale interview, 16 May 1984.
72. Ibid. and letters, Edward Lansdale to C.T.R. Bohannan, 16 January, 26 February 1979, Bohannan Collection.
73. Memorandum, Edward Lansdale to Bernie Yoh, 16 July 1984, and letter, Stanley Karnow to Edward Lansdale, 25 May 1978, Lansdale Personal Papers.
74. Letter, Edward Lansdale to C.T.R. Bohannan, 26 February 1979, Bohannan Collection.
75. Letter, Edward Lansdale to C.T.R. Bohannan, 1 August 1979, Bohannan Collection. Also see letters, James L. Collins to Edward Lansdale, 16 April 1979; S. T. Williams to Edward Lansdale, 22 May 1979; Edward Lansdale to James L. Collins, 23 April 1979; memoranda, Maurice Matloff to panel members, 17 May 1979, and Edward Lansdale to review panel, 6 June 1979, Lansdale Personal Papers.
76. Letter, Edward Lansdale to C.T.R. Bohannan, 10 March 1980, Bohannan Collection.
77. Lansdale memorandum, "Questions re El Salvador," 26 February 1981, Lansdale Personal Papers.
78. Letter, Edward Lansdale to C.T.R. Bohannan, 9 January 1982, Lansdale Personal Papers, and Lansdale interview, 19 December 1984.
79. Lansdale interview, 19 December 1984.
80. This episode reconstructed from Lansdale interview, 19 December 1984, and letters, Edward Lansdale to Peter C. Richards, 14 December 1983, Richards Collection, and Edward Lansdale to Hubert H. Roberts, 4 October 1983. Mr. Roberts generously shared a photocopy of his letter with me.
81. Lansdale interview, 19 December 1984.
82. Letter, William E. Colby to Edward Lansdale, 7 February 1986, Lansdale Personal Papers; and William E. Colby, "The Ten Greatest Spies of All Time," in Whittingham, Almanac of Adventure, p. 165.
83. Edward Lansdale, "Some Thoughts About Central America," 10 May 1983, Lansdale Personal Papers.
84. Lansdale interview, 19 December 1984.
85. Lansdale interview, 16 May 1984. And see Stone, "The Special Forces in 'Covert Action.' "
86. Letter, Edward Lansdale to Hubert H. Roberts, 4 April 1984. Mr. Roberts generously shared a photocopy of his letter with me.
87. F. Andy Messing, Jr., interview, 29 June 1987. Messing is executive director for National Defense Council, an organization founded by General John Singlaub, who was fired by President Carter when he spoke out against the president's plans to reduce American troop strength in Korea. He has

subsequently become an indefatigable organizer: of the Coalition for World Freedom (1985), formed to "disseminate information and counteract disinformation" about the cold war, and the Institute for Regional and International Studies, which provides intelligence and psywar training to Salvadorian military personnel and Nicaraguan Contras. Singlaub is also involved with the Refugee Relief International Center, Inc., and is president of the U.S. Council for World Freedom and chairman of the World Anti-Communist League. Lansdale was a "private sector adviser" for the National Defense Council and met Lieutenant Colonel Oliver North at its Singlaub Panel II meeting in 1985. See letter, F. Andy Messing, Jr., to Edward Lansdale, 28 November 1984, Lansdale Personal Papers, and Hilarion M. Henares, Jr., "Make My Day!" *Philippine Daily Inquirer,* 17 November 1986.

88. Pat Lansdale interview, 23 June 1985.
89. Letter, Benjamin Franklin Cooling to Edward Lansdale, 7 June 1985, Lansdale Personal Papers.
90. *New York Times,* 24 February 1987.
91. *Washington Post,* 24 February 1987.
92. *Philippine Daily Inquirer,* 25 February 1987.
93. *Washington Post,* 26 February 1987.
94. *Philippine Star,* 26 February 1987, and letter, Dorothy Bohannan to Cecil B. Currey, 11 March 1987.

BIBLIOGRAPHY

DOCUMENT COLLECTIONS

Bohannan, C.T.R., Papers of. The Hoover Institution for War, Revolution and Peace, Stanford University. Palo Alto, California. [Cited in Notes as Bohannan Papers.]

Bohannan, Dorothy. Collection of letters to and from Edward G. Lansdale. Manila, Philippines. [Cited in Notes as Bohannan Collection.]

Currey, Cecil B. Collection of letters to, from, and about Edward G. Lansdale; copies of many of his mimeographed speeches; and related Lansdale materials. Lutz, Florida.

Dulles, John Foster, Papers of. Dwight D. Eisenhower Presidential Library. Abilene, Kansas. [Cited in Notes as Dulles Papers.]

Lansdale, Edward G., Papers of. The Hoover Institution for War, Revolution and Peace, Stanford University. Palo Alto, California. [Cited in Notes as LP, THIWRP.]

Lansdale, Edward G. Personal Papers of. Material left in his home upon his death. McLean, Virginia. [Cited in Notes as Lansdale Personal Papers.]

———. 201 Personnel File. United States Air Force. [Cited in Notes as Lansdale 201 file.]

Philippine Guerrilla Movements. Federal Records Center. Suitland, Maryland.

Richards, Peter C. Collection of letters to, from, and about Edward G. Lansdale and analyses of Philippine politics. Manila, Philippines. [Cited in Notes as Richards Collection.]

Williams, Samuel Tankersley, Papers of. The Hoover Institution for War, Revolution and Peace, Stanford University. Palo Alto, California. [Cited in Notes as Williams Papers.]

PRINTED GOVERNMENT DOCUMENTS

Gravel, Mike, Ed. *The Pentagon Papers: The Defense Department History of United States Decisionmaking on Vietnam*. 5 vols. Boston: Beacon Press, 1971.

U.S. Congress, Senate. Select Committee to Study Governmental Operations with Respect to Intelligence Activities. *Alleged Assassination Plots Involving Foreign Leaders: An Interim Report*. 94th Congress, 1st Session. Report

No. 94-465. Washington, D.C.: Government Printing Office, 20 November 1975. [Cited in Notes as Church Report.]
U.S. Congress, Senate. Select Committee to Study Governmental Operations with Respect to Intelligence Activities. *Foreign and Military Intelligence.* 94th Congress, 2nd Session. Washington, D.C.: Government Printing Office, 1976.
U.S. Department of Defense. *United States–Vietnam Relations,* 1945–1967. 12 vols. Washington, D.C.: Government Printing Office, 1971. [This work is the Department of Defense version of the Pentagon Papers.]

INTERVIEWS

By Cecil B. Currey
Baker, Joseph. 23 June 1985; 3, 4, 26 May 1987.
Banzon, José. 30 July 1985.
Bohannan, Dorothy. 27 July 1985; 18 July 1986.
Chavez, Manuel J. 15 January 1986.
Colby, William E. 24 June 1985.
Conein, Lucien. 24 June 1985; 3, 4, 27 May 1987.
Davis, Spence. 30 January 1986.
Deutch, Michael. 24 June 1985.
Doran, John. 11 November 1985.
Ellsberg, Daniel. 23 September 1985.
Espino, Romeo. 21 July 1986.
Gilday, William. 22 May 1986; 4 June 1986.
Glazer, Charles. 29 July 1985; 19 July 1986.
Johnson, Joseph. 29 January 1986.
Justiniano, Medardo. 25 July 1985.
Lansdale, David. 11 November 1985.
Lansdale, Edward G. 15, 16, 17 February 1984; 16, 17 May 1984; 29, 30 November 1984; 17, 18, 19 December 1984; 12 November 1985.
Lansdale, Patrocinio Yapcinco Kelly (Pat). 23 June 1985.
Lansdale, Peter. 11 November 1985.
Lansdale, Phil. 20 September 1985.
McCarry, Charles. 13 November 1985.
Manahan, Manuel. 24 July 1985.
Messing, F. Andy, Jr. 29 June 1986.
Mojica, Proculo L. 28 July 1985.
Navarro, Edmundo. 25 July 1985.
Novales, Vicente O. 27 July 1985.
Paschal, Henry. 29 July 1985.
Phillips, Rufus C. 26 May 1987.
Quintos, Antonio A. 26 July 1985.
Redick, Joseph. 19 December 1984.
Richards, Peter C. 23 July 1985.
Roberts, Hubert H. 13 July 1985.
Telesco, Lee. 21 July 1986.
Valeriano, Emma. 26 July 1985.
Ward, W.T.T. 11 November 1985.

Yepez, Ceferina. 27 July 1985.
Zaldarriaga, Frank. 26 July 1985.

With Edward G. Lansdale by Others
Alnwick, Major. Department of History, United States Air Force Academy. United States Air Force Oral History Program. 30 April 1971.
Gibbons, William, and Patricia McAdams. 19 November 1982.
Gittinger, Ted. Lyndon Baines Johnson Presidential Library, Austin, Texas. 5 June 1981.
Morse, Harold. *Honolulu Star-Bulletin.* 7 January 1984.

LECTURES AND SPEECHES BY EDWARD G. LANSDALE

"Counter-Guerrilla Operations in the Philippines, 1946–1953." 15 June 1961. Seminar with Lapus, Valeriano, Justiniano, Bohannan, and Lansdale. Special Warfare School, Fort Bragg, North Carolina. Mimeographed, 74 pp. Copy in author's possession.
"The Free Citizen in Uniform." 1 November 1960. Army Civil Affairs School, Fort Gordon, Georgia. Mimeographed, 7 pp. Copy in author's possession.
"Fundamentals for Americans." 13 June 1959. Military Government Association, Shoreham Hotel, Washington, D.C. Mimeographed, 6 pp. Copy in author's possession.
"The Insurgent Battlefield." 25 May 1962. Air Force Academy. Mimeographed, 9 pp. Copy in author's possession.
"Introductory Comments on the Huk Campaign." 15 June 1961. Counter-Guerrilla Seminar, Fort Bragg, North Carolina. "Speeches," USDOD, OSD, Box 45, LP, THIWRP.
"Lessons Learned: The Philippines, 1946–1953." 26 September 1962. Interdepartmental Course on Counterinsurgency, Foreign Service Institute. Copy in author's possession.
Library Lecture. 19 November 1984 (2:00 P.M.). University of South Florida, Tampa.
Military History Lecture. 19 November 1984 (8:00 A.M.). University of South Florida, Tampa.
"Military Psychological Operations." Part I. 7 January 1960. Armed Forces Staff College, Norfolk, Virginia.
"Military Psychological Operations." Part II. 29 March 1960. Armed Forces Staff College, Norfolk, Virginia.
"People's Wars: Three Primary Lessons." 15 January 1973. Air War College, Maxwell Air Force Base, Montgomery, Alabama. Published in *Vital Speeches of the Day,* pp. 357–361.
"Southeast Asia." 3 December 1958. Army War College, Carlisle Barracks, Pennsylvania. Mimeographed, 8 pp. Copy in author's possession.
"The True American." 3 June 1960. No indication of intended audience. Mimeographed, 6 pp. Copy in author's possession.
"The U.S. Military in Non-Military Warfare." 23 July 1959. Panel with Darcy, Heyward, Bonesteel, and Lansdale. National Strategy Seminar, National War College, Fort McNair, Washington, D.C. 7 pp. Copy in author's possession.

"Vietnam." 23 November 1964. Southeast Asian Studies Program, Yale University. Mimeographed, 11 pp. Copy in author's possession.
"Vietnam: Goons, Clerks and Patriots." N.d. [post-1965]. No indication of intended audience. Mimeographed, 14 pp. Copy in author's possession.
"Vietnam: A Test of American Understanding of Revolution." 8 August 1964. No indication of intended audience. Mimeographed, 12 pp. Published as "Viet Nam: Do We Understand Revolution?"

UNPUBLISHED MANUSCRIPTS

Adelstein, Jon. "Something Extra and Special." Master's thesis, Department of History, Stanford University, 1985.
Iversen, Joan. "The Ugly American: A Bestseller Re-Examined." Copy courtesy of Iversen.
Kushner, Rose. "The Quiet American Comes Home." Lansdale Personal Papers.
———. "The Quiet American Returns to Saigon." Lansdale Personal Papers.
Lansdale, Edward G. "The Lansdale Family." Rough-draft typescript, 39 pp. Alexandria, Virginia. November 1971. Lansdale Personal Papers.
———. "Military Policy in Underdeveloped Areas." Box 12, LP, THIWRP.

ARTICLES

Farrell, Barry. "The Ellsberg Mask." *Harper's* (October 1973).
Karnow, Stanley. "On Duty, 'Dirty Tricks,' and Democracy." *Potomac Magazine, Washington Post* (10 December 1972). Reprinted as "Lansdale," *Stars and Stripes* (14 January 1973).
Kushner, Rose. "General Dirty Tricks." *Washingtonian* VII, 6 (March 1972).
Langguth, A. J. "Our Policy-Making Men in Saigon." *New York Times Magazine* (28 April 1968).
Lansdale, Edward G. "Comrades." *Bulletin of the American Historical Collection* (April–June 1984).
———. "People's Wars: Three Primary Lessons." *Vital Speeches of the Day* XXXIX (1 April 1973).
———. "Still the Search for Goals." *Foreign Affairs* (November 1968).
———. "The Story Ramon Magsaysay Did Not Tell." *Orient* VII, 8 (August 1963).
———. "The Report the President Wanted Published." *Saturday Evening Post* (20 May 1961).
———. "Two Steps to Get Us Out of Vietnam." *Look* XXXIII (4 March 1969).
———. "Viet Nam: Do We Understand Revolution?" *Foreign Affairs* (October 1964).
Lasco, Jack. "America's Deadliest Secret Agent." *Saga* (March 1967).
Palm, Edward F. "Novels of Vietnam and the Uses of War Literature." *Marine Corps Gazette* (November 1986).
"Philippine Chamber of Industries Policy Statement on Laurel-Langley Agreement." *Progressive Review* (January/February 1965).
Prouty, L. Fletcher. "The CIA's Saigon Military Mission." *Freedom* (December 1965).

Shalom, Stephen R. "Counter-Insurgency in the Philippines." *Journal of Contemporary Asia* VII, 2 (1977).
Stone, Peter H. "The Special Forces in 'Covert Action.' " *The Nation* (7–14 July 1984).
Thanh, Phan Chan. "The Man Sentenced to Death by Ho." *Thoi Nay* (1 September 1967). Transcript in Lansdale Personal Papers.

NEWSPAPERS

Christian Science Monitor
Honolulu Star-Bulletin
Komsomol Pravda, Moscow
London Telegraph
London Times
Manila Chronicle
Manila Times Journal
New York Herald Tribune
New York Times

Philippine Daily Inquirer, Manila
Philippine Star, Manila
St. Petersburg (Florida) *Times*
Stars and Stripes (U.S. armed forces)
The American Opinion (John Birch Society)
Washington Post
Washington Star

SECONDARY ACCOUNTS

Abaya, Hernando J. *The Untold Philippine Story*. Quezon City, Philippines: Malaya Books, Inc., 1967.
————. *Betrayal in the Philippines*. Quezon City, Philippines: Malaya Books, Inc., 1970.
Abueva, José Velosa. *Ramon Magsaysay: A Political Biography*. Manila: Solidaridad Publishers, 1971.
Agee, Philip Burnett Franklin. *CIA Diary: Inside the Company*. Suffolk, England: Penguin Books, Ltd., 1975.
Agoncillo, Teodoro A., and Milagros C. Guerrero. *History of the Filipino People*. Quezon City, Philippines: R. P. Garcia Publishing Company, 1973.
Asprey, Robert B. *War in the Shadows: The Guerrilla in History*. 2 vols. Garden City, N.Y.: Doubleday and Co., Inc., 1975.
Avancena, Rose Laurel, and Ileana Maramag. *Days of Courage: The Legacy of Dr. José P. Laurel*. Manila: Vera Reyes Publishers, 1978.
Bardsley, Charles Wareing. *Dictionary of English and Welsh Surnames (with Special American Instances)*. Baltimore: Genealogical Publishing Company, 1968.
Bowman, John S., Ed. *The Vietnam War: An Almanac*. New York: World Almanac Publications, 1985.
Browne, Malcolm W. *The New Face of War*. Indianapolis: Bobbs-Merrill Company, Inc., 1965.
Chaffard, George. *Indochine: Dix ans d'indépendance*. Paris: Calmann-Levy Publishers, 1964.
Charlton, Michael, and Anthony Moncrieff. *Many Reasons Why: The American Involvement in Vietnam*. New York: Hill & Wang, 1978.
Cincinnatus [Cecil B. Currey]. *Self-Destruction: The Disintegration and Decay of the United States Army During the Vietnam Era*. New York: W. W. Norton and Company, 1981.
Cline, Ray S. *Secrets, Spies and Scholars*. Washington, D.C.: Acropolis Books, Ltd., 1976.

————. *The CIA Under Reagan, Bush and Casey: The Evolution of the Agency from Roosevelt to Reagan.* Washington, D.C.: Acropolis Books, Ltd., 1981.

Colby, William E., and Peter Forbath. *Honorable Men: My Life in the CIA.* New York: Simon & Schuster, 1978.

Committee of Concerned Asian Scholars, The. *The Indochina Story: A Fully Documented Account.* New York: Pantheon Books, 1970.

Constantino, Renato. *The Making of a Filipino.* Quezon City, Philippines: Malaya Books, 1969.

Corson, William. *The Armies of Ignorance: The Rise of the American Intelligence Empire.* New York: The Dial Press, 1977.

————. *The Betrayal.* New York: W. W. Norton and Company, 1968.

Critchfield, Richard. *The Long Charade: Political Subversion in the Vietnam War.* New York: Harcourt, Brace and World, Inc., 1968.

Crisol, José M. *The Red Lie.* Manila: Bureau of Printing, 1954.

Dawson, Alan. *55 Days: The Fall of South Vietnam.* Englewood Cliffs, N.J.: Prentice-Hall, Inc., 1977.

Detzer, David. *The Brink: The Cuban Missile Crisis, 1962.* New York: Crowell Publishing Company, 1979.

Don, Tran Van. *Our Endless War: Inside Vietnam.* San Rafael, Calif.: Presidio Press, 1978.

Dooley, Thomas. *Deliver Us from Evil.* New York: Farrar, Straus and Cudahy, 1956.

Doyle, Edward, Samuel Lipsman, and Stephen Weiss. *Passing the Torch: The Vietnam Experience.* Boston: Boston Publishing Company, 1981.

Drinnon, Richard. *Facing West: The Metaphysics of Indian-Hating and Empire Building.* Minneapolis: University of Minnesota Press, 1980.

Duncan, Donald. *The New Legions.* New York: Pocket Books, 1967.

Fain, Tyrus G., Katharine C. Plant, and Ross Milloy, Eds. *The Intelligence Community: History, Organization and Issues.* New York: R. R. Bowker Company, 1977.

Fall, Bernard. *The Two Viet-Nams: A Political and Military Analysis.* New York: Frederick A. Praeger Publishing Company, 1967.

Fernandez, Alejandro M. *The Philippines and the United States: The Forging of New Relations.* Quezon City, Philippines: University of the Philippines Integrated Research Program, 1977.

FitzGerald, Frances. *Fire in the Lake: The Vietnamese and the Americans in Vietnam.* Boston: Little, Brown and Company, 1972.

Freemantle, Brian. *CIA.* Briarcliff Manor, N.Y.: Stein and Day, 1983.

Gettleman, Marvin E. *Vietnam: History, Documents, and Opinions on a Major World Crisis.* New York: Fawcett Publications, 1966.

Gibson, James William. *The Perfect War: Technowar in Vietnam.* Boston: Atlantic Monthly Press, 1986.

Greene, Graham. *The Quiet American.* New York: Viking Press, 1955.

Harrison, James Pinckney. *The Endless War: Fifty Years of Struggle in Vietnam.* New York: The Free Press, 1982.

Hunt, E. Howard. *Undercover: Memoirs of an American Secret Agent.* New York: Berkley Publishing Co., 1974.

Kahin, George McT., and John W. Lewis. *The United States in Vietnam.* New York: The Dial Press, 1967.

Kalb, Marvin, and Elie Abel. *Roots of Involvement: The U.S. in Asia, 1784–1971.* New York: W. W. Norton and Company, 1971.

Karnow, Stanley. *Vietnam: A History.* New York: Penguin Books, 1983.

Kerkvliet, Benedict J. *The Huk Rebellion: A Study of Peasant Unrest in the Philippines.* Berkeley: University of California Press, 1977.

Kintner, William R. *The Front Is Everywhere.* Norman: University of Oklahoma Press, 1950.

Kirkpatrick, Lyman B., Jr. *The U.S. Intelligence Community: Foreign Policy and Domestic Activities.* New York: Hill & Wang, 1973.

Krepinevich, Andrew F., Jr. *The Army and Vietnam.* Baltimore: The Johns Hopkins University Press, 1986.

Ky, Nguyen Cao. *Twenty Years and Twenty Days.* New York: Stein and Day, 1976.

Lachica, Eduardo. *The Huks: Philippine Agrarian Society in Revolt.* New York: F. A. Praeger Publishers, 1971.

Lansdale, Edward G. *In the Midst of Wars: An American's Mission to Southeast Asia.* New York: Harper & Row, Publishers, 1972.

Lartéguy, Jean. *Le mal Jaune.* Paris: Presses de la Cité, 1962. Translation, *Yellow Fever.* New York: E. P. Dutton & Company, 1965.

Leary, William M., Ed. *The Central Intelligence Agency: History and Documents.* Tuscaloosa: University of Alabama Press, 1984.

Lederer, William J., and Eugene Burdick. *The Ugly American.* New York: W. W. Norton Publishing Co., 1985.

Leites, Nathan, and Charles Wolf, Jr. *Rebellion and Authority: An Analytic Essay on Insurgent Conflicts.* Chicago: Markham Publishing Company, 1970.

Manchester, William. *American Caesar: Douglas MacArthur, 1890–1964.* Boston: Little, Brown and Company, 1978.

Marchetti, Victor, and John D. Marks. *The CIA and the Cult of Intelligence.* New York: Alfred A. Knopf, 1974.

Mecklin, John. *Mission in Torment: An Intimate Account of the U.S. Role in Vietnam.* New York: Doubleday and Company, 1965.

Millette, Allan R. *A Short History of the Vietnam War.* Bloomington: Indiana University Press, 1978. Foreword by Edward G. Lansdale.

Peterson, A. H., G. C. Reinhardt, and E. E. Conger, Eds. *Symposium on the Role of Airpower in Counterinsurgency and Unconventional Warfare: The Philippine Huk Campaign.* Santa Monica, Calif.: The Rand Corporation, 1963.

Pomeroy, William J. *An American Made Tragedy: Neo-Colonialism and Dictatorship in the Philippines.* New York: International Publishers, 1974.

————. *The Forest: A Personal History of the Huk Guerrilla Struggle in the Philippines.* New York: International Publishers, 1963.

Powers, Thomas. *The Man Who Kept the Secrets: Richard Helms and the CIA.* New York: Alfred A. Knopf, 1979.

Prados, John. *The Sky Would Fall: Operation Vulture — The U.S. Bombing Mission in Indochina, 1954.* New York: The Dial Press, 1983.

Prouty, L. Fletcher. *The Secret Team: The CIA and Its Allies in Control of the United States and the World.* Englewood Cliffs, N.J.: Prentice-Hall Publishing Co., 1973.

Ranelagh, John. *The Agency.* New York: Simon & Schuster, 1986.

Ransom, Harry Howe. *Central Intelligence and National Security.* Cambridge: Harvard University Press, 1958.

Raskin, Marcus G., and Bernard Fall, Eds. *The Viet-Nam Reader: Articles and*

Documents on American Foreign Policy and the Viet-Nam Crisis. New York: Random House, 1965.

Rocolle, Pierre. *Pourquoi Dien Bien Phu?* Paris: Flammarion Publishers, 1968.

Romulo, Carlos P., and Marvin M. Gray. *The Magsaysay Story.* New York: The John Day Company, 1956.

Rositzke, Harry. *The CIA's Secret Operations: Espionage, Counterespionage, and Covert Action.* New York: Reader's Digest Press, 1977.

Rostow, Walt Whitman. *The Diffusion of Power: An Essay in Recent History.* New York: Macmillan Publishing Company, Inc., 1972.

Scheer, Robert. *How the United States Got Involved in Vietnam.* Santa Barbara, Calif.: Center for the Study of Democratic Institutions, 1965.

Schlesinger, Arthur M., Jr. *A Thousand Days: John F. Kennedy in the White House.* Boston: Houghton Mifflin, 1965.

Shaplen, Robert. *The Lost Revolution: The Story of Twenty Years of Neglected Opportunities in Vietnam and of America's Failure to Foster Democracy There.* New York: Harper & Row, 1965.

————. *The Road from War: Vietnam, 1965–1970.* New York: Harper & Row, 1970.

Sihanouk, Norodom, and Wilfred Burchett. *My War with the CIA: The Memoirs of Prince Norodom Sihanouk.* New York: Random House–Pantheon, 1973.

Smith, Joseph Burkholder. *Portrait of a Cold Warrior.* New York: Ballantine Books, 1976.

Smith, R. Harris. *OSS: The Secret History of America's First Central Intelligence Agency.* Berkeley: University of California Press, 1972.

Solberg, Carl. *Hubert Humphrey: A Biography.* New York: W. W. Norton and Company, 1984.

Stavins, Ralph, Richard J. Barnet, and Marcus G. Raskin. *Washington Plans an Aggressive War.* New York: Random House, 1971.

Steinberg, David J. *Philippine Collaboration in World War II.* Ann Arbor: University of Michigan Press, 1967.

Stevenson, William. *Intrepid's Last Case.* New York: Ballantine Books, 1983.

Syjuco, José G. *The Press in the Republic of the Philippines: Its Role and Activities.* Manila: Philippine National Defense College, 1968.

Szulc, Tad. *Compulsive Spy: The Strange Career of E. Howard Hunt.* New York: The Viking Press, 1974.

Taber, Robert. *The War of the Flea: A Study of Guerrilla Warfare, Theory and Practice.* New York: Citadel Press, 1965.

Taylor, Charles. *Snow Job: Canada, the United States and Vietnam (1954–1973).* Toronto: Anansi Publishers, 1974.

US Intervention in Philippine Politics: The Historical Record. Manila: Katipunan ng Bagong Pilipina, 1978.

Vietnam: A Historical Outline. Hanoi: Xunhasaba Publishers, 1966.

Westmoreland, William C. *A Soldier Reports.* Garden City, N.Y.: Doubleday Publishing Co., 1968.

Whittingham, Richard, Ed. *Almanac of Adventure: A Panorama of Danger and Daring.* Chicago: Rand McNally & Company, 1982.

Wise, David, and Thomas B. Ross. *The Invisible Government.* New York: Random House, 1964.

Wyden, Peter. *Bay of Pigs: The Untold Story.* New York: Simon & Schuster, 1979.

INDEX